# Special Event Production

This must-have guide to special event production resources looks deep behind the scenes of an event and dissects what it is that creates success. It is an extensive reference guide to the technical details of producing an event, large or small. It provides thorough, in-depth explanations of entertainment, décor, lighting and audio systems, visual presentation technology, special effects, staging, and temporary outdoor venues.

This new edition includes:

- New content on: the latest in audio, lighting, A-V technology, industry safety standards, experiential entertainment, special effects, décor, staging and set design, and tent technology, for both indoor and outdoor events.
- Updated and new real-life case studies.
- New Industry Voice features in each chapter, including interviews with industry experts from around the world.
- Comprehensive coverage of venues, staging, rigging, lighting, video, audio, scenic design and décor, CADD, entertainment, special effects, tenting, electrical power, fencing, and sanitary facilities in a variety of indoor and outdoor event settings.
- Enhanced online resources including: PowerPoint lecture slides, checklists, glossaries, additional questions and challenges, and web links.

Incorporating pedagogical features, this easy-to-read book is packed with photographs, diagrams, flow charts, checklists, sample forms, and real-life war stories. The vast varieties of A-V technologies, indoor and outdoor venues, décor, and staging are presented. This is a must-have resource for event planners, managers, caterers, and students.

This text is part two of a two-book set; also available is *Special Event Production: The Process* (978-1-138-78565-6). This book analyzes the process—the planning and business aspects—to provide a unique guide to producing a variety of events from weddings to festivals.

**Doug Matthews** has over 30 years' experience in the events industry. For 19 years he owned an award-winning production company based in Vancouver, Canada, followed by lecturing at a local university. He continues to deliver guest lectures and to write on subjects concerning the industry.

# Special Event Production

## The resources

**Second edition**

Doug Matthews

Routledge
Taylor & Francis Group

LONDON AND NEW YORK

Second edition published 2016
by Routledge
2 Park Square, Milton Park, Abingdon, Oxon OX14 4RN

and by Routledge
711 Third Avenue, New York, NY 10017

*Routledge is an imprint of the Taylor & Francis Group, an informa business*

© 2016 Doug Matthews

First edition published by Butterworth-Heinemann 2008

*British Library Cataloguing in Publication Data*
A catalogue record for this book is available from the British Library

*Library of Congress Cataloging in Publication Data*
Matthews, Doug.
   Special event production. The resources / Doug Matthews. —
2nd edition.
      pages cm
   Includes bibliographical references and index.
   ISBN 978-1-138-78568-7 (hbk) — ISBN 978-1-138-78567-0 (pbk) —
   ISBN 978-1-315-76770-3 (ebk)    1. Special events—Planning.
   2. Special events industry.   I. Title.
   GT3405.M375 2015
   394.2—dc23                                              2015011910

ISBN: 978-1-138-78568-7 (hbk)
ISBN: 978-1-138-78567-0 (pbk)
ISBN: 978-1-315-76770-3 (ebk)

Typeset in Iowan old style
by Keystroke, Station Road, Codsall, Wolverhampton
Printed by Ashford Colour Press Ltd.

The world is not yet exhausted; let me see something tomorrow which I never saw before.

Samuel Johnson
English author, critic, and lexicographer (1709–1784)

# Contents

| | | |
|---|---|---|
| *List of figures* | | *xiii* |
| *List of tables* | | *xvii* |
| *Preface* | | *xix* |
| *Acknowledgements* | | *xxi* |

| | | | |
|---|---|---|---|
| **1** | **Entertainment** | | **1** |
| | 1.1 | Defining entertainment | 2 |
| | | 1.1.1 Form in entertainment | 2 |
| | | 1.1.2 Reasons for entertainment | 5 |
| | | 1.1.3 Content in entertainment | 10 |
| | 1.2 | Staging entertainment | 28 |
| | | 1.2.1 Number of performers or acts | 28 |
| | | 1.2.2 Scheduling and timing | 29 |
| | | 1.2.3 Using the event space | 32 |
| | | 1.2.4 Building the show | 37 |
| | | 1.2.5 Beginnings, segues, and endings | 39 |
| | 1.3 | Working with performers | 44 |
| | | 1.3.1 Mindset | 44 |
| | | 1.3.2 Creature comforts | 44 |
| | | 1.3.3 Unique preparations and performance needs | 45 |
| | | 1.3.4 Communications | 47 |
| | | 1.3.5 The special case: celebrities | 48 |
| | | 1.3.6 Risk and safety | 49 |

| | | | |
|---|---|---|---|
| **2** | **Décor** | | **53** |
| | 2.1 | Design theory | 54 |
| | | 2.1.1 Elements of design | 54 |
| | | 2.1.2 Principles of design | 60 |
| | 2.2 | Categories of décor | 64 |
| | | 2.2.1 Backdrops | 64 |

|                |                                                      |     |
|----------------|------------------------------------------------------|-----|
| 2.2.2          | Themed sets                                          | 64  |
| 2.2.3          | Props                                                | 66  |
| 2.2.4          | Furniture                                            | 66  |
| 2.2.5          | Linens and napery                                    | 69  |
| 2.2.6          | Drapery                                              | 71  |
| 2.2.7          | Banners and signs                                    | 74  |
| 2.2.8          | Tension fabric structures                            | 82  |
| 2.2.9          | People and other creatures as décor                  | 83  |
| 2.2.10         | Floral décor                                         | 84  |
| 2.2.11         | Inflatables                                          | 87  |
| 2.2.12         | Technology as décor                                  | 90  |
| 2.2.13         | Other unique décor                                   | 92  |
| 2.3            | Considerations for the setup and strike of décor     | 94  |
| 2.3.1          | Prior to the event                                   | 95  |
| 2.3.2          | At the event                                         | 96  |
| 2.3.3          | After the event                                      | 96  |

**3   Audio systems**                                                  **99**

| 3.1   | Acoustic theory and its application to the event space        | 100 |
| 3.1.1 | What is sound?                                                | 100 |
| 3.1.2 | Sound propagation and its relationship to the event space     | 102 |
| 3.2   | Uses of an audio system                                       | 104 |
| 3.2.1 | Audio for speech                                              | 104 |
| 3.2.2 | Audio for entertainment                                       | 105 |
| 3.3   | Main audio system groups and their components                 | 106 |
| 3.3.1 | Input group                                                   | 106 |
| 3.3.2 | Mixing and Processing group                                   | 119 |
| 3.3.3 | Output group                                                  | 125 |
| 3.4   | Signal flow and equipment locations in the event space        | 135 |
| 3.4.1 | Signal flow                                                   | 135 |
| 3.4.2 | Equipment locations                                           | 136 |
| 3.5   | Pre-event sound check and system operation during the event   | 137 |
| 3.5.1 | Pre-event sound check                                         | 137 |
| 3.5.2 | System operation during the event                            | 139 |
| 3.6   | Risk and safety                                               | 142 |

**4   Visual presentation technology**                                 **145**

| 4.1   | Purpose of visual presentations                               | 146 |
| 4.2   | Content in visual presentations                               | 146 |
| 4.2.1 | Setting goals and content for the show                        | 148 |
| 4.2.2 | Choosing equipment and personnel                              | 149 |
| 4.2.3 | Putting it together                                           | 150 |
| 4.3   | Visual sources                                                | 151 |
| 4.3.1 | Still image files                                             | 151 |
| 4.3.2 | Pre-recorded digital video                                    | 153 |
| 4.3.3 | Live video and image magnification (IMAG)                     | 157 |

|  |  |  |
|---|---|---|
| 4.3.4 | 4K and 8K ultra-high-definition (UHD) video | 160 |
| 4.3.5 | Projection mapping | 161 |
| 4.3.6 | Interactive content | 167 |
| 4.3.7 | The Internet | 168 |
| 4.4 | Control and distribution | 168 |
| 4.5 | Projection equipment | 170 |
| 4.5.1 | Types of projectors | 170 |
| 4.5.2 | Key specifications for projectors | 172 |
| 4.5.3 | Edge blending and warping | 177 |
| 4.6 | Display equipment | 179 |
| 4.6.1 | Plain screens | 179 |
| 4.6.2 | Monitors | 182 |
| 4.6.3 | Videowalls | 184 |
| 4.6.4 | LED screens | 184 |
| 4.6.5 | Teleprompters and confidence monitors | 186 |
| 4.7 | Equipment setup and operation | 187 |
| 4.7.1 | Setup | 187 |
| 4.7.2 | Operation during the event | 188 |
| 4.8 | Risk and safety | 190 |
| **5** | **Lighting systems** | **193** |
| 5.1 | Objectives of event lighting | 194 |
| 5.1.1 | Visibility | 194 |
| 5.1.2 | Relevance | 194 |
| 5.1.3 | Composition | 195 |
| 5.1.4 | Mood | 196 |
| 5.2 | Qualities of light | 196 |
| 5.2.1 | Intensity | 197 |
| 5.2.2 | Distribution | 197 |
| 5.2.3 | Color | 197 |
| 5.2.4 | Direction | 200 |
| 5.2.5 | Movement | 201 |
| 5.3 | Lighting instruments | 202 |
| 5.3.1 | Construction of luminaires | 202 |
| 5.3.2 | Types and uses of luminaires | 206 |
| 5.4 | Event lighting design | 214 |
| 5.4.1 | Conceptual design | 215 |
| 5.4.2 | Practical design | 215 |
| 5.4.3 | Physical design | 218 |
| 5.5 | Between concept and execution | 221 |
| 5.6 | Lighting control | 221 |
| 5.6.1 | Dimming system | 221 |
| 5.6.2 | Control protocol | 222 |
| 5.6.3 | Control console | 225 |
| 5.7 | Lighting setup and operation | 225 |
| 5.7.1 | Lighting setup | 226 |
| 5.7.2 | Lighting operation during the event | 228 |
| 5.8 | Risk and safety | 229 |

| | | |
|---|---|---:|
| **6** | **Special effects** | **232** |
| 6.1 | What are special effects? | 232 |
| 6.2 | Types of special effects | 233 |
| | 6.2.1   Streamers and confetti | 234 |
| | 6.2.2   Fog, smoke, and haze | 234 |
| | 6.2.3   Lasers | 238 |
| | 6.2.4   Fireworks and pyrotechnics | 242 |
| | 6.2.5   Atmospherics | 253 |
| | | |
| **7** | **Staging and set design** | **257** |
| 7.1 | The language of the stage | 258 |
| | 7.1.1   Styles of stage | 258 |
| | 7.1.2   Stage directions | 259 |
| 7.2 | Types and construction of stages | 259 |
| | 7.2.1   Manufactured decks and support systems | 261 |
| | 7.2.2   Custom stages | 262 |
| | 7.2.3   Mobile stages | 263 |
| | 7.2.4   Accessories for stages and other optional structures | 264 |
| 7.3 | Placement and sizing of stages | 268 |
| | 7.3.1   Horizontal size | 268 |
| | 7.3.2   Vertical size | 269 |
| 7.4 | Stage draping | 272 |
| | 7.4.1   Backdrops | 272 |
| | 7.4.2   Masking curtains | 273 |
| | 7.4.3   Stage skirting | 273 |
| | 7.4.4   Front curtains | 273 |
| 7.5 | Stage sets and set design | 274 |
| | 7.5.1   Design procedure and criteria | 275 |
| | 7.5.2   Construction and installation of the set | 275 |
| 7.6 | Risk and safety | 277 |
| | | |
| **8** | **Tenting** | **279** |
| 8.1 | Why use a tent for a special event? | 280 |
| 8.2 | Styles and configurations of tents | 280 |
| | 8.2.1   Traditional tent styles | 280 |
| | 8.2.2   Hybrid and unique tent styles | 282 |
| | 8.2.3   Modern tent technology | 284 |
| 8.3 | Tent accessories and options | 288 |
| | 8.3.1   Tops | 288 |
| | 8.3.2   Sidewalls | 288 |
| | 8.3.3   Gutters | 288 |
| | 8.3.4   Doors | 288 |
| | 8.3.5   Lighting | 288 |
| | 8.3.6   Liners | 289 |
| | 8.3.7   Flooring | 289 |
| | 8.3.8   Heating, ventilation, and air conditioning (HVAC) | 289 |

8.4  Setup considerations                                        292
     8.4.1  Site and site survey                                 292
     8.4.2  Weather and time of day                              293
     8.4.3  Installation                                         294
8.5  Risk and safety                                             297
     8.5.1  Pre-occupancy inspection                             297
     8.5.2  Occupancy permits                                    297
     8.5.3  General safety regulations and standards             299

9  Miscellaneous technical resources                             301

9.1  Electrical power                                            301
     9.1.1  Determining electrical service requirements          302
     9.1.2  Electrical distribution                              304
     9.1.3  Portable power                                       307
     9.1.4  Electrical safety considerations                     308
9.2  Trussing                                                    309
     9.2.1  General truss design                                 309
     9.2.2  Ground-supported truss configurations                309
     9.2.3  Truss safety                                         310
9.3  Rigging                                                     314
     9.3.1  Overview                                             314
     9.3.2  Rigging equipment                                    315
     9.3.3  Rigging safety                                       319
9.4  Other temporary structures                                  321
     9.4.1  Scaffolding                                          321
     9.4.2  Bleachers                                            322
     9.4.3  Fencing and barriers                                 324
     9.4.4  Sanitary facilities                                  328

Index                                                            334

# Figures

| 1.1 | Origins of human entertainment | 2 |
|---|---|---|
| 1.2 | Evolution of entertainment genres | 3 |
| 1.3 | Example of strolling performers as decoration | 8 |
| 1.4 | Connecting with the audience | 13 |
| 1.5 | Extreme beam | 16 |
| 1.6 | Example of contemporary choreography | 23 |
| 1.7 | Example of large touchscreen technology | 26 |
| 1.8 | Order for multi-group setup and sound check onstage | 31 |
| 1.9 | Example of a technical act requiring detailed setup | 33 |
| 1.10 | Possible auxiliary stage locations in a typical hotel ballroom situation | 34 |
| 1.11 | Central main stage with auxiliary stages | 35 |
| 1.12 | Possible options for using floor space as a performing area | 36 |
| 1.13 | Pacing: sample show energy level over time | 38 |
| 1.14 | The Sparklers, a unique interactive and technical percussion act using LED lighting | 42 |
| 2.1 | Example of an unusual form | 55 |
| 2.2 | Color and color schemes | 59 |
| 2.3 | The golden proportion | 60 |
| 2.4 | Example of fantasy Alice in Wonderland backdrop | 65 |
| 2.5 | Examples of props | 67 |
| 2.6 | Examples of event lounge furniture | 68 |
| 2.7 | Examples of dining chairs and square and round dining tables | 69 |
| 2.8 | Examples of drapery at weddings | 74 |
| 2.9 | Examples of different event entrances | 77 |
| 2.10 | Examples of tension fabric structures | 83 |
| 2.11 | Examples of floral décor | 85 |
| 2.12 | Examples of inflatable décor | 91 |
| 3.1 | Sound wave causing a change in air pressure | 100 |
| 3.2 | Reflection and absorption of sound waves from a large surface | 103 |

| | | |
|---|---|---|
| 3.3 | Diffraction of sound around obstacles | 104 |
| 3.4 | Effect of different temperature gradients on sound waves | 105 |
| 3.5 | Main audio system groups and signal flow | 106 |
| 3.6 | Microphone operating principles | 108 |
| 3.7 | Microphone directionality | 109 |
| 3.8 | Balanced and unbalanced cables and connectors | 110 |
| 3.9 | Examples of vocal and speech microphones | 113 |
| 3.10 | Examples of instrument microphones | 114 |
| 3.11 | 3-to-1 rule | 115 |
| 3.12 | Bluetooth active direct input box | 119 |
| 3.13 | Example of analog mixer (Mackie CFX20.MkII) and individual channel strips | 121 |
| 3.14 | Example of a digital mixer (MIDAS PRO6) | 123 |
| 3.15 | Example of onstage digital interface unit | 125 |
| 3.16 | Speaker design and operation | 128 |
| 3.17 | Examples of speakers | 129 |
| 3.18 | Example of a distributed speaker system | 129 |
| 3.19 | Example of a flown speaker system | 130 |
| 3.20 | Example of a flown speaker system with front fill speakers | 130 |
| 3.21 | Example of a flown speaker system with delay speakers | 131 |
| 3.22 | Example of speaker placement for a typical event with stage entertainment | 131 |
| 3.23 | Example of speaker placement for lateral coverage | 132 |
| 3.24 | Example of vertical line array of speakers for large area coverage | 133 |
| 3.25 | Typical traditional band stage plot with monitor requirements | 134 |
| 3.26 | Signal path and equipment locations for typical event audio system | 136 |
| 3.27 | Corporate event audio control | 140 |
| 4.1 | Example of a multimedia presentation | 147 |
| 4.2 | Visual presentation flow | 151 |
| 4.3 | Comparison of video resolutions/aspect ratios | 155 |
| 4.4 | Main video camera position for IMAG | 159 |
| 4.5 | Example of projection mapping | 161 |
| 4.6 | Conference session produced by the Mills James Group | 165 |
| 4.7 | Examples of projectors | 175 |
| 4.8 | Edge blending | 178 |
| 4.9 | Screen aspect ratio and effect on displayed image | 182 |
| 4.10 | Large LED screen used as a stage backdrop | 185 |
| 4.11 | General visual presentation setup and signal flow | 189 |
| 5.1 | Example of elements and principles of good lighting design | 196 |
| 5.2 | Lighting color wheel | 198 |
| 5.3 | Illustration of additive and subtractive color mixing in light | 199 |
| 5.4 | Direction in lighting | 200 |
| 5.5 | General construction details of a conventional luminaire | 203 |

| | | |
|---|---|---|
| 5.6 | Lighting accessories | 204 |
| 5.7 | General construction details of an LED luminaire | 205 |
| 5.8 | Examples of conventional luminaires | 208 |
| 5.9 | Examples of LED luminaires | 209 |
| 5.10 | Examples of moving luminaires | 211 |
| 5.11 | Lighting the World Cup closing ceremonies | 213 |
| 5.12 | Examples of practical lighting design | 217 |
| 5.13 | Example of a 2D event lighting plot | 222 |
| 5.14 | Signal path and equipment locations for event lighting control | 224 |
| 6.1 | Example of confetti launch—Bayer Anniversary, 150 Years | 235 |
| 6.2 | Example of haze used to enhance lighting | 237 |
| 6.3 | Examples of laser effects | 240 |
| 6.4 | Archangel team preparing for a show | 244 |
| 6.5 | Outdoor fireworks display | 247 |
| 6.6 | Live fire choreography—Fire Swing | 248 |
| 6.7 | Example of foam used at a party | 254 |
| 7.1 | Thrust stage | 258 |
| 7.2 | Proscenium stage | 259 |
| 7.3 | Arena stage | 260 |
| 7.4 | Stage directions | 260 |
| 7.5 | Examples of different stages | 262 |
| 7.6 | Example of mobile stage | 263 |
| 7.7 | An example of Barkley Kalpak staging | 266 |
| 7.8 | Stage height determination for a standing audience | 270 |
| 7.9 | Stage height determination for a seated audience | 271 |
| 7.10 | General locations and names of stage drape components | 274 |
| 7.11 | Examples of stage set design | 276 |
| 8.1 | Traditional tent styles | 281 |
| 8.2 | Hybrid and unique tent styles | 285 |
| 8.3 | Examples of modern tent technology | 287 |
| 8.4 | Tent accessories | 290 |
| 8.5 | Example of a scaled CADD tent site plan | 293 |
| 8.6 | Tented events | 295 |
| 9.1 | Single-phase electrical connections | 305 |
| 9.2 | Typical three-phase power connection and distribution equipment | 307 |
| 9.3 | Examples of ground-supported truss configurations | 311 |
| 9.4 | Glastonbury Festival | 313 |
| 9.5 | Rigged truss lines | 317 |
| 9.6 | Rigging trim heights | 318 |
| 9.7 | Examples of scaffolding structures for events | 323 |
| 9.8 | Examples of fencing and barriers | 325 |

9.9    Simple FOSB configuration                                                         327
9.10   FOSB with finger                                                                327
9.11   Example of cages and wave-breakers                                             328
9.12   Portable toilet requirements for an 8-h event (total attendance up to 30,000)   330
9.13   Portable toilet requirements for an 8-h event (total attendance 30,000 to 100,000) 331

# Tables

| | | |
|---|---|---:|
| 2.1 | Linen sizing chart | 70 |
| 3.1 | Sample of wavelengths at different frequencies | 101 |
| 4.1 | Summary of common projector resolutions | 173 |
| 4.2 | Recommended projector brightness | 174 |
| 5.1 | Interaction of colored light with colored pigment | 199 |

# Preface

This book and its accompanying volume, *Special Event Production: The Process*, were first published in 2008 in response to a need for a compilation of knowledge that could span the gap between information that was too technical and thus suitable only for technicians, and information that was too general to provide enough useful material to make a student "job-ready," or to provide a handy reference for mid-career professionals. By all reports, the books have achieved what was intended of them; in fact they have achieved it internationally.

When Routledge approached me to write revised editions, I quickly realized just how much had changed in not only special events, but also the world in the years since 2006 when I was in the process of writing those original books. Indeed, at that time there were no smartphones or tablets and the mobile environment we take for granted today was still the stuff of science fiction. Climate change and sustainability were barely beginning to be of concern in the planning of events. The digitization of most technical areas of events was starting slowly, but digital audio and lighting consoles were far too expensive for most industry suppliers to acquire. Most video was still on tape and too complex for individuals to edit.

Most of the changes have been positive for the industry. At the same time, though, there have been some rough spots. Competition has increased dramatically. Questionable ethics still abound. Risk management has improved but still not to the level it should be, as witnessed by the far too numerous serious accidents that have occurred around the world at events of all sizes. Last but not least, the very feasibility of many government and corporate events has been called into question because of the lack of perceived return-on-investment, particularly in tight economic times. We as event producers need to be able to defend our purpose and we can only do that by keeping abreast of all changes as they pertain to our industry.

The changes, both the positive and negative ones, were strong enough reasons to make me realize that an update was definitely required. In this second book, *Special Event Production: The Resources*, as before the emphasis is on the technical aspects of event production and those resources that are at the very heart of a successful event. While things have not changed to any great extent in areas such as entertainment, there have been orders of magnitude advances in visual presentation technology such as ultra-high-definition video and projection mapping, LED technology in lighting, mobile applications in everything, and the list goes on. There are no new chapters in this volume, but there are extensive updates to bring all these advances into the knowledge base of producers and would-be producers in specific areas.

As I said in the original versions of the books, they are purposely not intended to duplicate the many excellent references that have already been written about the field of event management and event planning, where details of the basic responsibility areas may be found. Instead, they concentrate solely on event production. They are not entry-level "how-to manuals" for those who are still trying to decide whether this industry is the right career path; they are for those who have already made that decision and are some years along the path. The emphasis in these books is on reality: real-life war stories that prove that even the best producers make mistakes and that is just part of the learning process; real-life production challenges that are intended to place the reader in the position of an actual producer; and a continuous stress throughout on the importance of compliance with safety standards and best practices of risk management. Whenever possible, reference is made to not only North American standards and regulations, but also to those in the United Kingdom (UK), Europe, and Australia, with the occasional reference to those in other countries. Finally, one new feature has been added in every chapter in response to a call for an even greater international flavor to the books, called the "Voice of the Industry." These voices constitute interviews I have conducted with some of the most respected and experienced event producers and specialists in the world, in which they explain and opine about the current and future state of affairs of the industry through their own eyes.

I hope you enjoy the learning experience and continue to invent ever more creative, astounding, and memorable special events.

Doug Matthews
March 2015
Vancouver, Canada

# Acknowledgements

As the second volume in the two-part compilation of knowledge that explains to the world what special event production is all about—the first being *Special Event Production: The Process*—this book required substantial contributions from many sources.

The following people deserve special mention for their assistance in completing this work:

My publisher, Routledge, and in particular Commissioning Editor Emma Travis, and Editorial Assistant Philippa Mullins.

The "Voices of the Industry," special events industry experts who graciously gave of their time to humor me and answer my questions about the state of the industry in their various countries and fields of expertise:

- Ms. Archie Archer, Founder and Managing Director, Contraband International Ltd., London, United Kingdom, www.contrabandevents.com/—Chapter 1;
- Ms. Leslee Bell, Founder and Partner, Décor & More Inc., Toronto and Calgary, Canada, www.decorandmore.com/, and Mr. Martin da Costa, CEO, Seventy Event Media Group, Mumbai and Delhi, India, www.seventyemg.com—Chapter 2;
- Mr. Tim Lang, Vice President, Operations and Finance, Proshow Audiovisual Broadcast, Vancouver and Calgary, Canada, www.proshow.com, and Mr. Bruce Johnston, Director, JPJ Audio Pty Ltd., Sydney and Melbourne, Australia, www.jpjaudio.com.au—Chapter 3;
- Mr. Bryan Campbell, Director of Technology, MJx, the Mills James Experience Group, Columbus, Cincinnati, and Cleveland, Ohio, USA, http://millsjames.com—Chapter 4;
- Mr. Ofer Lapid, Founder and Managing Director, Gearhouse SA (Pty) Ltd., Cape Town, Johannesburg, and Durban, South Africa, www.gearhouse.co.za—Chapter 5;
- Mr. Kelly Guille, President, Archangel Fireworks Inc., Winnipeg, MB, Canada, www.archangelfireworks.com—Chapter 6;
- Mr. Michael Reese, Executive Vice President Creative, Barkley Kalpak Agency, New York, NY, USA, www.bka.net—Chapter 7;
- Mr. Mike Holland (CEO of Chattanooga Tent Company, www.chattanoogatent.com) and Mr. Tom Markel (President of Bravo Events Expos Displays, www.bravoeventrentals.com) on behalf of the Tent Rental Division, Industrial Fabrics Association International (IFAI), Roseville, MN, USA, www.ifai.com—Chapter 8;

- Mendip Dictrict Council (MDC), Licensing Authority for the Glastonbury Festival, Pilton, Somerset, England, www.glastonburyfestivals.co.uk—Chapter 9.

The many contributors of photographs and information from around the globe.

The thousands of students, teachers, and event practitioners worldwide who have purchased the first edition and for those in the future who hopefully will do the same with this edition, thus validating the need for such a body of knowledge in printed form.

My wife, Marimae, for her patience and encouragement.

Thank you.

Chapter **1**

# Entertainment

## LEARNING OUTCOMES

After reading this chapter, you will be able to:

1. Understand and describe the different forms of entertainment.
2. Understand the primary reasons why entertainment is used in special events.
3. Understand what comprises content in entertainment, from both the audience and performer points of view.
4. Describe and analyze what makes a good performance in the five main genres of entertainment.
5. Plan an effective entertainment program.
6. Understand how to work with performers.

*If man is a sapient animal, a tool making animal, a self-making animal, a symbol-using animal, he is, no less, a performing animal, Homo performans, not in the sense, perhaps that a circus animal may be a performing animal, but in the sense that a man is a self-performing animal—his performances are, in a way, reflexive, in performing he reveals himself to himself. This can be in two ways: the actor may come to know himself better through acting or enactment; or one set of human beings may come to know themselves better through observing and/or participating in performances generated and presented by another set of human beings.*

*(Turner, 1988, p. 81)*

This statement by renowned anthropologist Victor Turner succinctly summarizes what special event entertainment is all about: communication. It is about live performers understanding their craft well enough to be able to communicate powerful messages, be they subtle or obvious, to their audiences. The successful delivery of a well-designed entertainment program can evoke strong feelings, emotions, and memories, and can affect many of our senses. Indeed, it is the one part of an event people may remember long after the event is over. In that sense, it is arguably the one resource that can make or break the event.

Although many event producers purport to be experts in the field of entertainment (are we not all critics?), it is a complex field. Our goal in this chapter is to make it easier to understand. In doing so, we will explore: how entertainment is defined; how to effectively stage an entertainment program; and finally, how to work with performers. Along the way, we will delve into physiology, psychology, and creativity. By the end, all the pieces should fit together, making it easier for producers to create, plan, and execute a successful and exciting program, and more than anything, to understand why they are doing it.

## 1.1 Defining entertainment

Properly defining entertainment requires us to understand the whole package, the sum of the various components that go into making up a complete presentation. Any given entertainment, whether a single performer or a multi-act extravaganza, can be fully defined by an analysis of three components or characteristics: form, reason (or "use" by another definition), and content. We will examine each of these defining characteristics separately.

### 1.1.1 Form in entertainment

To really define form, we need to first briefly contemplate the origins of performance. Although it would be nice to have foolproof evidence of the beginnings of human performance, such may never be the case. What we do have, based on current research, is a general knowledge of past eras or time periods during which the archaeological evidence strongly suggests that certain genres of performance were either just beginning or were clearly fully developed.

To start at the true beginning, physiologically, it is not hard to understand that humans were capable of utilizing two basic modes of communication: vocalization and physical movement. These were not always present. It is believed that one of our related ancestors, *Homo heidelbergensis*, had developed a hypoglossal canal of sufficient size and construction to be able to create actual speech by at least 500,000 years ago (Tattersall, 2006).

On the physical side, the best evidence for movement resembling modern humans lies with early footprints found in Laeotoli, Africa, of a much more distant relative, *Australopithecus*, who seemed to walk with a bipedal gait similar to today's version of humans. Those preserved footprints are 3.5 million years old (Feder, 1996).

We now must take a leap of faith based on logic and posit that at some point in the unrecorded distant past, these basic communication skills, vocalization and physical movement, further developed into the beginnings of entertainment, as illustrated in Figure 1.1.

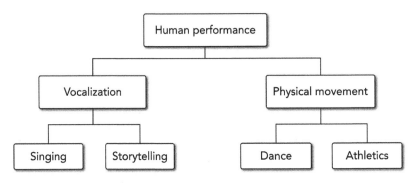

Figure 1.1 Origins of human entertainment

Courtesy of Doug Matthews

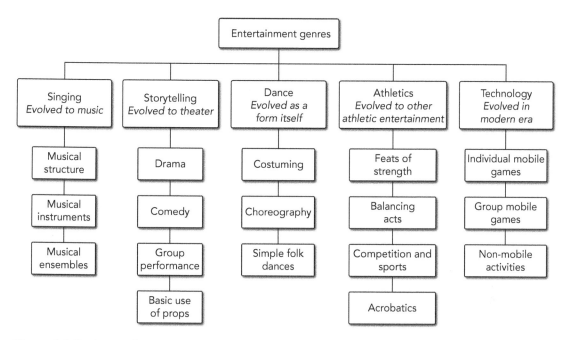

Figure 1.2 Evolution of entertainment genres

Courtesy of Doug Matthews

Whether these all occurred at the same time is both unknown and unlikely; however, we have to start somewhere, and lacking prehistoric archaeological evidence, this is the best place. It is also not illogical to speculate that this process was taken a step further over time, so that each of the basic forms of entertainment in Figure 1.1 probably evolved into the more complex forms outlined in Figure 1.2, to which has also been added technological entertainment from the modern era.

This, then, can be the starting point for defining form in entertainment. Form is actually another word for genre, but with the addition of sub-genres and categories. The use of form helps us understand the makeup of the entertainment itself and allows for ease of cataloguing. The proposed classification system outlined below is not necessarily the only one or the right one, but it is one that allows for easier understanding of how genres are related to each other, and it is the only one that follows most logically from the origins of each form of entertainment.

### 1.1.1.1 Genres and categories

Again, it seems logical to follow the original evolution of entertainment as outlined in Figure 1.2 and base form on that. We thus arrive at the following primary genres and sub-genres:

- Music. Music in general can be considered a primary entertainment genre with sub-genres of vocal and instrumental.
- Theater. Beeman (1993, pp. 381–383), among others, has attempted to codify theater itself into a number of different genres based on the type of media used, the performers, and the content. However, his approach does not look at all entertainment genres together, thus making it difficult to arrive at any sort of common classification. I propose here that theater include the sub-genres of comedy, tragedy, and general speech. This allows for the inclusion of keynote speakers and similar spoken theatrical presentations that we use in special events.

- Dance. Throughout my own experience of working with every type of dance in special events, the sub-genres break down easily into cultural (e.g. folk, ethnic, traditional by other names), ballet, and modern or contemporary (e.g. tap, jazz, hip-hop, ballroom).

- Other athletic entertainment. This primary genre covers all other physical entertainment and includes the two sub-genres of sports and physical entertainment (e.g. acrobats, jugglers, magicians, stunt people, and stilt walkers). It thus includes most modern variety acts.

- Technology. The expanding use of mobile devices plus the development of increasingly sophisticated lighting, touchscreens, visual presentation technology, and music have led to the creation of unique forms of entertainment with technology as the "performer" or "performance medium." See Section 1.1.3.3.5 for more information.

In order to further define any given form of entertainment, we need to add non-performative classifications that allow the form to be specified exactly. These we can term categories, as follows:

- Size. Size places the entertainment form in the context of a group performance. The sub-categories of size are large group (i.e. more than ten), small group (i.e. less than ten), and solo.

- Prop-assisted. This covers a wide range of possibilities and breaks down into sub-categories of large props and small props. Examples could be stilts (i.e. large props) for a stilt walker, balls and knives (i.e. small props) for a juggler, roller blades (i.e. small props) for a roller blade demo team, and even mobile devices such as smartphones or tablets (i.e. small props). It could even include human-controlled electronic or technological displays (e.g. lighting, lasers, music).

### 1.1.1.2 Classifying and cataloguing entertainment forms

Of course, any of the genres, sub-genres, categories, or sub-categories can be combined with any others to arrive at a specific entertainment form. This can work in reverse as well, taking an entertainment form and tracing it back to its primary genre, sub-genres, and categories. Let us look at some examples:

- A juggler. The primary genre is other athletic entertainment, sub-genre physical entertainment, size category solo, and prop-assisted category small props.

- Rock band with a vocalist. The primary genre is music, sub-genres instrumental and vocal, size category small group.

- Musical comedian. This would be a combination primary genre of music with sub-genre instrumental and theater with sub-genre comedy, size category solo.

- A steel drum band accompanying limbo dancers. This would also be a combination of dance as the primary genre with sub-genre cultural and music with sub-genre instrumental, size category small group, and finally prop-assisted category of small props (e.g. the limbo bar).

- A keynote motivational speaker using a laptop computer onstage. The primary genre would be theater, sub-genre general speech, size category solo, prop-assisted category small props.

Using this system, any given entertainment form can be defined and, if need be, catalogued. Many entertainment agencies and event producers use their own system of cataloguing entertainment using slightly more familiar terms, although the end result is still the same. All the acts available somehow need to be catalogued in order to be retrieved easily when needed. Some of the more common categories used by producers and agents are:

- Celebrity talent. This includes nationally and internationally known performers, who can be singers, musicians, comedians, speakers, or any of the other genres.

- Musical variety. This includes comedy music, background music such as instrumentalists and soloists, symphony orchestras, and marching bands.
- Dance bands. This can be everything from duos to big bands.
- Variety. These are the unusual types of entertainers such as jugglers, magicians, ventriloquists, clowns, stilt walkers, and Cirque-type acrobatic acts. Comedians are sometimes categorized with this group.
- Cultural or ethnic. This group includes Native Indian, Asian, Latin, and all other cultural performances that stress heritage.
- Interactive. This covers anything in which the main goal is for people to participate such as virtual reality games, teambuilding activities, table acts (e.g. fortune tellers, caricaturists, handwriting analysts), and strolling acts who interact with people.

Rutherford-Silvers (2012) has an extensive list of entertainment resources, most of which can be categorized according to the genre and category system proposed above.

It is really only by classifying and cataloguing entertainment forms that entertainment as a resource can be useful. Most event producers and entertainment agents have enormous databases of performers of every conceivable form. Without a cataloguing system, easy retrieval is almost impossible, but it is invariably required when an event proposal must be prepared on short notice. Although most producers devise their own system for cataloguing, the genres and categories outlined above may be a good starting point.

As discussed in Chapter 11 of *Special Event Production: The Process*, most producers will probably use a relational database of some sort, either web-based or on their desktop. These programs are very sophisticated and are customizable to suit individual company needs. An alphanumeric cataloguing system of some sort (like any library) can be set up to catalogue entertainment genres for easy retrieval. The system proposed above easily lends itself to that. For example, a dance band with a vocalist might have the initial letters "MIVSS" for "music instrumental and vocal, small group size." After that could come the name of the group (possibly abbreviated) and/or a number that might indicate the date they were posted in the database. A combination entertainment form may have two or more catalogue numbers to allow them to be part of different lists. This is useful when, say, a comedy act is also a musical act, and both may be called upon for different events, so they need to be listed as both genres. These are only very rough examples but the concept is that a catalogue number is what permits easy retrieval using the search function of the database program. Of course, other necessary information for the performers must be included, such as contact information (e.g. name, phone, email, and address) and details of the act itself (e.g. what it includes, length of normal show, standard cost, rider requirements, and promotional material). Considering that this is at the heart of what makes entertainment resources effective, it is well worth spending time to develop an effective system.

## 1.1.2 Reasons for entertainment

The reason for any given entertainment concerns the overall message delivered by a performance. It is the "why" question answered. The performance must satisfy the audience and client and deliver the promised results based on the original reason for the entertainment. For special event production purposes, the audience's interests are usually represented by a single person (e.g. a client or event manager) or a small number of persons (e.g. an organizing committee) during the planning process, and it is this person or these persons who must articulate the reason for the entertainment to the producer. Here, then, are the main reasons we produce entertainment shows for special events:

### 1.1.2.1 Education

A powerful reason is the imparting of knowledge to an audience; it may be based entirely on learning or may be a small part of a larger show with multiple goals. Here are some typical examples that have proven successful in my own and my colleagues' experiences:

- Scripted show. This occurs when entertainment is used with the main goal of providing—or helping to provide—knowledge to the audience. I have done this for a scripted variety show format in which we created a show that told part of the history of Canada through segments that incorporated singing, dancing, comedy, and acting, thus telling the audience in an interesting way about the country's history. Another way is to partially script a show to augment a corporate presentation and to thereby explain more about the company goals, such as for a sales meeting, or for the explanation of a complicated concept. I have done this through the use of improvisational comedians who performed semi-scripted, humorous problem scenarios for an audience of financial planners who then had to workshop solutions for the scenarios presented. To do this successfully requires a talented scriptwriter and quite likely a good theatrical director as well, so it may not come cheap.

- Existing act. Knowledge may also be imparted through the inclusion of performers who use education as part of their act, such as cultural dance groups who explain the origins of their dances (e.g. Chinese, Native American, African), storytellers, or handwriting analysts (personal knowledge), among many. My company frequently used a world champion gold panner who would not only teach guests how to gold pan, but would also teach the history of gold panning and gold rushes while they were doing it.

### 1.1.2.2 Physically moving people

There is no more impressive method of physically moving crowds than to have them follow highly visual and loud performers. Using a marching band or other noisy entertainment to lead people can save considerable time, especially with a large audience, and can be a nice segue from a reception to dinner or between event segments. In my career I have used marching bands, Swiss alpine horns, drum groups, color guards, cowboys on horses, fanfare trumpets, a town crier, stilt walkers, a Chinese lion, Dixieland bands, dancers of various types, clowns, old cars, and more I can't remember. In almost all cases, guests automatically followed the entertainment without having to be told what to do, thus making my job as a producer a little easier (not to mention negating the need for a costly add-on audio system in a remote location).

Following musical performers or noisy acts is not the only way to move people. Also possible is creative hosting. For example, we once designed an Evening in Paris night for an important client at which we used a dozen male and a dozen female dancers dressed in traditional French attire and all very outgoing. They greeted and cheered guests as they arrived and individually escorted each guest to their table, then appeared later to perform a can-can dance routine after which they went into the room full of seated guests to bring them up to the dance floor. Don't forget that these are all just different ways to create that *"experiential event"* that has become popular, as described in Chapter 2 of *Special Event Production: The Process*.

### 1.1.2.3 Emotionally moving people

Psychologists define the primary emotions as fear, anger, sadness, joy, surprise, disgust, and contempt. An emotion is considered a response to stimuli that involves characteristic physiological changes—such as increase in pulse rate, rise in body temperature, greater or less activity of certain glands, change in the rate of breathing—and tends in itself to motivate the individual toward further activity (Emotion, 2004). People tend to confuse emotions with feelings and even psychologists are not united in definitions: "By one estimate, more than 90 definitions of 'emotion' were proposed over the course of the 20th century" (Plutchik, 2001, p. 344). For simplification, we will assume that emotions are the primary ones stated above and feelings are what emanate from these. For example, one might feel guilty about not contributing to a charity for starving children as a result of watching a movie that stirs the emotion of anger in the observer because so much food is being wasted due to corruption in poor countries. One might feel exhilarated and proud because of the emotion of joy experienced when hearing one's national anthem played as an Olympic champion stands on the podium. Any performance that is able to trigger strong emotions and subsequent feelings, to stir the audience inside, will be memorable, no matter what the performance genre (e.g. music, dance, comedy, acting). Emotional content is a direct reflection of the skill of the performers in choosing appropriate material, combined with their abilities to deliver it. We will explore this in depth in the next section.

I was once given the task of providing after-dinner entertainment for a black-tie gala of a national association. The organizer and her committee were not too happy with my suggestion of a harmonica player as they thought it was not befitting the occasion; however, because they were longstanding clients, they allowed me to proceed. The show went very well and after it, several people came up to me and thanked me profusely because they were moved to tears by the performance, which had managed to hit them deep inside. The choice of performer was purposeful, in that he had a tremendous ability to deliver emotionally charged songs (his own) that I knew would work. He was also adept at playing over 20 different mouth instruments and had won numerous awards.

### 1.1.2.4 Motivating and inspiring people

Motivating an audience is distinctly different from emotionally moving them, although they will undoubtedly experience some strong feelings when being motivated. As opposed to only trying to stir inner feelings, motivation's goal is to give the audience a reason to take some action. This might be to buy a product, to improve one's life, to become closer to God, to work harder, to give to charity, to sell more cars, or a host of other reasons. Motivational entertainment takes emotional performances and adds a specific message and call to action. For example, if one is producing a fundraising event for special needs children, the entertainment might incorporate a moving song performed live by an onstage celebrity with video clips of the special needs kids in the background. At the end, a request is made for donations. For more excellent examples of this type of persuasive entertainment, one only has to watch the many charity telethons that raise millions of dollars annually. Almost any form of entertainment can achieve motivation if the content and timing are correct. Other examples of when it might be used are for incentive groups and teambuilding activities (e.g. with drum circles), for sporting events (e.g. with cheerleaders or loud rock music), and for conference opening and closing sessions (e.g. with motivational speakers). Inspirational entertainment differs from motivational entertainment primarily by the fact that there is not necessarily any call to action, only a general uplifting of the spirit.

### 1.1.2.5 Decoration

A novel and frequent use of entertainment in events is as decoration. The performer(s) take on the persona of decorations that can be either stationary or moving, interactive or inactive. Costumed living statues, interactive entertainers (e.g. stilt walkers, mimes, dancers, and others in themed costumes who move amongst guests anywhere but on a stage), and look-alikes are typical of decorative entertainment.

My company produced many events using this form of entertainment. At some, we placed dancers in spotlighted statuesque poses amongst tables as guests entered an event space. Once all were seated, the

Figure 1.3 Example of strolling performers as decoration

Courtesy of Designs by Sean, www.designsbysean.com

dancers then gradually came out of their poses and began an introductory dance routine. At another beach party event, we actually hired bodybuilders to pose and lift weights as if on "Muscle Beach." Many examples exist of this type of reason for entertainment. See also Section 2.2.7 of Chapter 2, and Figure 1.3.

### 1.1.2.6 Announcing, introducing, or advertising

For this use, performers may announce, introduce, and advertise people, products, services, and activities. These reasons are lumped together because the concept for each is similar. Some examples best illustrate this concept:

- Celebrities as masters of ceremonies.
- Herald trumpets to sound a call to dinner, to introduce another segment in an event, or to draw attention to a speaker.
- A personalized video greeting from a celebrity as part of a product introduction.
- Strolling robots used at a trade show to draw attention to a particular booth or product.
- A magical reveal created by a magician for introducing a product or person.
- Fireworks at midnight used to introduce the New Year.

Perhaps the best results occur when producers get creative with off-the-wall concepts. Here are some examples from my own personal experience, and hundreds more are being devised by many of today's event companies:

- We once introduced a new Vancouver to Boston airline service by photographing a Paul Revere character riding a horse in front of a taxiing 747 while holding a huge banner announcing the service.

- One of our clients (a gas company) made the front page of the local newspaper when we dressed up two actors as a new baby and Father Time and had them lighting a giant 15 ft tall gas torch like an Olympic flame (it was an Olympic year), just before New Year's.
- For the introduction of a simulator computer game near Christmas one year, we provided about a dozen Santa Clauses all playing the game at a bank of computers, an advertising gimmick that successfully drew a lot of attention and garnered press coverage.
- A new dollar coin was introduced using an 18 ft diameter helium flying saucer inside a convention center ballroom that made a surprise entry flying over the heads of assembled guests and dropping a giant replica of the coin onstage to a VIP speaker who proceeded to make a speech about the occasion.

### 1.1.2.7 Creating ambience

Particularly in theme events, establishing the right ambience for the event is one of the first considerations producers have. The ambience can be so much more than static décor or lighting, even if the lighting is automated. Adding other sensory input in the form of live entertainment helps to set a living mood. This can be done for any number of reasons, such as providing an atmosphere for easy discussion, for conducting business, or for relaxing. The proper choice of music can accomplish this with perhaps a jazz trio that enables unstrained conversation. As a side note, the importance of establishing and maintaining this relatively quiet ambience should not be passed over lightly. At far too many special events, the background noise level is excessively high, caused by poor room acoustics but exacerbated by music that is supposed to be background but is too loud. Some event managers tend to believe that volume equates to having a good time which in turn equates to a successful event and they could not be more wrong. In the majority of corporate events, guests attend because they want to dialogue with long-lost colleagues, and in many such events, to consummate business deals. This cannot be done if talking is uncomfortable.

At the other extreme, atmosphere can be high energy. For example, a group of paparazzi greeting guests at the event entrance sets a lively ambience. One prime example from my own experience was adding to a beach party ambience by having a surf band enter the party in an authentic "Woodie" complete with honking horn, surfboards, and girls in bikinis.

### 1.1.2.8 Rewarding performance and for image purposes

Frequently, producers are called upon by clients to "just give me something really good." This would seem to yield the conclusion that not all entertainment needs to have a deep reason. Realistically, there usually is one if the event manager or client is asked the right questions. For example, an incentive client may make just that statement, although the real reason for the entertainment is as a reward for top sales people (i.e. meaning motivational content). Likewise, a client may not state a reason but in reality wants to impress his or her clients by providing great entertainment.

If budget presents a problem, producers may have to find performers or perhaps a single act, who can deliver an all-round package at a reasonable price. Such performers tend to exhibit three key characteristics. First, they are absolutely perfect at their craft (entertainment form) whether it is music, comedy, dance, athletics, or any combination. Second, they incorporate a component of comedy into their act and make it seem natural and spontaneous, not forced. Typically, though, it has been rehearsed, proven, and refined over the course of time. Third, they incorporate a component of audience participation into their act, again making it seem unrehearsed and spontaneous, and again it will have been proven to work over the course of dozens or hundreds of performances. Such acts, in my experience, regularly receive standing ovations and make producers and clients look good.

Celebrity performers can also be ideal as rewards or as image enhancers, especially for a corporate image. For clients with good budgets, this is undeniably the best way to gain prestige.

Once the reasons for entertainment are known, as expressed by the client, it is time to turn attention to the chosen performers and allow them to develop the content necessary to achieve the goals set by the client and producer.

### 1.1.3 Content in entertainment

Content is the last of the three characteristics (form, reason, content) that define entertainment.

Beeman (2002) states,

> *performance is the means—perhaps the principal means—through which people come to under-stand their world, reinforce their view of it and transform it on both small scale and large scale. It can be employed for conservative and for revolutionary uses. As a conservative force, it reinforces the truth of the world and enacts and verifies social order . . . As a transformational force, performance behavior has the power to restructure social order through the persuasive power of rhetoric, and through the power of redefinition of both audience and context.*

What he is saying is that it is content that drives the success of the performance.

It is in the content of entertainment programs that special events—particularly private corporate events—and the relationship of performer(s) to audience differ from most other platforms for performers (e.g. concerts, TV). First, in many cases, performances are restricted to short segments for any individual performers or acts, often 15 min or less, necessitating an informed selection of material on the part of the performer(s) that will provide the desired content and will meet the goals of the client. Second, audiences are captive in that they have paid for their attendance at the event, the primary purpose of which may very well not be to observe entertainment. Third, they are watching the performances with no prior knowledge of the performers or content and have not had any previous opportunities for evaluation (i.e. they must rely on the skills of the main client or event producer to make informed choices on their behalf). Fourth, audiences have often been subjected, in a positive or negative manner, to lengthy proceedings prior to the entertainment program, including the use of alcohol, which can inhibit their objective appreciation of the performance. Finally, the performance setting in terms of acoustics, visibility for all audience members, staging, rehearsal opportunities, and timing is not always as ideal as in other platforms for performers, which can, in turn, place undue stress on the performers. It is under these constraints that performers must operate with their advertised and expected skill and aplomb.

Success all boils down to this. The performer must deliver the expected content to an audience that is presumably untrained in the art form, under the constraints explained above. Whether this is achievable will depend on the choice of material and the manner in which it is delivered. It is the producer's job to act on behalf of the client to ensure that this is done effectively. Therefore, it behooves the producer to understand what makes a good or bad performance, to become in essence an entertainment critic. We begin by trying to "get into the head" of a performer, looking at why one would choose this profession, and then looking at the general ways that performers connect with audiences. We finish this section by actually becoming performance critics and analyzing what makes a good performance in the different genres.

### 1.1.3.1 Why performers perform

Loosely interpreting the pioneering work of Turner (1988) and later of Schechner (2002), performance in complex societies is a three-phase process consisting of a rehearsal period (*proto-performance*, from Schechner), a performance period, and a cooling-down or post-performance period (*aftermath*, from Schechner). These periods form the core of performers' existences, and although they move occasionally outside the phases, they inhabit them most of the time if performing is their chosen profession. It is a lonely place to be, especially during the rehearsal period, a place where the only feedback may be a mirror, a director's or choreographer's comments, the playing back of a recorded song, or a spouse's friendly encouragement. Validation comes with group rehearsals and eventually from a real audience. Why, then, would anyone choose such an existence? There are several reasons:

- To enter *flow*. Czikszentmihalyi (1974, pp. 35–36) and later Turner (1988, p. 54) are credited with bringing the term flow into the lexicon of psychology. Flow refers to "an interior state which can be described as the merging of action and awareness, the holistic sensation present when we act with total involvement, a state in which action follows action according to an internal logic, with no apparent need for conscious intervention on our part." Most performers at some point in their careers will experience this. If they are highly trained, it will undoubtedly occur on a regular basis. For the performer, it is a very desirable mental state, somewhat metaphysical and even transcendental. For them, it is a feeling of wanting to remain in the moment. It happens particularly with group performances and only when members are completely in synch and performing together, each sensing what the others are doing as if they were a single, totally blended unit. It does not happen for every performance and it does not necessarily happen for an entire performance. When it does, however, it is magical for the performer.

- To connect with the audience. Connecting with an audience is the ultimate validation for their existence that performers seek. It means that first, the audience has indeed received the message, and second, the art form and method of delivery are appreciated. Most of the time, this will be either sensed by, or obvious to, the performers (e.g. through the audience's rapt attention or applause/laughter at appropriate times). Of course, negative connection is also possible and if it is obvious to them, the performer must make immediate changes to try to re-establish a positive connection.

- To receive recognition. What better job satisfaction can there be than the instantaneous gratification obtained by sustained applause or a standing ovation? For performers, this beats the endless pushing of paper in an office, the constant struggle to climb the corporate ladder, and the frustrations of company personality clashes. The occasional accolade letter or annual corporate personnel reviews do not come close to the ecstatic screams of an adoring audience. Why else would aging rockers like the Rolling Stones still be performing after 50 years? They certainly do not need the money!

- To receive remuneration. Unfortunately, performers have to live and, unlike the Rolling Stones, most of those who work in special events are not highly paid, contrary to the opinion of some uninformed clients and the general public. While the psychology of performing may be their main reason for choosing this career path, they do need to be compensated for doing it.

### 1.1.3.2 Connecting with the audience

Beeman's statement about performance being the means "through which people come to understand . . . and transform [their world]" (Beeman, 2002) can only happen if the performer can connect with the audience. Although performance strategies vary amongst genres and amongst individual performers, there appears to be a more or less universal set of criteria that combine to define the skill set necessary for an effective performance: charisma or stage presence, technical proficiency, and choice and interpretation of material. We will explain these in detail.

#### 1.1.3.2.1 CHARISMA

Webster's dictionary defines charisma as "a special charm or allure that inspires fascination or devotion." Beeman (2002) suggests it is "the ability to engage and hold the attention of an audience." In other words, it is stage presence. It is not necessarily a gift performers are born with, but more often a skill that must be nurtured and developed. How, then, can good stage presence be achieved? Most top performers with charisma use one or more of the following techniques. For simplicity, we will use a single performer for explanations but the same information applies to group performances.

- Placement. Being close to the front edge of the stage (*downstage*) brings the performer into a seemingly more intimate relationship with the audience. Likewise, working the entire downstage area including both corners ensures that as much of the audience will be brought into this relationship as possible.

- Eye contact. Periodic direct eye contact with audience members is considered very positive and enhances the feeling of intimacy. Again, this should not always be front and center but vary from side to side as well. Done too much, however, eye contact can get distracting, so the default look should be slightly over the heads of the audience.

- Facial expressions. This is one of the more difficult skills to master for good stage presence. Basically, the facial expression of a performer should mirror the material that is being performed: sad song = sad expression, upbeat song = smile, and so on. Of course, in comedy this theory falls apart as it is often the incongruity of mixed emotions that wins the laugh. However, even in this situation it is necessary to master the correct expression (think the exaggeration of Jim Carrey). Usually the expression of choice is the smile, especially in special events where the audience must almost always leave with a feeling of having had a good time.

- Costuming. No matter what the circumstances of the performance, good costuming is essential in helping to establish a professional look. Too often this is the last thing that performers—and producers—think about. Even if the trite, all-black ensemble must be used, it should be made clear to performers that shoes must be polished, dresses and pants must be pressed, and everything must be immaculately clean. Costuming is all about first impressions, just as it is in job interviews, and poor costuming onstage is magnified a hundred-fold thanks to lighting and the fact that the performer is the focus of all attention. If possible, something bright, unusual, or attention-grabbing should be used rather than black, within the bounds of good taste dictated by the event. Liberace, Michael Jackson, Elton John, Cher, Prince, Madonna, Kiss, Empire of the Sun, Katy Perry, Lady Gaga, and many others were and are masters of this aspect of performing.

- Interaction with other performers. In some situations that do not include group interaction as a choreographed or rehearsed part of the performance, onstage performer interaction can signal to the audience that the performers are having a good time and help to transfer that feeling to the audience. Examples might be when two guest singers work spontaneously together or when musical band members interact.

- Audience participation. This is one of the most powerful and effective ways to gain audience support and enhance charisma. It is not, however, only a simple matter of asking the audience "how they are doing." The more rehearsed and controlled the situation, the more effective it will be. Participation can take place in the audience (i.e. offstage) or it can take place on the stage. By going into the audience, a performer is in the audience's territory and had better be well prepared for anything that may happen. Therefore, for this type of situation, all circumstances should be covered. That means that a set routine should be rehearsed (e.g. exact dialogue and participation actions), with escape plans for any eventuality, be it vocal inappropriateness (e.g. audience member swearing at the performer or no reaction at all), or physical abuse (e.g. audience member grabbing or touching the performer inappropriately). Proper technical preparation must be in place as well (e.g. adequate audio and lighting). Just "winging it" when a performer is in the audience makes the performance appear amateurish.

  Audience participation onstage brings the audience into the performer's territory and puts the performer more in control of the situation, although removing some of the intimacy of direct contact with a larger portion of the audience. Onstage participation can take several forms: rehearsed, unrehearsed, controlled, and uncontrolled. Once again, the more rehearsed and controlled, generally the better will be the performance. By rehearsed is meant that the routine is tested and perfected over the course of many performances (including all jokes, questions, and dialogue) so that the outcome is more or less standard, thus defining what may be considered a controlled situation. This type of routine might include anything from a set of questions and answers between performer and audience members (still in their seats) to an entire onstage performance by a group of audience members (e.g. dance number, hypnotism show, victims of a pickpocket, ventriloquist's dummy). At the other extreme is the completely unrehearsed and uncontrolled situation. Someone is invited to the stage to sing a song or to be interviewed by the performer. Because the routine has not been rehearsed and never been done before, or perhaps tried once successfully (without rehearsal), the performer assumes that it will be successful again. Unfortunately, human nature often turns ordinary people into caricatures once they get on a stage and they suddenly want to take over a microphone or act up for their friends (one of the basic rules of performing is never give the microphone to someone else unless it is rehearsed). This is not a situation that engenders a performer to the audience, but rather it makes the performer look even more inexperienced. I once employed a celebrity performer before he became famous who thought it would be a good idea to invite a friendly guest to the stage. The guest was drunk and refused to leave the stage, resulting in our having to find several very burly guests to remove him physically from the stage. It was embarrassing for the performer and undoubtedly became a valuable lesson for him on his road to the top.

See Figure 1.4 for an example of good audience interaction, people cheering at an open-air concert at the Usadba Jazz Festival in Moscow.

Figure 1.4 Connecting with the audience

Copyright: dacosta/123RF Stock Photo

### 1.1.3.2.2 TECHNICAL PROFICIENCY

We will deal with this aspect of performing in much more detail in Section 1.3.3. when we analyze the different entertainment genres. However, let us look here at some of the universal considerations for technical proficiency. To some extent, technical proficiency is a reflection of the audience's knowledge of the genre. If a violin virtuoso is hired for a corporate dinner, will the audience appreciate the performer's virtuosity because of only the performance or because of the association of the performance with the name of the performer? Will a performance by a Beatles clone band receive a standing ovation only because of the perfect delivery of the material or because of the stage presence of the performers and the fact that everyone in the audience likes Beatles songs? These are difficult questions to answer, and the results are never consistent. Perhaps rather than trying to analyze what makes a technically proficient performance, it is easier to analyze the universal difficulties encountered by performers in striving to achieve proficiency, as postulated by Beeman (2002).

- Pushing. This is the obvious effort shown in the interpretation of symbolic materials. This effort can be seen by the audience and can distract them from finding the message of the performance. An example might be the exaggerated facial expression and body movements of a singer trying to interpret a love song, or a jazz musician trying too hard to impress by overplaying.

- Losing concentration. If the performer is not totally engaged with the task of performing, it can also provide a distraction. Examples here might include the distracting glances of dancers at each other that are not part of a performance, unnecessary dialogue between band members, or inappropriate facial expressions as part of the material presented.

- Underpreparation. The lack of adequate preparation and rehearsal makes it impossible to present material in a smooth and spontaneous way. This is usually obvious and takes the form of forgotten lines in scripts, incorrect dance moves, wrong notes in music, and such.

- Overpreparation. Similarly, too much rehearsal or preparation de-humanizes the performance, and makes it less believable. Many seasoned performers believe that once they stop feeling the butterflies and nervousness before a performance, they will no longer be good at their craft. There is some truth to this in that experienced performers can sometimes appear to be performing by rote and without feeling.

### 1.1.3.2.3 CHOICE AND INTERPRETATION OF MATERIAL

How well material for a show is chosen and interpreted will be partly determined by how successfully the producer has conveyed to the performer the goals of the event—especially the message to be delivered (see Chapter 2 of *Special Event Production: The Process*)—and the demographics of the audience. At one end of the spectrum, as noted by Beeman (2002),

> *the performance may fail due to miscalculation of context, resulting from several causes. The performer may misread the audience, and present something that they already know and will be bored with, or that is so esoteric that they cannot comprehend it. Another possibility is presenting offensive material, or material that is insulting to persons of importance. The performer may also misread the circumstances of the performance and present material that is inappropriate, although the same material might be effective on other occasions [e.g. off-color comedy that works in a club but not in a corporate environment—author].*

At the other extreme, the successful choice and interpretation of material may lead the audience to mutually share the experience of flow that the performer is feeling. This is the ideal situation and it often results in the standing ovation so sought by performers. An audience member might experience this physically as a lump in the throat or a shiver down the spine, both indications that the performance has touched very deep emotions and feelings.

Armed with adequate knowledge of the event and the audience, the performer can make informed decisions on content and interpretation based on several considerations:

- Relationship of the material to audience demographics. Demographics, of course, refer to age, sex, language, occupation, and special interests. Appealing to only one or two aspects of demographics rather than their totality can mean choosing incorrect material. For example, assuming that anyone over 50 only likes big band era music is an incorrect assumption because that demographic grew up in the rock and roll era. Assuming that because another culture may not be as demonstrative as North Americans they will not like audience participation is incorrect because they may enjoy it as much as anyone. It helps in this regard to determine what sort of entertainment has worked for a particular audience in the past so that this can be integrated with knowledge of their demographics.

- Relationship of the material to the reasons for the event and the message to be delivered. Although this may seem obvious, it is not. Often, a client may tell a producer that they only want a great show. It may be necessary to read between the lines of this statement. It may mean that because the event is an incentive for sales persons, there should be some subtle inclusion of the company products in the show. Perhaps it becomes a customization of comedy material, a slight changing of song lyrics or the dedication of a song to the company president, or a small sign, logo, or corporate colors that become part of an act. This simple gesture of going beyond expectations can turn the show into a success, based purely on a knowledgeable interpretation of the event's goals.

- Universality of material. If evoking emotions is desired, nothing does it better than using subject matter that has universal appeal. This includes good versus evil, family values, love and honesty, striving to improve, and patriotism. Music or stories with any of these as their main theme will almost always be greeted with positive audience reaction. For example, a performance my company once gave for Canadian troops serving the United Nations in Cambodia climaxed with a series of patriotic songs that turned the audience into a screaming and ecstatic mass of fans totally at one with the performers.

- Suitability for the genre. This essentially means that a performer should exercise caution if choosing material that may cross genres. For example, if a popular song evokes memories of teen love, will a satirical, comedic form of the same song be successful? Can dance be turned into theater, can dramatic theater be turned into physical comedy, can serious subject matter be made humorous, and so on? Examples of this include: *West Side Story*, a Broadway musical form of Shakespeare's *Romeo and Juliet*; *Wicked*, a Broadway musical about the witches of Oz; and *Life is Beautiful*, an Oscar-winning film that played the holocaust for laughs.

- External enhancement of the performance. Any performance can usually be enhanced by technical wizardry. Proper lighting cues (e.g. fading stage lights to black after a routine or performance segment and waiting exactly the right amount of time before fading back up), proper audio (e.g. using the correct microphones and speaker placement), special effects (e.g. pyrotechnics, confetti cannons, fire, performer-controlled lasers), or augmenting the show with dramatic visuals on large screens can add to the effectiveness of the performance. Experienced performers know this and usually have certain audio and lighting requirements for their shows. For those who do not, a producer should consider adding them to a show whenever possible. Figure 1.5 illustrates a performer interacting with laser beams.

- Interpretation. Also sometimes considered as the style of the performer, this involves many factors and its success is often governed by the audience's personal tastes. Successful interpretation usually means that the audience empathizes with the performer or performance situation. Zillman (2006b, p. 154) states, "With regard to the type of presentation, it seems likely that the effective impact on an observer increases with the fidelity of the portrayal of the circumstances that foster emotion in a model." In other words, the more realistic the performance, the more an audience will empathize and so take on the same emotions as the performer. A life story dramatically told, a piece of music played from the heart with a story that the audience relates to (e.g. teenage angst), a dance with a story line using a protagonist and

Figure 1.5 Extreme beam

Courtesy of T. Skorman Productions, Inc.

antagonist, will all bring the audience to more strongly empathize. Timing also plays a role in interpretation. Beeman (2002, p. 90) defines it as "the ability to display symbolic elements precisely at a time when they will most effectively convey an intended meaning." This can mean minutely pushing (i.e. coming in a fraction of a second early) or holding back (i.e. coming in a fraction of a second late) on such things as musical phrasing, dance moves, or dramatic statements, or even the very slightest but subtle change in facial expression. Finally, freshness and spontaneity or the ability to "display symbolic materials in novel and unexpected ways" as Beeman (2002, p. 90) says, are additional means by which the audience's attention may be captured. Playing a song in a style not used before (e.g. turning a ballad into an upbeat reggae piece) or creating a musical about the tearing down of the Berlin Wall are two examples of such new approaches.

### 1.1.3.3 Analyzing performance

Before performers are chosen for special event entertainment, someone must decide which act is right for the particular event (i.e. it matches the reasons and goals for the event, the audience demographics, etc.). This task invariably falls to the event producer who must make an informed decision about the quality and value of the act and their ability to deliver on advertised promises. The key phrase here is "informed decision." This means that the producer must understand what makes a good or bad performance and further extrapolate that performance into a successful—perhaps modified—performance for the special event being planned. It has been my experience that although many producers come from entertainment backgrounds, many do not, and as a group, producers are ill-informed and under-educated about what constitutes a good or bad performance in entertainment of all genres. It is hoped that this section will help to ameliorate this situation, albeit even if only in a small way. In Figure 1.2 we postulated that entertainment has evolved into four main forms, namely music, theater, dance, and other athletic performance, plus more recently technology as performance. Now we must become critics of these forms and learn how to properly analyze performance within each one.

## 1.1.3.3.1 MUSIC

At the risk of oversimplifying a complex subject, we will attempt to review the most important aspects of musical performance as they pertain to special events. These can loosely be divided into technique, psychology, and presentation:

- Technique. Whether vocal or instrumental, good technique is necessary for good performance. Music schools and competitions abound that critique technique, but not too many producers are aware of it. Here is a list of the important evaluation criteria:
  - Pitch and harmony. For instrumentalists, this begins with a well-tuned instrument. For vocalists, it refers to their vocal range (typically soprano and alto for females, and tenor, baritone, and bass for males), and whether they can move effortlessly though their range. It further refers to the ability of the musician or vocalist to hit the correct notes within musical phrases without wavering to one side or the other of the target note's pitch. For vocalists, the ability to harmonize or correctly sing different notes of a chord when in a group situation is essential to a smooth-sounding performance. Note that this analysis refers to our Western major and minor scales and not to the many other scales with differing intervals that exist in other cultures.
  - Rhythm and tempo. This refers to the appropriateness of the rhythmic interpretation of the piece, and how well the musician, group, or vocalist sustains the rhythm through complex passages. For example, if it is a samba, can the group and vocalist keep to the rhythm even when the words to the song get complicated and may not be right on the beat? Tempo refers to the ability of the musicians and vocalists to keep time. In other words, do they speed up or slow down when playing or singing, rather than maintaining constant timing?
  - Dynamics. Dynamics means relative loudness. Good technique is reflected in a wide range of dynamics from very soft to very loud, which leads to an improved interpretation of the music.
  - Tone quality. By tone is meant the clarity and quality of an instrument's sound or the quality of a voice. Good tone is generally smooth throughout an instrument's or a voice's entire range with no harshness anywhere. For vocalists, this can also be affected by the type of resonance used (i.e. does the voice seem to come from the head, chest, or throat and which is most effective?).
  - Practical technique. For musicians, this refers to manual dexterity and flexibility and how well difficult passages appear to be played. If they are played with ease, then dexterity is good. For vocalists, practical technique also involves proper breath control and diction. For proper breath control, the vocalist uses the abdominal muscles and diaphragm to control breath and push out air from the very bottom of the lungs rather than using the throat muscles and only the top part of the lungs. Proper diction means that the words to a song are clear and easily understandable. If they are not, poor diction is likely the cause (in spite of some vocalists claiming that the audio system is to blame). Jones (2001) has a good review of damaging vocal techniques for those interested.

- Style. Style refers to the style of music and how well a musician or vocalist can consistently interpret it. For example, can they give a consistent and non-mechanical rendition of New Orleans jazz, reggae, country and western, baroque, big band, rock, or other styles? Not all professional musicians can effectively interpret all styles of music equally. More importantly, interpretation in the case of vocalists refers to their sensitivity to the words.

- Psychology. It is well known that music profoundly affects human beings on a deep, emotional level. How it does this is studied in the vast field of music psychology. We will be limiting discussion to only a few pertinent concepts that may help in the analysis of musical performance at special events:

  - Sonic entrainment. Goldman (2000, p. 218) explains entrainment as "an aspect of sound that is closely related to rhythms and the way these rhythms affect us. It is a phenomenon of sound in which the powerful rhythmic vibrations of one object [e.g. a dance band—author] will cause the less powerful vibrations of another object [e.g. an audience member—author] to lock in step and oscillate at the first object's rate." Furthermore, within our own bodies, "our heart rate, respiration and brain waves all entrain to each other." To make a long story short, it is possible, although not proven conclusively through rigorous scientific research, that playing music at certain frequencies may induce entrainment of an audience's brain waves. In other words, the comment that "this music is hypnotic" may not be far from the truth. It is also a plausible—but not completely proven—explanation for the popularity of music with a particularly good beat (e.g. techno dance music, rap, reggae, etc.). Musical performers who understand this concept can construct their programs to take advantage of it (e.g. techno dance music with the same rhythm or heavy beat). One very popular example of sonic entrainment at work is a participative drum circle.

  - Excitation transfer. As postulated by Zillman (2006a, pp. 222–223), this concept basically translates into the fact that there is residual excitation created whenever a realistic portrayal or situation occurs that generates an arousing emotional response in an audience. Although studies have been done mostly for cinematic presentations, it is not unreasonable to make a logical leap to music and theatrical drama or comedy. Some examples that have been found by Zillman are that residual arousal from scenes of distress can facilitate subsequent sexual excitement, and residue from fearful scenes can intensify feelings of sympathy and support. Transferring this to music could lead to residual strong emotions after a powerful song about death which in turn could heighten the effect of a subsequent song that might be about love, or an upbeat rock song. Generally, excitation transfer is best the closer together the two scenes, or supposedly in the case of music, the songs. In other words, the more unarousing the songs that are placed in between the emotionally strong ones, the less will be the residual effect. In summary, it is best to keep music strongly emotional and the stronger are the emotions generated, the closer together the music should be for maximum effect.

  - Tonal sensitivity. Campbell (2000, p. 91) uses this term when he states, "With the introduction of electronic sounds, our tonal sensitivity is evolving. We are learning not to judge new sounds as evil and uncharged." In the same article, he also makes the point that other cultures such as Chinese, Indian, and Balinese have music that uses quartertones and microtones (i.e. sounds that are not in our Western scale and which our Western ears are unaccustomed to hearing), and that these have been entering Western music for the last few decades. In short, with new cross-cultural music and new electronic music, we had better be aware of these new sounds and learn to adapt to them. Astute musicians are already creating new music with them. Thus, producers should be aware of such new sounds and not be too quick to judge them as inappropriate for events or simply as poor musicianship.

- Presentation. Our earlier discussion of charisma did not fully explore the totality of musical presentation, especially in a group situation. For musical groups used in special events, there are other criteria to consider. Here are some pertinent questions:

  - Is the group one that relies on reading music (e.g. a symphony orchestra)? If not, as in the case of a dance band, is the group *off-book*? In other words, have they committed their entire stage presentation musical repertoire to memory? Usually, the best dance bands for special events will have been together long enough to have done this. It makes for a more professional, spontaneous presentation and removes unsightly music stands from the stage. It also enables the group to make sudden changes to their set lists without any problems. In addition, all vocalists must know their material by memory.

- Is the group capable of moving directly from one song into the next (with no pauses) in a logical sequence that builds to a climax at the end of their set or program? This is in keeping with our previous discussion about excitation transfer and sonic entrainment.

- Does the group or musical show successfully set up an inviting and exciting environment around them or in the total event space? An exciting environment means that they themselves, rather than the producer, have considered costumes, staging, backdrops and room décor, audio, specialized lighting, special effects, and choreography.

- Is the group capable of changing direction in their material based on audience reaction? As a simple example, if nobody is dancing to a band, can they switch gears and play slower or faster music?

- Do all members of the group buy into the show? In other words, are they all smiling—or frowning—at the same time, do they all project charisma, do they all make coordinated moves, do they know exactly when and where to play for solos or group parts, and are they obviously having fun? If any of these things are absent, they may have to change members, rehearse more, or reconsider their approach to the show.

### 1.1.3.3.2 THEATER

In this section, we are concerned with dramatic acting, comedy, and speaking (e.g. keynote speakers), as well as the effective use of the stage for them. For special events, pure acting and full theatrical presentations are rare, but smaller scripted acting and speaking segments are often worked into a larger variety or musical stage show. Again, because this is such an extensive field, we will attempt to only mention the parts most relevant to special events:

- Theatrical direction. There are some fundamental elements to watch out for when evaluating the presentation of a play or any staged entertainment. They include:

  - The use of props. Clutter in the form of too many props should be avoided and the strategic center stage position should never be occupied by large props. Props should be varied in color, theme, and material in order to avoid monotony. Set pieces should be placed in at least three horizontal planes (e.g. foreground, middle, and background) to create the illusion of depth. Finally, the rules of good design should apply to the overall arrangement of props so that the entire composition is visually pleasing (Bloom, 2001; Pollick, 2002).

  - Blocking. Blocking is the choreography of actors' movements throughout a play. It is the job of the play's director to determine where the actors should go, or in the case of special event entertainment, where the performers should go, actors or otherwise. Some key points to note from Bloom (2001) are:

    - the upstage (toward the back) position is always the strongest when two or more actors are working;
    - a downstage actor looking at the audience is also in a strong position;
    - standing is a stronger position than sitting;
    - intimate moments require closeness of the actors and if they are shared moments, they are best done with the actors in profile to the audience;
    - powerful actions require more stage space;
    - movement should be minimized when complex language or difficult concepts are being presented;

- the eye attaches more importance to the center of the stage and so any movement away from here should be deliberate and express change or it will be purposeless;
- Western audiences read the stage from left to right so entrances and exits should follow that pattern;
- compositionally, when more than a single actor are onstage, diagonals or any arrangement other than a straight line works best; and
- as a rule of thumb, every audience member should be able to see at least one actor's face at all times.

As mentioned, these guidelines can also apply to any staged presentation of entertainment whether actors, comedians, variety acts, or musical shows.

- Drama and acting. There are many schools of acting and even kinds of acting. Schechner (2002, p. 148), for example, has broken acting into five kinds: realistic, Brechtian, codified, trance, and objects (masks, puppets). In our daily lives in North America, we are subjected to a bombardment of realistic acting in movies and television, so that is the type we will concentrate on in this section. Again, we are most concerned with analyzing performances so are interested in what constitutes a good performance. In special events, this will likely manifest itself on a regular basis as keynote speaker presentations. Here are some things to watch for in good actors and presenters (note that where referenced to Stevenson, the quotes are courtesy of Doug Stevenson, Story Theater Method, www.storytelling-in-business.com, 1-719-573-6195. (All Rights Reserved. Printed with permission from author)).

  - They do not become distracted by the audience or let the audience's body language keep them from staying centered. All their concentration is on playing the part. In other words, they "own the role" (Stevenson, October 2004).

  - They understand the importance of language and use it to evoke imagery and emotion. The language is in complete congruence with the topic and what is being said. It is first about communicating, not about actual words or their meanings. This understanding includes the use of verbal language (i.e. the words), vocal language (i.e. rhythm, tempo, volume, inflection, attitude, silence), physical language (i.e. physical movement and non-verbal cues), and emotional language (i.e. the actor's feelings and emotions) (Stevenson, June 2005).

  - They know how to use their voice. The most effective speaking pitch range is in the 2,000 to 4,000 cycles per second frequency band. Anything lower tends to "discharge" the listener and detracts from the presentation (Wilson, 2000). The voice must also be clear and easily heard with good breath control (see Section 1.1.3.3.1).

  - They use tempo to illustrate anxiety or tension by speeding up their speaking, and to illustrate shock or confusion by slowing down.

  - They understand how silence speaks by using it after delivering a profound or thought-provoking statement to allow the audience to process the concept and hopefully learn or be transformed. Stevenson (January 2005) makes the following comments when teaching speakers, "You must determine in advance where in your presentation you are going to say something powerful, profound or stimulating. After you say it, pause and let it sink in. Let your audience speak. Give them time to talk to themselves. You've just made a powerful or provocative statement. Hopefully you were standing still when you said it. Movement during powerful statements distracts from their power. After you make the statement, stand still for three seconds. Let the words hang in the air. Then, as if to gather your thoughts, turn and walk slowly to the right or left four or five steps. You may keep your eyes on the audience or bring them down into a private rumination. This movement fills another three to five seconds. Keep in mind, you must fill all silences with thought and/or emotion."

- They are good storytellers. They use "in and out" (i.e. in and out of first person character) moments of personal stories to illustrate their presentations. The "in" moments are short bursts of first person acting out of a story (Stevenson, January and June 2005).
- Their presentations are precise and replicable. Although there may be some spontaneity due to changing audiences, their presentations are precisely honed and rehearsed when it comes to delivering the key points. This replicability includes full content, jokes, gestures, tempo, volume, moments of silence, spirit, and emotion. The speech can be given anywhere at any time and it will remain the same. "Winging it" and "ad libbing" are never options (Stevenson, 1999).

- Comedy. Before being able to analyze comedy, one has to understand its structure and the importance of delivery. According to Beeman (2000), the structure of humor involves four stages, "the *setup*, the *paradox*, the *dénouement*, and the *release*. The setup involves the presentation of the original content material and the first interpretive frame. The paradox involves the creation of the additional frame or frames. The dénouement is the point at which the initial and subsequent frames are shown to coexist, creating tension. The release is the enjoyment registered by the audience in the process of realization and the release resulting therefrom." Here is a simple joke to illustrate, told by famous comedian Red Skelton, from Raymond (2015):

> *A fellow told me he was going to hang-glider school. He said, "I've been going for three months." I said "How many successful jumps do you need to make before you graduate?" He said, "All of them."*

In this case, the setup is the first two sentences, which establish a situation. The third sentence is the paradox, which helps to fix a set of assumptions in the minds of the audience (i.e. that a certain number of hang-glider flights would be required to pass the course). The fourth sentence is the dénouement (the *punch line*), and the one that is the surprise, that points out the incongruity of the whole situation. The release is the expected laughter of the audience. By laughing, the tension created by the paradox is released. Generally speaking, setup lines should be short (i.e. no more than one or two short sentences) and punch lines should end with a punch word if at all possible. In the case above, the punch word is actually a short but very effective phrase, "All of them," which makes this a strong joke.

Of course, part of the structure of comedy is the subject matter, the concept. Typical comedians will spend many hours making notes of life's situations and making lists of funny ideas and phrases that can be further refined through ridiculous combinations. For comedy at special events, subject matter is often extremely important because audiences may be cross-cultural or from specialized occupations. Obviously, different cultures may not understand certain jokes and specialized occupations may prefer tailor-made material. Off-color material is normally not part of special event comedy unless specifically requested. Most good standup comedians will go into their show with jokes loosely based on subject matter. If one set does not work, they may switch to another. The first part of their show is usually devoted to ascertaining how the audience will react to certain jokes based on subject matter.

Delivery is what makes comedy successful. It involves rhythm, tempo, volume, inflection, and timing, besides all of the traits we examined earlier on charisma and stage presence. Similar to the excitation transfer we discussed in music psychology, comedians may try to build on successful jokes by either adding more incongruities and further punch lines to a good joke or by adding more jokes at a faster pace. In doing so, they may incorporate higher or lower volume in their voices, different facial expressions, and body movements. Timing, though, is the key to delivery. A short pause before the punch word or line can make the joke.

In delivering jokes, comedians may also use different types of comedy. According to Stevenson (September 2005), there are 29 disciplines of comedy, including self-deprecating humor, hyperbole (extravagant exaggeration), the tongue-tie, physical comedy, alliteration, plays on words, characterizations, and many more. Most good comedians use at least one of these disciplines in their acts.

The best judge of any given comedy show is the audience, and as with all of the entertainment genres, watching them rather than the stage will give the biggest clue as to how successful a comedy show will be.

### 1.1.3.3.3 DANCE

There are numerous sub-genres of dance and we could fill several books trying to analyze all of them. The sub-genre most often encountered in special events is contemporary jazz dance and for the sake of brevity, that is the one on which we will concentrate. Analysis of jazz dance involves an understanding of choreography and technique.

- Choreography. Choreography uses the three basic elements of dance: space, time, and energy (Roston, 2000). Space includes both vertical and horizontal planes. In the vertical plane, choreographers will use low level moves (i.e. on the floor) to lower the energy level, medium level moves (i.e. standing) to travel in the horizontal plane and to work in different patterns, and high level to add energy and more spectacular moves such as leaps and lifts (Roston, 2000). All choreographers have different styles and will use space in different ways, but most will vary all three levels for variety and to match the mood or energy level of the music. Cooper (1998) discusses how the changes and shifts in vertical and horizontal planes are like "moving sculptures," some of which emphasize the individual line of the dancers through symmetrical and asymmetrical patterns (i.e. different placement of group shapes and sizes in the horizontal plane). She suggests the need for artistic variation in the number of dancers onstage, noting that too many dancers too often can look tedious. Obviously, in any group patterns or movements, all dancers must be precisely and exactly placed and move precisely together as a single unit.

  Time, according to Roston (2000), "encompasses speed, rhythm, and syncopation of movements. For example, when dancers freeze in a position, they 'stop' time." For variety, some sections can be performed in half time (twice as slow) or in double-time (twice as fast). Also, *canons* can be used. Roston (2000) explains how: "A choreographic canon requires dancers to perform an identical phrase at specific intervals – 8, 12, or 16 counts apart, for example. Canons work best when the movement changes levels, remaining at each level for a while." Generally, the more variety, the more interesting will be the routine.

  Energy "relates to the quality of the movement" (Roston, 2000). For example, leaps and lifts add energy, funky and upbeat jazz or hip-hop demands explosive energy, and rapid movement from upstage to downstage can add energy. Slower music (e.g. ballads, blues) usually requires soft and expansive qualities (Roston, 2000). Again, variety will always be perceived as more interesting. Any routine should have a beginning, middle, and end and should build toward a climax, while always reflecting the lyrics and energy level of the accompanying music.

  Powers (2011) also suggests considering contrast and musicality in choreography: "Contrast the numbers of dancers onstage. Use tension/resolution dynamics. Use space, silence, freeze-frames and voids for contrast." Likewise, from a musicality standpoint, the suggestion is to "match musical breaks, accents, lyrics and crescendos/diminuendos with physical versions of the same."

  Figure 1.6 is a fine example of contemporary choreography making use of space and energy.

- Technique. Diane Buirs—a creative director, production supervisor, and choreographer with extensive experience in England and Canada, including several Royal Command performances—offers some enlightening comments on dance technique. She breaks down technique into essentially four components: flexibility, strength, focus, and placement.

  Although probably not noticeable by the audience, poorly developed flexibility and strength can cause a dancer to be unable to make the necessary moves. Lack of flexibility, for example, can result in improper foot placement or limb movement. Underdeveloped strength can result in an inability to gain

Figure 1.6 Example of contemporary choreography

Copyright: evdoha / 123RF Stock Photo

the elevation required for good leaps and lifts since leg strength and deep knee bends (*pliés*) control takeoff and landing.

Focus is both psychological and physical. Psychologically, a dancer must want to leap. In addition, when physically leaping the dancer must lead the leap with an *eye line* that indicates the direction of the leap, by placing the head in a slightly higher position. Likewise, in turns or spins, the dancer must properly *head spot* to maintain balance and proper limb position.

Finally, placement necessitates that the dancer knows exactly where and how to position his/her body at all times.

Although not critical parts of technique per se, both endurance and overall appearance also play a part in successful dance. Endurance can only be gained by constant practice but can be assisted by alternative forms of physical activity including other forms of dance, getting proper rest, and maintaining a good diet. Appearance dictates that costumes, hair, and makeup must be perfect so that there are no distractions to the performance (D. Buirs, personal communication, June 10, 2014).

Varsity (2014) contains a lot more on technique, including information on body alignment, leaps, jumps, and turns. However, it should be noted that good technique is an extensive subject and can also depend on the type of dance involved.

#### 1.1.3.3.4 OTHER ATHLETIC ENTERTAINMENT

This genre includes so much variety that specific analysis is virtually impossible. Some examples of athletic or physical entertainment, besides sports, include stilt walkers, acrobats, trampoline artists, illusionists, clowns, mimes, face and body painting, fire eaters, hypnotists, jugglers, knife throwers, living statues, mascots and costumed walkaround characters, motorcycle and bicycle trick acts, pickpocket artists, puppeteers, rollerbladers, stuntmen, and many others. For most of these, their success is dependent on several key criteria:

- Originality. Many of these acts have intense competition in their particular sub-genre. To stand out, they must be very original. Jugglers, for example, cannot just get by with juggling three or four balls; now they have to juggle chain saws, lamps, handkerchiefs, bottles and other unusual items all at the same time. Illusionists can no longer amaze an audience by using Houdini's trunk illusion; they have to do it with a completely new twist (e.g. escaping from the trunk while underwater or some such idea). Living statues can no longer just stand or sit; they have to incorporate some unique movement or audience interaction into their performance.

- Costuming. Outrageous and "over-the-top" are the new guidelines for costuming in this genre. Flashy, creative, and colorful costuming is becoming normal, and is one of the few ways that performers can stand out from the crowd.

- Audience interaction. A lot of these types of acts have managed to get by in previous times by just doing their act. An example might be stilt walkers who may have been well costumed but really had no other skills with an audience other than walking around looking pretty. Now, it is almost required that most of the acts have good personal interaction with an audience. This is often not only the ability to speak to them in a friendly manner, but also to incorporate other skills such as comedy, balloon sculpting, or magic. Again, an example might be stilt walkers who can also deliver creative comedy routines in their interaction with the audience. Furthermore, acts that can do both roving sets and stage shows are more valuable and stretch a client's entertainment dollar.

- Skill. Fortunately, in this genre most audiences have seen so many examples in their lives that formal analysis of skill is not necessary. They know what is good and bad just by their experiences. Acts that do not measure up in terms of advanced skill simply do not get the business. Acrobats have to jump, contort, fly, twist, and maneuver themselves in ever more intricate ways, puppets have to be more outrageous, stuntmen have to perform as if they were in a Jackie Chan movie, bicycle trick acts have to balance on more bikes going faster, and so on. Before any such acts are hired, they should be seen ideally before another audience so the audience's reaction can be observed. Again, watching the audience and not the act is the best way to analyze their capabilities.

### 1.1.3.3.5 TECHNOLOGY AS ENTERTAINMENT

In Chapter 11 of *Special Event Production: The Process*, we discussed the future of technology and how it might affect the world of special events. That future is now upon us, as technology begins to fuse with entertainment and other previously separate specialties. I believe this has come about as a result of three phenomena: the popularity of experiential events, *gamification*, and *crowdsourcing*. One other technological advancement will also have enormous implications for special events and that is *robotics*.

Experiential events are those that emphasize immersing event attendees in the moment. Rather than being passive onlookers, they become active participants, and in some cases help to control the outcome of the event. Gamification is "the use of [video] game thinking and game mechanics in non-game contexts to engage users in solving problems. Gamification techniques strive to leverage people's natural desires for competition, achievement, status, self-expression, altruism, and closure" (Gamification, 2014). This is usually done through rewards like points or achievement badges. Most studies on gamification find positive effects from it (Hamari et al., 2014). Crowdsourcing is the practice of obtaining needed services, ideas, or content by soliciting contributions from a large group of people, and especially from an online community, rather than from traditional employees or suppliers. In special events, this group of people can be considered the audience or event attendees.

When these three phenomena are put together, what emerges are mobile and other unique applications for special event entertainment. While the field is barely in its infancy, there are developments on several fronts and they appear to fall into three categories: individual mobile device-based games, group mobile device-based games, and non-mobile device-based activities. Note that these terms and categories are my own and may very well be displaced in the future by others.

- Individual mobile device-based games. In these games, the platform (e.g. smartphone or tablet) acts as the participant along with the individual or very small group. Minimal input is contributed to the larger group of which the individual or very small group may be a part. Examples include:
  - ice-breaker apps for meetings and events in which individuals take photos of themselves and share them with each other;
  - individuals draw their own visions of the conference's key message;
  - individuals draw one another and answer questions about each other (see www.magencydigital.com for more examples of the last three types of games);
  - Global Positioning System (GPS) scavenger or treasure hunts. These types of games use the built-in GPS receiver in cell phones and tablets to help guide and navigate participants on a pre-determined geographical route. Typically, individual participants or teams are given tablets pre-loaded with software to use in the game as opposed to using their own devices. Challenges may involve a search for objects or places outdoors, answering questions, creating photo or video reports along the way, drawing pictures, interacting with people, etc. They are often used as teambuilding activities. Prizes may be awarded for the top teams in various categories. Examples may be found at www.wildgoosescotland.co.uk and http://eventplatform.ru/en/.
- Group mobile device-based games. These games or activities tend to be crowdsourced applications in that the wisdom of the entire audience is encapsulated in the outcome. Individuals contribute to the larger group. This is the form that is the most experiential and no doubt where most growth will occur because it offers more social interaction. Some examples include:
  - live audience voting in answer to group questions;
  - quiz and buzzer audience games (i.e. like a TV game show);
  - creative team collaboration much like the old flip chart concept but instead using tablets and phones;
  - multi-player gaming in which all attendees participate simultaneously in a game projected on a large wall or screen using their smartphones (http://buzzy.io);
  - DJ dance songs chosen ahead of time by guests using mobile devices and an app called Rockbot (https://rockbot.com). At an event, Rockbot screens provide even more social engagement, so guests can see what other partygoers have selected, and vote up their songs and even try to play similar music choices. They can easily share the songs and interactivity through social media, too, with instant links to their accounts and pages (Rosenbaum, 2014);
  - attendees using their smartphones as event lighting by downloading an app before the event and at the event the phones' lighting is synchronized to performed music through "audio calibration tones" received by the smartphones (Bailly, 2013 and http://whamcitylights.com);
  - audience members using their mobile devices to control part of a musical performance, actually the opposite of the music controlling the phones (Hödl et al., 2012); and
  - creation of original group music using smartphones and/or tablets as actual instruments (Wang, 2009; Wang et al., 2010; and http://mopho.stanford.edu).
- Non-mobile device-based activities. There is an increasing number of ingenious developments in which the physical dynamics—gestures—of audience members rather than mobile devices can control a performance outcome. Here are some examples:
  - the popular Angry Birds game on a large scale in which the audience controls the game (on a large screen) using their voices, first done at a Formula 1 race in Singapore (Vilpponen, 2011);

Figure 1.7 Example of large touchscreen technology

Courtesy of Molly Galler

- a technological version of the old "choose your own adventure" stories in which the audience controls the outcome of a movie using hand waving gestures (www.audienceentertainment.com);
- stage lighting controlled by how hard an audience dances on the dance floor (Jagadeesh, 2013);
- future concepts using large touchscreen technology combined with touch, gestural interaction, and maybe device interaction hold great promise for amazing special event entertainment, using wall-sized—and possibly flexible—touchscreens (A. Scott, personal communication, May 27, 2014; Wong, 2011; Bourzac, 2014). Not only walls, but floors and dining tables will become interactive entertainment centers (CSE1, 2013) (see Figure 1.7 showing a large touchscreen display in which the roses had to be wiped away to reveal the castle); and
- holographic projection, while not dependent on human gestures, represents great potential for event entertainment (CSE2, 2013) in the form of actual stage presentations from stars both alive and dead.

Finally, robotics is beginning to be noticed as more than a novelty. For example, Amazon is using thousands of robots in warehouses, self-driving vehicles will soon be the norm, and robots now deliver fresh towels at the Aloft Hotel in Cupertino, California. As if that's not enough, an entertainment robot named Sopo can play games with you, dance, collect trash, and serve drinks (Sinha, 2014). The implications for using such robots in special events are mind-boggling.

Since this section deals with the analysis of content in entertainment, at present there is precious little experience and history available to judge the quality of any performance or game based on technology. It appears that the concept may end up as a specific niche in the events industry in which companies provide these games as their sole raison d'être, because the technology is both expensive and theoretically complex. For example, in the case of team games using GPS, there is often the need to provide teams or individuals with pre-loaded tablets, which necessitates a large outlay of capital. Second, and as an example, it may be too large a task for a company that currently specializes in A-V to also handle the programming of a group-based game, as well as possibly providing the expensive surface(s) that the game must be played on. Thus, only a caution can be expressed at this time and that caution is for producers to work with specialist companies in these types of gaming. Indeed, several have already been referenced in this section.

---

### PRODUCTION WAR STORY

#### Love those cats

I had a friend whose talent we often bought. His name was Gary and he supplied animals of every description for the movies. Out of the blue one day, he came to our office.

"Doug, Doug, I've got some big cats in town for a movie." He could barely contain his excitement. "They're only here for three weeks. If you want, I could bring them to one of your events. Do you have anything on the go?"

I thought for a moment. "Yeah, I might have. A big convention in Whistler in two weeks. Tell me about the cats."

Gary had a bushy, handlebar moustache that bounced when he talked and blue eyes that twinkled when he was excited. Everything was bouncing and twinkling today. "Oh, you won't believe this," he said. He showed me some fuzzy Polaroid photos. "Aren't they beautiful? The little tiger cub's only two months old. The panther's a juvenile, still not full grown. I have handlers who can stay with them. Your clients will love them. They can even pet them. Think of it. It'll blow them away."

His timing couldn't have been better. We were in the middle of putting the finishing touches on the entertainment for a convention with the theme "Around the World in Eighty Hours," a takeoff on the Jules Verne classic, *Around the World in 80 Days*. The last night was to be a wildly creative offering of entertainment from the various countries Phileas Fogg and Passepartout visited on their trip. The animals would be perfect for India.

"Let's do it," I said. "The handlers will have to dress up as Hindus and stay at their post for about four hours. It's a reception and buffet, so the guests will be circulating." I knew my client would like the once-in-a-lifetime opportunity.

It was 10 min to doors opening for the Around the World extravaganza. I waited with the handlers and cats, who sat docilely on the floor. The handlers were stroking them. Gary was right. They really were beautiful. The baby tiger was perhaps 3 ft long. He had enormous paws. The panther was about 4 or 5 ft long with silky black fur and gleaming eyes. The night was going to be an unforgettable experience.

The tiger's handler was a young guy. He looked fairly strong. The panther's handler was a petite blonde. I had to ask her the question.

"Are you sure you can manage him?"

"Oh, yeah, no problem," she said. "He knows me. We're buddies."

Stop worrying, I thought. Everything will be fine.

We sat in silence for a few more minutes, admiring the animals and watching the wait staff bring their final loads of fresh food to buffet tables around the room. Then it happened.

A waiter with a tall cart full of dishes bumped the cart over a power cable taped across the floor. The rattling dishes broke the stillness.

I used to watch Tarzan movies as a kid and often wondered what it would be like to be jumped by a jungle cat in the wild. At that moment, I was given a pretty good idea. You wouldn't stand a chance. The panther could have been a rocket. I'd never seen any living thing move so fast. In less than a breath he was on top of the cart and accelerating toward a table. He pounced. The table crashed to the floor, breaking dishes and spreading linens and cutlery all over.

His handler said in a high-pitched, childlike voice, "Oh my god! He's never done that before." She started to sprint across the room, losing ground to the cat's Mach 2 slink.

The panther reached the stage at the far end of the room and slowed down. She caught up, grabbed his leash, and dragged him back, speaking softly to him, "Bad kitty. You be good from now on."

I wasn't entirely convinced that would be enough to keep him calm for the whole night.

Luckily, nothing else was damaged, but by now, everybody was in panic mode. The wait staff were running all over, gathering up broken dishes and resetting the smashed table. The catering manager shouted at me, "This could be a disaster." His eyes were wide. He looked terrified. "You can't keep the animals here."

I took a deep breath. "Listen," I said, "the client's been looking forward to this. Let me just tell him there's a slight delay and the doors will open in five minutes."

"I don't know," he said. "It could still be dangerous."

"The handlers tell me what happened was really unusual. They're convinced the cats will be fine," I lied.

He reluctantly agreed, and five minutes later the doors opened.

The cats were the hit of the party. Everybody got to pet them. Thousands of photos were taken. My client was ecstatic. He never knew what happened.

I sweated bullets for 4 h.

(Courtesy of Doug Matthews)

## 1.2 Staging entertainment

Having defined the entertainment to be used, we now turn our attention to its effective presentation. In Section 1.1.3, we discussed the content of a performance from the standpoint of the performer in isolation. To now use this content effectively in a show, we must consider it in the context of other event parameters, namely the audience, the layout of the event space, the staging available or possible, the scheduling and timing, including length of the performance, technical support, and any required interaction with other acts or performers.

### 1.2.1 Number of performers or acts

Special event entertainment can be simple in presentation, such as a single act that has no requirements for rehearsals or special technical support. There is a fixed show length, a certain start time, and the show proceeds with little fanfare, particularly if the event is being held indoors. For example, a dance troupe might come fully prepared for their performance with costumes and backing music on a CD or flash drive. They may not even require a rehearsal. Likewise, an outdoor event, such as a festival, may have a series of simple acts between which there is little or no interaction. They arrive, they set up and sound check at the appointed time, and no rehearsals are required. More often than not, however, special event shows involve more than a single act and frequently include scripts, complex rehearsals, technical support, and unique staging. In these cases, considerably more preparation and planning is needed to stage a successful show.

For a show with multiple acts, it is possible to create the illusion of a coordinated presentation through the use of common theatrical elements such as costuming or music. For example, if a show—let us say an 80s show—is being presented that consists of a comedian, a dance troupe, and a dance band, all scheduled to perform at different times in the event schedule, they can be tied together by common costumes and music from the 80s. The comedian can be linked by a costume and some reference to the 80s in his material.

For most other shows with a number of acts, there may be a requirement for a full script, rehearsals with all performers and technical support, and the need to integrate the show into a larger program of speeches and/or awards.

Given all the event parameters (e.g. schedule, location, budget, demographics of audience), at some point during initial event planning, the producer and client will have to decide whether a single act, multiple acts, or a scripted show format works the best in achieving the event's goals and translating the reason for, and message of, the event into a meaningful entertainment program.

## 1.2.2 Scheduling and timing

For stage presentations, in terms of timing there are typically two options: one is a single continuous show and the other is a show divided into multiple segments.

### 1.2.2.1 Single continuous show format

A single show, particularly for corporate events, rarely exceeds 50 or 60 min in duration. This is because the audience has often been subjected to prior extended and unrelated event segments, namely reception, dinner, speeches, or award presentations, and lacks the necessary stamina for a longer show. Shows containing overly esoteric material should also be avoided in the interests of keeping the audience's attention. If a single continuous show has multiple acts of short duration, there is a much better chance of success due to the variety presented, in that more of the audience is likely to enjoy at least one of the acts. With a single act, there is a greater possibility of some of the audience not appreciating it.

### 1.2.2.2 Segmented show format

Fortunately, the problem of sustained audience attention can be minimized in several ways. Rather than having a single continuous show after dinner at the end of a long event, dividing the entire show into short segments performed between meal courses works well. A show of this type can be divided up yet still maintain a story line providing that there is a simple link or explanation between segments, such as a script with a Master of Ceremonies (MC) voiceover that can tie them together. The duration of such segments should be no longer than 5–10 min during which the event space must be completely clear of wait staff and food. This requires close coordination between the producer and catering or banquet manager in order to ensure all tables are cleared from the previous course and the following course is not served until the entertainment segment is complete. The other advantage this method of presentation has is that it permits an extended period for stage changeovers without the audience having to wait. This further enables all presentations to take place from a single stage instead of multiple ones if required. All presentations do not necessarily have to take place between all the courses. The timing is entirely at the discretion of the producer and the client. Perhaps one at the very beginning of the event as guests arrive or as they sit down to dinner followed by only one more after dinner is all that is needed for a varied program.

This method also is an excellent means to inject interest into a lengthy standup reception event at which guests might otherwise only stay for a short time. Given periodic and unique entertainment segments at 15 or 20 min intervals throughout a reception can add an element of surprise that will make guests want to stay.

A segmented show has another dimension to it when a performance is sustained for a longer period of time. By this is meant a form of entertainment that is not used for a stage show per se, but rather strolls around or is stationary for a long period. Examples include solo musicians or a group of musicians (e.g. a dance band) who are hired either to provide background music during dinner and/or a reception, or to provide continuous dance music, or other performers with sustained performances. Examples here include table acts such as caricaturists, graphologists (handwriting analysts), tattoo artists, and fortune tellers, or strolling physical performers such as sleight-of-hand magicians, jugglers, mimes, stilt walkers, costumed characters, and such. At some point, all these types of performers will need breaks, so they should be built into the schedule in such a way that not all are taking breaks at the same time. We will deal more with this aspect in the next section about working with performers.

### 1.2.2.3 *Show setup and sound checks*

The last but by no means least critical aspect of scheduling and timing, excluding the show content itself, is the time and method of setup, sound checks, and rehearsals for performers. If the show is at all complex and involves several acts that are dependent on each other (e.g. a live musical group backing up dancers, a musical group playing *stings* or musical play-ons and offs for awards, a comedian interacting with an MC, or a multimedia show as a component of the entire presentation), then at least one full technical rehearsal with audio, lighting, A-V, and complete performance, should be scheduled. Without one, the show has an increased likelihood of failure and an amateurish appearance. In special events, there is only one chance to get it right and for a complex entertainment show, that one rehearsal is critical.

For shows with unconnected entertainment presentations, a full rehearsal is usually not required; however, full setup and sound checks are still needed. If performances are to take place from a single stage and there are multiple acts sharing the stage during the course of the show, then there is a correct and efficient way to execute the setups and rehearsals for all the groups, and that is to work in *backward performance order*. This means that the last act scheduled to perform will set up and sound check first, followed by the second to last act, and so on down to the first act which sets up and sound checks last in the production schedule. When the last act has completed setup and sound check, the stage is *spiked* or taped with small "Xs" that indicate the correct placement for pieces of equipment (e.g. amplifiers, microphones, monitors), and then their equipment is *struck* and stored, usually beside the stage on one side in reverse order to their scheduled performance so that their equipment is farther from the stage than the act before them. This same procedure is followed until all acts have completed setup and sound check. The last act to set up and sound check is thus the first act to perform and when their sound check is complete, their equipment remains onstage. When the actual performance time comes, and the first act's performance is over, the equipment is removed, usually to the other side of the stage. The next act's

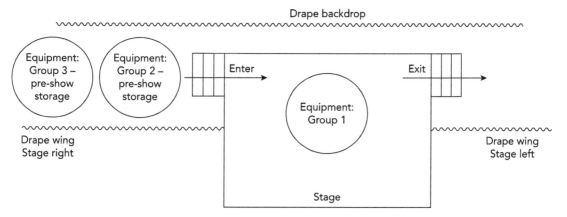

Figure 1.8 Order for multi-group setup and sound check onstage

Courtesy of Doug Matthews

equipment is then setup, the group performs and exits in the same manner, and so on until the final act. In the same way, the performers themselves will enter from one side of the stage and exit from the other in order to avoid confusion, usually from stage right to stage left. Figure 1.8 illustrates what this coordinated approach to setup and sound check looks like, with locations indicated for pre-show equipment storage after setup and sound check. Note the group numbers refer to the order in which the groups will perform in the program.

The length of time that setups and sound checks take is invariably underestimated by producers and especially by clients. Here are some considerations for each of the primary genres of entertainment:

- Theatrical presentations. For most standup comedians, all that is required is a microphone sound check, as they normally come prepared with their material. This will take about 5 min. An improvisational comedy troupe may require wireless lavalier or wireless headset microphones that will have to be individually tested and equalized, which will take somewhat longer, approximately 10 min per person. Other theatrical presentations and speeches such as for keynote or motivational speakers or MCs may take longer as they typically require a check of their PowerPoint presentations or scripts either with their own laptop computer at a lectern onstage, with another remotely controlled computer, or with a teleprompter. As well, their microphones—which again may be wireless lavalier, wireless headset, wireless handheld, or wired—will have to be equalized and set up as discussed in Chapter 3. This can take up to 30 min or more per speaker if the speaker insists on a full run-through of their presentation.

- Dance. Most dance troupes come with their music on CDs or flash drives and may require a short rehearsal to the music so they can become accustomed to the event staging. This may be one song or routine rehearsed one or more times, or their entire dance program, depending on: the quality of the stage surface and the ease with which they can maneuver; their ability to adequately hear their music (i.e. how well audio monitors have been placed on or near the stage); and how much their choreography must be changed to match the staging situation (e.g. the ease of their entrances and exits, the distance to the green room, the route to travel undetected by the audience from one side of the stage to the other, usually backstage). Sometimes this can take as little as 5 or 6 min for a single dance routine with an uncomplicated stage setup, to over 60 min for a complex dance program in which the dancers must perform several routines one after the other, complete with costume changes and travel between stage sides backstage, or must enter and exit through the audience. It can become even more complicated if the dancers are performing to live music and/or backing up singers, because then the entire show must be rehearsed onstage. Whenever this type of show is being performed, it is preferable to allow at least 2 to 3 h for rehearsal.

- Music. Whenever live music is a part of a show, especially if the musical group is a large one or if they are accompanying other performers, sufficient time must be allowed for setup and sound check. As discussed in Chapter 3, the audio needs of a musical group can be quite complex. In addition to the main audio system, there is also the full monitor system that must be balanced and equalized for all musicians. It is the monitor system that often takes the most time to check as it is critical that each musician be able to hear exactly what he or she must in their individual monitors, whether *in-ear* or onstage, as there is no other way for them to tell if they are playing correctly for the other musicians. As well as the sound check, the preceding setup itself may take a long time due to the need for the musicians to be conveniently positioned onstage for audience visibility and for visual connection with each other. A minimum of 30 min and ideally 60 min should be allowed per musical group for complete setup and sound check.

- Other athletic and variety performers. Most other acts will have unique setup and sound check requirements. Hypnotists, jugglers, physical comedians, magicians, acrobats, and similar acts all must be given time to become accustomed to the stage and the space in which they will be working. Stage magicians, often called illusionists, may need considerable preparation time to construct their illusions and place them in exact positions onstage. Acrobatic and Cirque-type performers may need time to check the rigging for their act and to rehearse their act in its entirety. Jugglers and hypnotists may need to try out the stage and ensure there is sufficient space for their act. The list goes on. Usually, an average of 30 min should be allowed for this type of act, longer if it is known to be complicated, such as a magic show with large illusions.

- Technological entertainment. This is so new that there are no standards or suggested methodologies for pre-show preparation. Suffice it to say that equipment should be tested in its entirety to ensure that all connections and cues for music or lighting are working. Acts incorporating some form of technology are expected to increase dramatically in the near future, not just because the technology is there, but because most modern audiences have now seen all the different forms of traditional entertainment.

Figure 1.9 shows a unique and quite technical act of "dancing fabrics" that requires a fairly extensive setup, including special lighting and fans. They would need sufficient setup and rehearsal time to ensure that everything worked properly.

With any show, no matter how many acts or how complex, there should also be an opportunity made to review lighting during the rehearsal time, as this enhances any show in terms of establishing a mood and assisting in segues between acts (e.g. fading to black after an act ends). It may also be critical if actors must hit marks onstage within a certain focused light's beam, or if performers will be moving around the audience—or offstage as with aerial acts—and need to be seen with followspots.

### 1.2.3 Using the event space

Considering that an event space is three-dimensional, it makes logical sense to stage as much of the entertainment in as much of the space as possible. After all, the audience occupies a considerable amount of that space, so why should they not all be given equal opportunity to have an optimum view of the show, rather than place it all on a single main stage that only those close enough can see well? Indeed, if space and budget permit, it is preferable to use one or more auxiliary stages for short segments of entertainment. This has several advantages. First, it permits more of the audience to feel included, thus endearing the performers to them. Second, it permits easier main stage changeovers without undue attention so that the

Figure 1.9 Example of a technical act requiring detailed setup—Pas de Deux

Courtesy of Contraband International Ltd., www.contrabandevents.com/

show in its entirety becomes more seamless. Just as with stages, so too can doors play into the show. Having performers enter and exit from many doors rather than the same one all the time, allows the audience more opportunities to feel part of the show by being close to the performers. This can be done with any of the stage setups below.

### 1.2.3.1 One main stage against a wall

We begin this discussion by assuming that there is always the option of a single stage against a wall with no other stages. This is still the most common method of presenting entertainment. The advantages include: lower costs for staging, audio, and lighting; one central focal point; lower costs for stage décor; and generally easier coordination of stage presenters and entertainment. However, adding auxiliary stages greatly improves the performer–audience connection and adds an exciting and more professional approach to the entire show. Figure 1.10 illustrates some optional locations that may be used in addition to a main stage in a typical hotel or conference center ballroom for an event. One or more of these stages can be used in the course of a single show. For example, a large act requiring a lot of stage area can be confined to the main stage while other smaller acts may be interspersed on one or more of the auxiliary stages. This works particularly well in a situation such as an event in which there is a dinner followed by a main stage presentation (e.g. speeches, awards, or show) followed by a dance band. It allows for the dance band to set up and prepare silently while the main stage activities are still ongoing, but allows for an instantaneous, seamless transition to dancing once the main stage activities are complete. Of course, there must be a dance floor already in place in front of or near the auxiliary band stage. This also brings up a second advantage to using two stages in a main stage/dance band situation, and that is it prevents a large gap between audience and performers if there is only a main stage that must be used for a show preceding a dance. This is a deadly situation for any performer because it disconnects the audience from the performer and sometimes this disconnection cannot be repaired sufficiently, causing the main stage show to "bomb." This setup is especially bad for comedy. Note that in any case where there

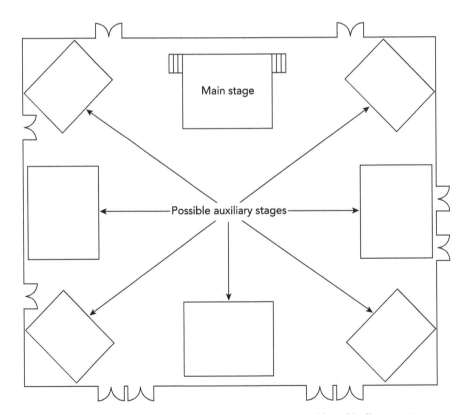

Figure 1.10 Possible auxiliary stage locations in a typical hotel ballroom situation

Courtesy of Doug Matthews

is more than one main stage, each of the auxiliary stages requires a separate technical setup for audio and lighting, although both systems may be tied into and operated from their respective main consoles and console location.

### 1.2.3.2 One main stage centrally positioned

Although a little awkward for technical setup in that lighting and audio must be multi-directional, a centrally located stage can be very impressive for focusing audience attention. Its big advantage is that it puts most of the audience on more of an equal footing than a stage against a wall. Technically, the multi-directionality can best be handled using flown audio and lighting systems or a box trussing system around and over the main stage. Some of the extra work involved in the setup of the lighting, in particular, may soon be overcome through the use of wireless lighting (see Chapter 5). The disadvantage of a central stage is that any stage changeovers as part of a continuous show are viewable by the audience unless there is some intervening or distracting activity such as a meal course or unless there are auxiliary stages, thereby making the show a little less seamless. Figure 1.11 diagrammatically illustrates a central stage with some possible options for auxiliary stages. Of course, with a central stage, if the event is a sit-down dinner then dining tables have to be placed around the outside of the stage. Interestingly, this situation can also be achieved by having the dining tables and hence the audience on risers around the outside of the space with the central stage replaced by a central floor space as the performing area, although this requires considerable time, effort, and expense for renting and setting up risers of differing heights with safety railings installed. This setup resembles the old Greek amphitheater setting.

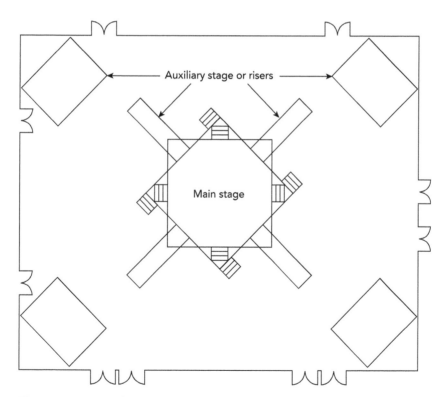

Figure 1.11 Central main stage with auxiliary stages

Courtesy of Doug Matthews

### 1.2.3.3 Floor space as a performing area

Entertainment need not be confined to a stage. Often, for greater visibility and audience interaction, it is preferable to use floor space. This situation arises for performers who find stage work awkward, such as large processions with giant puppets and stilt walkers, and costumed characters, marching bands, and certain types of athletic acts (e.g. bicycle stunt riders, roller bladers, gymnasts). For these acts, space can be designed in and amongst tables or around the periphery of a room. Of course, this can also be combined with one or more stages for even more variety in presentation. When performers are moving about a larger area, however, they require adequate lighting and this usually takes the form of one or more followspots so that they may be lit equally on all sides and the entire audience may see them clearly. They might also require wireless microphones if there is any spoken or sung component to their performance. Figure 1.12 illustrates some possible options for the use of floor space for performing. Almost any combination of floor areas and staging is possible and really a matter of how creative producers wish to be.

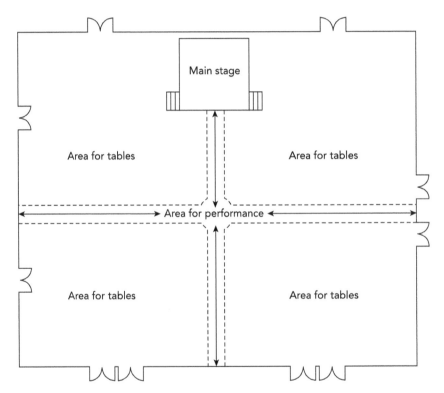

Figure 1.12 Possible options for using floor space as a performing area

Courtesy of Doug Matthews

### 1.2.3.4 Vertical space as a performing area

Although theater productions have used vertical space for literally hundreds of years, it has only been since Cirque-type acts started being used in special events in the late 1990s that performances using the third dimension have become increasingly popular. This has necessitated more emphasis on proper risk assessment and proper rigging. We discuss these topics in detail in Chapter 8 of *Special Event Production: The Process* and Chapter 9 of this book respectively. Acts of this genre include aerial silks, bungee, ropes, hoops, and trapeze, among others, and all require rigging plus a circular safety area beneath the performing location that is clear of people and objects. This may be on the floor or on a stage. The one consideration that always presents a creative challenge is finding a way to place performers in position prior to their act without drawing undue attention from the audience. This can often be done by using a distraction at another stage or with a roving performer to keep audience focus away from the aerial act. As with any roving performers, aerial acts require special lighting consideration. Usually followspots work well for these acts, but at least two may be needed to adequately light all sides unless the act takes place over a stage that is being viewed from only one direction.

## 1.2.4 Building the show

Although a show relies on talented performers and exciting acts to be successful, it needs the loving, guiding hand of a masterful choreographer or director to pull them together into a finished product. Lynnette Barkley, of event production company Barkley Kalpak Associates in New York, has staged over 200 musicals and plays as an award-winning choreographer and director. About this process, she advises,

> *Piece by piece the materials are pulled together, as scripts, arrangements, designs, floor plans, and costumes are developed. The show is rehearsed, tweaked, massaged, and adjusted to create a theatrical arc. Within that arc, you want balance, flow, pace, build, and surprises.* Balance – a variety within the music and staging so that it is never monotonous. *Flow – seamless transitions and segues from one moment to the next.* Pace – keep it moving, even within a beautiful ballad, there is an underlying energy that must be maintained. *Build – making sure each moment is enhanced from the moment before it.* Surprises – never allow the audience to anticipate the next moment – keep their interest with variety and the unexpected.
>
> *(Barkley, 2004, p. 10)*

Let us briefly examine each of these:

It does not matter if the show consists of a single act or multiple acts in a variety format; all these elements can and should be used. As Vancouver-based choreographer Diane Buirs states, "The audience needs to have a relationship with the performers as soon as possible from the outset of a show" (D. Buirs, personal communication, June 10, 2014). This can be done by having balance in subject matter (e.g. a comedian who can discuss multiple topics); in repeat small appearances by the same performers but in different costumes or roles (e.g. dancers returning with different styles of dances and costumes); in different musical styles (e.g. an a cappella vocal group that varies singing styles among barbershop, Gregorian chant, and R&B); and in working different parts of the stage and the event space (e.g. using the entire stage or different stages, corners of the room, or different entrances).

We discuss flow in Section 1.2.5 in the context of beginnings, endings, and segues (different from the psychological interpretation discussed in Section 1.1.3.1). The key to flow is not to have any "pregnant pauses" in a show. As soon as one act or performer finishes, the next is already coming onstage to perform, or indeed becomes part of the preceding act and moves directly into their performance with no abrupt start and end. This can be done by using different parts of a stage for one act and another part for the next act, or by using entirely different stages or parts of the room. It can also be done by musical transitions. These are often especially written for a live orchestra or band and can involve no more than several bars of modulated key changes that correspond to stage changeovers. It can also be done by using audio effects operated by the audio engineer in the form of pre-recorded sound tracks such as fanfares or short musical interludes. Lighting can help to effect the changes and the flow of the show by changing colors, light levels (e.g. fading to black at the end of a dance number), direction, or focus (see Chapter 5).

Surprises are what help to keep audience interest and connection with performers. Sometimes, surprises can be very endearing to an audience. A wacky character that only appears for a minute, a wild costume, an entrance from a totally unexpected location, a prop or object that becomes part of the show, or a waiter who turns into a performer are all surprises that are beyond the audience's concept and expectations. Special effects also fall into this category and we will be explaining them in detail in Chapter 6.

Pace and build tend to work together in that they represent the overall energy level of the show. Pace is concerned with timing and the ability of the performers to sustain the audience's attention throughout the show. For example, it can be a fast-paced or slow show. For most special events, the overall pace must generally be fast. There can be short periods when it slows down, but no more than about two in a typical short 45 min show. Fast-paced does not necessarily mean that all songs have to be up-tempo or that all gags have to be delivered in rapid-fire mode. What it does mean, however, is that changeovers, performance styles, the number of performers onstage, the lighting levels, colors, and amount of automation all cannot be static for too long but must be efficiently and purposefully changed. Any slowing down is for an audience breather and only serves to bring them back refreshed and ready for even more. Likewise, build refers to being able to consciously relate to and improve upon what went before this point in the show. This is particularly significant toward the end of the show. There cannot be any "down time" very close to the end, as Diane Buirs cautions, but rather a gradual build in energy level so that the show finishes on a high note that might incorporate all the performers, complete with special effects, all backed up by the strongest song of the show and/or the delivery of the key message of the event.

As an example to illustrate pace and build, Figure 1.13 depicts a hypothetical plot of the energy levels from one to ten of a typical 45 min corporate event stage show. Let us assume that this show includes a contemporary dance troupe, a comedy variety act, and a small musical group with three lead vocalists that is also used to back up the dancers. The dancers would open the show strongly, backed by the band with what is called a *production number* in which all dancers and perhaps one or two of the vocalists are onstage

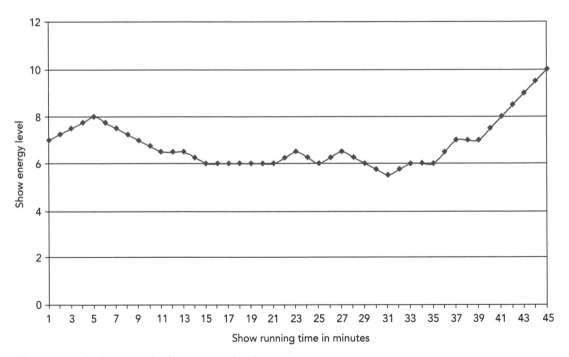

Figure 1.13 Pacing: sample show energy level over time

Courtesy of Doug Matthews

(minute 0:00 to about 5:30). The singers and band might stay onstage for another one or two songs (minute 5:30 to 10:00). The comedy variety act could then take over, perhaps entering through the audience while the band exits the stage, and they perform for about 20 min (minute 10:00 to 30:00). The band returns with perhaps one vocalist or alternatively a single dancer for a solo routine (this is the breather number for the audience before a final build, minute 30:00 to 33:00). The remaining vocalists then return for perhaps two or three songs (minute 33:00 to 42:00) before the final, high-energy production number with the entire dance troupe, full band, vocalists, and perhaps even the variety act if they can be choreographed into the routine (minute 42:00 to 45:00). This would be a show with relatively fast pacing, variety, and a good build to the finale.

Being cognizant of how a show should be structured is the first step to success. The second is knowing the right people to make this happen. Although producers may decide to tackle this on their own if they feel they have the talent, it is never a bad idea to seek out exceptional choreographers or directors with theater experience to help the process. Now we will turn our attention to what really makes the difference: beginnings, segues, and endings.

### 1.2.5 Beginnings, segues, and endings

"Visualize this thing you want. See it, feel it, believe in it. Make your mental blueprint and begin." So said Robert Collier (2015), and nothing could be truer when it comes to staging entertainment. A good producer will coordinate acts. A great producer will coordinate a concept. It takes effort on the beginning, the segues (smooth transitions) between acts, and the ending to coordinate a concept. It is more than simply throwing acts onstage one after the other in the right order. A method of introduction is required to begin, a method of acknowledgement is required to end, and a method to tie all the acts together with segues is required to produce a show that exudes professional finesse.

#### 1.2.5.1 Beginnings

The question of how to introduce a show or individual acts is always a challenge for any type of entertainment. The beginning of the show is the first impression and sets the tone for what will follow. Let us look at the possible options for beginning a show, whether it is a single act or scripted show comprising many acts:

- Live introduction. This comes in two forms: professional or amateur MC, the amateur form often being the client or a client representative. Although it saves money, using an amateur MC, even with the insistence of a client, can be a disastrous way to start a show. Why is this? First, the amateur usually has no formal training and very little public speaking experience, thereby making a demonstrative, expressive, showbiz-type introduction highly unlikely, rather more likely very stilted. Second, there is a good possibility that, because the amateur is not familiar with the act, the introduction will probably be read, making it sound completely unnatural. Third, invariably a name is mispronounced or left out entirely. Professional MCs, on the other hand, will ensure none of these happen because they will check scripting and voice intonation, and will ensure that all names are pronounced correctly.

- Onstage introduction or voiceover. Onstage introductions have their place and seem to work well if the MC is familiar with the audience or if the event is not too formal. Otherwise, it can appear to be unnatural and outdated, resembling the old vaudeville days and the stiffness of Ed Sullivan. It may work if there is only a single act and no need to continually keep popping up to the stage to introduce multiple acts. Otherwise, a voiceover or *God-voice* using the house audio system and a microphone set up at the *front-of-house* (FOH) position (audio control console position) gives a very professional feel to introductions and can allow for proper voice inflection and intonation by a professional MC reading a script. In fact, it is the best form of introduction when a script must be read. It also allows for clean stage changeovers and segues between acts when there are multiple acts, eliminating messy entrances and exits of performers and MC at the same time. For example, it permits the stage to go dark while one act exits and the next act takes the stage, during which time the MC can read the scripted intro at a speed suitable to allow the stage changeover. Thus once the intro is finished, the act is completely ready to begin on the last word of introduction, with no pauses.

● No introduction at all. With the advent of more theatrical-style shows in special events that incorporate multiple acts and a story line, a beginning fashioned after the theater can lend a professional feel to the production. House and stage lights can be dimmed or *ballyhooed* (i.e. moved excitingly), a musical introduction can be employed, and the event can begin with no spoken introduction, thereafter just being allowed to flow one act into the other, with lights and/or music being used for scene or act changeovers. The success of this approach usually depends on the strength and understandability of the story line in combination with the strength of the overall presentation of the acts and how well they relate to the storyline and reason for holding the event. If there is no obvious connection or if the connection is too esoteric, there is a chance that the point of the show will be lost on an audience with other distractions (e.g. alcohol, conversation), so the totality of the show should be considered before deciding that no spoken introductions are required.

### 1.2.5.2 Segues

Segues or transitions between acts are what glue the show together. As producers like to say, they are what make the show "seamless." They depend on a number of factors, including where the stage(s) and performance spaces are located, where doors are located for entrances and exits, where the green rooms are located, what lighting is available, whether there will be act introductions (e.g. onstage or voiceover), what other event programming may be before or after the act (e.g. another act and what type it is—speeches, meal course, awards, auction, and such). Sometimes, exact segues cannot be finalized until the entire event setup is complete and the producer has a chance to check where and how acts will get to and from the stage(s). Here are some possibilities for segues:

● Verbal introductions and acknowledgements by a live onstage MC or by a voiceover. As explained, a live onstage MC tends to make for a disjointed show due to the need for him or her to continually take to the stage for short periods. It also means that any exits or entrances by performers are seen by the audience and, if they are not clean, will give the show an amateurish appearance. A voiceover allows for lighting to be used to hide stage transitions so they can be done in the dark. In the end, it depends on personal preference. It may also depend on whether the live MC is a celebrity, in which case it makes sense to have that person seen as much as possible, or if the MC is a comedian who can continue with an act as part of the transition.

● Changing audience focus. This requires that the producer employ a method to distract the audience while acts are in transition. It often is used when there are not going to be any verbal introductions. If there is only one stage used for performances, it may mean that acts enter the event from a door at the farthest end of the venue and make their way up to the stage through the audience, either interacting with them (the audience) or performing in some way as they move, thus allowing sufficient time for the previous act to exit cleanly and unseen from the main stage. It may also mean changing focus to an auxiliary stage or performance area (e.g. a section of floor, an aerial act suspended from the ceiling) if there is more than one stage so that the main stage may be changed over.

● Interaction of acts. This is the most theatrical of any method of transition. It means that either the producer or the acts in the show must devise a short, scripted interplay that will, in itself, become the transition between them. For example, comedians might call on a dancer to join them onstage for some simple banter, which in turn leads to the start of a dance routine that enables the comedy act to exit. A band playing an opening overture might be stopped midstream by a comedy musical performer who then joins the band and begins his act accompanied by them. There are endless possibilities, with the only requirement being the willingness of the acts to cooperate and take the time to rehearse together. Of course, this often necessitates extra remuneration to them.

### 1.2.5.3 Endings

The ending is what leaves a lasting impression and will be the strongest memory the audience carries away. Much like the beginning, it cannot be simply allowed to happen on its own with no forethought. Whether the show is a single act or multiple acts, there must be an acknowledgement of them, ideally as a voiceover or an onstage acknowledgement. This is the opportunity to bring all the performers back onstage in a professionally choreographed ending with properly rehearsed bows. It is worth taking the time to gather all acts together at the sound check and have a short rehearsal of this ending so it appears rehearsed and planned. The audience will always appreciate that a little extra effort above and beyond the call of duty has been given to the show. If it is too awkward to acknowledge each individual act after they complete their portion of the show, then this final bow is that opportunity.

What about encores? They present a unique and unpredictable case in that every show is different. It is usually the producer's call whether an act or acts return to the stage for an encore performance. This can depend on several factors. The most important one is obviously audience reaction. An extended standing ovation is the best thanks that any performers can be given and usually means an automatic encore if they have the material. At least one strong song or routine should be kept at the ready for this. However, if applause is sustained but there is no standing ovation, the decision is a little harder. I used to watch for signs such as shouts of "More!" or rhythmic clapping before I would bring an act back. Another factor is show length and how long the show—and the event (e.g. dinner, speeches, awards, etc.)—have already lasted. If it has been a marathon of 4–6 h, it may not be worth extending the show, no matter how good it has been. It is best to "leave them wanting more." How long should an encore be? Not long is the best answer. If it is for a musical act ideally one song, with two at most if the show has been fairly short (e.g. 30 to 45 min). Anything longer has a negative effect on the audience and they sense they are being "milked" or forced to enjoy against their will.

Beginnings, endings, and segues are all a matter of timing, of knowing the exact second when to begin to act or play, and the exact second when to stop. It means that as the applause is just starting to die out for the previous act, the next act begins (or is introduced), not after the applause is over and not too soon during it, but just at the moment that "feels right." It follows from this statement that for great segues, all performers must know where to be and when to be there so that there is no last-minute panic before taking the stage. This is covered in more detail in Chapter 9 of *Special Event Production: The Process*.

**VOICE OF THE INDUSTRY**

**An interview with Ms. Archie Archer**

Founder and Managing Director, Contraband International Ltd.
London, United Kingdom
www.contrabandevents.com

In ten short years, Archie Archer has grown her company from a single employee operating out of a North London flat to an entertainment agency with global reach, and one of Britain's most successful event businesses. Contraband International Ltd. now provides over 6,000 performers for over 1,500 events each year all over the world. They employ 11 full-time staff and annually gross in excess of £2 million. Archie has been named as one of the top 100 most influential people in the UK events industry by *Event Magazine* in 2011, 2012, 2013, and 2014.

**Figure 1.14** The Sparklers, a unique interactive and technical percussion act using LED lighting

Courtesy of Contraband International Ltd., www.contrabandevents.com/

**DM**: You have an amazingly large and varied roster of acts. How do you scout out new acts and how do you determine if you will represent them?

**AA**: Most acts now approach us as a result of referrals from other performers or because of our reputation. We receive about 20 emails per day from acts wanting us to represent them, and the calls come from all over the world. We are very discerning about who we represent and only accept top-quality, highly original acts. They must have at least ten corporate clients already, many testimonials, and high-quality videos or CDs. When possible, we also review them live in a special performance area of our office.

**DM**: How do you catalogue your talent roster?

**AA**: We actually use our web site as our main roster. It has all the details about each act, including still images, videos, and technical riders. We keep the confidential information about them on an Excel spreadsheet.

**DM**: How do you charge for your services?

**AA**: We contract separately with clients and with performers and charge a markup on the performers.

**DM**: How extensively do you customize an entertainment program or show for clients?

**AA**: Although some of our shows are booked as complete packages, we do not customize shows. Everything is off the shelf and our business model is strictly on volume. If a show needs more, we will pass it to business colleagues who provide that service. We are almost never asked for complete custom shows.

**DM**: Do you or your staff attend all events at which you have booked entertainment? If not, how do you decide which ones to attend?

**AA**: It is physically impossible for us to attend all events. There are just too many. If there are multiple acts at an event, we may send a manager to look after them.

**DM**: Do you have any suggestions about how to treat performers and acts before, during, and following their performance?

**AA**: The main thing to remember is that performers are people. I have had clients who won't even consider giving performers a glass of water, but others who will offer them a full meal. We have had enough experience that we now include a section in all our client contracts about what is required for performers, including green room details and food.

**DM**: Do you also subcontract and coordinate other event components such as audio, lighting, A-V, décor, staging, or special effects?

**AA**: No, we spell out in client contracts what is required for tech and the client is then responsible for obtaining it.

**DM**: What are some of your most popular acts for events such as teambuilding (corporate), conferences, award ceremonies, weddings, and festivals?

**AA**: The big trend right now is technology—for example, LED acts such as The Sparklers and the Pas de Deux dancing fabrics. Also, we have found that the popular Cirque-type acts of the recent past have now moved toward other performance sporting acts such as 3 Run, three guys who do parkour, free running, and martial arts.

**DM**: How—and why—do you see the entertainment industry in the UK, especially as it pertains to special events, changing over the next five to ten years?

**AA**: Our events industry is affected by the economy. When the recession started, spending dried up and events were canceled as clients like the banks couldn't be seen to be spending the money. In 2014 we've seen great growth in the market and the economy feels back to pre-recession confidence. For us personally we've never been busier in the history of the company and I see this on a huge upward trend due to our growth in international business.

## 1.3 Working with performers

It is amazing how many clients I have encountered in my career who treat performers like lower class hired help. They wonder why they are so expensive (e.g. "Why is so-and-so charging $1,000 for 30 minutes. I'm in the wrong profession."), they wonder why they need two hours to set up and sound check (e.g. "It's only a dance band with some singers. Why all the fuss?"), they wonder why they need coffee and sandwiches and a comfortable changing room (e.g. "That is going to cost $300 extra and it is not in my budget. You will have to cover it."), and then they wonder why the show was not very good! I am hoping that producers and their clients of the future will read this section and reconsider this way of thinking. The reasons should become obvious as we progress through the section and consider the key points in working with performers from their perspective.

### 1.3.1 Mindset

Mindset—zone—headspace. These terms describe a utopian psychological state inhabited by performers, elite athletes, motivational speakers, and anyone who must be at their absolute peak of ability performing before a live audience. It is a place where their body, mind, and spirit meet in harmony in readiness for the task at hand. Only those who have visited this place can understand how necessary it is to find it in order to give a successful performance.

Different performers have different ways of achieving this state. Some pace, some pray, some joke, some drink coffee, some intently review scripts, some practice, some stretch or do exercises, some just talk, but everyone does it, either consciously or subconsciously. Indeed, some performers have onstage personalities completely different from their offstage personalities and people are often astonished by this. Really, it is only their inhabitation of a performing mindset that is happening. If the two personalities are extremely different, then performers may need some extra time to get into that performing mindset.

Anthropologist Turner (1988, pp. 54–55) understood what is happening. Any performance, as he noted, involves "frame, flow, and reflection." By "frame" he was referring to "that often invisible boundary around activity which defines participants, their roles, the 'sense' or 'meaning' ascribed to those things included within the boundary, and the elements within the environment of the activity." In other words, for our purposes, this frame is an event entertainment show. Performers recognize that the show is a distinct activity outside the norm of everyday life, and can be treated as such, so that they are free to be who they want or need to be. They can only get to this state by being given time to be on their own away from distractions.

What does this mean for producers? It means that performers, no matter who they are, must be given quiet time before their performance, on their own, to find the right frame of mind. Therefore, it behooves the producer to provide such an environment. This topic is listed at the very top of this section because it is considered the most important aspect of working with performers.

### 1.3.2 Creature comforts

Along with the need to provide a welcoming environment is a need to provide creature comforts for performers. This will mean some standard amenities in the form of:

- Changing rooms. Also called *green rooms*, these are areas or actual rooms in a venue—or perhaps a tent at an outdoor event—set aside for the use of the performers only. They can take many forms. I have had to put performers in everything from presidential suites to tiny washrooms. Ideally, they should be heated, well lit, and large enough to comfortably contain all the performers. They should also be close to the performing areas or stage(s). If possible, washrooms should be close by and not require performers to be seen by the public or the audience when visiting them. Finally, if there are multiple performing groups, or single groups with both sexes, different rooms should be assigned to each group or to each sex, out of respect. At the very least, if separate rooms are not possible, a single large room can be divided using pipe and drape. Occasionally, some groups such as dance troupes require secondary quick-change or preparation areas close to the stage where they will be performing. This can be a small curtained area behind or beside the stage, which should be well lit and invisible to the audience.

- Other amenities. Common sense dictates that if it is a changing room, then performers will need something to hang their clothes on, as well as other amenities to assist them in preparing to go onstage. This means that sufficient chairs, tables, movable clothes racks, coat hangers, mirrors, and electrical outlets for hair dryers, razors, and other appliances will be needed for all the performers.

- Refreshments. Although refreshments are not always a necessity, they are especially appreciated if performers must remain onsite at an event for a period of 2 h or more, including their performance time, but are virtually a necessity if this period extends over a meal hour. Although they do not have to eat the same six-course meal that the event guests will be fed, they will expect and appreciate at minimum a substantial sandwich tray, along with perhaps crudités and cookies, plus a selection of water, soft drinks, juice, and coffee. They should not expect any alcoholic beverages although occasionally one drink may be allowed after their performance as long as they will not be driving and consumption takes place out of sight of the event guests. Food or drinks should never be consumed by performers in front of event guests or by taking food or drinks prepared for the guests, without the very clear and express permission of the client or event producer.

It should be noted that all the amenities listed, particularly refreshments, also apply to technical personnel working onsite at the event (e.g. audio, lighting, A-V technicians, and stage managers) if they will be there over meal hours, which is often more likely to happen for them than for performers. They will also need the changing space as they must change from their work clothes into more formal attire for the event itself and may need to change back to work clothes after the event for the strike.

### 1.3.3 Unique preparations and performance needs

Inexperienced producers cannot always understand why performers prepare in certain ways. To understand this, one first has to understand that a special event is a temporary and shifting performance situation. It is one that has unusual demands for performers, including: the need to often shorten or rearrange their performance to suit the length of the overall show, sometimes at a moment's notice; the need to wait for extended periods of time, often well past the stated performance start time; and the need to begin their performance immediately when called, having prepared themselves completely notwithstanding any lengthy wait. Because of this, every performance genre has unique needs.

#### *1.3.3.1 Musicians and vocalists*

Musicians and vocalists anywhere in the world have common needs because music is a universal language. As well, many instruments have their own quirks to deal with. Here are some of the common considerations, not including technical needs (e.g. audio and lighting), for musical performers:

- Vocalists. Vocalists need to warm up their voices alone and together and can only do this in a room where they and others will not be disturbed. They also need water onstage, normally in individual glasses and without ice in order to keep lubricated and hydrated. Water can be delivered to the stage and placed in an inconspicuous location before the performance begins.

- Musicians. Many musicians—and vocalists—belong to the American Federation of Musicians (AFM) or "union" and must abide by their regulations, which stipulate maximum play times and minimum fees for contracted types and lengths of performances. For example, technically the union maximum time that a musician or group can play is 90 min before taking a break. This must be borne in mind when the event is planned, especially if a client expects a continuous performance of a dance band or musician playing background music. Most breaks should last no longer then 15–20 min, often depending on the length and energy level of the preceding performance. Typical dance band or background music sets last from 45 to 60 minutes.

- Equipment and instruments. Musicians also require time to perform last-minute tuning of their instruments (guitars, violins, other stringed instruments, and woodwinds are particularly susceptible to going out of tune when the ambient temperature varies even slightly) before taking the stage or beginning their performance. Some instruments require a lot of warming up, such as bagpipes, and pipers or pipe bands will expect an area out of audible range of any guests to warm up, tune, and practice. Acoustic pianos (e.g. uprights, baby grands, or full grands) need to be tuned after extensive moving (slight moving is acceptable without tuning) such as being lifted onto a stage, and this should be done prior to a sound check. It usually takes about 2 h. Musicians, especially symphony musicians, require music stands and lights for these stands, and they do not always bring their own, so this question has to be settled prior to contracting.

### 1.3.3.2 Actors, comedians, and speakers

The biggest concern for this group is remembering their lines, so they need a quiet area to reflect and review. Their second concern is getting into character and this also requires a quiet space away from distractions. Occasionally, they may have special props that are used as part of their performance and that must be pre-placed on the stage prior to the performance.

### 1.3.3.3 Dancers

Dancers must have their bodies in perfect working order to perform. Hence, they need a green room or area large enough to warm up with stretching exercises and perhaps to do last-minute run-throughs of their routines. This might be extremely important if their performance space (i.e. stage area) is not as planned or not the size that they were initially told, and they have to make last-minute adjustments to choreography onsite. To the chagrin of choreographers everywhere, this happens far too often in special events due to lack of communications between producers and performers. Dance troupes will often bring CD players to their events to do these run-throughs. Dancers will also need to adjust their routines for entrances and exits and may have to make several unobtrusive visits to the stage area to determine how to do this once all dancers are onsite prior to their performance.

### 1.3.3.4 Other athletic and variety entertainment

This group encompasses all other variety-type entertainment and their needs run a broad gamut. Some of the more common ones used in special events are jugglers, magicians, hypnotists and mind readers, stilt walkers, acrobatic acts, table acts, fire performers, a variety of cultural performers, occasionally animal acts, and more recently, acts depending on technology. Many of these have props (e.g. jugglers, fire performers, magicians) that may need pre-placing onstage prior to their performance. Some such as fire performers or magicians using flash pots and indoor pyrotechnics (see Chapter 6), need fire extinguishers close by with operators at the ready, as well as a safety zone clearly demarcated. Stilt walkers need assistance negotiating doorways and stairs (some can use them, some cannot, but they should be avoided if possible). Table acts (caricaturists, body massage, graphologists, temporary tattoo artists, fortune tellers, cardsharps, and others) normally only need an area with good lighting but may also require their own tables and chairs for guests, plus some water for themselves. Acrobatic acts are similar to dancers in that their bodies are their performing instruments and they must stretch and warm up, often immediately before taking the stage, so a heated space near the stage may be needed (this is important for contortionists especially). In the occasional jurisdictions that still permit animal acts at special events, special care and thorough risk management assessments are required, as well as safety enclosures and areas for the animals to heed the call of nature, preferably not inside on a carpet! In my career, some of the funniest and scariest moments have involved animals and they have invariably been the hit of any show, but they also must be treated humanely and with the utmost respect. Technological acts such as musicians interacting with an audience's mobile devices may need to pre-place equipment and run through its operation. Others such as sand artists may require special light tables to be pre-placed and checked. These types of acts are becoming more prevalent and all have unique requirements.

Those athletic and variety acts that perform onstage have varying average lengths of shows: 5–6 min for acrobatic acts and fire performers; 5–15 min for animal acts; 15–30 min for jugglers; 30–45 min for magicians if using large illusions; 60–90 min for hypnotists; and up to 60 min for large cultural performances. Those that are roving or table acts have average performance durations that are more a function of their physical and mental stamina than anything else: 20–30 min for jugglers or stilt walkers; 30–40 min for sleight-of-hand magicians; and up to 2 h for table acts. For most, a break of 15–20 min is expected after these performances and then they are able to perform another set of the same length.

## 1.3.4 Communications

Regular communication with performers is critical for optimum performances. This begins with the first phone call, moves to a contract, and ends with the performance.

### 1.3.4.1 General

From the very first request to use their services, performers will be expecting to know: the time, date, venue, and address of the performance; duration of the performance(s); type and theme of the event; who or what precedes and follows them in the show or event program; audience size; and audience demographics (ages, genders, nationality, languages, type of business or organization). Of course, remuneration will also be discussed and tentatively agreed upon. From this information, the performers will be able to adjust and mold their shows to relate to the audience and event parameters. They may also want to know, prior to contracting, what amenities will be provided, including green rooms with their own needs considered as outlined above, costume or attire requirements, where and how load-in will take place, rehearsal and/or sound check details, and whether parking fees will be covered. There may also be a number of other considerations that need to be confirmed such as eating and drinking policies, book-back policies, whether performers' guests are allowed at the event, and such.

### 1.3.4.2 Contracting and followup

We discuss contracting at length in Chapter 6 of *Special Event Production: The Process*, and Sonder (2004) goes into some detail about it, as does Rutherford-Silvers (2012). Suffice it to say, all the performance details discussed during initial contact and any leading up to the contract need to be put into the contract with the performer, including such things as overtime performance and remuneration policies, payment schedules, and cancellation policies. Along with the contract, a tentative event schedule and show running order, plus a floor plan and *stage plot*, should be sent to the performer or act so that they have the latest information.

The time between the contract date and performance date can be lengthy, often months. Producers sometimes forget that they need to keep performers informed of changes to a show. Start times, rehearsal and setup times, and show length changes can all affect an individual act's ability to give an optimum performance. Therefore, any changes to the event that impact on the show should be given to all performers whenever they occur, right up to the performance date. A day or two out from the event itself, all performers should be called and all performance details re-confirmed. It is at this time that the load-in information, green room assignments, parking details, meal arrangements, and setup and sound check expectations are provided in their final form.

### 1.3.4.3 At the event

As we have alluded to throughout this section, performers must be treated with courtesy and respect. Nothing can undermine this more than having them frustrated on arrival at an event site by a locked door and no visible way to enter the event space. They must be given exact directions about how to load-in and enter the venue, or navigate through an outdoor event and fencing. Sometimes this entails getting though security barriers such as doors with pass codes or live security guards. If it is impossible to give them codes to enter a venue, then someone must be assigned to meet them at a specific location on arrival. Otherwise, there is a chance that they will be late for setup, sound check, or rehearsal. Luckily, cell phones can help to prevent this possibly embarrassing situation. Once onsite, they should be escorted to their green room, or if it is not ready, at least to a location where they can temporarily leave valuables and equipment safely.

From the moment they arrive onsite to the time they perform, they must be kept fully informed of what is happening at the event, including any changes to their start time or to the length of their show. As they will undoubtedly be confined to the green room once setup, sound check, and rehearsals are over, this means regular updating of their estimated performance time. I personally like to give approximately 60, 30, 15, five, and one min warnings. At the 15 min mark prior to their performance, they should be moved to their standby location at or near the stage or other performing area, such as an entrance door, to await their cue to enter.

After their performance, they should be personally thanked and paid. If the show was great, they should be told, but if it was not, this is not the time to dwell on the negative. This can be saved for later discussion as they will usually clearly understand what went wrong without being told.

### 1.3.5 The special case: celebrities

Celebrities draw people to events. However, while they are wonderful as a draw, they can be expensive to accommodate and sometimes come with complex contract riders outlining technical and personal requirements. These last may extend to the type of transportation, accommodations, and meal arrangements that are acceptable, but may go much farther and detail green room requirements, some of which can get into the ridiculous. Often, fulfilling riders costs as much or more than the basic contract. However, most are quite reasonable and result from years of experience and often inadequate treatment at the hands of inexperienced show producers and promoters. See www.thesmokinggun.com/backstage for some examples, both reasonable and extreme. Sonder (2004, pp. 183–184) also discusses this topic. McGarey (2004), formerly of Axtell Productions in Atlanta, USA, has spent many wonderful hours and days working with celebrities. She offers the following advice:

- Determine your client's budget up front. You simply must know whether you are buying a Cadillac or a Ford before you start shopping!
- Determine whether a meet and greet is key to the success of the event. If so, you will need to do your homework to see which artists are gracious and eager to accommodate. Much better than to find out the day of the show that they will only meet for five min and permit five photographs! Yes, this has actually happened.

- Determine the type of act that will best suit your client.

- Obtain a list of available acts in the price range desired. Remember the cost can easily double or even triple when rider requirements and expenses are added in.

- Present the list to your client asking them to narrow their choices to the top three (in order please) so that you can do your homework to nail down exact bottom line prices (including production at the intended location). I normally do a line item cost analysis for each of the three acts.

- Be sure your client understands that availability is good "at this writing" since most celebrity acts will not hold dates until a written offer is in their hands! This way, if the client procrastinates and loses their first choice, you cannot be held responsible.

- Be sure that your client understands that once the written offer is made, they are committed! I've had to demand a minimum 50 percent payment on more than one date where the client changed their mind after the written offer was made. In some cases, a full 100 percent payment was made after a decision to cancel the order. When you play with the big boys, there is very little room for mind changing without penalty!

- Be sure that you have access to the venue no later than the morning of an evening event. Better yet, if possible, try to negotiate a setup time the night before. This can give you the breathing room you need in case of technical difficulty the day of the show.

- Be sure to schedule a production meeting the day before your celebrity event with all the key players including hotel or venue contacts, sound and lighting contractors, A-V supplier, decorators, caterers, and ground arrangements personnel. Provide each of them with a contact list so that in case you are not available at a critical time, they can call the person needed to address the problem.

- Stay calm. The day of the screaming, out-of-control producer is past! You will gain much more respect from your client and your co-workers if you work through each challenge without throwing around a lot of attitude. Delegate responsibility from the beginning so that you will not be inundated with trivial questions on event day. Once sound checks are done, you should be able to relax and enjoy the event along with everybody else!

We have spent a lot of time in this chapter discussing entertainment from the performer's perspective, and that has been on purpose, because so many books and articles consider only the entertainment consumer's perspective. In summary then, given that the performers for a special event have been treated well, that they have been fully informed of the reason for the event and the content they must deliver, and that all other preparatory concerns have been satisfied, what can the event producer or manager expect in return? First, because the vast majority of performers follow this calling out of sheer love for their craft, they can be expected to deliver a professional performance filled with emotion and passion. In more practical terms, it should be delivered on time, be of the correct length, and communicate the messages and content discussed and contracted prior to the event. Stage attire and costuming should be of the highest quality, deportment should be respectful at all times before, during, and after the show, and language and content should be above reproach. Any performer who is incapable of fulfilling and meeting these minimum expectations should not be seriously considered for future employment in special event entertainment.

## 1.3.6 Risk and safety

Most of the risk associated with performers and entertainment in general, assuming that all the technical equipment is correctly used, surrounds their being where they should be at the right time, and performing according to their contract for the length of show promised. Therefore, as discussed throughout this chapter, if contracts are followed and performers treated appropriately, there should normally be no risk involved from their side. From my personal experience, the most risk has been associated with having performers arrive on time and knowing where to go. Even with the best directions and allowing enough time for getting lost, traffic jams, or parking problems, there were still instances when fate intervened and a performer was late. Producers sometimes have to accept that probabilities tell you that this is inevitable. However, having a backup plan such as rearranging the order of performances, or calling an alternate performer is always a good idea, as is keeping a list of performer contact information at the ready while onsite.

The physical safety of performers and the audience is paramount as well. Ignoring the obvious crowd management problems of large concerts, which we deal with to some degree in Chapter 9, there may be potential for harm depending on the performance content. For example, I once became an onstage volunteer for a strong man act and ended up standing on his shoulders thinking to myself, "I sure hope you have liability insurance, my friend." Usually, these types of audience participation routines are relatively harmless but just in case, producers should ensure that such an act has a contract holding the producer harmless for any injuries incurred to audience members, that the act carries sufficient commercial and general liability (CGL) insurance, and that the act names the producer as an *additional insured*. On the other side of the coin, performers may get injured just moving through an audience or venue or by an audience member. These cases are covered by Workers' Compensation and producers should again ensure that all acts and performers are registered for coverage by providing copies of their certificate of registration. Double-checking routes that performers will use in getting to or from a stage or in performing their act is critical, especially with respect to trip hazards and proper lighting, as is the safety of any overhead rigging for performance. Other risks are covered in the applicable technical chapters of this book.

## PRODUCTION CHALLENGES

1. Briefly describe the different forms of entertainment.
2. Name six reasons for entertainment. Give examples of an event that might be organized for each reason.
3. You have a client who would like to motivate and educate his company's sales force by means of cutting-edge, experiential entertainment. Research online and suggest four different options for mobile device-based entertainment that would achieve this and explain how it could be done.
4. You are to produce an entertainment show for a standup reception for 3,000 convention attendees in a large convention center ballroom. The event lasts 3 h and your client would like to keep the attendees there for as long as possible. Plan a show that will be exciting and highly visual and that will keep attention for the full event. Suggest at least three different layouts for stages or performance areas and how the entertainment could be staged for maximum effect.
5. An awards show for which you are the producer will have periodic entertainment segments throughout the event, including performances by a standup comedian, a backup band for the awards program, a three-member female vocal group, and a keynote speaker. Detail the concerns that must be addressed in looking after these performers and suggest ways to take care of them throughout the event, which will last for 5 h (6:00–11:00 pm). They will all have had to be at a rehearsal at 4:00 pm and will need to stay on the premises from then until the end of the event at 11:00 pm.

## REFERENCES

Bailly, N. (2013, June 26). The Future of the Live Concert Experience, Part 1. *iQ Innovation Everywhere*. Retrieved May 27, 2014, from http://iq.intel.com/the-future-of-the-live-concert-experience-part-1/.
Barkley, L. (2004). Building a Show from Scratch: From Inspiration to Execution. *Hot Tips for events that SIZZLE* (pp. 7–11). Vancouver: Total Event Arrangements and Meeting Network.

Beeman, W.O. (1993). The Anthropology of Theater and Spectacle. *Annual Review of Anthropology, Vol. 22*, 369–393. Retrieved May 18, 2006, from www.brown.edu/Departments/Anthropology/publications/Theater.pdf.

Beeman, W.O. (2000). Humor. In Alessandro Duranti (Ed.), Linguistic Lexicon for the Millenium, *Journal of Linguistic Anthropology, Vol. 9, No. 2*. Retrieved May 18, 2006, from www.brown.edu/Departments/Anthropology/publications/Humor.htm.

Beeman, W.O. (2002). Performance Theory in an Anthropology Program. In N. Stuckey and C. Wimmer (Eds.) *Performance Studies as a Discipline* (pp. 85–97). Carbondale: Southern Illionois University Press.

Bloom, M. (2001). *Thinking Like a Director: A Practical Handbook.* New York: Faber and Faber, Inc.

Bourzac, K. (2014, January 3). Nanomaterials Could Enable Large, Flexible Touch Screens: 3M's new silver nanowire films could lead to large, interactive, and ultimately flexible displays. *Materials News.* Retrieved May 28, 2014, from www.technologyreview.com/news/523221/nanomaterials-could-enable-large-flexible-touch-screens/.

Campbell, D.G. (2000). The Overtones of Health. In Don Campbell (Ed.) *Music: Physician for Times to Come* (pp. 89–94). Wheaton: The Theosophical Publishing House.

Collier, R. (2015). Robert Collier Quotes. *Goodreads.* Retrieved May 29, 2015, from www.goodreads.com/author/quotes/257221.Robert_Collier.

Cooper, S. (1998). *Staging Dance.* London: A & C Black Limited.

CSE1. (2013). GESTURETEK Brings Tech to Life. *CanadianSpecialEvents.com.* Retrieved June 17, 2014, from http://canadianspecialevents.com/8038/gesturetek-brings-tech-to-life/.

CSE2. (2013). Holographic Projection – Fiction is Now Fact. *CanadianSpecialEvents.com.* Retrieved June 17, 2014, from http://canadianspecialevents.com/8752/holographic-projection-fiction-is-now-fact/.

Czikszentmihalyi, M. (1974). *Beyond Boredom and Anxiety.* San Francisco: Jossey-Bass.

Emotion. (2004). *The Columbia Encyclopedia, Sixth Edition.* New York: Columbia University Press. Retrieved April 27, 2006, from Questia database: www.questia.com/PMqst?a=o&d=101242680.

Feder, K.L. (1996). *The Past in Perspective: An Introduction to Human Prehistory.* Mountain View: Mayfield Publishing Company.

Gamification. (2014, May 25). In *Wikipedia, The Free Encyclopedia.* Retrieved 17:57, May 26, 2014, from http://en.wikipedia.org/w/index.php?title=Gamification&oldid=610051977.

Goldman, J.S. (2000). Sonic Entrainment. In Don Campbell (Ed.) *Music: Physician for Times to Come* (pp. 217–233). Wheaton, IL: The Theosophical Publishing House.

Hamari, J., Koivisto, J. and Sarsa, H. (2014, January 6–9). Does Gamification Work? – A Literature Review of Empirical Studies on Gamification. *Proceedings of the 47th Hawaii International Conference on System Sciences.* Hawaii, USA.

Hödl, O., Kayali, F. and Fitzpatrick, G. (2012). Designing Interactive Audience Participation Using Smart Phones in a Musical Performance. *International Computer Music Conference Proceedings, Vol. 2012* (pp. 236–241). Ann Arbor: Michigan Publishing.

Jagadeesh, K. (2013, June 20). Futuristic Stage Radiates Light and Creates Visuals Based on How Hard You Party. *Storylines About the Future.* Retrieved May 28, 2014, from www.psfk.com/2013/06/dancing-powered-stage.html#!QWe3m.

Jones, D.L. (2001). Damaging Vocal Techniques. *The Voice Teacher.* Retrieved May 22, 2014, from www.voice-teacher.com/damaging.html.

McGarey, D. (2004). Creative Ways to Reap ROI From Your Entertainment Program! *Hot Tips for events that SIZZLE* (pp. 65–72). Vancouver: Total Event Arrangements and Meeting Network.

Plutchik, R. (2001, July). The Nature of Emotions. *American Scientist, Vol. 89,* 344. Retrieved April 28, 2006, from Questia database: www.questia.com/PMqst?a=o&d=5000081731.

Pollick, M. (2002). Basic Stage Blocking Techniques for Play Directors. *Pagewise.* Retrieved May 23, 2014, from www.wy.essortment.com/stageblocking_rbua.htm.

Powers, R. (2011). Suggestions for Choreographing a Dance. *Stanford Dance.* Retrieved May 23, 2014, from https://socialdance.stanford.edu/Syllabi/Choreography.htm.

Raymond, T. (2015, February 4). Red Skelton on Hang Gliding. *Red Skelton: Good Night and God Bless – America's Crown Prince.* Retrieved June 1, 2015, from http://red-skelton.info/articles/jokes/red-skelton-hang-gliding/

Rosenbaum, L. (2014, January). Let Guests DJ Your Events with their Smartphones. *Bar & Restaurant Marketing Insights.* Retrieved May 28, 2014, from http://blog.rockbot.com/blog/let-guests-dj-events-smart-phones.

Roston, J. (2000, June). So You Want to Choreograph. *Dance Spirit*. Retrieved May 23, 2014, from www.dancespirit.com/backissues/may_june00/feature01chorg.shtml.

Rutherford-Silvers, J. (2012). *Professional Event Coordination*. Hoboken, NJ: John Wiley & Sons, Inc.

Schechner, R. (2002). *Performance Studies: An Introduction*. London: Routledge.

Sinha, P. (2014, September 30). Get a Friend Other Than Just an Entertainment Robot: Sopo. *StockNewsDesk*. Retrieved January 12, 2015, from http://stocknewsdesk.com/friend-entertainment-robot-sopo-1217399.html.

Sonder, M. (2004). *Event Entertainment and Production*. Hoboken, NJ: John Wiley & Sons, Inc.

Stevenson, D. (1999). Acting Technique. Colorado Springs: Story Theater International. Retrieved May 18, 2006, from www.storytheater.net.

Stevenson, D. (2004, October). The Paradox. *Story Theater Newsletter, Vol. 5, No. 9*. Colorado Springs: Story Theater International. Retrieved May 18, 2006, from www.storytheater.net.

Stevenson, D. (2005, January). Let the Audience Speak. *Story Theater Newsletter, Vol. 6, No. 1*. Colorado Springs: Story Theater International. Retrieved May 18, 2006, from www.storytheater.net.

Stevenson, D. (2005, June). The Four Types of Language. *Story Theater Newsletter, Vol. 6, No. 6*. Colorado Springs: Story Theater International. Retrieved May 18, 2006, from www.storytheater.net.

Stevenson, D. (2005, September). Get More Laughs. *Story Theater Newsletter, Vol. 6, No. 8*. Colorado Springs: Story Theater International. Retrieved May 18, 2006, from www.storytheater.net.

Tattersall, I. (2006, September 19). How we came to be HUMAN. *Becoming Human: Evolution and the Rise of Intelligence. Scientific American*, Special Edition, 67–73.

Turner, V. (1988). *The Anthropology of Performance*. New York: PAJ Publications.

Varsity. (2014). Dance Technique. *Varsity*. Retrieved May 23, 2014, from www.varsity.com/event/1170/dance_technique.

Vilpponen, A. (2011, September 26). Rovio and Uplause Premiered Angry Birds Crowd Game at Formula 1 GP Singapore. *Arctic Startup*. Retrieved May 28, 2014, from www.arcticstartup.com/2011/09/26/rovio-and-uplause-premiered-angry-birds-crowd-game-at-formula1-gp-singapore.

Wang, G. (2009). *Designing Smule's iPhone Ocarina*. Stanford, CA: Center for Computer Research in Music and Acoustics (CCRMA), Stanford University.

Wang, G, Essl, G. and Penttinen, H. (2010). *Do Mobile Phones Dream of Electric Orchestras?* Stanford, CA: Center for Computer Research in Music and Acoustics (CCRMA), Stanford University.

Wilson, T. (2000). Chant: The Healing Power of Voice and Ear. In Don Campbell (Ed.) *Music: Physician for Times to Come* (pp. 11–28). Wheaton: The Theosophical Publishing House.

Wong, R. (2011, February 9). World's Largest Touchscreen can Detect up to 100 Touch Points at Once. *DVICE*. Retrieved May 28, 2014, from www.dvice.com/archives/2011/02/worlds_largest_14.php.

Zillman, D. (2006a). Dramaturgy for Emotions From Fictional Narration. In J. Bryant and P. Vorderer (Eds), *Psychology of Entertainment* (pp. 215–238). Mahwah, NJ: Lawrence Erlbaum Associates, Inc.

Zillman, D. (2006b). Empathy: Affective Reactivity to Others' Emotional Experiences. In Jennings Bryant and Peter Vorderer (Eds.), *Psychology of Entertainment* (pp. 151–181). Mahwah, NJ: Lawrence Erlbaum Associates, Inc.

Chapter **2**

# Décor

**LEARNING OUTCOMES**

After reading this chapter, you will be able to:

1. Understand and explain design theory, specifically the elements and principles of design, and how they relate to event décor design in a three-dimensional space.
2. Describe the different categories of décor and how they can be used in a special event.
3. Understand the importance of correctly planning for the setup and strike of décor at an event.

Special events are emotional and sensory experiences. The more an event can appeal to the emotions and the five senses, the more memorable and successful it will be. People attend events to be transported into an environment that is different from their everyday life, whether it is a concert, a championship football game, or a formal dinner. Frequently, these events are held in what would ordinarily be venues that are not conducive to such a fantasy environment unless they are transformed through the magic of well-designed décor. Successful event décor design takes talent and considerable thought to be effective. It has become a specialty in itself and the designer is a key member of the production team, with the producer and designer working together to bring the wow factor of décor into the event.

This wow factor often takes the form of a theme event. This chapter is intended to provide knowledge of the resources that may be used to create such an event without detailing what might go into any specific theme, as several other authors (Malouf, 1999; Monroe, 2006; Goldblatt, 2014) have given excellent interpretations of the process.

In this chapter, we will review design theory and how good event décor designers use it, we will explore the main categories of décor that designers use for events, and finally, we will discuss the myriad details that a designer and a producer must consider when integrating a décor setup into the event production schedule. This is not intended to be an exhaustive treatment of this subject, but only enough to acquaint producers with the essentials.

## 2.1 Design theory

Design theory crosses all artistic boundaries. Whether it is interior decorating for a home, planning for a store window display, landscaping, creating a web page, or conceiving a stage set for a rock star's world tour, similar theory comes into play. Design theory incorporates *elements* of design and *principles* of design.

### 2.1.1 Elements of design

These are the raw ingredients of design. They are very general but form the basis of the design in that different functional or visual effects can be achieved by working with them. Although they are sometimes called by other names in different artistic disciplines, we will examine each one and how it relates specifically to event décor. Several excellent resources explain most of these in detail (Gatto et al., 2000; Lovett, 1999; Saw, 2001; and Skaalid, 1999).

#### *2.1.1.1 Space*

Three-dimensional space is the most obvious element of design that one notices when first walking into a large room such as a convention center hall or a hotel ballroom with nothing in it. Space is something we cannot touch but it touches us. It surrounds us and envelops us, and any other object in it. Luckily, we are able to sculpt it and change its appearance, and therein lies one of the secrets of good décor design. That cold, cavernous hall can be changed from an empty, echoing void into a warm, intimate dining room and theater. The challenges faced by an event designer, unlike artists in other disciplines, are that this transformation must be temporary, it must be accomplished relatively quickly, and it must make use of all three dimensions in the most effective manner.

Making use of space effectively means being aware of negative and positive space. Positive space is where shapes and forms occur within the three dimensions. Negative space is where they are absent. For the designer, this necessitates striking a balance between the amount of negative and positive space. Novice event designers often mistake three-dimensional décor as being a combination of wall coverings (the two dimensions of height and length or width) and tables, chairs, and centerpieces (the two dimensions of length and width with minimal height). They neglect to extend into the third dimension in both cases, thus leaving too much negative space in one dimension. For example, the vertical plane can be better filled by using very high table centers extending up from the tables, or by using ceiling-mounted, matching décor pieces extending down from the ceiling above the tables. Likewise, extending themed props outward into the room from murals or wall coverings can fill the horizontal plane. In this way, all three dimensions are more effectively utilized.

One key point must be made that is well known by good designers, and that is that in any event space indoors or outdoors (where the vertical dimension is infinity!), people quickly fill the bottom 6 ft (1.8 m) of the vertical dimension. That means any décor placed below this level is virtually ineffective and will not be noticed. The general rule of thumb is to place all essential décor above eye level (i.e. above approximately 5–6 ft from the floor or ground).

Accomplishing quick three-dimensional event space transformation necessitates the designer being aware of the raw materials available that can be set up easily. Some of the latest décor pieces that enable this to happen will be discussed in Section 2.2, and include large inflatables, tensile fabric structures, banners, and murals or backdrops.

Having reviewed what can be done with a space, it is also necessary when first analyzing an event space to be aware of what is already there. Three-dimensional architectural or other elements, such as columns, obstructive corners, overhanging balconies, unmovable furniture or practical fixtures (e.g. bars, fixed seats, tables, or open kitchen), might require some sort of work-around, as may doors and windows. The key point here is that the designer wants to avoid any extra costly construction or time-consuming cover-ups of these elements in order to achieve the desired design. Rather, it is better to work with them and incorporate them into the design. Likewise, unsuitably patterned or colored wallpaper, carpets, and lighting can clash with a designer's concept and may have to be brought into the design to be successful.

### 2.1.1.2 Form

Form is the basic tangible element of design. In two-dimensional disciplines such as painting, it is known as *shape* and is made up of combinations of basic rectangles, triangles, and circles. In three-dimensional design, such as event décor design, the forms take on volume and mass, and the combinations of shapes are limitless. Geometric forms such as boxes, cones, balls, tubes, and many others are used to create event décor. By combining the basic geometrical forms in different ways, new free form or abstract shapes emerge.

With the advent of new materials in recent years, designers have realized that event décor can be revolutionized by incorporating unique design forms that can be erected and taken down easily, inexpensively, and efficiently. Examples include tensile fabric décor, air tubes, and the integration of structural-type forms such as scaffolding or trussing, with fabrics and lighting. These are often used to transform mundane shapes into attention-grabbing, colorful sculptures.

In terms of the practical use of forms for events, if they are intended to be functional, forms should be appropriate for their intended use. In terms of the use of forms for pure design, varying shapes adds excitement to the overall design, such as combining new table and stool shapes with other forms (e.g. perhaps wildly shaped inflatables), but still keeping within the event's color scheme and theme in all the forms. We will be exploring color and themes later in this chapter.

Form can be truly spectacular. See Figure 2.1.

Figure 2.1 Example of an unusual form

Courtesy of Moss Exhibits, www.moss-exhibits.com

### 2.1.1.3 Line

As a design element, line has two meanings. The first and most obvious is that it serves to outline form and separates it from the surrounding space. For example, one might say that an automobile, a dress, and a piece of furniture have nice lines, meaning that their shapes, as defined by their *outlines*, are well designed.

The second meaning of line is an abstract one. It describes the separation between areas of change, when objects are aligned, or when the repetition of objects creates visual movement. The line leads our eye from one point in the overall design to another, and thus helps to unify the design by bringing various objects together. Furthermore, the direction of the abstract line has more subtle, inherent meanings. Horizontal lines suggest calmness, vertical lines suggest a potential for movement, and diagonal lines suggest actual movement, giving vitality to the design.

### 2.1.1.4 Texture

Texture is the surface quality of form. It is always present in three-dimensional space because everything has a surface. The term is often misused to refer only to rough surfaces, but it can mean smooth like the surface of a mirror, coarse and rough like burlap, or variations in between. Actually, texture can be either tactile (i.e. the actual physical feeling of an object's surface) or visual (i.e. the illusion of a surface's texture in two dimensions, exemplified by the angle of light falling on a surface in a photo). In special events, we deal primarily with tactile texture.

Two other terms are related to texture. The first is *ornament*. Ornament is an extension of texture and gives visual interest to the form. For example, an ornament may be a single logo on a plate or cup, it may be the chrome bumpers on an old 1950s car, or it may be the decorative top of a Corinthian column. If ornament is repeated on a surface, it becomes a *pattern*. It should be noted that an ornament is normally physically attached to, and part of, a surface.

The second term associated with texture is *accessory*. An accessory is an addition to a form, and is physically separate from it, although it could appear to be part of it. For example, it may be a napkin ring, a chair tie, or in the case of our 1950s car, simulated leopard skin seat covers.

In designing events with texture in mind, it is considered good practice to vary textures and hard goods, while still keeping within the event color scheme and theme, as with variations in forms. For example, variations in linens and soft goods could encompass mixing crushed velvet table covers with smooth spandex chair covers. Variations in hard goods could mean using a mixture of metal, wood, stone, and plastic, all in the same event.

### 2.1.1.5 Value and light

Value is considered to be one of the main elements of design, even though it is related to color. It refers to the relative lightness or darkness of a certain area within a space. For an event, this is also related to the amount of light in that certain area. Variations in value (*value contrast*) can be used for emphasis (a *principle* of design) to create a focal point in a room. Depending on the color and texture of a form in an event space, the amount of light thrown on it can also highlight the *color contrast* of the object against its background.

### 2.1.1.6 Color

Color, like space, is all around us. It is unquestionably the most powerful design element for event décor. Because we deal extensively with color theory in Chapter 5 on Lighting, we will focus our attention in this chapter on color meaning and the various color schemes that may be used with décor to create an event environment. In doing so, we will demonstrate how color may be used to dramatize an effect, tie a variety of objects together, create a subtle understated look, or create a mood.

### 2.1.1.6.1 COLOR MEANING

To fully understand how important color is in event design, one should have a basic knowledge of how color affects us as human beings. This enters the realm of *design psychology*. It affects our bodies and it affects our minds, but our culture and sex determine how we interpret it. An examination of the meaning of color will assist us in making the correct choices for event color schemes. Here is a review of how we interpret colors, courtesy of Color Wheel Pro (www.color-wheel-pro.com/), which is a software tool that helps one create harmonious color schemes based on color theory (QSX Software Group, 2014).

- Red. Red is the color of fire and blood, so it is associated with energy, war, danger, strength, power, determination as well as passion, desire, and love. Red is a very emotionally intense color. It enhances human metabolism, increases respiration rate, and raises blood pressure. It has very high visibility, which is why stop signs, stoplights, and fire equipment are usually painted red. This color is also commonly associated with energy, so it can be used when an event involves games, cars, items related to sports, and high physical activity.

- Orange. Orange combines the energy of red and the happiness of yellow. It is associated with joy, sunshine, and the tropics. Orange represents enthusiasm, fascination, happiness, creativity, determination, attraction, success, encouragement, and stimulation. To the human eye, orange is a very hot color, so it gives the sensation of heat. Nevertheless, orange is not as aggressive as red. Orange increases oxygen supply to the brain, produces an invigorating effect, and stimulates mental activity. Orange is the color of fall and harvest. Orange has very high visibility, so it can be used to catch attention and highlight the most important elements of design.

- Yellow. Yellow is the color of sunshine. It is associated with joy, happiness, intellect, and energy. Yellow produces a warming effect, arouses cheerfulness, stimulates mental activity, and generates muscle energy. Yellow is often associated with food. Bright, pure yellow is an attention-getter, which is the reason taxicabs are painted this color. When overused, yellow may have a disturbing effect; it is known that babies cry more in yellow rooms. Yellow is seen before other colors when placed against black; this combination is often used to issue a warning. Yellow can be used to evoke pleasant, cheerful feelings. Yellow is very effective for attracting attention, so it can be used to highlight the most important elements of a design. Light yellow tends to disappear into white, so it usually needs a dark color to highlight it. *Shades* of yellow are visually unappealing because they lose cheerfulness and become dingy.

- Green. Green is the color of nature. It symbolizes growth, harmony, freshness, and fertility. Green has strong emotional correspondence with safety. Dark green is also commonly associated with money. Green has great healing power. It is the most restful color for the human eye; it can improve vision. Green suggests stability and endurance. Sometimes green denotes lack of experience; for example, a *greenhorn* is a novice. Green, as opposed to red, means safety; it is the color of free passage in road traffic. Green can be used in any event that has a component of nature as part of the theme, or with any component that concerns money or wealth, such as the color of gaming tables.

- Blue. Blue is the color of the sky and sea. It is often associated with depth and stability. It symbolizes trust, loyalty, wisdom, confidence, intelligence, faith, truth, and heaven. Blue is considered beneficial to the mind and body. It slows human metabolism and produces a calming effect. Blue is strongly associated with tranquility and calmness. It can be used in any event that involves air, sky, water, or sea. As opposed to emotionally warm colors like red, orange, and yellow, blue is linked to consciousness and intellect. Dark blue is associated with depth, expertise, and stability; it is a preferred color for the corporate world. When used together with warm colors like yellow or red, blue can create high-impact, vibrant designs; for example, blue-yellow-red is a perfect color scheme for a superhero.

- Purple. Purple combines the stability of blue and the energy of red. Purple is associated with royalty. It symbolizes power, nobility, luxury, and ambition. It conveys wealth and extravagance. Purple is associated with wisdom, dignity, independence, creativity, mystery, and magic. Purple is a very rare color in nature; some people consider it to be artificial. Light purple is a good choice for a feminine design in events.

- White. White is associated with light, goodness, innocence, purity, and virginity. It is considered to be the color of perfection. White means safety, purity, and cleanliness. As opposed to black, white usually has a positive connotation. White can represent a successful beginning. It can be used for events using high-tech or futuristic themes. White is an appropriate color for charitable organizations and hence, non-profit events; angels are usually imagined wearing white clothes. It can also be used as a neutral color to offset others in an event color scheme. White has a negative connotation in some Asian cultures, as it is associated with death.

- Black. Black is associated with power, elegance, formality, death, evil, and mystery. Black is also associated with fear and the unknown (e.g. black holes). It usually has a negative connotation (e.g. blacklist, black humor, Black Death). Black denotes strength and authority; it is considered to be a very formal, elegant, and prestigious color (e.g. black tie, black limousine). Black gives the feeling of perspective and depth, but a black background diminishes readability. Black contrasts well with bright colors. Combined with red or orange, other very powerful colors, black gives a very aggressive color scheme for an event.

### 2.1.1.6.2 COLOR SCHEMES

In Chapter 5, we explore color theory in detail, specifically how colors are mixed in the *visual color wheel* (also called the *lighting* or *RGB [red, green, and blue] color wheel*). In this chapter, we will examine the *pigment color wheel* (also called the *mixing color wheel*), and how the colors in it can be used alone or in combination to create attractive event color schemes, because most décor is constructed of pigment-based materials.

In traditional color theory, there are three pigment colors (i.e. colors found in paint and fabrics) that cannot be mixed or formed by any combination of other colors. These are red, yellow, and blue, known as primary colors. All other colors are derived from these. Secondary colors are formed by mixing the primary colors, and are green, orange, and purple. Tertiary colors are formed by mixing the secondary colors and are yellow-orange, red-orange, red-purple, blue-purple, blue-green, and yellow-green. All these colors can be represented in a color wheel for pigments, as in Figure 2.2 (left).

As opposed to the pigment color wheel, the visual color wheel is based on the primary colors red, green, and blue (RGB). The RGB primaries are used for computer monitors, cameras, scanners, and such. The secondary triad of the visual (RGB) wheel is cyan, magenta, and yellow (CMY), which is a standard in printing. Also, the human eye contains RGB receptors (QSX Software Group, 2014), hence the name "visual." Because of this fact, many artists believe that the visual RGB color wheel should be used instead of the traditional pigment (RYB) wheel to create visual complements, and indeed they

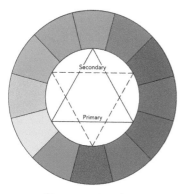

Pigment color wheel

Split complementary color scheme

Figure 2.2 Color and color schemes

Images courtesy of: left—Doug Matthews; right—Blueprint Studios, www.blueprintstudios.com

are occasionally used in events. However, for the purposes of this chapter we will stick to the pigment color wheel.

Given the color wheel and the meaning of color, we can now proceed to develop specific event color schemes. There are six classic color schemes: monochromatic, analogous, complementary, split complementary, triadic, and tetradic (QSX Software Group, 2014):

- Monochromatic. In this scheme, one *hue* is dominant and variations in lightness and darkness of the single hue are used. The scheme looks clean and elegant but lacks contrast. It is relatively easy to manage, and works well with neutrals such as white or black.

- Analogous. These are related colors from a pie-shaped section of the color wheel, usually colors adjacent to each other. It is always a good idea to strive for one color to be the dominant one and allow the others to enrich it. This scheme is relatively easy to create but lacks contrast, although it is very rich.

- Complementary. This scheme uses colors that are *complementary* or directly opposite each other on the color wheel. It offers the highest contrast of any of the color schemes, but is harder to balance than others. The best results are achieved by placing warm colors against cool ones.

- Split complementary. This is a variation of the complementary scheme and uses a single color combined with the colors adjacent to its complementary. It provides high contrast but is harder to balance than the monochromatic or analogous schemes. It is best to choose a single warm color and place it against cool colors. Figure 2.2 (right) shows such a scheme using lighting, linens, and chairs. It features gold-yellow against magenta and blue-purple.

- Triadic. Any three hues equally spaced on the color wheel can form a triadic color scheme. This scheme looks very balanced and offers strong visual contrast and richness. It is best to choose one color to be used in larger amounts than the others and to subdue the use of gaudy colors.

- Tetradic. This is the richest of all the color schemes. It brings together two pairs of complementary colors. While offering more variety, it also is the hardest scheme to balance and for this reason, it is recommended that one color be chosen as the dominant one and set against the others. This is about as far as most event designers will go in working with color schemes, as anything more can easily become an unattractive jumble.

## 2.1.2 Principles of design

While the elements of design are the raw ingredients, the principles of design provide flexible guidelines for the effective combination of these elements. Once again, they transcend all artistic disciplines. They include proportion, balance, rhythm, emphasis, and harmony.

### 2.1.2.1 Proportion

Proportion is the relationship between *size* and *scale*. Size is absolute. It is how large—or small—an object (form) is and is a measurable quantity. Scale is relative. It refers to how small or large an object seems to be in relation to the space it occupies. For example, for an event in a large room or outdoors, the décor will need to be of very large "size" because the "scale" of the event space is very large. If the ceiling is 50 ft (15 m) from the floor, a 4 ft (1.2 m) high banner will be lost (i.e. out of proportion) when suspended from it. This vertical height will demand a banner of at least one-third of the total height (16.7 ft or 5 m, a ratio of 1:2) to be in good proportion and aesthetically pleasing. Likewise, an overly large décor piece in a very small room will be out of proportion because the size of the piece does not match the scale of the event space.

One interesting aspect of proportion is the *golden* or *divine proportion*. This refers to a ratio of sizes between two objects that is 1:1.62. It is represented by the 21st letter of the Greek alphabet, Phi (Ø). Although adequate explanations are scarce, it turns out to be the most pleasing ratio of sizes used not only in human designs but also in the natural world. For example, the ratio of a violin's neck to the length of the violin body is 1:1.62. The distance between the edge of some butterflies' wings to the first colored mark compared to the distance to the center of its body is 1:1.62. Figure 2.3 demonstrates this ratio in a comparison of simple gray bars. The most aesthetically pleasing one is the one with a ratio of light to dark of 1:1.62. Good art, photography, interior design, and advertising, among others, all recognize this ratio, although sometimes not overtly. There is no reason why it cannot be applied to the three-dimensional space of an event. Hence, the ideal height for the banner in our example would probably be just over 19 ft (5.7 m) instead of 16.7 ft (5 m), also dependent of course on its width, the readability of its graphics, and the total number and placement of other pieces of décor.

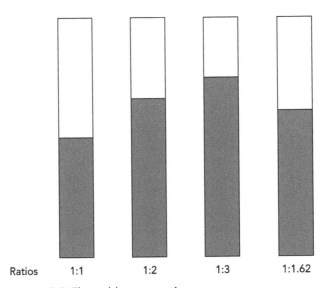

Figure 2.3 The golden proportion

Courtesy of Doug Matthews

When working with event décor, some other general rules also apply. When in doubt about the exact proportion, oversize almost always impresses. Why? Because having décor larger than the scale demands gives the psychological impression that there is more of it, and it is usually easier to take some away than to add some at the last minute. Second, for visual variety, it can be more interesting to mix the scale in patterns if there will be more than one pattern. For example, large patterns in table overlays could be mixed with smaller patterns in chair covers.

### 2.1.2.2 *Balance*

Visual balance is related to the size of objects (forms) and also their value, such as lightness or darkness, termed *visual weight*. One part of a design should appear equally weighted or visually balanced with another. There are three categories of balance:

#### 2.1.2.2.1 SYMMETRICAL BALANCE

This is usually considered to be mirror image balance, meaning that in two dimensions, both sides of the design are identical. It can also mean that both sides of a design are equal in terms of numbers, colors, and sizes of objects or forms (Skaalid, 1999). In three dimensions, symmetrical design is more difficult to achieve, particularly in an event space where doors, windows, and other features may prevent perfect symmetry. In general, symmetrical balance is more formal and orderly, and "conveys a sense of tranquility, familiarity or serious contemplation" (Howard Bear, 2014). Typical symmetrical balance at an event would refer to both sides—or even four quarters—of a venue being decorated with identical numbers and sizes of props in close to similar positions in the space, although the subject matter and material need not be the same. Approximately equal color value would also enhance the symmetry.

#### 2.1.2.2.2 ASYMMETRICAL BALANCE

This is considered to be informal balance. Each design half is different yet appears to be of equal importance visually. As Skaalid (1999) states, this is achieved when:

> *several smaller items on one side are balanced by a large item on the other side, or smaller items are placed further away from the center . . . than the larger items. One darker item may need to be balanced by several lighter items. It is usually harder to achieve [than symmetrical balance] because the artist must plan the layout very carefully to ensure that it is balanced.*

Sometimes, by intentionally avoiding balance, a designer can "create tension, express movement, or convey a mood such as anger, excitement, joy, or casual amusement" (Howard Bear, 2014).

#### 2.1.2.2.3 RADIAL BALANCE

The third type of balance is radial balance in which all elements radiate out from a center point (although not all designs are exactly circular). "It is very easy to maintain a focal point in radial balance since all the elements lead your eye toward the center" (Skaalid, 1999).

### 2.1.2.3 *Rhythm*

Rhythm in design refers to the manner in which one's eye is drawn into the design. Some designs:

> *move you throughout in a connected, flowing way much like a slow, stately rhythm in music. Others move you from one place to another in an abrupt, dynamic way much like a fast, staccato rhythm in music will give you the impression of movement.*

> *(Skaalid, 1999)*

Rhythm is produced through *repetition* and *transition*:

> *Repetition is the use of the same element more than once. Transition is the relative change in size from large to small; the gradation in color from light to dark, from dull to bright, and from color to color; and in texture from rough to smooth or coarse to fine.*
>
> (Adler, 1998)

### 2.1.2.4 Emphasis

Emphasis, also known as *dominance*, is all about controlling the attention of a viewer. According to Adler (1998),

> *it creates a focal point or center of interest within the design and attracts the eye to a central outstanding feature or idea to which all else is subordinate. One kind of line, shape, direction, texture, or color needs to dominate or the design falls apart.*

Emphasis is achieved through *contrast*, *placement*, or *isolation*.

#### 2.1.2.4.1 CONTRAST

Contrast can be by color or value (i.e. lightness or darkness). Generally, bright colors of the same hue stand out more than dull colors (value), but different colors that are the same value do not stand out as much from each other. Contrast can also be by shape and texture. A single geometric shape, for example, will stand out against a backdrop of free-form shapes, a vertical line against horizontal lines, and a silver truss grid against a painted wall.

#### 2.1.2.4.2 PLACEMENT

Correct placement of décor in the context of a special event is key to creating a focal point. In the three dimensions of a special event, creating one or more focal points becomes a design challenge due to the many options available. Let's look at what can affect the placement of décor to create a focal point:

- Type of event. This will be the first determinant in choosing a focal point. For example, if the event is a dinner with only dining tables in a room, multiple focal points could be created as spectacular, 8 ft tall table centers each individually lit from above. If the event is an awards show with a stage, the main focal point will have to be the stage and most effort should go into designing an attractive and practical stage set. If the event is a standup reception with multiple buffets, the decorating effort should go into making the buffets the focal points in order to attract guests to them, best done by designing very tall and well-lit buffet centerpieces. Perhaps it is an interactive event in which there are multiple themed rooms or areas. In this case, it would be best to design entrance décor, perhaps in the form of themed vignettes, to lead guests to that location. Finally, if it is an outdoor event such as a festival with large crowds spread out over a large area, the focal points will necessarily have to be extremely high and well-lit in order to act as "beacons" for people to go to them. These might be tents with large banners on top, stages with huge graphics over speaker wings, an entrance with a tall arch, and so on.

- Number of attendees. We have briefly mentioned the necessity of placing décor above the average height of a human being in our initial section on space as a design element. Again, this is a factor in designing a focal point. Anything that is intended to be a focal point will have to be above this height. One interesting exception is that the floor can be a focal point. This can be done by using certain lighting effects like *gobos* or *automated lights* on the floor, by using a colored *light-emitting diode* (LED) dance floor, or by placing actual décor on the floor. Many great designers have used a variety of floor coverings to achieve a certain effect. These have included live rose petals for a romantic setting, sawdust for a western theme, peanuts for a Cuban-themed restaurant or a baseball theme, leaves for an outdoorsy theme, artificial turf for a sports event, sand for a beach theme, and many more. In these cases, the number of attendees becomes irrelevant.

- Budget. If money is tight, there are key areas that, if decorated well, will still make a focal point. In approximate order of descending importance, these are:
  - Stages. If there is no more at an event than a performance stage—or multiple stages—it can be made a focal point by the simple placement of a drape or curtain behind it to offset the action onstage from the wall or scenery behind. This is often the only focal point for many corporate meetings, conferences, and outdoor festivals.
  - Entrances. An appealing entrance gives a good first impression and sets the theme for the entire event.
  - Tables. If the event involves a sit-down meal, attractive dining tables can override all other décor as a focal point. High, well-lit table centers and well-chosen table linens can draw the eye immediately to them. This also applies to buffet tables.
  - Corners. If budget allows after the other key areas have been decorated, then we move to corners where décor vignettes can be built out of props or backdrops, then subtly illuminated. These work well for themed events.
  - Walls. Now the budget gets bigger. Wall coverings in the form of murals, complete draping, or wide-screen projections can form spectacular focal points but are expensive.
  - Ceilings. Finally, ceiling draping, hangings (e.g. banners or inflatables), complete coverings, or ceiling lighting can be focal points and complement the other décor. They tend to be costly due to the extra time and labor involved for installation.

Once the focal point has been established by placement, what is noticed next as either part of that same point, or the next focal point, is governed by *proximity, similarity,* and *continuance* (Saw, 2001). Proximity refers to the fact that near or overlapping objects will generally be seen next. For example, if the main focal point is a stage set with a large graphic, the panels surrounding the graphic will be seen next. Similarity means that an object that is of the same color, size, and/or shape will be seen after the nearest one. In our stage set, if a frame surrounds the graphic and there are other frames surrounding A-V screens, they will be seen third. Continuance means that if the primary object points or looks at another object, it can direct the viewer's attention. This could be especially important in the design of multimedia shows. In the case of our stage set, if there are two A-V screens with similar frames, the image on one could be used to direct the audience's attention to the second screen, or to any other object on the stage or in the event. See also Section 7.5 of Chapter 7 on Set design.

### 2.1.2.4.3 ISOLATION

This is fairly obvious as a method of controlling emphasis. Everyone is acquainted with the giant inflatables used for advertising. A giant Elvis on top of a used car dealership is a very obvious example of how isolation can work to create a focal point. Similarly, for an outdoor event, a stage strategically placed with no other similar stages or décor of comparable size near it will be the focal point.

### 2.1.2.5 Harmony

"Harmony is achieved when different forms and colors have a feeling of unity" (Skaalid, 1999). In essence, for an event it is an almost intangible sense that the design is complete and that all the elements and principles have been successfully followed. It is pleasing visually and psychologically.

## 2.2 Categories of décor

A successful event designer not only has to know design theory, but must also be intimately familiar with the ingredients that can be used to put the theory to practical use and build the design. By this we mean the actual décor itself. There are almost endless choices for décor with new inventions added annually. To assist with understanding what they are, we will break these choices down into categories and explain what each one is and how the types of décor within it can be used.

### 2.2.1 Backdrops

In the special event world, backdrops (also called *murals*) are used for theming. By definition, they are often used as backdrops for stages (where they make excellent focal points) and as decorative murals mounted on, or in front of, walls. Because of their size, sometimes measuring over 50 ft (15 m) in width and up to the ceiling of a venue in height (i.e. approximately 22 ft or 6.7 m), they are ideal for creating a total surround, themed environment. Realism is often enhanced by the addition of smaller props to extend out into the third horizontal dimension in front of the backdrop.

Although in the past most backdrops were constructed of canvas and the designs used oil-based paint, today they are constructed of lightweight, 100 percent polyester and the designs are airbrushed on. In the past, the old painted canvas was subject to drying and cracking whereas today's lightweight polyester cotton material with better paints applied can be easily folded and transported without any damage. Today's material also receives fire retardant treatment as standard procedure. Most backdrops are constructed with a top sleeve and/or fabric ties that allow for easy suspension on pipe and drape hardware (horizontal poles supported by vertical poles), trussing, or any other horizontal support available in a venue. Some newer themed backdrops are painted onto smaller horizontal sections that can be joined together vertically by means of heavy-duty zippers to form larger murals, thus providing flexibility for fitting into venues with differing ceiling heights.

Correct lighting is the key to a backdrop having optimum decorative power. Even lighting over the entire surface of the backdrop is recommended to eliminate shadows. Luminaires are best placed well downstage— or in front—of the backdrop surface to avoid any burning of the fabric. Figure 2.4 illustrates a fantasy backdrop in use as a main décor component of a themed dinner. Note how it creates a total environment feel, particularly with the color-coordinated lights and tables.

### 2.2.2 Themed sets

Set pieces for special events generally mean large décor pieces. Sets have traditionally been designed as part of theatrical stage productions, but they have actually been part of special events for centuries. One spectacular early event near the beginning of the third century BCE was a dinner held in an immense tented pavilion in Alexandria, Egypt, and hosted by Pharaoh Ptolemy II. The pavilion was decorated:

> *on either side with beams concealed by tapestries with white stripes draped voluminously about them; between the beams were painted panels set in order. Of the columns four were shaped like palm trees, but those which stood in the middle had the appearance of Bacchic wands.*
>
> (The Deipnosophistae of Athenaeus, Book V, trans. 1928)

Other parts of the set included gold tunics, silver and gold shields, paintings, 25 ft long gold eagles in the ceiling, couches, and much more.

Indeed, one of the most famous theatrical set designers, turned special event producer, was Leonardo da Vinci. He staged many theatrical spectacles for royalty during the Renaissance and was especially adept at creating mechanical devices as part of sets. Examples include sets designed as mountains and earth that

Figure 2.4 Example of fantasy Alice in Wonderland backdrop

Photo provided by Backdrops Beautiful®, www.backdropsbeautiful.com

opened up to reveal hell and a self-propelled, mechanical lion that actually took steps then opened its chest to reveal lilies (Laurenza et al., 2006, pp. 185–187).

Shortly after da Vinci died, in 1520 at the famous Field of the Cloth of Gold meeting between Henry VIII of England and Francois I of France, theming was very much on display. The English built a temporary palace for the occasion,

> *in four blocks with a central courtyard, each side over 300 ft long. The only solid part was a brick base about 8 ft high. Above the brickwork, the 30 ft walls were made of cloth or canvas on timber frames, painted to look like stone or brick; a slanting roof was made of oiled cloth painted the color of lead to give the illusion of slates. Contemporaries commented especially on the huge expanse of glass, which made visitors feel they were in the open air. Red wine flowed from two fountains outside.*

> *(Nurse, 2007)*

Not unlike those of the 16th century and even before, sets today tend to be constructed of wood with various adornments such as window frames, signs, mock stairs and doors, or roofs. Although spectacular if used in the right space, these sets can be extremely cumbersome to set up, and nowadays they are often rejected in favor of lightweight fabric décor, backdrops, lighting, and projection technology. There is, however, still a place for them in events such as trade shows and often as spectacular focal points on a stage or room entrance. They also work well if setup time is not at a premium, in a large space with high ceilings, especially if an element of realism is sought.

Set pieces are usually constructed of thin wooden plywood sheets affixed to a wood frame (together called *flats*), painted realistically on their front surfaces or covered with material, and supported by triangular wooden bracing screwed into the frame, upon which sandbags or other weights are placed to hold them sturdy and upright. They can also be supported by L-shaped steel brackets, especially good for two-sided scenic flats. Part of the difficulty with using sets for special events is that they are large and this can pose problems if venue access is difficult or tight, especially freight elevators and hallways where the pieces must be carried. As with backdrops, realism may be enhanced by the addition of smaller props in and around the larger set. More detail on sets is provided in Chapter 7.

### 2.2.3 Props

Prop is a shortened version of the word *property* and derives from theater terminology, wherein *stage properties* constitute the smaller items that are used by actors in a play. This terminology has also crossed into the movie industry as well as special events. In theater, props have traditionally been divided into three categories: set props, hand props, and decorative props.

Set props are considered to be larger movable items not built into a stage set, such as furniture, floor lamps, rugs, stoves, tree stumps, and others (Gillette, 2000). We can categorize these items similarly in special events but include much larger items such as classic columns, cars, wagons, models, machinery, and others. They often are used to embellish large sets or backdrops as described above. In my personal event career, I have utilized a great variety of unique large props in events, such as large model trains and airplanes, boats of varying sizes, antique cars and hot rods, real race cars, real western buckboards, robots, miniature space ships, jukeboxes and pinball machines, and totem poles. Set props, if used correctly, especially authentic ones like jukeboxes or antique cars, can become good focal points for an event, often acting as a surprise component. They work best when combined with thematically matching large sets as described above (e.g. a western buckboard placed within a false-fronted western street scene), so that the realism of the scene is enhanced. As with backdrops, due to their size and attractiveness, these items demand proper lighting, as well as safekeeping and adequate insurance, since many are on loan or rented from private collectors.

Hand props are smaller items that are literally handled or carried by actors. Decorative props are ones that enhance a setting visually but are not actually handled by actors (Gillette, 2000). In special events, these two categories tend to be lumped together as *small props*. Sometimes they are handled by guests at the event, sometimes they are handled by performers, and sometimes they are pure decoration with nobody touching them. Typical small props are such items as mock ice cream sodas and old signs at a 1950s diner, surfboards at a beach party, carved masks at a northwest coast native potlatch, a suit of armor at a medieval feast, a real ice carving as a table center or as a larger sculpture, or an old movie camera at an Academy Awards-type dinner.

Often, real props cannot be found and replicas must be made or new creations manufactured. Suffice it to say that any and all materials are used, including Styrofoam (e.g. simulating large boulders), *Foamcore* (simulating many different shapes in lightweight material), wood, metal, Plexiglas, rubber (e.g. knives, swords), and plastic (e.g. those fake ice cream sodas). Designers will either make them themselves or sub-contract to have them built as required for a specific event. The current thinking in props is that they must be very real and purposeful, ideally with an interactive element (Rothstein-Kramer, 2013).

Figure 2.5 illustrates two different prop categories. On the left are several buffet table centers for a Cirque-themed event using decorative small props. Note that these centers also provide dramatic focal points in the event space. On the right is an example of a large set prop, an Asian archway used as an event entrance.

### 2.2.4 Furniture

Not that long ago, the only furniture at an event consisted of dowdy dining and buffet tables in standard shapes, and unimaginative dining chairs so ugly that they begged to be covered up. Fortunately, that has all changed. Furniture has finally become décor by itself, and much of it begs to be exhibited in its naked form, rather than being hidden. There are essentially two main categories of furniture that are used in events: specialty lounge furniture and bars; dining tables and chairs. For purposes of this discussion, office furniture will be omitted even though it may sometimes be part of a larger event or trade show.

Decorative small props        Large set props

Figure 2.5 Examples of props

Images courtesy of: left—Cindy Raider of Nat Raider Productions Inc., www.natraider.com, and Fotografika, www. fotografika.ca; right—Décor and More, www.decorandmore.com/

### 2.2.4.1 Specialty lounge furniture and bars

The increasing appeal of lounge furniture appears to have come from two directions. On one hand, budget crunches resulting from the economic downturn of 2008 "have resulted in a trend away from full-seated [more expensive] events to hors d'oeuvres and cocktails served in stand-up environments" (Beurteaux, 2012). On the other hand, event organizers seem to have finally realized that many people use such events to network, and often to make critical business decisions. To not have enough high and low tables for drinks and light food as well as insufficient seating (as in older event scenarios of the 1990s and early 2000s) means unhappy attendees and an unsuccessful networking environment. Using lounge furniture also permits an easier division of the event space into different purpose-designed areas, such as networking, dinner, and/or dance.

Almost any style, color, or material is available for easy chairs, ottomans, and sofas, including vintage, modern, rustic, and specially themed. Some are also internally lit by LEDs. Tables open up the possibilities even more, with traditional coffee and end tables to LED tables in programmable colors being available from numerous rental companies now specializing in only event furniture. Most companies also offer a wide range of accessories to complement the tables and chairs, including mirrors, cushions, rugs, and occasionally florals. Such furniture can thus bring both subtle theming and event colors into the event décor mix without a lot of extra cost coming from other props or from extra room lighting.

Bars and liquor displays have really blossomed as unique décor focal points, especially those using LEDs. They can be large, small, or modular for a custom look.

See Figure 2.6 for examples of modern event lounge furniture.

### 2.2.4.2 Dining tables and chairs

Once upon a time in special events . . . there were only four choices for dining tables, and they were all round. Events—corporate ones especially—would be held almost exclusively in hotel or conference center ballrooms and the catering departments of those hotels and conference centers would own a stock of round, foldable dining tables varying from 48 in. (120 cm) in diameter to 72 in. (181 cm) in diameter and capable of comfortably seating between six and ten people. Occasionally, an adventurous event producer would attempt the extraordinary and ask for rectangular dining tables, often to be told there were not

Lounge furniture (USA)

Lounge furniture (India)

Figure 2.6 Examples of event lounge furniture

Images courtesy of: top—Extraordinary Events, www.extraordinary events.net; bottom—Seventy Event Media Group, www.seventyemg. com

enough for the number of guests. Heaven forbid! It was considered sacrilegious to mix table types, so it would be back to the good old rounds. These tables were hideously ugly and had to be covered at the very least with unimaginative white table linens, and for the then adventurous producer, occasionally black if he or she could scrounge enough linens that looked reasonably similar from various sources.

Likewise, dining chair choices were limited to the hotel's vast stock of uncomfortable and almost as ugly conference chairs that doubled as dining chairs. Although they usually at least color-matched the hotel's overall décor scheme, they often did not match an event's décor in any way. That's about the time that spandex chair covers and accompanying chair bows—and spandex table covers—came onto the scene in order to make some semblance of a coordinated overall event color scheme.

Fast forward about 15 or 20 years. The choices now are almost limitless. Although the tried and true dining rounds and hotel/conference chairs are still available in abundance, many event producers choose to go farther afield and rent dining tables and chairs, as well as linens (as we will see in the next section). These rental items are much more conducive to creating a personalized, custom event. Flexibility in styles, colors, and sizes is becoming the new norm.

Tables run the gamut of styles, from heavy, period Napoleonic to ultra modern clear Plexiglas with LED-lit pedestals. Sizes vary from intimate square tables for four, to large rectangular tables for 14, with rounds and ovals covering everything in between. There are even sectional tables that can be made in varying sizes and shapes, from a triangle to a hexagon. Except for the clear ones, the tables come in many different colors and materials, most of which are designed to be beautiful in their own right and seldom need covering up with linens, although many designers still do for the best overall themed look. Oh, yes, and now it is no longer considered to be in poor taste to mix table styles and sizes. As long as the main theme is maintained, it is much more "progressive thinking."

Chairs—at least the rental ones—have undergone a similar transformation in sizes, styles, materials, and colors. Wooden Chivari chairs are still popular, but they are now facing strong competition from some creative newcomers such as Chameleon Chairs® (www.chameleonchair.com) with changeable styles, cushions, and covers all designed specifically for that chair line instead of for generic chairs. Even LED-lit dining chairs are appearing (www.cortevents.com). There is no doubt that many more inventions for chairs and tables will appear in the near future. Figure 2.7 illustrates some of these new tables and chairs.

Figure 2.7 Examples of dining chairs and square and round dining tables

Images courtesy of: left—Chameleon Chairs®, www.chameleonchair.com, MGM Mirage, and Dahl Photographers; right—Chameleon Chairs®, www.chameleonchair.com, Art of the Party Design, and Patrick Parenteau

## 2.2.5 Linens and napery

Arguably the category of décor that has revolutionized the appearance of special events more than any other over the last 25 years has been fabrics, particularly fabrics associated with dining. Dinner tables with stark white tablecloths and practical but ugly chairs have been replaced by free-form structures with shapely fabric table and chair covers of every imaginable color and design, creating event venues bursting with energy and life. Cavernous convention center halls have now become fantasy environments. The choices and uses of different fabrics increase each year.

Linens and napery include tablecloths, table runners, table overlays, table skirting, chair covers, chair sashes or bands, napkins, tray and tray stand covers, and placemats. The options of material, sizes, colors, and patterns available are almost endless, making it easy to coordinate a color scheme or event theme. As an example, some of the materials available in most of these products include polyester, spandex, cotton, damask, crushed velour, satin, lace, burlap, and denim. Prints vary from red and white checks to themes of space, sports, stars and stripes, racing, leopard, jungle, and many more. These fabrics are used to cover almost every type of table and chair, including round dining and cocktail tables, rectangular dining or buffet tables, serpentine tables, regular dining chairs, Chivari chairs, fold-up chairs, and stools. Table 2.1 details linen sizes generally required to properly fit the most common table sizes.

Table 2.1 Linen sizing chart

| Table size | Seating | Cloth size | Drop point | Skirting required | Overlays |
|---|---|---|---|---|---|
| Round | | | | | |
| 30 | 2–4 | 90 | 30 | 8 | 48/54 |
| 36 | 4 | 90 | 27 | 9.5 | 48/54 |
| 42 | 4–5 | 90 | 24 | 11 | 48/54 |
| 48 | 6 | 72 | 12 | 13 | 54/72 |
| | | 90 | 21 | 13 | 54/72 |
| | | 100 | 26 | 13 | 54/72 |
| | | 108 | 30 | 13 | 54/72 |
| 54 | 6–8 | 72 | 9 | 15 | 54/72 |
| | | 90 | 18 | 15 | 54/72 |
| | | 100 | 23 | 15 | 54/72 |
| | | 108 | 27 | 15 | 54/72 |
| 60 | 8–10 | 72 | 6 | 16 | 72/82 |
| | | 90 | 15 | 16 | 72/82 |
| | | 100 | 20 | 16 | 72/82 |
| | | 108 | 24 | 16 | 72/82 |
| | | 120 | 30 | 16 | 72/82 |
| 66 | 8–10 | 72 | 3 | 18 | 72/82 |
| | | 90 | 12 | 18 | 72/82 |
| | | 100 | 17 | 18 | 72/82 |
| | | 108 | 21 | 18 | 72/82 |
| | | 120 | 27 | 18 | 72/82 |
| 72 | 10–12 | 90 | 9 | 19 | 82 |
| | | 100 | 14 | 19 | 82 |
| | | 120 | 24 | 19 | 82 |
| | | 132 | 30 | 19 | 82 |
| Rectangular | | | | | |
| 36 x 36 | 4 | 54 x 54 | 9 | 13 | |
| | | 82 x 82 | 23 | 13 | |
| 48 x 48 | 4 | 54 x 54 | 3 | 17 | |
| | | 82 x 82 | 17 | 17 | |
| 30 x 48 | 4–6 | 60 x 96 | 15 x 24 | 14 | |
| 30 x 72 | 6–8 | 60 x 96 | 15 x 12 | 18 | |
| | | 72 x 120 | 21 x 24 | 18 | |
| 30 x 96 | 8–10 | 72 x 120 | 21 x 12 | 22 | |
| | | 72 x 144 | 21 x 24 | 22 | |
| | | 90 x 156 | 30 x 30 | 22 | |

For these sizes, note the following:

- Table size refers to table diameter in inches for round tables and the width and length in inches for rectangular tables.
- Cloth size refers to the cloth diameter in inches for round tables and the cloth length and width in inches for rectangular tables.
- Drop point refers to the point below the tabletop where the cloth ends, in inches. For rectangular tables the points are the drop below the sides followed by the drop below the ends. The formula to find the drop point is:

$$\text{Drop point in inches} = \frac{\text{Cloth size in inches} - \text{Table size in inches}}{2}$$

- Skirting refers to the total length of skirting required to fully skirt the table (in feet) with one extra foot added for safety. The formula to find the total length is:

$$\text{Length of skirt in feet} = \frac{\text{Table size in inches} \times 3.1416}{12} + 1$$

- Overlay dimensions are in inches and refer to the size of a square overlay (dimension of a single side) that will at minimum fully cover the table surface. For many, two options of sizes are given, separated by a slash.

One important consideration when working with linens, especially chair covers, is that installation can take much more time than expected, particularly if the covers must be individually fitted and if the chairs also require the addition of sashes or bands. It should be determined at the outset by the designer who will be doing the installation (and strike) of these items, either catering staff or decorating staff, and the appropriate labor planned. Venues do charge for the installation of linens so costs should be compared.

Care must be taken when handling linens in order to keep them unwrinkled. Normal packing and transportation will necessarily result in fold lines. If these are unsightly, then they are best removed through steaming, especially if they are synthetics made of polyester or nylon, such as lamés and organzas. Sometimes, however, steaming is wasted because most of the linen's area ends up being covered by tableware and the only part of chair covers seen are the backs. Linens do wrinkle when held by a hand though, so wait staff in particular need to be made aware.

See Figure 2.7 for examples of coordinated linens and chairs.

## 2.2.6 Drapery

Thanks to an array of sturdy and flexible support hardware, drapery has become commonplace as an attractive and inexpensive means to isolate stage areas and to hide equipment and undesirable sections of a venue. In addition, drapery fabrics are used extensively in decorating entrances, ceilings, walls, and augmenting other décor pieces such as props, furniture, and backdrops. We will examine the main uses and types of drapes and materials.

### 2.2.6.1 Stage draping

Event managers frequently neglect to consider what a stage presentation will look like when a stage is placed against a bare wall. Because the stage is relatively low in height, it tends to get lost against the larger area of wall behind it. For this reason, to assist in creating a focal point, placing a simple drape backdrop behind the stage can make a tremendous difference. Besides the need for creating a focal point, sight lines in a venue often necessitate drapery being used to *mask* or hide backstage areas and equipment such as lighting and A-V equipment. We will cover stage draping in detail in Chapter 7.

### 2.2.6.2 Room draping

Drapery is often used to dress up, divide, or hide other areas of an event besides the stage. For example, it may be swagged over entrance doors to give a classy appearance when guests arrive, it may divide a trade show into separate booth areas, it may hide changing and technical areas, or last but not least, it may be suspended from ceiling-mounted piping or trussing to form floor-to-ceiling masking of the entire venue walls and the ceiling itself. This drape, in one form or another, plus its associated support hardware, is known generically as pipe and drape. There are two main considerations when planning to use pipe and drape: the method of support or hardware, and the type and amount of fabric. Parts of this section have come from Whitacre (2014).

#### 2.2.6.2.1 METHOD OF SUPPORT

The hardware for mounting drape from the ground consists of steel base plates, vertical pipes, and horizontal pipes. The horizontal and vertical pipes are usually made of aluminum.

- Base plates. Base assemblies include a heavy square steel plate with up to nine screw holes into which is screwed a short pin over which the vertical pipe is fitted. Base weights vary from 6–62 lb (2.7 kg–28 kg), with the most common being 35 lb (15.8 kg) for an 18 in. x 18 in. (45 cm x 45 cm) plate. The higher weights are used for higher drapes. Pins vary from 4–8 in. (10–20 cm), again with the higher ones used for higher drapes. Sandbags of 25 lb (11.3 kg) are often added to the base assemblies for extra support, with two bags necessary for 22 ft (6.7 m) high drapes.

- Vertical pipe. Although some vertical pipes are of fixed height (typically used for trade shows), most are fully slip-lock adjustable from 3–5 ft (1.0–1.5 m) up to 14–26 ft (4.2–7.8 m).

- Horizontal pipe. These are fully adjustable with button click stops and incorporate metal hooks at each end that slip into the slotted openings in the vertical pipes (uprights). They are capable of holding light and heavy fabrics. The rule of thumb is to use a horizontal that is 1 ft (0.30 m) less than the desired hanging length of drape.

#### 2.2.6.2.2 FABRIC

There is a wide range of options for drape material. The two defining overall categories are opaque and non-opaque. Opaque drapes are most often used to mask off room areas like walls or kitchens and are the material of choice for stage and A-V draping. They include:

- Velour. This is the most common theatrical and event drape. It is a medium weight woven polyester fabric that is full of texture, bright with luster, and feels luxurious. It comes in various weights from 14–25 oz/yd (396–708 g/m), the most common being 16 oz (453 g). It has a nap so all sections must be hung the same way.

- Encore. Now replacing velour, Encore is a wrinkle-resistant, brushed polyester velour with no nap. Its weight is 22 oz/yd (624 g/m).

- Supervel. This is a lightweight, brushed polyester velour with a dappled finish and that comes in vibrant colors. It responds very well to up lighting. Its weight is 8 oz/yd (227 g/m) and it has the best inherent flame retardancy of any fabric.

- Muslin. Natural Muslin is an un-bleached, lightly woven cotton-like polyester fabric that gives a warm, sophisticated, and clean look to any event space. For want of a better description, it is similar to a bed sheet—and does wrinkle. The weight is 7 oz/yd (198 g/m).
- Commando Cloth. Also known as Duvetyn (Duvetyne), it comes in three weights: 8 oz, 12 oz, and 16 oz/yd (227, 340, 453 g/m), and is a flame retardant, 100 percent cotton fabric with a brushed matte finish. It is used for budget draperies and masking.

Non-opaque, or semi-transparent, drape is typically cheaper than opaque and often used with opaque drape for a layered effect. For example, black Encore or Supervel can be used as a mask for walls and transparent sheers can be arranged as an inner layer. If lights are used behind the inner, transparent layer, the effect is highly dramatic. Another unique but classy look is the use of *swags*. Swags are pre-made in order to make them look the best and can also be used over the top of an outer layer. The different types of non-opaque drape include:

- Sheers. For an elegant special effect, polyester sheers may be used alone or as an overlay. Sheers are popular for ceiling draping, and they respond well to lighting. This is the lightest of all drape material at 3 oz/yd (85 g/m).
- Banjo. This is a lightweight, polyester fabric with a slightly shiny finish, usually used for trade show booth dividers. The weight is 7 oz/yd (198 g/m) and it comes in many colors.
- Show Taffeta. Also known as Velon or Show Plastic, taffeta is a budget-driven, waterproof vinyl drapery that comes on a roll ready to hang. It has a matte finish with slight texture and perforation between drapes. It comes in many colors and can reach heights of 150 ft (45 m). Liner coverage helps prevent transparency.

Of critical importance in making drape look its best is the fullness. Fullness adds depth, richness, opacity, and improves sound suppression. Fullness is achieved by gathering the drape along its width. A completely flat look is 0 percent fullness, often used with Muslin. The most common fullness is 50 percent, so that for a 10 ft wide drape, 15 ft of width must be ordered. Thirty percent fullness is weak and 100 percent is very rich. This is most often used with lightweight drape such as Show Taffeta or Sheers (can even be up to 200 percent), and would mean that for a 10 ft wide drape, 20 ft would need to be ordered for 100 percent fullness.

The actual hanging of drape is normally achieved using pockets or sleeves sewn into the upper hem of the drape. Bottom hems also allow for straightening and flattening some drape such as Muslin. The horizontal pipes are inserted through the sleeves and the drape manually gathered along the horizontal pipe to obtain the desired fullness. Double horizontal bar setups are also available for layering (i.e. with inner sheers as described above), as are special clips for extra support.

Another method of hanging drape is using a theatrical tie-on method. Drape tie methods used may be a standard grommet and tie, where the tie and grommet hole are visible unless a clove hitch is used, and once tied, the drape ties must be rolled to hide the ties from the audience side of the drape. Blind ties are another drape top finish that allows for drapes to be tied to a pipe without the audience seeing the grommets and ties (Pipe and drape, 2014).

To complete a theme if budget permits, effective ceiling treatment can be spectacular and swagged draping is often the means to accomplish this. Because of the heights and weights, the material used for ceiling treatment is usually lightweight sheer, voile, or satin made from 100 percent polyester. The material is typically suspended from trussing, piping, or wires that have previously been rigged from ceiling hanging points. As a cautionary note, ceiling draping can be very time-consuming and labor-intensive, and also must be accomplished while there are no interfering obstacles such as dining tables or chairs underneath.

This means that it must usually be done before any other equipment or décor has been set up for the event, often in the early morning hours.

See Figure 2.8 for examples of drape installations at weddings.

Draped walls and ceiling

Draped entrance

Figure 2.8 Examples of drapery at weddings

Images courtesy of: left—Drape Kings, www.drapekings.com and Timmester Photography, www.timmesterphoto.com; right—Seventy Event Media Group, www.seventyemg.com

### 2.2.7 Banners and signs

Material and printing technologies are now at the point where gigantic, crystal-clear photo reproductions and graphics can be printed on a variety of durable materials and suspended from large buildings or other structures, both indoors and outdoors, to be viewed from great distances. These are not the old-style painted billboards, but superior quality, easy-to-install signage. These banners and signs have become commonplace in the special event world as décor and signage at trade shows, exhibitions, sporting events, and festivals, not to mention all types of smaller events. We will review the different materials available for signs and banners, the methods of printing, the requirements for graphic artwork, and finally, the methods of suspension.

#### 2.2.7.1 Materials

Materials for signs and banners are varied, with some long-lasting fabrics that are suitable for indoor or outdoor use, and many flexible or rigid options. All materials used for graphic displays need to be tested for fire safety and should come with a fire certificate, especially for fabric prints. The following list is a summary of materials, applicable methods of printing, and sizes generally available (some provided by Signable Inc., 2010), although these can and do change frequently:

##### 2.2.7.1.1 SPECIALTY FABRICS

- Canvas. Heavy material with coarse texture and stiff look, matte finish. Up to 16 ft 4 in. (4.9 m) wide. Screen and digital printing, or hand painting.
- Knit polyester. Cost-effective fabric with glossy, mesh-like finish, indoor/outdoor. Up to 60 in. (151 cm) wide. Screen or digital printing.

- Polyester. Matte finish, indoor. Up to 60 in. wide. Screen or digital printing and appliqué.

- Satin. Lustrous, elegant, indoor. Up to 60 in. wide. Screen or digital printing.

- Sunbrella. Durable, high quality, indoor/outdoor, multiple colors. Up to 60 in. wide. Can be screen-printed.

### 2.2.7.1.2 FLEXIBLE SUBSTRATES

- Mesh. Economical indoor/outdoor, multiple colors, multiple styles, good for windy areas such as for fence covers. Up to 16 ft 4 in. wide. Seaming will create larger sizes. Comes in different weights. Screen or digital printing, hand painting, computer-cut vinyl letters or graphics.

- Nylon. Rich look with bold, saturated colors, indoor/outdoor, many colors. Up to 60 in. wide. Comes in different weights. Screen and digital printing, or hand painting.

- Polyethylene. Cost-effective indoor/outdoor, many colors, short-term use. Up to 60 in. wide. Comes in different weights. Screen or computer-cut vinyl printing.

- Static Cling Vinyl Film. A PVC film that sticks/clings to smooth gloss surfaces such as glass, smooth plastic, and shiny metal surfaces. It sticks to these surfaces without any adhesive and can be removed without leaving behind any residue. It is ideal for a variety of graphics, craft, and decorative applications such as signs, decals, window graphics, door covering, protective masking and more. Screen or UV printing.

- Vinyl. Economical indoor/outdoor, smooth finish, multiple colors. Up to 16 ft 4 in. wide. Seaming will create larger sizes. Comes in different weights. Screen or digital printing, appliqué, hand painting, computer-cut vinyl letters or graphics.

### 2.2.7.1.3 RIGID SUBSTRATES

- Acrylic. Also known by the trade name of Plexiglas. Due to the high thermal expansion and contraction rate of acrylic, it is best mounted using an extruded aluminum frame (usually custom made to size). Vinyl may be applied—including translucent vinyls—for backlit signs. Thicknesses vary and sizes range from 49 in. x 97 in. (1.5 m x 2.9 m) to 75 in. x 100 in. (2.3 m x 30.3 m). Some typical uses include backlit ground signs, backlit fascia signs, and pylon signs. It is popular in some of the LED furniture mentioned in this chapter.

- Aluminum. Lightweight, durable sheet metal, variety of thicknesses, can be coated to any color. Up to 5 ft x 10 ft (1.5 m x 3 m) sheets. Screen or digital printing, hand painting, computer-cut vinyl letters or graphics.

- Coroplast. Lightweight, corrugated plastic, indoor/outdoor, many thicknesses and colors, good for short-term use. Up to 5 ft x 10 ft sheets. Screen or digital printing, hand painting, computer-cut vinyl letters or graphics.

- Gatorboard and Foamcore. Durable, lightweight paper and foam product, many thicknesses, several colors. Up to 5 ft x 8 ft (1.5 m x 2.4 m) sheets. Screen or digital printing, hand painting, computer-cut vinyl letters or graphics.

- Magnetic. Ultra magnetic material is a thin film of vinyl on top of a magnetic sheet for mounting to metal surfaces. Screen printing or vinyl graphics. This material comes in rolls 24 in. (60 cm) wide in thicknesses of 0.030 in. (0.75 mm). Some typical uses include fridge magnets and vehicle signs.

- Masonite. Light, less durable, cost-effective pressed wood, variety of thicknesses, can be coated to any color. Up to 5 ft x 10 ft sheets. Screen or digital printing, hand painting, computer-cut vinyl letters or graphics.

- Polycarbonate. Also known by the trade name of Lexan. Polycarbonate is an extremely strong, shatter-resistant material. It is usually used where the opportunity of breakage is possible. Vinyl may be applied—including translucent vinyls—for backlit signs. Polycarbonate comes in white or clear. Thicknesses vary and sizes range from 49 in. x 97 in. (1.5 m x 2.9 m) to 75 in. x 100 in. (2.3 m x 30.3 m). Some typical uses include backlit ground signs, backlit fascia signs, and pylon signs.

- Plywood. Durable wood, indoor/outdoor, variety of thicknesses, can be coated to any color. Sometimes known as Crezon. Up to 5 ft x 10 ft sheets. Screen or digital printing, hand painting, computer-cut vinyl letters or graphics.

- PVC. A smooth, hard plastic material, available in various standard colors such as red, blue, yellow, green, white, and black but not in all thicknesses. The most popular thickness is 0.125 in. (3 mm). Sheet sizes up to 5 ft x 10 ft. Typical uses include trade show displays and light duty industrial signs.

- Showcard. Coated cardboard paper product, variety of thicknesses and colors. Up to 40 in. x 60 in. (100 cm x 151 cm) sheets. Screen or digital printing, hand painting, computer-cut vinyl letters or graphics.

- Sintra. Durable indoor/outdoor plastic, many thicknesses and colors. Up to 5 ft x 10 ft (1.2 m x 2.4 m) sheets. Screen or digital printing, hand painting, computer-cut vinyl letters or graphics.

- Styrene. Cost-effective indoor/outdoor plastic, white only, different thicknesses. Up to 4 ft x 8 ft sheets. Screen or digital printing, hand painting, computer-cut vinyl letters or graphics.

## VOICE OF THE INDUSTRY

### Interviews with Ms. Leslee Bell

Founder and Partner, Décor & More Inc.
Toronto and Calgary, Canada
www.decorandmore.com

### and Mr. Martin da Costa

CEO, Seventy Event Media Group
Mumbai and Delhi, India
www.seventyemg.com

This chapter's Voice of the Industry looks at where décor has come from and where it will be going in countries on opposite sides of the globe.

Leslee Bell founded Décor and More in 1989 and since its inception has successfully cultivated it into Canada's largest and most awarded design and décor company, garnering over 50 national and international awards in the process, and employing over 30 people.

Martin da Costa is recognized as one of the pioneers in the high-end special events industry in India. His multi-award-winning company, Seventy EMG, with offices in Mumbai and Delhi, produces some of the most exclusive weddings, fundraising benefits, luxury brand experiences, and festivals in Asia.

**DM**: How have you seen décor change over the last five to ten years? Not the flash in the pan hot ideas, but the trends with staying power?

**LB**: Décor is ever-changing and ever-evolving. After 9-11—and SARS for Canada—then with the economic recession, the field of décor was hit the most. Over-the-top ostentatious events went to streamlined modern, eco-friendly, and urban for anything corporate. The days of hard prop sets

Figure 2.9 Examples of different event entrances

Images courtesy of: left—Décor and More, www.decorandmore.com/; right—Seventy Event Media Group, www.seventyemg.com

were diminishing and being replaced by a "look" or a "feel" rather than a theme in corporate Canada. Our typical Canada Coast to Coast themed dinners, so synonymous with conferences, were being replaced by food stations that articulated iconic props in an urban design with the chosen medium being ice, or metal, or even sculptured florals.

Nowadays, experiential is a major buzzword. People not only want to be entertained, but to be engaged as part of a performance. Characters—we term "decortainment"—serve as greeters, visual sign pieces to an event. If we use a large 15 ft feathered Caribana costumed character, it is 100 percent décor and 100 percent entertainment, stretching décor dollars for greater ROI.

For corporate, the formal sit-down dinner—unless an awards evening—is being replaced by a clubby scene with high volume, soft seating and stroll-about experiential food stations. Within the last year spending has been on an upswing. Every party wants their "aha" moments so that guests can "Tweet" and "Instagram."

Florals over the last ten years have gone from lush and opulent to structural and dramatic. We are now doing a melange of both—lots of show but with architectural lines for drama.

Only recently did we hear so much hype about the pantone shades of the year. With huge social media impact and Pinterest and Olio, every home DIY [do-it-yourself] guru knows about the "in" colors of each year.

Over the last six or seven years, beaded crystal drape, first seen at the Oscars, made its way into many events, fashioned into hanging "shimmiliers" (a form of chandelier made from beaded drape with no internal light source) where projected light dances off them and gives incredible drama.

Linen suppliers are providing copious choices in texture, finish, bling, and appliqué—with multi layering added if budget permits.

**MdC**: The Indian marketplace has seen some quite dramatic changes in décor sensibilities over the past decade, at least at the top end of the Private Function, Wedding and Special Event business. The very large-scale sets based on Rajashtani, Bavarian, and Louis XIV palaces, Bollywood dance sets, and temples that we used to design and build on a regular basis are slowly being replaced by an emphasis on a gentler, more holistic design aesthetic. The focus these days for the clients at the trendy leading edge of the market has been a shift to more understated luxury. As a client from one of India's most powerful industrial houses disarmingly told me a few weeks back, "Everyone knows we're rich. There's no need to trumpet it at large. Let's design this wedding so that my guests are amazed at the detail at every level—design, hospitality, travel, catering." One of the trends here in India has been to re-locate events out of the major urban centers to destinations like Udaipur, Venice, Florence, and Versailles purely in order to take advantage of the architecture already present. The implications have been two-fold: one, absolute numbers of guests at large Indian functions have decreased, certainly at the top end of the market; and two, florists, choreographers, and set dressers have dramatically increased in importance.

**DM**: Have there been unique trends within certain event genres such as weddings, corporate, fundraisers, and festivals?

**LB**: Weddings [in Canada] have not been affected by the economy the way that corporate events have, and those companies who had a nice balance between social and corporate fared best. Milestone moments like weddings, bar and bat mitzvahs still had either modest or higher budgets with the mid-range almost disappearing. Brides or families were justifying the expenditures on a "once in a lifetime event," so even as contracts were signed, more and more last-minute additions were the norm. Also, the once elitist event chair has been lowered in price so much it is mainstream. Chair accessories have been added, skirts, bustles, cinched lace back sheaths, florals, rhinestone buckles are all add-ons for the "dress to impress" chair. In fact in some circles, the chairs are better dressed than the guests in them.

Fundraisers wanted more and more for less and less, advocating great exposure. This is the worst reason to invest. [A décor company should] invest time and energies into an event because you believe in the cause.

**MdC**: Indians are stretching their ambitions globally, and are increasingly traveling to destinations that would have been unthinkable a decade ago. One of the largest Indian weddings of 2014–15 took place at a Palace/Fortress deep in the Umbrian countryside for example.

Clearly though, the trend here is echoing a more generalized, worldwide focus on events that fit beautifully into their surroundings. The days of re-imagining a Belgian sports center into a Bollywood set with the addition of miles of crenellated plywood battlements and thousands of square meters of pink fabric are long gone. Clients are much happier with designing events in and around a heritage site or spectacular natural surrounding. In a sense, it is a sign of the growing design maturity of luxury Indian clients.

**DM**: How do you see décor changing over the next five to ten years?

**LB**: Décor is evolving yearly; nothing is stagnant. From a company that still has one of our skills as large set and set piece design, we are looking at smaller and smaller element pieces that travel well and assemble easily onsite into large sets. With warehouse space at a premium for most companies, large oversized sets cannot be stored for years. Either they are a one-time use, or they are readily repurposed and built from component pieces that allow for that in their original design.

Painting on fabric and digital artwork are perfect when clients have multi-city events. This is only getting bigger in the industry as technology improves.

In the last decade, digital mapping has come of age, electro-luminescence, LED component walls, dance floors, and stages are all front and center. Entertainment in illuminated light costumes or sound-activated shirts for wait staff are the perfect countdown for a New Year's Eve event, taking center stage as mixed media form a new product.

More and more clients want grand reveals, whether a launch, an intro of an MC or President, or just the first glimpse of an event space. Exploding walls, mist screens, the lowering down of a main stage, smoke, Kabuki drop, fireworks, or traveler draping are all used to create the mystery and hype clients want.

I believe the next ten years will place sound and light as a major "paintbrush" at events, coloring and changing the room over and over. A good lighting director will be imperative to the success of an event. Depth, motion, mood, and a great vision are all achieved by lighting. What Disney has mastered in "digital mapping" will be the direction of lighting going forward.

We are sitting on the cusp of a new era of design we call "The Chocolate Fluoride Theory," where two diverse designs are played off each other in harmony. Phrases like industrial chic, rustic elegance, modern country, upscale grunge, or shabby chic are the future of irreverent design, which encourages you to understand the rules of design in order to break them . . . break them by juxtaposing the right elements for a totally new look.

What 2025 looks like, none of us know . . . it could look like the 80s revisited, it could look very futuristic—almost sci-fi—but whatever it is, it will begin evolving today, kind of like a kaleidoscope, and with each turn of the lens a new pattern occurs, and re-occurs with each new shape tumbling into place. The key to ever-evolving design is to keep turning the lens and never staying stagnant. It will be interesting to hear what people in 2025 think of design in 2015. . . .

**MdC**: Technology as décor has existed for some time, certainly in the special events and festivals that Seventy EMG promotes and designs. In the corporate space (e.g. launches, conferencing, exhibition stand design, etc.), it has become a staple of the décor aesthetic. Holograms, 3D mapping, and [large] projection have become commonplace in the work we do. Where the design and set have to communicate a specific brand message, technology will continue to dominate décor briefs; in the luxury special event space, less so. The emphasis is on a more natural, ambient enhancing décor aesthetic, linked to the use of a venue's innate beauty as the dominant trend in India outside of the festival party/corporate space.

### 2.2.7.2 Printing methods

Many options exist for getting graphics and photos onto materials. Here is a brief listing and what they can do:

#### 2.2.7.2.1 DIGITAL PRINTING

Digital printing techniques are generally used for printing short-run graphics, especially banners and signs for special events. The three main processes are regular photo printing, inkjet or UV printing, and dye sublimation or fabric printing. The assistance of Image Options and the Freddie Georges Production Group in California is gratefully acknowledged in compiling the information in this section (M. Salmon and F. Georges, personal communications, February 2006).

- Regular photo printing. This uses a traditional style processor to produce photo panels that are then laminated with a variety of offerings for finish. Printing with this method requires a high-resolution image of 150–300 PPI at full size be provided to the printing company. In order to work with smaller files, it is possible to proportionally downsize the file given to the printing company to 300–600 PPI at half the final print size. Note that PPI refers to the resolution of a photograph in a digital file, while *dots per inch* (DPI) refers to the resolution of a photograph from a printer.

- Inkjet or UV printing. This method is slightly lower in resolution but costs less for printing large graphics. Heated dies with raised images press a thin plastic film carrying colored pigments against the paper. The pigments transfer from the film to the paper; heat and pressure assist in the bonding process. Using new UV flatbed printers allows graphics to be printed directly onto substrate material instead of printing on paper first then laminating and mounting the print onto the substrate, thus saving on labor and material. Files for the inkjet print process should be 75–150 PPI.

- Dye sublimation printing. Sublimation is a process that imprints color on a variety of surfaces using heat and pressure. Sublimation is performed by using specially formulated inks printed on paper, and then applying the print to receptive surfaces. Unlike screen-printing, the sublimation process produces permanent images that will not crack or fade. Dye sublimation is cost efficient and popular for short-run customization of fabrics. Special logos, pictures, and designs can easily be created or scanned into the computer. Transfer paper can be generated and custom prints finished in a matter of minutes. Files for this process should also be 75–150 PPI.

A fairly recent outgrowth of digital printing is *variable-data printing* (VDP), also known as variable-information printing (VIP or VI). It is a form of printing in which elements such as text, graphics, and images may be changed from one printed piece to the next, without stopping or slowing down the printing process and using information from a database or external file. It holds promise for special events in which certain graphics must remain on signage while other details change, examples being the changing daily schedules of conferences or festivals.

### 2.2.7.2.2 SCREEN PRINTING

Screen printing is a very old process that is the most economical method of producing thousands of images from a single one onto a variety of substrates, especially textiles such as nylon, cotton, wool, silk, and canvas. Ink is expressed through a stretched fabric mesh by a squeegee blade to reproduce the original image onto the substrate below. It is ideal for such things as multiple advertising banners and signs (e.g. for a festival or large public event).

### 2.2.7.2.3 APPLIQUÉ

Appliqué is a decorative design made of one material attached to another (e.g. sewn or glued). This can be very attractive for single designs for special events but does not make sense for large runs of signs or banners.

### 2.2.7.2.4 HAND PAINTING

Like appliqué, hand-painted designs are great for one-off pieces of decorative artwork, but prohibitively expensive for multiple copies. Occasionally, hand-painted designs have made their way into special events, especially for such unique items as T-shirts, clothing, or other artwork created by well-known artists as part of an event entertainment program or fundraising auction.

### 2.2.7.2.5 COMPUTER-CUT VINYL

This refers to small lettering and graphics that are cut out of sheets of vinyl with adhesive on one side, using special cutting machinery controlled through a computer interface. These letters or graphics are then applied to larger banners or signs of almost any material that will allow them to adhere.

### 2.2.7.3 General requirements for graphic artwork

In addition to the resolution sizes mentioned for graphics in the section on printing methods, there are several other general requirements that most printing companies have (M. Salmon and F. Georges, personal communications, February, 2006). Knowing what they are will save time and effort for designers, producers and managers:

- Vector files (e.g. file formats for what is known as *line art*, including logos and geometric shapes, such as EPS and SVG), produced by such software as Adobe Illustrator and Corel Draw, are ideal for large format reproductions because they can be scaled to larger sizes without losing any image resolution. In other words, one can start out with a small image file and it will be just as good when blown up.

- Raster files (e.g. file formats for photographs, such as TIFF, BMP, GIF, and JPEG), produced by such software as Adobe Photoshop, are dependent on resolution and require higher resolution files if the image is to be blown up to a large size.

- Files should be provided with all editable elements, including fonts and actual images.

- Color references should be included for consistency. This means giving the printing company color matching *PMS numbers*. PMS stands for Pantone Matching System, which designates every color in a standardized industry set by a unique number. Alternatively, there should be enough time allowed for a proof of all files before final printing is done.

- Color model. Most printing companies require color images or files to be in the *CMYK color format* rather than the *RGB format*. "The CMYK color model (process color, four color) is a subtractive color model, used in color printing, and is also used to describe the printing process itself. CMYK refers to the four inks used in some color printing: cyan, magenta, yellow, and key (black). Though it varies by print house, press operator, press manufacturer, and press run, ink is typically applied in the order of the abbreviation.

  The 'K' in CMYK stands for *key* because in four-color printing, cyan, magenta, and yellow printing plates are carefully *keyed*, or aligned, with the *key* of the black *key plate*. Some sources suggest that the 'K' in CMYK comes from the last letter in 'black' and was chosen because B already means blue. However, this explanation, although useful as a mnemonic, is incorrect.

  The CMYK model works by partially or entirely masking colors on a lighter, usually white, background. The ink reduces the light that would otherwise be reflected. Such a model is called *subtractive* [as opposed to the RGB model which is additive—see Section 2.1.1.6.2] because inks 'subtract' brightness from white" (CMYK color model, 2014).

- Printed image resolution or DPI must be adjusted for viewing distance. If the originating file resolution in PPI is high, usually the resulting printed image will be better, but not always. An 8 ft x 10 ft (2.4 m x 3 m) image on a wall does not need the same DPI at full size as a 2 ft x 3 ft (0.6 m x 0.9 m) image. The smaller image will probably be viewed from 1 to 8 ft (0.3–2.4 m) away, whereas the larger image will probably be viewed from 6 to 25 ft (1.8 m–7.5 m) away. A simple formula can be used to determine an approximate resolution for the final image as follows:

$$\text{Standard Resolution in DPI} = 300/\text{Viewing Distance}$$
$$\text{High Resolution in DPI} = 600/\text{Viewing Distance}$$

In other words, if a blown up 8 ft x 10 ft photo will be viewed from a 10 ft distance in a trade show booth and the highest resolution possible is needed, the DPI would be 60. A good rule-of-thumb is to provide raster (image) files at 72 DPI for the final output size.

### 2.2.7.4 Methods of suspension

Most fabric banners and signs are constructed with a method of suspension built in. These methods are simple and usually consist of one of three types: a stitched hem with a metallic grommet and hole at corners and key points along a hem to allow for rope, wire, plastic, or other ties to be inserted; a series of fabric ties stitched to the banner along the top and/or bottom hems to allow the banner to be tied onto a support; and a sleeve or pocket stitched to the top and/or bottom hem of the banner to permit horizontal support poles such as those used with draping to be inserted.

Actual suspension mechanisms vary considerably. For larger fabric banners, a horizontal pole inserted in the top sleeve of the banner is the preferred method and allows for the easiest installation on large structures or from ceilings or trusses. A horizontal pole inserted into a bottom sleeve helps to keep the banner hanging straight. Fabric ties are also used. For smaller signs, especially ones made from rigid or semi-rigid material, there are a great many different freestanding support bracket and sign holder combinations available. Occasionally, male and female Velcro patches placed on the back of signs and on the mounting surfaces work well for temporary signage, as do flexible magnets (e.g. like refrigerator magnet material) on the back of the signs if they will be mounted on metal surfaces.

### 2.2.8 Tension fabric structures

Since the early 1990s, interior tension fabric structures have revolutionized special events. By definition, the fabrics used are stretched (i.e. tensioned) into a final shape in one of two ways: the first is by anchoring lines tied on one end to reinforced corners of the fabric and on the other end to an architectural structural component such as a wall, ceiling, or floor; the second is by forming around a freestanding or self-forming structure made of aluminum, PVC (polyvinyl chloride, a widely used plastic), or fiberglass tubing. The freestanding structures are supported by vertical poles (pipe and drape hardware) that fit into heavy metal bases for anchoring. For indoor use, the fabric is typically nylon spandex (also called Lycra®, or elastane in Europe) that can be cut into limitless shapes, colors, and sizes, and can be imprinted with graphic designs (e.g. advertising, logos, photos) using a dye sublimation or silkscreen process. Because of the nylon, it is stretchable in four directions. Single-color tension fabrics, especially white, are perfect for use as projection media for video and multimedia, and for lighting effects, and are so used in many event applications.

Fabric structures are most impressive when well lit. According to Debra Roth of the fabric structure design firm, The Originators, and indeed one of the first designers in the industry:

> the best form of lighting is front and up lighting because it causes the structures to glow. LED lights are the standard because of their low cost, battery power, and safer cool operation, and the fact that they can safely be used for inner lighting of the structures.
>
> (D. Roth, personal communication, June 30, 2014)

She also mentions that such structures are coming into their own as photo backdrops. The designs "elicit an emotional response . . . [they] make people want to take photos precisely because they're taking images worth sharing."

Interior tension fabric structures are popular for creative trade show booth design especially with large graphics, stage set design, delineating event spaces and pathways, and focal points in an event space. Several firms provide both custom design and ready-made shape rentals.

Figure 2.10 illustrates two different tension fabric structures, one used as a 140 ft tunnel entrance (note the photo being taken), and the second used as a trade show booth with printed graphics.

Besides indoor uses, tension fabric structures play a major role in the latest designs of tenting but are constructed of more durable, weather-resistant material that we will be discussing in Chapter 8 on Tents.

Tunnel entrance

Trade show booth

Figure 2.10 Examples of tension fabric structures

Images courtesy of: left—The Originators, http://originatorsdesign.com; right—Moss Exhibits, www.moss-exhibits.com

### 2.2.9 People and other creatures as décor

There is nothing that raises the participation level and excitement of an event more than having the action amongst the guests. If the guests are the action, or at the very least interact with the action, they feel empowered and tend to enjoy the event more than if they are only observers. This is the ultimate in the "experiential" concept. One way to do this is by using people as décor. People—and creatures—as décor can take three forms: functional, interactive, and decorative.

Functional refers to using the actual participants in the event as décor. These include wait staff, bar tenders, technical personnel, and guests. It is relatively easy to rent costumes for technical personnel, wait staff, and bar tenders. Add guests to the mix of costumed participants and suddenly a venue is transformed into a sea of moving decorations. Costuming in this manner has several advantages. First, costuming is relatively inexpensive when compared to other décor. Second, even a simple hat can transform the most reticent guest into a gregarious personality. Third, setup time is non-existent.

Interactive refers primarily to entertainment and the different forms that can interact with guests in thematic costumes or as special characters. This includes robot characters, strolling celebrity look-alikes, magicians, stilt walkers, jugglers, musicians and others in theme costumes, and table acts such as caricaturists, graphologists, and fortune tellers who can be in character and costume but interact from a fixed position. Figure 2.12 illustrates an interactive performer in a balloon costume.

Besides people, this category can include other creatures, specifically animals. Until not so long ago, before animal rights advocates pushed for changes in municipal laws, animals were a popular highlight of events. My company frequently put a variety of live Canadian wild animals on decorative display for guests, such as bear cubs, cougars, eagles, moose, and deer, and sometimes more exotic ones like pythons, panthers, tigers, and spiders. Two necessary conditions that we always insisted on were that they be properly caged or penned for safety and that qualified handlers be present at all times. Although this form of display is rare now, if and when it is still possible under the strictest of safe, sanitary, and humane conditions, it can represent a unique opportunity for guests to interact with creatures they would never see close up. Although we had the occasional sanitary mishap, because precautions were taken, no guests or animals were ever harmed.

Decorative refers again to entertainment but in this case not as interactive. Decorative entertainment is there to actually be visual and to be a passive part of the décor. Although the performers may move, they generally do not interact. Examples are living statues and performance art.

### 2.2.10 Floral décor

Nothing evokes memories or joyful gasps from guests on first entering an event than the scent of fresh flowers in bloom. In keeping with the designer's dictum to use the five senses, nature never fails when called upon to assist.

Many volumes have been written about floral design and many schools and classes exist. Because of this, we will not go into detail about floral design in this section. See Malouf (1999) and Monroe (2006) for excellent treatments of this subject. However, we will briefly refer to how and where florals may successfully be used in events and review general guidelines for integrating their use into event production.

### 2.2.10.1 Where and how is floral design used?

Nature has endowed humans with a love of flowers. Our senses of smell and sight react to them in a positive way, very seldom negative. For this reason, their use is almost unrestricted, and a special event is no exception. For the remarkable, memory-evoking scents mentioned above, real flowers arranged creatively and timed to bloom at the event cannot be beaten. Also running a close second visually, but without the scent, are silk and artificial flowers. If seasonal flowers are not available and/or if maximum impact is required for minimal budget, either a design using all artificial flowers or a combination of real and artificial can work well. Also not to be forgotten are other forms of plants categorized with florals, such as trees, mosses, grasses, cacti, and vines, all of which can be real or artificial. Armed with this knowledge, let's now look at where and how both these types of florals may be best used.

#### 2.2.10.1.1 PART OF EVENT FOCAL POINTS

Earlier in the section on design we discussed the principle of emphasis, or creating a focal point, and referred to several locations within an event space that would be considered focal points. Some of these form perfect settings for the use of florals to achieve this emphasis. These include tables (dining and buffet), entrances, stages, and corners, or décor vignettes. Floral arrangements placed in these areas will be the most obvious.

- Entrances. Colorful, large, surrounding, and aromatic are the key words when placing florals at entrances. Large vases with high, full arrangements and colored but hidden lighting work well. Topiary trees with pin lights work, as do many other possibilities. The idea is to be spectacular since the entrance is the first impression of the event.

- Dining tables. For many events in which a meal is served, the dining tables occupy the largest proportion of the event space, so to use this space and that above the tables makes sense if visual impact is sought. High table centers with a floral component extending as much as 6–10 ft (1.8–3.0 m) above the table surface can be truly spectacular. Heights should be adjusted to accommodate sight lines for guests if they must view a stage or presentation of some sort, as must conversational barriers in the form of lower table centers. Usually, a short table center should be under about 1 ft (30 cm) in height while tall centers can extend much higher as long as their bases are narrow and guests can still see each other across the table. Indeed, a long, low center can be just as effective as a tall one—and allow for better sight lines. See Figure 2.11 (top).

- Buffet tables. The guidelines for dining tables do not apply to buffet tables. For buffets with a floral component, spectacular is the way to go. High, wide, and oversize is best if space permits, because each is a focal point. Interestingly, in keeping with today's emphasis on "green events," even food is being used as décor, especially as centerpieces on buffets and dining tables.

- Stages. Florals are often used to dress stages. Typical placements are on downstage corners, upstage corners, as rows along the downstage edge, as rows along the upstage edge or under a backdrop, in front of lecterns, or on the floor in front of the stage. Generally, any of these arrangements should be large and oversize as long as they do not obstruct sight lines of the audience. This is because distances to the stage are often large and what at the front of a room may appear large will appear very small 200 ft (60 m) away at the back of the audience. Also, these arrangements are isolated and as such need to be large to create an impact and to help focus attention. See Figure 2.11 (bottom).

Floral table centers

Floral stage décor

Figure 2.11 Examples of floral décor

Images courtesy of: top—Designs by Sean, www.designsbysean.com/; bottom—Seventy Event Media Group, www.seventyemg.com/

- Corners or décor vignettes. Florals can become part of décor vignettes in isolated locations such as corners or smaller themed rooms. Again, scent, color, freshness, and size determine how effective the arrangement will be.

### 2.2.10.1.2 TOTAL ENVIRONMENTS

Probably the ultimate in event design with florals is to completely transform the event space using florals. Good event designers can use all three dimensions to do this. Consider the impression created by filling the ceiling with hanging vines and subdued lighting for a jungle atmosphere, completely covering the floor with rose petals to instill a candlelit dinner with an ambience of romance, or covering the walls with giant floral murals. What the designer is really doing is using architecture to advantage, and instead of trying to match or coordinate with the room colors or designs, is choosing to ignore the designs and create a totally new space.

Alternatively, if the architectural design is so unique and attractive, it may invite the designer to bring florals into it without disturbing the basic aesthetic, but rather augmenting it. I have seen this done in an 800-year-old Norman cathedral in England in which floral arrangements were creatively worked into doorways, windows, pews, and other sections of the cathedral.

### 2.2.10.1.3 ON PEOPLE

The act of wearing flowers has always been an important one for human beings, whether it is as an expression of love as with corsages or boutonnieres at weddings, or simply as an expression of individualism as in hair bands of the "free love" generation. This begs the question, "Why not more?" Indeed, event designers have already been there in some very unusual ways. People can become décor unto themselves and florals can be the way to do it. Actors or dancers so costumed can stroll around or be part of a specially designed "living garden" concept. Individuals have also been used as buffet table centerpieces and have become part fruit or vegetable and part human, the so-called "talking centerpiece." Combined with props, this concept makes for some very interesting approaches.

### 2.2.10.2 General guidelines for integrating florals with event production

To successfully integrate floral design with an overall décor design and to accomplish the installation of florals at an event in a timely fashion that fits into the production schedule, there are some key points with which a producer or event manager should be familiar:

- Florals can and should be integrated with any theming in keeping with the event's overall décor design. This is mentioned because the floral supplier is often not the overall event décor designer. Themed props and other décor should be considered to be part of the design, whether it is table centers, stage arrangements, people as décor, or entrance décor. Props can be added to florals or florals can be added to props. For example, this can include using miniature cars in a floral table centerpiece for a racing theme, old wine barrels or giant oversized wine bottle props as part of a wine-tasting event integrated with a floral vineyard, or adding large classical urns of florals on top of tall Greek columns on a stage at an awards ceremony.

- Sufficient time and space must be allowed for final preparations of florals onsite. This means having a room or large vacant area set aside to do the final builds of table centers or the final arranging of large pieces. This room should preferably have access to fresh water and be well lit but out of direct sunlight.

- The floral designer must communicate with the producer, and vice versa, in order to obtain florals that match the event design and that can be obtained for optimum freshness in that particular season. This communication should include a discussion of the temperature of the event environment in order to time the arrival and setup of florals to minimize harm to them. Flowers should be delivered the day of the event, a few hours before the start time. They are often one of the last things to be set up, after the rush of lighting, room décor, table placement, and linens. Because the temperature of the venue can never be predicted, it's possible that the flowers could wilt quickly once the event begins—although not common under normal circumstances—and the freshest flowers possible are required. Fresh out of the florist's cooler or off the design table works best because both situations will help prolong the florals' lifespan. An example of a hot venue in which one should be careful about adding florals too soon is a summer tent that can get incredibly warm inside. If you can't avoid the risk of storing the florals before the event or even overnight, they must be kept cool (not cold) and out of the sun. The venue contact person should be asked if they can be kept temporarily in the venue's empty fridge. Some types of flowers will die in the cold, like delicate orchids, but others will appreciate the cold.

- Static floral designs must be properly illuminated. This can include everything from individually lighting table or buffet centers with pin spots or automated fixtures, to subtle hidden ambient lighting of entrance or corner vignettes. A meeting of the lighting designer, décor designer, and producer is essential to accomplish this. Sufficient space should be allowed on buffets or around vignettes and other arrangements to allow for lighting, ideally from overhead using small *PAR* lamps or remote-controlled LED lamps (see Chapter 5).

- Finishing touches are critical to successful florals. Edges and the underneath of floral designs have to be finished with embellishments such as moss, grass, sand, or dirt or at least a neat enclosed border.

## 2.2.11 Inflatables

The term inflatables covers a number of different products: air- and helium-filled regular latex balloons; balloons made out of foil and other materials in regular and odd shapes; reinforced poly air tubes; and other oddly shaped blowups made of various materials such as foil, latex, and lamé. Inflatables have been a staple of event décor for a long time, and with new concepts coming along regularly, will continue to be. We will briefly examine each type of inflatable and how it can be used.

### 2.2.11.1 Balloons

The lowly balloon is the grandfather of inflatables. Balloons are ideal as decoration when one wants to create a whimsical look, or for any festive event such as a carnival, a life celebration like a birthday and bar mitzvah, or a grand opening. Balloons come in every color and style imaginable. Surface finishes include metallic foil, jewel tones, solid, and at last count, up to more than 30 types and names, each with at least one or more shapes. They can be filled with helium to float or with air to hang. However, recent restrictions in the helium supply in the United States have caused helium prices to rise so that most balloon companies now do about 90 percent of their balloon décor on pre-built frames using air-filled balloons (Masori, 2013). The following are some of the most common types used in events:

- Animal balloons. These are the long, narrow balloons used by entertainers to create animals, flowers, and other sculptures. Also called pencil or twisty balloons, they are made of latex, a form of rubber. Animal balloons are used in small sculptures and as embellishments in helium-filled balloon bouquets or clusters on tables and around rooms.

- Foil balloons. Often incorrectly called Mylar (a trademarked name for a certain type of polyester film) balloons, the balloon industry refers to them as foil balloons because they are made of nylon sheet, coated on one side with polyethylene and metallized on the other. They are generally used in bouquets, sculptures, or clusters.

- Giant balloons. This refers to balloons that are greater than about 16 in. (40 cm) in diameter. The smaller sizes are usually latex, the larger made of vinyl. They are most often used to make a visual statement over tables or as the tops to balloon columns.
- Round balloons. These are the standard latex balloons that are most used in balloon bouquets, arches, clusters, and drops. They come in a variety of finishes and diameters. They are often customized by imprinting with logos or names.
- Odd shapes. Other common shapes of latex balloons include:
  - Airships. Same shape as a blimp but small.
  - Crescent. Shaped like a crescent moon.
  - Flying saucer. A flat, round balloon with a nozzle coming off the edge at an angle. It spins as it deflates.
  - Geos. Donut-shaped or flower blossom-shaped.
  - Hearts. Heart-shaped, sometimes made of foil.
  - Knobbies. Long skinny balloons that inflate into a series of bulbous segments, rather like a caterpillar.
  - Link-o-Loons. Type of balloon that has an extra tail on the end so that it can be tied to others in chains.
  - Megaloons. Large foil balloons in the shape of numbers and letters.
  - Mouse head. Shaped like a cartoon mouse head.

Balloons can be used in several novel ways for event décor. The common ones include:

- Arches. Arches are built by tying helium-filled round balloons to strong (e.g. 50 lb) fishing line and weighting the line down at both ends using attractively wrapped bricks or other weights. They can also be made using framing and air-filled balloons. Arches can be single balloon or multiple balloon spirals. If used with a mixture of colors, the effect of a spiral arch can be quite spectacular. Arches are perfect for covering vertical space at an event as a grand entrance or over entire areas of a room or stage. Multiple arches of decreasing size on the same vertical plane can be used together to create a backdrop or wall cover, or multiples of the same size on a horizontal plane can be spaced to create a tunnel effect. The opposite of arches in the form of balloon swags can be created using air-filled balloons suspended from the ceiling.
- Columns. Columns are built of air-filled round balloons supported by an internal PVC frame or of freestanding, helium-filled balloons. Most columns are topped with a large helium-filled, giant round balloon. As with arches, multiple colors used in a spiral effect works well. Columns are very effective in key locations in an event space, such as the edge of dance floors, the corners of rooms, or the corners of stages.
- Clusters or bouquets. These are arrangements of helium-filled round balloons often mixed with some of the differently shaped ones, and tied to decorative ribbon, then weighted down. They can also be supported by air-filled balloons. They are commonly used as table centers in which they can also be mixed with small props, flowers, custom Foamcore cutouts, or fabrics, or they can be stand-alone centers themselves. Large bouquets or clusters can be freestanding around a room as well, and of any height. They are good for augmenting arches in key locations such as entrances, stages, or dance floors.
- Ceilings, floors, and walls. Masses of free or structurally supported balloons can be used to cover ceilings, floors, or walls.
- Sculptures. Giant three-dimensional depictions of life-sized machines, buildings, animals, people, logos, and artwork constructed entirely of balloons can be impressive. These are often suspended from a ceiling or freestanding, and attractively illuminated to act as a décor focal point in an event. They are usually

constructed out of air-filled round balloons, but can bring in other shapes and types as well. Similar two-dimensional art can be used to fill walls and built using a preformed frame and small 5 or 6 in. balloons.

- Balloons as clothing. Very small sculptural balloons are used to create entire dresses. This can be highly imaginative and add a wild new dimension to people as décor. Even more interesting is Paintloon. The brainchild of fine artist and body painter Bella Volen from Bulgaria and balloon artist and designer Guido Verhoef from the Netherlands, it is a combination of fine art, body painting, and balloon sculpting. Using latex modeling balloons, objects, and accessories, complete costumes are made that create an extension of the body paint or add surfaces for the fine artist to paint on. The body thus fully merges with additional parts into one design. If used on a professional dancer then combined with music, this creation can bring a unique form of performance art to an event. See Figure 2.12 (bottom right).

For any of the creations listed above, the balloons may be augmented with rope light or pin lights woven throughout the bouquets or sculptures, by external illumination, or even by small, battery-powered LED lights placed inside some of the balloons.

Using masses of balloons, certain special effects can be created. These include:

- Reveals. This is industry terminology for an effect that hides an object or person and then instantly reveals them using a special effect. Balloons can do this in several ways, including:
  - An exploding wall in which air-filled balloons are arranged close together as a wall supported by an internal PVC framework and hiding the person/thing. At the appropriate moment, key balloons with small charges in them are exploded and the entire wall instantly falls apart revealing what is behind.
  - A floating reveal in which a similar wall of helium-filled balloons is created but anchored to a supporting bottom frame. At the key moment, the frame support is loosened and the balloons float up to reveal what is behind.
- Drops. A large number of air-filled balloons is enclosed in a light netting and suspended from a ceiling with a length of filament or string coming down to the floor in a key location. At the appropriate time, the string is pulled releasing the netting and the balloons fall. Like any special effect, this is best timed to emphasize a key point in an event or program. This same effect can also be achieved by building an upside down pillar and filling it with small air-filled balloons capped with a giant one. Once the giant one is released (ideally as an exploding balloon), the insides spill out.
- Releases. This involves releasing dozens—or even up to thousands—of helium-filled balloons into the air at once, usually timed to be a strategic component of an event. Although impressive, due to environmental concerns releases have come under severe restrictions. Most municipal authorities have special regulations as do aviation authorities. Both would need to be consulted prior to any such release.

There are several insider tips about balloon décor that every producer and designer should know in order to get the most out of the balloons (L. Jones, personal communication, June 28, 2014):

- Air-filled balloons are best for long-term displays due to the fact that air molecules are heavier than helium and do not escape as rapidly. Air is generally good for up to seven days and helium for 24 h. However, a helium retention product called "Hi Float" can be used to coat the inside of helium balloons to make them last up to five times longer.
- Oxidation dulls the outside finish of balloons, particularly jewel tones (transparent balloons), so the length of display time should also be judged by the appearance of the balloons based on this oxidation. If a longer term is needed, a different choice of finishes should be made.
- Nitrogen makes a good inflation medium as an alternative to air when large quantities of small balloons are required. This makes for quick inflation due to the high pressure in the nitrogen tank.

### 2.2.11.2 Airtubes®

Invented by Doron Gazit of Air Dimensional Design, Airtubes are long, tubular inflatables, best used when an abstract display is needed. They fill visual space very well and can be used to wind around permanent or temporary architectural structures, both indoors and outdoors, such as buildings and bridges, scaffolding and fences, stages and columns. Airtubes are constructed of heavy, flame-retardant polypropylene and are sold in long rolls of flat uninflated material. They must be unrolled and cut to length before installing in their uninflated state. One end is then attached to a high-powered, steel-encased, 110 V, 3 amp fan that must constantly blow air to keep them inflated, and the other end is sealed. They can remain inflated indefinitely. They are available in inflated diameters ranging from 4.5 in. (11.3 cm) to almost 18 in. (45 cm), and multiple colors.

### 2.2.11.3 Other blowups and air-supported décor

The ingenuity of inventors combined with strong new materials has resulted in a plethora of different inflatable and air-supported products that can be used for event décor. One such inventor, Ashley Ramage, president of UK and San Francisco-based Blowupthings, takes a distinctly refreshing approach to the design of events using inflatables. Because of the ability of inflatables to do so much with so little, he likes to take an event space and use it to "enhance, conceal, or distract, and also to arrest people's sensibilities; in other words, make them stop and think" (A. Ramage, personal communication, March 28, 2006). He has made walls, suspended décor, stage backdrops, and trade show booths out of unique, customized inflatables and is on the cutting edge of this expanding category of décor. His and most of the other new inflatables also coming from inventors such as Gazit are made of lightweight fabrics other than latex, such as rip stop nylon, and most require an electric-powered, low voltage fan to keep them inflated, and/or at least one external suspension point. Some of these exciting products include:

- Architectural pieces such as stage backdrops, entranceways, and trade show booths for indoor use.
- Giant portable movie screens as large as 100 ft x 45 ft (30 x 13.5 m) for outdoor use.
- Smaller air- or helium-filled abstract shapes for hanging or mounting on the ground. Many are lit internally for extra attention.
- Wearable inflatable products to permit a human interactive component to be added. Some are not wearable but are guidable by humans because they are so large (e.g. a full-sized parading elephant, http://spacecadets.com). Some are strictly for fun like inflatable ball suits, similar to the older sumo wrestling suits, and some are just decorative.
- Wind-movable products such as Fly Guys®, another invention from Gazit of Air Dimensional Design, that come in heights up to 60 ft (18 m) and require two fans to keep inflated and moving. Note that they need to have dry weather if used outdoors.

See Figure 2.12 for examples of unusual inflatable décor.

### 2.2.12 Technology as décor

Similar to what was explained in Chapter 1 about technology as entertainment, mobile and other technology is playing a major role in re-shaping what we think of as event décor. Advances are happening quickly and new ideas surface every year. Here are some that are potentially destined for greater things:

- The use of large screen projection to create an atmosphere for an event in the form of still images (photos) or video that cover entire walls. There will be more about this in Chapter 4. See Figure 2.6, which also includes a wide-screen projection covering an entire wall.

Freestanding cones
and suspended stars

Flower petals

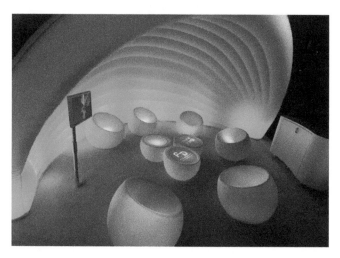

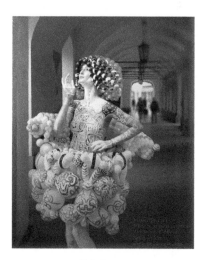

Freestanding ice cave

Paintloon

Figure 2.12 Examples of inflatable décor

Images courtesy of: top left and right—Air Dimensional Design, www.airdd.com; bottom left—Blowupthings, www.blowupthings.com; bottom right—Bella Volen, www.bella-volen.com

- The creation of an artistic iPad "wall" in which individual attendees contribute to a physical wall of iPads to build a single image (www.magencydigital.com), a new consideration for event décor.
- The projection of drawings and designs from attendee smartphones or tablets onto a café wall or other projection surface (http://buzzy.io), again a possible component of event décor once further developed.
- Interactive wallpaper that can be programmed to monitor its environment and control lighting and sound. A hand can be run across this wallpaper to turn on a lamp, play music, or send a message to a friend. The wallpaper is flat, constructed entirely from paper and paint and can be paired with a paper

computing kit whose pieces serve as sensors, lamps, network interfaces, and interactive decorations (http://highlowtech.org/?p=27).

- The use of mobile devices (smartphones, tablets) to control event elements. Even now, smartphones are being used to control lighting. As illustrated in Chapter 3 of *Special Event Production: The Process*, the unique aerial sculptures of Janet Echelman are designed to be illuminated by lighting controlled by audience smartphones.

And these are just the beginning . . .

---

### PRODUCTION WAR STORY

**A premature surprise**

A beautiful and highly creative balloon wall was installed in front of the band stage that would magically burst and reveal the band once it was time to dance. It would be an incredible ending to an evening of good food, fun, and camaraderie. Unfortunately, someone forgot to tell Mother Nature. The room was fully encircled by floor-to-ceiling windows looking out to the west and this event was held late in June near the day when sunlight lasted until very late in the evening. The event day was quite hot and the sunlight beamed through the windows, eventually making its way to shine on the balloon wall. Just as dinner was underway, we heard the first explosion, followed in fairly rapid succession over the course of the next 20 minutes by a periodic, unrehearsed exploding balloon wall that was soon left in tatters, ragged pieces of balloons hanging from the wall supports like broken flesh. Although somewhat comical while happening, this premature balloon wall explosion did not make our client very happy. The balloon experts were called in and the remaining pieces of the wall were dismantled to leave a clean look, but the damage had been done.

In this case, communication with the client was immediate and consisted of an apology and an explanation. This was a situation that could only be described as a true Act of God. It may have been avoidable but we were never sure exactly how. During the site inspection days before, the weather was cloudy and an estimate was made of exactly where the sun would be at a certain time and whether it would strike the balloon wall. This was only a guess and even with this, nobody—even the balloon experts—expected or anticipated that the sunlight would overheat the balloons and their tethers, which we could only surmise expanded at different rates and caused the premature explosions. The client was not charged a penny for the wall and seemed to be happy with that settlement, but nothing could bring back the planned excitement that had been lost.

What lessons were learned? This was a difficult case. The most obvious one that we learned was not to use a balloon wall or any balloon structure in situations where weather—or excessive heating or cooling of any sort—could be a factor.

(Courtesy of Doug Matthews)

---

### 2.2.13 Other unique décor

Every year, someone invents a new type of décor that does not fit within the categories laid out in this book, so more than likely we will not have covered it all. However, in an attempt to bring it all in, here are some other categories that do not fit the traditional mold.

### 2.2.13.1 Nature as décor

The ancient world was considered to be composed of the elements earth, air, fire, and water. Special event designers still use these elements in various ways. Fire is still popular in the form of candles or as entertainment. Earth and sand are sometimes used in floral displays or artificial beaches. Water is used for florals and sometimes in special displays for boats and in the form of ice carvings. All of it can enhance any event if used properly. However, some cautions pertaining to risk management are in order:

- Candles, especially tall ones, tend to drip wax and should never be used in a drafty room. Furthermore, all flammable material in close proximity should be treated with flame retardant or the candles should not be used at all. Tall candles on candelabra are particularly susceptible to drafts and if flame is used, it should be sustained by gas and not the candle itself. Many events have moved away from real flame candles to battery-operated ones.

- Earth or sand, especially in large quantities such as for an indoor artificial beach and beach volleyball games, can be a nightmare for venue staff to clean up. It almost always requires several large dump trucks full of sand to provide enough. The event will likely be a big success providing arrangements have been made for cleanup before the event is finalized.

- Ice carvings are spectacular when sculpted by a master. There are even companies that carve to music as a form of entertainment. Carvings can be used as food dishes, bars, table centers, buffet centers, and just plain décor focal points. The cost usually depends on the size, which is governed by the number of standard ice blocks that will be used. They must be delivered just before the event begins and will last at least 2 h or so and still look good. However, they do require proper lighting and proper drainage, whether it is a small tray placed beneath a table center or larger trays on a buffet for a giant ice carving. For ponds and other water displays, tarpaulins or waterproof ground sheets should be used as well as leak-proof containers.

### 2.2.13.2 Other sensory décor

Up to this point, we have mostly concentrated on only two of our senses, sight and touch. A successful event will encompass all the senses if possible, and that is where other sensory décor comes in. Apart from food (our sense of taste), which is usually the purview of catering, there are two other senses we need to think about.

#### 2.2.13.2.1 SMELL

The Proust effect, or Proustian memory, named after French author Marcel Proust who first described it in writing in the early 1900s, is the phenomenon of a particular smell or odor bringing a memory to mind. It has been proven that the part of our brain that handles memory is the same part that interprets smells, so we have a built-in link. Thus, smell is a very powerful sense and one that can lead directly to an emotional interpretation of time and place. It has not been used to its full potential as part of special event décor, but the tools are available to use it.

Certainly, the catering side of an event uses appropriate food choices to stimulate our olfactory receptors, but artificial scents are also available to help. There are several companies that provide different scents to retailers to stimulate sales, and to events to create sensory environments. For example, North Carolina-based ScentAir offers over 1,000 scents ranging from environmental ones like ocean, rain, sagebrush, and redwood forest, to exotic and unusual ones such as musty, oily machinery, and dinosaur breath. They are delivered using a dry-air technology that releases a fragrance from undetectable locations such as ceilings, without sprays, aerosols, or heated oils. A single scent delivery system is very small, operates on adapted 110 VAC, covers up to 4,000 ft$^2$ of space, and even includes a motion sensor. A scent cartridge lasts up to 300 h.

### 2.2.13.2.2 HEARING

Several authors talk about *soundscaping* for events (Goldblatt, 2014; Rutherford-Silvers, 2012) and how it adds to the experience of being encompassed by a total environment. Put simply, soundscaping is the ability to control the aural environment at an event. Certainly, there are event sounds that cannot be controlled such as people (talking, eating, moving, etc.), but other ambient sounds can be. It is included in this section because it should be considered as part of the event designer's arsenal of décor options.

There are two main ways to control the aural environment: live sound, such as musical groups or people making real-time sounds through an audio system, and recorded sound. It's easy to say to the audio engineer, "Just put on some mellow walk-in music" or "Crank up the volume when they start dancing." This is not soundscaping and it is far from properly controlling the aural environment. Successful control considers timing, volume, and content, and often must be coordinated with other resources such as lighting and catering.

Timing means that a conscious effort has to be made to change the ambient sounds at pre-determined moments at an event. For example, a popular form of entertainment for convention opening ceremonies in Vancouver has been a West Coast Native Talking Stick Ceremony, and our company produced many. During walk-in, we would carefully choose appropriate new age music with an environmental flavor such as flutes with light drumming at a low volume to set the mood, then at the start of the ceremony, we would dim all the house lights and initiate a grand entrance with the room dark and only the sound of crashing thunder and the rain forest for ambience. The thunder was at a volume high enough to shake the floor, thus creating a realistic feel, and demonstrating the power of dramatically changing volume at a precise moment to gain attention.

Volume is also important when sounds are being played in the background to only create ambience. Many events have been ruined because volume was not controlled. Whether it is the sound of ships' foghorns set amongst a rolling fog and a gangplank at an event entrance, or a live quartet playing background jazz, either one could be too high or too low to be effective if not continuously monitored. It is necessary to monitor guest reactions to background sounds by physically being where the sounds are. The audio engineer or producer has to literally go to the entrance or walk amongst the diners to see if people can hear or are complaining about volume. People-watching is critical to successful soundscaping.

Content, as we have discussed in Chapter 1, is arguably the most powerful variable in generating emotional and physical reaction to entertainment. This is where many producers do not take enough time to consider what the effect of sound will be. This is particularly true of background music or other sounds. Let us take an example of a sports-themed event in which guests walk around to different themed rooms to participate in activities and partake of different foods. Consider a "baseball room." What would be more conducive to an exciting and emotional reaction in that room, background rock music or playback of a live radio broadcast of a world series winning game, complete with play-by-play action and the sound of the cheering crowd? If you had been watching that game 20 years ago, wouldn't the radio broadcast bring back more memories than simply rock music? Time needs to be taken to choose content.

## 2.3 Considerations for the setup and strike of décor

Setting up or installing décor can be a stressful undertaking, not only for the designer but also for the event producer who must coordinate with venue staff and other suppliers. There are literally hundreds of details that have to be considered and probably equally as many things that can go wrong. Of course, every event and every type of décor presents unique problems and challenges, so it is virtually impossible to predict or list every one. Throughout setup, however, constant monitoring for potential risks and safety hazards is essential. Although there are no specific safety or design standards for décor, many venues have a number of restrictions on what can and cannot be done. Monroe (2006, pp. 104–105, 109, 133, 174–175) outlines several potential risk areas for the various types of décor, such as structural stability, flame retardancy, and toxicity. Producers should be fully aware of all restrictions on décor and of all potential risk by thoroughly reviewing the event décor plan with the designer. Here are some of the general considerations necessary prior to and at the event:

## 2.3.1 Prior to the event

These happen from the moment the event is being considered right up until move-in, and include safety and risk concerns:

- A preliminary site inspection should be made by the producer and designer to ascertain:
  - Load-in access from the loading dock to the event space, including exact measurements of the freight elevator if there is one, sizes and lengths of any connecting corridors, door sizes, timing restrictions to movement of décor caused by necessity to go through public areas.
  - Accessibility of the actual loading dock, including size and number of docks, whether there is a ramp, parking restrictions for trucks and/or parking areas.
  - The number, location, and load rating of ceiling *hanging points* in the event space if rigging and suspended décor will be used.
  - The location(s) and rating of house power in volts and amps, plus which outlets are on which circuits.
  - The location of doors and windows and any effect daylight might have on event décor and lighting.
  - The exact measurements of the event space and preliminary locations for décor placement, and if a scaled floor plan is available that may be translated into CADD (computer-aided design and drafting).
  - Whether there will be any stages, tables, dance floors, or other furniture in the space, plus the planned number and sizes of everything.
  - Who will be responsible for providing ladders or scissor lifts and qualified operators.
  - Any restrictions on scheduling caused by other activities in the same or adjoining space, including noise restrictions.
  - Any restrictions on nailing, screwing, or otherwise affixing décor to venue property.
  - Any pertinent restrictions relating to fire and the flammability of décor.
  - Requirements for cleanup before and after the event and whether it will be done by contracted decorators or by venue staff.
  - Existing venue color scheme and whether it must be covered or can be worked into the event color scheme.
  - Availability of dedicated preparation areas or rooms for décor staff such as florists.
  - Availability of a crew break area and availability and cost of refreshments.
  - Planned setup schedule for venue staff such as power tie-in, stage setup, and table placement.
  - Any restrictions from the venue for strike of décor after the event, including loading dock accessibility, noise, or staff assistance.
- The designer should create a preliminary décor design plus a rough floor plan using the venue information and all the resources necessary, and/or incorporate the rough plan into the overall floor/site plan on CADD.
- The designer should create a setup schedule of deliveries and timing for all suppliers that should be reviewed by the producer for integration into the overall production schedule and for possible cost savings by using existing suppliers such as lighting who can light décor as well as stages.

- The designer should calculate staff needs for setup and strike based on the approved schedule ensuring that sufficient staff plus a contingency factor are included.
- The designer should review and plan for all necessary tools, including portable electric saw, screw gun and electric drill and selection of drill bits, duct tape in a variety of colors, 50 ft (15 m) measuring tape, hammers, variety of nails and screws, glue gun and glue, zap straps, pencils, paper, and paint, brushes, and cleaner if onsite painting is to be done. If sets and hard props form a large part of the décor, it can be useful to have a carpenter onsite for last-minute changes.
- The designer should arrange for all transportation for setup and strike.
- The designer and producer should review safety procedures and risk, including:
  - Any setup or strike procedures that could incur a risk or injury to workers, event staff, clients, or venue staff and ensure all involved are aware of the hazards.
  - Safety attire (e.g. steel-toed boots, hard hats, gloves, safety vests) and that it will be used by setup and strike personnel as required.
  - Flame retardancy rating of all materials.
  - Support mechanisms for all décor and whether they will adequately and safely carry the weight of that décor.
  - Qualifications for equipment operation if designer personnel will be operating it, such as scissor lifts.
  - All WCB (Workers' Compensation Board) certificates are current and payments are up to date.

### 2.3.2 At the event

These happen during onsite setup and strike:

- The producer and designer continuously monitor all work for safety, risks, and adherence to regulations.
- The producer and designer continuously monitor setup schedule and liaise with venue staff immediately to overcome problems as they arise.
- The producer and designer ensure all décor setup is coordinated with other suppliers such as lighting and A-V to ensure they can work around each other and that their components fit the décor as planned (e.g. lighting décor).
- The designer should ensure finishing touches are applied to all décor elements, such as:
  - Edges of floral displays are finished with moss or grass or edging.
  - Any battery-operated equipment has new batteries.
  - All electrical cords for décor are taped down safely, preferably using duct tape in the color of the venue carpet or floor.
  - All electrical hazards such as lights close to flammable material are moved to safety.
  - Any support mechanisms for large décor such as pipe and drape hardware for backdrops or wooden bracing for set pieces is hidden by other décor, specially manufactured returns, or drapes.
- The producer and designer together should conduct a final "idiot check" at least 1 h prior to the event commencing to ensure there are no safety hazards and all décor as planned and contracted is in place.

### 2.3.3 After the event

Mention must be made at this point of the importance to plan for décor strike after the event. This is a time, usually very late at night, when many problems occur, often unseen by either the producer or the designer as new crews are in place to accomplish the strike. For this reason it is absolutely necessary for the designer and producer to do the following:

- Establish crew call times for strike.
- Assign a supervisor for strike.
- Give special instructions about the handling of all décor and the exit routing out of the venue.
- Provide the supervisor with venue and client contact information. This will ensure that the strike is smooth and coordinated.

## PRODUCTION CHALLENGES

1. You have a client who wants you to produce an event in which the venue is completely transformed into a jungle. Suggest three different ways to cover the walls, including methods of support or mounting for the décor.

2. You and your designer are having a debate about which color scheme will best combine richness and high contrast for an event. What would be your choices as the best two schemes and why? Which would be easier to coordinate?

3. You and an event designer are brainstorming ideas for table centers for a theme of "The Old West Meets the 21st Century." What are three different types or combinations of types of décor that could be used to depict this theme? How high would you make the table centers if the diners will be watching a stage show and how high if they will only be eating dinner followed by dancing to a DJ?

4. You are attending an initial meeting with a potential client who wants a 1980s Rock and Roll event. Describe some specific creative décor for her that would appeal to all five senses and would sell her on using your company to produce the event.

5. Give ten items that should be discussed with a venue manager before proceeding to organize the décor setup for an event, and explain why they must be agreed upon and finalized ahead of time.

## REFERENCES

Adler, L. (1998). *Centerpieces and Table Decorations*. Cooperative Extension Service. University of Kentucky, College of Agriculture. HF-LRA.093. Retrieved June 25, 2014, from www2.ca.uky.edu/hes/fcs/factshts/hf-lra.093.pdf.

Beurteaux, D. (2012, April). Event Furniture for Every Style. *In Tents*. Retrieved June 9, 2014, from http://intentsmag.com/articles/0412_f2_style_furnished.html.

CMYK color model. (2014, October 14). In *Wikipedia, The Free Encyclopedia*. Retrieved January 26, 2015, from http://en.wikipedia.org/w/index.php?title=CMYK_color_model&oldid=629554131.

Gatto, J.A., Porter, A.W. and Selleck, J. (2000). *Exploring Visual Design: The Elements and Principles*. Worcester, MA: Davis Publications.

Gillette, J.M. (2000). *Theatrical Design and Production: An Introduction to Scene Design and Construction, Lighting, Sound, Costume, and Makeup, Fourth Edition*. New York: McGraw-Hill Higher Education.

Goldblatt, J. (2014). *Creating and Sustaining a New World for Celebration, Seventh Edition*. Hoboken, NJ: John Wiley & Sons, Inc.

Howard Bear, J. (2014). Symmetrical Balance. *Desktop Publishing*. Retrieved May 5, 2014, from http://desktop-pub.about.com/od/designprinciples/l/aa_balance1.htm.

Laurenza, D., Taddei, M. and Zanon, E. (2006). *Leonardo's Machines: Da Vinci's Inventions Revealed*. Newton Abbot, Devon, UK: David & Charles.

Lovett, J. (1999). Design and Colour. Retrieved June 9, 2014, from www.johnlovett.com/test.htm.

Malouf, L. (1999). *Behind the Scenes at Special Events: Flowers, Props, and Design*. New York: John Wiley & Sons, Inc.

Masori, S. (2013). *The Event Planner's Essential Guide To Balloons*. CreateSpace Independent Publishing Platform.

Monroe, J.C. (2006). *Art of the Event: Complete Guide to Designing and Decorating Special Events*. Hoboken, NJ: John Wiley & Sons, Inc.

Nurse, B. (2007). The Field of the Cloth of Gold. *Alecto Historical Editions*. Retrieved June 11, 2014, from www.alectouk.com/The%20Field%20of%20the%20Cloth%20of%20Gold.htm.

Pipe and drape. (2014, May 28). In *Wikipedia, The Free Encyclopedia*. Retrieved 02:49, June 17, 2014, from http://en.wikipedia.org/w/index.php?title=Pipe_and_drape&oldid=610482374.

QSX Software Group. (2014). Color Meaning. Retrieved June 3, 2014, from www.color-wheel-pro.com/color-meaning.html.

Rothstein-Kramer, S.L. (2013, September/October). Propped Up. *Special Events*. Retrieved June 9, 2014, from http://viewer.zmags.com/publication/f898b0fc#/f898b0fc/31.

Rutherford-Silvers, J. (2012). *Professional Event Coordination*. Hoboken, NJ: John Wiley & Sons, Inc.

Saw, J.T. (2001). 2D Design Notes: Part V: Design Elements. Retrieved May 3, 2014, from http://daphne.palomar.edu/design/part_v.html.

Signable Inc. (2010). Materials Explained. *Signable Inc*. Retrieved June 11, 2014, from www.1hoursigns.ca/info.html.

Skaalid, B. (1999). Classic Graphic Design Theory. Retrieved June 3, 2014, from www.usask.ca/education/coursework/skaalid/theory/cgdt/designtheory.htm.

Whitacre, D. (2014, January). *Pipe and Drape: From Basics to Brilliance and Everything In-Between*. Educational session presented at The Special Event, Nashville, TN, USA.

# 3

# Audio systems

After reading this chapter you will be able to:

1. Explain how the acoustics of an event space affect the quality of sound produced by an audio system.
2. Understand the primary uses of an audio system for special events.
3. Understand and be able to explain the general working of the main groups of equipment in a special event audio system and the components within these groups.
4. Know where in an event space the groups of audio equipment are normally located.
5. Understand the reason for an audio sound check and what it entails at an event.

Whenever an event has more than a bare minimum number of people in a small room (e.g. 100 people maximum, probably far fewer!), there will be a requirement for sound reinforcement in order that any speeches or entertainment can be heard. Poor sound quality can be catastrophic for an event, especially if an important speech cannot be understood or a high-cost celebrity artist's sound mix is totally inadequate.

Audio systems and their design tend to be one of several technical areas of specialization within the events industry that event planners and managers prefer to leave to the experts, often relying on the event producer to oversee the installation and operation of the systems. For that reason, the producer must understand the basic theory and functioning of these systems so that the optimum system can be designed for a specific event, and the best return-on-investment (ROI) made. This chapter will therefore explore the following key topics:

- Basic acoustic theory and how it is applied to the event space.
- Uses of an audio system.
- Main audio system groups, their components, and their basic theory of operation.

- Signal flow and equipment locations within the event space.
- The pre-event sound check and system operation during the event.
- Risk and safety.

Except where noted, the explanations, tables, and figures in Sections 3.1.1.1 through 3.3.1.1.6 are provided courtesy of Shure Inc. and used with permission.

## 3.1 Acoustic theory and its application to the event space

In order to understand why music or the spoken word can either be well heard or completely unintelligible, we must first understand the part that acoustics play in a venue and how they react to the room's architecture.

### 3.1.1 What is sound?

Sound is produced by vibrating objects such as musical instruments, loudspeakers, and human vocal cords. These vibrations in turn produce pressure variations in the air immediately adjacent to the object, which cause a wave effect of high and low pressure much like a wave in water. This is a sound wave and it travels through the air exactly like a wave in water, radiating outward from the sound source. A complete wave is a complete pressure change, or *cycle*, and takes the air pressure from rest, to maximum, to minimum, and back to rest again. Figure 3.1 shows how a wave forms alternating regions of rarefaction and compression as it radiates.

There are several important characteristics of sound waves that one needs to know in order to understand the basics of an audio system. They are frequency, wavelength, and loudness. The following explanations

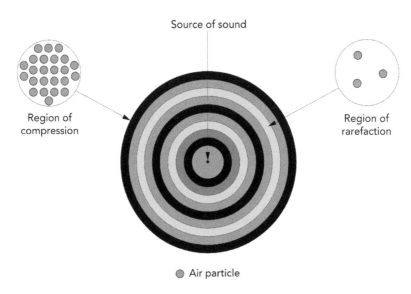

Air pressure is a maximum in the regions of compression
and a minimum in the regions of rarefaction.

Figure 3.1 Sound wave causing a change in air pressure

Courtesy of Doug Matthews

of these characteristics, unless otherwise noted, are provided by Shure Inc. and used with permission (Vear, 2011a).

### 3.1.1.1 Frequency

The frequency of a sound wave indicates the rate at which the sound pressure changes occur. It is measured in Hertz (Hz) or cycles per second, where 1 Hz equals 1 cycle per second. As an example, human hearing extends from about 20 Hz (very low sounds) to about 20,000 Hz or 20 kHz (very high sounds).

### 3.1.1.2 Wavelength

The wavelength of a sound is the physical distance from the start of one cycle to the start of the next cycle. Wavelength is related to frequency by the speed of sound, which at sea level is approximately 1,130 ft/s or 344 m/s. The following formula shows this relationship:

$$\text{Wavelength} = \frac{\text{Speed of sound}}{\text{Frequency}}$$

For example, for a 500 Hz sound source, such as the upper ranges of a tenor voice, the upper range of a tenor saxophone, or the middle to low range of a flute, the wavelength is 2.2 ft (i.e. 1,130 ft/s divided by 500 cycles per second). Of course, any particular frequency will have a unique corresponding wavelength. Table 3.1 gives some more examples of common frequencies and their corresponding wavelengths.

This relationship is important to know because shortly we will be discussing what happens when sound waves of certain lengths hit objects of a certain size.

Table 3.1  Sample of wavelengths at different frequencies

| Frequency (Hz) | Wavelength |
| --- | --- |
| 50 | About 23 ft or almost 7 m (low range of a bass drum) |
| 100 | About 10 ft or 3 m (low range of a tenor saxophone, mid range of a bass drum, low range of a bass male voice) |
| 1000 | About 1 ft or .3 m (upper range of a female soprano voice or mid-range of a flute and violin) |
| 10,000 | About 1 in. or 2.5 cm (the very highest notes of a pipe organ) |

Courtesy of Shure Inc.

### 3.1.1.3 Loudness

The loudness of a sound is directly related to the variation of air pressure, or in other words, the amplitude of the sound. The greater the pressure change or amplitude, the louder the sound. Loudness is commonly measured in *decibels Sound Pressure Level* (dB SPL); 0 dB is the threshold of hearing and at the other extreme, 120 dB is the threshold of pain. A loud rock band heard from 10 ft away is in the 110 to 120 dB range of loudness, and a quiet whisper is around 30 dB. Most special event environments are in the 80–110 dB range of loudness.

An additional property of direct sound is that it becomes weaker as it travels away from the sound source, at a rate governed by the inverse-square law. For example, when the distance increases by a factor of two (doubles), the sound level decreases by a factor of four (the square of two). This corresponds to a drop of 6 dB in sound pressure level, which is a substantial decrease. In contrast, ambient sound, such as noise and reverberation, is at a constant level everywhere in the space. Therefore, at a given distance from a sound source, a listener (or a microphone) will pick up a certain proportion of direct sound to ambient sound. As the distance increases, the direct sound level decreases while the ambient sound level stays the same (Lyons et al., 2008). A properly designed sound system can increase the amount of direct sound reaching the listener without increasing the ambient sound significantly as we will see later in this chapter.

### 3.1.2 Sound propagation and its relationship to the event space

Now that we know how sound waves are generated and travel through the air, the next thing to understand is that sound can actually be altered by its environment as it travels. There are four basic ways that this can happen: reflection, absorption, diffraction, and refraction. Let us examine each of them and relate them to the environment of a special event.

#### 3.1.2.1 Reflection

A sound wave can be reflected by a surface or other object if the object is physically as large as, or larger than, the wavelength of the sound. The reflected sound will have a different characteristic than the direct sound if all frequencies are not reflected equally.

Reflection is also the source of *echo*, *reverberation*, and *standing waves*. Echo occurs when a reflected sound is delayed long enough (i.e. by a distant reflective surface) to be heard by the listener as a distinct repetition of the direct sound. Considering the typical indoor special event environment, all but the very lowest frequencies (e.g. a bass drum) will normally be reflected by a room's walls and ceiling. If the room is a large one, such as in some conference centers, there may even be an obvious echo, particularly of low frequency sounds. Important to note, though, is that higher frequency sounds can be reflected by a lot more hard surfaces than the low frequency sounds. For example, again in our special event room, even dining tables, chairs, staging, and some items of décor will reflect higher frequencies, such as the human voice, or the high notes of instruments.

Reverberation consists of many reflections of a sound, maintaining the sound in a reflective space for a time even after the sound has stopped. For enclosed special event environments, particularly large ones like conference centers, this has the effect of making the listener feel that he is inside a giant cavern.

Standing waves in a room occur for certain frequencies related to the distance between parallel walls. The original sound and the reflected sound will begin to reinforce each other when the distance between two opposite walls is equal to a multiple of half the wavelength of the sound. This happens primarily at low frequencies. For example, in a small room that is, say, 60–65 ft (18–19.6 m) wide, a standing wave could form when the low notes of an electric bass are played. Let us look at how this works. At a frequency of, say, 90 Hz, one of the bass notes would result in a wavelength of about 12.6 ft (3.8 m). Half this figure is 6.3 ft (1.9 m). Therefore, with a width of 63 ft, the room would be a ten-times multiple of half the wavelength, resulting in a standing wave, or overly loud bass sound. This standing wave has to be eliminated during the sound check by adjusting the frequencies coming out of the main system speakers, a process called *equalization* (EQ) (see Section 3.5.1).

#### 3.1.2.2 Absorption

Some materials absorb sound rather than reflecting it. The amount and efficiency of absorption are again dependent on the frequency of the sound. Thin material such as acoustic ceiling tiles or clothing on humans

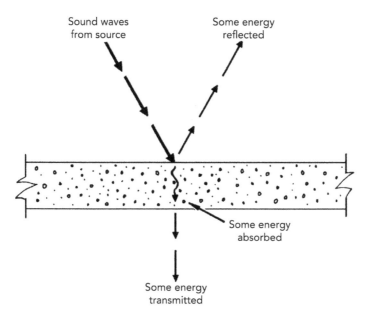

Figure 3.2 Reflection and absorption of sound waves from a large surface

Courtesy of JBL Professional, www.jblpro.com

will absorb middle to high frequencies, while thicker material such as pile carpets, padded furniture, and heavy velour drape will absorb lower frequencies (Figure 3.2). It is this absorption that helps to control reverberation in an event space. It is also the reason why the sound in a room will be completely different during a sound check when the room is empty, compared to during the event when the room is filled with people.

### 3.1.2.3 Diffraction

A sound wave will typically bend around obstacles in its path, which are smaller than its wavelength. The resulting effect in an event space is for low frequency sounds to fill a room while high frequencies tend to be blocked by most small objects, particularly people. That is why audio engineers place large bass speakers (low frequencies) on the floor, as they will be heard everywhere in the room, even with people sitting or standing in front of them. Likewise, the middle and high frequency speakers will be placed either on top of the bass speakers or, ideally, flown from the ceiling in order to be in a position to reach the entire audience without these frequencies having to go through the audience (see Figure 3.3). As an example, from the table of wavelengths (Table 3.1), if an acoustic trio of flute, bass, and guitar are playing for a standup reception in a crowded room with only a localized, small audio system to amplify them, as one gets farther away from the trio in the crowded room, only the lower registers of the bass will be heard because the shorter wavelengths of the other instruments will be stopped by the people in the room.

### 3.1.2.4 Refraction

A sound wave will bend if it must pass through a change in air density. This is most apparent outdoors, particularly at large distances, when the sound from loudspeakers passes through temperature and wind

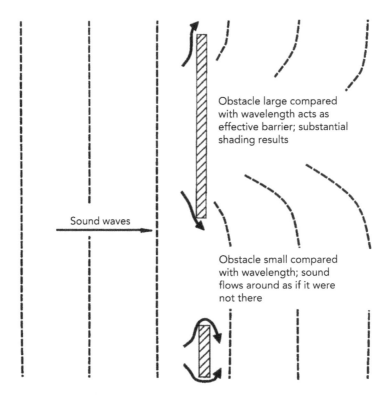

Figure 3.3 Diffraction of sound around obstacles

Courtesy of JBL Professional, www.jblpro.com

gradients (see Figure 3.4). As well, there is more sound attenuation in drier air (i.e. lower relative humidity) for frequencies above 2 kHz. This means that high frequencies will be attenuated more with distance than will low frequencies (Eargle, 1999).

In summary, the audio quality at an event will depend on the dimensions of the room, the materials present in walls and other structures and equipment, the number of audience members, the seating or standing arrangements of the audience, the layout of the room, whether or not audio system speakers will be flown or mounted on the floor, and finally, whether the event is outdoors or indoors.

## 3.2 Uses of an audio system

Armed with knowledge of acoustic theory, we now turn our attention to the actual audio system and how it is used to amplify the human voice and the sounds of musical instruments or recordings for special events. Patil et al. (2000) have provided parts of the explanations in this section.

### 3.2.1 Audio for speech

Often if speech is the main component of an event, the audio system takes on a different appearance from that for a concert or musical entertainment stage show. It must provide extremely crisp and clear reproduction of the spoken word. The spoken word generally demands specific types of microphones and speaker systems that are different from those used for music. Microphones, which we will explore in

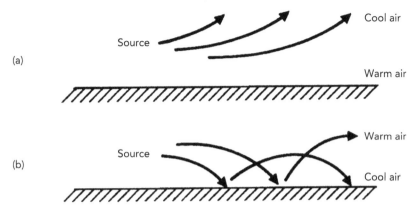

Figure 3.4 Effect of different temperature gradients on sound waves

Courtesy of JBL Professional, www.jblpro.com

depth shortly, are primarily of four main types when the spoken word is to be amplified. These are wireless handheld, wireless lavalier, wired lectern, and wired handheld microphones. Occasionally, wireless headset microphones will also be used, but these tend to be more for a theatrical setting that uses the spoken word.

What is called a *distributed system* of speakers is most often used for speech, at least in smaller venues. This type of system consists of multiple smaller speakers that amplify mid-range voice frequencies. These speakers are placed on stands distributed usually around the periphery of the event space. This distribution permits clear sound coverage throughout the audience without any single location being too loud. It presents a more appealing and unobtrusive look to the equipment, and one that does not block sight lines. It is also better suited to improving the sound quality of the range of speech frequencies in acoustically challenging spaces with a lot of hard, reflective surfaces (e.g. glass-walled buildings), as the placement of speakers allows for easier adjustment of critical frequencies and generally less reverberation to eliminate. Finally, it permits what is known as more *gain before feedback*, which essentially means that sound attenuation is not as serious and the volume may be increased without feedback. Speech generally does not need speakers for sub frequencies below about 80 Hz., although for a warmer and fuller sound, some audio engineers add small *sub-woofer* speakers (also called *bass bins*) near or even under the stage to handle the very low to mid-range frequencies.

### 3.2.2 Audio for entertainment

Most special event entertainment, particularly musical acts and bands, operates within a much more demanding range of frequencies than the spoken word, as well as with a large fluctuation of loudness levels. An audio system must deliver clearly and audibly to an entire audience, no matter how large, everything from quiet whispers to loud rock music, and from high-pitched violin solos to booming bass lines. This wide range of frequencies and volumes can come from many different sources, some live, some already amplified, and some pre-recorded. To do this acceptably requires a much larger variety of microphones and a different package of speakers with different capabilities than those systems used only for speech.

Microphones used for entertainment include wireless handheld, wireless lavalier, wireless headset, wired handheld, plus a wide variety of specialized wired and wireless ones for picking up musical instrument sounds.

Speakers for entertainment must be able to amplify frequencies covering the entire spectrum of audible sounds. This cannot be done acceptably by any single type of speaker as for speeches. The spectrum of frequencies has to be amplified using at least two or even three different types of speakers. These speaker systems, especially the bass bins used for low or sub frequencies, tend to be large, cumbersome, and intrusive to sight lines, and must be placed judiciously within the event space to keep this sight line intrusion to a minimum. Likewise, the speakers that amplify the middle and high frequencies are better placed as high above an audience as possible in order to avoid reflection, absorption, and diffraction of the higher frequencies. Therefore, they usually perform better *flown* or rigged from the ceiling—or from special trussing if outdoors—if the venue structure and setup times permit. Both sound quality and sight lines are improved by doing this. If the event space is very large, with an audience that extends a significant distance back from the stage, *delay speakers* are also needed to compensate for the time delay in the sound reaching the rear of the audience. These are also best flown.

In addition to the larger speaker groupings, musical entertainers usually require a monitor system so they can hear themselves and the other musicians play. This system may be quite complex. It consists of a number of different monitors (e.g. small, floor-mounted speakers and increasingly, in-ear monitors) and *mixes* which combine certain performers and instruments into one monitor. The monitor mixing board is normally positioned beside the stage and is typically operated by a dedicated, trained *monitor engineer*.

## 3.3 Main audio system groups and their components

An audio system includes three groups: Input group, Mixing and Processing group, and Output group, each with its own set of equipment components and standard locations (Patil et al., 2000). See Figure 3.5. Let us take a long look at each one and try to explain exactly what all this equipment does and how it works.

### 3.3.1 Input group

It might help in gaining an understanding of an audio system by thinking of the entire system as the flow of an audio signal, much like a river, from its origin as a sound wave from an instrument, a voice, or a recording, downstream toward its final destination, the ocean, otherwise called speakers. The sound wave, at its origin, is converted to an electrical signal within the first main group of sound system components called the Input group, most of which is normally located on the stage at a special event. This group consists of a number of standard pieces of equipment, all of which, in some manner, convert sound waves into electrical signals. They are:

- wired vocal and instrument microphones;
- transmitters of wireless microphones;
- direct input boxes or DIs;

Figure 3.5 Main audio system groups and signal flow

Courtesy of Doug Matthews

- keyboard mixers;

- onstage CD/DVD players, tablets, computers, Internet;

- CDs, DVDs, USB flash drives, tablets, computers, Internet, and audio inputs from video or PowerPoint located near the main mixer.

Except for wireless microphone transmitters and the other inputs located near the main mixer, these are all connected to a common onstage connector or junction box. This box forms one end of the *snake* or cable between the stage and the Mixing and Processing group (where the main mixer is located). Since the resultant electrical signal from this equipment is the essence of the audio system, we will first examine each of these components and explain how this conversion takes place.

### 3.3.1.1 Microphones

A microphone is:

> *a generic term that is used to refer to any element which transforms acoustic energy (sound) into electrical energy (the audio signal). A microphone is therefore one type from a larger class of elements called* transducers, *devices which translate energy of one form into energy of another form.*
> *(Davis and Jones, 1990, p. 113)*

The most important characteristics of microphones for live sound applications are their operating principle, frequency response, and directionality. Secondary characteristics are their electrical output and physical design. It is these five characteristics that an audio engineer uses to choose the appropriate microphone for a specific event application, such as speeches or picking up the sounds of certain instruments. The choice of microphone based on these characteristics can mean the difference between a successful event and audio disaster. Event producers should be aware of the choices available and what they mean.

In this section we will cover all the characteristics of microphones, as well as how to correctly position them and finally, examine the design and use of wireless mic systems for special events. The explanations and figures in sections 3.3.1.1.1 through 3.3.1.1.4, except where noted, are provided by Shure Inc. and used with permission (Tapia, 2008; Vear, 2011a; Lyons et al., 2008).

### 3.3.1.1.1 OPERATING PRINCIPLE

The operating principle describes the type of *transducer* inside the microphone. A transducer is a device that changes energy from one form into another, in this case, acoustic energy into electrical energy. It is the part of the microphone that actually picks up sound and converts it into an electrical signal. The operating principle determines some of the basic capabilities of the microphone. There are several such principles:

- Dynamic microphone. This type of microphone employs a thin plastic diaphragm that vibrates in response to a sound wave and in turn sets up an electrical signal in a small, attached coil of wire (*voice coil*) within a magnetic field created by a small permanent magnet. This type of microphone is extremely robust and is the most widely used in special events (Figure 3.6 left).

- Condenser microphone. This type of microphone employs a thin metal diaphragm mounted in front of a metal *backplate* and this entire miniature assembly (otherwise known as a *condenser*) is continuously charged electrically. When the sound wave hits the front diaphragm, the space between the two diaphragms changes and the resultant electrical signal also changes. The power used to maintain the continuous electrical charge within the microphone is known as *phantom power* and is provided by a

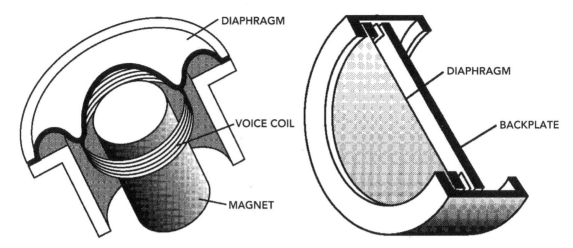

Figure 3.6 Microphone operating principles: left—dynamic; right—condenser

Copyright Shure Inc., used with permission

mixing board that actually sends the small voltage required (typically 12 to 48 V DC) back through the microphone cable to the actual microphone. Condenser microphones are more complex and costly than dynamic microphones, and are not as robust, but are more sensitive and provide a smoother, more natural sound, especially at higher frequencies (Figure 3.6 right).

- Others. Other principles include an *electret condenser*, a *ribbon*, a *carbon*, and a *piezoelectric* type of microphone, all with unique characteristics. Davis and Jones (1990, pp. 114–116) provide excellent explanations of these types, most of which are seldom used in special events.

### 3.3.1.1.2 FREQUENCY RESPONSE

This determines how the microphone sounds. It refers to the *sensitivity* of the microphone over a certain frequency range. A microphone whose output signal is equal at all frequencies has a *flat* frequency response, and is typically used to reproduce instruments with a wide range of frequencies such as guitars or pianos. One whose response has dips or peaks in signals at certain frequencies has a *shaped* response, and is typically used for close-up vocals.

### 3.3.1.1.3 DIRECTIONALITY

This is the sensitivity of the microphone to sound relative to the direction or angle from which the sound arrives. The three basic directional types of microphone are *omnidirectional*, *unidirectional*, and *bi-directional*:

- Omnidirectional. This microphone has equal pickup sensitivity from all directions around it, a full 360 degrees (Figure 3.7 left). This means that the sound source does not need to be directly in front of it to be heard. It is used, for example, as a type of lectern microphone when there might be several speakers at a lectern, none of whom may be standing directly in front of the microphone, such as in an awards show with several winners of an award all surrounding the lectern. It is important to remember, however, that omnidirectional microphones can pick up ambient room sound as well and thus can be more susceptible to feedback.

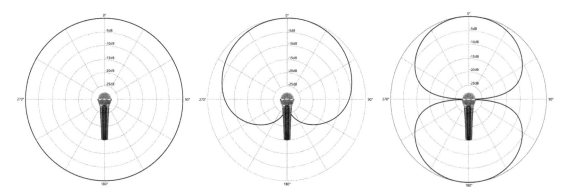

Figure 3.7 Microphone directionality: left—omnidirectional; center—unidirectional; right—bi-directional

Courtesy of Doug Matthews and Microphone, 2014

- Unidirectional. This microphone is most sensitive to sound arriving from on-axis and less sensitive to sound arriving as it moves off-axis (Figure 3.7 center). This type of microphone will allow higher gain levels (i.e. higher input volume) before feedback becomes a problem. There are two types of unidirectional microphones that derive their names from their pickup patterns. *Cardioids* (upside-down heart-shaped pickup pattern) have a 130-degree pickup angle in front. *Supercardioids* have a 115-degree pickup angle. The lower the angle, the less is the susceptibility to feedback.
- Bi-directional. This microphone is the last form of directional microphone. It has a pickup angle of 90 degrees, so that it essentially picks up sound coming from directly in front of it or directly behind it (Figure 3.7 right). It is not used much in special events but more in studio recording situations.

### 3.3.1.1.4 ELECTRICAL OUTPUT

The output of a microphone is usually specified by *output level*, *impedance*, and *wiring configuration*. These determine the proper electrical match of a microphone to a given sound system:

- Sensitivity. Remember that small electrical signal that is generated by the microphone when a sound wave reaches it? That small signal is called the sensitivity, *output level*, or *microphone level*, and is measured in millivolts. It generally falls between 0.1 mV and 100 mV, depending on the intensity of the sound and the type of microphone. If a signal voltage is small (i.e. if a sound is faint or distant from the microphone), it may be of similar level to the level of noise in the circuit (e.g. thermal noise from amplifiers, hum, hiss, clicks). Microphone level signals therefore must be amplified to what is called *line level* before being processed or routed onwards in order to overcome the effects of unwanted noise. This is done in the mixer, to be discussed later, but the line level voltage is approximately 1 volt.
- Impedance. The output impedance of a microphone is roughly equivalent to the *electrical resistance* of its output: 150–600 ohms for low impedance (low Z) and 10,000 ohms or more for high impedance (high Z). For practical purposes, low impedance microphones can be used with cable (snake) runs of 1,000 ft (300 m) or more with no loss of quality, while high impedance types lose high frequencies with cable runs greater than about 20 ft (6 m). Most microphones used for special events are low impedance.
- Wiring configuration. Finally, the wiring configuration may be *balanced* or *unbalanced*. A balanced output carries the signal on two conductors (wires with shield). The signals on each wire are the same level but opposite polarity so that only the difference between the two signals is amplified and any unwanted noise is rejected, since it is identical in each wire. On the other hand, an unbalanced microphone output

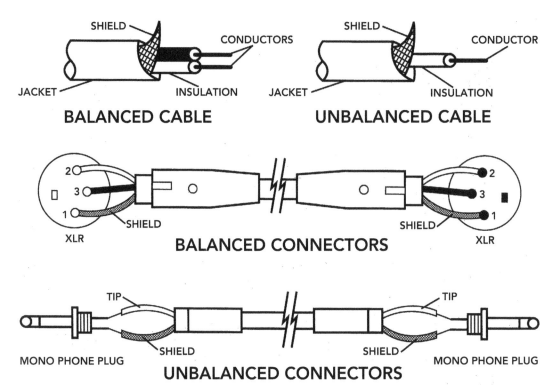

Figure 3.8 Balanced and unbalanced cables and connectors

Copyright Shure Inc., used with permission

carries its signal on a single conductor (plus shield), which in turn amplifies any unwanted noise pickup up by the conductor (wire). Unbalanced microphones and cables can never be recommended for long cable runs, or in areas where electrical interference is a problem. Therefore, for the sake of the best sound quality, nearly all special event sound reinforcement systems use balanced, low-impedance microphones. See Figure 3.8 for a representation of balanced and unbalanced cables and connectors.

### 3.3.1.1.5 PHYSICAL DESIGN, TECHNIQUE, AND PLACEMENT

The physical design of a microphone is its mechanical and operational design. Types used in special event sound reinforcement include handheld, lavalier, headset, overhead, stand-mounted, instrument and instrument-mounted, and surface-mounted. Most of these are available in a choice of operating principle, frequency response, directional pattern, and electrical output depending on the intended application. The correct selection of microphones is essential to good sound at a special event. The audio engineer must understand all details of the sound source in order to select the right microphones.

Proper techniques for using microphones, as well as the correct placement of those microphones, no matter what the application, are also critical to avoid feedback and other potential problems. This is an area that is often overlooked in special events and it can result in disastrous audio problems. It is also an area about which many event producers are blissfully ignorant. We will review the main microphone designs, consider the optimum technique for using each design, and review the basic placement for optimum sound quality. Most of the explanations and diagrams in this section, except where noted, are provided by Shure Inc. and used with permission (Lyons et al., 2008; Vear, 2011b; Waller et al., 2012):

- Handheld microphones. These come in both wired and wireless types and are normally used for speeches and by vocalists. The desired sound is the voice; the undesired sounds may be other talkers and, in the case of a musical group, other instruments, voices, or amplifiers. Dynamic microphones are the ones most often used in special events as they are more robust and will withstand frequent handling. The preferred frequency response is shaped, the directional pattern is usually unidirectional, and the output is balanced low impedance. See Figure 3.9 for an example of a handheld, wired microphone.

  Good technique for handheld microphone use includes:
  - holding the microphone at the proper distance for balanced sound (4–12 in. for speech; touching the lips or 3–4 in. away for vocals);
  - aiming the microphone toward the mouth, ideally somewhere between the nose and mouth;
  - using a pop filter to control breath noise;
  - controlling loudness with the voice rather than moving the microphone;
  - using a microphone stand (for wired or wireless types) to reduce handling noise if the speaker or vocalist does not need to move around.

- Lavalier. These come in both wired and wireless types. The desired sound source is a speaking voice; undesired sounds include other talkers, clothing and movement noise, and loudspeakers. A condenser lavalier will give the best performance but only when phantom power is available. Otherwise, a dynamic is the choice. The most common directional pattern is omnidirectional but it may lead to more ambient noise. The frequency response is specially shaped to compensate for off-axis placement (e.g. speaker's head turns away from the microphone) and the output is balanced low impedance.

  Placement of lavalier microphones is critical. They should be as close to the mouth as practical, usually a few inches below the neckline on a lapel, tie, or lanyard, or at the neckline on a woman's dress, and never underneath any clothing. When they are used in theater applications on actors, they are best placed on or near the hairline, with the best method of holding it in place to be determined by the wig master. For this purpose, lavaliers come in white and tan colors to be more inconspicuous, and with an array of mounting pins and clips. Figure 3.9 gives an example of a lavalier microphone.

  Good technique for lavalier microphone use includes:
  - not breathing on or touching the microphone or its cable;
  - not turning the head away from the microphone;
  - speaking in a clear and distinct voice.

- Headset. These come in wired and wireless forms, unidirectional and omnidirectional, condenser or dynamic, and with a choice of frequency responses. Most newer models have a lightweight frame that sits on the ears and wraps around the back of the head, with a short boom arm that holds the microphone at the corner of the mouth. They are the preferred microphone (especially unidirectional, wireless) for use in special events entertainment, in particular when a performer must both move and speak at the same time. They are used extensively for dancer/singers and for other variety performers moving around the stage (e.g. jugglers, physical comedians). The big advantage to these microphones is that they are directly in front of, and close to, the sound source, resulting in optimum sound quality with minimum feedback possibilities. Figure 3.9 gives an example of a headset microphone.

- Overhead. In the temporary world of special events, overhead microphones are rarely used except in venues that enable mounting of them above the stage area, such as in theaters. These microphones are most often condenser types, with unidirectional, cardioid pickup, and flat, wide-range frequency response. They are balanced, low impedance, and high sensitivity due to the distance from the sound source(s). Physically, they consist of a small condenser element mounted on a short gooseneck, which then leads to a thin cable that can be up to 20 or 30 ft (6 or 9 m) long. Figure 3.9 gives an example of an overhead microphone.

In these cases, if the desired sound reinforcement is of a large area of the stage (e.g. for a special play with multiple actors/performers), placement would be for the upstage area with the microphones suspended 8–10 ft (2.4–3 m) above the stage and aimed upstage. The pickup areas should not be overlapped.

- Lectern mounted. Although most of the standard microphone types may be mounted on microphone stands, it is the lectern type of microphone that we are concerned with here. These are normally wired and are used exclusively for the human speaking voice. Undesired sounds include nearby loudspeakers, rustling papers, and ambient noise (e.g. ventilation, traffic, reverberation). Both condenser and dynamic microphones are used, with condenser types providing the most unobtrusive design with the highest quality. The frequency response is flat within the range of the human voice (100 Hz to 10 kHz), the directionality is usually unidirectional cardioid but can be omnidirectional depending on how much movement there will be by the person speaking or how many persons may be sharing the lectern, and the sensitivity should be in the medium to high range since the sound source may be low and occasionally distant from the microphone. Most of these types of microphone are small and mounted on a gooseneck (Figure 3.9).

Good technique for lectern microphone use includes:
- maintaining a fairly constant distance of 6–12 in. (15–30 cm) from the microphone;
- not blowing on the microphone or touching the microphone mount when in use;
- not making excessive noise with materials on the lectern;
- speaking in a clear and well-modulated voice.

- Surface mounted. Also known as boundary microphones, these types can be used for speech in a boardroom meeting setting or equally well to pick up stage floor sound as in the case of tap dancers. They are low profile in appearance, condenser in principle, and have unidirectional cardioid or omnidirectional pickup patterns, with varying frequency response and sensitivity depending on the application (Figure 3.9). They are placed either on a conference table for meeting applications, or usually on the downstage edge of a stage or dance floor for best pickup of performance applications.

- Instrument and choral group microphones. Because of the range of frequencies and tone qualities (*timbres*) exhibited by musical instruments, there is no single microphone that will work for all instruments (or choral groups). Critical in the decision of which microphone to use are the directional output and dynamic range of the instrument. With respect to directional output, a musical instrument radiates a different timbre in every direction, essentially resulting in different timbres coming from different parts of the instrument. It is thus difficult to find the exact location for microphone placement; however, generally speaking, a close placement minimizes feedback and gives the best gain. Dynamic range refers to the instrument's range of volume from softest to loudest. Loud instruments such as drums or amplified guitars are best handled by dynamic microphones with moderate sensitivity, but soft instruments such as flutes or violins are best with condenser microphones with high sensitivity.

Waller et al. (2012) provide extensive recommendations for choral and musical instrument mic placement but here are some very general guidelines that work in most live performance situations:
- Choral groups and large musical ensembles. Use flat response unidirectional microphones, ideally condenser for best quality, placed 1–3 ft (0.3–0.9 m) above and 2–4 ft (0.6–1.2 m) in front of the first row of singers, aimed toward the middle row of the group, and approximately one microphone per 10–15 voices. Similar techniques can be used for large musical ensembles with one microphone per section. Soloists should have a small condenser clipped to the instrument. See Figure 3.10 for an example of a choral mic.
- Electric guitar or bass amplifier. Dynamic cardioid microphone placed 1–4 in. (2.5–10 cm) from the loudspeaker pointed toward the center of the speaker cone. See Figure 3.10.
- Drums. Good coverage can be achieved with four microphones—usually dynamic—quite easily: one overhead of cymbals, one overhead of tom-toms, one overhead of snare, and one in front of bass/kick drum. See Figure 3.10 for an example of a kick drum mic.

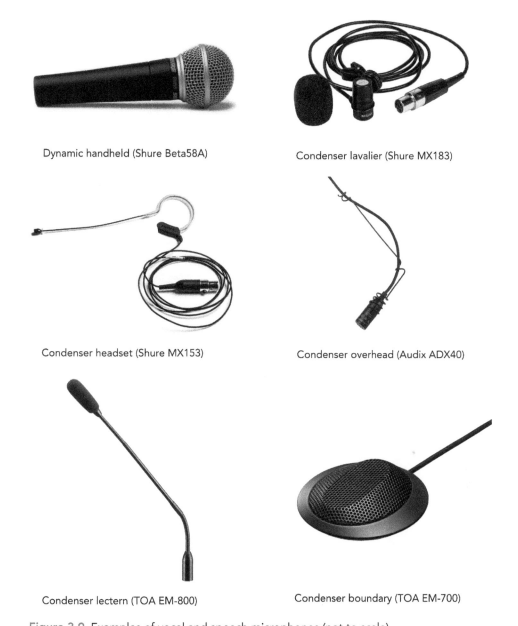

Dynamic handheld (Shure Beta58A)

Condenser lavalier (Shure MX183)

Condenser headset (Shure MX153)

Condenser overhead (Audix ADX40)

Condenser lectern (TOA EM-800)

Condenser boundary (TOA EM-700)

Figure 3.9 Examples of vocal and speech microphones (not to scale)

Copyright Shure Inc., used with permission, and courtesy Audix Corporation and TOA Corporation as per labels

- Upright bass. A condenser microphone placed about 6 in. in front of the bass just above the bridge works best.
- Piano. For a grand piano, one flat response, cardioid condenser microphone placed roughly 12 in. (30 cm) above the middle strings and 8 in. (20 cm) from the hammers will suffice. For an upright piano, a similar microphone should be placed just over the open top above the treble strings.
- Woodwinds. A unidirectional cardioid, or supercardioid, dynamic microphone works best placed a few inches above the bell and aimed at the sound holes (mounted on a stand). Alternatively, a

miniature condenser microphone clipped to the instrument and aimed at the bell yields excellent sound quality. Figure 3.10 illustrates a typical small condenser mic used for this purpose.

- Brass. A similar setup and choice works for brass instruments as for woodwinds. A dynamic unidirectional microphone placed 1–2 ft (0.3–0.6 m) in front of the bell or a small condenser microphone clipped onto the bell.

- String quartet. For violins and violas, a miniature condenser microphone clipped to the instruments near or on the chin rest works best; for cellos, a stand-mounted condenser microphone aimed at the bridge about a foot away.

Condenser ensemble (Audio-Technica Artist Elite® AE5100)    Dynamic for guitar and other amps (Shure SM57)

Dynamic kick drum (Shure Beta52A)

Condenser clip-on for woodwinds and strings (Audio-Technica ATM350)

Figure 3.10 Examples of instrument microphones (not to scale)

Courtesy of Audio-Technica U.S. and Copyright Shure Inc., used with permission

### 3.3.1.1.6 GENERAL RULES FOR MICROPHONE PLACEMENT

Based on acoustics and the effects of using multiple microphones in a performance situation, there are some general rules that help in deciding where to place microphones. They are:

- 3-to-1 rule. This basic rule-of-thumb states that, for multiple microphones, the distance between microphones should be at least three times the distance from each microphone to its intended sound source. See Figure 3.11.

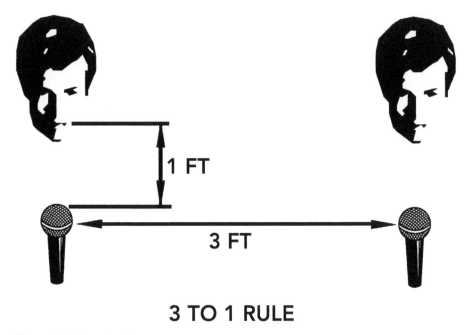

Figure 3.11  3-to-1 rule

Copyright Shure Inc., used with permission

- Potential acoustic gain. Also called gain before feedback, this determines how high the volume can be turned up before feedback occurs. It is a mathematical relationship involving the distances between sound system components, the number of open microphones, and other variables. The resultant calculations tell us the following about microphone and audio system component placement:
  - Microphones should be placed as close as practical to the sound source.
  - They should be kept as far away as possible from loudspeakers.
  - Loudspeakers should be placed as close as possible to the audience.
  - The number of microphones should be kept to a minimum.

### 3.3.1.1.7 WIRELESS MICROPHONE SYSTEMS

A unique but important adaptation of the microphone as described up to now is the wireless microphone. Wireless mics eliminate the need for cables, so performers are no longer tethered to a sound system or tripping through messy performing environments. The characteristics of the microphone are all the same as for any microphone, but with one notable exception. The electrical signal produced by the workings of the microphone is converted into a radio signal that is broadcast by a transmitter to a receiver (usually across the event space or room to near where the mixer is located). This principle is called *frequency modulation* (FM) and is identical to that used by commercial radio stations. The combination of transmitter/ receiver thus replaces the microphone cable.

Physically, the transmitter can take three forms. One is a small box, called a body or beltpack that can be clipped to a belt or otherwise attached to the user, and the microphone is connected to the beltpack via a small, thin wire. This form is most often used with lavalier or headset microphones for someone who must move around a lot, such as a keynote speaker or singer who also dances. It is also used for clip-on instrument mics (e.g. that can be attached to stringed or brass/woodwind instruments) and via a cable plugged directly into an acoustic guitar or electric guitar/bass. The second form of transmitter is built into the body of the microphone itself and is used almost exclusively for speeches and for vocalists. The third form is a *plug-on* transmitter designed to attach directly to a typical handheld microphone, effectively allowing many standard microphones to become wireless. The transmitter is contained in a small rectangular or cylindrical housing with an integral female XLR-type input connector. All wireless transmitters, whether inside the actual mic or inside the beltpack, require batteries, so any good audio engineer will have spares on hand.

The receiver end of the system converts the radio signal back into an electrical signal and a regular audio cable connects the receiver output to the mixer, where the microphone is assigned a separate channel as for any wired microphone.

Wireless microphones operate in two main frequency bands, very high frequency (VHF) from 49 to 216 MHz, and ultra high frequency (UHF) from 450 to 952 MHz. The VHF frequencies are shared with walkie-talkies, radio-controlled toys, and other consumer electronic gadgets, thus making the wireless equipment using these frequencies prone to *radio frequency interference* (RFI). It is for this reason that most serious special event applications use only UHF wireless systems. A combination of larger frequency range, smaller antennas (i.e. UHF is less than half the size of VHF), and dramatic radio circuitry advances have all but eliminated VHF systems from the current landscape. Present UHF systems offer much greater performance capabilities than historical VHF systems and at comparable or even lower cost. However, there is still the possibility of interference from such devices as cell phones in the upper range of UHF wireless operation (Vear, 2011b).

It should be noted that each wireless microphone must be assigned an individual frequency, which means that no two microphones can share the same frequency, and each microphone must have its own transmitter and receiver. The transmitter and receiver should always be placed in line of sight of each other for proper functioning.

Wireless mics are now also moving into digital format. The highest level of digital implementation uses a fully digital transmission path. The input signal is digitized in the transmitter and remains in the digital domain until the receiver output. It is even possible to output a digital signal from the receiver to subsequent digital equipment. Benefits of an all-digital wireless approach include both improved audio quality and improved radio transmission (Vear, 2011b).

## PRODUCTION WAR STORY

### The latest and greatest

I was waiting backstage with Canadian country music star Michelle Wright as a spitfire auctioneer rambled through a long list of items, getting the audience pumped. Michelle was up after him.

Out front, my own audio engineer, Chris, was assisting Michelle's personal engineer, Danny, in getting ready for the show. Danny had brought in a very compact digital mixing console. I had heard the two of them talking about it earlier during a rehearsal.

Whereas the old-fashioned analog one Chris used was about 6 ft wide, Danny proudly boasted about the extensive capabilities of his new 2 ft wide board.

"It can pre-record all the settings for the show. All I have to do is plug it in and the show's ready to go—virtually no rehearsal. It's been with us for this whole tour with Michelle, all over North America. Absolutely no problems."

Chris looked envious.

Danny continued, almost rubbing it in. "Everything can be recorded on a disk and I just insert it into the board. I carry around a separate disk for each different arena we play in."

Because of the "wonder board," the rehearsal was over in less than an hour, much more efficient than the normal 2 h or more.

As I watched the auctioneer ramble on, I received an excited call from Chris over the intercom.

"Doug, we have to delay the show start as long as possible."

"Why? What happened?"

"We just had a power surge and it fried all the settings for Michelle's show that were on the disk. Danny has to re-program the entire show into his board."

"Crap. How long will that take?"

"Dunno. Could be half an hour."

"Well, I don't think we have that long, maybe 10 min at best. I'll try to get the auction stretched out a bit. Keep me posted."

I looked over at Michelle. Her long, dark hair outlined her appealing features. She smiled and shifted from one foot to the other. I had to say something to her. I knew how performers hated waiting.

But not the whole truth. I liked her smile too much.

"Uh, Michelle, we're going to be a bit longer before show start. There are more auction items than we first thought."

"OK, no problem," she said. She was more patient than many others I knew.

I asked the auctioneer to extend and then spent the next minutes worrying whether he would run out of things to auction before the audio was ready. After 7 or 8 min, I could sense that keeping the auction going any longer would kill the show. The audience was getting impatient. We had to go.

"We need to start in 2 min," I signalled to Chris. "Is Michelle's show ready?"

A long, silent pause.

"No, Danny says it will take way too long to get all the cues back into the board. He's going to run it live."

I knew what this meant. Danny would have to monitor all the board settings continuously and use the first minutes of the show to set absolutely every single level on the board from scratch—the same thing that was normally done in the course of a 2-h rehearsal on an analog board. The likelihood of tremendous sound problems was very high, screaming feedback being one of the worst.

I cued Michelle. She had no idea what had happened, and I didn't tell her.

Unbelievably, other than a few motions from her to Danny to change monitor levels, the show was flawless—at least from my viewpoint. No question they were pros.

The client loved the show and never knew about the power surge and audio panic that had occurred. We were lucky.

Afterwards, I went back out front and talked to Chris, who had basically witnessed an hour of intense panic as his companion in the audio world fought to control Michelle's show. He had a big grin as he whispered in my ear, "I'm kinda glad I still have the old stuff. It's reliable as hell."

Danny departed with a brief thanks and goodbye. He never said another word about his new digital board.

From then on I viewed new technology with trepidatious optimism—and a healthy respect for the tried and true.

(Courtesy of Doug Matthews)

### 3.3.1.2 Direct input boxes (DIs) and other stage inputs

To review, there are three factors that determine the output of a microphone: the signal level, the impedance, and the wiring configuration. These same factors are also important for all other instruments and electronics feeding signals into the mixer via the snake. In the case of instruments or devices such as electric guitars, keyboards, keyboard mixers, DVD players, laptop computers, tablets, and even smartphones, the electronic signal that is created by these instruments or devices is higher than the signal created by a microphone and is at what we previously described as line level.

Recalling our previous discussion, unbalanced wiring configurations (e.g. quarter inch phono plug) are capable of carrying a line level signal a short distance (less than 20 ft or 6 m) whereas a balanced configuration (e.g. XLR cable) is capable of carrying a low, microphone level signal a long distance (1,000 ft/300 m or more). Certain instruments (e.g. guitars, keyboards, keyboard mixers) produce output signals that are already at line level. This means that if these signals were to be fed directly into a mixing console—and there are inputs that accept line level signals—there would be a significant amount of noise and poor sound quality due to the length of cable that would be required to get the signal from the instruments to the mixer in almost every special event situation. For example, in a typical event, the stage is on one side of the room and the mixing console is on the other, sometimes as far as 100 or 200 ft (30 or 60 m) away, enough distance to degrade a line level electronic signal. This is where a DI or *direct input* or *injection box* is used.

A DI is, in its most simple terms, a transformer that takes a line level signal (high impedance and unbalanced) and transforms it down to a lower or microphone level signal (low impedance and balanced) so it can be transported along that extended length of cable (the infamous snake) to the mixer and still arrive in good condition via an XLR connector at either end. A *passive* DI is one that is constructed of components such as capacitors and resistors, and an *active* DI is one that is constructed of active electronics such as integrated circuits, and must have continuous power applied from a wall outlet or battery. Active DIs tend to be less susceptible to hum and have more flexibility with types of inputs.

The other main purposes of a DI are to balance the signal and to independently feed the same signal to a separate onstage amplifier (such as a guitar or keyboard amp) at the same time as the signal goes to the main PA system.

In most real event situations with musicians, it is, however, more normal to use a microphone for an electric guitar or electric bass amplifier rather than putting the signal through a DI, which tends to take away some of the warmth of the sound. On the other hand, a DI is used for acoustic guitars and also for an electronic keyboard mixer output.

For other onstage devices such as turntables for DJs, laptop computers, tablets, and smartphones, there are DIs available with the appropriate input receptacles (e.g. USB). Most recently we have seen the advent of Bluetooth wireless DIs with the ability to accept *radio frequency* (RF) signals from a device (e.g. tablet, smartphone) and output them to low impedance, balanced signals and then to the mixer via an XLR cable (Figure 3.12).

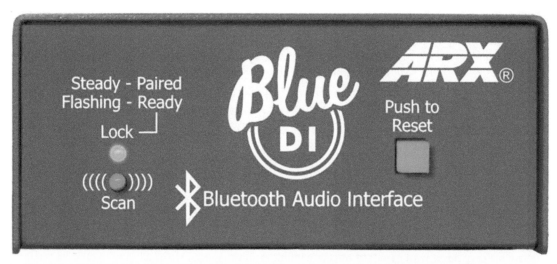

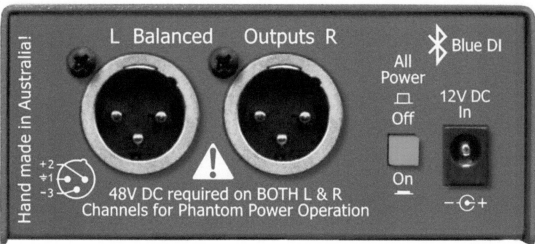

Figure 3.12 Bluetooth active direct input box: top—front, input side; bottom—back, output side

Courtesy of ARX®, www.arx.com.au

### 3.3.2 Mixing and Processing group

This important group of equipment is normally located directly in front of the main stage and at least 30 ft (9 m) away and across the room or event space.

The purpose of this group is to increase the strength of, and to manipulate, individual signals arriving from the Input group via the snake, integrate them to create the best sound possible, and then send it as a package back to the Output group via the snake. The group includes:

- the house console or mixer;
- effects;
- the snake (although not technically part of this group, it is included so that it can be explained properly).

### 3.3.2.1 *The mixer*

Also called a sound, house, or audio *console* or *board*, the mixer to the uninitiated eye looks like the bridge of the Starship Enterprise; something to be feared and far too complicated for the average event producer to comprehend. Once the basics of design and operation are known, however, the mixer ceases to hold as large a fear factor. In this section, we will explain the layout of a traditional analog mixer and then look at its modern counterpart, the digital mixer.

#### 3.3.2.1.1 ANALOG MIXER

The job of the mixer is really quite simple. It—with the guiding hand of a good audio engineer—performs the following tasks:

- Provides a separate channel for each input. Every single microphone (both wired and wireless), DI, CD/ DVD player, keyboard mixer, computer, smartphone, and piece of sound-producing equipment onstage is assigned a separate input channel on the mixer. Mixers are usually identified by the number of input channels they have, with standard mixers coming in four, eight, 12, 16, 24, 32, 48, and 54-channel versions. Inputs are mic level (XLR) or line level (quarter inch phono plug).
- Increases or *normalizes* the strength of the input signal. The mixer converts the input signal, if required, from the small microphone level (in the order of millivolts) to line level (0.1–2 V), so that all inputs have approximately the same signal strength before they move on.
- Sends the input signal of each channel to monitors if desired.
- Integrates effects. It manipulates the sound of each channel and of the entire mix.
- Combines all input signals into a final mix and sends the signal on to the Output group via the snake.

Let us now look at how the audio engineer uses the controls available on each separate channel. This is the actual "mixing" of the individual signals. Here is a brief explanation of how each control works and what it does. For purposes of illustration, we will use an older, basic analog mixer's channel strips (Mackie CFX20.MkII) as a guide (Figure 3.13), starting from the top of the strip.

- Trim or gain control. This controls a *preamplifier* or *preamp* built into the mixer. It boosts the input signal from microphone level to line level, or otherwise adjusts the signal strength to bring it to the same level as all others.
- Auxiliary send (AUX). This feature allows a channel to send a signal to an external device, such as stage monitors or an effects unit, and then accept the return of the modified signal. By using this option, audio engineers can use their own effects units or devices to customize the sound instead of being limited to using only the effects that the audio mixer offers.

  This particular mixer has specific sends for effects (EFX) after the pre-fade listen (PFL). We will cover effects in Section 3.3.2.2.
- PFL (or pre-fader). This button enables the audio engineer to check that the signal is present, at the right level, and of suitable quality before it goes to the fader (volume control) for the channel.
- EQ. This refers to equalization of bands of frequencies. The engineer can boost or diminish a particular frequency band for the individual channel to improve the sound quality of that channel. For example, the bass frequency band can be reduced on a lavalier microphone to reduce clunking sounds, or the high frequency band can be reduced to prevent *sibilance* (excessive hissing through a microphone).
- Pan. This adjusts the amount of individual channel sound heard through the left or right speakers. Although each channel is actually in mono, this adjustment enables the simulation of stereo.
- Mute button. This mutes or silences the particular channel to prevent unwanted noise from impinging on the mix.

Figure 3.13 Example of analog mixer (Mackie CFX20.MkII) and individual channel strips

- Assign. Also known as the bus section, this assigns the input microphone or channel signal to the main output channels of the mixer, which can be anywhere from two to eight (for this mixer).
- Fader. This controls the individual signal or channel level (volume) sent to the output of the mixer. Note that the individual channel signals sent to monitors and effects (i.e. via aux send) are sent before the channel fader so such things as monitor mixes (e.g. guitar wanting to hear more piano or vocals in his monitor) or the quality of individual vocal or instrument sounds are not affected when a channel fader is moved.
- Solo button. This isolates the channel signal so that it can be heard by itself. This is useful for such things as cueing CDs or other device playbacks.

Once effects have been integrated, the individual channels are combined into one signal that is controlled by two stereo faders (left and right) usually on the right side of the mixer, and sent to the Output group and speaker system.

In an analog mixer, every channel, bus, preamp, EQ, and other component mentioned above is comprised of physical circuitry (e.g. wires, resistors, potentiometers, and switches). If there is a large number of separate channels required, this makes such a mixer very space reliant and cumbersome. On the positive side, analog mixers are easier to understand and operate. Because of this ease of use, analog mixers still hold a percentage of the professional audio market. Digital mixers, however, are becoming more the norm.

### 3.3.2.1.2 Digital mixer

Digital mixers are nothing but a replacement for the large analog mixers described above. According to Tim Lang of Proshow Audio Visual Broadcast in Vancouver, Canada, once events require more than about 16 channels of input, digital mixers begin to make sense, and are used for almost all of these larger events (T. Lang, personal communication, August 12, 2014).

The main difference between digital and analog mixers is that the analog signals from microphones and other inputs are converted to a digital signal through what is known as an *analog-to-digital converter* (ADC) either before they enter the snake (see Section 3.3.2.3) or shortly after entering the mixer, usually right after the preamp. Also, with digital mixers, all effects described in Section 3.3.2.2 are built into the mixer, as well as dynamics control (e.g. compressors and gates) and output processing (e.g. equalization and time delays). This means that a great deal of extra equipment is not required and setup time is reduced. Most professional digital mixers have add-on modules so that a small mixer can be increased to 96 channels or more with little space added. Such modules may be placed anywhere in the event space and need not be together onstage. The beauty of digital mixers is that individual channel settings can be pre-set, memorized, and instantly recalled when required. They can also be managed as any number of groups with common requirements using *voltage control amplifiers* (VCAs) so that at the touch of a single button, a group of several channels can be brought up on a monitor to allow adjustments to be made to those channels. Finally, most are remotely controllable via proprietary apps for tablets, smartphones, or computers.

By design, at first glance digital mixers appear nothing like analog mixers and every manufacturer's design is different. However, in concept they are the same. On the MIDAS PRO6 console of Figure 3.14, for example, the input channel controls are still there on the left hand side of the mixer (twelve), and also on the right hand side (four) to enable two completely different operators, designated as Areas A and B. The functions described above for each channel are hidden behind buttons and can be recalled instantly onto the main monitor screen and can then be individually adjusted. The center portions contain: channel grouping mix options controlled by VCAs; auxiliary sends (e.g. to effects or monitors); monitor mixes; and output faders. Some mixers like the PRO6 have color-coding of buttons to assist with operation.

Any and all settings can be stored and instantly recalled later from a USB stick, thus saving considerable time in sound checks if the same mixing is required in different venues (e.g. as with a touring band). Storage, transportation, and setup are naturally much easier; however, operation requires a longer learning period.

### 3.3.2.2 Effects

Effects help to thicken or modify the audio signal that is going through the system. They are normally added by setting up what is known as an effects *loop* in which an individual channel signal is sent from the mixer via the auxiliary send. The signal is then routed through a number of different effects. In an analog mixing setup, the hardware that creates these effects is all mounted on what is known as a *rack* (just another term for a vertical arrangement of individual effects boxes in a traveling road case). Once the signal has had the effects added, it is returned to the mixer either pre- or post-channel fader. In a digital mixing setup most if not all of the effects—and more—are available and applied from within the mixer itself, meaning the external rack is not required.

The effects that are most commonly used in special event audio systems are:

- Delay and echo. Echo is exactly that. It simulates the sound of a natural echo. Delay is basically the same. It is done by adding a time-delayed signal to the signal output. This produces a single echo, but multiple echoes (delay) can be achieved by feeding the output of the echo back into its input. Delay times from a few milliseconds to several seconds are common.

Figure 3.14 Example of a digital mixer (MIDAS PRO6): top—front view; bottom—rear view

© Copyright 2013. MUSIC Group IP Ltd., www.midasconsoles.com

- Reverberation (reverb). This is used to simulate the acoustical effect of sound in large rooms or concert halls, in particular the sound from all sources including reflected sound. It gives the impression of being in a very large space. It can be done digitally to lengthen the actual reverberation time within a small room to give it the feel of sound within a large room.

- Chorus. Chorus simulates the effect of more than one person singing. In other words, it can make a solo vocalist sound like two or more vocalists. It is achieved by adding in an echo to the original input signal; however, in this case, the echo's delay is continuously varied.

- Flanging and phasing. These are similar effects and are variations of the chorus effect. They make the sound appear to "whoosh" or pulsate.

- Noise gate. This is used to prevent unwanted pickup of background noise such as hissing or extraneous stage noise. It can be set to a certain threshold level so that any audio signal below that level will not pass through the gate, the result being a quiet channel.

- Compressor. A compressor simply reduces the difference between the loudest and quietest parts of a piece of music by automatically turning down the gain when the signal gets past a pre-determined level. In this respect, it does a similar job to the human hand on the fader—but it reacts much faster and with greater precision. In a loud environment, say, for example, a special event dinner, quieter passages will get lost unless the audio engineer "rides" the channel fader for that instrument or vocalist to boost the volume during those quiet passages. The volume then needs to be reduced to prevent distortion or feedback when the instrument or vocalist gets loud again. A compressor allows the volume to be left at the "boosted" level by reducing the peaks (loud parts) by a preset amount so they don't cause distortion. Two controls common to compressors are *threshold* and *ratio*. The threshold determines at what point the compressor function activates, and the ratio controls how much the signal is compressed (Sigismondi, 2008). The compressor allows much more control by the audio engineer, and negates any reason for a vocalist—or person speaking—to move a microphone to control the volume level.

Once all effects have been added to the mix, the signal is routed to the final output of the mixer and the main speaker volume level controlled directly from the master fader on the output panel of the mixer. It is normally comprised of one stereo or two single channel faders that correspond with the left and right main house speakers. It can also include outputs that correspond to monitor mixes for onstage performers.

### 3.3.2.3 *The snake*

The purpose of the snake is simply to act as an extension cord that connects all the signals on the stage to the equipment the audio engineer uses at the audio console position, usually at least 30 ft (9 m) across the room or event space from the stage. Traditional audio snakes use analog technology and consist of a large diameter cable containing multiple wires (XLR cables). These wires—one for each channel—carry the audio signals from one location to the other. At one end of the cable is a large junction box, or *snake box*, with low impedance (i.e. XLR) female receptacles for connecting each of the audio sources (e.g. microphones and DIs). The other end of the cable splits into individual multiple plugs again for connection to the mic preamps and line inputs of the mixing console.

Some snakes also allow for a number of return signals to come back through the snake, such as for monitor mixes; however, for best audio quality, it is recommended not to use these returns (in analog snakes) for the mixer output going to power amps, and hence to main speakers, as feedback can occur due to *coupling* of signals going to and coming from the mixer (Davis and Jones, 1990, p. 289). In summary, analog snakes are bulky, heavy, expensive, and don't always provide the best possible audio quality.

Now, however, the snake, like everything else, has become digital. The benefit of the digital snake is that it eliminates long analog audio signal transfers and the signal degradation that always comes along with them. This is accomplished by converting audio signals to digital at the stage position (typically actually beside the stage) within the snake box—sometimes referred to as an *input-output* (I/O) *box* or *interface* by some manufacturers—which allows them to be transferred hundreds of feet with absolutely no loss in sound quality. Since multiple digital signals can be transferred over a single lightweight cable, the enormous bulk of the analog snake's multi-channel cable is also eliminated. The stage unit may also feature a number of audio outputs for signals sent back to the stage from the mixing console (e.g. amplifier feeds for main and monitor speakers). See Figure 3.15.

At the mixer end of the digital cable, there may be a requirement to convert the digital signal back to analog if it is going into an analog mixer (yes, the two can be compatible). This is accomplished by another similar unit to that onstage except it contains a *digital-to-analog converter* (DAC). The separate signals are then patched into the mixer using standard XLR cables. If the mixer at the receiving end of the digital snake is a digital mixer, then the cable is patched directly into the mixer and reconversion of the one digital signal into separate ones is done internally using the mixer's software.

The actual lightweight cable is called *Enhanced Category 5 Ethernet patch cable* (CAT5e). It is very small in diameter, lightweight, and uses connectors similar to those for a telephone, but a bit more robust. Depending on the brand, up to 56 or more channels can be carried on this cable for up to 100 m (330 ft) or more with little degradation. Category 6 (CAT6) is the next generation, arranging the wire pairs within the cable jacket differently than CAT5e. CAT6 cable is flatter and a bit less flexible than CAT5e. Many

**Figure 3.15** Example of onstage digital interface unit

Images courtesy of: left—Roland Corporation; right—etherCON CAT6 Cable © Neutrik® AG 2014

people use "CAT5" as a generic term for any Ethernet-style cable. See Figure 3.15. The methodology of transporting audio signals via a digital CAT5e or CAT6 cable is known as *Audio-over-Ethernet* (AoE).

There are drawbacks to Ethernet cabling and digital snakes, however, as Lang of Proshow Audiovisual Broadcast notes:

> *They are very susceptible to damage and the promised longer runs have not materialized without extra repeaters. As well, they are technologically complex. However, they work well for fixed installations and for large concert setups. We continue to use mostly analog snakes.*
>
> *(T. Lang, personal communication, August 12, 2014)*

What's next? Wireless connectivity is coming—soon! Using a wireless protocol designed for A-V—and there are several coming onto the market—all an audio engineer will have to do is set up the stage end of the snake and the mixer end without running any cable between the two. Even better, up to 512 channels can be run using this protocol, more than enough for almost any special event one can imagine. In addition, fiber optic cable is replacing Ethernet for longer runs up to 100 km or more.

### 3.3.3 Output group

This group is comprised of the audio system components that represent the final destination of the original audio signal that began way upstream as a sound wave going into a microphone on the stage. The equipment includes:

- A frequency equalizer system for the main sound, located as an independent unit near FOH, or within a digital mixer, or within a *speaker processor*.
- A limiter for the main sound, located as an independent unit near the stage, or within a digital mixer, or within a speaker processor.
- Crossovers to divide up frequencies going into the power amplifiers, located as an independent unit near the stage, or within a digital mixer, or within a speaker processor, or within the speakers themselves.
- Power amplifiers, located either near the stage or within the speakers themselves.
- The main speakers, located on, above, or near the stage.
- The entire monitor system, also including equalization, amplifier, and stage monitors, located either near the stage or at FOH.

The purpose of this group is to prepare and deliver the output signal from the main mixer to the main or house speakers. The signal is first adjusted by the house equalizer and then by the limiter. The signal is then routed back through a snake to the main stage area where it is divided up by crossovers into frequencies that correspond to the different main or house speakers, amplified, and finally fed into the speakers. Let's examine how each of these components achieves this:

### 3.3.3.1 Equalizer

This equalizer system works exactly the same as the one for each individual channel except that this one adjusts the frequencies going to the main speakers in the house or event space after the audio signal has already been adjusted for each channel. In other words, this particular equalizer adjusts the entire mix.

The equalizer placed at the output of the mixer—and in digital mixers usually within the mixer itself, or in many cases in a speaker processor unit near the main mixer—is used primarily to control the frequencies that are affected by the room or event space itself. For example, we earlier discussed the problems with low frequencies being dominant in a room by virtue of the fact that they "bend" around small objects and are thus not absorbed as much as higher frequencies. Because of this, they can be minimized through the use of an equalizer at the output of the mixer, just as the high frequencies that tend to be absorbed by people filling the room can be boosted. This is especially important when a sound check is done in the afternoon before an event and before the room is filled with people. At the time of the event, with more people, the room behaves differently acoustically and the equalizer can compensate for this.

### 3.3.3.2 Limiter

A limiter is a specialized form of compressor (see the earlier section on effects) that uses a very high ratio to prevent any signal from surpassing the level set by the threshold. A limiter is primarily used as an overall system protection after the equalizer, while compressors are typically used on an individual channel basis, although the actual hardware usually combines the two functions. Most digital mixers now incorporate a limiter, or it can be found as a separate control within a speaker processor unit near the main mixer.

### 3.3.3.3 Crossovers

Crossovers are electrical devices placed in the path of the audio signal after the limiter. Their purpose is to divide up the audio signal into separate outputs of mid-, low-, and high-range frequencies. These separated signals are then routed to the appropriate speakers that are designed for them. *Passive* crossovers are located inside *full-range* speaker cabinets (i.e. speakers that cover all frequencies) and do this by dividing the signal after it leaves the power amplifiers. They tend to be inefficient in that all the speakers are working from the same power source, and the low-range speakers, which require more power, will rob power from the higher range frequency speakers.

*Active* crossovers are located outside the speaker cabinets and before the power amplifiers. In this way, they make it possible to power the low-, mid-, and high-range speakers from different power amplifiers. This is a much more efficient use of power and enables the system to provide a more powerful and full sound covering all frequencies equally. It does, however, require more equipment and expense. It is the system of choice for most special events with complex audio requirements and large audiences. However, increasingly nowadays, powered, full-range speakers are being used for more intimate events and these speakers contain both active crossovers and power amplifiers.

Most digital mixers also include active crossovers or, if not located within the speakers, they can be found in the same speaker processor unit that controls the limiter and EQ functions. Occasionally, they may be located near the stage along with separate power amplifiers.

With respect to the current digital technology, for small to medium-sized events, Tim Lang of Proshow Audiovisual Broadcast in Vancouver, Canada, states that the digital mixer at FOH typically handles the job of the limiters, crossovers, and EQ in most instances. However, when it comes to larger events, concerts, or touring shows, it is more likely that a separate unit called a speaker or effects processor, as mentioned above, will be used. The processor is normally located at the FOH position and handles the limiter, crossover, and EQ functions rather than the digital mixer or, as in the "old days," a group of individual units, each with a separate job (T. Lang, personal communication, August 12, 2014).

### 3.3.3.4 Power amplifiers

The purpose of the power amplifiers is to boost the low voltage line level signal coming from the limiter (or from the equalizer if there is no system limiter) to a higher voltage output signal capable of efficiently driving the loudspeakers. Power amplifiers are functionally simple units. All amplifiers have a set of line-level inputs and a set of speaker-level outputs. Most have a power switch and volume controls as well.

Appropriately, the power rating of an amplifier is its most important statistic. It is measured in *RMS watts* (root mean square, or RMS, is a mathematical expression used to describe the level of a signal) and should match the power-loading capabilities of the speaker it is driving. For example, for special event situations, it is not unusual to have amplifiers rated at 400 W or higher to amplify all the instruments and microphones. However, the matching speaker system must also be able to handle at least that amount of power.

It should be noted here why exactly so much power may be needed. The answer is quality and clarity of sound. If the required level for comfortable listening for a musical stage show is only 20 W, but there is a musical peak in the performance that is twice as loud, the laws of physics demand that the amplifier will require ten times the power to make the music seem twice as loud. In other words, the amplifier must be capable of delivering 200 W of power to the speakers. Otherwise, the music will sound distorted and fuzzy. Not only that, but the speakers may also be damaged if the amplifier is incapable of providing that power level.

### 3.3.3.5 Main speakers

Speaker design and the choice and placement of the correct speakers within the event space are critical to audio quality.

#### 3.3.3.5.1 DESIGN

A loudspeaker (speaker) is the final destination of the original sound wave that started onstage with a microphone or other electronic device. It simply converts the electrical signal back into mechanical energy in the form of a sound wave. The signal activates an electromagnet attached to the speaker frame. This electromagnet in turn generates a magnetic field that corresponds in intensity to the frequency and loudness of the electrical signal emitted by the amplifier. The variation in this magnetic field causes a *voice coil*, which is attached to the rear of a flexible cone-shaped diaphragm (also called a *membrane* and constructed of paper or synthetic material), to move the cone forward and backward in a pattern that mimics the frequency and loudness dictated by the electrical signal (Gillette, 2000).

Figure 3.16 (a) is a simple drawing showing basic speaker design, and Figure 3.16 (b) shows how the electromagnet moves the cone to produce a sound wave.

Speakers are generally classified as low frequency (*woofers*), with a frequency range from approximately 20 to 1,000 Hz; middle frequency (*mid-range*), with a frequency range from approximately 500–5,000 Hz or more; and high frequency (*tweeters*), with a frequency range from approximately 5,000–20,000 Hz.

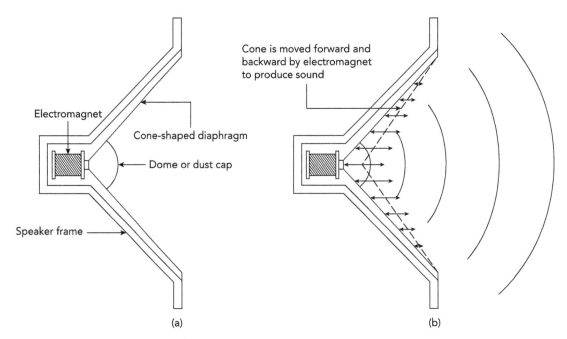

**Figure 3.16** Speaker design and operation

Courtesy of Doug Matthews

Most manufacturers make speakers that combine the middle and high range of frequencies into ones that cover about 30 or 40 Hz to 20 kHz. These are referred to either as *mid-high* or full-range speakers. Only the very low frequencies below about 80 Hz occasionally need reinforcement in event situations, especially for concerts or musical acts, and these speakers are called *subs* or *sub-woofers*, although most manufacturers' speakers in this category cover a range from about 30–50 Hz to about 220–250 Hz.

Most low frequency speakers are of a cone-type design while the mid- and high-range speakers incorporate both a unique horn design called a *pressure driver* that uses a thin metal diaphragm, and a *horn* that helps to direct the sound in a particular direction and pattern because of its unique shape.

Speakers can be *active* (i.e. with their own built-in amplifiers—also sometimes called *powered* speakers) or *passive* (i.e. no built-in amplifier). Most speakers in the larger audio systems for special events are passive, although the sub-woofers are active. However, according to Tim Lang of Proshow Audiovisual Broadcast in Vancouver, Canada, the use of powered speakers is increasing, with at least 50 percent or more of those used in corporate events being powered (T. Lang, personal communication, August 12, 2014).

Speaker cabinets are also designed to enhance the specific frequencies of the speakers they house. For example, bass speakers may incorporate sound-absorbing material to reduce reflections within the cabinet since the low frequencies tend to radiate in all directions. In general, cabinets help to reinforce the low frequencies and to smooth out the quality of the bass response. Mid and high frequencies radiate outwards at about 180 degrees or less, so less cabinet design is required, although most speakers for these ranges have their backs covered with thin material to avoid interference from the vibrations of lower frequencies. Figure 3.17 illustrates a full-range speaker (left) and a sub-woofer (right), both without their front grilles.

Figure 3.17  Examples of speakers (not to scale)

Courtesy of JBL Professional, www.jblpro.com/www/home

### 3.3.3.5.2 PLACEMENT

Speaker placement is also critical depending on the type of event, whether there will be only speeches or mainly musical entertainment, the size of the audience, and the size and construction of the venue or event space. Placement must be made with at least a general understanding of the acoustics of the space.

In the case of an event in which there are only speeches, there are several options for speaker placement. The one that achieves best consistent sound quality throughout the event space is a distributed system. This system uses a number of full-range speakers on tripod stands placed around the space so that full coverage is obtained. For a richer sound, as previously described, it may also include small sub-woofer speakers beside or under the stage (for frequencies below 80 Hz). It is good for a relatively small space and audience. See Figure 3.18. Note that this is a side view of the space and shows only one row of speakers

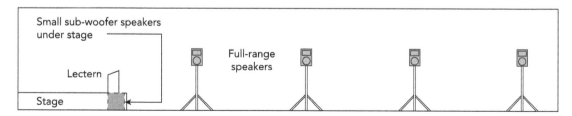

Figure 3.18  Example of a distributed speaker system

Courtesy of Doug Matthews

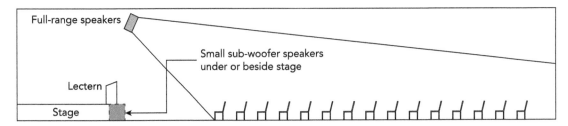

**Figure 3.19** Example of a flown speaker system

Courtesy of Doug Matthews

down one side of a wall in a 100 ft (30 m) long room. This arrangement would be duplicated down the near wall with perhaps one or two speakers across the back wall as well.

Figure 3.19 is a second option for speaker placement. It uses a flown system from a ceiling-mounted truss that points a cluster of full-range speakers at the audience so that all seats are covered by the dispersion of the sound. Additionally, sub-woofers are generally placed under or beside the stage. In most situations, there would be two or more sets of speakers mounted on the same truss over the stage so that equal coverage could be maintained across the space.

Occasionally a situation will arise that requires audience seating closer to the stage, usually because event managers want to seat the maximum number of persons in the room. If the sound system is flown, this requires that an additional set of flown speakers be aimed at the front few rows of seats, as in Figure 3.20. An optional way to achieve the same thing is to either place one or two sets of the same full-range speakers on stands at the front of the room to cover this part of the audience, or place even smaller fill speakers (such as monitors) on the downstage edge of the stage pointing at the front rows of the audience.

If the event space is large and extends back from the stage more than 80–100 ft (24–30 m), there is usually the need to provide what are known as delay speakers. These are exactly the same types of full-range speakers except that there is a programmed delay to the sound that emanates from them in the order of milliseconds. This delay compensates for the sound coming from the speakers nearest to the stage and reaching the audience's ears at a time after it would reach them if a delay were not built in. Thus, all sound reaches audience members farther from the stage at exactly the same time. These delay speakers also compensate for sound degradation at distant points in the event space caused by reverberation, points at which the level of reverberation and the direct sound level (i.e. the sound coming directly from the speakers vs. reflected sound) are approximately equal. Farther back in the room from this point the sound quality will be poor and speech especially becomes less intelligible. Figure 3.21 illustrates the installation of such delay speakers in a long room.

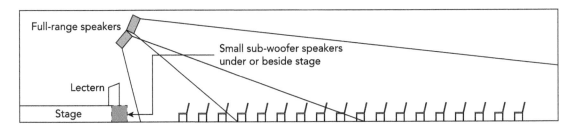

**Figure 3.20** Example of a flown speaker system with front fill speakers

Courtesy of Doug Matthews

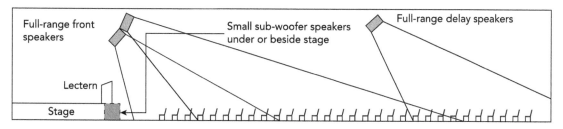

**Figure 3.21** Example of a flown speaker system with delay speakers

Courtesy of Doug Matthews

In the case of entertainment, as mentioned in Section 3.2.2, the range of frequencies is much more than for ordinary speech. Because of this, large sub-woofers are demanded. These are typically placed near the stage and immediately to either side. They do not normally have to be flown because, as explained in the section on acoustic theory, low frequencies tend to bend around obstacles and therefore can cover an entire room with objects such as people in the way. Figure 3.22 illustrates how a typical event dinner might look from a side view showing such speaker placement.

One final concern in speaker placement is lateral coverage. The above placements can cover short and long rooms, but what if the room or event space is very wide? This is usually solved by arraying several speakers on the same horizontal plane but facing different directions in order to obtain coverage across the room. The exact amount and quality of coverage will depend in the end on speaker design and angle of speaker placement. Figure 3.23 illustrates this type of placement from a top view of the same event situation as in Figure 3.22.

### 3.3.3.5.3 LINE ARRAYS

The last point for discussion on speakers concerns larger indoor or outdoor events, mainly concerts with large audiences. The term "array" has already been mentioned above in explaining the use of multiple similar speakers placed in a horizontal plane in order to achieve horizontal coverage. An array of speakers is also used to cover large distances and large audiences in the vertical plane. This is known as a *line array*. A line array is a set of speakers arrayed in the vertical plane to create what appears as a straight line when viewed from the front. However, arrays can take several forms when viewed from the side: straight, simple curve, "J" shape, and spiral. Although the "J" shape has been used a lot, in fact the spiral shape gives better coverage. For example, a line array can be used to cover the entire vertical plane within a stadium from roof to floor.

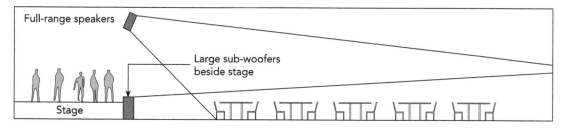

**Figure 3.22** Example of speaker placement for a typical event with stage entertainment

Courtesy of Doug Matthews

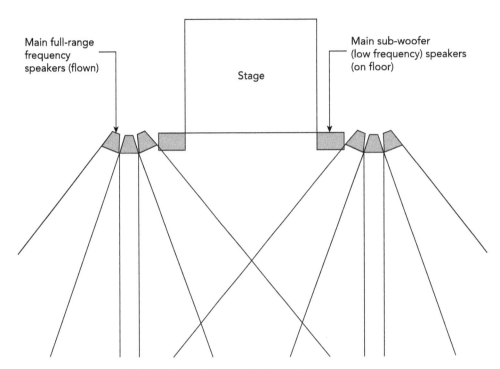

Figure 3.23 Example of speaker placement for lateral coverage

Courtesy of Doug Matthews

The majority of systems used in vertical line arrays are specially designed for that use alone. The individual speakers generally cover a wider frequency range than other types, usually from about 40 Hz to 18 or 20 kHz. Often sub-woofers are added for events involving entertainment in order to cover the very low frequencies below 30 Hz. These may be mounted on the ground or flown with the line array. Line array speakers are also designed for wider horizontal coverage, usually about 90 degrees in the horizontal plane, but some can go up to 120 degrees.

The decision on number of speakers, curvature of the speaker array, and type of speakers is determined based on the size of the venue or event space, the audience size, the extent of coverage needed, manufacturer's specifications, and other variables. Manufacturers typically provide a spreadsheet or custom program to design arrays. The design process starts by entering the dimensions of the room and the required sound pressure level. The program then suggests the number and arrangement of boxes. Alternatively some programs require the number of boxes to be entered and it will predict the resulting sound pressure levels in different parts of the room.

Once designed, the speakers are hung from rigging points on a support structure such as trussing constructed as a stage roof. The individual speaker boxes of the array may be connected one at a time or rigged together on the ground and then pulled up using *chain motors* (see Chapter 9 for more details about chain motors and rigging). One benefit of using a manufacturer's line array design is that special mounting and flying bracketry comes with the speakers, making this process much more efficient. As the array is lifted, individual box angles are adjusted to match the array prediction program. If height or lack of rigging points does not permit flying the speakers, the speakers are typically stacked on the stage or on sub-woofers using a custom stacking frame. Stacking of line arrays is common in smaller venues and in temporary

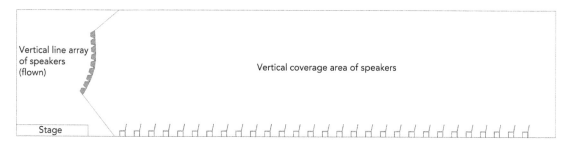

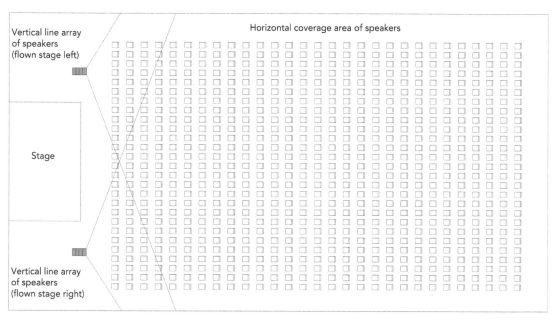

Figure 3.24  Example of vertical line array of speakers for large area coverage

Courtesy of Doug Matthews

installations. Compared to flown speakers, they require less vertical dispersion to cover front to back and the resulting array will have little curvature (Line array, 2014).

Recent developments have led to floor line arrays for improved coverage in smaller venue situations. The speakers comprising these arrays are much smaller than for the large event setups.

Figure 3.24 illustrates a line array setup in side and plan views. Figure 3.26 also shows line arrays.

### 3.3.3.6 Monitor system

The main purpose of monitors is to allow performers onstage to hear what all the other performers are singing, what other instruments are playing, or what backup music is being played to accompany a performance or program. If an event is held in a small room with very few people in the audience, there is probably no need for any stage monitors since anyone onstage will be able to hear what is going on directly from the main speakers. However, when an event gets to any significant size in terms of audience, or the event space or venue itself becomes large, there will be a need for monitors—typically small, wedge-shaped speakers sometimes called *wedges*—to allow onstage performers to hear everything else that is happening on the stage. Often for many special events the audio system is quite modest, even with multiple performances onstage in a large venue. Perhaps there is a choreographed dance show, or perhaps a few speeches followed by a four- or five-piece combo for dancing, or perhaps a multimedia show with PowerPoint slides accompanied by a choir. In all these cases, there is probably no need for more than two to four monitors onstage at any time.

In these cases, monitors and their mixes can be controlled entirely from the main FOH mixer. Most analog mixers have auxiliary sends located on each input channel. This means that the signal from that channel can be sent to an auxiliary output channel on the mixer, thereby creating separate mixes for onstage monitors that are sent back through the snake to the stage. Unfortunately, in an analog mixer, the number of different mixes is limited by the number of auxiliary output channels on the mixer. Once the number of mixes required exceeds the number of auxiliary output channels, a separate monitor mixer is needed. For example, if there is a large band playing with several instruments, lead vocals, and backup vocals, there may be quite a large number of separate mixes desired by the band. The lead vocalist, for example, may want to hear only the keyboard and bass players with a little bit of the backup vocals; the drummer may only want to hear the bass, guitars, and keyboard; the keyboardist may only want to hear the lead vocalist, guitars, and drummer, etc. In this type of situation, with complex monitor mix requirements, the monitor mix must be located beside the stage. See Figure 3.25 for an example of a typical band's stage plot for exactly this type of situation.

In the case of digital mixers, most have multiple auxiliary sends—some as many as 32 or more—allowing all monitor mixing to be done at the main FOH mixer. However, even with this possibility, larger bands will probably opt for a monitor mix close to the stage if for no other reason than better communication. In almost all cases, though, the monitor mixer itself will be digital.

It should be noted that many musical groups and performers now prefer to work with in-ear monitors (IEMs) that are simply one-way ear bud speakers much like those available with portable music players

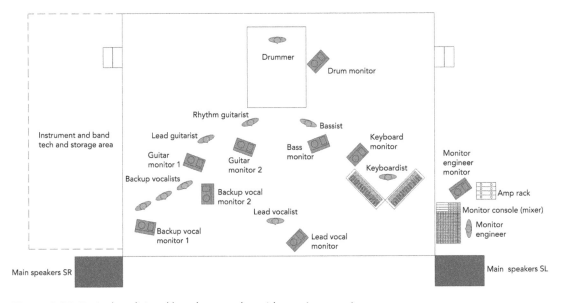

Figure 3.25 Typical traditional band stage plot with monitor requirements

Courtesy of Doug Matthews

and smartphones. This personal monitor system may be either wired or wireless. From the output of the mixer, the audio signal goes to a transmitter, which converts it to an RF signal. A beltpack receiver, worn by the performer, picks up the RF signal and converts it back to an audio signal, all very similar in principle to wireless microphones except in reverse. At this stage the audio is then amplified and output to the earphones. Personal monitors eliminate large monitor speakers and remove onstage clutter. The most practical benefit to personal monitors is that performers can have direct control over what they are hearing. While still relying on the sound engineer to make fine adjustments, personal monitor systems give the performer some ability to make broad adjustments, such as overall volume, pan, or the ability to choose different mixes. If everything in the mix needs to be louder, instead of giving a series of complex hand gestures to the monitor engineer, the performer can raise the overall volume directly from the beltpack (Sigismondi, 2009). Indeed, some manufacturers also have complete small individual mixers for each performer, thereby eliminating altogether the need for any master monitor mix beside the stage or even at the main FOH mixer position.

The monitor mixer—if needed—and the associated equipment are essentially identical to the main mixer and its related equipment, except that the output ends up at a number of different monitors onstage instead of the main house speakers. Because the same principles apply as for the main audio system, the monitor system will not be explained in detail.

## 3.4  Signal flow and equipment locations in the event space

Now that we have examined in detail all the main groups that comprise the audio system, let's go back and review exactly how the audio signal flows and follow it from beginning to end in a diagram.

### 3.4.1  Signal flow

Let us follow the actual signal flow with assistance from a more comprehensive diagram, Figure 3.26, in which colored text indicates components of each group, red for the Input group, green for the Mixing and Processing group, and blue for the Output group. The lines with arrows indicate the path of the audio signal.

To review, the audio signal:

- begins onstage with the Input group, through: microphones where it is converted from a sound wave into an electrical signal, instrument DIs, guitar amp, keyboard mixer, or other devices such as computers;
- goes into a snake box that sends the signal to the main mixer and possibly also to a separate monitor mixer beside the stage;
- is processed in the Mixing and Processing group, by the main FOH mixer where it is raised in strength by a preamp, and has various effects added (for each individual channel);
- goes from the mixer into the Output group, via a speaker processor in which a house equalizer adjusts frequencies, a house limiter controls maximum strength, and house crossovers split it into different frequency bands;
- goes back through the snake to the power amplifiers that boost its strength and send it to low frequency speakers/sub-woofers (usually floor-mounted) and full-range speakers (usually flown from trussing) that convert it back into sound waves.

The signal going to the monitor mixer is handled in almost exactly the same way as the signal going to the main house mixer, with identical components.

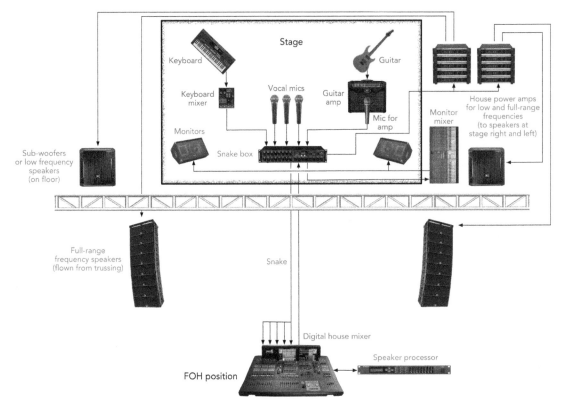

**Figure 3.26** Signal path and equipment locations for typical event audio system (not to scale)

Courtesy of Doug Matthews

### 3.4.2 Equipment locations

In the same way, let us review exactly where in the event space all the audio equipment is located, again with reference to Figure 3.26.

- Input group. In special event applications, almost all the Input group of equipment is located entirely onstage. This includes vocal and instrument microphones, instrument DIs, keyboard mixers, and occasionally onstage CD/DVD players or even computers that are controlled by performers. Other components of the Input group are found often at the house mixer location. These may include USB flash drives, CD/DVD players, computer audio output signals (used in multimedia presentations), video audio outputs, receivers for onstage wireless microphones, and voiceover microphones for MCs.

- Mixing and Processing group. This equipment, including main house mixer and effects rack, is located at the FOH position which, particularly in the case of special events with complex entertainment and musical stage shows, should be at least 30–100 ft (9–30 m) directly across the room or event space from the stage. The general rule of thumb, as suggested by Davis and Jones (1990, pp. 190–191), is that the console should not be closer to any of the main speakers than the distance between the two mains (left and right), and no farther than twice the distance between the two mains. It is not absolutely necessary to have the console at the same height as the stage. In fact, it may be preferable to have it on the floor to avoid the amplification of low frequencies by the riser structure, which would be required if it were raised. Often, due to the restrictions of space and the room layout, it is not possible to have the FOH location in front of the stage, but rather at the side of the room somewhere. This is not ideal and means that the audio engineer must continually monitor the sound by walking to the center of the room to listen for proper balance. Unfortunately, this is one of the negatives of the event business.

As mentioned in Section 3.3.2.2, most effects are now contained within the main mixer if it is digital, so external effects racks are no longer required at the FOH position as they were in the past with analog systems.

The third member of this group, the snake, is what connects the Input group to the Mixing and Processing group. There are several options for locating it, whether it is an analog or digital snake. The snake box is usually at the side of the stage near the monitor mixer. The ideal routing of the actual cable from an audio standpoint is in a straight line on the floor between the stage and FOH. If the event is a dinner or standup reception of some sort, however, this can make it a serious trip hazard. It should therefore be matted if possible with a solid mat with yellow warning markings or at the very least with a rubber mat, again with yellow or caution cross-taping. Otherwise, the safer route is also in a straight line but across or through the ceiling, which negates any matting and avoids trip hazards, but increases setup time. The third option is to route the cable around the perimeter of the room. This means that it must either go over doorways, or across the floor in the doorways. The better choice is over the doors but if it must go across the floor, it again must be matted with either a solid cable mat (best) or a large rubber mat.

- Output group. The components of this group have several different locations which are usually as follows:

  - House equalizer and limiter. These are always located near the FOH console position. If a digital mixer is used, they are usually contained within the mixer or within a speaker processor.

  - Crossovers and power amplifiers. These are usually located on or near the stage and, if there is a monitor engineer, close to him, although the crossovers can be placed at the FOH position. Again, if a digital mixer is used, the crossovers are usually contained within the main mixer or within a speaker processor. The power amplifiers may be separate units, or nowadays more frequently contained within the individual speaker cabinets.

  - Main speakers. The locations and number of these can vary depending on the type of event, the size of the audience, and so on, as explained in Section 3.3.3.5.2. Figure 3.26 is just a general scenario. However, there will always be a set of speakers near the main stage, usually at the outside edges.

  - Monitor system. In a simple event, regardless of whether the system is digital or analog, monitors will probably be controlled from the FOH position. In a complex event, the entire monitor system will be located on either stage right or left and there will be a separate technician called a *monitor engineer* assigned to it full-time.

## 3.5 Pre-event sound check and system operation during the event

In this section we examine what the audio engineer does during sound check and during the actual event.

### 3.5.1 Pre-event sound check

Most audio systems, no matter what the size, are run in essentially the same way. Whether it is a small meeting with simple speeches and an audience of 100, or a stadium rock and roll concert, the operating principles of the audio system are similar. Once the basic components of microphones, snake, mixer, effects, equalizer, amplifiers, and speakers are set up, then it is necessary to carry out a sound check and proceed with system operation.

What is the purpose of the sound check and why does it take so long? This is perhaps one of the most misunderstood—but absolutely necessary—tasks that must be carried out for a special event to run without technical glitches, especially one with a large audience and complicated audio requirements. Event producers must understand that sufficient time has to be allotted to accomplish it. One to two hours—or more—are not unusual for a complete check.

A thorough sound check is done for several reasons:

- Testing the system. Because of the number of components in most systems, initial testing must be done slowly and in the right order so no damage is done to components, mainly speakers. Before the system is turned on at all, the crossover points (i.e. specific frequencies) must be set for all the speakers so that signal power is not too great for the speakers. After this, the system components are turned on in the general order of: effects, EQ, mixer, and amplifiers. This is done with all volume and gain controls set to zero and most other knobs at a neutral position on the mixer. Following this, the individual speakers (mid/high then low) are tested to ensure that only the correct frequencies are coming through them.

- Setting EQ. The main reasons for using EQ (specific frequency adjustment) in an audio system are to prevent feedback and to help create a desired sound. Of these, feedback is of the most concern and the one annoying problem that can keep cropping out throughout an event if this procedure is not done properly. The procedure is done in exactly the same way for main speakers and for monitors. The preferred method is to use an analyzer system that compares the output of the console with what is heard coming out the main speakers via calibrated microphones in the audience. After going to all this trouble, there may still be a problem with feedback due to the different acoustics in the venue once all the event attendees are present, so EQ usually needs to be monitored continuously during the event.

- Adjusting individual channel signals. From this point on during the sound check, the band or performers should be present so they can provide information to the audio engineer as to the acceptability of their sound. For this exercise, individual channel signal inputs are tested separately. For example, the lead vocalist's microphone is tested by first turning the gain control on that channel up until *clipping* or signal cutoff is shown by a light on the mixer channel. The gain is then turned down just below this level and remains there with no further adjustment during the event. From then on, the only adjustment is to the individual channel faders. The purpose of doing this is to get the maximum possible clear signal from each input source. Once this is accomplished for all channels, then the main mixer faders can be turned up and the individual channel faders adjusted to obtain a suitable overall mix coming out of the main speakers. Most audio engineers will assign a name to each channel at this time on a piece of tape and sometimes will set a preliminary level indication as well for each channel. On a digital mixer, the crude tape is often replaced by color-coded buttons. This entire process can take quite a long time with a large band, so that time must be built into the event schedule.

As a quick review, here is the relationship amongst the different volume controls on the mixer:

- The gain control adjusts the signal as it comes into the mixer.
- The channel fader adjusts the signal level as it leaves the individual channel on its way to the main fader.
- The main fader adjusts the entire level of all signals as they leave the mixer on their way to the amps and main speakers.

- Setting monitor mixes. This is a procedure that in theory is very simple. The musicians onstage decide who wants to hear which of the other performers (either instruments or vocals or both) and then those specific channels are combined in the monitor mixer to create a specific mix that is sent to that person's individual monitor. If there are only one or two mixes required, as with a small band, then this mix procedure can be handled by the main mixer using the auxiliary send channels. If there are too many mixes for the main mixer, then, as described earlier, a separate monitor mixer must be set up beside the stage and an audio technician assigned to mix the monitors full-time during the event. Of course, every musical group has different requirements so there is no set mix that can be described. What should be remembered, however, is that although the procedure is simple in theory, in practice it can be the most time-consuming part of the sound check. Event producers should keep this in mind.

In the case of musical groups, Tim Lewis of Proshow Audiovisual Broadcast in Vancouver, Canada, states how important it is to have a band that is organized for the sound check and especially for setting mixes. He cites one group that uses a method of going through the monitor mix procedure one musician at a time by having that musician play while all others raise their hands until their individual mix is perfect. This saves considerable time overall and is one of the best ways to accomplish the procedure if in-ear monitors are used (T. Lewis, personal communication, August 12, 2014).

Of course, as mentioned in Section 3.3.3.6, if a personal monitor system is used, especially in combination with digital mixing, much of this time-consuming procedure can be eliminated.

- Setting up effects. This is usually the last part of the sound check and is done to enhance or improve overall sound quality rather than to cover up mistakes or poor musicianship. If you recall those effects racks—or equivalent digital mixer software—and all the possible effects such as reverb, chorus, flanging, and such, this is the time that they are brought into play. The procedure is really just a balancing act in obtaining a nice sound using a combination of the individual channel effects send knob and the master effects send knob (both on the main mixer), plus the effects mixture controls and the effects level knob (both on the individual effect units—or digital mixer).

Now that the sound check is complete, it's time to open the doors and start the event—after crew dinner break, of course!

### 3.5.2 System operation during the event

If the sound check has been done properly, there is not too much to worry about for the audio engineer in terms of maintaining levels. However, if the event is complicated and will involve speeches, followed by entertainment, followed by a band, and most of the channels of a large mixer are being used, then he/she must be constantly vigilant. He/she will need to do some or all of the following during the event:

- Adjust individual channel faders on the mixer to minimize feedback and to isolate speeches (i.e. turn off all channels except the speech microphone).
- Adjust individual channel faders for instrumental solos, backup vocalists, or other inputs such as computer backing tracks, voiceover microphones, video, or PowerPoint feeds.
- Prevent feedback by adjusting house EQ and main mixer and individual channel faders.
- Adjust effects as needed for best sound quality.
- Maintain house volume to an acceptable level for the audience and client.
- Adjust monitor levels and fine-tune monitor mixes as requested by the performers (this task may be assigned totally to a separate monitor engineer).

This, then, is the essence of special event audio systems. Although technology changes constantly, the basics remain the same. Understand them and the new technology will become much easier to follow.

---

### VOICE OF THE INDUSTRY

**Interviews with Mr. Tim Lang**

Vice President, Operations and Finance, Proshow Audiovisual Broadcast
Vancouver and Calgary, Canada
www.proshow.com

### and Mr. Bruce Johnston

Director, JPJ Audio Pty Ltd
Sydney and Melbourne, Australia
www.jpjaudio.com.au

For over 20 years, Proshow Audiovisual Broadcast has served the corporate, political, and media special events market in Canada and the United States. They have made a highly respectable name for themselves working with such luminaries as the Dalai Lama, Queen Elizabeth II, George W. Bush, Bill Clinton, Pope John Paul II, Bill Gates, Elton John, Diana Krall, Paul Simon, Paul Anka, and a host of others. Their VP of Operations, Tim Lang, has been with the company since its inception.

Bruce Johnston is widely recognized as one of the foremost audio engineers in the world. His company, JPJ Audio, covers the concert, theater, festival, TV, and corporate markets, with particularly extensive experience in concert touring in Australia. Since 1970 they have worked with a literal "who's who" of pop and rock, a very small sample of which includes Rihanna, Katy Perry, Fleetwood Mac, Santana, Pearl Jam, Cher, Dave Matthews, Green Day, Jack Johnson, Pink, John Mayer, and Alicia Keys.

Figure 3.27  Corporate event audio control

Courtesy of Proshow Audiovisual Broadcast, www.proshow.com

**DM**: What are some of the major changes you have seen in the use of audio in special events in the last five to ten years?

**TL**: First, of course, is the introduction and widespread use of digital mixing boards. Their quality and ease of use has increased so that most events are now using digital mixers. This has allowed for shorter setup times, smaller space requirements for audio gear, smaller trucks, fewer crew, and ultimately better audio quality at a lower cost.

A second major change is in the continuing advancement of line array speaker technology, leading to ever smaller sizes while increasing quality and power. This has led to better sound quality and coverage, and better audience sight lines and reduced visual obstructions.

Lastly, a negative one. There has been a proliferation of low-quality, cheap equipment flooding the industry. I refer to it as the commoditization of audio-visual. It simply does not have the robustness or good engineering that the top-level gear does. Clients who are not knowledgeable may opt for paying less and are often disappointed with the results. Also, increasing competition means that many A-V companies do not have good maintenance policies and engineering support for their equipment, again leading to disappointed clients.

**BJ**: I guess the biggest change is the usage of the digital console. It's everywhere now, from the small in-house club to major events and touring . . . Another big change is the way systems are networked and you can see what is going on from end to end. On top of that, most of the system control is digital which allows a lot of last-minute changes if a client wants to send sound to some particular area . . . I'm also seeing that audio is taking a back seat to the lighting and video budgets on these shows.

**DM**: What changes do you see coming in event audio over the next five to ten years?

**TL**: Line arrays will continue to improve, becoming smaller, cheaper, and of better quality. Wireless technology will also continue to improve. Digital mixers will continue to get cheaper while adding more and more features and capabilities.

**BJ**: I feel that the digital age is really upon us now and we will see everything being digital across the board. At the high end most systems are now networked and there's a load of pressure on audio technicians to have a good understanding of networking, etc. . . . There seems to be a lot of pressure on audio companies and the fees they are getting, so I see a lot of re-systemizing to help make systems less labor intensive and in the end cheaper to put out to a show. Fiber [optic] distribution systems are starting to take off and as they become less costly I would say most systems in the future would all be on fiber. I'd say soon the smaller digital boards would have all the plug-ins that the large expensive boards have. Hopefully we see a drop in the costs of digital consoles . . . Also we are going to start to see a lot more use of WiFi products.

**DM**: From your experience working with both event planners and event producers (producers generally being more technical than planners), what would you say is the minimum knowledge base for both in terms of event audio systems?

**TL**: They need to understand the different approaches to sound reinforcement. They need to understand venue infrastructure requirements for their desired level of production: the number, location, and rating of rigging points; power availability; what setup times are required and what it means if venues squeeze clients for time. They need to understand the effects of audience size on sound reinforcement, for example what is the best speaker arrangement for a certain size of audience and type of event.

**BJ**: I guess it would be good if they had a basic understanding of how we go about things. I don't think it's a must, but it certainly helps when you start discussing schedules and timings, etc. Otherwise they start thinking we can get this all up and running in an hour or so. Also it does help when they do in fact understand what they want sound wise. From my experience, most have a general understanding I guess through working their way up the ladder themselves. It certainly helps when they do.

## 3.6  Risk and safety

As with most of the technical subjects covered in this book, producers must be concerned with risks involved in the operation of audio equipment and with the safety of their own or contracted personnel and event attendees. We begin by providing current known North American and other audio equipment operation and safety standards, as follows:

- *IEC 62368-1* (in the United States, and Europe with *EN* prefix) and *CAN/CSA-C22.2 No. 60065A-03 (R2012)* (in Canada): *Audio/Video, Information Technology and Communications Technology Equipment, Part 1 – Safety Requirements.*

- *ANSI (American National Standards Institute) E1.8 – 2012: Entertainment Technology – Loudspeaker Enclosures Intended for Overhead Suspension – Classification, Manufacture and Structural Testing.*

- Cooper, D.C. (Ed.) (2014). *The Event Safety Guide: A Guide to Health, Safety and Welfare at Live Entertainment Events in the United States.* New York: Event Safety Alliance of USA, Inc./Skyhorse Publishing. Of particular note are Chapters 9 through 15 regarding worker and work site safety. Note also that this publication is an intentional and cooperative upgrade of *The Purple Guide to Health, Safety and Welfare at Music and Other Events* from the United Kingdom.

- Other ANSI standards with respect to rigging for audio systems that must be flown are available from www.plasa.org.

These standards apply specifically to the general design and use of this equipment in an entertainment context, although the Event Safety Guide applies also to worker safety. Not listed here is the myriad of design standards that apply to individual pieces of equipment. However, most of these are covered within UL 60065. It should be noted that for Canada and the United States, this equipment is certified by Standards Development Organizations (SDOs) in each country (see Chapter 8 of *Special Event Production: The Process* for an explanation of these organizations). In the United States, the main SDO for audio equipment is the Underwriters Laboratories Inc. (UL) and in Canada, the Canadian Standards Association (CSA). Producers should be extremely cautious of allowing suppliers to use any equipment that does not bear a certification sticker with either of these marks on it. There is every chance that it may be of substandard quality or built by an individual with little knowledge of the standards required. In other words, it could be hazardous not only to health but also to the proper functioning of all other equipment to which it is connected. Indeed, as with other standards, it is advisable to mandate the use of only UL or CSA certified equipment within production supplier contracts.

In terms of personnel safety when using audio and A-V equipment, the OSHA (Occupational Safety and Health Administration) and WCB guidelines in the United States and in Canadian provinces, respectively, must strictly apply. Associated with them must be strict adherence to the *National Electrical Code* in the United States and the *Canadian Electrical Code* when working with any electrical equipment in either country, which is essentially all audio and A-V equipment. Again, it is recommended that adherence to these standards be mandated in all supplier contracts.

For other countries (limited list), here are the general starting points for worker health and safety standards:

- United Kingdom. Health and Safety Executive (HSE), www.hse.gov.uk.

- European Union. European Agency for Safety and Health at Work (EU-OSHA), https://osha.europa.eu/en.

- Australia. Safe Work Australia, www.safeworkaustralia.gov.au/sites/swa/pages/default.

- India. National Policy on Safety, Health and Environment at Workplace, Ministry of Labour and Employment, Government of India, www.ilo.org/wcmsp5/groups/public/---asia/---ro-bangkok/---sro-bangkok/documents/policy/wcms_182422.pdf.

- South Africa. *Act No. 85 of 1993: Occupational Health and Safety Act* as amended by *Occupational Health and Safety Amendment Act, No. 181 of 1993*, www.labour.gov.za/DOL/downloads/legislation/acts/occupational-health-and-safety/amendments/Amended%20Act%20-%20Occupational%20Health%20and%20Safety.pdf.

As well, certain risk mitigation techniques that ensure flawless event execution are employed regularly by audio specialists based on their experience. Tim Lewis, the owner of Proshow Audio Visual Broadcast in Vancouver, Canada, and Bruce Johnston with JPJ Audio in Australia offer recommendations from their experience (T. Lewis, personal communication, August 12, 2014; B. Johnston, personal communication, September 4, 2014):

- Redundancy. For every event on which he works, Lewis has what he calls a Catastrophic Backup Plan. He analyzes the audio requirements for the event and looks at what might cause a worst-case scenario or "catastrophe." By his definition, a catastrophe is having the audience leave because the event cannot continue. He then plans the amount of additional equipment required to prevent that from happening. For example, if a VIP or keynote speech is lost, the event is over. If a band cannot be heard, the show or dance is over. Depending on what that catastrophe is, the extra equipment might be a small powered house mixer, twin lectern microphones (or running an extra microphone cord to the lectern), additional lavalier microphones, obviously many extra batteries for wireless equipment, additional handheld wireless microphones, extra CD/DVD players and computers, extra cables and power supply, and so on. The decision centers around what the event can do without and still survive. Lewis further stresses that the decision should be based on maintaining the highest level of professionalism and never on the cost.

  Johnston echoes Lewis's concern with respect to redundancy in equipment: "What we try and do at JPJ Audio is have enough spares to get us out of any issues that might arise. We always carry extra microphones, leads, and power. With our rigging we always supply an extra chain motor. I guess that's the same with the monitors as we always send extra wedges out. We do send out spare diaphragms and the odd speaker for 'just-in-case' issues . . . We also tend to supply a similar opening act console to the main act even if it's on the same digital console [note that Johnston specializes in touring concert acts]. If we are at a regional/out in the country show we will send a spare console as it would be just too hard to sort it out if we did have an issue."

- Ambient effects. Producers need to be cognizant of what is happening in the event space and with other equipment. Lewis points out that ambient noise from other equipment can be problematic for audio quality. For example, fan noise from projectors, moving lights, and air conditioning can be quite high and can interfere with audio quality, thus squeezing the available *headroom* or amount of gain available before feedback. It is far better when it comes to ambient noise to turn the noise off rather than turn the audio system volume up, according to Lewis, even if it is only for a very short period during a key moment in a speech or the event program.

- Technical capabilities of personnel. In audio, there can be specialists in mixing audio for widely different types of events. For example, some audio engineers are trained and experienced in mixing rock and roll at concerts, some have only experience with corporate speeches, some have experience with theatrical presentations, and many more. According to Lewis, it is essential for producers to ensure from dialogue with audio subcontractors that the experience of the engineers provided matches the audio needs of the event.

A combination of these tips, compliance with safety and design standards, and a well-thought-out list of risks and their solutions for the particular event should alleviate most potential problems for producers in the audio area.

## PRODUCTION CHALLENGES

1. You are managing an event in a large indoor venue with all glass walls and a very high ceiling, in addition to quite a number of large structural columns. Explain generally why the acoustics are bad in this venue.

2. A keynote speaker has been hired for a conference opening general session. Besides speaking for 30 min, this person also plans to sing several songs to backing music tracks on his iPhone as part of his presentation. Suggest three options for microphones for this person and why they may or may not work for him.

3. Your client is dumbfounded by the apparent complexity of the digital mixer that your audio engineer has just unloaded and set up on the venue wall opposite the main stage. She expresses concern that such equipment is needed for the 12-piece band and three vocalists backing your headline celebrity act, and the simple series of PowerPoint and video presentations that precede the show. Not wishing to appear ignorant, you try to explain its function. What will you say about the various capabilities of the mixer and why a lot of channels are needed?

4. Research and explain the benefits of completely converting an audio system to digital technology.

5. An important corporate event has speeches followed by a short 20 min entertainment show to end the evening. There are 400 guests at the black tie dinner in a 150 ft long x 90 ft wide x 20 ft high (45 m x 27 m x 6 m) room. What are two types of, and possible locations for, a speaker system for this event?

6. Your client is concerned about the length of time required for a show's sound check. Explain what takes place during the sound check and why it is required for a good show.

## REFERENCES

Davis, G. and Jones, R. (1990). *The Yamaha Sound Reinforcement Handbook, Second Edition.* Milwaukee: Hal Leonard Corporation.

Eargle, J. (1999). *JBL Professional Sound System Design Reference Manual.* JBL Professional.

Gillette, J.M. (2000). *Theatrical Design and Production: An Introduction to Scene Design and Construction, Lighting, Sound, Costume, and Makeup, Fourth Edition.* New York: McGraw-Hill Higher Education.

Line array. (2014, June 2). In *Wikipedia, The Free Encyclopedia.* Retrieved July 10, 2014, from http://en.wikipedia.org/w/index.php?title=Line_array&oldid=611162862.

Lyons, C., Vear, T. and Pettersen, M. (2008). *Audio Systems Guide for Meeting Facilities.* Shure Incorporated.

Microphone. (2014, July 9). In *Wikipedia, The Free Encyclopedia.* Retrieved 15:54, July 14, 2014, from http://en.wikipedia.org/w/index.php?title—icrophone&oldid=616167280.

Patil, A., Rabbitt, J. and Waldrop, D. (2000, August). Act I: Scene II – Lighting & Sound Elements. *Seminar Workbook: Event Solutions Expo 2000*, pp. 59–93.

Sigismondi, G. (2008). *Audio Systems Guide: Music Educators.* Shure Incorporated.

Sigismondi, G. (2009). *Selection and Operation: Personal Monitor Systems, Third Edition.* Shure Incorporated.

Tapia, C. (2008). *Audio Systems Guide: Theater Performances.* Shure Incorporated.

Vear, T. (2011a). *Audio Systems Guide: Houses of Worship.* Shure Incorporated.

Vear, T. (2011b). *Selection and Operation: Wireless Microphone Systems.* Shure Incorporated.

Waller, R., Boudreau, J. and Vear, T. (2012). *Microphone Techniques: Live Sound Reinforcement.* Shure Incorporated.

# Chapter 4

# Visual presentation technology

## LEARNING OUTCOMES

After reading this chapter you will be able to:

1. Understand the purpose of creating a visual presentation.
2. Understand content and why and how a multimedia show is created using visual presentation technology.
3. Describe the different visual sources used in presentations.
4. Describe the signal path and how the visual signal is manipulated as it travels from source to final projection.
5. Describe the different types of display and projection equipment.
6. Understand what happens during the setup and operation of visual display equipment at a special event.

The "tag team" of audio and visual equipment (A-V) can sometimes be confusing because it encompasses so much technology. Because the audio needs of a complex entertainment program are very different from a meeting consisting mainly of speeches, audio has a separate chapter in this book, and only the visual component of A-V will be the subject of this chapter. (We will refer to visual presentation equipment, for purposes of simplicity, as A-V.) In truth, many companies offer both audio and visual equipment because they are both interrelated.

As with all other technologies, visual presentation equipment is advancing rapidly. It is the goal of this chapter to take a point in time and to explain the current theory of operation of this equipment and how the equipment is used in special events. We will therefore concentrate on the following topics:

- purpose of visual presentations;
- content in visual presentations;
- visual sources;
- control and distribution;
- projection equipment;
- display equipment;
- equipment setup and operation;
- risk and safety.

## 4.1 Purpose of visual presentations

"There is nothing worse than a brilliant image of a fuzzy concept." So said famous photographer Ansel Adams. All the most advanced equipment and largest screens in the world will not make an event successful if the purpose of the visual presentation is not fully understood by all concerned before the event is designed (see Chapter 2 of *Special Event Production: The Process* concerning event design). Clients, producers, and equipment suppliers must be in perfect synchronization. The choice of projection and display equipment, the location of equipment, the length of the presentation, and most importantly the content of the presentation are all impacted by the purpose of the presentation.

For example, one of the most common purposes is for educational meetings and conferences in which the presentation is primarily for speaker support. In this case, there are often no more than one or two supporting screens designed either as part of a stage set or off to one or both sides of a stage. Occasionally, smaller monitors may be used throughout the venue depending on the venue design and ease of actually seeing the speaker and stage. Projection equipment may consist of no more than one or two digital projectors for PowerPoint and content may be entirely provided by the presenters.

On the other hand, if the purpose of the presentation is to augment an entertainment program, such as 3D projection mapping, then the possibilities become endless and limited only by budget. Frequently now, with the advent of high-intensity projection systems, A-V is being incorporated into almost every event, even outdoors. Visual elements such as computer animations, slides or still images, and video are projected onto fabric, ceilings, walls, the sides of buildings, and even water as part of event décor, part of the entertainment, or part of strategic messaging. Such imaging may be stored not only on CD/DVD players, but computers, smartphones, tablets, or even the Internet. For complex shows, content is the key and considerable time must be devoted to programming it, either by the producer or by a specialist in the medium.

## 4.2 Content in visual presentations

Not all presentations are or will be simple. More frequently with advancing technology, several technical areas are combined in visual presentations in order to convey the message of the event. We have all seen recent Olympics opening and closing ceremonies in which the latest large screen projection technology is combined with entertainment, special effects, and creative staging in order to tell a story. As would be expected, this scenario is spilling over into private and corporate events as well as other public events. This has traditionally been known as a *multimedia presentation*. Before we look at the actual equipment used in visual presentations, let us delve a little deeper into content, because unless content is right, an expensive visual presentation—and indeed the event itself—can fall flat on its face.

What, then, is a multimedia presentation? According to at least one definition, it is "the use of computers to present text, graphics, video, animation, and sound in an integrated way" (Beal, 2014). Herein lies the problem. On one hand, the expectations of those more attuned to working with computers, such as A-V companies and anyone under the age of 50, are for a multimedia show to incorporate mainly computer technology and video. On the other hand, those of a generation able to remember the 1960s associate multimedia with the influential work of Andy Warhol in his groundbreaking 1966 performance "Exploding. Plastic. Inevitable," which was then termed "multimedia" and combined the rock music of the Velvet Underground with cinema and performance art. Arguably, this was the true beginning of not only the visual aspects of the psychedelic phenomenon, but also of adding visual content in the form of lighting effects, video, and IMAG to concert performances.

To be sure, multimedia can encompass all these influences, but to get it right, the producer has to have very clear goals at the outset of the project in order to meet the expectations of the client and audience. To do this, let us consider that there are two types of multimedia presentations: traditional and non-traditional. The traditional, contrary to the influences explained above, includes only the simplest of presentation content and equipment, such as basic video, still images, PowerPoint on a screen, and a live presenter, but with minimal interaction between the audience and speaker or audience and the visuals themselves. Only the speaker interacts with the visuals (e.g. by changing slides). The non-traditional, more contemporary presentation may include not only video and PowerPoint, but also newer technology (e.g. water screens, LED screens, 3D projection mapping, touchscreens, and live streaming content from the Internet) along with special effects, live human performances, and possibly audience interaction using mobile devices. See Figure 4.1 illustrating an event (Russia Day, 2014) in which water effects, lasers, fireworks, video, lighting, and live stage performances were all incorporated into a multimedia show.

Figure 4.1 Example of a multimedia presentation

Courtesy of Petr Ushanov, http://petrushanov.livejournal.com

It is this second form of multimedia presentation, like the one originating with Warhol, that we are concerned with in this section. As Warhol said at the time of his 1966 presentation, "We all knew something revolutionary was happening. We just felt it. Things could not look this strange and new without some barrier being broken" (McNeil and McCain, 2006, p. 16). Of course, what everyone had experienced was the emotional power of combining visuals and performance. That is the secret to getting a message across with multimedia, the power of emotion. Here are some tips on doing it right:

### 4.2.1 Setting goals and content for the show

To start with, multimedia can be expensive. There is always a temptation that "more is going to make it better." That is why it is necessary to understand and discuss with all concerned what the exact goal of the presentation is before the project is launched. There may not be a reason for using three or four live video cameras if two will do. Perhaps the show is not complicated enough to warrant pre-recording and synchronizing everything to disc. As with entertainment and décor, the sensory experience is being heightened through the addition of more exciting visual stimuli and audio effects, so these stimuli had better get the point across in the most efficient manner possible. This means a close examination of the goals. Some of the more common goals of a multimedia presentation include:

- improving the understanding of a particular message, such as corporate goals or strategic marketing;
- motivating sales forces;
- evoking emotions in order to more easily sell a service or product, or motivate the audience to take some action;
- educating in a cultural or spiritual context.

Once the goal has been determined, it then requires creative sessions with the producer and A-V supplier to decide what sort of show content should be developed. The combinations are almost endless, but here is some food for thought based on the above generic types of goals:

- If there is to be a specific message such as a corporate sales goal, will the company president be part of the show and will he or she be able to, or want to, deliver the message without help from additional images or video? Will signage suffice for a message or must extra pizzazz be added? Will he or she need to use PowerPoint with perhaps a laptop computer or tablet near or on the stage?
- If the goal is motivational, how is it best delivered? This is where the list of possibilities is long. Cheerleaders, motivational keynote speakers, upbeat dance routines, bands, celebrity acts, magicians, cirque shows, and many others have been used as live entertainment together with motivating slides, videos, projection mapping, special effects (e.g. fireworks, lasers), and automated lighting. Who will write the script and direct the show?
- Does the show require an emotional appeal or impact and how will that best be achieved? This can sometimes be done by using a pre-recorded video clip with good scripting, videography, editing, and perhaps suitable emotional background music. On the other hand, it might be better achieved more dramatically with a live performance, especially if the performers are good at eliciting emotion from audiences (e.g. the drama of a Shakespearean actor, the flawless performance of a professional ballerina, the power of a 100-voice choir, etc.), which in turn can be augmented with other visuals such as still images, or short video clips.
- If the goal is to tell a story or educate, what length is the show to be (shorter is always better, in the order of five to ten minutes or so)? Is it too cerebral to be effective as a multimedia presentation (most presentations work best if the message is fairly straightforward)? Will it need extensive scripting and rehearsing? All these can take extra time and money. Often, telling a story requires intensive research for, and editing of, still and video images in order to make them suitably relevant to the subject, in order

to achieve the emotional impact sought, and in order to make them clear and of high enough resolution to be effective.

- In any of the scenarios, will there be live video and how many cameras will be needed?

## 4.2.2 Choosing equipment and personnel

Once content has been determined, then equipment and personnel must be planned. The options once again are almost limitless, but usually end up being restricted by budget. Here are some points to consider:

### 4.2.2.1 Screens and projection surfaces

If there is only one stage and all the presentations are intended to be from there, is there any sense to have auxiliary screens or monitors elsewhere in the venue or is the audience small enough that they will be fully engaged with a large screen or projection surfaces at or near the stage? Typical screen setups for large, seated audiences include: a large stage backdrop screen(s) with occasional smaller screens as part of the larger one(s); corner screens set diagonally across the front corners of the venue, usually flanking the stage; and supplementary screens for large audiences sometimes flown on trussing partway down a long venue. Not used too often are side screens. If the screens are close to the stage and there will be performances, their visibility will be influenced by any light spillage from stage lighting, so the entire show will also have to be reviewed with the lighting designer. As well, any stage performances may have to be restricted to only the downstage area if there is front projection, due to the possibility of shadows falling on the screen surface from the performers.

Is the presentation to be outdoors during the daytime? In this case, LED screens might be the best solution because of their brightness and ability to overcome the competition from sunlight (see Section 4.6.4). Also, if there is to be a lot of audience interaction in the form of either touchscreens, mobile devices used as input, or body gestures as input, then extra consideration must be given to the proximity of the screen(s) to the audience.

### 4.2.2.2 Projectors

The main concern for projectors is whether they are used for front or rear projection and what brightness is needed, depending on the ambient light. Also required is the distance to the screens or projection surfaces and the material of the surfaces. The show does not necessarily have to be on only traditional screens. It can be partly on other surfaces like water screens, fabric, tables, walls, ceilings, floors, streets, buildings, and décor components as mentioned earlier. Lens focal length is also critical, and is influenced by the final decision on projector placement. Front projection in a large venue, for example, may very well be from a projector suspended from a lighting truss. The truss location is decided based mainly on lighting concerns and so the projector lens has to be chosen to ensure optimum projection from this location. For massive 3D projections outdoors, projectors may have to be mounted on the roofs of buildings, so not only is projection distance important, but so are obtaining the proper authorization, weather-proofing, scheduling, potential setup problems, and risk management.

### 4.2.2.3 Video cameras

Section 4.3.3 deals at length with IMAG and the use of video cameras. Suffice it to say that prior to embarking on a multimedia show if part of it is to be live, the number of cameras and the exact locations of the cameras must be determined. Usually, for best results and to enable a creative variety of shots, at least two cameras, one stationary, and one roving, are required.

### *4.2.2.4 Personnel*

Personnel are chosen based on the complexity of the show. They may include:

- Technical director to call the camera shots and video switches from a central location, usually FOH.
- Camera operator for each camera plus a *grip* for each roving camera (see Section 4.3.3.4).
- *Shader* or switcher operator to operate the signal processing, switching equipment, and video recorders at the FOH position. This position will also typically have one *preview monitor* per camera, and one preview monitor for the final signal before it goes to projection equipment, so the operator can ensure what will be viewed on the final display has the correct color balance, resolution, and size.
- One or more computer operators depending on the number of computers and the complexity of software and digital images used as part of the show. Each computer will have a monitor for previewing images before sending them to the switching hardware. The location is usually backstage with the rest of the A-V equipment for the show.
- Possibly an extra technician to assist with complex tasks and equipment problems.

### 4.2.3 Putting it together

Putting a multimedia show together means more than just showing up with a collection of discs, USB flash drives, PowerPoint, computer, and video cameras. A good multimedia show is a full-blown work of art, much like a musical composition or a stage play. It requires a story line, a script, performers who are professional, good production support, and extensive rehearsals and technical run-throughs. In many cases, the job of writing and scripting a story line falls to the show producer who must interpret the goals of the show set by the client and deliver a stunning multimedia performance that gets the point across. This may be, in its simplest form, just a series of PowerPoint slides interspersed with video clips or guest speakers, but put together in a logically flowing format. On the other hand, it may be an actual story written from scratch that is used as an analogy to deliver a message. This might involve actual scripting. It might involve researching for, selecting, and editing still and/or video images. It might involve specialized programming for large screens or 3D mapping. It might involve auditioning and contracting appropriate live entertainment to supplement and emphasize the message. It might be very short or it might extend over an entire event.

Whatever the case, it is helpful to treat visual sources such as live or recorded video and still images as another form of performer, albeit with some limitations but many capabilities. In this way, the technology can be fit into the story line whenever it will improve the delivery of the message, particularly the emotional side. This means that the show must be built as any entertainment program, with a logical flow to a climax, using all the disparate elements. Chapter 1 of this book and Chapters 2 and 9 of *Special Event Production: The Process* discuss the creation of such a show in detail.

My company created many multimedia shows, but one sticks in my memory as an example of the intricate mixture of such disparate elements. The concept was to use an original Native American legend as an analogy to the historic rise and success of the client company. My task was to write the story, find the performers, choose the background music and much of the imagery, and rehearse the show with my A-V colleagues who also assisted with video selection, still image and video editing, and putting it all together with the appropriate equipment. We ended up with a complete three-act play that was performed on three different stages throughout dinner, each stage with a separate large screen as a backdrop. The play was narrated by an old chief whom we had to pre-record in a studio and whom we placed behind a *scrim* where he sat by a campfire telling the story. The logistics were complex to say the least, and the timing of the entire visual component with live dancers, rhythmic gymnasts, giant puppets, stilt walkers, and backing imagery was a challenge. It called for an experienced show caller (see Chapter 9 of *Special Event Production:*

*The Process*), a well-written script broken down into logical segments with accompanying cues for music and visuals down to the second, and video clips that were accurately edited.

Once it is determined that an event requires some sort of visual presentation, whether just a basic PowerPoint presentation backing up a keynote speaker, or a full-blown, no-holds-barred multimedia extravaganza, then it's time to delve into the equipment required. While the majority of visual presentations will be coordinated by an A-V company, it is still useful for any producer to have a basic understanding of the equipment and its capabilities. To that end, what we are going to attempt in this chapter is to translate a world of complex jargon and equipment into a logical pattern. Computer, video, projection, and display technologies are undergoing a quantum leap in capabilities. Much of the older analog technology is rapidly becoming obsolete and being replaced by its digital equivalent. For this reason, the chapter will concentrate solely on digital technology.

In order to make this chapter understandable, we will follow a visual presentation from start to finish, from its basic initial visual source to its final destination as an image displayed for an audience. Along the way, we will examine the most common equipment currently in use, paying particular attention to how this equipment transforms our initial source into the projected image. In general, a presentation will follow a path similar to that in Figure 4.2.

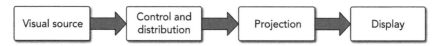

Figure 4.2  Visual presentation flow

Courtesy of Doug Matthews

## 4.3  Visual sources

In the good old days of the 1980s and 1990s—and earlier—most of the projected visuals for special events came from 35 mm slides played back on Kodak carousel projectors. Sometimes, for complex shows, several banks of such projectors could be found mounted on scaffolding behind a screen. Likewise, for many technical or scientific presentations, an overhead projector could be found in front of a screen with a real person assigned to change the acetate transparencies whenever required by the presenter. For the more sophisticated events, analog video might have been used and played back using a VHS or other format tape player, with the actual projector being mounted either in front of or behind the screen. Generally speaking, the overall quality of any of these types of presentations was not what today's event attendees are accustomed to experiencing.

To begin, we will review and explain the main sources of information for visual presentations, starting with the simplest and ending with the most complex.

### 4.3.1  Still image files

Most still images that will be projected will be photographs or graphic illustrations, and the key considerations here are image size, image resolution, and file format.

#### 4.3.1.1  Image size

Most photographic or other still digital images will originate from a digital camera or a scanner, and will in all likelihood be too large or too small in size for a suitable onscreen presentation. How the image will appear onscreen is a factor of both the computer it was processed on and the projector that will display it.

Assuming that the intention is to fill the screen with the image, in a photo-editing program like Adobe Photoshop the original image should be cropped to the size desired to fill the screen. In other words, if it is desired to show the entire width of the photo onscreen, then the entire width of the computer screen should be filled, so for example, assuming the computer screen resolution is 1,024 x 768, then setting the image width at 1,024 pixels (px) will result in the entire width of the photo being projected and fitting perfectly onto the screen. If the image is a vertical one, then the same applies, so the image should be sized to 768 px in the vertical dimension depending on the computer resolution. It is preferable to crop in a photo-editing program rather than in PowerPoint because PowerPoint only resizes without reducing the image file size. Note that for higher resolution images from some of today's digital cameras, computers will automatically downsize the image size to fit on the computer monitor. Unfortunately, keeping that resolution—and corresponding large file size—will not necessarily result in a better image onscreen. That is a function of the projector resolution (see Section 4.5.2.1).

### 4.3.1.2 Image resolution

For onscreen presentations, the best resolution is 72 to 100 PPI and this is what should be set when cropping the photo in the photo-editing program. This allows for optimum clarity and minimum file size.

### 4.3.1.3 File format

The enemy of effective smooth presentations is excessive file size as it slows them down. The preferred file format for projection is JPG (also called JPEG). This is a *compressed* file format, which means that it consumes less memory yet still delivers good quality. When saving re-sized files, the highest quality JPG option should be chosen. Although JPG files are the best for photos, a file format called GIF is best for images that have blocks of solid color like graphs or clip art. Like JPG, it does not take up excessive memory.

### 4.3.1.4 Text and non-photographic material

For non-photographic screen presentations within PowerPoint, there is a fundamental caution that what looks good on a computer screen may not look good on a large screen. Font types and sizes should be basic (e.g. Arial or Times New Roman fonts) with a minimum of bullets on a slide, these being large bullets. Contrast is best achieved with white or yellow text on a dark background. Finally, for logos or other graphics, it is best to avoid web-sourced, low resolution versions and opt for an original version from the artist if possible. See the discussion above for image resolution and sizing.

### 4.3.1.5 Other image improvements

Because projectors tend to darken images, it is better to increase the brightness during the initial editing process. Using the same photo-editing software (e.g. Photoshop), the brightness should be increased to more than would be appropriate for best viewing on the computer monitor but not enough to distort image details. Contrast between darks and lights should also be turned up as well as *saturation*. Finally, the image color profile should be converted to sRGB for best compatibility with the projector.

### 4.3.1.6 Storage of digital still images

Most still image files or slide show files like PowerPoint will be stored on USB flash drives, CDs/DVDs, or laptop computers for delivery to the event and the A-V engineer. Before delivery, the producer should determine that all files can be read by the host computer's software used for the show (i.e. that the host computer has a compatible and current version of PowerPoint or other slide show program) or that all necessary connections are available for such options as running the presentation from an onstage laptop computer. It is wise to store a copy of any presentation and all image files online for easy access and download in case of emergency or loss of data.

## 4.3.2 Pre-recorded digital video

Thanks to smartphones, tablets, and the incorporation of high-quality video technology in every level of consumer camera, video is now an integral—and some might argue necessary—part of almost every special event. Whether the video originates from a mobile device, a video camera, a CD/DVD, or the Internet, producers and A-V engineers must have the necessary equipment available to successfully play back all these forms. Although the technology can be daunting, this section will attempt to simplify it to the point that any producer may be able to effectively communicate a client's needs with the A-V subcontractor. Once again, to take a relevant point in time, we will only be concerned with digital video.

By definition, "video is an electronic medium for the recording, copying and broadcasting of moving visual images" (Video, 2014). When we talk about video at the source, we are talking about two methods of playing it back for an audience. The first is from a stored video file pre-recorded on a DVD, computer, SD card, or other medium, and the second is as a magnified image (*IMAG* or *image magnification*) on a screen taken directly from a camera or multiple cameras recording live action. In this section we deal only with pre-recorded video and will cover IMAG in the next section.

In order to easily follow the path of the video image from the source to the screen as in Figure 4.2, we must first fully understand how video works. The two main areas of concern for video to arrive at the final pre-recorded product (i.e. a visual source) are image acquisition and recording/storage.

### 4.3.2.1 Image acquisition

Since the optical front end of a digital video camera is almost identical to that of a digital still camera, we will not be concerned about the optics in this section but will concentrate on the electronic nature of the video signal.

Video cameras incorporate sensors that convert incoming light to an electronic charge then convert the charge into a voltage. The voltage is digitized, stored in memory as an image, and then displayed on the camera's *liquid crystal display* (LCD). Until recently, all video cameras used *charge-coupled device* (CCD) sensors. The advent of *complementary metal oxide semiconductor* (CMOS) technology changed this, however, and now the overwhelming majority of cameras have CMOS sensors, for the simple reason that they are easier to produce and hence cheaper to manufacture. They are also capable of higher shutter speeds than CCD cameras. It should be noted that the amount of detail recorded by a sensor is determined by the number of pixel sensors on its surface.

Unlike digital still images in which the structure of the image is the same anywhere in the world, digital video has been influenced by television with the result that various groups of countries have dictated that digital video signals created within a camera—and played back by projectors and display equipment—must conform to certain structural standards. There are currently four standards in use: Advanced Television Systems Committee (ATSC), mainly in North America, Mexico, and South Korea; Digital Video Broadcasting

(DVB), mainly in Europe, Africa, Asia, and Australia; Integrated Services Digital Broadcasting (ISDB), mainly in Central and South America, Japan, and some of Southeast Asia; and Digital Terrestrial Multimedia Broadcast (DTMB), mainly in the People's Republic of China, Hong Kong, and Macau. Fortunately, there is considerable compatibility among the standards, although still enough differences to cause concern if a video created on one system (i.e. in a camera using those standards) must be played back on another. The standards cover the following key aspects related to the acquisition of the video signal by a camera:

- Frame rate. Like a movie camera, a video camera takes a specific number of still pictures or *frames*, every second (i.e. *fps*, the *frame rate*). This, of course, is how the illusion of motion is created. For most video, this frame rate is either 25 or 30 fps. Which rate is used is dependent on the display standard—and the relevant equipment—in use in the particular country in which the video is recorded and played back. For example, one of the main remaining differences between ATSC and DVB standards is frame rate, with 25 in the case of DVB and 30 in the case of ATSC. Most professional video cameras, however, are capable of shooting at both frame rates.

- Scanning and interlacing. For a video to be displayed on a screen, each frame must be "painted" on the screen or display surface. The method of doing this is called *scanning*. It started with the original video formats that were designed for use with *cathode ray tube* (CRT) televisions (analog type) on which the picture was displayed by an electron beam that projected one horizontal line of information at a time as it literally swept across the screen from left to right and top to bottom. The method is still in use today with digital video although the technology to actually imprint the image on the screen surface is complex and not related to this topic. We will delve into it a little in Section 4.6 on display equipment.

  Today there are two methods of video scanning, *interlaced* and *progressive*. An interlaced display is one in which the horizontal scans skip every second line and return to the top to fill in the missing lines. This helps to smooth out motion and flicker. A progressive display is one in which each frame includes all the scan lines rather than every second one. The result is a much higher perceived resolution. To summarize what this means, to be effective as a device to accurately portray the motion recorded by the video, a television display or a monitor, for example, therefore has to produce at least 25 (or 30 depending on the standard) full-screen pictures per second (i.e. 25 or 30 full scans) to match the 25 frames taken by the video camera. Video sources that are listed with the letter "p" are called progressive scan signals, while sources that are listed with the letter "i" are called interlaced. Examples of these would be 480p, 720p, 1080p, 480i, or 1080i. The numbers listed before the "p" or the "i" represent the number of scan lines the video source uses to reproduce the video, in other words, the resolution. This is one standard which is supported by both ATSC and DVB.

- Resolution. For digital video, resolution is the number of horizontal pixels per scan line combined with the number of scan lines (i.e. vertical pixels), and the frame rate. These are expressed as combinations of three numbers and a letter indicating whether the scan is interlaced or progressive, as described above. For example, all standards support *high-definition television* (HDTV) resolutions up to 1,920 x 1,080p60 (i.e. 1,920 px per scan line, with 1,080 scan lines in a progressive scan at 60 frames per second, where the resolution of the display screen or television is 1,920 px wide by 1,080 px high). They also support the older, lower quality resolution of *standard definition television* (SD). See Figure 4.3.

- Aspect ratio. Aspect ratio is the ratio of the width of a video or TV picture to the height, in other words the actual shape. Although there is no universal standard for aspect ratio, the most common ratios are 4:3 and 16:9. Traditional analog televisions and computer screens were all 4:3, but the newer HDTV models and almost all new computer screens are 16:9. These can easily be seen by the screen resolution set up on a computer in terms of horizontal and vertical pixel counts. For example, a common resolution for analog video is 1,024 x 768 or 4:3, but for digital such as the HDTV mentioned above, it is 1,920 x

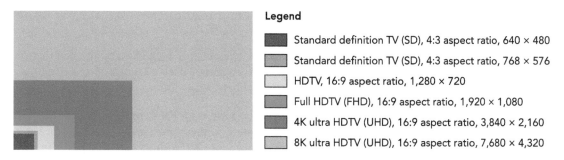

**Legend**

Standard definition TV (SD), 4:3 aspect ratio, 640 × 480

Standard definition TV (SD), 4:3 aspect ratio, 768 × 576

HDTV, 16:9 aspect ratio, 1,280 × 720

Full HDTV (FHD), 16:9 aspect ratio, 1,920 × 1,080

4K ultra HDTV (UHD), 16:9 aspect ratio, 3,840 × 2,160

8K ultra HDTV (UHD), 16:9 aspect ratio, 7,680 × 4,320

**Figure 4.3** Comparison of video resolutions/aspect ratios

Courtesy of Doug Matthews

1,080 or 16:9. Unfortunately, when a video made on one system must be transferred to another system, there will necessarily be a loss of some of the actual picture if moving to a smaller size (e.g. HDTV to NTSC, an older analog standard), like trying to watch a full-screen version of a wide-screen movie specially formatted for an old 4:3 analog TV set, or requiring a smaller picture if moving to a larger size. This effect is also illustrated in Figure 4.9 later on in the chapter. Once again, most video cameras have the option of shooting in either 4:3 or 16:9.

The actual size of a video image displayed, however, is not necessarily restricted to these dimensions. In special events, with current panoramic projection technology, images covering entire walls may be projected and appear seamless, even though they are composed of multiple projected video images. See Section 4.5.3.

Figure 4.3 compares different TV/video resolutions for different display standards and illustrates the aspect ratios of these common standards. We will be discussing the ultra HDTV in a later section.

- Color encoding. Besides information about the size and resolution of the video picture, the video signal must also contain information about the color (known as *chrominance* in video parlance) and brightness (known as *luminance*). This is done by adding a small "packet" of information about the color and brightness to each line scanned. The way in which the color information is stored and carried with the other information is extremely complex and differs with each of the standards. The color and brightness information are then decoded at the receiving end (e.g. television set) by built-in electronics. The differing color encoding methods are one reason why video connectors are different for different types of video.

It should be mentioned that the standards also cover the recording of audio tracks and the transmission of video signals (including audio) via mobile devices, satellite, and cable.

### 4.3.2.2 Recording and storage

Digital video requires a tremendous amount of storage capacity for the signal to be recorded and stored in its entirety on a *medium* (e.g. card, disk, tape—more about this later). For example, uncompressed 1,080i HD video recorded at 60 fps eats up 410 GB per hour of video. Likewise, the audio tracks recorded with the video take up a lot of storage space, although nowhere near as much as the video signal. For this reason, the video and audio information must be reduced in size to allow for more efficient storage. This process is called *compression* and the software that does it is referred to as a *codec* (coder-decoder or compressor-decompressor). This software is found within the video camera itself and it "compresses" the information;

it is also found within any playback unit (e.g. computer) and there it "decompresses" the information, basically turning it back into the full video signal.

Once the information has been compressed, it is placed in a "container," much like a zip file, and then all of this is stored on a medium (all accomplished within the video camera itself). Let us look at each of these in turn:

- Codec. The most common compression method used currently is MPEG-4, sometimes referred to as H.264 or MPEG-4 AVC (*Advanced Video Coding*). It is found in most professional cameras. H.264 is perhaps best known as being one of the video encoding standards for Blu-ray Discs; all Blu-ray Disc players must be able to decode H.264. It is also widely used by streaming Internet sources, such as videos from Vimeo, YouTube, and the iTunes Store; web software such as the Adobe Flash Player and Microsoft Silverlight; and also various HDTV broadcasts over terrestrial (ATSC, ISDB-T, DVB-T, or DVB-T2), cable (DVB-C), and satellite (DVB-S and DVB-S2). It is thus truly compatible with all the main digital video standards (H.264/MPEG-4 AVC, 2014). While there are other codecs (e.g. Theora, VP8, DV, etc.) for consumer and proprietary professional cameras, this is the one most commonly used.

  A codec is also applicable to the audio signal recorded with the video. Common audio codecs include MP3, AAC, and Vorbis.

- Container. Basically, a container is what we associate with the file format. Containers "contain" the various components of a video: the stream of images, the audio, and anything else. For example, you could have multiple soundtracks and subtitles included in a video file, if the container format allows it. Examples of popular containers are OGG, Matroska, AVI, and MPEG.

  One of the benefits to the MPEG-4 AVC codec is that it acts as video codec, audio codec, and container all in one. The file name for the MPEG-4 container is often called MP4 or .m4v.

- Medium. This refers to the actual recording medium on which the container and its contents (compressed video and compressed audio) are stored. As with a still image digital camera, digital video cameras typically have similar cards. Examples include SD card, P2 card, Memory Stick, and others. This card can then be removed from the camera and the contents loaded into a computer (i.e. video and audio decoded) for further editing and processing.

### 4.3.2.3 Video editing

What we have described above really only gets to first base as far as creating a final video for an event. All the action takes place within the video camera but most people wishing to use a video in an event, such as a keynote speaker, will need to edit the raw footage down to something manageable and make it more attractive, perhaps adding fancy transitions between scenes, music, a voiceover, still images, and titles. Unlike the early days of video when a full studio was required to do this, almost anyone with a computer can now accomplish it with video-editing software.

From lower end programs such as iMovie to heavy duty professional programs like Adobe Premiere Pro or Final Cut Pro X, high-quality final edited videos can be produced at home. The programs read the input video using a card reader (e.g. SD card reader built into the computer). They accept a wide variety of video file formats (i.e. the "container" that holds the compressed video and audio information) and with their own built-in codecs, decode the compressed information for editing. Such formats might include MPEG-4 (.m4v), DV stream (.dv), Flash Video (.flv), Microsoft AVI (.avi), Windows Media (.wmv), QuickTime Movie (.mov), and many others.

Once editing is complete, the video is compressed again into any one of a number of similar file formats using the software's codecs. It can then be stored on different media such as USB flash drive, CD/DVD, or Blu-ray disc, using hardware built into the computer, or alternatively exported using WiFi or cable to the Internet (e.g. YouTube, Vimeo, etc.) or a mobile device (e.g. smartphone or tablet). The finished video is most likely to be given to the A-V engineer at an event as either an edited file on a USB, DVD, Blu-ray disc, or on a personal device (e.g. laptop, smartphone, tablet). From this the engineer must ensure that the video is playable and that the necessary playback equipment is available (i.e. clean computer with software installed that can read and play the video for projection).

### 4.3.3 Live video and image magnification (IMAG)

Nothing makes an audience feel closer to the action than live video. Rock concerts, award shows, meetings, and conferences use this technology extensively. Image magnification is simply the projection on a large display, usually a screen, of whatever action is taking place onstage or elsewhere, and being filmed or videotaped by one or more live cameras. It applies well to events that have an audience of more than 400 or 500 persons, and in venues that are very long and narrow, placing much of the audience at a distance from the stage. A live video presentation requires the consideration of four key aspects: equipment choice, camera location(s), lighting, and personnel.

#### 4.3.3.1 Equipment

The video camera is the first consideration. For purposes of this discussion, we will concentrate on only professional digital video cameras, sometimes called camcorders. In Section 4.3.2.1 we discussed how these cameras acquire the video image. Fortunately, today's cameras are extremely versatile. They can record from the older standard definition (SD) of 480i/p or 576i/p right up to full high definition (HD) 1,080i/p and also at either 50 or 60 fps, which makes them compatible with any of the current world standards. Quite simply, they can be used anywhere.

Professional cameras also come equipped with remote control that allows the iris, black balance, white balance, and chroma (color) adjustments to be made remotely by another person. It is thus possible for another person to completely control the quality of an image on a screen without the cameraperson having to worry about it.

Of course, to get the live image to a projector and screen entails the camera being physically connected to a video mixer and *switcher* and then to the projector (more about this in Section 4.4). Pro cameras have one or two outputs or physical connections—remember this is not the storage medium, which is something different, as explained above. The most common is a 75 ohm ($\Omega$) *Bayonet Neill–Concelman* connector (BNC). This type of connector carries both the audio and video signals according to *serial digital interface* (SDI) standards established by the *Society of Motion Picture and Television Engineers* (SMPTE) (i.e. along an SDI cable). Most consumer cameras use the *High-Definition Multimedia Interface* (HDMI) interface and connector.

Also necessary is a good tripod for stability, equipped with a solid *head* that allows for *pan* (movement on the horizontal axis) and *tilt* (movement on the vertical axis) functions, and a *spreader* to keep the tripod legs in position.

#### 4.3.3.2 Locations

Prior to the event, a decision will have to be made on the number of video cameras needed to cover the action. Often, if everything is taking place only in relatively fixed positions on a stage, one camera will suffice mounted on a tripod in a fixed position. The location of this position will be critical, with a position as close to the action as possible generally being the best. However, the decision will be impacted often by audience visibility of the action, as "close" usually means placing the camera and operator on a riser in the middle of the venue mere feet (meters) from the stage, in turn obscuring some of the audience's view and often blocking foot traffic to and from many of the seats. An option to this position is one at the rear of the venue, most likely on or near the technical riser. The disadvantage of this position is that it requires a longer lens which, coupled with the placement on a riser, can lead to shakiness of the final image caused by even the slightest movement of the riser, but the advantage is a shorter cable run. If possible, for optimum viewing, the height of any camera riser should take the camera on its tripod up to the eye level of any person onstage.

If there is action taking place in the audience, if there is action taking place in more than one position onstage (e.g. award winners are coming to the stage while someone is still announcing, or multiple entertainers are working at the same time), if there are multiple focal points (e.g. multiple stages), or if there is a desire to shift the focus between different points of view purely for excitement and a more professional look, then more than one camera will be required. A two-camera shoot with one camera in a fixed position and one roving can often provide an adequate option with switching between the two points of view for excitement. More cameras naturally provide more creative options. One big advantage of live video, and particularly of using more than one camera, is that the event can be recorded for posterity for later TV viewing or even for selling or giving away copies of the event video.

The most interesting shots for live entertainment are usually from the side of the stage or from a hand-held camera onstage. An additional stationary or hand-held camera in front of the stage can take care of lead singers or shots from the audience's perspective.

For speakers or awards presentations, a single camera in front of the stage, either stationary or roving, can usually cover all that is required, although a second camera adds interest and can be used for over-the-shoulder shots as in interview situations.

See Figure 4.4. This image illustrates just such a camera position in front of the stage at an awards show. Also note the camera, a professional video camera (Sony). From this position an SDI cable (BNC connection) runs along the floor to the FOH position where the video signal goes through a switcher and is projected as IMAG.

### 4.3.3.3 Lighting

Correct lighting for live video is a high-priority production consideration. Because video cameras have much lower contrast or dynamic ranges than the human eye (e.g. 100:1 compared to 100,000:1), the lighting needs to be much brighter (i.e. higher color temperature of around 3,600 Kelvin) and the contrast between subjects (e.g. entertainers or speakers) and background (e.g. black stage backdrop) in order for the video images to look realistic and not be too dark. As will be explained in Chapter 5, this is best done with a combination of unfiltered light that provides at minimum a *key light* from one side, a *fill light* from 90 degrees to the key, and a *back light* to help visually separate the background from the subject. The lighting director or supplier will need to know that live video is planned so that the correct color temperature luminaires are provided and placed in the appropriate locations for the shoot.

### 4.3.3.4 Personnel

For a professional live video presentation and IMAG, certain key personnel are required. They include:

- The director. This is the person who calls for camera shots and communicates with the technical director who actually works the controls on the switcher (see Section 4.4). These positions are often combined. The ability to think three to five shots ahead while communicating this information to the rest of the video team is the most important quality of a director, combined with knowledge of transition and shot

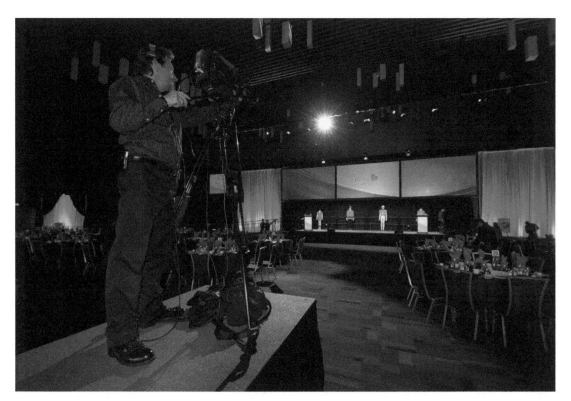

Figure 4.4 Main video camera position for IMAG

Courtesy of Doug Matthews

selection so as to enhance—not distract from—dance, drama, awards presentations, or whatever is happening onstage. Directors need to specify what shot is up, what is next, and what camera those shots are coming from, starting with the camera number and then describing the shot succinctly. A common type of instruction might be, "Standby two." This informs the technical director and camera operators that camera two is about to be selected as the live camera. The technical director would bring this shot up in the preview monitor, and camera two's operator would make sure his shot was stable. "Cut two" would instruct the technical director to perform a cut to that camera. "Dissolve two" would instruct the technical director to perform a dissolve transition to camera two.

- The camera operator(s). The operator (op) is the person through whose eyes the audience sees. Even given the same direction, two camera ops will see and shoot somewhat differently. A good eye and an ability to concentrate and quickly follow directions are necessary for this position.

- The shader. While the video director, technical director, and camera operators are all focusing on the shots and transitions between shots, another person, called a video engineer or shader, watches each shot as it is put on standby, and adjusts its color and brightness to match the previous shot. This is done through a *camera control unit* (CCU) which powers the camera and remotely controls camera settings. The shader may also be given the responsibility of operating DVD players or computers when pre-recorded footage is to be shown.

- A grip. The grip makes sure camera cables don't tangle and follows the camera operators around to do this.

### 4.3.3.5 *Timecode*

"A *timecode* is a series of numbers generated in a controlled sequence by a timing system. In video and other recorded media, timecode can be added to a recording in order to facilitate logging, synchronization, file organizing, and searching" (Wavelength Media, 2014). It can be very useful when editing and combining multiple live videos (i.e. IMAG) from an event for posterity. As a simple example, it is the best way to ensure videos from different cameras are synchronized for speech or music. Professional cameras and video recorders are equipped with timecode generators and readers.

> *Timecode can be overlaid on a video image or it can be hidden as data only. In either case every single frame of the video is marked with a unique timecode number. Video timecode follows the format: HH:MM:SS:FF, which means hours:minutes:seconds:frames. For example:*
>
> *00:00:01:00 = 1 second*
> *00:01:00:00 = 1 minute*
> *01:37:14:07 = 1 hour, 37 minutes, 14 seconds and 7 frames*
>
> *The first three numbers are the same as normal clock time so they have maximum values of 23, 59, and 59 respectively. The last number counts the number of video frames since the previous whole second, so [its] maximum value depends on the frame rate of the video system. In a system that uses 30 frames per second (fps), the maximum range is therefore 00:00:00:00 to 23:59:59:29.*
>
> *(Wavelength Media, 2014)*

### 4.3.4  4K and 8K ultra-high-definition (UHD) video

New industry buzzwords are 4K and 8K ultra-high-definition video and TV. What are they? Quite simply, they represent full HD (FHD) taken to a new level of resolution. 4K provides a resolution of 3,840 x 2,160 pixels, or four times as much detail as 1,080p FHD. In the movie business, the 4K resolution refers to 4,096 x 2,160. Going further, 8K provides a resolution of 7,680 x 4,320 pixels, or 16 times as much detail as FHD. Fortunately for future equipment compatibility, both 4K and 8K remain at the 16:9 aspect ratio. See Figure 4.3 for a comparison of these resolutions.

It should be noted that 4K has been around for a few years; the first commercially available 4K camera for cinematographic purposes was released in 2003, several major motion pictures have been shot in 4K since 2009, YouTube began supporting 4K for video uploads in 2010, 4K home theater projectors have been on offer since 2012, and consumer 4K televisions are already selling for under $1,000.

What does this mean for the future of video in special events? First, if 4K is to act as a visual source for events—and it surely soon will, both as live and edited video—it means new equipment and standards. New equipment includes specialized cameras to shoot at the new resolution. It also includes projectors capable of accepting the new signal, as well as the associated codecs. It means larger screens, because the higher pixel density of a 4K panel also enables one to get much closer without the grid-like structure of the image itself becoming visible. This means one can comfortably watch a much larger screen from the same seating position as for an FHD panel. Currently all available 4K UHD TVs are in excess of 50 in. (Rivington, 2014). Again, Figure 4.3 gives an idea of the increase in screen size possible to clearly see the same image from UHD video compared to FHD video. The potential for stunning graphics and panoramic screen videos at special events, especially in smaller venues, is thus very exciting.

At the time of writing, UHD standards from all the standards groups were still under development, although narrowing in on a new codec called *High Efficiency Video Coding* (HEVC)/H.265. There are also few consumer computers with the graphic card capacity to edit video files of this size, and cable does not yet have the bandwidth to deliver 4K. Obviously, there is still a way to go. Of course, the challenges of dealing with the sheer size of files leave the successful use of 8K in special events still farther in the future.

### 4.3.5 Projection mapping

Projection mapping is another exciting source of visual material for special events. From early experiments in the theater through the *son et lumière* shows originating in the 1960s, projection onto large and unusual surfaces has always fascinated audiences. Today's versions far surpass those early shows. Although it goes by several names (e.g. older terms like video mapping or spatial augmented reality), 3D projection mapping is the art and science behind creating projected visual effects on three-dimensional objects. "Mapping" visuals to fit an object creates the illusion that the light cast by the projector is actually emanating from the object itself. It is best known for outdoor projection mapping on a building, featuring specific content designed to highlight the building's architectural features (e.g. outlining windows, tracing bricks, and effects where content builds and collapses). This type is sometimes called *architectural mapping*. It has been used on surfaces that range from Egyptian temples, historic castles, and mosques to cars and everything in between. 4D mapping extends 3D by utilizing additional sensory effects to heighten and accentuate illusions. This includes temperature, scent, interactive controls, fireworks, and water effects.

Figure 4.5 illustrates a projection mapping installation in which a hotel's wall appears to be crumbling. This was a relatively small project at the Westin Kierland Resort & Spa in Arizona, United States. Created by a project team from PaintScaping, it used only a single Christie Roadster HD 18,000 lumen projector.

Figure 4.5 Example of projection mapping

According to specialist mapping company Christie Digital Systems USA, Inc., "The big driver behind projection mapping projects is using compelling visuals, blended with stories, information and even calls to action, to create profound experiences" (Christie Digital Systems USA, Inc., 2013). However, the finished product is not as simple to create as it looks. There are several important considerations for a successful mapping project, and we will review them so producers at least have a basic knowledge when clients come asking for this amazing technology. The information in Sections 4.3.5.1 through 4.3.5.3 has been provided courtesy of Christie Digital Systems USA, Inc., copyright 2013. All rights are reserved.

### 4.3.5.1 Show content and objectives

Projection mapping involves a considerable amount of time and money to build a show. It is essential to understand both the objectives of the show and the audience if the best technical and creative work is to be done.

- Objectives. The outcome can be generating excitement and viral buzz about the public launch of a new consumer product or brand. But it can as easily be an effort to help make an audience aware of a milestone—like a centennial—and reflect that in visuals that make people both appreciate and understand the significance. It can be a monumental statement or used to help create or complement an environment, such as ambient visuals for a party. In those cases, the visuals are intended as accents that energize the space and set a tone but are not intended as focal points.
- Audience. Many questions need to be asked and explored about the audience for a projection mapping project. These include:
  - How large is the crowd? Are they seated or standing? How far back will they be?
  - How wide is the viewing zone and will those at the sides see the visuals properly?
  - Does the performance include audio and if so, what's the audio delivery technology?
  - Is this a scheduled performance that people come to watch with a hard start and finish or is it intended as continuous ambient material? Or something else?
  - Do the content plans and objectives make sense for the composition of the expected audience and the tone of the event? (e.g. Is what's planned appropriate?)
  - Are there any aspirations to make the event interactive with audience participation through gestures, sound, or other means?

Once these questions are out of the way, then the actual content can be considered. It begins by gaining a complete understanding of the structure that will act as the display surface.

### 4.3.5.2 Structure and location

Before any creative programming can begin, the structure being mapped must be studied thoroughly as well as the surrounding area so that camera positions can be determined. Some of the considerations include:

- Characteristics of the structure. How will its contours, shades, and physical properties affect the ability to deliver a compelling visual spectacle? Traditional projection works with flat, planar surfaces that offer uniformity and a surface optimized for visuals. Projection mapping is almost invariably applied to surfaces that are not flat or uniform, or in some cases, even solid. Projections have been done successfully on vapor screens created by water jets.

  Ancient castles, cathedrals, and massive, complicated, and modern structures present endless variations in surfaces, color, and dimension. A castle will have different types and shades of stone, as well as crenels, merlons, slits, hoardings, rounded towers, and curtain walls that somehow have to be unified for a cohesive visual presentation.

If the surfaces are outside, the color may change when it rains and make a light surface dark and the projection muted.

Ultra-modern structures, like the sails of Sydney's iconic opera house or cylindrical curves of New York's Guggenheim Museum, present a uniform color palette, but are anything but flat, requiring precision scaling, warping, and blending (see Section 4.5.3).

Even the tall, rectangular modern office towers in city centers around the world present challenges. They're usually flat and uniform, but the glass of the office windows—or the full tower façade—can't reflect light. Projections pass through unless the glass gets a layer of reflective film or scrim.

Finally, the sheer scale of the targeted surface will dictate how many projectors, and what kind of lighting power, will be needed.

- Site conditions. Technology and creativity can overcome the characteristics of most structures and objects targeted for projection mapping projects, but a thorough site inspection at the start of any project is essential.

Both the technical and creative leads (part of the projection mapping company team) need to inspect the site and the environmental and physical conditions that can affect the presentation and technical operations.

Those considerations include:

- the amount of ambient, surrounding light;
- obstructions on the projection path, such as trees, streetlights, and power poles;
- for live performances, the movement of people potentially in the projection path;
- the distance, location, and height of projector positions, which informs decisions on the brightness and number of projectors needed, as well as the lenses and media devices;
- power availability;
- weather conditions, not just temperatures and moisture, but wind as well (note that mapping can work in rain but not snow);
- rooftop access or line of sight window access.

- Local approvals. Projects in public spaces will almost invariably be subject to the rules and regulations of local governments, and those can vary considerably even within the same metropolitan area.

Bylaws affecting advertising, lighting, noise, temporary structures, public gatherings, traffic, and parking may all affect not only the scale of a project, but also whether it will even be allowed. It may take multiple approvals, because of jurisdictional rules and coverage, to get approval for one event.

Involving someone on the project team familiar with the local government and its regulations is often critical to executing a project, particularly on the planned timeline.

- Timelines. Every project is unique, but more time for planning, development, and execution tends to have direct ties to excellence.

Projection mapping projects have been pulled off in as short a period as one week, but industry experts prefer to have much more time to fully deliver on objectives, as well as control costs and minimize chaos. The most ambitious projects can take a year or longer from the idea stage to the event launch. Some have taken many years in planning and approvals.

Integrators and staging companies can often respond on relatively short notice, but what truly takes time is the creative. Minutes of motion graphics and video can require weeks or months of work to take through the idea stage, storyboard concepts, drafts, revisions, rendering, and testing.

In rare cases, creative is available that readily translates to the targeted projection surface. But projection mapping done well is much more than finding a massive surface to run broadcast or online creative. The best projects use structures as so much more than screens.

Local approvals can also stretch timelines because of paperwork, process, and even public hearings.

### 4.3.5.3 Budget

Brighter projectors and software are steadily reducing costs on projects by illuminating a broader surface with fewer projectors and either automating or greatly simplifying many of the planning and setup tasks—like alignment—that historically have required many man-hours. But some things such as creative costs can't easily be resolved through technology.

The good news is that the producers of most projects—unless they are designed to be permanent—can limit capital costs by renting the projectors, related technology, structures, and other gear required to execute an event.

Once a site survey is done, an experienced producer will have the knowledge and tools to estimate how many projectors will be needed and what supporting infrastructure is required onsite. The producer, creative director, and client need to then collaborate and reach decisions on the breadth and complexity of the creative, which will help arrive at an estimate on those costs.

Because of the complexity of projection mapping projects, and since no two projects are alike, each installation requires careful budgeting so that costs can be contained while achieving a spectacular show. Depending on the requirements, an installation may also require as much coordination and equipment as a major public concert in an urban area.

However, experience is showing tangible returns in ways such as earned media from both mainstream and social media. The buzz from big events has direct monetary value. The organizer of a massive projection event in Moscow for Russia's Alfa-Bank suggested, for example, the overall costs were in line with a month-long national TV and outdoor ad campaign, but probably much more effective in media terms.

### 4.3.5.4 Software and equipment

Mapping relies on specialized software that can alter and distort projection content in real time, allowing the creation of mapping effects that work over and around architectural idiosyncrasies. Popular mapping software includes D3, Resolume Arena, VDMX, and Madmapper. Often, the programming is done on a stand-alone *media server* designed for highly reliable playback for a show. It includes mapping software for content mapping. Popular brands of media server include Pandora's Box and the Hippotizer. The term "media server" may alternately be used to refer to a conventional computer running mapping software.

Other main equipment consists mainly of projectors. Projection mapping may use as few as one or two projectors to as many as 30 or more for a single project. Most large-venue projectors used in projection mapping are 20,000 *lumens* or brighter. They also accept up to 4K UHD video signals. These projectors are by no means easily portable, topping out at anywhere from about 160 to 300 lb (72.6 to 136.8 kg) in weight and up to almost 5 ft (1.5 m) in depth. Input typically comes via BNC and HDMI connections from cameras, Ethernet for networking with other projectors, and *Video Graphics Array* (VGA) or *Digital Visual Interface* (DVI) for connecting to host computers. See Section 4.5 for more information on projectors.

Quite often, projectors must be stacked on scaffolding and protected from the weather. Power may need to be from portable units brought in for the project (see Chapter 9 for more details on portable power and scaffolding). These setups may have to go in awkward locations like the tops of buildings opposite the surface used for projection, hence the need for extensive pre-planning.

If there is one important recommendation from this section, it is that any mapping project be handled by a company that specializes in it since it is far too complex to be done by most A-V suppliers, although they may be able to supply the projectors and associated connection hardware.

## VOICE OF THE INDUSTRY

### An interview with Mr. Bryan Campbell

Director of Technology, MJx, the Mills James Experience Group
Columbus, Cincinnati, and Cleveland, Ohio, USA
http://millsjames.com

With the Mills James Group for 18 of the company's 30 years, Bryan Campbell has devoted his career to the creative use of technology. Mills James is one of the largest and most comprehensive independent production companies in the United States. Its staff numbers more than 150 professionals in their three facilities, with training and experience that covers the full range of creative, electronic, and theatrical production disciplines.

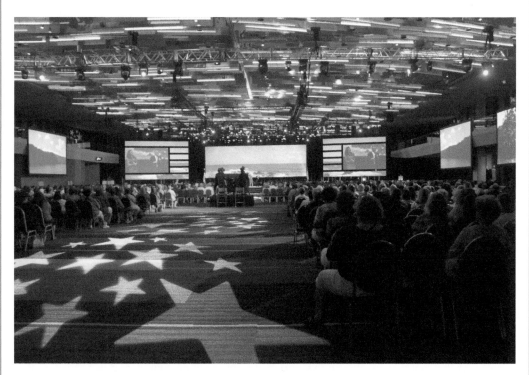

Figure 4.6  Conference session produced by the Mills James Group

Courtesy of Mills James

**DM**: What are some of the major changes you have seen in the use of video in special events in the last five to ten years (e.g. wide screen, edge blending, projection mapping, switching technology, etc.) and how have these affected the industry?

**BC**: Technical innovation has made integrating video into special events much more practical and impactful in the last five to ten years. Costs have fallen dramatically and equipment now is smaller, more flexible, and easier to use. Multiple screen surfaces, wide screens, LED screens, projection mapping, and custom projection surfaces have allowed more creative ways of sharing visual content with the audience. Instead of the presentation being just a much larger version of a computer screen, we turn it into an experience. Display surfaces that wrap around the audience help to involve attendees and make them feel more like a participant than a viewer.

High-definition cameras, graphics, video playback, and projection allow for greater detail, stunning imagery, and a level of control of the video image that was only dreamed of a decade ago. No longer is a video image projected on a screen as part of a set, video **is** the set so the look and feel of the room can change instantly in an infinite variety of ways. In many cases the size of a display can actually be reduced due to greater clarity, and we are using video where it couldn't be a consideration a few years ago. HD has allowed high-quality wide-screen content to be produced at much lower cost. And video post cards are being used as "save-the-date" announcements and invitations.

One of the biggest changes is in mobile engagement. People are always looking at their screens, so instead of telling people to put away their phone we now remind them to turn on their phones as part of the event. Social media, texting, and real-time display of collaboration and participant polls in the venue and on display surfaces involve the audience further in a presentation. Using mobile devices for voting allows for real-time collaboration and feedback in what otherwise might have been a one-way message.

**DM**: What changes do you see coming in event video over the next five to ten years?

**BC**: Advances in LED technology will allow for more compact projection and improved color rendering over non-Xenon lamp sources. Better tools will be available for mapping projection images on dimensional surfaces. But since integrating video throughout an event is no longer technically or cost prohibitive, I think just like mood lighting, "Mood Video" will fast become the dominant special event design tool, with video covering every surface within a guest's view. In events of the future, we will walk on video and we will sit on video. Buffet linen will actually be made of flexible Organic LED (OLED) video screen material that can instantly change color, pattern, or images. Event performers will wrap themselves in video wear and become flexible design elements. Video will drive the event experience and make distance irrelevant allowing global participation.

**DM**: From your experience working with both event planners and event producers (producers generally being more technical than planners), what would you say is the minimum knowledge base for both in terms of event video? In other words, how much should they understand the equipment and what it does?

**BC**: They should both understand the different types of video technology, what differentiates it, and when it's appropriate. An event producer needs to understand more about how it actually works, as they need to be able to talk about content, work on cueing, and will likely "call" the show. They need to be able to intelligently discuss appropriate timeframes for creating content and how much content costs to produce. They need to be able to serve as a liaison between client and artists. So it stands to reason that the more you know and understand video the more effectively you'll create with it.

### 4.3.6 Interactive content

In Chapters 1 and 2, we discussed the increasing use of mobile applications as both entertainment and décor. In many of these cases, this required the projection of crowd-sourced material from smartphones or tablets on a display surface, either a screen or a wall. While very much still in its infancy, this technology is expected to grow quickly. These mobile apps are therefore at the point in their evolution where they now become visual sources themselves.

This section explores how that can be done. For example, with an audience polling application, how do the results get instantly posted onto a screen? Or for a participative audience game, how does it get projected onto a screen in real time? Here are some of the possible sources for display and how that display is accomplished.

#### 4.3.6.1 Audience response systems

Audience response and polling have been around for several years but have only recently been applied using smartphones and tablets rather than proprietary and dedicated voting keypads. The scenarios in which polling is most used are in a classroom teaching situation and in a conference venue as part of a conference speaker's presentation. Most such current systems are software-based and rely on WiFi or *General Packet Radio Service* (GPRS) signals (i.e. cell phone networks). Audience members must download an application for their smartphones or tablets that works with special *audience response software* (ARS) that the presenter loads on his/her computer. The ARS collects participant data, displays graphical polling results, and exports the data to be used in reporting and analysis. Usually the presenter can create and deliver the presentation with the ARS software, either as a stand-alone presentation platform or as a plug-in to PowerPoint or Keynote. A standard projector and connections would suffice to project the presentation.

#### 4.3.6.2 Live audience gaming

Of course mobile gaming has been extremely successful on an individual device basis. But what if a client wants to let the entire audience play the game at once? There are some companies that have developed such capabilities and there is much more to come. Let's take a brief look at how some of these games work:

- Multiple choice and simple questions. The simplest of gaming is just a takeoff from audience polling, for example trivia-type games that require multiple-choice answers. This can be extended to create teams but still uses the same basic software. Many of these still use proprietary keypads emitting RF or *infra-red* (IR) signals, which require base stations to accept the incoming signals. However, mobile device-based games are software-driven, the technical setup is straightforward, and only the host computer needs to be connected to the projector. Again, these use either WiFi or GPRS signals.

  A slight variation on this technology uses separate wands that have different colors painted on each of two sides instead of keypads or smartphones. Video cameras in front of the audience record the colors displayed by the audience and feed the results to a computer program that either chooses an answer or moves something onscreen based on audience response.

- Gesture recognition and motion tracking. Gesture recognition gaming involves the use of hand, arm, leg, and finger movements as well as facial expressions to control software. It is essentially the reverse of showing a video to an audience in that it relies on taking a video of the audience and feeding their movements into a program that interprets them in order to make decisions for the movement of something like racing cars or even "Angry Birds" on a large screen or other display surface. There are limited such games presently in existence but the number is expected to grow as gesture recognition software improves and moves beyond 2D into 3D, which typically would require a camera positioned to record gestures in the third dimension (e.g. mounted on the ceiling above the audience as well as in front of the audience) (Strickland, 2012). Other than the regular connections between cameras and computers, no special hardware is required, only very sophisticated software.

- Connected play. Connected play advances the software to beyond simple questions answered on mobile devices or body gestures and integrates actual games played on multiple audience devices. This software allows those multiple inputs to be displayed onscreen for the entire audience to see. This could include drawing software that displays designs on a wall or full video games. Again, projector connection should be straightforward from one or more computers as this is mainly software-driven. In some cases, proprietary hardware may be required to capture WiFi signals before processing them in the software. This is somewhat similar to the concept of *second screen* in which TV viewers—or event attendees for that matter—can interact with regular TV programs or with event speakers through their mobile devices as they watch (Second screen, 2014).

### 4.3.7 The Internet

One important source of visuals for events is the Internet. Such things as podcasts, Skype, Facetime, YouTube, and others have made the Internet ubiquitous in our daily lives and created additions to presentations for such people as keynote speakers and educators. Most of these types of pre-recorded or live videos will be from a unique computer, either a presenter's or one provided by the A-V company. This has more or less replaced old-style videoconferencing with its multiple video cameras. The only requirement is for the receiving computer to be connected to the projector via a mixer/switcher so that the entire audience can see the conversation or pre-recorded video.

## 4.4 Control and distribution

With the plethora of different visual sources possible at a special event, all with potentially different signal types and standards, there has to be some method of controlling the various inputs and ensuring they get mixed or displayed on the right screens or devices at the right time. Fortunately, what used to be a mass of separate specialized equipment has now been integrated into a single unit known as a *digital video mixer* or switcher. Some models integrate only video signals while others also incorporate a small audio mixer. For purposes of this discussion, we will deal with the switcher portion of the equipment since audio was covered in Chapter 3.

A switcher has several key functions that used to be separate. They include:

- Splitting signals. This function allows any given signal to be fed to two or more displays while maintaining original signal quality. An example might be in a classroom setting with an instructor's computer and multiple monitors for students, or for a special event that has a number of monitors in different rooms. It is accomplished with a *video distribution amplifier* (VDA).
- Scaling. A *video scaler* is a system which converts video signals from one display resolution to another; typically, scalers are used to convert a signal from a lower resolution (e.g. 480p standard definition) to a higher resolution (e.g. 1,080i high definition), a process known as *upconversion* or *upscaling* (by contrast, converting from high to low resolution is known as *downconversion* or *downscaling*) (Video scaler, 2014).
- Scan conversion. This is also built-in hardware that converts a video signal into a format compatible with a specific type of display. For example, it can convert different analog or digital video signals into a signal compatible with a particular projector or large monitor.
- Compositing. This feature is a creative one. It allows such things as the application of layers to the image such as a picture-in-picture, keying a graphic over the top of the image, or putting a logo in a corner of a screen.

- Switching. The actual switching for which the device was named enables multiple video and audio signals to be selected and sent to one or more display devices. These switchers accept audio/video signals from a range of input sources—computers, cameras, DVD players, tablets, etc.—and route the output to different destinations, such as projectors and monitors.

In summary, the latest and greatest of these mixer/switchers are capable of accepting HD and SD video, both interlaced and progressive, video of different standards, computer inputs, live camera inputs, mobile device inputs, and more. Likewise, they can output to projectors, monitors, video walls, mobile devices, the Internet, and recording devices (occasionally built-in). They can also program transitions and effects as well as creative input for split screen displays and edge blending for wide screens. As if that were not enough, they can memorize settings for later recall.

## PRODUCTION WAR STORY

### The deadly screen wipe

It was the middle of a keynote address to a major conference about human interaction and training. Several of the 500 audience members had already begun to doze off as the PowerPoint slides rolled on. The speaker was nearing a critical juncture in his speech. It was deadly serious.

I was at the back of the room sipping coffee and talking to someone. I had ceased paying attention to the presentation, as all I had to do was ensure that the A-V components functioned properly, which included the audio, lighting, and projector systems. Everything appeared to be well under control, that is until a collective guffaw arose from the suddenly wide-awake audience.

The speaker stopped mid-sentence. He looked stunned.

"Was that what I think it was?" he asked the audience as he glanced over his shoulder at the screen behind him.

Amidst the snickers I heard, "Yup." "It was." "Oops." "That was weird."

Feeling a little dumb, I asked, "What happened?" to a woman in the last row of seats.

"You mean you didn't see that?" she answered. "A silhouette of a nude dancer cartwheeled across the screen just as the speaker was going to give us the main message. It was hilarious. A bit of bad timing, though. Someone's going to be in trouble."

I glanced up and realized that someone was me.

Up until that time, I had only known my client as an easygoing, affable woman. Apparently she had another side, and that side was clearly broadcast by the expression of rage on her face. Within seconds she was at the control desk.

"What the hell was that?" she asked. "It was inexcusable." Her face was red and she was shaking. This didn't look good.

My video technician, who controlled the PowerPoint projection, looked sheepish. "Sorry, I pushed the wrong button." At least he was smart enough to own up to it, since he was the only one at the controls. I knew I should have been watching him more closely.

My client's gaze drilled through me. "You make bloody sure that doesn't happen again. I don't want any more glitches."

By now the humor of what had happened struck me and I had trouble stifling a giggle as I responded, "We will. No problem." The irony of the blunder was that it might very well cement the speaker's message in the audience's memory better than anything could, but I didn't offer that viewpoint to my client.

A couple of minutes later, I retreated to a distant corner and laughed out loud. The juxtaposition of the serious presentation with the crazy screen wipe just wouldn't leave my mind. Someone, though—and probably something—had to be sacrificed.

I never hired the video technician again. But, being a businessman and wanting to *stay* in business, I offered my client a substantial discount and an apology. Her response was unusual.

"Tell you what," she said. "Why don't you just bill us for the entire amount and then give your discount to our charity?"

"Great idea." I'd never thought of that as a way out. "I will."

A week later I received an accolade letter and a nice jacket with the charity's logo on it. Apparently, they liked my "proactive mindset."

I learned a lesson about supervision—and how easy it is for technology to turn against you—but I still chuckle about the screen wipe.

(Courtesy of Doug Matthews)

## 4.5 Projection equipment

Following our initial simple signal path illustrated in Figure 4.2, the next step after the visual source has been processed in the mixer/switcher is projection of the visual image. This section deals with the case in which the projection technology is separate from the display technology. In other words, we are concerned with how a video/data projector—or simply "projector"—is able to project an image on a screen, a wall, or other surface that has no inherent display technology itself.

Projector technology, like all others, is advancing rapidly. Projectors may be required to project full HD video, 4K HD video, 3D projection mapping projects, or even simple PowerPoint slide shows. It is helpful if the event producer is able to understand the basics of today's projectors in order to better choose the right one for a client's needs and to better understand the job of the A-V company. To help with this we will look at projector types and capabilities.

### 4.5.1 Types of projectors

There are four main types of video and data projectors currently in use: LCD, DLP, LED, and Laser projectors. Each has advantages and disadvantages, based on the technology. Sections 4.5.1.1 through 4.5.1.3 are provided courtesy of eBay (eBay, 2014).

### 4.5.1.1 *LCD projector*

These projectors utilize *liquid crystal display* (LCD) technology. An LCD is a thin, flat display device made up of any number of color or monochrome pixels arrayed in front of a light source or reflector. The technology is used in watches, smartphones, and other electronic devices.

Most LCD projectors use 3 LCD technology, a patented system that combines three liquid crystal displays. An image is created in a multistep process, which begins with the light source providing a beam of white light. The white light is passed to three mirrors (called *dichroic mirrors*) that are specially shaped to reflect only a certain wavelength of light. In this case, the mirrors reflect red, blue, and green wavelengths. Each beam of colored light is then fed to an LCD panel, which receives an electrical signal that tells it how to arrange the pixels in the display to create the image. All three LCD panels create the same image, but they have different hues because of the colored light passing through the panel. The images then combine in a prism, creating a single image with up to 16.7 million colors that is passed through the lens and projected onto the screen.

LCD projectors have been around since the 1980s, and the technology is more reliable than film projectors. However, they may still require maintenance, as pixels can burn out and dust particles can interfere with image quality. On the other hand, LCD projectors have no moving parts, as DLP projectors do, and they are generally less expensive than their DLP counterparts. They also support setups in larger rooms where a greater projection distance is needed, because they are compatible with zoom lenses and lens shifts.

### 4.5.1.2 DLP projector

*Digital light processing* (DLP), a technology developed by Texas Instruments, forms the core of this type of projector.

In DLP projectors, the image is created by 2 million microscopically small mirrors, no wider than one-fifth the width of a human hair, laid out in a matrix on a semiconductor chip, known as a *Digital Micromirror Device* (DMD). Each mirror in this chip is capable of independent adjustment, moving toward or away from the light source to create a dark or light pixel. At this point, however, the image is in grayscale. Color is fed to the DMD by a beam of light that passes through a spinning color wheel before it reaches the chip. Each segment of the color wheel delivers one color. Basic color wheels support red, blue, and green, whereas more advanced color wheels support cyan, magenta, and yellow. While these chips can create up to 16.7 million colors, a DLP projector with a three-chip architecture can deliver up to 35 trillion colors. A three-chip DLP projector uses a prism to split light from the lamp, and each primary color of light is then routed to its own DLP chip, then recombined and routed out through the lens.

DLP projectors require less maintenance than LCD projectors because they have a filter-free and sealed chip design, which means dust can't settle on the chip and cause an image spot. They are effectively immune to color decay. Furthermore, they are not subject to the misalignments that can occur in LCD projectors with a three-panel design, which require each panel to be in perfect position to combine the image at the proper angle. They are also better for live video and other moving images. However, DLP projectors with slower color wheels may give off a rainbow effect; flashes of color that appear on the screen, like rainbows. There is also some fan noise and lamp replacement can be expensive. However, the introduction of LEDs and lasers as light sources has eliminated all these disadvantages to the point that DLP projectors are now the most prevalent in the higher-end market (see the next two sections).

### 4.5.1.3 LED projector

*Light-emitting diode* (LED) projectors—sometimes known as *lamp-free*—are defined not by the display technology used, but the lighting. In fact, some DLP projectors with *solid-state illumination* technology are actually LED projectors. Another type of projector, the *pico projector*, commonly uses LED technology as well. Pico projectors are essentially handheld devices that use LCoS (*liquid crystal on silicon*, which is similar to an LCD panel but reflective rather than transmissive) or DLP technology. In these cases, the projector replaces the traditional lamp with longer-lasting and more efficient LEDs, colored in red, green, and blue.

In DLP projectors, this also replaces the color wheel technology, instead letting the red, blue, and green LEDs shine directly on the DMD chip.

> The LEDs in an LED projector have a much longer life than traditional projector lamps, rated at 10,000 or even 20,000 h as opposed to 1,000 to 5,000 h. As such, the LED light source is meant to last the entire life of the projector without ever needing to be replaced. This is a big advantage because replacing traditional lamps can be a major expense in projector maintenance. There is no warm-up or cool-down time needed because the LEDs are much more energy efficient than traditional light sources, and they are also much quieter. This reduces maintenance and operating costs.
>
> (eBay, 2014)

See also Section 4.6.4 for more explanation of LEDs.

### 4.5.1.4 Laser projector

In a modern laser projector,

> red, green, and blue laser beams each fall upon a separate spatial light-modulator chip. For each of these colors, the corresponding spatial light modulator determines, for every pixel of every frame, how much light of that color gets reflected through the projector optics to the screen. The path length for each colored beam from the modulator chip to the projection optics must be the same, so that the three images focus on the same plane.
>
> (Beck, 2014)

Due to the special features of laser projectors, such as a high depth of field, it is possible to project images or data onto any kind of projection surface, even non-flat. Typically, the sharpness, color space, brightness, and contrast ratio are higher than those of other projection technologies. Future laser projectors are expected to have brightness well over 50,000 lumens, up to a 12-yr life for the light source, a much higher frame rate, and overall low maintenance (Beck, 2014).

## 4.5.2 Key specifications for projectors

For special events, projectors need to do many things, from projecting PowerPoint text in a small, darkened meeting room for 30 people, to projecting DVD movies or live video in an open-air, day-lit stadium for an audience of 60,000. No single projector will handle all these situations and the choice will depend on the key specifications of the projector, these of course being driven by the design technology discussed above. Listed below are these key specs.

### 4.5.2.1 Resolution and aspect ratio

Projectors use rows of pixels to make the images seen onscreen. The clarity of the image depends on how many pixels are projected and it is measured by projector resolution. The resolution that is built into the projector is dependent on the technology discussed previously and is called the projector's *native resolution*. It is measured as the number of pixels across the screen and then down the screen and the ratio between the two numbers is the aspect ratio. For example, many consumer projectors have native resolutions of 1,024 x 768 or 1,600 x 1,200. What this means is that the projector will itself scale any image it receives from a computer to its native resolution. Thus, if the file it receives is 4,000 px x 3,000 px, it will scale it down to 1,024 x 768. Although projectors will accept resolutions other than their native resolution, for example displaying an HD video at 1,920 x 1,080 resolution on a 1,024 x 768 XGA projector, the best viewing will be at the native resolution because the projector must scale up or down to be able to show

Table 4.1 Summary of common projector resolutions

| Aspect ratio | Native resolution | Projector class | Application |
| --- | --- | --- | --- |
| 4:3 | 1,024 x 768 | XGA | Excel-type spreadsheets and detailed graphics (e.g. architectural drawings). |
| 16:10 | 1,280 x 800 | WXGA | Good for use with wide-screen laptops. Inexpensive alternative to XGA. |
| 4:3 | 1,400 x 1,050 | SXGA | CADD applications or high resolution graphics. |
| 16:9 | 1,920 x 1,080 | Full HD | High resolution, detailed information, especially video-heavy content. Good for live events, concerts, trade shows, large venues. |
| 16:10 | 1,920 x 1,200 | WUXGA | High resolution, detailed information, especially video-heavy content. Good for live events, concerts, trade shows, large venues. |
| 16:9 | 4,096 x 2,160 | 4K HD | Large format still or video projections on walls, giant screens, and innovative architectural spaces outdoors or indoors. Format is for 4K movies as compared to 4K video at 3,840 x 2,160, which will still display. |

other resolutions and this can result in a loss of quality. Scaling down is usually less problematic than scaling up or, simply put, "a larger video signal with more information will look good on larger screens and anything smaller. Conversely, a smaller image will only look good on a smaller screen. It doesn't have enough information to upscale properly" (Shreve, 2013). However, if a mixer/switcher is used, any scaling will probably be done with it, but it is always best to try to match the visual source resolution with the projector resolution.

Table 4.1 summarizes the most common projector aspect ratios, resolutions, projector classes, and applications.

### 4.5.2.2 Brightness

The brightness of a projector is measured in lumens, a term discussed in Chapter 5 that indicates the *intensity* of a light source. In the case of a projector, this is the lamp or other light source. In fact, technically speaking, "brightness" is the measure of light leaving a surface being illuminated and is not measured in lumens but in foot-lamberts, so this can be a source of some confusion.

The venue size (i.e. audience size), screen size, and ambient light are what will determine the brightness required. Most professional projectors for business uses are in the 2,000 to 5,000 lumens range, which is good for large venues and relatively subdued ambient lighting. If the lighting approaches daylight (e.g. in an outdoor stadium or brightly lit room), a higher rating is required. Some high-end professional projectors are available with 35,000 lumens for just these conditions. Table 4.2 provides a helpful summary of recommended projector brightness levels for certain ambient conditions, audience sizes, and screen sizes (4:3 aspect ratio only).

Table 4.2 Recommended projector brightness

| Room size < 100 people | Screen size (diagonal dimension, 4:3 aspect ratio) | | | | | | Room size > 100 people |
|---|---|---|---|---|---|---|---|
| Lumens | 72 in. | 100 in. | 120 in. | 150 in. | 200 in. | 240 in. | Lumens |
| 1,500 | | | | | | | 2,500 |
| 2,000 | | | | | | | 3,000 |
| 2,500 | | | | | | | 3,500 |
| 3,000 | | | | | | | 4,000 |
| 3,500 | | | | | | | 4,500 |
| 4,000 | | | | | | | 5,000 |
| 4,200 | | | | | | | 5,200 |
| 4,500 | | | | | | | 5,800 |
| 5,000 | | | | | | | 6,500 |
| 5,200 | | | | | | | 7,000 |
| 5,800 | | | | | | | 7,700 |
| 6,500 | | | | | | | 10,000 |
| 7,000 | | | | | | | > 10,000 |

| | | | |
|---|---|---|---|
| N/A | Degraded or unacceptable | Average | Lights set for note-taking; windows open to interior |
| Low | Little or no ambient light | Bright | Skylights/windows open to exterior; no shades |
| Some | Dimmed lights or leaking blinds | Ultra | Overabundance of light as in an arena or stadium |

Some useful rules of thumb for estimating brightness requirements are also provided by Lewis Sound and Video Professionals:

- Increase projector brightness if the projector will be more than 25 ft from the screen.
- Decrease brightness if the projector will be less than 12 ft from the screen.
- Increase brightness by 1000–2000 lumens for room capacities of 400 or more.
- Increase brightness by approximately 25% for 16:9 installations.

(Lewis, 2013)

### 4.5.2.3 Contrast ratio

This is the ratio between the brightest white and the darkest black and complements brightness. The higher the contrast ratio, the clearer the image will be. Room light impacts contrast so a higher ratio is better if the room will be well lit during projection. A contrast ratio of 1,500:1 is good, but 2,000:1 is considered excellent. Most projectors used in special events are well above even this level. However, because of the lack of any standardized method for measuring contrast ratio, it is considered to be of minimal use when comparing projectors.

### 4.5.2.4 Weight and portability

Projectors come in a diverse range of sizes and weights. The smallest and most portable are *handheld projectors* (also called *pocket projectors*, *mobile projectors*, pico projectors, or *mini beamers*). Besides being self-contained themselves, this technology also applies the use of an image projector inside a mobile device (e.g. smartphone, digital camera, tablet) and allows digital images to be projected onto any nearby viewing surface. While they are unlikely to be used for large projection at special events, as their brightness (e.g. typically 100 or fewer lumens) and maximum screen size (e.g. maximum 80 in. or 203 cm) are too low, there is a definite possibility that the technology could morph into personal and crowd-sourced mobile gaming at events. These projectors weigh in the neighborhood of 1 lb (454 gm) or less, and are about 4–6 in. (10–15 cm) in their longest dimension. They fit in the palm of one's hand. See Figure 4.7 right.

It is in the mid-size range that most event projectors fall. These are the ones you might see mounted at the rear of, or in front of, a screen. Usually, especially if front projection is used, they are mounted on trussing above the audience. They are very portable and usually weigh in the order of 5–35 or 40 lb (2–18 kg), with their longest dimension being in the order of 12–20 in. (30–50 cm). See Figure 4.7 center.

The behemoths of the projector world are large venue projectors, those with brightness levels in the range of about 10,000 to 40,000 lumens. These are the ones most likely to be used for wide-screen video with edge blending, 4K video, and projection mapping. Although at the lower end of size and brightness they are reasonably portable (i.e. 25 lb, 11 kg), at the upper end they are far from it. For example, a 40,000-lumen Barco HDQ-2K40 large venue model weighs 463 lb (210 kg) and its longest dimension is about 40 in. (103 cm). It would need more than two people to carry and install it. See Figure 4.7 left.

Barco HDQ-2K40                ViewSonic Pro8520HD                Optoma Pico PK320

Figure 4.7  Examples of projectors (not to scale)

Images courtesy of: left—© Barco; center—ViewSonic, www.viewsonic.com; right—Optoma Technology Inc.

### 4.5.2.5 Connectivity

Critical to the success of any presentation using a projector is the ability of the projector to accept the information from the source—and often several sources simultaneously. The source may be video, data, or any combination of the analog or digital information we have already discussed, although most nowadays will be digital. In the higher-end projectors used in special events, connectivity can happen in a variety of ways.

### 4.5.2.5.1 ANALOG CONNECTIONS

For the odd occasion when older analog video is brought to an event, most projectors accept the following types of connections:

- Composite video. This is the most basic and lowest quality type of connection. It carries all the video information (color, brightness, synchronization) on a single, yellow RCA or composite cable. It is typically used to hook up a standard VCR and stereo equipment.
- RF or BNC. This is another form of a composite cable and can be changed to an RCA type with a simple adaptor. It is the type most often found on professional video equipment rather than RCA. The physical connection is more secure because it uses a twist lock.
- Separate video (S-video). This type of connector splits the video signal into two separate components: luminance (brightness) and chrominance (color). It is typically found on most high-end televisions, all videodisk players, camcorders, digital cable, and satellite set top boxes, and older standard VHS VCRs.
- Component video. With this type, the video signal is split into three components and three separate, color-coded cables: the Y cable (green) carrying luminance, image detail, and synchronization information; the Pb or Cb cable (blue) carrying color information; and the Pr or Cr cable (red) also carrying color. This connection gives a superior image over composite or S-video connections, and is most often found on high-end DVD players and HDTV tuners.
- RGBHV. These cables look identical to simple composite cables, but the RGBHV cable splits the video signal into five cables: for color into red, green, and blue; and two more cables to carry the sync for the signal (horizontal and vertical sync). RGBHV connectors are found on most high-end professional monitors and some HDTV decoders. Cables can be either BNC or RCA.
- Video Graphics Array (VGA). The 15-pin VGA connector is found on many video cards, computer monitors, and high-definition television sets. On laptop computers or other small devices, a mini-VGA port is sometimes used in place of the full-sized VGA connector.

### 4.5.2.5.2 DIGITAL CONNECTIONS

Most video sources for special events will be digital. Generally, projectors accept the following types of digital connections:

- Serial Digital Interface (SDI). SDI is a *broadcast quality* digital video connection, serving SDTV and HDTV (standard and high-definition) digital standards at 1,920 x 1,080 resolution. SDI is a high-speed connection of most commonly 270 Mbps that is carried on one *coax* cable with a BNC connector. Higher speeds of 1.485 Gbit/s exist for HD-SDI (high-definition) connections, 2.97 Gbit/s for the newer *dual link* HD-SDI and the most recent *3G-SDI*. It is good for long cable runs.
- Digital Video Interface (DVI). This is a video display interface used to connect a video source, such as a computer, to a computer monitor or projector. It is a multi-pin connector that was designed to maximize the visual quality of digital display devices such as flat panel LCD computer displays and digital projectors. It can transmit digital streams at speeds up to 5 Gbps. There are several versions in existence, all with slightly different pin configurations, that are capable of connecting analog or digital devices. They are: DVI-D for digital devices only; DVI-A for analog devices only; and DVI-I for digital

and analog devices. An important point to note here is particularly applicable for smaller events in which there may only be a projector and computer present (e.g. in a classroom situation). If mixing PC and Apple equipment, an adaptor may be required to take the signal from the *Thunderbolt* connector on the Apple/Mac to the DVI input for the projector—or for a stand-alone monitor—as most projectors do not accept the Mac signal directly. Most PCs, however, do have either DVI or HDMI.

- High-Definition Multimedia Interface (HDMI). An extension of DVI, this is an uncompressed, all-digital audio and video connection system. It is the first connection to handle all audio, video, and control data. Type A is a 19-pin connector and Type B is a 29-pin connector designed to support resolutions higher than 1,080p. HDMI is used with an increasing variety of digital equipment, including DVD players, digital audio or video monitors, computers, and digital TVs (e.g. plasma, LCD, etc.). It provides excellent image quality.

### 4.5.2.6 Other features of projectors

Projectors have come a long way in a very short time and most now have the following features as part of the package. It is useful to know what they can do:

- Zoom lens. This is useful if the exact placement of the projector cannot be controlled. In fact, many have optional lenses with different focal lengths, allowing more flexibility in placement.
- Keystone correction. This corrects for rectangular distortion caused by positioning the projector away from the central axis of the screen or projection surface.
- Remote control. Most now have remote control capability over focus, keystone, power, page up or down, color mode, freeze, resize, menu, onscreen pointer, and other features. Many projectors are now also operated with wireless technology.
- Front or rear projection. Many projectors have the capability of projecting from the front or rear of screens.
- Power consumption. The low-end, lower brightness projectors only consume in the 300 to 400 watt power range; however, the higher-end, brighter projectors can consume up to 8 KW of power. This is important to know when planning for power requirements for an event. See Chapter 9 for more details about electrical power.

### 4.5.3 Edge blending and warping

Two recent technological advances having a major impact on special events are projector *edge blending* and *warping*. Both are software-based, with the software typically housed within either a separate processor or the projector itself, especially higher-end models.

### 4.5.3.1 Edge blending

This software allows horizontal arrays and/or vertical stacked arrays of projectors to blend their images together in an infinite number of ways. For example, an extremely wide image can be created by projecting a smaller part of it with each separate projector and blending the edges of the separate images softly so that the division between the images is not noticeable. The same can be done with vertically stacked projectors for a higher overall image. In this way, immense wide-screen projections are possible, covering entire walls—or even a complete surround—of the event space. Likewise, similar projections are possible as stage backdrops in which there may be a number of completely different images required to be seen. In this case, for example, an IMAG image of a keynote speaker could be combined with an image of his PowerPoint slides on the same screen, and even another IMAG of the audience's reaction to his speech, the concept being that of a *picture-in-picture* (PIP). All these could be combined with hard or soft edges.

Edge blending and large screens have essentially replaced older, more cumbersome *video walls* for special events, and are having a similar effect on event décor, rendering large physical décor and sets almost obsolete.

Figure 4.8 illustrates how edge blending works. In this example, four projectors have been ceiling-mounted in front of a 16:9 proportion screen (note the image is backwards and being viewed from the rear) and are projecting four different quadrants onto the screen, each also 16:9 in proportion. The middle vertical and horizontal strips shaded in yellow represent the regions in which edge blending takes place. The actual full image resolution can be determined by subtracting the image blending region pixels from the total vertical or horizontal pixels of both projectors in the vertical or horizontal plane respectively. The resulting full image appears seamless.

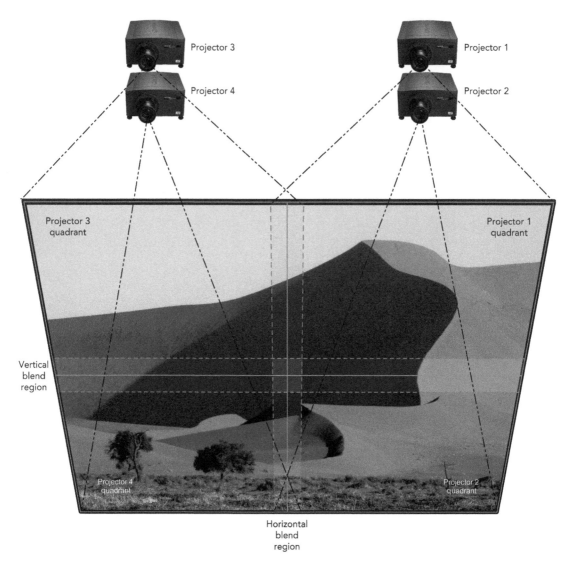

**Figure 4.8** Edge blending

Courtesy of Doug Matthews

### 4.5.3.2 Warping

Image warping is the process of digitally manipulating an image such that any shapes portrayed in the image have been significantly distorted. Warping is used for correcting image distortion so that a correct image is displayed. The software enables images to be projected onto curved screens or other oddly shaped surfaces such as domed ceilings, curved building walls, tensile fabric structures, and such. The most obvious uses are in real simulators used for training (e.g. aircraft, trains, cars, and trucks) and immersive rides, both of which utilize curved screens, and also projection mapping (see Section 4.3.5).

## 4.6 Display equipment

The final step in the process outlined in Section 4.2 is displaying the image(s) of the visual source. There are many ways to do this and we will look at each one in order to help in making the right choice for a special event. The main equipment choices for display are:

- plain screens;
- monitors;
- videowalls;
- LED screens;
- teleprompters and confidence monitors.

### 4.6.1 Plain screens

Undoubtedly what comes to mind as a first choice for displaying images is a projection screen. Screens are used more than any other display medium in special events. There are several concerns that must be addressed before deciding on a particular screen.

### 4.6.1.1 Front or rear projection

This is the first decision that must be made for any event. Each type of projection has advantages and disadvantages:

- Front projection. This takes up far less space than rear projection, and is particularly good if the projector is truss or ceiling-mounted, thus eliminating any chance of screen interference caused by people walking in front of the projector. However, there is a greater chance of light interference from other ambient sources such as stage or house lighting, and there may also be audio system interference from projector fan noise. Generally speaking, front projection is less difficult to set up.
- Rear projection. This eliminates chances of audience members casting shadows on the screen when walking in front of the projector and it is less prone to ambient light interference. However, it may require a large area behind the screen for projector setup and this area must often be cordoned off and even curtained off to minimize light spillage on the projector and screen from external doors. Using a mirror with the projector can decrease the area required for rear projection setup; however, the mirror must be *front-surfaced* to eliminate double images.

Note that for either front or rear projection, screens may be suspended from ceilings or trusses for better viewing. Supplemental or *delay* screens are frequently added in positions part way down a large venue if the viewing distance from the back of the audience is too far to the main screens(s).

### 4.6.1.2 Types of screen support and mounting

Because special events are temporary, almost all requirements for screens will mean that the screens must be portable in some form, unless the event takes place in a location with a permanently installed screen, such as an arena, auditorium, classroom, or theater. This section deals with the types of screens and support systems available for temporary, portable use.

There are four main types of screens that are available:

- Tripod. These are for front projection only. The fabric pulls up and out of a metal cradle, with the top of the screen being attached to a movable vertical support rod. The base is made of three foldable legs (i.e. the tripod). They are available only up to approximately 8 ft x 8 ft (2.4 m x 2.4 m) in size and are best used for presentations in small rooms or spaces with audiences under approximately 150 people. Size ratios are typically 16:9, 4:3, and 1:1.

- Pullup or floor. These are similar to tripod screens except that the support base is more compact and stands closer to the floor, making the overall screen appearance a little more professional. The screen itself also pulls up and out of a metal cradle mounted right on the base at the floor level, again attached to a vertical metal support rod. Some screens pull up past the bottom of the screen for better viewing and have a black portion or material under the screen itself. Sizes vary up to about 10 ft x 7.7 ft (300 cm x 230 cm) and ratios are 16:10, 16:9, 4:3, or 1:1 depending on the manufacturer.

- Modular. Sometimes known by the brand name Fast-Fold®, these are tensioned screens that feature a foldable aluminum frame and a soft screen surface which attaches to the frame via push studs, tensioning the surface for an extremely flat projection screen. The screen may be used for front or rear projection depending on the screen material. Legs may be adjusted to various heights and the screens may also be flown if required, usually with a more rigid truss-type frame. They are available in sizes up to about 40 ft (130 m) in width and ratios of 16:10, 16:9, 4:3, and 1:1, depending on the manufacturer. These screens are the most commonly used in special events, particularly corporate and private ones in hotels and conference centers.

- Ultra-wide. With the advent of HD video, ultra-wide screens up to 150 or 200 ft (45 or 60 m) are becoming available, typically in increments of 50 ft (15 m) wide or so, and heights of 30 or 40 ft (9 or 12 m). These screens are made of soft material similar to that of Fast-Fold®, and are mounted on trussing with piping weighting down the bottom. They are joined and stretched to eliminate wrinkling. Chain motors rigged from the ceiling allow them to be raised or lowered for dramatic reveals and surprises (D. Clark, BC Event Management, personal communication, August 17, 2014). Another mounting method is *lace and grommet* that literally ties the screen to a tubular metal frame. Masking material is used to cover the lacing and act as a screen border.

### 4.6.1.3 Screen surface and material

In front projection, matte white surfaces, by far the most popular, offer excellent definition for finely detailed images, such as computer text. Smooth silver or white pearlescent surfaces provide particularly bright images best for video or computer projection, but are prone to *hotspotting*. Glass beaded surfaces offer a brighter image with some sacrifice of sharpness. They are intended for general video and film projection use, but are not recommended for computer data. *Lenticular* surfaces are designed for video and slide projection and for rooms with side light from windows. They work by focusing projected light that would otherwise be disbursed on the vertical axis onto the horizontal where it can be viewed. In the same way, ambient side light that would otherwise mix with the projected image is reflected away. Gray screens, a fairly recent innovation, are good for front projection. Their high-contrast gray offers a high resolution image and enhances the depth of blacks while maintaining the quality of lighter colors. The low gain rating of 0.8 provides this type of projection screen with a wide 180-degree viewing degree, but requires it to operate in an environment of low ambient light (Bamboo AV, 2011).

In rear projection situations, there are several coatings and screen materials designed for specific situations. Most standard surfaces are best for rooms with a relatively narrow seating cone and good lighting control, with specialty surfaces available when viewing angles will be wide or lighting high. Rear screen fabrics are translucent and allow the image to pass through from behind. They attach only to Fast-Fold® frames.

### 4.6.1.4 Other features and concerns

Understanding several other features of screens may help in making the right screen choice:

- Gain. This is the ability of a screen to gather light from a projector and direct it to a certain location. A high gain screen can be important in situations where room lights must remain high for note-taking or discussion, particularly if those lights wash onto the screen surface. Gain varies with screen surface. Most matte white screens are rated at a gain of about 1.0, and most glass beaded screens provide a gain of about 2.5. Lenticular surfaces are rated from 1.5 up to about 3.0, and rear screens offer gains up to 5.0.

- Viewing angles. No matter what a screen's stated viewing angle, seating an audience outside a 90-degree cone has inherent problems that no screen will overcome. At angles greater than 45 degrees from a line perpendicular to the center of the screen, images appear distorted, with objects looking taller and thinner than they should. Thus, most screens are designed to focus projected light back to an audience within that 90-degree cone, and images viewed from beyond that will appear quite dim.

- Screen dressing. By *dressing* is meant finishing off the screen installation with defining borders, usually black drape. These give it a professional appearance, mask the support framing, assist in giving the perception of a brighter image, and help to mask any setup behind the screen, especially for rear projection. Most professional screens come with black borders anyway, but the addition of short drapery sections along the top and bottom of the screen along with full screen height drape on either side finishes the setup properly. Obviously, the side draping can extend as far as required in any direction by adding panels.

### 4.6.1.5 Determining screen size

Correct screen size is determined be using a general formula. Find the distance to the last row of seats and divide by eight to determine the screen height, then apply the aspect ratio of the media you will be using to arrive at the screen width. Usually this is 4:3 for computer or video images, but may be 16:9 for HDTV formats. For example, if the last row of seats is 70 ft (21 m) from the screen, then the height should be approximately 8.75 ft (i.e. 70/8 = 8.75), or for the closest screen size, 9 ft (3 m). Using the 4:3 ratio will then give a screen width of 12 ft (i.e. 9 x 4/3 = 12) or 3.6 m. Note that the first number in screen sizing is the screen height and the second is the width. One caveat that goes with the above formula for determining screen size is that if the images are finer in detail than simple graphics, the guiding number of eight changes to six for reading spreadsheets or text, and to four for detailed drawings like CADD. Finally, the minimum distance from the screen to the first row of seating should be at least two times the width of the image on the screen, and the bottom of the screen should be at least 40–48 in. (100–120 cm) above the floor.

In helping to determine the exact screen size, it should be noted that the most common aspect ratios in screen sizes are 4:3 (video format), 16:9 (HDTV format), 16:10 (wide format), and 1:1 (square format). The effect of using a screen size not matched to the aspect ratio of the projected image is shown in Figure 4.9. Note that this same effect will be apparent with monitors as well (see Section 4.6.2).

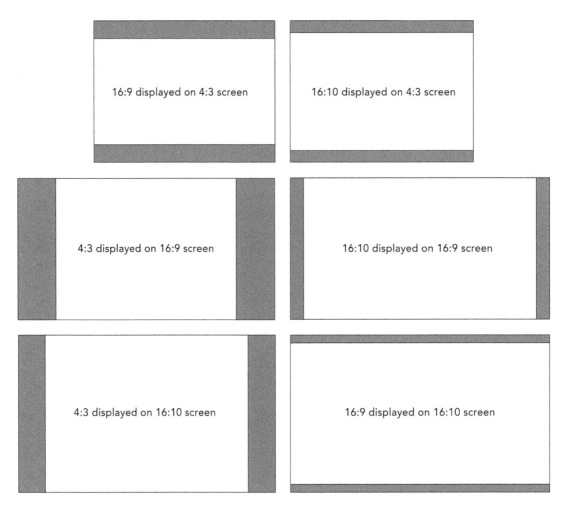

Figure 4.9 Screen aspect ratio and effect on displayed image

Courtesy of Doug Matthews

For many rental screens (e.g. Fast-Fold®), movable horizontal or vertical bars can be used to correct for the wrong screen aspect ratio.

### 4.6.2 Monitors

Monitors can be thought of as combinations of projectors and screens. For special events they are often used in small venues and as supplementary displays to larger screens to cover sections of audience that the screens cannot cover in large venues (e.g. at the front of an audience not within the viewing angle of the main screens). In terms of appearance, the monitors used for events are no different than consumer monitors.

Monitor technology is changing rapidly. Presently, there are four technologies commonly used in special events: LCD, OLED, plasma, and touchscreen.

- LCD. Similar in theory to LCD projectors, LCD monitors are the most widely used monitors today. They consist of liquid-crystal-filled pixels inserted between two polarizing filters. A backlight source generates light which passes through the filters. The electrodes control the flow of current which passes through the liquid crystals and aligns them in a particular direction. The alignment of the crystals, controlled by the electrodes, sets the intensity and color for the light which will pass through the second filter and will hit the screen. LCD monitors are lightweight, consume little power, and have good contrast and brightness. Diagonal sizes are now more than 110 in. (277 cm) and capable of accepting 4K UHDTV.

- Organic Light-Emitting Diode (OLED). This is a thin-film LED technology (see Section 4.6.4 and Chapter 5) in which the emissive layer is an organic compound, sandwiched between two thin-film conductive electrodes. In essence, it is a screen and projector all in one piece of extremely thin, flexible material. This technology lends itself to the actual printing of the light-emitting screen using ink-jet printers, a fact that renders it cheaper to manufacture than any other existing technology. OLEDs and their newer versions, polymer OLEDs (PLED), phosphorescent OLEDs (PHOLED), top-emitting OLEDs (TOLED), and flexible OLEDs (FOLED), all have a greater range of brightness, colors, and viewing angles (e.g. approaching 180 degrees) than any other technology. This means they will be able to be used in such things as clothing and portable displays. They are already evident in smartphones, tablets, and digital cameras. Advantages include faster response times, small size/thickness, better power efficiency, and good viewing angles. Diagonal sizes are now up to 77 in. (194 cm) and increasing, again for 4K UHDTV.

- Plasma. Plasma monitors are flat, lightweight surfaces covered with millions of tiny glass bubbles. Each bubble contains a gas-like substance, the plasma, and has a phosphor coating. The bubbles can be considered as the pixels, each pixel-bubble having three sub-pixels: one red, one green, and one blue. When it is time to display an image signal (RGB or video), a digitally controlled electric current flows through the flat screen, causing the plasma inside the designated bubbles to give off ultraviolet rays. This light in turn causes the phosphor coatings to glow the appropriate color. Advantages include superior contrast ratio, wide viewing angle, and high refresh rate. Diagonal sizes have reached over 152 in. (383 cm) but in spite of this and their superior quality, plasma monitors seem to be losing the competitive battle and may not be around for long.

- Touchscreen. A touchscreen is actually not the monitor itself but a separate layer or panel placed on top of the monitor, and so can be applied to the types of monitors described above. It has a grid of light beams or fine wires on the screen. It lets the user interact by the touch of a finger rather than typing on a keyboard or moving a mouse. The user enters data by touching icons or menus identified on the screen. There are different types of touchscreen technology. The most common types are *resistive, surface wave*, and *capacitive*:

  - Resistive. This panel has two layers of thin, electrically conductive material facing each other. A change in electrical current occurs when it is pressed and the layers touch. The input can be processed by a computer. These monitors are the most popular types of touchscreen monitors used today. They are usually not affected by dust or liquids, which makes them very reliable.

  - Surface Acoustic Wave (SAW). These monitors use ultrasonic waves to process input from the screen. These waves flow over the touchscreen. The wave is absorbed and processed by computer when a person touches the pad.

  - Capacitive. These screens are coated with indium tin oxide. This material provides continuous current across the screen. The current can be measured by the processor when the panel is touched. These screens have high clarity and are not affected by dust.

Other touchscreen technologies include *infrared acrylic projection, optical imaging, dispersive signal*, and *acoustic pulse recognition*; however, resistive and capacitive are the most used presently. Touchscreens are continually increasing in size, and are now in excess of 82 in. (206 cm). It is expected that their use will probably increase in special events, particularly with increased gamification.

### 4.6.3 Videowalls

Videowalls are high-end image display systems consisting of multiple monitors (cubes) placed in various configurations such as 2 x 2 (e.g. four monitors with an overall aspect ratio of approximately 4:3), 3 x 4 (e.g. 12 monitors with an overall aspect ratio of 16:9 or HDTV size), and almost any other combination desired. The monitors are especially constructed for this type of display and are designed to be stacked together. The monitors use the same technology as found in other projection systems (e.g. LCD, plasma). The technology basically takes video, digital data, and/or computer graphics input and feeds it into a processor that manipulates and splits the signal to allow it to go to one or more monitors. Almost limitless possibilities are available for uniquely displaying the image or combinations of images. The advantages of a videowall include constant high resolution and brightness no matter to what size the image grows. Unfortunately, because of the setup time and complexity, multiple video projectors and screens are now replacing videowalls in most special event situations, although videowalls continue to thrive in more permanent installations like trade show booths, shopping centers, and control rooms.

### 4.6.4 LED screens

In its most simple form, an LED is a semiconductor device that emits light when electricity is passed through it. This effect is a form of electroluminescence. The color of the emitted light depends on the chemical composition of the semiconducting material used. LEDs are also explained in Chapter 5. Before we go any further, it is worth noting that LEDs can have two different purposes. On one hand, they can be strictly light sources, as with projectors (see Section 4.5.1.3) and conventional event lighting (Chapter 5). On the other hand, they can be display devices, as in the case of the OLED monitors mentioned above, but more importantly as larger screens for indoor and outdoor use. Such screens have now become ubiquitous in permanent displays for advertising, stadia, arenas, bars, and many other venues. They also see temporary use in concerts, special events, and other types of entertainment. Although they had been used before, one of the most impressive pioneering examples was their use in large format in the opening and closing ceremonies of the 2008 Beijing Olympics. Because of their increasing importance, LED screens deserve a little more explanation. The two primary considerations when choosing a screen are the design technology and the specifications and features.

#### 4.6.4.1 Design technology

In an LED screen, like a monitor, the screen corresponds to the computer screen driving it, and there are two slightly different technologies involved in creating the display:

- Direct In-Line Package (DIP). This technology uses discrete red, green, and blue diodes stamped into a pre-drilled *printed circuit board* (PCB) using a process known as *through-hole mounting*. The legs are then soldered onto pads on the opposite side, which can be done by hand or with machines. This complete module forms a single pixel. Screens formed from these modules are mostly used in large outdoor applications because of their lower resolution, lower cost, brightness, and high contrast.
- Surface-Mounted Diode (SMD). This is an encapsulated LED that has all three colors of diode in a slim tube that is soldered directly onto a circuit board printed with *solder pads* instead of having mounting holes drilled into it. SMDs can be made smaller and placed closer together since they're only mounted onto one surface of the board. Because of this, they are able to have smaller *pixel pitches* (see Section 4.6.4.2 below) and much closer viewing distance (InnovisionLED, 2014). They are used mostly for indoor applications but are also making inroads into outdoor signage. See Figure 4.10 for an example of a large LED screen with SMD technology used as a stage backdrop.

Figure 4.10 Large LED screen used as a stage backdrop

Courtesy of Showmax Event Services, www.showmaxevents.com

### 4.6.4.2 Specifications and features

The choice of screen will also be influenced by certain specifications and features:

- Pixel pitch. This is the distance between screen pixels in millimeters. The lower the pitch, the closer the screen can be viewed without appearing to be pixelated. Pixel pitch typically ranges from 4 mm up to 20 mm for indoor LED displays; for outdoor displays, pixel pitch can range from 10 mm to 34 mm or higher. There is a trade-off, however. Generally the lower the pitch, the higher the number of pixels and also the higher the cost.

- Pixel density. Also called *LED density*, this is a measure of how many pixels there are in a given area of screen. Sometimes this can be "per square foot"; sometimes it can be "per screen panel." Because LED screens are made differently by different manufacturers, the pixel layout on a panel may indicate that there is a high pixel pitch, but when the pixel density is also taken into account, the resulting resolution may not be as high as another screen with the same pixel pitch. Put more simply, the higher the pixel density, the more pixels in a given area and the better the screen will look. It will also last longer because it can be driven at a lower current and temperature.

As an example, one provider, Showmax Event Services in Vancouver, Canada, builds special event screens in which each panel measures 20¼ in. x 20¼ in. (51 cm x 51 cm) and weighs 25 lb (11 kg).

Each panel uses a 6 mm pixel pitch and has a density of 6,400 pixels per panel, which is incredibly high resolution. It can be viewed with no pixelation from only 12 ft (3.6 m) away. Using these panels, larger screens of varying sizes can be built easily. Unlike videowalls, the panels are seamless when placed together (D. Sabina, personal communication, May 27, 2014). See Figure 4.10, in which the screen was 40 ft (12 m) wide x 8 ft (2.6 m) high.

- Brightness. This is another specification that will help in choosing the right screen. Brightness is measured in Nits or *candelas per square meter* ($cd/m^2$). For indoor use, a brightness of 800–2,000 Nits is adequate, but for outdoor use, it should be between 3,500 and 5,000 Nits. LED screens do tend to lose brightness after extended use.

- Refresh rate. "The refresh rate of an LED screen is the number of times in a second that the LED screen hardware draws the data. This is distinct from the measure of frame rate in that the refresh rate for LED screens includes the repeated drawing of identical frames, while frame rate measures how often a video source can feed an entire frame of new data to a display . . . On LED screens, increasing the refresh rate decreases flickering, thereby reducing eye strain. However, if a refresh rate is specified that is beyond what is recommended for the LED screen, damage to the display can occur" (Vegas LED Screens, 2014). A normal refresh rate is in the order of 400 Hz, and a high rate is considered to be 1,500–2,000 Hz. Flicker generally disappears above 1,000 Hz.

- Other features. Some desirable features include:
  - a quiet fan for low noise;
  - dual signal cables for fail-safe operation;
  - easy panel replacement to avoid non-working segments of screen. The panels described above can be "hot-swapped" in under 5 min;
  - seamless panels.

In summary, LED screens are improving in quality, size, and cost at a rapid rate, and are now even being incorporated into soft fabrics. They are incredibly bright, modular, easily scalable, and present unlimited creative possibilities for set and scenic design for special events.

### 4.6.5 Teleprompters and confidence monitors

A teleprompter is the modern version of the old theatrical cue cards used to help with the speech of someone onstage. A modern teleprompter is a display device that prompts the person speaking with an electronic visual text of a speech or script, by sending the script to a flat panel that is projected up to one-way mirror glass that in turn reflects the writing directly at the eye level of the presenter. The glass is specially coated so that the audience can see right through it and cannot see the text.

A teleprompter system usually requires three or four components to function: a dedicated host computer and operator, although it can also be controlled by the onstage speaker; prompting software that can reverse and variably scroll the text; and a teleprompter display device with mirror hood. Nowadays, prompters can also use smartphones or tablets as the source, via an application.

Teleprompters come in several different versions: a hooded version that can be placed directly onto the front of a camera for TV or onscreen personalities so that it appears they are speaking directly to the camera; a floor-mounted panel with eye-level prompter glass used for executive presentations from a stage (sometimes called a *presidential teleprompter*); and a stage-mounted prompter that looks much like an audio monitor that can be used for singer lyrics or speaker text, called a *confidence monitor*.

For special events, the executive-type teleprompter is most often used. With such a teleprompter, from the perspective of the audience, it appears as though the speaker is speaking extemporaneously with only pre-planned glances to the notes on the lectern. The eye contact with the audience assists the speaker to connect in a relaxed demeanor and with confidence.

## 4.7 Equipment setup and operation

Once the use and format of the presentation is determined, the producer and A-V supplier must decide on the optimum equipment for the job, using combinations of the available projection and display options, and then proceed to setup and operation.

### 4.7.1 Setup

Like audio and lighting, visual presentation equipment can involve a time-consuming setup due to the requirements to occasionally fly projectors and screens, the need for dark time to check colors and alignment, and especially due to the need for rehearsing complex cues and switching. In order to ensure the right equipment and locations are chosen, here are the most important questions a producer must ask an event manager or client:

- How many attendees are there and what is the room layout? If this is a classroom setting, then more people can be accommodated within the space and there will likely be no obstructions to sight lines. This means that screens need to go only at the front of the room. If a dining setup, then attendees will be facing all different directions and projection to different locations in the room may have to be considered. If the event is in multiple rooms simultaneously, then smaller monitors in each room might be appropriate.
- What size of projection system is needed? If there is a large spread-out audience, that means a larger screen size. The formula for screen size given in Section 4.6.1.5 may be used.
- Is projection to be rear or front? As explained in Section 4.6.1.1, each has advantages and disadvantages.
- Are sight lines to the screens clear or is there a possibility of any obstruction caused by people walking in front of a projector or of table centers or architectural elements (e.g. columns) being in the projection path? If so, then a decision must be made to change either the projection system or the event design.
- Do presenters need support in the form of remote control or cabling for laptop computers near the stage?
- Is a teleprompter or confidence monitor required for speaker or MC scripts and, if so, is there sufficient unobstructed space for it near the stage?
- If IMAG is being used, where will the camera(s) be placed in order to obtain a good picture yet cause minimal obstruction to audience sight lines?
- Is there appropriate technical support at the venue in the form of electrical power, ceiling hanging points with an acceptable load rating, and easy and early room access?
- Is the budget sufficient to do the job?

Once the answers are known and equipment chosen, the setup can proceed. It involves the following tasks:

- Preparation of all equipment takes place in the shop. If there is a multimedia show, some pre-programming may be required, as may the loading of special software on a computer.

- Equipment is delivered and loaded in.

- Regular screens, LED screens, and monitors are positioned and set up, either flown or floor-mounted. They are then dressed with drapery material as required. Display equipment requiring it is connected to electrical power.

- Switching hardware, preview monitors, show control computers, and Blu-ray/DVD players are set up backstage—or at the FOH position if that is where control will be—and connected as required. This equipment is tied into electrical power and Internet if required. Audio from the switching hardware or devices is tied into the main audio mixer in and out. Intercom is set up between the switcher position, all camera operators, and any additional technical personnel controlling equipment. Internet connections are tested. See Figure 4.11.

- Projectors are positioned and set up, either on projector carts, scaffolding, or ceiling-mounted from trussing or other supports. Correct cabling is then run from the projectors to the switching position. Electrical power is connected to projectors.

- Speaker support equipment, such as teleprompters, confidence monitors, onstage computers, and/or remote control devices, is set up, connected, and tested.

- Video cameras, if used, are positioned, electrical power is connected, if possible, for all stationary cameras, and cabling is run from the cameras to the switching position.

- Cameras are tested and balanced for color; projector alignment is finalized; LED screens and monitors are aligned, color-corrected, and tested; switching between sources is checked; preview monitors are checked; and all audio feeds in and out of the switching hardware are checked for levels.

- An event and/or show talk-through or rehearsal normally takes place after all this has been done in order to ensure all cues are correct. This is especially important if the show involves a combination of verbal and recorded cues, as with a multimedia show that might include live performers and lighting or special effects.

Figure 4.11 outlines the general layout of visual presentation equipment at an event and the routing of signals from their sources to their final display.

Note that in the setup of Figure 4.11, a recording is being made of the event so all video signals from the switcher and audio signals from the house audio mixer must be routed through a special unit that synchronizes video and audio so nothing is out of synch (e.g. lips moving on the video but not synchronized with the audio).

### 4.7.2 Operation during the event

Operation of visual presentation equipment during an event can be complex and stressful. It requires an intimate knowledge of the equipment and its capabilities as well as a thorough understanding of the event and show running order with all the cues involved. See Chapter 9 of *Special Event Production: The Process* for more about show production schedules and running orders. Assuming a complex show environment, the following represent the most important tasks of the A-V team:

- Providing live camera coverage of the event according to the cues and shots called by the technical director.

- Adjusting the color, resolution, and format of all live and pre-recorded video before screening.

- Adjusting and correcting all still images before screening.

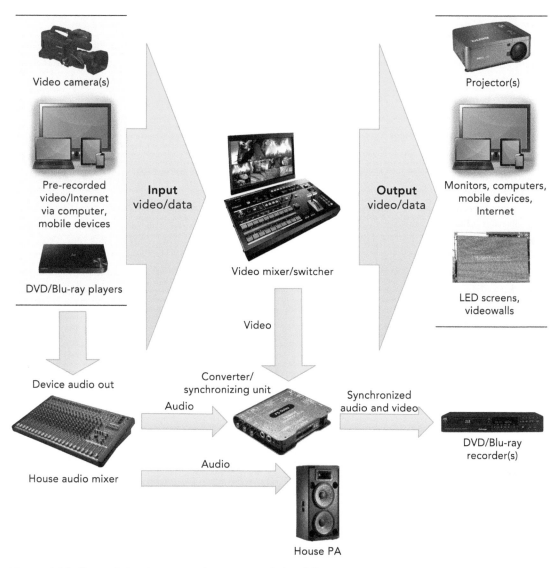

Figure 4.11  General visual presentation setup and signal flow

Courtesy of Doug Matthews

- Previewing and switching all visual presentation sources before screening according to cues given by the technical director.
- Adjusting audio levels going to and returning from the main house audio mixer.
- Running video recorders.
- Communicating with lighting and audio engineers to ensure levels of audio and lighting work smoothly with the visual presentation.

As with décor and lighting, a plan for equipment strike after the event must be coordinated with the other suppliers (partly because A-V equipment is often part of the trussing used for lighting and audio), the event manager, and venue personnel to ensure conflicting tasks are minimized.

## 4.8 Risk and safety

Visual presentation equipment is highly complex and evolving rapidly, yet standards still apply to its safe design and use. In this regard, Chapter 3 lists both audio and visual presentation equipment standards, and the same comments apply as for audio (see Section 3.6 of Chapter 3).

As with audio, risk mitigation techniques that ensure safe and professional event execution are employed by knowledgeable visual presentation specialists. Tim Lewis of Proshow Audiovisual Broadcast in Vancouver, Canada, again offers the benefit of his extensive experience (T. Lewis, personal communication, August 12, 2014):

- Redundancy. As with the audio system, this is critical. There is a significant failure rate of CDs and DVDs provided by suppliers (e.g. performers) and presenters, especially when trying to play them in different recorders. Lewis usually dubs a CD or DVD brought to him onto a trusted format and plays it in his own fully checked-out machine. He may also bring a second brand of recorder if there is any doubt that there may be trouble playing CDs or DVDs, especially if the requirement is very high profile, as when it is part of a VIP presentation. For PowerPoint presentations, he is insistent on redundancy and always provides a minimum of two computers onsite at the A-V console position, and all presentations are loaded onto the two computers. Each computer is equipped with a CD/DVD burner for quick copying when necessary.

  He also provides at least one additional projector that can be quickly hooked up and used with front projection off a cart in case a flown or floor-supported show projector goes down. He stocks a wide variety of lenses with differing focal lengths for all projectors in order to work in event situations that may not allow sufficient space either behind or in front of screens. In this way, there are far fewer restrictions on space placed on the venue and the client.

- Equipment quality. Lewis is especially cognizant of problems that can occur with personal laptop computers provided by presenters. He does not allow presenters to use their own computers onstage or even at the console position, instead preferring to load presentations onto his own pristine computers that are equipped with the latest version of all software (e.g. PowerPoint and Windows). To alleviate presenter stress, he provides top-of-the-line remote cueing hardware that uses RF signals and has built-in laser pointers. As well, he provides a confidence monitor near the lectern for the presenter. He notes that his preference is a small monitor attached to a microphone stand that sits just below the lectern top out of audience sight lines, making it less obvious than a presentation teleprompter.

  For video, Lewis refuses to use less than professional, TV quality equipment, notably cameras. He insists on using only highly skilled video camera operators, preferably with a lot of television experience, as well as a good video director with similar training. As he says, "Bad camera operation can destroy an IMAG presentation."

- Effects of other equipment. Similar to the ambient noise effects mentioned in Chapter 3, other equipment might interfere with visual presentations. For example, moving lights should never be mounted on the same truss as projectors because motion is transferred to the projectors with obvious consequences.

- Professionalism. Personnel make all the difference. Lewis insists on only providing highly trained technicians with a professional approach to the event (as with the camera ops). He recommends that all personnel be briefed before any event that such things as idle chatter and improper comments should never be part of the show, especially on intercom. Focus must be maintained at all times.

As with audio, these tips plus compliance with safety and design standards and a thorough analysis and documentation of the specific event's risks should minimize most potential problems.

## PRODUCTION CHALLENGES

1. A client company wishes to project images and videos during an event that celebrates the company's 50-yr history. Included are old photographs, VHS videos, and one of the original telephones they used. What would have to be done to this archival material to make it presentable on a screen and what equipment could be used to project it?

2. Explain frame rate, interlacing, resolution, and aspect ratio as they pertain to video.

3. An opening ceremony for a major 5,000-person conference is taking place in a football stadium. You need to cover the event with IMAG and the screen will be the stage backdrop. The rear-most seating is 300 ft away. The largest screen obtainable to you is 20 ft in width. Suggest solutions so that the entire audience will be able to see the proceedings and explain how to calculate the screen sizes to be used.

4. You have been asked to produce a 15-min projection mapping presentation on the side of your city's 100-yr-old city hall. The gray concrete building has a lot of inset windows, Corinthian columns, and a large domed roof. The only place to set up the projectors is from the top of a six-storey parking garage across the street and exposed to the elements. It is winter and there is a chance of snow. What must you consider to obtain approval for the show and also generally what equipment is required?

5. For the kickoff to a corporate dinner, you have been asked to recreate the inside of a 1960s-era nightclub, complete with psychedelic images, music, and lighting as a 5-min multimedia presentation. Suggest some visual sources to do this and possible ways that it could be accomplished including equipment or surfaces to be used for projection and display.

## REFERENCES

Bamboo AV. (2011). The Importance of Choosing the Right Screen Surface. *The Different Types of Projection Screen Surfaces*. Retrieved August 18, 2014, from www.bambooav.com/the-different-types-of-projection-screen-surfaces.html.

Beal, V. (2014). Multimedia. *Webopedia*. Retrieved August 21, 2014, from www.webopedia.com/TERM/M/multimedia.html.

Beck, B. (2014, February 22). Lasers: Coming to a Theater Near You. *IEEE Spectrum*. Retrieved August 21, 2014, from http://spectrum.ieee.org/consumer-electronics/audiovideo/lasers-coming-to-a-theater-near-you.

Christie Digital Systems USA, Inc. (2013). *The Book of Transformations*. Christie Digital Systems USA, Inc.

eBay. (2014, April 15). Understanding the Differences between LED, LCD and DLP Projectors. *eBay*. Retrieved August 6, 2014, from www.ebay.com/gds/Understanding-the-Differences-between-LED-LCD-and-DLP-Projectors-/10000000177630814/g.html.

H.264/MPEG-4 AVC. (2014, June 25). In *Wikipedia, The Free Encyclopedia*. Retrieved 20:57, July 25, 2014, from http://en.wikipedia.org/w/index.php?title=H.264/MPEG-4_AVC&oldid=614330777.

InnovisionLED. (2014, March 18). THE DIFFERENCE BETWEEN SMD AND DIP LEDS. *InnovisionLED*. Retrieved August 19, 2014, from www.innovision-led.com/?p=1069.

Lewis. (2013). Projector Brightness. *Lewis Sound and Video Professionals*. Retrieved August 8, 2014, from www.lewissound.com/projectorbrightness.html.

McNeil, L. and McCain, G. (2006). *Please Kill Me: The Uncensored Oral History of Punk*. New York: Grove Press.

Rivington, J. (2014, July 18). 4K TV and Ultra HD: Everything you need to know. *techradar*. Retrieved July 28, 2014, from www.techradar.com/news/television/ultra-hd-everything-you-need-to-know-about-4k-tv-1048954.

Second screen. (2014, August 11). In *Wikipedia, The Free Encyclopedia*. Retrieved 21:48, August 26, 2014, from http://en.wikipedia.org/w/index.php?title=Second_screen&oldid=620751885.

Shreve, D. (2013, November 8). Does Size Matter? *productionMatters v2*. Retrieved August 25, 2014, from http://blogs.wayne.edu/lighting/2012/11/08/does-size-matter/.

Strickland, J. (2012, February 10). How 3-D Gestures Work. *HowStuffWorks.com.* Retrieved August 1, 2014, from http://computer.howstuffworks.com/3-d-gestures.htm.

Vegas LED Screens. (2014). LED Screens and Refresh Rate. *Vegas LED Screens.* Retrieved August 19, 2014, from www.vegasledscreens.com/faq/80-led-screens-and-refresh-rate.html.

Video. (2014, July 8). In *Wikipedia, The Free Encyclopedia.* Retrieved 20:39, July 23, 2014, from http://en.wikipedia.org/w/index.php?title=Video&oldid=616026110.

Video scaler. (2014, April 8). In *Wikipedia, The Free Encyclopedia.* Retrieved 21:26, August 4, 2014, from http://en.wikipedia.org/w/index.php?title=Video_scaler&oldid=603255455.

Wavelength Media. (2014). Video Timecode. *Mediacollege.com.* Retrieved August 25, 2014, from www.mediacollege.com/video/editing/timecode/.

Chapter **5**

# Lighting systems

**LEARNING OUTCOMES**

After reading this chapter you will be able to:

1. Explain the objectives of event lighting.
2. Understand the qualities of light and how they can be manipulated for specific purposes in a special event.
3. Describe the basic capabilities of the main types of lighting instruments used for special events.
4. Understand how effective event lighting is achieved through proper design.
5. Understand how event lighting is controlled.
6. Explain the requirements for an efficient event lighting setup.
7. Understand and explain what a lighting operator does during an event.

Lighting is yet another of the rapidly changing technical fields in special events. Used for meetings, rock and roll concerts, outdoor architectural highlights, and every type of special event, lighting can be costly, frustrating, and power-hungry, yet still provide an amazing component to an event. It is one of the primary ways to achieve emotional impact, especially if done by an experienced professional lighting designer (LD).

For special events, good lighting design should enhance the event experience without drawing too much attention to itself as a separate entity. This is accomplished by understanding from the outset exactly for what purpose the lighting will be used, what types of lights will be used to achieve this purpose, and how the design will be carried out. Although most producers subcontract to a lighting company, they should ideally understand what equipment is available and how it works in order to provide the best lighting design for the available budget. In this regard, this chapter will discuss and illustrate the following topics:

- objectives of event lighting;
- qualities of light;
- lighting instruments;
- event lighting design;
- what happens between concept and execution;
- lighting control, setup, and operation;
- risk and safety.

## 5.1 Objectives of event lighting

When people enter a special event, they are entering a new environment, an environment that has been purposefully transformed into one that is different from their normal one. This new environment can be as simple as a darkened room with a single spotlight on a keynote speaker onstage, or a room that has been changed into an undersea wonderland. In both cases, lighting plays an influential role in the success of the transformation. It is in this transformation that the objectives of event lighting lie. These objectives include:

- visibility;
- relevance;
- composition;
- mood.

We will examine each one to see how it can influence the transformation of an event space.

### 5.1.1 Visibility

Considered the most fundamental function of event lighting, visibility simply means that for an event audience to clearly understand what is going on within the event space, they must be able to see the action or the appropriate décor. Although this may seem obvious, it is amazing how many producers fail to understand the importance of *selective visibility*. By selective, we mean that "well-lit" does not translate into turning all the house lights up full and leaving them there for the duration of an event. Selective means lighting only what an audience needs to see when they need to see it.

For example, if the only activity happening on a large stage is a keynote speaker at a lectern, then there is no need to light the entire stage, but rather just the speaker himself. In this way, the focus of the moment is on the speaker, and the audience is not distracted by anything else onstage. Likewise, if a 40 ft (12 m) wide, decorative painted mural is placed against a wall, it should be fully lit in order to be seen and to be an effective component of the themed décor; however, if it only covers half the wall, there is no reason to light the other half.

Although visibility presumes that certain objects or people will be lit, its effectiveness is not solely dependent on the intensity of the lighting. It is also affected by contrast, size, color, and movement of the object(s) being illuminated, as well as the distance of the light source from the object and the condition of the eyes of the observer.

### 5.1.2 Relevance

Stage lighting specialists sometimes refer to this objective as naturalism, style, or even structure. According to Williams (1999), this means that the lighting design should provide a sense of time and place through the use of such items as simulated sunlight or moonlight. In event lighting, it really is more than this because a special event often comprises more than what is happening onstage.

For example, in a large special event that has different eras themed in different rooms, relevance might mean: strobelights, lasers, and smoke in a futuristic setting; simulated gas lamps in a Victorian setting; lots of colored neon in a 1950s setting; and simulated fire in a prehistoric setting, all of which could be used to light décor or simply to add to the relevance of the theme by using these means to actually light just the room itself.

At the same time, if there is action taking place within those settings, perhaps in the form of themed entertainment, that action might also have to be lit in a way that is relevant to the dynamics of the action within the theme. For example, a futuristic dance troupe might be accompanied by high-energy automated lighting moving in time with the music, a Victorian singer might be lit by old-time stage footlights, a 1950s diner scene with characters from *Happy Days* might have a mirror ball, and a prehistoric cave campfire scene with actors might use low light level amber tones to illuminate the scene with moving fire images on the cave wall.

## 5.1.3 Composition

Composition refers to how effective the LD has been in helping to create an overall event environment. The lighting should take into account the same design tools and design elements that a decorator would use and, in fact, should be designed in conjunction with the décor design. For example, here are possible considerations within each of these groups:

### 5.1.3.1 Design elements

As with décor, the design elements are:

- Space. Are all three dimensions effectively illuminated? (e.g. Does lighting cover walls and ceilings—and even floors?) Is lighting used to actually "fill" the space by using smoke or haze that will reflect the light beams?
- Form. Does the lighting design enhance the form of objects? (e.g. Are they made to look attractive? Do they become focal points? Are they more three-dimensional as a result of using proper lighting to create depth?)
- Line. Are the lines of objects made to be part of the whole design? (e.g. Does rear lighting effectively separate a dark-suited speaker from a black velour stage backdrop?)
- Texture and ornament. Does the lighting bring out the texture in objects?
- Light. Is the light intensity too high or too low?
- Color. Does the lighting design complement the event's overall color scheme?

### 5.1.3.2 Design principles

Similarly, the design principles are:

- Proportion. Is the lighting of different event components in proportion to each other? (e.g. Is a large décor vignette lit by big lights and another lit by small lights?)
- Balance. Is the lighting design symmetrical or asymmetrical? This applies especially for stage lighting.
- Rhythm. Is there a repetitive pattern in the lighting or are there smooth transitions between colors?

Figure 5.1 Example of elements and principles of good lighting design

Lighting by Images by Lighting; photo by Elizabeth Solano for John Solano Photography; event designer Ed Libby; event coordination and design by Levine Fox Events

- Emphasis. Is there a lighting focal point or is lighting used to illuminate a decorative focal point?
- Harmony. Does the overall lighting design create a comforting, or harmonious feeling, particularly in conjunction with other décor?

Figure 5.1 illustrates several design elements and principles. Note the even lighting of the entire space, the texture of the stage backdrop brought out by the lighting, the consistent color scheme, and the overall balance and harmony of the design.

### 5.1.4 Mood

Mood refers to how lighting affects the psychological reactions of the audience at an event and how it reinforces the emotional tone of a themed venue or of a stage performance. This is often done by using an appropriate color—or changes of color—to elicit an emotional reaction, as outlined in Section 2.1.1.6.1 of Chapter 2. However, it can also be accomplished by other means, such as using automated lights for excitement or combining lighting with various special effects to strengthen the effects and add to the emotion. We will discuss this in more detail in Section 5.4.

## 5.2 Qualities of light

Before committing to a design of any sort, the LD must first understand the actual qualities of light itself. In other words, how can this "raw material" in the form of a light beam emanating from a fixture be manipulated to achieve the desired look? The qualities of light that the designer is able to manipulate are:

- intensity;
- distribution;
- color;

- direction;
- movement.

We will discuss each of these in turn.

### 5.2.1 Intensity

In simplest terms, this refers to the strength of a light source. However, there are some other relative measurements that are also associated with a light source and what happens when the light is projected over a distance and strikes an object.

*Intensity* is the strength of a light source (e.g. the actual lamp inside the light fixture), or the light output. It is measured in lumens (lm) or candelas (cd). *Illuminance* is the light level actually falling on the surface of an object being lit. It is measured in lux (metric) or foot-candelas (Imperial) where 1 ft-cd = 10.76 lx (lux). *Brightness* is the effect of light leaving the surface of an object being illuminated. It is what the human eye actually sees. It is affected by the intensity of the light source, the distance from the source to the object, and the properties of the object (e.g. color and texture). It is measured in foot-lamberts (ft-L). These three measurements are related mathematically by the *inverse-square law*, $E = I/D^2$, where $E$ is the illuminance in foot-candelas, $I$ is the intensity in lumens, and $D$ is the distance in feet between the sources and the point of calculation on the surface.

Generally speaking, objects that appear bright draw more attention to themselves. Because of this, it is the job of the LD to ensure that those objects needing attention, whether they be performers or decorative, are appropriately bright.

### 5.2.2 Distribution

Distribution refers to the manner in which light strikes a surface and reveals an object.

It can be applied to how objects appear, in that they might be softly lit as part of a larger scene with light that has no sharp edges. On the other hand, they may be individually lit with a small, sharply defined, single light beam.

On another level, distribution can be applied to the appearance of light that uses an image projector of some sort, such as a *gobo* in front of an *ellipsoidal* fixture (to be discussed in more detail later in the chapter) or an actual projector. These in turn produce certain desired images on a surface such as a wall or scrim.

On a third level, distribution can be applied to the shape of a light beam itself when viewed through smoke or haze effects.

### 5.2.3 Color

As with the design tools of event décor, color is the most noticeable and strongest quality of light. Indeed, all light is colored, and white light is simply a mixture of all visible wavelengths (colors) between infrared and ultraviolet radiation on the electromagnetic spectrum. One of the keys to good lighting design is a thorough understanding of color. We begin with some definitions.

Hue is the pure form of a color with no white, black, or gray added. *Tint* is the mixture of a hue with white. Shade is the mixture of a hue with black. *Tone* is the mixture of a hue with black and white (gray). It is sometimes also called value (see Chapter 2). Saturation refers to the amount of hue in a color mixture. For example, a pure red color (like fire-engine red) would be said to have a high saturation of red.

In the world of lighting, the color wheel takes on a slightly different appearance from the color wheel associated with décor (which uses pigments). For light, the primary colors are red, blue, and green. The secondary colors

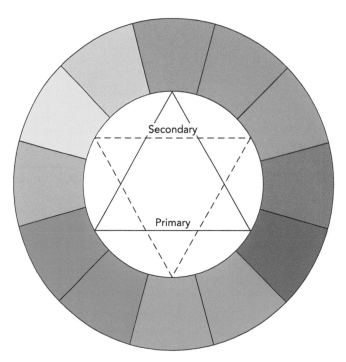

Figure 5.2 Lighting color wheel

Courtesy of Doug Matthews

are yellow (mixture of red and green), cyan (mixture of green and blue), and magenta (mixture of red and blue). Figure 5.2 illustrates a lighting color wheel (also called a visual or RGB color wheel).

The two differing color wheels, the one for pigment as described in Chapter 2, and the one for light, are often confusing since they do not make logical sense when mixing colors. Technically, as pointed out by Fitt and Thornley (2002, pp. 22–23),

> the lessons learned from mixing the colors of paint are somewhat different to those for mixing the colors of light. It has to be realized that light is the source of all color, but pigments in paint [or in dyed fabrics] are simply reflections or absorbers of parts of the light that illuminates them. If a beam of red light and a beam of green light are superimposed the result is yellow. On the other hand, if we mix red and green paint, we get rather a nasty looking 'brown black' color. When using light, all spectral colors can be created by adding various component parts of red, green, and blue light and the system used is called 'addition,' ultimately creating white. Pigments derive their colors by subtracting parts of the spectrum, therefore the system with pigments is called 'subtraction' and ultimately creates black.

For special events, the LD is frequently called upon to not only light stage performances, but also decorative elements. These are particularly sensitive to the interaction between the hues of light and pigment hues, since most décor is pigment-based (e.g. fabrics, painted surfaces, costumes). Table 5.1 illustrates the interaction between the two types of color, and can serve as a guide for what a decorative element or person looks like when subjected to a certain color of light (Fuchs, 1929).

To add to the confusion, additive and subtractive color mixing are also found in the lighting world alone. Additive color mixing refers to the combining of two or more colors to form a new color. As illustrated in

Table 5.1 Interaction of colored light with colored pigment

| Color of Pigment | Color of Light | | | | | | | |
|---|---|---|---|---|---|---|---|---|
| | Violet | Blue | Blue-Green | Green | Yellow | Orange | Red | Purple |
| Violet | Deep violet | Dark violet | Dark violet | Violet | Dark brown | Dark brown | Dark gray | Dark violet |
| Blue | Light blue | Deep blue | Light bluish gray | Light blue | Dark bluish gray | Black | Gray | Blue |
| Blue-Green | Dark blue | Very dark blue | Dark bluish gray | Dark green | Greenish blue | Dark greenish brown | Black | Dark blue |
| Green | Bluish brown | Light olive green | Light greenish gray | Intense green | Bright green | Dark green | Dark gray | Dark greenish brown |
| Yellow | Scarlet | Greenish yellow | Greenish yellow | Greenish yellow | Intense yellow | Yellow orange | Red | Orange |
| Orange | Scarlet | Light brown | Light brown | Light brown | Orange | Intense orange | Intense orange red | Scarlet |
| Red | Scarlet | Purplish black | Dark maroon | Maroon | Bright red | Orange red | Intense red | Red |
| Purple | Reddish purple | Dark violet | Maroon | Purplish violet | Light brown | Maroon | Reddish brown | Deep purple |

Courtesy of www.rosco.com/canada/technotes/filters/technote_1.asp

Figure 5.3 (left), the combining of red and blue light sources, for example, will produce a new color, magenta. Subtractive color mixing refers to the filtering of light. When light passes through a single colored *gel* or filter, only the wavelength corresponding to the color of the filter will pass through it. Figure 5.3 (right) illustrates this concept.

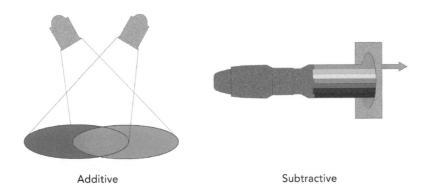

Additive                                        Subtractive

Figure 5.3 Illustration of additive (left) and subtractive (right) color mixing in light

Courtesy of Doug Matthews

The last important concept of color in lighting design is the meaning of color. As outlined in Chapter 2 when we discussed décor, every color has certain emotions attached to it. It is these emotions that the LD tries to enhance in order to make his design more effective.

### 5.2.4 Direction

For special event lighting, there are three areas of concern with respect to lighting direction: stage and entertainment lighting, décor and theme lighting, and ambient lighting. In all cases, the effect of directional lighting is similar, but the desired outcome may be different. Let us examine the different directions that may be used to light people or objects and then see what the differences may be, using Figure 5.4 as a guide.

#### 5.2.4.1 *Front lighting*

We begin with front lighting (Figure 5.4A). Although this direction gives the best visibility, it also tends to make objects and people appear "flat." For lighting people and stage shows, this is one direction that is absolutely necessary so the audience can see what is happening onstage. Generally speaking, in almost every instance of special event entertainment, some component of continuous front lighting will be needed, even if it is not fully bright or not white. On the other hand, for ambient lighting and theme décor lighting, front lighting is not always desirable. If lighting walls, for instance, to achieve a general mood, direct

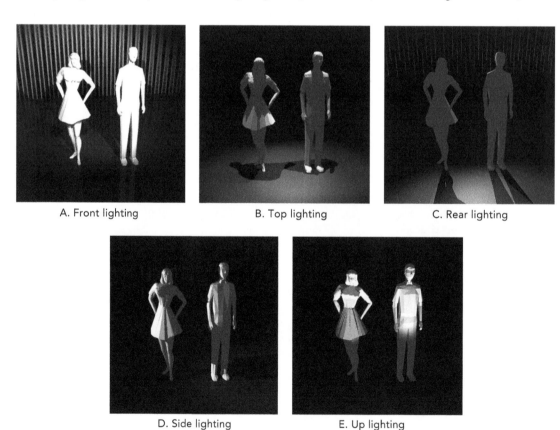

A. Front lighting          B. Top lighting          C. Rear lighting

D. Side lighting          E. Up lighting

Figure 5.4  Direction in lighting

Courtesy of Doug Matthews

lighting is less desirable than up lighting as it tends to highlight the flaws in the wall. However, if a large painted mural is part of the décor, front lighting may be the right choice in order to give the best visibility and render the mural scene more realistic. The same would apply if the front lighting is a gobo and a clear, proportionally correct pattern is required to be seen on the wall.

### 5.2.4.2 Top lighting

The next direction is top lighting (Figure 5.4B). For people, this adds shadows to faces but also adds nice highlights to hair and shoulders, which onstage can help to separate people from backgrounds. For décor purposes, top lighting is often used to light table centers with pin spots or automated fixtures, to give crisp, undistorted beams of light throughout the event space. It is also used for highlighting décor vignettes and for floor lighting.

### 5.2.4.3 Rear lighting

Rear lighting (Figure 5.4C) is very useful for adding dimension to people or objects onstage and for separating them from the background. Similarly, for décor it can help to add a third dimension and make a display seem more "alive."

### 5.2.4.4 Side lighting

Side lighting (Figure 5.4D) is highly desirable in some form when lighting people onstage as it also adds dimension and makes the body shape more obvious (e.g. facial features). In the same way, it can add shape to décor. However, when lighting flat décor as in the case of murals, it tends to highlight flaws in the surface and is not recommended.

### 5.2.4.5 Up lighting

The final direction for lighting is under or up lighting (Figure 5.4E). When used to light people, this is associated with a ghoulish, macabre effect as seen in movies and is not desirable unless it is being used for a special effect. However, for décor, especially for ambient lighting, it is one of the most effective directions, particularly for uplightng walls, ceilings, and backdrops.

### 5.2.5 Movement

A related aspect of direction is *movement*. Movement indicates any change in lighting that gives life to the lighting and brings it closer to the natural world. It is usually of timed duration and can include:

* a change in direction;
* a change in color;
* a change in intensity;
* a change in distribution, such as the appearance of different gobos from the same fixture;
* the movement of an offstage light such as a followspot or automated fixture.

According to Williams (1999),

> *movement may be rapid or very subtle, slow and imperceptible. Such may be the case of a designer that provides a slow shift in sunlight from one side of the stage to the other throughout the duration of a play. The audience may not notice the shift; however, they often may 'feel' the result of the change emotionally . . . Up until recently, movement was probably the least utilized quality of light by the stage LD. This all changed in the 1980s when the automated lighting fixture was born. The modern automated fixture can now move physically – directing its beam*

*from one part of the stage to another [or any other area within the event space]. In addition, the automated fixture can 'move' from one color or effect to another, at any speed. The changes and combinations of intensity, form, distribution, color, and movement are endless.*

There will be more on automated lights in the next section.

## 5.3 Lighting instruments

Depending on where one works, lighting terminology differs. In North America, a lighting instrument is also called a *fixture* or *unit*. In Britain, it is known as a *light fitting* or *lantern*. In the engineering and architectural communities and the rest of the world, it is known as a *luminaire*. This will be our common term for the remainder of this chapter.

In this section, we will be discussing the basic construction of luminaires, the different types, and what each is used for in special event lighting.

### 5.3.1 Construction of luminaires

Like audio systems and video, lighting is in the midst of major evolutionary changes. Constantly advancing LED technology has resulted in the slow but inevitable replacement of most conventional luminaires with their LED counterparts, especially in many high-end events and concerts. Because there is still a place for conventional luminaires in lower-end events and permanent installations, in this section we will examine how both conventional and LED luminaires are constructed.

#### 5.3.1.1 Conventional luminaires

All the terms defining a lighting instrument mentioned above refer to a "package" that is comprised of the following components:

- Outer housing. This is a metal or plastic, specially shaped container that houses the whole instrument and prevents light from spilling to undesired locations.
- Lamp. This is the source of the light. Similar to an everyday household light bulb, lamps are normally made up of a glass or quartz envelope, a base, and a filament (usually made of tungsten and powered by electricity) surrounded by a gas (called a *gas discharge lamp*). Depending primarily on the gas used within the bulb, the light produced may vary slightly in its *whiteness*. This variation is an indication of different color *temperatures*. The only real significance of different color temperatures is that if luminaires with different temperatures are being used for lighting a specific scene, then different gels will probably need to be used to achieve the same apparent color. We will discuss gels in more detail shortly.
- Lens. This is a curved, glass plate that is positioned at the front of the luminaire to give the light beam emanating from the lamp its characteristic shape. Most lenses are curved a certain way to make the beam either narrow or widely dispersed, and with *hard* or *soft* edges for effect. Generally speaking, the greater the curvature of the lens and the smaller the focal length (distance from lamp to lens), the greater will be the dispersion of light. This wide angle of the beam is known as the *beam angle*, defined as the point in the cone of light emitted by the luminaire where the light level is diminished by 50 percent when compared with the level in the center of the beam. Note that not all conventional luminaires have separate lenses. PAR lamps (*parabolic aluminized reflector*—see below), for example, incorporate reflector and housing as a single unit with the lamp attached to one end and the size of the beam determined by the length of the housing.
- Reflector. Inside the luminaire, the lamp produces light that emanates in all directions, including to the rear of the luminaire. In order to increase efficiency, a curved reflector is placed at the rear of the

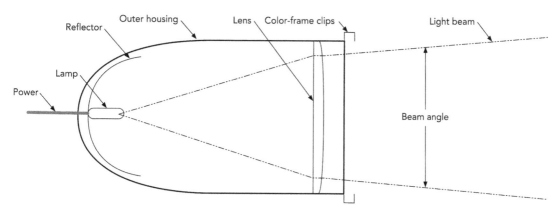

**Figure 5.5** General construction details of a conventional luminaire

Courtesy of Doug Matthews

luminaire that takes the excess light and re-directs it toward the lens. There are various reflector designs for each of the different types of luminaire and they play an important part in the intensity and shape of the light coming from the luminaire.

See Figure 5.5 for a depiction of a generic conventional luminaire.

- Accessories. In addition to the four main components of construction, most luminaires also come with accessories that improve their performance. They generally include some or all of the following:
  - Lamp socket. This is a socket designed to accept the specific lamp.
  - Electrical cord and connector. These tie into the lighting circuitry.
  - Mounting yoke with a pipe or "C" clamp. The mount allows the luminaire to *pan* (rotate horizontally 360 degrees) and *tilt* (move vertically up and down), then to be securely locked into place on an overhead truss or pipe support.
  - Color-frame clips. These metal clips, fitted to the front of the luminaire, accept a lightweight metal or heat-resistant fiber holder (*color frame*) for colored *gels* (filters), *donuts*, *barn doors*, or *gobos* (image projection). A colored gel is typically made of plastic or glass and comes in a large selection of colors. A gel normally serves three purposes: to correct for the color temperature of a specific lamp, thereby allowing uniform light all over a surface; to provide drama and effect in lighting décor or performers; and to diffuse or soften light (e.g. uplighting walls). A donut is a metal plate used to increase the clarity of patterns in an *ellipsoidal reflector spotlight* (ERS) by reducing halation and sharpening the image. A barn door is a metal apparatus fitted on the front of a luminaire using the clips. It has independently adjustable flaps that are used to control light spill. A gobo stands for *go-between* and refers to a small metal cutout incorporating a pattern that can be projected onto any surface. This enables the luminaire (typically an ERS, to be explained later) to act as an image projector. Gobos come as stock patterns from a number of manufacturers or they can be customized into names, company logos, black and white or color photographs and graphics, and almost any pattern desirable. See Figure 5.6 for an illustration of these accessories.

### 5.3.1.2 LED luminaires

We have touched on light-emitting diodes in previous chapters but never really explained what they are. LEDs are basically just tiny light bulbs that fit easily into an electrical circuit. Unlike ordinary incandescent

Color frame and gel

Gobo

Barn doors

Donut

Figure 5.6 Lighting accessories (not to scale)

Courtesy of Doug Matthews

bulbs, they don't have a filament that will burn out, and they don't get especially hot. They are illuminated solely by the movement of electrons in a semiconductor material, and the color of the resulting light is determined by the magnitude of that movement (Harris and Fenlon, 2014).

There are several important advantages that LEDs have over conventional luminaires that have made them very attractive for event lighting, including: faster cycling time; more light per watt; smaller size; changeable colors within a single luminaire eliminating the need for color filters/gels; no dimming circuits required; lower heat radiation; lower operating cost; longer life, typically 50,000 h vs 1,200 h; and easier focusing ability. These advantages make LEDs the luminaires of choice as more events concentrate on "going green" (see also Chapter 12 of *Special Event Production: The Process*). There are few disadvantages and the main one, higher acquisition cost, is rapidly disappearing as the technology improves and becomes more competitive.

The design of an LED luminaire is quite different from a conventional luminaire as described above. Let's examine the components of one:

- Housing. Unlike the general "can" shape of a conventional luminaire, an LED luminaire's housing is typically metal, shaped to dissipate heat rather than to form the light beam. Ironically, "although LED lighting systems do not produce significant amounts of radiated heat, LEDs still generate heat within the junction [i.e. the movement of electrons within the semiconductor], which must be dissipated by *convection* and *conduction*. Extracting heat from the device using *heat sinks* [i.e. that part of the metal housing designed to conduct heat away from the LEDs] and by operating LEDs in lower ambient temperatures enables higher light output and longer life of the device" (Bullough, 2003). Because of this, most LED luminaires are much shorter than conventional luminaires.

- Light source. This, of course, is the LED itself, or rather an array of individual LEDs. Some designs incorporate arrays of individual LEDs of separate colors (e.g. red, green, blue, white), while others incorporate arrays of individual LEDs that generate all colors, or simply plain white. Unlike the position of lamps in conventional luminaires at the back of the housing, LEDs are placed near the middle of the housing.

- Lens and reflector. Individual LEDs usually incorporate their own lenses in this type of luminaire. Thus, if there is an array of 14 LEDs, there would be 14 separate lenses. They also incorporate their own individual reflectors, so instead of having one large reflector at the back of the housing, there would be 14 separate reflectors, one built into each LED light package. Many LED luminaires add a separate lens in front of the LED array that moves back and forth or "zooms" within the housing, which allows adjustment of the beam angle from narrow to wide.

- Power supply/driver. This is built into the housing and essentially integrates the *DMX signal* (see Section 5.6.2 for an explanation of DMX) with electrical power and controls the functions of the LED array.

- Control panel. This is normally found on the outside rear of the housing and consists of an LCD display that has menu options for such things as setting the individual address of the luminaire.

- DMX in/out. These are two DMX connection points, one female and one male, that permit the luminaire to be *daisy-chained* (linked together) with other luminaires so that all can receive the proper DMX signal.

- Accessories. Most LED luminaires also incorporate many of the same accessories as conventional ones (e.g. mounting yoke and color-frame clips for the same purposes as conventional) because they still must provide the same functionality.

See Figure 5.7 for a depiction of a generic LED luminaire.

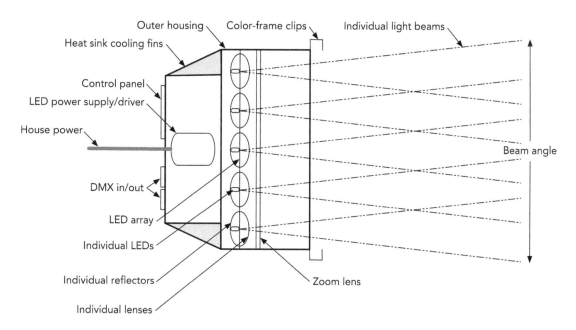

Figure 5.7 General construction details of an LED luminaire

Courtesy of Doug Matthews

## 5.3.2 Types and uses of luminaires

Being highly competitive, the lighting industry has produced a plethora of luminaires with various trade names, many with the same capabilities. Additionally, there is interaction among the TV, movie, theater, and special events industries, each with their own preferences for certain luminaire types, which contributes to the confusion. We will attempt to cut through this confusion by categorizing and explaining the most common types of luminaires used in the events industry. Some of the lesser-used ones will be omitted in the interest of keeping to the point. The main categories of luminaires are:

- conventional;
- LED;
- moving;
- digital;
- specialty.

### 5.3.2.1 Conventional luminaires

These are fixtures basically designed as shown in Figure 5.5. They have a single light source and a beam whose shape is dictated by the lens and construction of the housing. They can only be fixed in one position so are controllable by manually aiming them where wanted. They can only provide a single color of light but can be dimmed using separate hardware. The most common ones include the following:

- Ellipsoidal Reflector Spotlight (ERS). One of the true workhorses of the lighting industry, the ERS also goes by the names *Source Four* (as marketed by ETC—Electronic Theater Controls), *Leko* (as marketed by Strand Lighting), and *profile*, a term in common use in the UK. It is the most sophisticated of conventional instruments. Its beam shape is round and uniform with a hard edge, and various lenses inside the changeable barrels control the size of the beam. Some units are focusable so that an image can be projected, and *framing shutters* allow the beam to be shaped to eliminate light spill onto projection screens, the audience's eyes, and such. The *lens trains* available provide beam angles ranging from very wide (50 degrees) to very small (5 degrees), an important consideration when choosing the right one for gobo projections at various distances. Options include *irises* to further reduce the beam spread, rotating pattern holders to make the projected images spin, and others. This is the best instrument to use with gobo patterns. Power requirements vary from 500–1,000 watts (W) and throw distances from 10–100 ft (3–30 m). Besides its use with gobos, it is a popular luminaire for isolating key areas and people onstage, such as a speaker at a lectern.
- Fresnel. This is one of the standard stage lighting instruments, especially in theaters. The Fresnel produces a characteristically intense, soft-edged beam created by the pebbled surface on the back of the Fresnel lens, named for its French inventor. For special events, it is typically used to provide large color wash areas onstage, and its soft beam edge easily permits blending of multiple beams and colors. Beam spread can be modified from spot to flood (about 15–70 degrees). Power requirements vary from 150–5,000 W with throw distances of 10–40 ft (3–12 m).
- PAR can. A PAR can is comprised of a PAR sealed beam lamp and a mounting fixture and base (the can). It produces a high-intensity narrow beam of light and is available in many different sizes and powers. The bigger the number with a PAR can, the bigger its size. Electric lamps used in PAR cans are sized by multiples of 1/8 in. To convert the PAR number to in., divide the lamp number by 8. Therefore, a PAR64 has an 8 in. diameter. A PAR64 is the most used such luminaire, especially for stage washes when flare and a very soft beam edge are not a problem. It is also commonly used as an inexpensive alternative for up lighting walls. Its power requirements are 500 or 1,000 W.

- Pinspot. Pinspots are very narrow-angle PAR lamps in a basic can-type housing. Beam spreads are very narrow and range from approximately 5 to 10 degrees. Pinspots come in power ranges of 75–1,000 W, and have a throw of 5–50 ft (1.5–15 m). They are sometimes referred to as *rain lights*. All PAR lamps for pinspots are low voltage and require transformers to transform the mains voltage (120 or 240 volts AC) to the proper lamp operating voltage. Usually, the transformer is incorporated into the rear of the fixture (Williams, 1999). Pinspots are useful for providing accents and highlights, and are particularly effective when all general lighting is dimmed down, allowing the pinspot(s) to highlight or draw attention to something (e.g. table centers in a dark ballroom).

- Followspot. This is a manually operated luminaire designed for following performers as they move about a stage or a venue. Modern followspot fixtures consist of a cylindrical housing 4–6 ft (1.2–1.8 m) in length, mounted on a telescopic stand with castered legs. They are usually fitted with a manual iris and a color filter changer. A followspot is designed to provide a hard beam edge. Controls often exist to soften the beam edge when required. Followspots are traditionally mounted as high as possible at the rear of an event space, in order to front light the performers if they are on a stage. The size of the room and the distance to be projected are the factors that determine the size and intensity of the unit to be used. Usually, they are 250–3,000 W in power, and throw 50–200 ft (15–60 m).

- Floodlight. Sometimes called a *cyclight* (after the technical term, *cyc* or *cyclorama*, for a stage backdrop in theater), this consists simply of an enclosed light source in a box with one open side. Floods are designed to provide a wide, even distribution of light over a large area. Typical beam angles range from 70 to 150 degrees. Most units come with a fixed beam angle, although a few units are adjustable between flood and wide flood. Wattages range from 500 to 1,500 W. Floodlights do not use lenses but some may have a clear protective safety glass. Floodlight fixtures are particularly well suited for lighting backdrops in a theater but have found their way into special events. Typically, a continuous row of floodlights is arranged above and parallel to the backdrop, at a distance of 3–10 ft (0.9–3 m) away. For additional interest and impact, a row of fixtures may be used to uplight the backdrop, from the floor, although front lighting is best if it is a scenic backdrop. Floodlights are also sometimes used for the lighting of scenery, to provide large area washes, and as work lights. Individual fixtures are commonly available in both scoop (round, open front) and box flood (square or rectangular, open front) designs (Williams, 1999).

- Audience blinder. "Not quite the slang name or use the manufacturers intended, but this is what audience blinders are generally used for—to illuminate or literally blind the audience" (Moody and Dexter, 2013). Generally, they consist of various configurations of PAR cans grouped in four to 20 or more lamps within a specially designed housing. Although they began in the touring concert world, they have made their way into special events. Using DMX control (see Section 5.6.2), they can be strobed in various patterns.

See Figure 5.8 for examples of all these conventional luminaires.

### 5.3.2.2 LED luminaires

These are fixtures basically designed as shown in Figure 5.7, with some modifications. These modifications have resulted in the development of LED versions of all the conventional fixtures except with more capabilities, smaller size, and much lower operating costs. Most of these fixtures have added the capability to operate off any of the world voltages so are useable anywhere. Here is a general breakdown of where the technology now stands:

- ERS. An LED ellipsoidal is a fairly recent development and the shape and optics of the fixture are almost identical to the conventional one, but the acquisition cost is considerably more. Savings come from the longer life of the LEDs and from the cooler temperature. For example, ellipsoidals are designed to project gobo patterns on surfaces. In the past such gobos have had to be made from

| ERS (Altman) | Fresnel | PAR can (Altman) | Audience blinders (Active Blue) |
| --- | --- | --- | --- |

| Followspot (Altman) | Floodlight (Altman) | Pinspot (CPS Group) |
| --- | --- | --- |

Figure 5.8 Examples of conventional luminaires (not to scale)

Photos courtesy of Altman Lighting, Active Blue, and CPS Group as per labels, and Doug Matthews (Fresnel)

heat-resistant material, usually metal, due to the heat generated by the lamp. With LEDs as the light source, such heat is non-existent and gobos can be made out of much cheaper material such as acetate, thus enabling the projection of such things as color images and almost any graphic at relatively low cost.

- Fresnel. Some Fresnels have not changed much in appearance but some are much more compact (i.e. thinner) than conventional Fresnels. They have the same characteristic beam spreads as conventional as well as continuous focusing, plus they have the added features of DMX control and are remotely controllable. The Fresnel lens remains in these fixtures.

- PAR can. LED PARs have LED arrays comprising varying numbers of red, green, blue, and occasionally white individual LEDs. They are normally fixed with a single beam angle like their conventional counterparts (usually 14 or 15 degrees), but some manufacturers offer filters to change the angle. They are programmable using DMX for color mixing—remember that conventional PARs could only have a single color using a gel—and many can strobe. Brightness is now equal to or better than conventional lights. Some are also much slimmer than conventional. Most come with a double yoke assembly that enables safe mounting on the ground or other flat surface as well as flying on trussing.

- Pinspot. LED pinspots now take on two different forms. One is as a DJ/club light with strobe features in a very narrow beam (e.g. 3 to 12 degrees) using programmable white or colored lighting. Of course, these can also be used for special events to add excitement at a low cost. The second form LED pinspots have taken is the more traditional one using only a single focus point, but with the added features of battery power and wireless infrared dimmable control, and throw distances up to about 30 ft (9 m). Some models have moveable heads via a gooseneck-type design. Unlike the DJ lights, these have been designed specifically for the special event market for ease of control, and also quick installation using strong magnets. The batteries last up to 14 h (see Figure 5.9).

- Followspot. LED followspots are about half the size of their conventional counterparts thus making them much more portable. Some are still fully manual, but others have options for either manual or DMX control. Colors are now changed at the push of a button as is dimming, although beam angle and diameter and focus are still manually controlled. Gobos can also be projected.
- Floodlight. Like the other LED luminaires, floodlights have added multiple capabilities. They are now usually referred to as *wash lights*, and come as either long, narrow *strips*, or larger rectangular *panels*. Most have DMX programmable strobing, dimming, and color mixing. Some are also sound-activated (e.g. strobing, dimming, and colors can be triggered by music), remotely controlled, and wireless, battery-driven.
- Audience blinder. Not too different in appearance from conventional blinders, LED units have multiple colors and individual LED control for colors, dimming, and strobing. They can also be sound-activated.

See Figure 5.9 for examples of some of the LED units described that are most changed in appearance and design from conventional luminaires.

### 5.3.2.3 Moving luminaires

In the history of the lighting industry, there is no invention that has revolutionized it more than moving luminaires.

> *Although automated fixtures (also called* moving lights, intelligent lights, *or* kinetic instruments*) have only been used in the special events industry since the late 1980s, the concept has been around since an original United States patent was issued to Herbert F. King of Newtonville, Massachusetts in 1928, for an 'automatic spotlight'.*
>
> *(Cadena, 2005)*

Real development, however, did not take place until the late 1980s and accelerated in the 1990s to the point where today, almost all special events, concerts, and stage performances with even modest budgets use them.

LED PAR can                    LED wash strip                    LED pinspots

Figure 5.9  Examples of LED luminaires (not to scale)

PAR can and wash strip © ADJ Products, LLC; pinspots courtesy of Fuel Lighting, http://fuellighting.com

The field has exploded in recent years and there are so many developments and companies making these products that it is impossible to keep up with them. There is, fortunately, some commonality among them:

- Features of moving luminaires. What are moving luminaires (automated fixtures)? Quite simply, they are the fusion of all the static luminaires that we have discussed into a single unit that can be remotely controlled. "The common feature of automated fixtures is movement, often very rapid: light beams pan the stage and event space, zoom in and out, change shape and color, diffuse and sharpen; gobos materialize, spin around, change pattern, then disappear" (Gillette, 2000, p. 353). Most such luminaires include a number of internal features, which can create almost endless combinations of effects:
  - *Color wheels* with dichroic lenses used to change the color of the beam (like having a variety of colored gels available).
  - *Pattern wheels* with gobos used to change the shape of the beam (like having many different gobo patterns to choose from).
  - Shutters used to *dim* or *strobe* the output (like using a strobelight or dimming the light).
  - Automated lens trains used to focus the beam (like a Fresnel lens).
  - Irises used to change the size of the beam.
  - *Gate shutters* to *square off* the beam (like using a highly focusable light with barn doors for a small or large area).
  - *Prisms* used for splitting the beam into three or five images, which can then be rotated.
- General principles of operation. As expected, these luminaires are complex in their design. Power requirements are typically 200–1,200 W—although LED versions are much less—and they operate on two main principles, *moving yoke* or *moving mirror*. The moving yoke principle achieves beam movement by using very precise electric *step motors* to control movement of the entire yoke and body of the fixture. The moving mirror principle achieves beam movement by reflecting the beam off a step motor-controlled mirror mounted on the body of the fixture. There are also numerous models of automated fixtures for the DJ/club industry that utilize the same basic designs but come in various forms and shapes that create differing effects. They are typically cheaper and less capable overall than the more sophisticated designs.
- LED versions. LED movable fixtures, sometimes called *moving heads*, are proliferating, particularly in the club market. The advantages include multiple colors without the need for a color wheel, lower power consumption, smaller size, and lower cost. Interestingly, rather than trying to exchange LEDs for conventional light sources (i.e. lamps) in a complex design, many companies have gone to moving LED fixtures that replace and extend the more simplified designs of individual traditional luminaires described above. For example, there are now *moving head wash* units with zoom capability (i.e. just a PAR can with extra capabilities), and also *moving head spots*, which are more a combination of a pinspot and an ERS, with gobo-projection capability. No doubt even more different combinations will arrive, some of which will prove popular for special events.

See Figure 5.10 for examples of moving luminaires.

### 5.3.2.4 Digital lighting

Digital lighting is the result of merging digital projection technology with automated lighting technology. This has produced products that are essentially moving projectors with the ability to project literally any type of digital graphic image, including digital photographs, computer graphics, and digital video, from one fixture onto any surface in a three-dimensional space. Not only that, but they also have the entire gamut of automated lighting features, typically those of a moving head wash unit. To do this effectively requires two light sources, one for the projector (usually a conventional lamp with a high lumen output), and one for the other automated features (usually banks of LEDs), together in the unit. Also, to utilize all the projector and lighting features requires a *media server*. A media server is "a sophisticated computer that stores video clips and still image libraries. It can be used to manipulate any of those images with color, effects, and image correction to surfaces (curved or flat) through digital light sources" (Moody and Dexter, 2013). Current models of digital lights now incorporate the server within the housing at the base of the fixture and it is controlled using *DMX digital protocol* (see Section 5.6.2) via XLR cables or another protocol called *Art-Net* via Ethernet cables.

Figure 5.10 also illustrates a digital fixture, the Robe DigitalSpot 7100 DT.

Moving yoke fixture
Vari-Lite VL4000 spot

Moving mirror fixture
Inno Scan HP

LED moving head
wash fixture Mac Aura

Digital fixture
Robe DigitalSpot 7100 DT

Figure 5.10  Examples of moving luminaires (not to scale)

VL4000 spot image courtesy of Philips Vari-Lite; Inno Scan HP copyright ADJ Products, LLC; Mac Aura courtesy of Martin Professional ApS; and digital fixture courtesy of Robe Lighting

### 5.3.2.5 Specialty lighting

Within the lighting industry, there are a number of specialized lights that are used frequently for events that do not fall exactly into the categories we have already discussed. These include:

- Blacklight. This light, an *ultraviolet* (UV) light source used to create special lighting effects with fluorescent materials, works best on light-colored material at low ambient light levels.

- Laser. Actually an acronym for *Light Amplification* by *Stimulated Emission* of *Radiation*, this word has become synonymous with a device that produces pencil-thin beams of coherent monochromatic light. It is used primarily for special effects and is discussed in more detail in Chapter 6.

- Strobelight. A *strobe* is a device that gives multiple rapid bursts of high-intensity light. Strobe lighting is almost always produced by a compact xenon strobe lamp activated by a power supply and timing circuitry. Strobelights can be simple low-power devices with fixed flash rates, or sophisticated devices triggered by a lighting control console at specific intervals. It should be noted that strobe lights set at certain frequencies might trigger epileptic seizures. They are now more often integrated with new luminaires (e.g. audience blinders) rather than single units.

- Searchlight. Manufactured in World War II to detect enemy aircraft at night, searchlights are still in use today for special events. Using a carbon arc light source, they are capable of projecting a wide, intense beam of light into the sky at night. Worth noting here is a series of spectacular Nazi rallies in Nuremberg, Germany, in the late 1930s (400,000 attendees), in which designer Albert Speer created a "cathedral of light" using 130 searchlights pointed straight up 8 km into the night sky. This was arguably the first real "light show" of the 20th century.

- Neon. Neon is a type of discharge lighting generated by a high voltage across two oppositely charged electrodes at opposite ends of a long, thin glass tube filled with neon gas. As the electrical charge flows between the electrodes, electrons collide with neon atoms causing them to give off energy in the form of visible light. Different colors can be obtained by mixing other gases, or by using fluorescent coatings. For special events and advertising, the glass tube is customizable and may be bent to form letters and different shapes. Small, battery-powered neon designs are popular as table centerpieces.

- Fiber optics. Optical fibers are long, thin strands of flexible glass approximately the width of a human hair. They transmit light through a thin glass central core that is covered with an optical cladding material that reflects the light back inside the core whenever the fibers bend. This in turn is protected by an outer plastic buffer coating. These fibers are used in special event applications as battery-powered, light-emitting bundles for centerpieces or small "sculptures," and as the main light source for star drops. See also Chapter 2 on Décor.

- String lights. Also known as miniature lights, pin lights, or fairy lights, these are the typical low voltage Christmas lights that now come in strings of 50, 100, and 150. They can be plain white or colored and can also be set up to twinkle randomly. They now usually incorporate LED lamps. The latest strings come in various shapes such as swags, tree wraps, netting, icicles, and curtains. For events, they work very well in large quantities used in foliage, trees, and florals, or with sheer draping.

- DJ club effects. What was once a popular addition to events was a mirror ball, a large plastic ball covered with small mirror pieces and motorized to rotate. When a spotlight—usually a pinspot—was focused onto the ball, specks of light were thrown around the room. This effect, and many other different patterns and colors, is now achieved by small moving luminaires intended for DJ events and clubs. Some are seeing their way into the special event market.

## VOICE OF THE INDUSTRY

### An interview with Mr. Ofer Lapid

Founder and Managing Director, Gearhouse SA (Pty) Ltd.
Cape Town, Johannesburg, and Durban, South Africa
www.gearhouse.co.za

At the age of 14, Ofer Lapid began his journey into the technical side of special events by assisting technicians loading audio and lighting gear in and out of the club below his parents' apartment in his native Israel. From there, everything was up: international touring with an Israeli band; moving to South Africa and freelancing with black bands and famous South African musician Johnny Clegg; stints with musical theater, ballet, and the movies; and finally starting and expanding his own businesses. Today, Gearhouse provides audio, lighting, A-V, set design, and other services to much of continental Africa. They employ 450 people, gross over 500 million rand ($50 million USD) annually, and even have their own self-funded, in-house training academy (Gearhouse Kentse Mpahlwa Academy) for underprivileged youth as a door into the industry.

Figure 5.11 Lighting the World Cup closing ceremonies

Courtesy of Gearhouse SA (Pty) Ltd. and Louise Stickland

**DM**: What are some of the major changes you have seen in special event lighting over the last five to ten years, particularly in South Africa?

**OL**: One thing to remember is that special events [as an industry] really have only been around for the last 20 years in South Africa so we started later than everyone else. We follow the UK and

European trends and we have noticed greater quantities of lighting instruments and much more sophistication at events. It seems that people [event managers] have lost touch with the fundamentals of lighting and instead just go for a lot of movement and rapid changes in the lighting of an event. Also, you now need a good background and training to operate modern lighting consoles.

**DM**: What aspects of event lighting design and the "raw materials" (i.e. the different luminaires and their capabilities) do you think are essential knowledge for event producers or event managers?

**OL**: They should know about scheduling for setup and teardown, about the power requirements for lights, and about the budget required for lights (i.e. the more lights and the more sophistication, the more crew, and hence the more budget needed). They should also have a general understanding of what lights are available and what their capabilities are, in other words, how they will affect a show. They need to know what kinds of lights can save money and still accomplish the show.

**DM**: Do you have any comments on event safety as it pertains to lighting, considering there have been so many accidents recently?

**OL**: Mainly, there are no internationally recognized, written safety standards and that is a concern. There should be worldwide standards. However, for now we try to keep up with what is available and are members of various safety organizations such as the Event Safety Alliance (ESA) in the USA and the Production Services Association (PSA) in the UK. A specific example of another concern I have is that most trussing structures for stages are made of aluminum and that is a problem because it would be better made out of steel, since aluminum breaks more easily.

**DM**: Where do you see event lighting in five to ten years from now?

**OL**: LEDs will continue to dominate, getting faster [moving heads]. Spots like the Vari-Lites will improve. Digital control will continue to improve.

**DM**: Do you have any other words of wisdom you would like to pass on to students entering the profession of event management, or any comments about the special events industry in South Africa?

**OL**: A production manager [producer] should understand what is involved in preparing equipment for an event, break down the entire process and watch for problems and faults in that process. Health and safety are very important throughout.

They [students] should try to acquire experience in as many different types of events as possible, including rock and roll, theater, and corporate. Take the time and make the effort to invest in their career and learn what a designer is trying to achieve with an event. They must remember that they [producers] are servicing the client and are not the stars.

## 5.4 Event lighting design

Williams (1999), in his extensive online explanation of stage lighting, states that a "lighting designer must be an artist. He must understand style, composition, balance, esthetics, and human emotion. He must also understand the science of light, optics, vision, the psychology of perception, and lighting technology." Williams wrote this with reference to lighting for the theater. Although the description of the LD is true, in the special event environment the luxury of a week or more to design and install a lighting configuration for a stage performance in a theater is not an option. Designers in events have only one chance and often no more than a cursory preliminary visit to the event venue before actual installation. Often, the design has to be completed in a rush, sometimes only a matter of days or even hours before installation. Besides this minimal timeframe for design, the installation must frequently be completed the day of, or at best the day before, the event itself. Focusing of luminaires and programming of automated fixtures is often accomplished literally moments before the doors to the event open. The event LD must therefore be able to design with the same artistic flare as the theater LD but must add an equal capability to be organized and to work under extreme pressure.

Steve Matthews, owner of Vancouver, Canada-based Innovation Lighting (www.innovationlighting.net), considers a complete understanding of the following topics to be critical for successful event lighting design (S. Matthews, personal communication, September, 2014—and a note of gratitude must be added to acknowledge his assistance in writing Sections 5.4.1 through 5.4.3):

- conceptual design;
- practical design;
- physical design;
- between concept and execution;
- lighting setup, control, and operation.

## 5.4.1 Conceptual design

Before beginning the design, the LD needs to know the purpose of the event and exactly what the goals for the lighting are in the mind of the event producer. The design will ultimately fail if both LD and event producer do not agree on these. For example, is the event's purpose to be an award show with a few simple presentations, or does the event producer expect a show with enough lighting pizzazz and excitement to rival the Academy Awards? Other key questions center around what is being lit, what concept the event producer has in mind, and whether only an ambience is needed or something specific must actually be illuminated. The categories of conceptual design include theme, ambience, and practical illumination:

- Theme. This refers to the enhancement of a specific event theme, usually decorative, through the use of lighting. It can vary from complementing a theme's colors, to lighting props, tables, walls, floors, and ceiling.
- Ambience. When we think of ambience, we often imagine a quiet restaurant with soft music in the background and candlelit tables. What we are trying to do when we talk about ambience is to set a mood for an event, something that makes us feel a certain way. For the special event LD, ambience is not quite so restrictive as creating that intimate restaurant mood. The event might not be a simple dinner. It might be a rock concert requiring high-energy, automated lights for a 20-something crowd or it might be a dinner and awards show for a 50-something group of academics. Obviously, the ambience required will be vastly different for these two extremes.
- Practical illumination. This refers to more of the plain, less creative use of lighting for such mundane items as stage backdrops, lecterns, IMAG and video, and guest speakers. The practicality concern goes back to our statement at the beginning of this chapter about selective visibility, in that an audience must be able to see only what they need to see when they need to see it.

## 5.4.2 Practical design

Keeping the three categories of conceptual design in mind, the LD moves on to practical design. Practical design forces the LD to consider how all the design elements and design principles that we discussed in Section 5.1 will be used to accomplish the goals set out by the event producer. Let us examine the practical applications of this theory.

### 5.4.2.1 Lighting for themes

Décor and event theming using light is a vast field with perhaps only a handful of truly gifted LDs in North America. When it is done well, it is usually the single event component that causes gasps from guests as they enter the event space. Some practical considerations that have proven effective for designers include:

- Using complementary colors for props, such as greens to enhance trees, and reds or ambers to enhance wood.
- Choosing the event colors at the outset with the event producer and trying to keep the lighting in those color families.
- Using lighting in conjunction with special effects, each to enhance the other. Examples include lighting along a path at floor level under fog, rapid automated light movement to enhance indoor pyro and confetti cannons, or lighting effects and gobo patterns on a *water scrim*.
- Using all the dimensions and surfaces within the event space. They can all be used for lighting: ceilings for cloud patterns or changing colors; walls for theme gobos or uplighting; floors for gobos, color washes, and wild movement. See Figure 5.12 (top).
- Striving for the unusual, such as: lighting under tables; unique lighting of table centers (not necessarily pinspots but battery-powered LEDs or mini lights); reverse lighting of the audience instead of the event space and walls; lighting of different event elements and theme prop vignettes at different times as the event progresses.
- Flying luminaires as much as possible in order to minimize clutter and distraction. For example, pinspotting table centers from above is effective and classy.
- Keeping instruments hidden from view and out of people's eyes.

### 5.4.2.2 Lighting for ambience

If this can be done very subtly, the effect is better and often can affect the mood of the event and of the guests. Some considerations that help to achieve the right mood, be it low key or highly exciting, include the following:

- Using indirect lighting for such things as walls, ceilings, pillars, and tables.
- Using the psychology of color. This means that colors used for lighting must be flattering to the attendees (stay away from cool colors that do not flatter the skin), yet must create a dramatic and desirable environment to be in. Refer to Section 5.2.3 for more information.
- Using color-changing instruments that can be programmed to change slowly over time and thus give a continuously new look and feel to the event every few minutes.
- Minimizing jolting contrast changes, such as a quick movement from purple to orange or yellow, or from red to blue, rather making it a more gradual, subtle movement through several colors.
- Generally keeping brightness levels low. See Figure 5.12 (bottom).
- Trying to avoid light spillage on unwanted or extraneous objects.

### 5.4.2.3 Lighting for specific needs

Most events have some element of the more mundane such as the need to light the company president giving his annual address or award recipients as they come onstage. Often, the mundane must be mixed with the need for ambience and theming, and it is necessary to plan for this well ahead of time since many luminaires can serve double duty, especially automated fixtures. Some of the considerations for practical lighting include the following:

Lighting for a theme

Lighting for ambience

Figure 5.12  Examples of practical lighting design

Images courtesy of: top—Innovation Lighting, www.innovationlighting.net;
bottom—Images by Lighting, ESPY's VIP Post Party produced by Silver Birches,
photographer Brian Callaway

- Lighting for live entertainment. Using front lighting is best to illuminate performers for visibility, but back lighting to create energy and to set the mood for the performance. The inclusion of automated fixtures on a back line is common in many high-energy performances. If a single performer or small group of performers is onstage, or especially going to be roving throughout the audience, one or more followspots is recommended. Depending on the type of performance (e.g. themed cirque-type show, comedy, dance, or music), a variety of front color washes is probably required so that the entire stage will be covered with even light, but also so that different onstage moods can be created for different segments of the performance. Typically, single luminaires (e.g. ERS or Fresnel) are used to isolate and focus on individual performers who may be important within a group, such as soloists in a band. The best way to provide for all contingencies in lighting a stage performance is to discuss in as much detail as possible the needs of individual acts and performers, and then ensure that the LD is able to provide for those needs with a sufficient variety and number of luminaires.

- Lighting for video. Using colored filters is not recommended, as the cameras require a common light color among all fixtures as well as a consistent temperature. Filters should only be used to correct for color temperature. Normally, lighting for the camera is bright and white. Cameras are less forgiving of color variations than is the human eye. Back light is also essential to create a visual separation between the subject and the background.

- Lighting for people other than entertainers. Front light coming from two sides helps to eliminate shadows. Complementary colored filters help to enhance the appearance of good health. Warm colors (pinks and ambers) improve the apparent health of the subject and cool colors (blues and lavenders) enhance the colors in clothing and sets (see again Table 5.1). Back lighting is also recommended, although not always necessary, again to separate the subject from the background.

- Lighting for attention. "Attention" generally refers to the use of flashy effects and new concepts in order to grab the attention of the audience, often in preparation for an important presentation or stage performance segment. Considerations include the following:

  - Projecting a logo as a gobo design is simple, inexpensive, and rewarding. Everyone likes to see their name in lights, and they can be projected on walls, ceilings, floors, screens, or any other reflective surface.

  - Automated lighting is an excellent way to add professional pizzazz and high-energy flash to an awards show or gala event. Using moving luminaires, or even more effectively digital lights as described earlier, allows unlimited combinations of graphics, gobos, lighting effects, and computer images to be used throughout a three-dimensional space.

### 5.4.3 Physical design

The physical design of the event lighting refers to how it will be accomplished. This is when the designer brings out his toolbox and puts the right luminaires in the right number in the right location and makes the magic happen. Primary considerations include the design of the venue itself, where and how the luminaires will be mounted, the number and variety of luminaires, and where and how lighting will be controlled.

#### 5.4.3.1 Venue physical characteristics

Every event space is different and an early site visit prior to designing the event lighting is essential. This enables the LD to mold the space with light. It also helps to establish the optimum number and types of luminaires to be used. The purpose of the site visit is to help the LD understand the following, especially if the event is to be held in an indoor venue:

- Shape of the room. Is it open, square, round, or oddly shaped and does it contain obstructions like pillars?

- Ceiling height and design. If the ceiling is too high or too low, lighting will be impacted and the effects either heightened or lessened, requiring either more or fewer luminaires. If large chandeliers or complex recesses form large parts of the ceiling, extra luminaires may be needed or a different approach taken. For example, lighting can be reflected off large crystal chandeliers without the chandeliers being turned on, to create spectacular colored ambient effects on the ceiling.

- Control of existing house and ambient lighting. Will daylight through windows or translucent ceiling material such as tenting be a factor in lighting design? Where and how is house lighting controlled and can a remote controller be used at a lighting control console position in order to save time and effort in turning house lights on and off?

- Stage position. Where will the stage or stages be positioned and how large will they be? Will there be one main stage and/or several satellite stages that need separate lighting or could one or two followspots be sufficient to light the satellite stages? Will there be a backstage area that requires work lights for performers or other technical personnel? Will there be elements of a stage set that require unique lighting? Often, these questions will require input from the event producer as well as the venue manager.

### 5.4.3.2 *Lighting support*

Luminaires must be mounted on something and in a location that provides optimum illumination to achieve the goals of the lighting design. Even though it could be directly on the floor or other surface (e.g. table, stage, or décor), the exact location, method of mounting and support, and tentative setup time required have to be determined well before the event takes place. The site visit is vital to establishing this.

- Location of lighting support. The LD will be asking a number of key questions during the site visit to best determine where the lights will be positioned:

  - Will lighting be flown (i.e. rigged from the ceiling) or ground supported on lighting trees or lifts? If flown, the designer must know the exact location of ceiling hanging points, how many there are, and what their load rating is. Flying lighting or audio is normally a much more expensive proposition than ground supporting it due to the additional work and time required, sometimes including the use of qualified union labor, extra time to rig the ceiling points, and time delay for other installation components such as décor and dining tables.

  - If trees or lifts are used, where should they be placed? Prime locations must be chosen to permit optimum lighting of stages and sets without blocking sight lines, without creating hazards to foot traffic, by eliminating lights in guests' eyes, and by minimizing cable runs.

  - Are there permanent obstructions in the venue? If there are pillars in the room or sets and other décor elements that might block the path of light from any luminaires, then the design must be changed or a new support method devised.

  - If followspots are to be used, where is the optimum location for them and will risers be required to elevate them to the required height?

- Ground-supported systems. Ground support can be simple or complex. Here are the possibilities in ascending order of complexity:

  - Placement on a surface. The simple version can mean actually placing the luminaires on the ground, floor, or other surface, such as a stage, table, audio speaker, or décor piece. In this situation, the luminaire is simply plugged into either a separate electrical circuit or into a dimmer circuit, focused, and controlled from the lighting console. Many luminaires today come with dual, movable yokes designed specifically for mounting on flat surfaces. Increasingly, luminaires of different designs are being equipped with long-life batteries enabling remote control using infrared (IR) or RF signals without any wiring.

  - Lighting trees. A second type of ground support uses *lighting trees*. These are simple aluminum structures comprising a horizontal bar to which the luminaires are clamped, usually from four to six fixtures such as Fresnels or PARs, and a vertical, adjustable, aluminum support pole with a tripod base. Trees are a good solution for lighting a simple and low-budget stage performance, and they also are good if setup time is minimal. The setup normally incorporates one tree on each side of the stage with luminaires from each tree cross-focused to light the entire stage in a wash.

- Genie lift-supported truss or *lift*. Continuing upwards in complexity, the next form of ground-supported system incorporates a special heavy-duty support machine called a *Genie® Super Tower™*, manufactured by Genie Industries. This machine is wheeled and vertically extendable, capable of supporting up to 800 pounds (363 kg) of weight, making it excellent for supporting a long *truss* line with many luminaires.

The remaining ground-supported systems—*rigging tower*, *ground-supported tower*, and *roof system*—are variations of designs constructed entirely out of metal trussing. Most of these are used in outdoor events, although they are occasionally found inside large venues like arenas or stadia where flying from high roofs is discouraged or difficult. Because of its complexity and the need for critical load calculations when mounting luminaires on it, we will deal with trussing in detail separately in Section 9.2 of Chapter 9.

- Flown systems. A flown system is one in which lighting trussing is attached to hanging points (mounting hooks or bolts stressed to carry a certain load) in a ceiling of a venue, usually by means of heavy-duty chains and pulleys or chains and a motor. Flown systems may also support audio speakers and audio-visual projectors on the same truss line as the lighting. Black masking drape is often used to hide the truss structure once the system is in place. The term "flown" can also refer to mounting luminaires on the larger, ground-supported systems mentioned above. Once again, this subject is discussed in Section 9.2 of Chapter 9.

### 5.4.3.3 Types of luminaires

Deciding on the number and type of luminaires to use is what makes a good LD and can make or break the effectiveness of the lighting design. Of all the instruments available from the lighting toolbox, the designer must choose the ones that will best achieve the event goals, including budgetary goals. In making this decision, the LD must review the following:

- Required intensity. How bright must each luminaire be to give the effect desired? Most lights come in multiples of 100 W power.
- Required color. What is being lit and how will it be affected by different colors? Are colors required to enhance the effect? The types of gels or gobos to use will be determined by the answer to this question. This question becomes less important with LED luminaires since most can project a variety of colors without the need for gels.
- Required coverage. How big an area must each luminaire cover? Will the budget allow for only eight luminaires to illuminate a 32 ft wide x 24 ft deep (9.6 m x 7.2 m) stage, or can more luminaires be added? The answers will determine the number and type of luminaires to be used.
- Required functionality. Is some high-energy pizzazz needed or just static lighting for a speech? Will the person or thing being lit be in motion? The more pizzazz, the more costly because moving luminaires will probably be used.
- Power. What will the total power consumption be? See Section 9.1 of Chapter 9 for more detail on power calculations.
- Cost. What is the budget for lighting?

### 5.4.3.4 Lighting console position

Most events require a location for the lighting operator and the lighting console(s). The last concern on the site visit is to determine where control will be and if technicians will be required to operate the lights during the event. Usually, the best location for controlling lighting is in the middle of the venue at the back of the event space, ideally directly opposite any performance stage (i.e. at the FOH position near the audio console); however, practicality does not always allow this. The designer must know the exact location in relation to power supplied in order to determine the length and routing of cable runs. In addition, the designer must know if the lit objects or people will be easily viewable, if there will be a raised platform for the control area, and if a remote house light control will be available at the console position.

## 5.5 Between concept and execution

What we have been doing up to this point in our discussion of lighting design is to follow a typical LD through the necessary steps and thought processes required to arrive at a tentative design for the special event. This design might include lighting for entertainment, for décor, or for architecture, and it might be either indoors or outdoors. Having now asked all the right questions and determined the type of lighting that is needed, the LD will return to his shop and take several more steps in preparation for setting up the event.

First, if the event is relatively complex, meaning that there will be a large number of different luminaires used, possibly mounted on a large truss structure, or in several different locations, the LD will choose the required luminaires and determine where they will be mounted based on an analysis of the answers to the questions asked previously. These choices will then be laid out on a *lighting plot* or *lighting plan*. This is simply a hand or CADD drawing of all the specific fixtures in their exact locations, drawn to scale and in relation to what they are lighting (e.g. stage or décor element). The drawing also indicates for each fixture its dimmer and channel assignments, the fixture number and type, and any and all accessories such as color filters required. For some events, an LD will draw a three-dimensional rendering of the lighting plan in CADD, which gives a very accurate visualization of the exact lighting effects, since the latest CADD software takes into account the types of lights and the amount of light, the various surfaces in the space including their reflectivity, and integrates it all into an accurate picture. Two of the more common programs now used for such three-dimensional representations are Vivien from Cast Group and Vectorworks from Nemetschek. CADD is also discussed in detail in Chapter 9 of *Special Event Production: The Process*.

See Figure 5.13 for a sample two-dimensional event stage lighting plot drawn in CADD. This is the lighting plot used for the event depicted in Figure 5.12 (top).

Second, and now with the lighting plot in hand, the LD will prepare a crew and installation schedule, along with power requirements, which will be passed to the producer, and then to the venue. In considering the crew required, often for complex events, the LD will not be the person present but instead the lighting crew will consist of one main operator (crew chief), possibly one programmer for automated fixtures, and one or more followspot operators. In addition, the LD—or the setup crew chief—will prepare all the necessary control and dimming equipment, the mounting and support hardware for the complete lighting installation, and load calculations for the rigging company if lighting is to be mounted on trussing.

## 5.6 Lighting control

The control system allows each luminaire to be controlled (e.g. dimmed, faded in and out, shut on or off, color changed, movement changed, gobo patterns changed, etc.) from a central location. It incorporates a dimming system, a control protocol, and a lighting control console.

### 5.6.1 Dimming system

In most event lighting situations, luminaires are not used constantly at full power but must occasionally be dimmed, faded, or turned off. This is accomplished by using dimmers.

In a traditional lighting setup in which only older conventional luminaires are used, each dimmer regulates one lighting circuit, or channel, allowing the attached luminaire's intensity to vary by altering the electrical

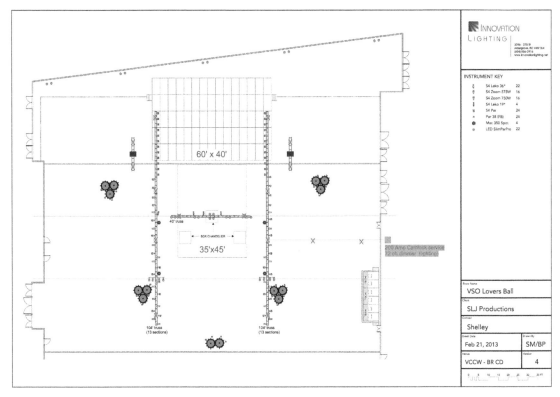

Figure 5.13  Example of a 2D event lighting plot

Courtesy of Innovation Lighting, www.innovationlighting.net

current sent to the luminaire. Each dimmer is designed to work to a maximum electrical load. For example, a 2,000 W dimmer might be loaded with two 1,000 W ERS spotlights or up to four 500 W luminaires (such as four PAR64s). This is an important point to remember. If one dimmer channel is assigned to one luminaire, only that luminaire will dim when the channel is used; however, if the dimmer channel is assigned to four luminaires, all four luminaires will dim at once when the channel is used. The LD will determine the best combinations of luminaires and dimmer channels in his concept and lighting plot.

A typical dimmer pack comprises several dimmer modules, all housed together. They may even be conveniently mounted on rolling racks, enabling the control of many lighting circuits. The dimmer packs are usually physically located in the event space close to the stage, or as close as possible to electrical power and ideally the luminaires as well. See Figure 5.14 and also Section 9.1.2.2 of Chapter 9.

Remember, what has just been described applies only to conventional luminaires that are not designed internally to be controlled by *digital multiplex* (DMX). With the advent of DMX, each luminaire can be individually controlled without the need for a dimmer pack. Let's look at exactly what DMX can do.

### 5.6.2 Control protocol

Control protocol refers to the language used to communicate between the luminaires, dimmers, and control console. In 1986, a new digital standard was created for the lighting industry called DMX (digital multiplex), with today's version being DMX512. The notation refers to a digital signal, which is a set of

512 separate channels or *intensity levels* that are constantly being updated at the rate of 44 times per second. Each channel/level has 256 steps divided over a range of 0 to 100 percent, and each set of 512 channels is defined as a *universe*. A DMX universe can be made up of many different devices that all use a set amount of channels. However, DMX512 has some limitations and must fall within the following limits:

- No more than 512 channels per universe.
- No more than 32 devices [e.g. luminaires] per universe connected in a daisy chain [however, this can be overcome—see below].
- The network cannot have cabling runs of more than 3,900 ft (1000 m) [this can also be overcome—see below]

(Seasonal Entertainment, 2012)

How does this all work? Think of an individual channel as being like a simple fader on an audio console with 256 steps. Such a channel can be used to control any number of variables because it has a unique, identifiable address. The DMX signal is sent from the control console along a single cable—specifically a 5-pin XLR type—to the luminaires which are connected in a daisy chain fashion, with DMX going into the first luminaire then out to the second, and so on to the end where there is a special terminator to stop the signal.

For a simple luminaire like a PAR can with minimal functionality, a single channel may just be used to dim the luminaire, which would equate to one device using one channel. For a more complex luminaire like an LED moving fixture, a single channel might control panning, another might control red color, another green, another blue, another the gobos, and still another a strobe function. In other words, the more complicated and functional the luminaire, the more channels will probably be required for maximum control of all functions. Thus it would be very easy to eat up the available channels in a single universe with far fewer than 32 devices/luminaires. Fortunately, there are ways around this.

The first way is to give two or more luminaires the same *base address*. The base address corresponds to one DMX channel and, for example, could be "001." If we assume that there are four luminaires that also each need three channels for controlling red, green, and blue colors, then the next three addresses would be "002 (for red), 003 (for green), and 004 (for blue)" for luminaire #1. For luminaire #2, if it was to be controlled independently, it would require "005" as its base address and "006, 007, and 008" as the addresses to control its red, green, and blue colors. However, by changing its base address to "001," the same as luminaire #1, when the faders on the console corresponding to red (e.g. fader numbers 2 and 6) are moved, **both** luminaires will fade in exactly the same manner. Even if more luminaires are added but all have the same base address (i.e. "001"), then they will all respond in the same manner to a control. In other words, by combining luminaires it is possible to control many more than 32 luminaires with one DMX universe.

The second way to add luminaires in a single universe is to use a DMX *splitter/repeater* or *opto-isolator* which can extend both cable distance beyond 3,900 ft (as the signal is regenerated and re-transmitted) and the number of devices on a single DMX universe. Each branch of a splitter/repeater can support up to 32 devices, so theoretically there is no limit to the number of devices controllable within a single universe. The splitter acts in a similar fashion as a router does for splitting an Internet signal (either by WiFi or hard wiring) and sending it to different computers/devices. It may be placed anywhere but is often found either near the lighting console or with the dimmer packs.

The last way to add luminaires is to increase the number of universes, and this can only be done by using a console that has more than a single "DMX Out," meaning that it can provide more than one DMX512 universe. For each additional "DMX Out," there are another 512 available channels.

The last point to understand about DMX512 protocol is that it can still control older conventional luminaires that are not equipped with DMX controllability, as described in Section 5.6.1. For example, dimming these luminaires can be done by running the DMX signal through a set of DMX-capable dimmers, again in a daisy chain setup, which will basically read the DMX signal then transmit it as a variable voltage to the conventional luminaires via a regular power cable. If there is more than one luminaire being dimmed, then a special cable known as *Socapex* bundles all the individual cables and carries them together to a position close to the actual luminaires, where an adaptor—also called a *splay*—once again splits them to go to the individual luminaires via separate wiring (see also Section 9.1.2.2 and Figure 9.2 of Chapter 9 for more details). They are then treated as a single device and dimmed together. Note that DMX-controllable luminaires must also be powered and they receive their power in exactly the same manner as the non-DMX-controllable luminaires (i.e. via regular power cables and/or Socapex).

Figure 5.14 illustrates DMX lighting control for both DMX and non-DMX-controllable luminaires. Note how the non-DMX-controllable luminaires on the left side are controlled from the console via dimmer packs—as explained above—while the newer luminaires on the right side that are DMX-controllable are controlled directly from the console via the DMX cable and daisy-chaining of the luminaires. All that comes from the dimmer packs for these luminaires (DMX-controllable) is power.

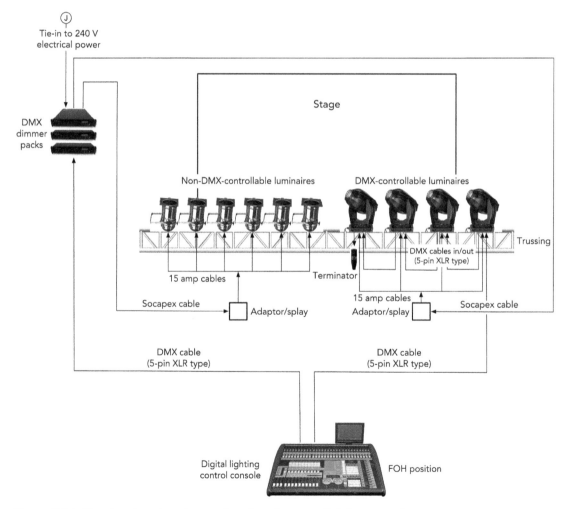

Figure 5.14 Signal path and equipment locations for event lighting control

Courtesy of Doug Matthews

The future for DMX control is exciting. While it will probably remain at the heart of lighting control for some time, there are improvements coming rapidly. *Remote Device Management* (RDM) is one such improvement. DMX uses only one-way communication (i.e. from the control console to the luminaires) to control lighting. RDM protocol will allow configuration, status monitoring, and management of devices in such a way that it does not disturb the normal operation of standard DMX512 devices that do not recognize the RDM protocol. In other words, RDM uses two-way communication and will still play nicely with DMX. This means that such tasks as setting the addresses for luminaires and configuring their functions can all be done remotely.

A second development already available is *Art-Net* or *ArtNET*. This is a control protocol that basically takes DMX signals and transports them using the Internet. Thus, signals can be sent in either of two ways, via an Ethernet cable (discussed in Chapters 3 and 4) or wirelessly via WiFi. When the signals must be read by a DMX device (e.g. a luminaire), they are converted back to that form using a special adaptor. The main advantage of Art-Net is considerably reduced cabling requirements and, as might be expected, there are already apps available that use it with tablets and smartphones for remote control.

### 5.6.3 Control console

This is the front end of the lighting control system. It is the equivalent in lighting to what the mixer is in audio. Simple stage lighting (i.e. conventional luminaires) can be controlled using a manual control console. This has a single level control or *fader* for each dimmer channel. It might also provide for two faders per channel, allowing the operator to set up two separate *scenes* (combinations of lights) and *cross-fade* (fade one scene in at the same time the other is fading out) between them.

More complex event lighting requirements will be handled by a *digital memory control console*. This is really just a computer with a complex interface built in. Most of these consoles are capable of storing dozens—or hundreds—of different scenes just as with an audio console, allowing for countless different "looks" to be created and programmed ahead of the event. For example, a low light level, cool-colored background for a musical ballad might be followed immediately by a high-energy rock dance routine requiring moving luminaires and warm colors, a change that is easily accomplished with pre-set scenes and fade times. Modern consoles also allow for *soft-patching*, or the assignment of more than one individual dimmer channel to a console channel. This allows more luminaires to be controlled as a logical unit than a single dimmer channel allows. Many of the higher-end consoles have more than one DMX universe, which simply means that they can handle 512 more separate channels for each DMX universe.

Most state-of-the-art lighting control consoles have fully automated fixture control built into them, including some form of *joystick* or moving control wheel. With the multiple DMX universes available, the many channels needed no longer pose a major problem. Newer consoles can also handle LED fixtures and video inputs (via a separate *video processing unit*), and operate off 120 V/60 Hz or 240 V/50 Hz, making them universally adaptable.

Finally, thanks to advancing technology, wireless lighting control is now possible in much the same way as wireless audio. Strategically placed transmitters and receivers send and receive the digital signal, eliminating long cable runs between the console and the luminaires, using the control protocol known as Art-Net discussed above.

## 5.7 Lighting setup and operation

Lighting often requires considerable time for setup due to several factors that render it different from other technical equipment. It is a labor- and time-intensive series of tasks that need to be done correctly or not only will the show be potentially poorly lit, but there may be a very real danger of physical injury to event attendees.

### 5.7.1 Lighting setup

In all but the simplest of events, invariably the lighting must be mounted on support trussing which must be *rigged* or suspended from a ceiling, if the event is indoors. Rigging (discussed in more detail in Chapter 9) has to be accomplished as the first of a long list of tasks in the setup process. Lighting is different because it must not only be rigged and suspended from trussing, but conventional fixtures must also be focused. This means that an extra trip up a special automated scissor lift or a ladder must be made once the trussing is in place, and because the lights are usually suspended over a floor area where other event elements might be placed such as dining tables or theater seating, this has to be accomplished while the venue is still empty.

Fortunately, most luminaires used in special events are DMX-controllable, thus eliminating some of the extra work of manual focus. However, if automated fixtures are part of the lighting plan, then a dedicated time for programming may also be required, ideally when nothing else is happening within the venue and it can be darkened. Working backwards, all these factors dictate that lighting be given special treatment in terms of allowed time for setup, especially since it is usually the first equipment to be installed. Unfortunately, sometimes this may only be accomplished at times when nobody else is working, such as between midnight and 6:00 am. For these reasons, and to determine crew numbers, the LD needs to know:

- how early they can get in for setup, possibly up to 48 h before the event;
- how long it will take to move equipment into the venue and room, including accessibility for trucks at the loading dock and availability of truck parking;
- who will be competing for floor space;
- whether "dark time" for programming of automated fixtures and focus time for conventional luminaires will be needed;
- how long the show is;
- what time equipment *strike* (teardown) will begin and what time it must be complete;
- if the venue is union run and if specialized workers such as riggers will be required;
- what is required in terms of equipment to comply with venue safety regulations (e.g. hard hats, steel-toed boots, and safety vests for workers);
- if any special permits or badging will be required.

---

### PRODUCTION WAR STORY

#### Learning on the fly

A few years ago I was working on a show for a very good client. My lighting designer had planned well for this show and the setup had gone amazingly well. We were completely ready well before doors and settling in for a fun evening.

Thirty minutes before the guests were to enter, my lighting operator came to me, his face completely white.

"I just got a phone call, my parents were in a bad car accident, I don't know what to do."

At this point all my crew had left, it was just he and I in the room, and I did the only possible thing at that moment, I told him to leave right away and take care of his parents. I would run the show.

The console we were using was a WholeHog 3; I was loosely familiar with its predecessor but had never used one of these before. I spent the next 30 minutes making sure I knew what was programmed and that I could access the most basic functions like room color and stage levels.

The doors opened and guests entered amidst "oohs" and "aahs" to a beautiful room. The night progressed and I was able to bring up stage lights for presenters, and lights for the band. I even got the back lights to color chase. Yes, I had everything figured out.

Dinner was over and the band was well into their set when I noticed that a couple of the band lights and some of the moving lights had gone out. Too many to be bulbs, in fact too many to be a simple breaker. Fortunately the dimmer rack was right beside me so I dove right in with my iPhone flashlight to figure out the problem. Two minutes of trouble-shooting confirmed my fears: we had blown a main fuse in the building power service. Options: call building maintenance to replace it—no, they'd take 30 minutes to get here and we'd have to shut everything down for them to fix the problem. Solution: repatch the dimmer and distro to hot up the barest minimum for the show to continue unhindered, while trying to reduce the load on the remaining two legs to prevent any more issues.

Great, we were up and running again—a little hamstrung, but the bulk of the evening was behind us.

The event was to end at midnight. Sure enough, at 11:00 pm I'm running a chase on the console when I lose the monitor. Great, just what I need, the console has crashed—or so I thought. I cycled the power off and back on. Nothing. Then my heart stopped as I realized the console was plugged into my distro panel. I looked up to find the majority of my stage lights had also shut off. This time it only took me a few seconds to figure out that I had lost another leg of power—on a 3-phase service—meaning that I only had one-third of my rig capacity left. This time it took some really fast and fancy repatching, plus using a few wall plugs and voila, the show was still running! I looked over at the two audio guys whose jaws had hit the floor by this point, simply shaking their heads asking how I had managed to keep the show running? I simply smiled back, held my breath and prayed for the show to end before my luck ran out.

Finally the stroke of midnight and the room lights came up. I spent a few minutes tidying up the console, and greeting the strike crew while telling them about my evening. Just as I was about to leave, the client walked up to me and thanked me up and down for a fantastic evening, everyone had a great time and the room looked amazing!

As if only noticing for the first time, she asked, "By the way, where's your regular operator? I hadn't expected to see you here."

"Oh, he had to leave so I decided to give this one a shot on my own." She had no clue that there was the slightest problem at any point through the night.

(Courtesy of Steve Matthews, Innovation Lighting, Burnaby, BC, Canada)

Once the answers are known, the setup can proceed. It involves the following tasks:

- Preparation of all equipment in the shop. Often this includes a pre-hang of luminaires on sections of truss in order to save time onsite.
- Delivery and load-in of equipment.
- Installation of *chain-falls* and *motors* (or pulleys) from the venue ceiling rigging points (see Section 9.3.2.2 of Chapter 9). These are used to support the lighting trussing.
- Construction of all trussing by piecing together the pre-hung sections, then attaching the completed trussing to the chain-falls.
- If the lighting is conventional and non-DMX-controllable, then also the following:
  - Tying dimmers and console into house power, or portable power if outdoors.
  - Attaching all luminaires to Socapex cables via six-outlet adaptors and running Socapex cabling through the trussing to the dimmers.
- Raising the trussing into place using the chain-falls and motors, being cautious to ensure that safety is paramount and that the trussing is level at all times.
- Running the main DMX cable from the dimmer packs located usually near the stage—or from DMX-controllable luminaires directly—to the lighting control console.
- Assigning all lighting channels and programmed sequences to individual console channels.
- Testing all channels and luminaires.
- Focusing and gelling all luminaires (if conventional and non-DMX-controllable).

If time permits, it is always a good idea to have the main lighting operator (usually the crew chief), automated fixture programmer if there is one, and any other techs such as followspot operators conduct a run-through of the event from *cue-to-cue* so that all the lighting looks or scenes for various show and event segments are known to the operators, to the TD, and also are approved by the event producer.

### 5.7.2 Lighting operation during the event

Lighting operation during the actual event may be simple or complicated, depending on whether or not pre-set scenes are used and whether or not the event calls for numerous manual changes to the lighting.

Up to this point, we have not mentioned much about lighting that is not used for the stage. However, many special events nowadays use lighting as a major component of décor. This means that a similar procedure must be followed for positioning and setting up décor lighting as for stage lighting. The big difference is that much of the décor lighting tends to be very subtle and hidden, often mounted on the ground and behind or inside props or fabrics. Just as with stage lighting, décor lighting can be pre-programmed for specific room "looks" such as gradual ambient lighting changes using wall up lighting to create a variety of moods. This can usually be accomplished by the main lighting operator in conjunction with the stage lighting, and is often controlled by the same lighting console.

Thus, for the event itself and stage performances, the lighting operator will be doing the following during the event:

- Monitoring ambient light levels for mood, including house lights.
- Monitoring stage lighting for unexpected stage requirements.
- Monitoring light spill onto other event elements such as multimedia screens.
- Either manually changing lighting scenes for stage needs or changing pre-set scenes based on rehearsed, verbal, or written lighting cues. Manual changes may require: turning lights on and off in time to music

if this function is not automated; fading to black at the end of stage performances or musical numbers, or on script cues; and changing colors, gobos, movement, brightness, and such for different needs.

- Giving cues to other lighting technicians such as automated lighting programmers and followspot operators.
- Maintaining communication with the TD or event producer to change lighting when needed and to be aware of changes to the event running order.

## 5.8 Risk and safety

Since it is the lighting company that usually provides the trussing for the luminaires and often for the audio gear (e.g. full-range speakers), it must also be the LD and lighting company that provide accurate load calculations for rigging, complete with exact luminaire locations on the trussing and the accompanying weights, along with the load data provided for any audio gear. Producers should demand that these calculations be made available when needed and certainly for record purposes should an insurance claim ever arise following the event. Concerning trussing, the lighting company should be fully conversant with all standards that apply to trussing and rigging as laid out in Chapter 9. Also with respect to rigging, knowing the correct *trim height* for any lighting trussing is essential to avoid last-minute panics to re-focus luminaires and raise or lower truss (see Chapter 9 for more on trim height).

Lighting does have unique equipment and once again, the use of only UL (Underwriters Laboratories Inc.) and CSA (Canadian Standards Association) certified equipment applies as much to lighting as to audio. In addition, *IEC 60598-1 Ed. 6.1: Luminaires – Part 1: General requirements and tests*, an international standard, covers classification, marking, mechanical construction, and electrical construction of luminaires in Canada, the United States, and other countries. Otherwise, lighting—and especially lighting control protocol—has several other currently known equipment standards and guidelines as listed below. Producers should ensure that lighting subcontractors are conversant with and follow these standards where applicable:

- *Canadian Standards Association (CSA) C22.2 NO. 166-M1983 (R2013): Stage and Studio Luminaires (for Canada).*
- *CAN/CSA-E598-2-17-98 (R2012): Luminaires – Part 2: Particular requirements – Section Seventeen – Luminaires for stage lighting, television and film studio (outdoor and indoor).*
- *ANSI E1.3 – 2001 (R2011): Entertainment Technology – Lighting Control Systems – 0 to 10V Analog Control Specification ANSI E1.11 – 2008 (R2013): Entertainment Technology – USITT DMX512-A, Asynchronous Serial Digital Data Transmission Standard for Controlling Lighting Equipment and Accessories.*
- *ANSI E1.17 – 2010: Entertainment Technology – Architecture for Control Networks (ACN).*
- *ANSI E1.20 – 2010: Entertainment Technology – RDM-Remote Device Management over USITT DMX512 Networks.*
- *ANSI E1.25 – 2012: Recommended Basic Conditions for Measuring the Photometric Output of Stage and Studio Luminaires by Measuring Illumination Levels Produced on a Planar Surface.*
- *ANSI E1.27-1 – 2006 (R2011): Entertainment Technology – Standard for Portable Control Cables for Use with USITT DMX512/1990 and E1.11 (DMX512-A) Products.*
- *ANSI E1.27-2 – 2009 (R2014): Entertainment Technology – Recommended Practice for Permanently Installed Control Cables for Use with ANSI E1.11 (DMX512-A) and USITT DMX512/1990 Products.*
- *ANSI E1.28 – 2011: Guidance on planning followspot positions in places of public assembly.*
- *ANSI E1.30-1 – 2010: EPI 23: Device Identification Subdevice.*
- *ANSI E1.30-3 – 2009 (R2014): EPI 25, Time Reference in ACN Systems Using SNTP and NTP.*
- *ANSI E1.30-4 – 2010: EPI 26. Device Description Language (DDL) Extensions for DMX512 and E1.31 Devices.*

- *ANSI E1.30-7 – 2009: EPI 29, Allocation of Internet Protocol Version 4 Addresses to ACN Hosts.*
- *ANSI E1.30-10 – 2009 (R2014): EPI 32, Identification of Draft Device Description Language Modules.*
- *ANSI E1.31 – 2009: Entertainment Technology – Lightweight streaming protocol for transport of DMX512 using CAN.*
- *ANSI E1.32 – 2012: Guide for the Inspection of Entertainment Industry Incandescent Lamp Luminaires.*
- *ANSI E1.35 – 2013: Standard for Lens Quality Measurements for Pattern Projecting Luminaires Intended for Entertainment Use.*
- *ANSI E1.36 – 2007 (R2012): Model Procedure for Permitting the Use of Tungsten-Halogen Incandescent Lamps and Stage and Studio Luminaires in Vendor Exhibit Booths in Convention and Trade Show Exhibition Halls.*
- *ANSI E1.37-1 – 2012: Additional Message Sets for ANSI E1.20 (RDM) – Part 1, Dimmer Message Sets.*
- *ANSI E1.41 – 2012: Recommendations for Measuring and Reporting Photometric Performance Data for Entertainment Luminaires Utilizing Solid State Light Sources.*
- *ANSI E1.45 – 2013: Unidirectional Transport of IEEE 802 data frames over ANSI E1.11 (DMX512-A).*
- *ANSI E1.48 – 2014: A Recommended Luminous Efficiency Function for Stage and Studio Luminaire Photometry.*
- *Application Guide for ANSI E1.3 – 2001, Lighting Control Systems 0 to 10V Analog Control Specifications.*
- Bennette, A. (2008). *Recommended Practice for DMX512: A Guide for Users and Installers.* Eastbourne, UK: PLASA.
- *Recommended Practice for Ethernet Cabling Systems in Entertainment Lighting Applications and the Supplement to the Recommended Practice for Ethernet Cabling Systems in Entertainment Lighting Applications,* available from http://tsp.plasa.org/tsp/documents/docs/EthernetPracticeAndSupplement.pdf.
- Other ANSI standards with respect to rigging for lighting systems that must be flown, available from www.plasa.org.

Updated information on these equipment standards and guidelines may be found by regularly checking the PLASA web site at www.plasa.org. PLASA is the lead international membership body for those who supply technologies and services to the event, entertainment, and installation industries.

Regarding personnel safety, the same OSHA and WCB worker health and safety standards and regulations apply for lighting personnel as they do for all others. Chapter 7 of *Special Event Production: The Process* refers to the controlling organizations for these standards in many countries. As well, compliance with the national electrical codes for the United States, Canada, and all other countries in which an event may be taking place is absolutely essential for lighting. Chapter 9 explains these in more detail.

With respect to performer and audience safety, Cooper (2014, pp. 190–191) deals with the need to test any flown luminaires in a performance situation before an event takes place to ensure their safe installation.

As with audio, redundancy and qualified personnel are considerations for lighting. Although changing or re-focusing lights mid-show is impractical in most event situations—unless full remote control is possible—bringing extra equipment such as spare dimmers, backup CD/DVD/flash drive with programs for a digital console, or even an entire lighting console for the more important lighting events should be considered as a hedge against complete lighting failure. As for trained personnel, producers should keep in mind that much of the new digital equipment (e.g. digital fixtures and lighting consoles) requires that technicians take specialized courses to operate it and also that programming it can literally take hours onsite prior to an event, depending on how many lighting cues there are. Allowances for programming and checks on technician qualifications should be made.

Event lighting is constantly evolving, at least equally as fast as any of the other technologies. The goal of this chapter has been to provide a snapshot of the technology at this point in time and to give the basics of how it all works. Further reading is encouraged to keep up to date in this exciting field.

## PRODUCTION CHALLENGES

1. You are an event producer planning for a corporate presentation by a company president who will be speaking from a lectern on a stage, accompanied by PowerPoint on a screen behind the speaker. Recommend the type of lighting you would use and from what directions you would light the speaker.

2. Your client has asked you, the producer, to prepare a technical plan for lighting an outdoor evening rock concert by Jimmy Buffet for 50,000 "parrot-head" fans. Suggest different types of lighting you might use and explain why, in terms of creating the right ambience and attention.

3. Suggest at least three ways in which gobos may be used at a special event, including where they would be projected and what type of luminaire(s) might be used to project them.

4. Briefly explain how non-DMX-controllable and DMX-controllable luminaires are controlled.

5. You are preparing the event production schedule for a large awards show and the venue catering manager has just informed you that the room will only be available from 10:00 am on show day rather than 1:00 am. You have a huge, flown lighting rig to set up—including a mixture of conventional and moving luminaire—and were counting on the extra time. Explain to the manager and to your client why the extra time is required and how the show might suffer if it is not available.

## REFERENCES

Bullough, J.D. (2003). *Lighting Answers: Light Emitting Diode Lighting Systems.* Troy, NY: National Lighting Product Information Program, Lighting Research Center, Rensselaer Polytechnic Institute.

Cadena, R. (2005, November). Automated Lighting. *Projection Lights and Staging News,* 75.

Cooper, D.C. (Ed.). (2014). *The Event Safety Guide: A Guide to Health, Safety and Welfare at Live Entertainment Events in the United States.* New York: Event Safety Alliance of USA, Inc./Skyhorse Publishing.

Fitt, B. and Thornley. J. (2002). *Lighting Technology: A Guide for Television, Film and Theater, Second Edition.* Woburn, MA: Focal Press.

Fuchs, T. (1929). *Stage Lighting.* Boston, MA: Little, Brown, and Company.

Gillette, J.M. (2000). *Theatrical Design and Production: An Introduction to Scene Design and Construction, Lighting, Sound, Costume, and Makeup, Fourth Edition.* New York: McGraw-Hill Higher Education.

Harris, T. and Fenlon, W. (2014). How Light Emitting Diodes Work. *howstuffworks.* Retrieved September 3, 2014, from http://electronics.howstuffworks.com/led.htm.

Moody, J. and Dexter, P. (2013). *Concert Lighting, Third Edition.* Burlington, USA and Oxford, UK: Elsevier, Inc.

Seasonal Entertainment. (2012). *Understanding DMX: It Really is That Simple!* Retrieved September 12, 2014, from www.seasonalentertainmentllc.com/pdf/UnderstandingDMX.pdf.Seao.

Williams, B. (1999). PART 1 – An Introduction to Stage Lighting. *Stage Lighting Design 101, Edition 2.d.* Retrieved September 9, 2014, from www.mts.net/~william5/sld/sld-100.htm.

Chapter **6**

# Special effects

## LEARNING OUTCOMES

After reading this chapter, you will be able to:

1. Understand what elements go into making a successful special effects display.
2. Explain in detail how the different types of special effects work, specifically: streamers and confetti; smoke, fog, and haze; lasers; display fireworks and proximate pyrotechnics; and atmospherics.
3. Understand and explain the safety concerns for all the special effects and what the related regulations and safety standards cover.

Today's event audiences demand creativity and cutting-edge ideas beyond the norm. Special effects (also called SFX, SPFX, or FX for short) are some of the most effective ways to leave a favorable impression with them and to make them feel they have been treated to something truly spectacular. At the same time, the events industry is under continuing pressure to maintain a high degree of safety and to minimize risk in the presentation of such effects. In this chapter we examine first what special effects are and how they can be designed for optimum presentation, followed by a thorough explanation of the most common types of effects used in events. Since risk management is one of the most important considerations in the decision to use special effects, we will also discuss the safety aspects of operation as they pertain to each type of effect.

## 6.1 What are special effects?

The term "special effects" has taken on several connotations in today's world. For most people, what immediately comes to mind and what seems to have become the default definition is movie special effects: computer-generated space travel; giant beasts; impossible movement; simulated disasters; and cartoon animation. Most of these, while possible in limited situations, are not what we use in special events. What then, do we use, and what is different about what we use compared to movie special effects?

Put simply, special effects used in special events are unusual and creative technological surprises timed to emphasize an event element. The main difference between our (special events industry) special effects and those of the movies is the fact that we use them for emphasis at strategic moments during the event. For the most part, they are not intended as the only entertainment, with notable exceptions such as a community fireworks show.

Admittedly, we borrow heavily from the movie industry in effects (e.g. artificial snow, wind, rain, and on rare occasions prosthetics, blood, and stunts) but we also borrow from some of the more ancient theatrical effects (e.g. fireworks, magic, and illusions), from computers (e.g. gesture control, gaming), from science (e.g. lasers, UV and black lighting, robotics, LEDs), and from older technology (e.g. balloon effects, streamers, confetti, bubbles). The influences are definitely varied and numerous. We often adapt these effects for our own use. Sometimes, they actually further evolve into other more fascinating inventions and effects (e.g. LED dance floors, lighting controlled by motion).

What about the actual presentation? According to Jaworski (2003), for a successful special effect presentation, one must consider four essential elements: surprise, whether the effects are remarkable, timing, and taste. The element of surprise is crucial and effects must not be "telegraphed." The surprise extends also to the type of feeling that needs to be elicited from the audience. For example, they can be alarmed and startled by fireworks, happy and uplifted by confetti and streamers, or energetic and excited by a combination of upbeat music and pyrotechnics.

Remarkable means that the effects stretch the imagination from the usual. They go beyond what an audience has seen to something they have not. Often this is through a combination of effects or a combination of entertainment and effects. For example, a regular show might simply use a stage presentation of entertainment and pyrotechnics. A better show might bring together interactive mobile content, pyrotechnics, lasers, and the stage presentation. However, by adding choreography to time the effects to music and then bringing all the elements in one at a time so that the show builds to a climax, the presentation rises to another level.

Timing the placement of effects tends to be intuitive. It is money wasted to place them at an inappropriate time during the event. It is also a waste of money to use them just for the sake of doing something different. They must be timed to coincide with a key moment in the event: the announcement of a location for the next year's event; the end of a song; the end or beginning of the event or show; the presentation of an award; and so on. It is usually the producer, in conjunction with the special effects expert, who decides the timing of the presentation.

Taste is mostly a matter of matching the client's vision with the producer's. It means that there must be a mutual understanding of what will work for both the audience and the producer and what show will incorporate the best effects based on knowledge of what is available to match those tastes.

## 6.2 Types of special effects

The list of special effects grows every year, with more colorful, bigger, noisier, higher, wider, denser, longer, and safer being some of the adjectives describing the never-ending innovations that cause hearts to skip beats. Although identifying the latest and greatest is a rapidly moving target, we will attempt to review and explain what the main ones are and how they are used. Some may seem obvious by their omission; however, that is either because they are very simple to use (e.g. bubble machines), or because we have reviewed them as part of other resources (e.g. automated lighting, mirror balls, stage curtain reveals like Kabuki drops, video effects).

### 6.2.1 Streamers and confetti

The term confetti refers to small pieces of paper in large quantities that are thrown by hand, launched by a special device, or dropped from a height. The term streamers refers to long pieces of paper spread in the same manner. The confetti and streamers used for events come in a multitude of colors, sizes, shapes, and paper types. The traditional and most common paper type is tissue paper that, being lightweight, is able to travel farther and dwell for longer in the air.

In terms of shapes and sizes, confetti is now available from ¼ in. (0.6 cm) diameter round shapes, to 3/4 in. x 2 in. (1.9 cm x 5 cm) rectangular strips, plus triangles and virtually any custom shapes. It also comes in shiny Mylar in different colors, but is difficult to clean up and does not travel as far as regular tissue paper confetti. Standard confetti is not colorfast so should not be used over diners or outside when it is raining or there is wet ground; however, it is obtainable from some dealers in biodegradable form that dissolves in the rain, making it perfect for outdoors.

Streamers are available in lengths ranging up to 100 ft (30 m), and widths ranging from ½ in. (1.3 cm) to 2.5 in. (6.3 cm), all in multiple colors. Like confetti, they also come in Mylar. The larger streamers are best used either outdoors or indoors when ceilings are very high. They can be used to simulate fireworks indoors. Both confetti and streamers can be made flame-resistant. Confetti and streamers may be customized with logos and graphic messages, as well as special shapes.

Confetti and streamer cannons—also called *launchers*—consist of long plastic or metal tubes or barrels that are filled with the densely packaged streamers or confetti and launched using a compressed carbon dioxide, air, or nitrogen cartridge or cylinder. These cannons come in various sizes from about a 1 in. (2.5 cm) to a 4 in. (10 cm) diameter barrel that can be up to 40 in. (100 cm) long, and even larger. They are capable of launching confetti and streamers anywhere from 30 ft (9 m) to 300 ft. (91 m) in the air. All are reusable in that they only require new charges of streamers and confetti and new compressed gas cartridges. Cannons come as handheld models as well as remotely triggered models via wireless or DMX protocol. They can be mounted on floors, overhead trussing, stages, and almost any surface. Some manufacturers have also developed much larger versions for bigger venues that are fed by separate units with larger capacity for confetti/streamers, and even a portable backpack version that carries extra charges. These larger versions are sometimes called *confetti blasters*. The blaster provides a continuous feed of confetti that is combined with air and compressed carbon dioxide in a venturi tube that shoots the confetti outwards for a total time of up to several minutes.

At present, there are no safety or other standards for confetti, streamers, or cannons and launchers, and no permit is required. The main caution is obvious and that is to not point them directly toward people.

See Figure 6.1 for an example of a stadium event using a large-scale confetti launch. Some of the cannons can be seen near the edge of the central crowd at the bottom of the picture.

### 6.2.2 Fog, smoke, and haze

To create "other-worldly" and dreamy looks, nothing beats fog, and to make light and laser beams sparkle and dance in the air, smoke and/or haze are a must. We will examine the main types of machines used to generate these effects.

#### 6.2.2.1 Fog

The older type of fog machine uses *dry ice*. These machines produce a low-lying, rolling fog effect by dropping solid carbon dioxide ("dry ice") into boiling water. Dry ice is very cold (–70 degrees Celsius) and will lose about 30 percent of its volume every day as the carbon dioxide sublimes back to a gas. The solid

Figure 6.1  Example of confetti launch—Bayer Anniversary, 150 Years

Courtesy of VOK DAMS Agency for Events- and Live-Marketing, www.vokdams.com

carbon dioxide is available in pellet or block form from industrial gas suppliers and can be stored in an insulated polystyrene container. The visible fog effect is actually water vapor. The carbon dioxide gas is invisible. Dry ice fog gives the "walking on clouds" effect.

More normally:

> *fog is created by pumping one of a variety of different glycol or glycol/water mixtures (referred to as fog fluid) into a heat exchanger (essentially a block of metal with a resistance heating element in it) and heating until the fluid vaporizes, creating a thick translucent or opaque cloud. Devices specifically manufactured for this purpose are referred to as* fog *machines.*
>
> *(Theatrical smoke and fog, 2014)*

These machines do not create the density or low-lying fog as well as carbon dioxide, but the:

> *effects can be simulated by combining a fog machine with another device designed specifically for this purpose. As the fog exits the fog machine, it is chilled, either by passing through a device containing a fan and dry ice, or by passing through a device containing a fan and compressor similar to an air conditioner.*
>
> *(Theatrical smoke and fog, 2014)*

Another spectacular fog effect is created by pushing liquid carbon dioxide through nozzles at high pressure in devices called *cryo jets*. They are used to generate fog bursts, which shoot dense white fog straight up into the air. They can be ganged together and controlled remotely but only work with regular 110 V switches. The carbon dioxide is pumped to each jet via a common line, much like a hose.

### 6.2.2.2 Smoke

To generate smoke, a glycol/water mixture is vaporized by heating under compression. Nearly all smoke machines work this way. Glycol or mineral oil *smoke guns* all work on the same principles although their size, precise method of operation, and the chemical used do vary. The basic principle is that a mineral oil or glycol-based substance is heated, atomizing the substance. This is then forced out of the machine under pressure. This produces a familiar "white cloud" effect, which rises and spreads throughout the air. Thicker smoke is produced by increasing the length of the smoke burst. As opposed to fog, smoke rises in the air and can obscure viewing depending on its density. To confuse matters, commercial smoke machines are often called fog machines or foggers.

### 6.2.2.3 Haze

*Haze effects refer to creating an unobtrusive, homogeneous cloud intended primarily to reveal lighting beams, such as the classic 'light fingers' in a rock concert. This effect is produced using a haze machine, typically done in one of two ways. One technique uses mineral oil, atomized via a spray pump powered either by electricity or compressed $CO_2$, breaking the mineral oil into a fine mist. Another technique for creating haze uses a glycol/water mixture to create haze in a process nearly identical to that for creating fog effects. In either case the fluid used is referred to as haze fluid, but the different formulations are not compatible or interchangeable. Glycol/water haze fluid is sometimes referred to as* water-based haze *for the purposes of disambiguation.*

*Smaller volumes of haze can also be generated from aerosol canisters containing mineral oil under pressure. Although the density of haze generated and the volume of space that can be filled is significantly smaller than that of a haze machine, aerosol canisters have the advantages of portability, no requirements for electricity, and finer control over the volume of haze generated.*

*(Theatrical smoke and fog, 2014)*

As may be apparent, the main difference between smoke machines and haze machines is in the volume produced, smoke being much more dense. The chemical fluids used to generate the effects are similar but as a caution, experts advise never to mix the fluids specified for a given brand of machine with that of another brand (Pea Soup Ltd., 2014).

Like confetti and streamer cannons, foggers, smoke machines, and hazers can be set off remotely using DMX controllers, similar to those used in lighting. See Figure 6.2 for an example of haze used effectively.

### 6.2.2.4 Safety of fog and haze

There are some contradictory problems with dry ice fog. The first is that it is very effective if air circulation is not good in that it remains close to the ground and does not dissipate quickly, making the effect more impressive. Contradicting this for health reasons is the need to disperse the fog through room ventilation so that concentrations do not get high enough to cause breathing problems. Fortunately, this is a small problem as most of the dry ice fog is water vapor and carbon dioxide does not reach toxic levels very quickly. However, it is a good idea to maintain ventilation and use the fog away from areas with high air flow, such as entrance doors, to avoid too rapid dispersion. Dry ice, due to its extremely cold temperature, must also be handled and stored safely. This includes the wearing of gloves when handling it and the use of heavily insulated containers for storing it. Dry ice machines also require a full-time operator to monitor the flow and to constantly feed the dry ice into the machine.

Fog machines and/or hazers should be tested in the event venue prior to the event. If there are smoke detectors then there is a very distinct possibility that one of these machines might set them off. There are many venues where they cannot be used because of the fire alarm systems installed. In fact, these devices

Figure 6.2 Example of haze used to enhance lighting

Pretty Lights at Red Rocks August 2013; Photo By Soren McCarty, mtnweekly.com

are now banned in many venues, or the fire department must stand by onsite for a large fee. If possible, smoke detectors should be disabled during—and only during—the effect. Again, however, the venue may charge for this service. They also may opt to stand by near the alarm system to monitor it rather than turning off the detection system, especially if the effect is a hazer that may be required for longer than fog in order to accentuate show lighting. If this is not possible, a test run is advisable. If in doubt, fog or haze should not be used because evacuation of the venue during the show is not the effect sought.

In relative terms, the ingredients used in fog and haze fluid are quite safe, but there is an ongoing debate in the entertainment industry about whether the output of the machines is safe or not. Indeed, a 2005 study found that short-term exposure to glycol fog was associated with coughing, dry throat, headaches, dizziness, drowsiness, and tiredness. This study also found long-term exposure to smoke and fog was associated with both short-term and long-term respiratory problems such as chest tightness and wheezing. Personnel working closest to the fog machines had reduced lung function results (Varughese et al., 2005).

It's a good policy to ensure that where fog or haze are being used in the vicinity of performers, it is kept to the minimum required to achieve the desired effect, and to post warnings. Other safety hazards include: the condensation of fog/haze back to fluid near the nozzle of the machine causing a slipping hazard; the nozzle of the machine, which is very hot, causing burns; and large amounts of fog/haze causing panic and disorientation in an audience.

In order to minimize the adverse effects of fog and haze, several international standards are available as guides, as listed below:

- *ANSI E1.5 – 2009 (R2014): Entertainment Technology – Theatrical Fog Made With Aqueous Solutions of Di- And Trihydric Alcohols.* This standard describes the composition of theatrical fogs or artificial mists that are not likely to be harmful to otherwise healthy performers, technicians, or audience members of normal working age. This standard is intended to be applied in theaters, arenas, and other places of entertainment or public assembly where theatrical fogs and mists are often used. It lists what is permissible in the fog or haze and how much can be there on a short- and long-term basis.

- *ANSI E1.14 – 2001 (R2013): Entertainment Technology – Recommendations for Inclusions in Fog Equipment Manuals.* The standard applies to the instruction manuals for fog-making equipment manufactured for use in the entertainment industry. In order to use fog safely and effectively, the user must have some general knowledge of the technology, have a clear understanding of how to operate the fog-making system, and be aware of the potential hazards related to the use of fog, and particularly the system that he or she is using. This standard is designed to establish guidelines for manufacturers to provide to the user the necessary information required for the safe and responsible use of fog equipment.

- *ANSI E1.23 – 2010: Entertainment Technology – Design and Execution of Theatrical Fog Effects.* This standard offers guidance on planning and carrying out fog effects so that recognized exposure levels are not exceeded, fire and egress hazards are not created, false alarms don't summon the fire brigade, and fog effects are executed as they are designed, performance after performance.

- *ANSI E1.29 – 2009 (R2014): Product Safety Standard for Theatrical Fog Generators that Create Aerosols of Water, Aqueous Solutions of Glycol or Glycerin, or Aerosols of Highly Refined Alkane Mineral Oil.* This is intended to help guide product safety testing laboratories in evaluating fog-making equipment for design or construction defects that might create unacceptable hazards. It is based on *ANSI/UL 998 – 2006, Humidifiers*, but has modifications to deal with safety issues peculiar to fog generators. Fog generators often are evaluated as heating appliances to assure they are not a fire or shock hazard. *ANSI E1.29* considers those issues, but also has safety tests for the fog generated.

- *Introduction to Modern Atmospheric Effects, Fourth Edition.* While not a standard per se, this is a revised version of a popular handbook on theatrical fogs. Illustrated and with more than twice as many pages as the first and second editions, the book gives the entertainment industry a factual presentation on all types of popular atmospheric fog effects. The section on using fog offers tips on putting fog where it will do the most good, lighting it effectively, working with fire alarms, and limiting exposure. The relative advantages and disadvantages of using time/distance tables and aerosol meters to ensure that exposure limits are not exceeded are discussed. It is available—as are the other standards—from the PLASA web site at http://tsp.plasa.org/tsp/documents/published_docs.php.

Producers should ensure that their subcontractors are familiar with these key documents if they intend to use theatrical effects at special events.

## 6.2.3 Lasers

As the International Laser Display Association states,

> There's no light like it: the most vivid, saturated color palette available; a contrast ratio unsurpassed by the best film and video technologies; the ability to reach out in three dimensions and shower an audience with cascades of beams or embrace them in waves of moving light. It's about enchanting an audience with dreamlike visions. It's about exciting crowds with visual effects that move faster than any other light-form.
>
> (ILDA, 2014a)

Lasers for special events consist of three main components: a light source (the laser itself), a projector, and software. We will examine these and then briefly discuss safety.

### 6.2.3.1 The light source (LASER)

*The word LASER is an acronym. It stands for Light Amplification by the Stimulated Emission of Radiation. By 'radiation', however, the acronym refers to a radiant vibration, not an emission of radioactive particles. In other words, the emissions of lasers are in the form of light . . . The lasers typically employed in events are called ion gas lasers, due to the fact that they utilize a gas or a mixture of gases as the lasing medium . . . The stimulation comes in the form of electricity, which excites the atoms of the gas: as the electrons in these atoms are given more energy, they tend to jump to a higher orbit. These unnaturally high orbits, however, don't last long, and the electrons fall back to their proper orbital shells, to be once again excited by the influx of electricity. It is this process of the electrons returning to their original orbits that creates the laser light we see. During this jump back down, the extra energy is released from each atom as a packet called a photon (light).*

*(Mueller, 2005)*

There are three general types of light show graphics lasers: low-power helium-neon (red), medium- and high-power argon (green-blue), and mixed-gas argon/krypton (red-yellow-green-blue).

### 6.2.3.2 The projector

The laser projector is the heart of the graphics system:

*Using tiny moving mirrors, a single beam of laser light can be moved so fast the human eye no longer sees the individual beam. Instead, the audience sees fans, cones, tunnels, or cascades of beams that fill the air. Specialized optics (diffraction gratings) can create sheets of light by splitting one beam into hundreds of individual shafts of light. Bounce mirrors can ricochet beams throughout a venue. Realistic wire-frame images can be projected onto walls, buildings, and even mountains to advertise products or tell a dramatic story. Wispy, cloud-like graphics called lumia can fill ceilings, and psychedelic abstract graphics can be created with eye-popping colors and contrast.*

*(ILDA, 2014b)*

### 6.2.3.3 The software

Laser show software is available for almost every personal computer, and there are even programs with their own custom computers. It is the software that creates the two main types of laser effects: aerials (sometimes called *atmospherics*) and animation projection or *graphics*:

- Aerials. The laser effect that most causes audiences to gasp with wonder and delight is the experience of seeing laser beams move through open air. Walsh (2005) describes how it is done: "These effects are called 'atmospheric' because they rely upon beams sculpting the atmosphere of the venue, with no projection screen involved . . . To help make the beams visible indoors, laserists often introduce particles into the air, usually using theatrical fog machines [these would more accurately be hazers since particulate smoke would be too hazardous to health] . . . If a laser beam is coming toward the viewer, the apparent brightness of the beam is increased. Beams that are perpendicular to the viewer are perceived as much less bright. Those going away from the viewer vary in apparent brightness depending upon the ambient light in the background. For creating successful beam shows, it is wise to plan the display as coming towards the audience."

- Animation projection. Dryer (2005) aptly describes animation projection created by *laser scanning*: "Animated Neon! That's an approximate description of laser scanning: the richly colored line-drawing quality of a neon sign set in motion with equal contrast and even greater color saturation. It's a medium

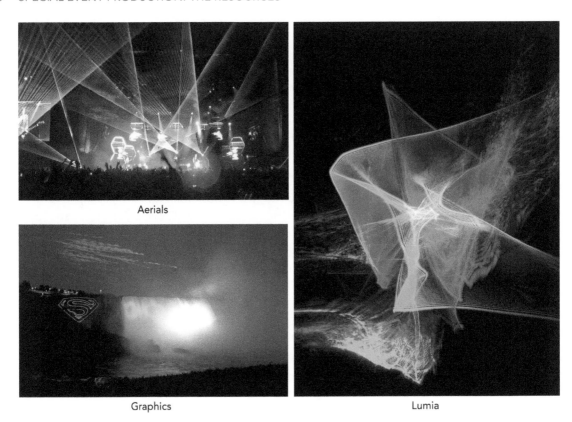

Aerials

Graphics

Lumia

**Figure 6.3** Examples of laser effects

Images courtesy of: top left—Muse at the Outside Lands Music and Arts Festival 2011 in San Francisco, photo by Edward Betts; right—Timothy Walsh, Laser Spectacles, Inc., and photographer Alan Kitchen; bottom left—Production Design International Inc., www.pdifx.com

that makes any message special. Laser scanners can project names, logos and animated imagery onto almost any surface including the side of a mountain, the curved dome of a planetarium, even a sheet of pulsating water . . . To do this, a laser produces a tiny linear beam of intense light that appears as a small dot when it strikes a surface. To make it move you have to 'scan' it by wiggling one or more mirrored surfaces. Once the dot of light moves fast enough, a phenomenon called *persistence of vision* causes your eye to perceive the movements of the dot as solid lines of light." This movement is achieved through a combination of the laser projector's hardware and special software.

See Figure 6.3 for examples of different laser effects.

### 6.2.3.4 *Laser safety*

According to the Australian Radiation Protection and Nuclear Safety Agency (ARPANSA):

> *The eyes and skin are the organs primarily at risk from exposure to laser light. Health effects from exposure to laser light are generally divided into two categories: radiation and non-radiation hazards. Radiation hazards include injury to the eyes and skin from direct exposure to the laser beam or any reflections. Momentary viewing of the beam from a Class 2 laser may cause temporary flash-blindness, similar in effect to viewing a photographic flash at close*

*range. However, unlike the photographic flash, a Class 2 laser can cause flash-blindness up to 50 m [165 ft] or more. Many non-radiation hazards arise from the use of lasers including electrical hazards, chemical hazards, burns from heated surfaces, production of fumes, vapors and airborne contaminants from materials within the beam.*

*(© Commonwealth of Australia 2013, as represented by the Australian Radiation Protection and Nuclear Safety Agency [ARPANSA])*

Also, according to Laser Spectacles, Inc. (2013):

*In many parts of the world, lasers used in laser shows are scanned directly into the audience and over their eyes (called* audience scanning*). If the laser beam is being scanned quickly enough, and the power density of the laser beam, or* irradiance*, is not too high, there will be no damage to the eyes, because the beam never settles in one spot for long enough to burn. However, if a failure in the scanning apparatus occurs, the beam will stop moving, and there is a great potential for damage to be done if anyone is in the way of the beam. Experienced laser safety officers must take measurements and perform calculations before shows of this type can go on. . . . The primary means of laser light show safety in the USA is provided simply by keeping the beam away from the audience. There are two rules for doing this: the '3 m (10 ft) vertical clearance' rule, and the '2.5 m (8.3 ft) horizontal clearance' rule. If there is an audience standing or seated in a given area, the laser beams used in a show must not drop lower than 3 m measured vertically above the surface that the audience is upon. Measured horizontally, the beams must not come any closer than 2.5 m to any place that the audience can reach. Audience barriers are required to ensure that the audience stays within this 'safe zone,' and danger/warning signs are required to be posted to inform people of the fact that laser radiation is present . . . To meet these distance requirements, laser light show companies must use simple devices called* beam stops*. Typically, a beam stop is a sheet of metal—or some other material that the laser can't burn through—that can be adjusted for different venues so that no matter how the beam is scanned, or if there is a scanning failure, it will not come any closer to the audience than the distances prescribed above.*

The best way that producers can ensure laser safety is to require laser companies to adhere to current international and North American standards on the use of lasers. The following list includes the most important of these standards as well as other safety guides:

- *IEC 60825-1:2014: Safety of laser products – Part 1: Equipment classification and requirements*. This is an international standard that introduces a classification system for lasers and laser products according to their degree of optical radiation hazard. Among other things, it also ensures, through labels and instructions, adequate warning to individuals of hazards associated with accessible radiation from laser products.

- *IEC 60825-1:2008: Safety of laser products – Part 3: Guidance for laser displays and shows*. This is an international guide that is a code of practice for the design, installation, operation, and evaluation of the safety of laser light shows and displays, and the equipment employed in their production. This guide is also intended for persons who modify laser display installations or equipment. The guide contains safety criteria for the protection of the public or persons in the vicinity of laser displays in the course of their employment. In some countries, there may be specific requirements, such as government permissions or notifications of shows, or prohibitions, such as against laser scanning of spectators without appropriate safeguards. This guide is not to be understood as in conflict with such requirements but merely to be supplementary.

- *ANSI Z136.1(2014): Safe Use of Lasers*. This US standard provides guidance for individuals who work with high-power Class 3B and Class 4 lasers and laser systems and also provides a practical means for establishing a laser safety program to protect the employer, facility, and personnel.

- *Code of Federal Regulations CFR 1040.10 (2000): Laser Product Regulation 21.* This is a US regulation that classifies lasers and also sets standards for testing, signage, and safety.
- *Center for Devices and Radiological Health (CDRH): FDA Laser Notice 50.* Part of the US Food and Drug Administration, the CDRH has issued *Notice 50* to allow laser manufacturers to comply with certain parts of *IEC 60825* and thereby try to eliminate the need for them to follow two separate sets of standards.

As well as these, the International Laser Display Association, ILDA (2014c), provides a very succinct and common sense list of basic principles with respect to staging laser shows plus further references to papers, articles, and safety standards. Chapter 21 of Cooper (2014) also contains some excellent tips on setting up and running laser shows for special events, as well as specific references to safety standards in the United States. Both are good starting points for learning about safe shows.

### 6.2.4 Fireworks and pyrotechnics

Fireworks were the earliest use of explosives known to man, invented in China in the 7th century. Such important events and festivities as New Year's and the Mid-Autumn Moon Festival were and still are times when fireworks are guaranteed sights. Nowadays, they can be seen around the world at festivals and regular celebrations, whether public or private. Chemically, they are classed as low explosive pyrotechnic devices in contrast to the infinitely more powerful high explosives such as TNT and the dynamites.

#### 6.2.4.1 Definitions

There has always been some confusion about the difference between fireworks and pyrotechnics. The pyrotechnics industry uses the following definitions:

- Fireworks. Any composition or device for the purpose of producing a visible or an audible effect by combustion, deflagration, or detonation, and that meets the definition of consumer fireworks or display fireworks.
- Pyrotechnics. Controlled exothermic chemical reactions that are timed to create the effects of heat, gas, sound, dispersion of aerosols, emission of visible electromagnetic radiation, or a combination of these effects to provide the maximum effect from the least volume.
- Theatrical Pyrotechnics. Pyrotechnic devices for professional use in the entertainment industry. Similar to consumer fireworks in chemical composition and construction but not intended for consumer use.

(APA, 2014)

For definition in the special events industry, there is now fairly common usage that interprets pyrotechnics as indoor, close proximity, smaller devices that create effects of relatively short duration (i.e. theatrical or *proximate pyrotechnics* as above), and fireworks as outdoor, distant, larger devices that create effects of relatively long duration (i.e. *display fireworks*).

#### 6.2.4.2 Classifications

In terms of classifications, there are very distinct differences. The US and Canadian governments have classified fireworks and pyrotechnics according to their potential hazards. The US government now classifies them according to their **shipping** hazards only, compared to the old system that classified based on **shipping** and **use**. The US system categorizes them as follows:

- Display fireworks (i.e. outdoor). Class 1.3G, with United Nations shipping category UN0335. This was the old Class "B" fireworks.

- Proximate pyrotechnics (i.e. indoor, theatrical). Class 1.4G and 1.4S, with United Nations shipping categories UN0431 and UN0432 respectively. This was the old Class "C" fireworks. Some may also fall under other classes, so all details of each class should be thoroughly understood.

The Canadian government's classifications are based on composition and roughly parallel the US categories. Class 7.2.2 represents display fireworks and Class 7.2.5 represents theatrical pyrotechnics. However, the United Nations shipping regulations for fireworks and pyrotechnics also apply in Canada.

In the UK (not Ireland), classifications are according to use and fall under Category 1 (for use indoors), Category 2 (for outdoor use in relatively confined areas), Category 3 (for outdoor use in large open spaces), and Category 4 (not intended for sale to the general public). Category 1 would generally correspond to proximate pyrotechnics and Category 4 to display fireworks. Specific details can be found in the series of standards published by the British Standards Institute (BSI), *BS EN 15947 – 1:2010*, through – *5:2010, Pyrotechnic articles. Fireworks, Categories 1, 2 and 3*. These standards specify details about categories, labeling, construction, and performance of the actual fireworks, but do not address safety or use.

For other countries, classifications vary and producers should check with the appropriate authorities in those countries if details are needed.

---

## VOICE OF THE INDUSTRY

### An interview with Mr. Kelly Guille

President, Archangel Fireworks Inc.
Winnipeg, MB, Canada
www.archangelfireworks.com

With over 20 years in the fireworks industry, Kelly Guille's designs have won praise for their innovative approach to the art of fireworks. He has led Archangel Fireworks Inc. to three international wins in as many years taking home top honors at the 2007 and 2008 HSBC Celebration of Light in Vancouver, British Columbia, and in 2009 at Les Grands Feux Loto-Québec in Québec City, both major international fireworks competitions. Kelly has also traveled with Team Spain to other fireworks competitions in Germany, Vietnam, and most recently Macau. Besides fireworks, Archangel supplies snow machines, bubble machines, cryo jets, and confetti for special events. We talked about the state of the special effects industry today.

**DM**: Have you seen any major trends or changes in the use of special effects for special events in the last five to ten years, particularly in Canada but also in other countries?

**KG**: Probably one of the biggest changes is the widespread use of lasers that came about as a result of price reductions over the last ten years. Also, I think pyrotechnics are being used more effectively and responsibly.

**DM**: What do you see coming in the next five to ten years in special effects for events?

**KG**: There will probably be changes to the formulation of pyro, in other words the chemical composition of the effects. This is due to environmental concerns and the need to make the products percholate-free [percholates are the oxidizers that produce colors in fireworks and that some studies have been found to be toxic in groundwater—author].

**DM**: With respect to safety, especially the safety of outdoor display fireworks and indoor proximate pyrotechnics, what specific safety regulations, standards, and/or guidelines do you as a company follow when providing pyro/fireworks in Canada and in other countries?

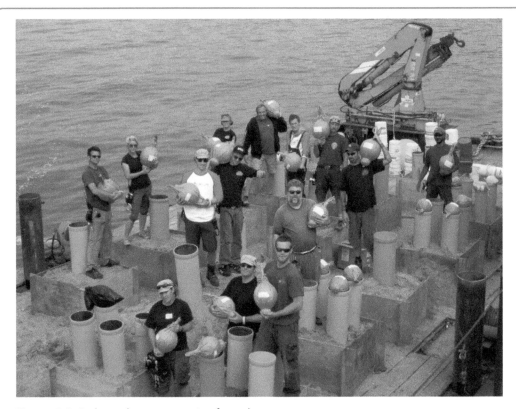

Figure 6.4  Archangel team preparing for a show

Courtesy of Archangel Fireworks Inc., www.archangelfireworks.com

**KG**: Canada has one of the strictest sets of regulations in the world. There are separate ones for display fireworks and for indoor pyrotechnics, both published by the ERD. In the USA, it is state by state. When we go anywhere outside of Canada we always work to the Canadian regulations due to their strictness, because in many countries there are no regulations at all.

**DM**: Have you or event producers/managers found that event liability insurance, especially for proximate pyrotechnics, is difficult to obtain, and if so, what have you done to make it easier to obtain?

**KG**: Insurance is as difficult to obtain as it is to afford. If you have enough money, you can get what you want. However, if you have a history without claims it is easier. We as a company have a policy that covers all our operations, all of which are considered high risk. Some fireworks insurers are now starting to team up to spread the risk around and lower the cost of insurance.

**DM**: Do you have any final words of wisdom for up-and-coming event producers/managers that would help to make your job easier? For example, is there a minimum knowledge base that they should possess to make it easier to understand, sell, and execute the various types of effects to enhance any special event?

**KG**: The toughest thing for fireworks companies is for the client or the person responding to an RFP to believe what the fireworks companies say. Sometimes the process [of creating a show] is not fully understood so there has to be an inherent trust on the part of the client [e.g. event manager/producer] that we will deliver the show we say we will.

### 6.2.4.3 Display fireworks (outdoor)

Display fireworks make the wonderful outdoor shows we have come to love and of which we never seem to tire. They are often the climax of special events, whether they are public festivals for 100,000 persons or private corporate events with 100 VIPs. The two most important aspects of their use are how they work and safety. There are three kinds of display fireworks: *high-level*, *low-level*, and *ground-level*.

#### 6.2.4.3.1 HIGH-LEVEL

The most impressive and best-known type of display fireworks are *aerial* or high-level fireworks. A single typical display or aerial firework is formed into a *shell* consisting of four components:

- Container or package. This is usually cardboard in the shape of a sphere or cylinder.

- Stars. Stars are the primary component of an aerial shell. They create the breath-taking flashes of color and light in fireworks displays. They are usually shaped into small spheres, cubes, or cylinders and are composed of coloring and binding agents. The way in which the stars are packed into the shells dictates the exploding shape they will adopt. Helmenstine (2014) gives a good explanation of how the color is achieved.

- Bursting charge. This is a packed, black powder charge at the center of the shell that is also sprinkled between the stars to help ignite them.

- Fuse. The fuse functions as a time switch to make the shells burst at the right altitude. It is lit at the moment of launch and after burning for a certain time, the fire reaches the bursting charge in the center of the shell. The length of the fuse differs according to the size of the package.

The shell is usually launched from a *mortar*. Mortars are generally made of *FRE* (Fiber-Reinforced Epoxy) or *HDPE* (High-Density Polyethylene). Some older mortars are made of sheet steel, but have been banned by most countries due to the problem of shrapnel produced during a misfire. The mortar also contains a lifting charge of black powder that explodes to launch the shell. When the lifting charge fires to launch the shell, it lights the shell's fuse. The shell's fuse burns while the shell rises to its correct altitude and then ignites the bursting charge so it explodes. Mortars range in size from 2 in. (5 cm) to 12 in. (30 cm) diameter but do come in diameters up to 16 in. (40 cm), the use of which requires special permission. See Figure 6.4 depicting a fireworks display being prepared. Note the large shells held by team members and the yellow and red mortars into which the shells will be placed.

There are also complicated shells that burst in two or three phases, called *multibreak shells*. They may contain stars of different colors and compositions to create softer or brighter light, and more or fewer sparks. Some shells contain explosives designed to crackle in the sky, or whistles that explode outward with the stars. Multibreak shells sometimes incorporate a shell filled with other shells, or they may have multiple sections without using additional shells. The sections of a multibreak shell are ignited by different fuses. The bursting of one section ignites the next. The shells must be assembled in such a way that each section explodes in sequence to produce a distinct separate effect. The explosives that break the sections apart are called *break charges*, and the *pattern* that an aerial shell paints in the sky depends on the arrangement of star pellets inside each shell. Both Brain (2000) and Fireworks (2014) provide good descriptions and illustrations of some of the more common effects and noises.

Occasionally, shells are launched into the air using *rockets*. A rocket can be considered as a "shell on a stick," which instead of being fired into the air from a mortar tube, is mounted onto a rocket motor to which a stick is attached. Cylindrical in shape, the rocket has a cone-shaped head filled with stars. Upon ignition, the gases from the propellant erupt out of the bottom of the cylinder and the rocket rises high into the air.

### 6.2.4.3.2 Low-level

Besides high-level fireworks, display fireworks are actually divided into two other categories. The first is low-level or *ground-to-air fireworks* that either perform below approximately 200 ft (60 m) or begin their display at ground level and rise to complete their effect. Some examples of low-level fireworks are:

- Candles or Roman candles. A candle is a cardboard tube that contains alternating layers of compacted black powder and single stars. When lighted, candles eject a series of colored stars one by one into the air and often emit a shower of glowing sparks between each shot.
- Cakes. A cake is a device consisting of a number of individual tubes of effects (e.g. comets, mines, etc.) set up together but not stacked as in a candle.
- Comets. This is an effect. A special composition pellet is propelled from a mortar or shell and produces a long tailed effect. Large comets are constructed much like aerial display shells, with attached lift charge ready for loading into mortars.
- Mines. This is a tubular device, comprised of a plastic bag containing a black powder lifting charge and a number of colored shells, balanced by a wooden or plastic base. The mine is designed to propel any number of items aloft: stars, whistles, and floating fireworks.

### 6.2.4.3.3 Ground-level

The last category is ground-level fireworks that function on the ground. Some examples of ground-level fireworks are:

- Fountains. Fountains are designed to project brilliant jets of sparks into the air much like a water fountain. Shaped like a cone or cylinder, the fountain's pyrotechnic composition is pressed into the case in the same way as for a rocket motor, but on a short rather than a long central cavity. Both gold and silver are common in colored fountains.
- Wheels and drivers. These are revolving pieces turned by drivers. Various effects can be attached to the wheel, such as colored lights and fountains. Horizontal wheels often have waterfall units and are positioned at the side of the barge or under water to form a "shower." "Catherine" or "pin" wheels are small wheels spinning on a pole.
- Gerbs. A gerb is a cylindrical preload intended to produce a controlled spray of sparks with a reproducible and predictable duration, height, and diameter. The pattern looks like a sheaf of wheat.
- Lances and lancework set pieces. Lances are small flares used in the makeup of portraits, flags, and mottos known as lancework set pieces. The outline is constructed on a wood lattice and a design picked out in appropriate colors of lances. According to Raymond Greenwood, past chairman of the Vancouver Fireworks Society that originally brought the Symphony of Fire to Vancouver, Canada, lancework is very popular for sponsored events because it allows for sponsors' logos and names to be more visibly identified with the show (R. Greenwood, personal communication, December 10, 2014).
- Waterfalls. Waterfalls are a series of gerbs (without nozzles) suspended fuse side down from a wire or rope strung between two points. The gerbs are all ignited simultaneously and produce a curtain of sparks.

Figure 6.5 illustrates a typical outdoor public fireworks display showing a clear distinction among high-level, low-level, and ground-level effects.

Greenwood from Vancouver also mentions that display fireworks are available for daytime shows that incorporate mostly smoke and noise but can also include flags and logos (R. Greenwood, personal communication, December 10, 2014). Perhaps not as impressive as at night but certainly an option if the event schedule will not accommodate a nighttime show.

Figure 6.5 Outdoor fireworks display

Courtesy of Doug Matthews

### 6.2.4.4 Proximate or theatrical pyrotechnics (indoor)

The use of explosions, flashes, smoke, or flames onstage is known as proximate pyrotechnics. Generally, pyrotechnics can be divided into categories based on the device's main effects, among them bangs, flashes, flames, or smoke. A basic proximate pyrotechnic device generally consists of a container to hold the materials (of an obviously hazardous nature), a fuel, and an oxidizer, as well as additives to increase the strength of the bang or the flash.

The best-known categories of proximate pyrotechnics are:

- Flash powders. Of all the effects used onstage, the flash effect is probably the most common. Most flash effects are created by igniting a fine-grained powder contained within a steel mortar. The resulting effect is a bright flash whose duration and color can be changed with various additives. The device in which the powder is typically used is called a *flash pot*. It should be noted that *flash paper*, unlike flash powder, is a form of *nitrocellulose* that burns quickly and completely with a bright flame, no smoke, and no ash. It is safe to use in handheld devices.

- Noise effects. A noise effect is often used in conjunction with either smoke or flash. It is created by igniting a suitable compound within a confined area.

- Airburst effects. These effects are intended to simulate outdoor aerial fireworks shells without hazardous debris. Airbursts are designed to be suspended in a lighting truss that is at least 6 (small airburst) to 8 (large airburst) meters (20–27 ft) above the ground. They produce a ball-shaped flash that is cool before reaching the lower levels or stage floor. There is very little smoke. An airburst that produces a flash of light and projects stars in all directions is called a *starburst*.

- Gerb effects. This effect is the same as the ground-level gerb. Gerb effects are widely variable, with plumes of usually silver or gold, durations of 0.5 to 30 s, and heights of up to 30 ft (9 m). Accompanying whistling and crackling sounds can be created as well. Waterfalls (upside-down gerbs without nozzles) are used extensively in proximate pyro.

- Line rockets. Also known as *grid rockets*, these are small whistling rockets that run along a steel cable. The cable must be securely fastened at each end, and is usually up to 50 m (167 ft) in length. The line rocket is attached to the line by a plastic tube, and takes between 2 and 4 s to travel the 50 m.

- Flame effects. Flames are always an impressive effect no matter how they are used. *Flame cannons* shoot gigantic fireballs up to 35 ft (10.6 m) in the air. *Flame bars* can be used to emit flames from various shapes, whether it's a flat bar, arch, or a custom shape. *Flame projectors* create a small tower of fire from a fixed point. Flames can also be colored. Flame effect machines are typically comprised of a canister containing flammable fuel (usually a propane/butane mix or a color-specific ethanol/methanol mix), an igniter, a nozzle, a box-like housing, and a control panel. Most are now controllable remotely by DMX.

- Fire. Live fire in other forms (e.g. torches, wands, finger-tips with special gloves) is sometimes used to create uniquely choreographed entertainment. Figure 6.6 illustrates a choreographed fire act.

Figure 6.6 Live fire choreography—Fire Swing

Courtesy of Contraband International Ltd., www.contrabandevents.com

### 6.2.4.5 *Fireworks and pyrotechnics safety*

Fireworks and pyrotechnics safety is extremely important. Most countries have stringent regulations that govern the permit requirements, setup, placement, loading, safe distances of audiences, cleanup, storage, and transportation of commercial display fireworks and indoor pyrotechnics. In this section, we will deal with safety only in the United States, Canada, and the UK. Producers in other countries should seek out their own applicable standards and regulations. As a start, it can be generally stated that the storage and transportation of display fireworks and proximate pyrotechnics are federally regulated, often through a country's explosive regulations. However, the actual safety of the displays or shows is typically not regulated but many guides are available.

#### 6.2.4.5.1 DISPLAY FIREWORKS SAFETY

In the United States, the most important documents are:

- *National Fire Protection Association standard NFPA 1123: Code for Fireworks Display (2014 Edition)*. This code contains information on how to set up and operate professional outdoor fireworks displays in order to prevent injuries to both the workers handling the fireworks and to the viewing audience, as well as to prevent fires that could cause property damage.
- *NFPA 1124: Code for the Manufacture, Transportation, Storage, and Retail Sales of Fireworks and Pyrotechnic Articles (2013 Edition)*. Although this has useful information on storage and transportation of fireworks, it is under review and has been temporarily withdrawn.

As well, Chapter 20 of Cooper (2014) provides extensive guidelines and checklists for performances in the United States.

In Canada, the comparable governing documents are:

- *SOR/2013 – 211: Explosives Regulations, 2013, Part 18 – Display Fireworks.* These federal regulations cover the acquisition, storage, certification, and use of display fireworks. These are regulations and thus enforceable by law.
- *Display Fireworks Manual, Second Edition, 2010.* Published by the Explosives Regulatory Division (ERD) of Natural Resources Canada, this is very comprehensive and contains extensive information on training and certification, fireworks and equipment, display site requirements, operation of the display, loading and firing fireworks, display dismantling, storage of fireworks, and transportation of fireworks.
- *Authorization Guidelines for Consumer and Display Fireworks: Authorization, Sampling, Composition, General and Detailed Requirements for Type F.1 and F.2 Fireworks (ERD 2010)*. These guidelines describe the safety requirements for the design and performance of display fireworks.

> "In the UK, responsibility for the safety of firework displays is shared between the Health and Safety Executive (HSE), fire brigades, and local authorities. Currently, there is no national system of licensing for fireworks operators, but in order to purchase display fireworks, operators must have licensed explosives storage and public liability insurance".
>
> (Fireworks, 2014)

There are two related guides for display fireworks:

- *HSE. (2006). Working together on firework displays: A guide to safety for firework display organisers and operators (also referred to as HSG 123)*. This provides guidance for display organizers on issues such as managing crowds safely and what to do if something goes wrong as well as giving safety advice for those who are responsible for setting up and firing the fireworks. How to clear up correctly after a firework display is also covered.

- *British Pyrotechnists Association (BPA) Display Guide: Guidance for organisers of professionally fired firework displays, Rev. 1.3 – October 2010.* This guide addresses changes in display design, rigging techniques, types of fireworks, risk assessments, and environmental concerns that have occurred since the publication of HSG 123 and should be read in conjunction with that document.

Event producers in any country contemplating using display fireworks should obtain a current copy of the applicable federal documents, as well as local state, provincial, county, or municipal regulations, which may differ throughout each country. Generally speaking, a producer who wishes to hold an outdoor fireworks display must have the following in their possession, either personally or through their official fireworks contractor:

- license or certification to work with display fireworks (typically state or federal);
- approval to purchase display fireworks (usually federal and/or state);
- permit to hold a fireworks display (usually the AHJ or *authority having jurisdiction*, such as local municipal fire, parks, or police department)—occasionally, the permit and approval to purchase are the same, depending on the jurisdiction;
- permission of land owner, lessee, or agent to hold a fireworks display;
- insurance of a minimum amount and type as specified by contract (i.e. the client/producer contract) and local regulations (usually the same organization that grants the permit)—the most common minimum amount now required is $5 million liability and reputable fireworks companies will have this;
- a site plan with complete details of crowd and fireworks locations, emergency access and egress, water locations, etc. (usually a requirement of the AHJ).

### 6.2.4.5.2 PROXIMATE PYROTECHNICS SAFETY

Proximate pyrotechnics can arguably be the most awesome of all special effects; however, they can also be extremely lethal. Since 2003, three nightclub fires in various countries (one in the United States, one in Argentina, and one in Brazil) that were started by pyrotechnics have caused the deaths of 530 people. It is little wonder that proximate pyrotechnics represent one of the areas of most concern for special event producers, particularly with respect to safety and the obtaining of liability insurance.

In the United States, the most important documents are:

- *National Fire Protection Association standard NFPA 1126: Standard for the Use of Pyrotechnics before a Proximate Audience (2011 Edition).* This standard provides requirements for the safe use of pyrotechnic special effects before a proximate audience at both indoor and outdoor locations to protect property, operators, performers, support personnel, and viewing audiences. Application includes use in conjunction with theatrical, musical, or similar performing arts productions in theaters, stadiums, concert halls, etc.
- *NFPA 1124: Code for the Manufacturing, Transportation, Storage and Retail Sale of Fireworks and Pyrotechnic Articles (2013 Edition).* As with display fireworks, this code provides historical information only as it has been temporarily withdrawn, with the next edition scheduled for 2017.
- *NFPA 160: Standard for the Use of Flame Effects before an Audience (2011 Edition).* This standard provides public safety officials, designers, performers, and operators of flame effects with the latest requirements for the protection of the audience, support personnel, performers, the operator, assistants, and property where flame effects are used.

Once again, Chapter 20 of Cooper (2014) provides extensive guidelines and checklists for proximate performances in the United States.

In Canada, the comparable governing documents are:

- *SOR/2013 – 211: Explosives Regulations, 2013, Part 17 – Special Effect Pyrotechnics*. These federal regulations cover the acquisition, storage, certification, and use of proximate or special effect pyrotechnics. These are regulations and thus enforceable by law.

- *Special Effect Pyrotechnics Manual, Edition 3, 2014*. Published by the ERD, this extensive manual covers certification, storage, pre-event planning and precautions, insurance, firing and show execution, post-event procedures, and transportation of special effect pyrotechnics.

- *Standard for Pyrotechnic Special Effects: Classification and Authorization – General and Detailed Requirements for F.3, 2008 Edition*. Also published by the ERD, this standard specifies the requirements for obtaining a Canadian product authorization and classification. In addition, it specifies what must be declared by the manufacturer or the manufacturer's representative. It also describes minimum requirements for the design, technical information, performance, primary package and labeling requirements, and corresponding test methods for the product.

The UK has no federal regulations currently available that apply to proximate pyrotechnics safety. As mentioned earlier, this responsibility rests with local authorities. However, there are guides that cover the basics, as follows:

- HSE. (2010). *The event safety guide (Second edition): A guide to health, safety and welfare at music and similar events (also referred to as HSG 195)*. Much like Cooper (2014) in the United States, this is the UK's event safety "bible" and contains a fairly comprehensive section on the planning and execution of a proximate pyrotechnics show.

- *Special or visual effects involving explosives or pyrotechnics used in film and television productions, HSE Entertainment Information Sheet No 16 (Revision 1), (2011)*. While this is intended primarily for the TV and movie industries, the guidelines are applicable for special events. They discuss personnel competencies, hazards, control, and the very basics of executing a show.

Again, and in general, any event producers contemplating using indoor pyrotechnics should obtain a current copy of, and be fully conversant with, the applicable federal documents, as well as local state, provincial, county, or municipal regulations which may differ throughout each country. To ensure proper risk management, event producers who wish to use indoor pyrotechnics must understand the following:

- Transportation. This is normally a federal regulation and producers should ensure that the pyrotechnics contractor is familiar with all requirements for the safe transportation of pyrotechnics products.

- Possession and storage. This is also typically a federal responsibility.

- Licensing and certification. This can be federal or state. Any producers who are planning shows with proximate pyrotechnics should always insist that the pyro contractor be fully certified.

- Permits. In addition to proper licensing or certification, a permit to hold the proximate pyrotechnics show on a specific date in a specific location is often required. Permit issuance is normally the responsibility of the AHJ, which is typically the local fire department. Like licensing, permitting regulations vary greatly, from none to stringent requirements that include licensing, insurance, pre-performance testing, and the hiring of a fire watch (generally a fireman who stands by during the performance to ensure that all necessary safety precautions are followed). Permits are frequently obtained by the contracted pyrotechnics company rather than the event producer. For cases in which actual fire and open flames are used, AHJ regulations vary widely and may be governed by the type of fuel used, such as gas or propane.

As with display fireworks, there are other safety items that should be addressed when a proximate pyrotechnics show is planned:

- Insurance. The insurance industry is very concerned about, and may not fully understand, the scope and importance of proximate pyrotechnics in special events. It has occasionally proven to be difficult for producers to obtain sufficient insurance for events that incorporate pyrotechnics, yet all local regulations, and universally most contracts, require insurance (the standard being $5 million liability). It is generally the responsibility of the fireworks contractor to provide this insurance and to name all parties as being *co-insureds*. According to Greenwood from Vancouver, some clients and even venues do not understand that the responsibility rests with the fireworks contractor to obtain this insurance (R. Greenwood, personal communication, December 10, 2014). It is up to that contractor to explain what is required and, as mentioned in this chapter's "Voice of the Industry," clients and venues must have an inherent trust in the company to do what they say they will do, and that includes taking all necessary safety precautions.

- Venue concerns. Indoor venues are also very worried about the disaster potential of indoor pyrotechnics. The venue must be given all the necessary information about the show and producers must ensure that any décor or stage set pieces and any flammable parts of the venue or the venue décor (e.g. drapes) are completely flame-treated and the performance moved to safe distances.

For producers, the key to the safe conduct of a pyrotechnics show is to completely understand and follow all federal, state/provincial, and municipal regulations, to be prepared with necessary documentation, and to cooperate fully with the appropriate authorities.

## PRODUCTION WAR STORY

### Three pretty vocalists and some very scary pyro

We were to culminate the formal segment of our railroad-themed dinner event with a pyrotechnic segue into an entertainment program beginning with three beautiful female vocalists. The segue was to begin with a costumed historical character, Lord Strathcona, striking a giant gold spike, a symbolic representation of both the past and the driving of the last spike. From the spike, a single line rocket would travel to the venue ceiling where it would hit a modern satellite, symbolizing the future, from which three more line rockets would travel down to the stage, ending up at the top of each of three magic reveal doors. From the doors would emerge the three vocalists through the smoke created by three flashpots, to begin their show, fittingly with the song, "Fire."

This all happened exactly as planned and was greeted by enthusiastic applause from the audience. However, there was a noticeable momentary uncertainty and slight staggering on part of the vocalists, as they emerged in their glamour through the smoke and began their first song somewhat hesitatingly, which was unusual as they had always been extremely professional onstage.

We learned from them after the show that they had feared for their lives as they stood behind the doors waiting to begin and watching the line rockets speed toward them. Of course, as soon as the rockets got to the doors, the doors opened and the flashpots were set off. In hindsight we realized that the flashpots had probably been loaded with too big a charge, as there seemed to be excessive smoke and much too loud an explosion. The vocalists, to their credit, soldiered on in spite of being terrified. What then was the problem? Since this was before the days of strict risk management assessments, we had not used a qualified pyrotechnician but another person who claimed to know the right charge to use in the flashpots. Also, we had failed to completely brief the vocalists about what to expect with these special effects. We were fortunate that the only result of this was a good story for the vocalists to tell their friends.

(Courtesy of Doug Matthews)

### 6.2.5 Atmospherics

This is the name applied to artificial snow, foam, bubbles, and water effects. Companies who deal in atmospherics, usually movie special effects firms, supply specialized machinery to create these natural elements. Although not used extensively in special events, there are occasions for atmospherics when they can add an element of realism to theme events.

### 6.2.5.1 Snow

Artificial snow can be an impressive special effect as a static part of set dressing or as a dynamic effect when falling from above. Thanks to the movie industry, there are now a number of different but highly effective ways to achieve these effects. Most artificial snow is made either of plastic, paper, or foam. Snow Business, a pioneering special effects company based in the UK, in fact makes over 200 different types of snow for various effects. The ones most commonly used for special events are the following:

- Falling snow. The most effective falling snow for special events is *evaporative snow*, made out of foam and blown out of snow machines with fans. The secret to this product is in the composition of the fluid that turns into "snow." In reality, the snow is really soap bubbles that are created when the snow fluid is blown through a modulator inside the snow machine. With modern machines, the size of the flakes and the fall time can be controlled by varying an onboard switch and adding an external fan respectively. These machines can be daisy-chained and controlled using DMX, and mounted on either the floor or on flown trussing. One large machine, for example, can cover an area up to 24 ft x 80 ft (7.2 m x 24.2 m). The choice of fluid affects the dryness of the flakes and hence the length of time before complete evaporation. The snow produced is biodegradable, non-toxic, and flame-retardant. Other falling snow that remains on the ground and can be blown with fans to create a storm effect is made of paper or foam, and while it looks very realistic, it must also be cleaned up after an event, unlike evaporative snow.

- Static or ground snow. For permanent snow cover on sets, stage, floor, or ground, there are many different compounds and styles. These include:

  - Paper snow in two basic versions: environmentally friendly paper snow with no chemical additives, to be used outdoors; inflammable paper snow for interior use. Paper snow can be ordered in various sizes and hues and it is stable and water-resistant.

  - Cellulose powder. Environmentally friendly and easy to clean, it does not require additional support surface priming, and looks like a thin layer of snow or frost, depending on the support surface.

  - Plastic snow. This is excellent for interior applications, photo shoots, etc. It is available in a great number of variants.

  - Starch snow. This is environmentally friendly and good for use in hard-to-reach locations as it does not require cleanup or removal.

- Polymer snow. This is very attractive and behaves like natural snow. It increases volume on contact with water, is excellent when footprints are required, and may be formed into snowballs. Consistency may be adjusted between light down and watery slush.

- Foam snow. The cheapest variety, this is excellent for a deep snow effect and for backgrounds with no action to focus on. It does not require cleanup.

- Sparkling snow. This may be added to all the other types of snow for bright sparkling reflections effect.

- Opalescent snow. This is plastic snowflakes giving a fairy-tale effect, used as an add-on for all the other types of snow.

(Bykowski and Gajzler, 2014)

Coverage with these types of snow can be achieved either by hand or by blowing or *flocking* it with special blowers. Some types also come as large *snow blankets* formed into rolls that can be placed by hand for realism. Note that some of these compounds are toxic and may cause eye, skin, and respiratory irritation. Data sheets should be reviewed for any such toxicity before use and warnings posted for guests or handlers.

### 6.2.5.2 Foam and bubbles

Actual foam, or more accurately concentrated soap bubbles, has become surprisingly popular for events. It is composed of similar compounds as evaporative snow but more concentrated. Although sometimes considered as *dry foam*, it is not dry but does have a water component, although there are variations in compounds to make it more or less watery. The foam products are non-toxic, hypoallergenic, non-staining, and environmentally friendly. The foam used for events is expelled out of large-volume cannons and can last for hours depending on the amount of human contact. Area coverage by a cannon can be up to 8,000 cu ft (227 cu m), deposited in less than 10 min. See Figure 6.7.

Figure 6.7  Example of foam used at a party

Copyright: olgavolodina/123RF Stock Photo

### 6.2.5.3 Bubbles

The venerable bubble machine is still as popular as ever, except now more modern. Today's machines are high volume and incorporate variable-speed fans. They can be floor-mounted or rigged on trussing and can be remotely controlled using DMX. The concentrated bubble fluid is non-toxic and biodegradable but may cause slight irritation to eyes, skin, and membranes if inhaled.

### 6.2.5.4 Water curtains

Water curtains, also called water scrims, are created by very narrow streams of water falling from distribution piping. The water is caught in a trough and re-circulated using pumps, back through the upper distribution piping. The distribution piping requires a truss to be set up for support. The curtain is then used as a projection medium for lighting, video, cinema, still, or laser images, although the projection is best from the rear due to the physics of projecting through water droplets. Water curtains have many different applications: backdrops or sets for stages; corridor water walkways; part of exhibition stands; and as part of reveal sequences in which it is possible to turn off individual sections of the water instantaneously, allowing cars, people, or any type of product to be uniquely revealed. Water curtains are sometimes called *rain curtains* although these tend to be smaller with fewer nozzles and used primarily as architectural enhancements.

At present, there are no known safety regulations or standards for the atmospherics described; however, possible risks might be water damage to materials or décor as a result of overspray or leaks, and some minor skin, eye, and respiratory irritation as mentioned.

---

## PRODUCTION CHALLENGES

1. Explain to a client why you do not recommend repeating a streamer cannon effect at the end of his presentation after doing it at the beginning. Suggest an alternative special effect ending.

2. You are planning to begin a stage show with thick fog rolling over the stage and disappearing over the downstage edge into the front rows of the audience. Describe how you would achieve this effect.

3. Explain the restrictions and cautions for a laser show according to international standards.

4. The local fire department demands that you obtain a permit for a large outdoor fireworks show that your client wants as a farewell for 5,000 convention attendees. It is to be held in one of the city's parks. The fire chief wishes to meet with you as this is the first time you have ever done such a show. List in detail all the applicable documents that should be included in your presentation and what you should know to convince him that you are aware of the regulations and risks involved.

5. You are planning a bar mitzvah for your son and would like to use some of the latest special effects popular with that age group. Research what is current and describe what you would use and where and how you would use these effects.

---

## REFERENCES

APA. (2014). Glossary of Pyrotechnic Terms. *American Pyrotechnics Association*. Retrieved October 7, 2014, from www.americanpyro.com/glossary-of-pyrotechnic-terms.

ARPANSA. (2013). Radiation Protection: Lasers. *Australian Radiation Protection and Nuclear Safety Agency*. Retrieved October 6, 2014, from www.arpansa.gov.au/radiationprotection/basics/laser.cfm.

Brain, M. (2000, June 30). How Fireworks Work. *HowStuffWorks.com*. Retrieved October 7, 2014, from http://science.howstuffworks.com/innovation/everyday-innovations/fireworks.htm.

Bykowski, J. and Gajzler, W. (2014). Snow. *Film Special Effects*. Retrieved October 9, 2014, from http://efektyspecjalne.pl/cms/?en_snow,6.

Cooper, D.C. (Ed.). (2014). *The Event Safety Guide: A Guide to Health, Safety and Welfare at Live Entertainment Events in the United States*. New York: Event Safety Alliance of USA, Inc./Skyhorse Publishing.

Dryer, I. (2005, October–December). Show Basics: Small Beam of Light Leads to Dazzling Images. *The Laserist, Vol. 16, No. 3*. Retrieved October 3, 2014, from www.laserist.org/Laserist/showbasics_2.html.

Fireworks. (2014, October 2). In *Wikipedia, The Free Encyclopedia*. Retrieved October 7, 2014, from http://en.wikipedia.org/w/index.php?title=Fireworks&oldid=628011098.

Helmenstine, A.M. (2014). Chemistry of Firework Colors: A Marriage of Art and Science. *About.com: Chemistry*. Retrieved October 7, 2014, from http://chemistry.about.com/library/weekly/aa062701a.htm?once=true&.

ILDA. (2014a). Discover Lasers: Why Lasers? *International Laser Display Association*. Retrieved October 3, 2014, from www.laserist.org/discover_lasers.htm.

ILDA. (2014b). Technology: How We Do It. *International Laser Display Association*. Retrieved October 3, 2014, from www.laserist.org/technology.htm.

ILDA. (2014c). Laser Show Safety – Basic Principles. *International Laser Display Association*. Retrieved October 6, 2014, from www.laserist.org/safety-basics.htm.

Jaworski, J. (2003). *The Secret to Creating Real "WOW" Power at Your Events*. Source and exact date unknown.

Laser Spectacles, Inc. (2013). Factors in Designing Safe and Legal Laser Light Shows. *Laser Spectacles, Inc.: Safety Issues*. Retrieved October 6, 2014, from www.laserspectacles.com/resources/safety-issues/.

Mueller, B. (2005, October–December). Show Basics: Making Light. *The Laserist, Vol. 16, No. 3*. Retrieved October 3, 2014, from www.laserist.org/Laserist/showbasics_4.html.

Pea Soup Ltd. (2014). Smoke Machines. *Pea Soup Ltd*. Retrieved October 13, 2014, from www.smokemachines.net/faqs.shtml.

Theatrical smoke and fog. (2014, September 14). In *Wikipedia, The Free Encyclopedia*. Retrieved October 1, 2014, from http://en.wikipedia.org/w/index.php?title=Theatrical_smoke_and_fog&oldid=625506068.

Varughese, S., Teschke, K., Brauer, M., Chow, Y., van Netten, C. and Kennedy, S.M. (2005, May). Effects of Theatrical Smokes and Fogs on Respiratory Health in the Entertainment Industry. *American Journal of Industrial Medicine, Vol. 47, No. 5*, 411–418.

Walsh, T. (2005, October–December). Show Basics: Atmospheric Effects Are True Showstoppers, Indoors or Out. *The Laserist, Vol. 16, No. 3*. Retrieved October 3, 2014, from www.laserist.org/Laserist/showbasics_1.html.

Chapter

# 7

# Staging and set design

**LEARNING OUTCOMES**

After reading this chapter you will be able to:

1. Understand the language of the stage that is shared between theater and special events.
2. Describe the three main types of special events stages and how they are constructed.
3. Describe the options and accessories available for stages.
4. Determine the correct horizontal and vertical sizes of a stage for a given purpose.
5. Describe the different types of stage curtains.
6. Understand how stage sets are designed and how they can be used to enhance a special event.

What is it about a stage that can cause exhilaration one minute and terror the next? Why is it that by physically raising a person or group of persons above the level of other people, the perception of that person or group by the other people instantly changes? Quite simply, over the centuries, we as human beings have come to subconsciously equate positions of power and higher social status than ourselves with a physical difference in height. Most political and religious leaders have always spoken publicly from raised positions or platforms, and hence we consider anyone who speaks or performs from such a position as special in our eyes. We attribute more credibility and importance to their utterances, whether those utterances are serious or humorous, true or false.

In this chapter, we examine not the psychology of being on a stage, but the humble construction of that structure that has been so supportive of human social and theatrical drama since ancient times. In so doing, we cover the following topics:

- language of the stage;
- types and construction of stages;

- placement and sizing of stages;
- stage draping;
- stage sets and set design;
- risk and safety.

## 7.1 The language of the stage

In special events, nowhere is our shared heritage with the world of theater more obvious than in staging, and we have borrowed extensively from theater terminology. The first instance of this is the style of stages, which goes all the way back to the ancient Greeks. The second important instance is in the directions for performers and those using the stage.

### 7.1.1 Styles of stage

There are three main styles of stages that are used in theater with accompanying similar, but modified, types in special events. It is useful to know what these are and how they are constructed:

- Thrust stage. The stage projects into, and is surrounded on three sides by, the audience. The fourth side contains the scenery or backdrop. Entrances to the stage may be made from backstage or through the audience and up onto the front of the stage (Figure 7.1). This type of stage most closely resembles the ones commonly used for special events, especially corporate events, although the backstage entrances are sometimes not used as there is no backstage area available, and usually the audience only surrounds the stage on one side (the front), unless space is in short supply. In this case, it is referred to as an *apron stage*. An offshoot or slightly different version of the thrust stage is the *catwalk* or *runway stage* that is just a narrower version of the thrust portion of the stage and that usually projects further into the audience, thus allowing for better audience viewing and interaction with performers. Figure 7.5 (left) is a unique example of a catwalk stage.

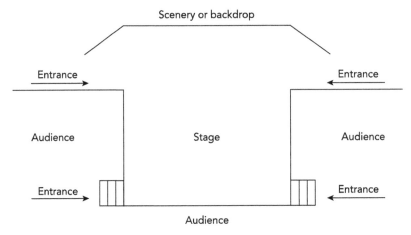

Figure 7.1  Thrust stage

Courtesy of Doug Matthews

- Proscenium stage. In this configuration, the audience watches the action through a rectangular opening (the *proscenium arch*) that resembles a picture frame. Scenery or a backdrop typically fills the space behind and upstage of the actors or performers. Entrances to the performing space are made from backstage

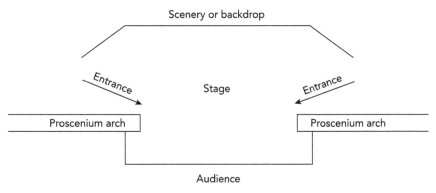

Figure 7.2 Proscenium stage

Courtesy of Doug Matthews

(Figure 7.2). This type of stage is most often found in modern theaters, but occasionally a reasonable facsimile is constructed for special events by using curtains to mask the backstage area that extend outwards to venue side walls from the fronts or near fronts of the stage. The proscenium arch per se, however, is non-existent.

- Arena stage. This type of stage—sometimes called a *theater-in-the-round*—is completely surrounded by the audience and any entrances must be made through the audience to the stage (Figure 7.3). Stairs to the stage may be placed in the center of each side, on corners, or any other location desired. In special events, this type of stage is most often found in concert settings; however, even there, the stage more often resembles a thrust stage configuration. Occasionally, an arena-type stage will be constructed for other special events, but audio, lighting, and sight-line challenges can pose problems. There are usually no scenic elements on this type of stage. See Figure 7.5 (right) for an example.

### 7.1.2 Stage directions

The second area of theater language that we share is stage directions. Production of an event with entertainment and action on a stage involves constant references to specific locations on the stage. To properly direct the action, whether it is the simple movement of lights, re-locating a microphone, or movement of people, all participants must understand the directions. It has become standard custom to give stage directions as if one is **on** the stage looking at the audience. Hence, *stage left* is to the left and *stage right* is to the right, *downstage* is in front, and *upstage* is behind a person on the stage. These same directions provide the reference if one is **off** the stage as well, for example a show caller directing lighting cues or managing talent. The terms *upstage* and *downstage* probably evolved in the 16th or 17th centuries during the era of *raked* stages which were purposely sloped stages built that way to create the illusion of depth. Figure 7.4 shows these directions.

## 7.2 Types and construction of stages

Temporary staging has come a long way from the rickety pageant wagons of Medieval England and the makeshift platforms of itinerant Commedia Dell'arte players in Renaissance Italy. Most staging used for special events today is one of three types: manufactured proprietary decks and support systems, custom stages, or mobile stages. We will examine each of these types and their construction, and then review common accessories for stages and other optional indoor structures.

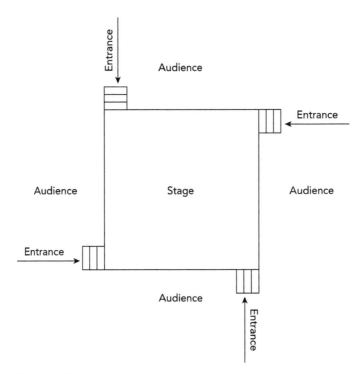

Figure 7.3  Arena stage

Courtesy of Doug Matthews

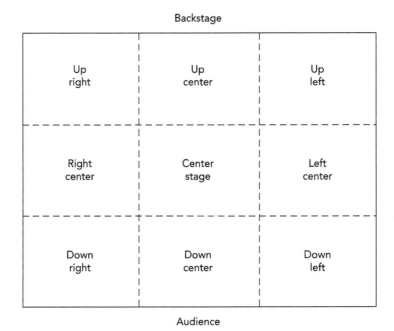

Figure 7.4  Stage directions

Courtesy of Doug Matthews

## 7.2.1 **Manufactured decks and support systems**

This type of stage comes in standard sizes of *decks* (sometimes called *risers* or *platforms*) that connect with each other to form larger surfaces (stages). Depending on the specific manufacturer and the design, they may have legs as an integral part of them or separate legs that attach to them. Typical rectangular deck sizes are 8 ft x 4 ft, 4 ft x 4 ft, and 8 ft x 6 ft. Less common are 2 ft x 4 ft, 2 ft x 8 ft, and 4 ft x 6 ft. These are North American sizes and comparable metric sizes tend to be slightly different (e.g. 244 cm x 122 cm, 122 cm x 122 cm, and 244 cm x 183 cm are the closest to the three most common sizes respectively). However, not all manufacturers make all the different sizes and, due to proprietary designs, decks from one manufacturer are usually not compatible with decks from a different manufacturer. This means that it is unlikely that a large stage could be built using decking from two different manufacturers. Some manufacturers have begun to make decks in unusual shapes that allow for a larger variety of overall stage shapes than traditional rectangles. Most manufacturers now also make 45-degree corner sections, both square and rounded, and some add semi-circles and triangles as well as other shapes. This, of course, increases the number of creative stage design possibilities immensely.

Manufactured decks typically consist of an extruded aluminum frame into which is fitted thick plywood sheeting, or a sandwich construction of cellulose honeycomb between thin sheets of plywood. Total thicknesses vary between about 3 and 4 in. (7.5 and 10 cm). Manufacturers usually offer optional surface treatment for the decks in the form of carpeting, varnished or unfinished wood, slip-resistant polypropylene, or fiberglass sheeting. Modern decking also has fixed holes or special fitting points in the top corners that will accept proprietary safety railings, as well as proprietary fittings on the underside for legs and supporting frames. Some decks are even reversible.

Supporting legs and frames for staging are as different as the riser surface shapes. Again, depending on the manufacturer, the legs may be fixed in height or have variable height settings. There are two reasonably standard height systems in use, one that works with 6 in. increments (e.g. standard leg heights of 6, 12, 18, 24, 30, 36, 42, 48 in.) and one that works with 8 in. increments (e.g. standard leg heights of 8, 16, 24, 32, 40, 48, 56, 72, and even 96 in.), with comparable European sizes (e.g. 200, 400, 600, 800, 1000 mm, etc.). Legs can be the only means of support, with a single leg supporting each corner, or they can be part of a larger frame system that incorporates horizontal and diagonal cross bracing. Many legs come with height-adjustable feet as well as more continuously variable height adjustments using cotter pins or special screws with indents at very small increments. Legs and frames are usually constructed of extruded aluminum. Some of the frames telescope and rotate for easier storage and some, besides telescoping, are permanently attached to stage decks for more efficient setup. Hotels and conference centers often purchase manufactured staging for use in special events, but event managers are usually charged for their setup and use.

These types of manufactured stages are often used for purposes other than entertainment or ceremonial. Thanks to the variety of leg lengths, they can be perfect for temporary tiered flooring for seating or dining to afford audiences or guests better visibility for action taking place on other surfaces, in effect putting the audience on the stage and the show on the floor.

Temporary circular stages are sometimes mounted on tracks and bearing assemblies and connected to motors that allow them to rotate. This is often seen in trade show situations to demonstrate products. It can also be very effective for entertainment presentations to achieve quick changes of stage sets; however, it is costly and for large stages must be strictly designed to permit sufficient loading and to determine the correct motor size.

Custom thrust stage                    Manufactured arena stage

Figure 7.5 Examples of different stages

Images courtesy of: left—Gearhouse SA (Pty) Ltd. and Chris Grandin; right—Gearhouse SA (Pty) Ltd. and ZooM Photography

### 7.2.2 Custom stages

The ingenuity of event producers and expectations of clients will always maintain a demand for customized staging, for shapes and sizes that are not achievable with manufactured systems. In this particular genre of staging, specialized staging companies come into their own. There are numerous companies in the industry that build stages out of wood and customize them with paint or other finishes and surface materials. Often these companies also provide complete set-building capabilities as well, which we will discuss in Section 7.5. The advantage of custom staging is that it can be built to fit into any space, of any size or shape, and of any theme or material. Some examples of situations where customized staging may be used are:

- For covering of awkwardly shaped or dangerous surfaces. This might be ground with rocks, gardens, or other obstructions that cannot be covered easily by manufactured staging, or that is at too great a slope. It might also include water such as swimming pools or lakes.

- To accomplish a unique design for an event. This is most often used in concert situations and for major award ceremonies where the set and stage design must be original and attention-grabbing. See Figure 7.5 (left).

- For large stages in situations where there is insufficient manufactured staging available or for which the rental of such staging would be excessively expensive. This might occur again in a concert setting or in a convention facility that does not own sufficient staging.

- To replace manufactured staging which may not be strong enough in a certain situation. For example, this might be to support heavy cars or trucks at a product launch.

- To fit a stage into an awkward space. If an event is being held in an unusual venue with architecture that does not lend itself to the standard rectangular staging, custom-fitted staging may be necessary, or if a client wishes a stage to fit into an irregular space.

- To extend an existing stage over existing seating in a theater or arena. This might entail constructing additional oddly shaped decking to butt against an existing stage, or to fit over seating that does not allow the regular spacing or fitting of support frames and legs of manufactured staging.

### 7.2.3 Mobile stages

Arguably the genesis of large outdoor concert stages began with the questionably engineered stage of Woodstock in 1969. Many of those outdoor stages are now in mobile form and capable of moving from one city to the next literally as the contents of, and an integral part of, large trailer trucks.

An entire series of easily erectable mobile stages is now available from several manufacturers in stage surface sizes ranging from about 24 ft x 20 ft (7.3 m x 6.1 m) to about 130 ft x 50 ft (39.3 m x 15.2 m). These stages are designed to fit entirely into, and as part of, a towable trailer. An onboard hydraulic system is used to literally fold the stage surface and roof into the trailer. These systems come equipped with trussing engineered to support full lighting and audio systems. Indeed, the largest stage mentioned above has a load rating of 75 tons (i.e. 150,000 lb or 56,000 kg). With most, there is a variety of accessories and options available, such as stage extensions, roof canopy extensions to cover equipment (e.g. lights on the trussing), stairs, ramps, safety rails, fire-retardant wind walls, vertical and horizontal banner supports, A-V screen support, generator, and heating and air conditioning. These mobile systems have greatly increased the efficiency of technical setups. See Figure 7.6 for an example of a fully erected 50 ft x 38 ft (15.2 x 11.6 m) mobile stage.

Figure 7.6 Example of mobile stage

Courtesy of Doug Matthews

### 7.2.4 Accessories for stages and other optional structures

Staging for special events is more than just decks and legs. Particularly with safety in mind, there are accessories that make for safer work on stages and easier access to them, specifically stairs, ramps, safety railing, and deck covering. As well, there are other indoor temporary structures that fit easier classification under staging options, namely dance floors and choral/band risers.

#### 7.2.4.1 Stairs

All stage manufacturers provide stairs that match their decking and leg heights in design and size. Some are equipped with wheels or casters that tilt out of the way when the stairs are in use. Most stairs have holes or attachment points to accept safety railing. For safety, the edges of stairs and stages are often marked with bright masking tape for better visibility.

#### 7.2.4.2 Ramps

Some manufacturers provide optional ramps for wheelchair and disabled access, including safety railing. Occasionally, custom ramps need to be built to provide this access. In North America, all such ramps must conform to ADA (Americans with Disabilities Act) *Standards for Accessible Design, Section 4.8*, which specifies slope, width, landing, and handrail requirements. The maximum gradient in North America and most of the rest of the world is 1:12, which equates to 1 foot of ramp for every inch of rise. For example, a 24 in. (60 cm) high stage would require a 24 ft (7.3 m) long ramp. Additionally, ADA limits the longest single span of ramp, prior to a rest or turn platform, to 30 ft (9 m). Ramps can be as long as needed, but no single run of ramp can exceed 30 ft, and no more than 10 m (33 ft) in Europe. The minimum width should be no less than 36 in. (91 cm), but 120 cm in Europe (Express Ramps, 2014; and DFPNI, 2006).

#### 7.2.4.3 Safety railing

In the interest of good risk management, it is becoming increasingly necessary to provide safety railing (also called *guardrails*) on access stairs, ramps, and the backs and sides of stages themselves. Although there are no regulations or standards for the special events industry, worker safety standards from the United States and Canada do provide guidelines that are met by most manufacturers. In the United States, *OSHA Code 1910.23(e)* states that railing should have a nominal height of 42 in. (100 cm) and be able to bear a load at the top in any direction of 200 lb (890 N). The Canadian standard (*SOR/86-304, Sec. 2.12*) mirrors the US, stating that the height range should be 900 to 1,100 mm (36 to 44 in.) and load rating 890 N. European/UK standards also are the same.

Most manufacturers meet these standards. Typically, safety railing is constructed of tubular steel and comes in heights of 39 to 42 in. (980 to 1,058 mm). It also comes in fixed or adjustable lengths, depending on the manufacturer. Most railing attaches to the stage surface in one of two ways: by fitting *spigots* into pre-drilled holes on the stage corners then placing the railing posts over the spigots; or by attaching a clamp or gripper-type adaptor with a spigot built onto it, to the stage surface that then accepts the railing post. Different railing designs have different load ratings and these should be checked before installation to ensure they are adequate for anticipated use and also meet standards. For example, one manufacturer (Prolyte) has two versions, one that is light duty and can resist only 30 kg/m (20 lb/ft) of horizontal loading, and one heavy-duty version that can resist 100 kg/m (67 lb/ft) of horizontal loading. Any event in a public area should have only heavy-duty railing with a high load rating installed.

### 7.2.4.4 Deck surface covers

Besides the finishes already discussed for stage surfaces, occasionally performers may demand that certain surfaces be provided for them. Dancers, especially ballet and contemporary, and some athletes, fall into this category. They require a surface that is forgiving yet is not too slippery and they may request a surface material generically known as a *Marley* carpet or flooring. The name comes from the company that originally manufactured it, but there are now different manufacturers with differently sized products.

This type of flooring is composed of a layer of mineral fiber interply sandwiched between two layers of thin PVC with a smooth finish. It comes in rolls of widths between 63 and 78 in. (1.6 to 2 m) and thicknesses between 0.04 and 0.10 in. (1.0 to 2.5 mm). The smallest thickness is also good for tap dance performances. The products come in a variety of colors and some even in woodgrain. It must be rolled out on top of an existing stage (hard surfaced, not carpeted) and taped together. If dancers must dance on an existing stage, their preference is normally a smooth wooden surface with no uneven joints. This may mean that joints between deck sections must be taped to cover irregularities.

### 7.2.4.5 Dance floors

Dancers may also request a hard surface for tap dancing that can often be provided simply by placing sections of wooden dance flooring on top of existing carpeted staging. Standard dance floors typically come in 3 ft x 3 ft, 2 ft x 4 ft, 3 ft x 4 ft, or 4 ft x 4 ft sections (depending on the manufacturer, although 3 ft x 3 ft or 91 cm x 91 cm is the most common) and interlock via tongue and groove aluminum edges on each section, sometimes with additional screws for extra safety. Outer edges have special bevel fittings to eliminate the possibility of tripping. Finishes are usually smooth varnished wood, or painted. Some have vinyl surfaces with simulated wood grain. Plexiglas surfaces and underlit LED floors are also available. Custom floors, like stages, can be made to almost any size and finish. There are a few manufacturers that make "sprung dance floors" which are really just shock absorbing, closed cell foam blocks that suspend the wooden floor above an existing, hard uncompromising surface.

If a dance floor is actually being used for dancing for guests—on the ballroom/meeting room floor, not the stage—the correct size must first be determined. One starts by using an educated assumption that only about 33 to 50 percent of the guests will be dancing at any given time. Next, the average area occupied by a single dancer (2 to 3 ft² per person) is multiplied by the number of people. Let us assume, for example, that the total number of persons attending an event is 500 and that it is a crowd that enjoys dancing so we can use the high figure of 50 percent of them being on the dance floor at any given time. This means the dance floor area required will be between 500 ft² and 750 ft² (depending on whether we use the 2 or 3 ft² per person assumption).

Using another assumption that the dance floor available is comprised of 3 ft x 3 ft sections (9 ft² per section), then the total number of sections of dance floor required will be 55 to 84 (i.e. 500/9 at the lower end of size, to 750/9 at the upper end of size). If we wanted to make a square dance floor, using the larger size for safety, then each side would be nine sections long, or 81 ft, for an actual total area of 729 ft². How did we arrive at this number? First, we calculated the square root of the maximum number of sections we need since we want a square dance floor (i.e. $\sqrt{84} = 9.17$), and the closest whole number to this is 9 so we will use nine sections per side.

Instead of opting for a square dance floor, if we want to match the width of the dance floor to the width of the stage and the stage is 24 ft across, then the width of the dance floor will be eight sections (24/3) since each section is 3 ft wide. Thus the length of the other side of the dance floor will be ten sections or 30 ft (i.e. 84 sections/8 sections = 10.5 **or** 750 ft²/24 ft = approx. 31.25 ft or ten sections of 3 ft wide flooring). Note that the numbers are rounded to obtain the closest number of sections, so that the final actual dance floor area will be 720 ft² (24 ft wide x 30 ft deep).

### 7.2.4.6 Choral and band risers

Frequently, events utilize large choirs or choral groups, concert bands, and symphony orchestras as part of their entertainment programs. These large musical groups usually require specially designed risers for their members in order for them to easily see their director/conductor, and for the audience to see all of them. These risers are positioned on top of the event staging, but occasionally may be placed directly on the floor. Although the risers may be custom-made, they are more often manufactured in standard sizes. These types of risers are constructed similarly to stage decks in that they have separate decks that are attached to legs (primarily steel) and support frames (steel or aluminum). They can be configured in rectangular or curved shapes using pie-shaped sections of decking. Usually, the deck rise is 8 in. and there are two, three, or four tiers in total, giving a total rise of between 8 and 40 to 54 in. (20 and 100 to 136 cm), depending on the manufacturer and whether the support legs are fixed height or fully adjustable respectively. Deck depths are usually 16, 18, or 21 in. (40, 45, or 53 cm) for choral risers and 36 or 48 in. (91 or 121 cm) for band risers, with widths being 6 or 8 ft (1.8 or 2.4 m) for band and 6 or 6.5 ft (1.8 or 2 m) for choral risers, although some are tapered. Deck surfaces are often reversible with one side being non-slip textured polypropylene and the other carpeted. Decks themselves are usually laminated honeycomb. The entire assemblies fold up or dismantle into individual sections and are portable. Some are equipped with their own wheels and, of course, safety railing is available.

## VOICE OF THE INDUSTRY

**An interview with Mr. Michael Reese**

Executive Vice President Creative, Barkley Kalpak Agency
New York, NY, USA
www.bka.net

With a Master of Fine Arts in theater design, Michael Reese has been a key member of the Barkley Kalpak team for over 11 years. BKA has won numerous awards for their creative corporate events and earned a well-deserved reputation for excellence. I spoke with Michael about how they do it.

Figure 7.7  An example of Barkley Kalpak staging

Courtesy of Barkley Kalpak Agency, www.bka.net

**DM**: Can you talk about how you approach set design and the idea of the "experiential event"?

**MR**: We bring people together for a shared experience to talk about something and often it is done as a story. It's important to remember that the design is saying something about the client's brand—their messaging—so you have to understand what they want to say. You have to ask a lot of questions. What's the vibe, or impact desired? What does the client want the audience to experience or feel? What story do they want to tell? What relationship do they want the presenter to have with the audience?

My personal style [for set design] is probably defined by using the fewest elements for the most impact. My work tends to be more sculptural and substantial. I had a design professor in grad school that talked about elegant solutions—use only what is necessary. And I've held onto that.

Also in the proposal or courting phase, I try to keep in mind that the clients want the Ferrari. Even if their budget is a station wagon, they want the dream. So we focus on the rendering quality, or the feeling of the experience, not just the ground plan showing how big the projection screens are and how many chairs fit.

**DM**: How has the event experience changed for audiences?

**MR**: First, there is a lot less live entertainment because of the perceived cost. This came about after the economic crash in 2008. The main thing that has filled the void has been networking, spending time with each other. There is also more of an emphasis on shared cultural experiences in which clients want to get attendees out of the ballroom and experiencing local culture.

**DM**: How has set design then changed over the last five to ten years as a result, in terms of materials, incorporating technology, and following standards for safety and sustainability?

**MR**: There is a focus on multimedia and video presentation. Ten years ago we weren't talking about screen resolution, picture-in-picture and video design nearly as much as we do now. There used to be more of a focus on the "theater" of the presentation space. It was even called "business theater." But now it's more about a personal connection; there is more of an attempt to be authentic, approachable. The designs are about supporting the presenter/attendee relationship. Safety is and has always been important. As we move to more authentic experiences in live events, the theatricality tends to have taken a back seat—which also relates to a sense of being needlessly expensive—so some of the safety concerns have been reduced. There's less "flying in a CEO from overhead rigging"!

**DM**: Can you give some examples?

**MR**: There is much less hardwood flat construction. Work tends to be more graphic with large format printing. There are also many more requests for wide-screen projection. The actual scenic design component has become minimal and there is more graphic design integrated into the multimedia. Often now, for example, we must move an onstage presenter in order to allow the screen presentations to be visible as they change. We are also seeing some gamification in which the audience becomes involved in the presentation. In fact, occasionally there is no screen at all and information is pushed directly to the mobile devices of attendees. However, there is a dark side to this and that is creating too much isolation when the main purpose is to bring people together for the shared experience.

**DM**: Regarding staging, do you tend to now custom-build stages more than before or just try to modify and work with manufactured staging?

**MR**: There are a lot of great rental solutions out there now, more than ever, and sometimes that's a great option. I actually think it's ego that prevents some designers from using more rental solutions. Just because you've seen it before, doesn't mean the clients or attendees have seen it before. I would say most of the time I'm using some rental elements blending with some custom fabrication for a personal and impactful (and budget-friendly) solution. You can usually make some version of a rental solution work in order to be cost effective for your client. If you want a 20 ft diameter stage, but the only rental stage around is 18 ft, you can usually make that work.

**DM**: Do you have any final words of wisdom to give students of event production that would make your job easier if they became your client? For example, is there say a minimum knowledge base they should possess with respect to staging and the process and cost of set design?

**MR**: Be as honest as possible with the requirements and the budget. It will only save you time and frustration.

We designers don't tend to have our own agenda. We only want to help the client have the best event they can—and have fun. It's a great opportunity to create something that has never existed before. And as much as possible leave the assumptions at the door. It doesn't always have to start with, "Where is the screen going to be?"

## 7.3 Placement and sizing of stages

In Chapter 1 we discussed placement of stages with respect to the effective presentation of entertainment. The same options hold true for all other types of presentations, namely against a wall, in corners, or in the center of a venue. For that matter, a stage or stages can be placed anywhere in a venue that is convenient for those using it and those viewing the onstage activities. What is a little more complicated is determining the correct size for the stage.

### 7.3.1 Horizontal size

Determining the correct area of a stage is sometimes more art than science. Unfortunately, event planners and managers often do not give it enough consideration. The horizontal area must accommodate any and all activities that will take place on it. Even though speeches may occupy 3 h and 55 min out of a 4-h program with only one speaker appearing at a time, but there is a finale with a 12-member dance ensemble, the stage has to be big enough from the outset to accommodate the dance ensemble. In other words, it must be large enough to allow for the activity that will require the most space, no matter how important or how long that activity is in relation to the rest of the staged program.

For most activities, there are no golden rules. Every performing group usually has a minimum size of stage that will accommodate their performance and they should be consulted prior to event setup to ensure that the properly sized stage is ordered. Generally, for speakers at a lectern, a minimum of 15–20 ft² (1.4–1.8 m²) is required. Unfortunately, if the event consists of only speeches by one or two persons at a time such as an awards ceremony, having a small stage might not automatically be the correct choice. The stage size in relation to the size of the venue and also in relation to the size of the stage set and any additional décor or A-V equipment must be taken into consideration. For example, if an awards ceremony is to take place with a stage set up in the middle of a 150 ft (45 m) long wall, and two large A-V screens with surrounding drape are to extend to the side walls on either side of the stage, it does not make good design sense to have a stage that is only 8 or 12 ft (2.4 or 3.6 m) wide as it is completely out of proportion to the remainder of the room's décor and the scale of the entire venue. The stage must reflect the correct proportion, and should be more in the order of about one-third of the total width of the venue or 50 ft (15 m) wide, in spite of the small number of persons occupying it at any given time. Part of the extra space may also be taken up purposely with a well-designed stage set.

In the case of musical groups, it is better to compute an accurate size of stage based on fairly static area requirements for individual musicians. The following guidelines will assist in calculating stage sizes for musical groups:

- Electronic rhythm instruments. 25–30 ft² (2.5 m²) per musician (e.g. guitar, bass, keyboards) including amplifiers and equipment.

- Acoustic instruments. 10–15 ft² (1.3 m²) per musician (e.g. brass, woodwinds, strings), including chairs and music stands.

- Drummer. 50–70 ft² (6 m²), including all equipment. Drummers are often elevated on a small riser, usually 8 ft x 8 ft x 6 to 12 in. high (244 cm x 244 cm x 30 cm), for better visualization.

- Spinet piano. 30 ft² (2.5 m²).

- Full grand piano. 100 ft² (9 m²).

- Vocalists. 10 ft² (1 m²) per vocalist if backup and not moving too much; 30–50 ft² (4–5 m²) per vocalist for a lead vocalist, and possibly more if part of a show band.

As an example using Imperial units, a five-piece regular dance band with a single lead singer, a drummer, a keyboard player, a bass player, and a guitarist, would require approximately 155–210 ft² of space using the variable area extremes from the above list. This would equate to a stage with horizontal dimensions of 16 ft x 12 ft (192 ft²) for the absolute minimum-sized stage, and at least three choices for the stage that would accommodate the band in a roomier manner. These possibilities would be 16 ft x 16 ft (256 ft²), 20 ft x 12 ft (240 ft²), or 20 ft x 16 ft (320 ft²), all assuming single riser dimensions of 8 ft x 4 ft. Since most musicians do not like to play beside a drummer but rather in front, and since a drum kit is approximately 8 ft deep, this means that the drummer occupies essentially the back or upstage 8 ft of the stage alone. Thus, there must still be at least 105 ft² of stage area remaining (155 ft² minimum less 50 ft² minimum for the drummer). If the stage size is 20 ft x 12 ft, that means there is only the front or upstage 4 ft remaining for the rest of the band to play on, a total of only 80 ft² of space (i.e. 20 ft wide x 4 ft deep, after subtracting the upstage 8 ft occupied by the drummer), which is inadequate. Therefore, the correct stage size should be 20 ft wide x 16 ft deep, which would leave an ample 160 ft² (i.e. 20 ft wide x 8 ft deep, after subtracting the upstage 8 ft occupied by the drummer) for the rest of the band. Although this sounds complicated, it is an exercise that a producer must go through if an adequately sized stage is to be provided for the entertainment planned.

In addition to drum risers for dance or show groups, larger musical ensembles such as symphony orchestras or big bands often specify tiered riser sections on top of the regular stage for the different orchestra sections, such as percussion, strings, brass, or woodwinds. The height and horizontal size of these risers is usually determined by the orchestra leader, and specified in their contract rider. Special band risers such as those described in Section 7.2.4.6 may need to be rented.

## 7.3.2 Vertical size

The first assumption in determining the height of a stage is that the special event is not being held in a venue with a permanent stage such as a theater. Otherwise, the height is dependent on the size of the audience, whether they will be sitting or standing, and whether the ground or floor is level (we will assume in this section that the surface is level). Standing audiences can occur for concerts, receptions, dances, trade shows, product launches, and others. Seated audiences can occur at dining events, award ceremonies, opening and closing ceremonies, meetings, and numerous others. We will deal with each of these.

### 7.3.2.1 Standing audience

In order to make an educated determination of the correct height for a standing audience, we must make some assumptions of human characteristic body dimensions and typical spacing between persons in a standing crowd. For purposes of this exercise only, let us assume that the average person is approximately 5 ft 11 in. (179 cm) tall and that in a standing crowd, people will tend to space themselves no closer than 2 ft (0.6 m) apart. Also, we must assume that persons in the crowd are able to maneuver themselves sufficiently to see over the heads of other persons two rows ahead of them (i.e. about 4 ft, or 1.2 m in front of them). If we further assume that at minimum any persons in the audience must see at least the top part of the head of an average person standing on the stage (near the front or downstage edge of the stage), then we can draw some sight lines to assist us with calculating the correct stage height that will relate directly to the size of the crowd. Figure 7.8 does just this. Note that at 25 ft (7.6 m) away from the stage, a person is able to see the top part of the head of someone onstage if the stage is 3 ft (1 m) in height. Likewise, at 50 ft (15 m) from the stage, the height must be raised to 4 ft (1.2 m) to achieve similar visibility and at 100 ft (30 m) away from the stage, the height must be at least 8 ft (2.4 m) for the same visibility. It is clear from this explanation that given a specific audience size and venue size, a stage should be constructed of sufficient height to enable the entire audience to view the stage in the worst case scenario. For example, even in the case of a standup reception at which there will be stage entertainment, the assumption must be made that during the entertainment, attendees will crowd the stage to the extent that they will be about 2 ft apart, even though when the entertainment is **not** on, this may not be true.

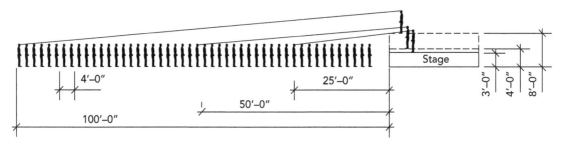

Figure 7.8 Stage height determination for a standing audience

Courtesy of Doug Matthews

### 7.3.2.2 Seated audience

For a seated audience, the height is also determined by the ability to see over the head of a person sitting directly across a table (if dining) or directly in front by two rows (if theater-style). We will illustrate the principle by using a dining situation in which diners are seated at 72 in. (1.8 m) diameter round tables, separated by 10 ft (3 m) center-to-center. Exactly the same principle applies as for the standing scenario, except that, because the distance from the observer to the person opposite is much greater than the critical distance in a standing crowd, the angle is lower and so the stage can be that much lower in height. Figure 7.9 illustrates the angles and can be used to calculate approximate stage heights. Once again, the worst case scenario must be assumed and if the tables are less than 72 inches in diameter (e.g. 60 in. or 1.5 m rounds) then the calculation must be rechecked. Note also that because of the low angle, a constant stage height may be used for the nearest 50 ft (15 m) to the stage before the stage height really needs to be increased, unlike the standing situation.

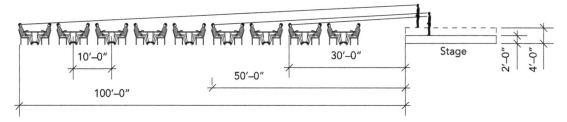

Figure 7.9 Stage height determination for a seated audience

Courtesy of Doug Matthews

It should be kept in mind that the variables in determining stage height are many (e.g. slope of ground if outdoors, proximity of audience members to each other, whether performers stay on mainly the downstage portion of the stage), so the above analyses are only intended to be general guidelines and not hard rules. Each situation will be different and in some cases, a lower stage might be adequate.

## PRODUCTION WAR STORY

### One small detail . . .

As part of a final night celebration for a large insurance convention, we were asked to produce a custom entertainment show in conjunction with the Sheraton San Diego. A professional, well-established technical production and staging company was also brought on board. This being the case, I felt that we would be in good hands.

As the Sheraton wanted this show to be completely custom, the technical production and staging company began developing a total custom stage for the performance and we were brought in early so that our performance needs would be considered in the development of the stage. Conversations during the planning and construction of the stage included our requests for concealed stage entrances on stage left, stage right, and center stage, as well as reminders that the floor of the stage must be constructed using wood, and then covered in Marley or some such surface to ensure safety for the show's dancers. We also took great care to indicate the kind of stairs to be used to ensure performer safety with their elaborate costumes.

Months were spent developing the show creative, building the costumes, producing the orchestral tracks, casting, and rehearsing the show. We maintained contact throughout this period with the technical producer, including a check of stage drawings.

On show day, we moved into the venue expecting the day to run smoothly. We had been rehearsing offsite, and had taken great care to ensure that the costuming would work despite the choreography and show staging. We were ready. The stage too seemed ready when we entered the ballroom. Everything we talked about seemed to be included, except the most important element of all, the wooden floor with a Marley surface atop. To save money, and unbeknownst to us, the technical producer had changed his mind due to cost and used a low-pile carpet as a stage surface instead of what we had requested.

Horrified due to the intricacy of the choreography and the safety of the performers, we immediately showed our concern, which was met in a most disagreeable manner by the technical producer.

Clearly in the wrong, he began to shout at us, insisting that the carpet would be fine, and that we were simply too demanding. He just did not agree that there was a problem other than the one we were creating.

Given that we had no more time to change the flooring and still be able to rehearse on the set, we determined that we would do the best we could under the circumstances, and dance on the carpet. We spent our onsite rehearsal time changing the choreography to work on carpet. This naturally only served to confuse the performers, who had spent weeks rehearsing.

What should have been a smooth, well-rehearsed performance ended up looking somewhat reckless and unrehearsed. We had spent tens of thousands of dollars and months preparing for this opportunity to wow our audience, and came up short thanks to a lack of communication on the part of the technical producer.

(Courtesy of Anthony Bollotta, Bollotta Entertainment, San Diego, USA)

## 7.4 Stage draping

Stages do not look good all alone. Because they are very short in stature when in a room full of people, they require higher embellishments to let people know where they are. For special events, this embellishment often takes the form of either draping or creative stage sets. In this section we will discuss the different types of stage draping.

### 7.4.1 Backdrops

Generally there are four types of fabric backdrops used for special event stages, apart from custom stage sets and technical backdrops like LED screens. These include the following:

- Regular drape. Drapes used for stage backdrops are usually constructed out of cotton or polyester *velour*, commando cloth, or Encore, the materials and support method for which are described in Section 2.2.4.2 of Chapter 2. Also as mentioned in Chapter 2, stages may have decorative murals as backdrops rather than plain drapes, or hard sets, and these can be further dramatized through the use of scrims (see below).

- Star drop. One unique fabric backdrop that has been around for some time but still finds use as a stage backdrop is a *star drop* or *drape.* This is a basic drape (e.g. velour) that has numerous small LED—or fiber optic—lights sandwiched between two layers of fabric. The lights come in color or white and the drapes themselves in a variety of sizes. The lights can be pre-programmed using DMX protocol and can fade or change patterns.

- Cyclorama or cyc. A cyc is a large curtain or wall, often concave, positioned at the back of the stage area. It can be made of unbleached canvas (larger versions) or Muslin (smaller versions), or seamless translucent plastic (often referred to as "Opera Plastic"). Traditionally it is hung at 0 percent fullness (flat). When possible, it is stretched on the sides and weighted on the bottom to create a flat and even surface. As seams tend to interrupt the smooth surface of the cyc, it is usually constructed from extra-wide material. Cycs are most often used for dramatic lighting effects.

- Scrim. A scrim in the theatrical sense as applied to special events is a gauze-like fabric made from cotton or flax: "Scrims both reflect and transmit light. This means that if a light from a front-of-house position is shone at a scrim, then both the scrim and everything behind it will be lit. This can lead to a variety of interesting effects.

- A scrim will appear entirely opaque if everything behind it is unlit and the scrim itself is grazed by light from the sides or from above.

- A scrim will appear nearly transparent if a scene behind it is lit, but there is no light on the scrim.

- A dreamy or foggy look can be achieved by lighting a scene entirely behind a scrim.

- If a light with a gobo is aimed at a scrim, the image will appear on the scrim, but also any objects behind the scrim will be lit by the pattern as well."

(Scrim, 2013)

For most special event situations, a scrim will probably remain static as part of the stage backdrop design, although in theaters they are rigged to be raised or lowered to achieve a dramatic effect on cue.

### 7.4.2 Masking curtains

The same regular drapery material used for backdrops is also used for *masking curtains* to hide parts of the stage and equipment. Masking curtains can be flat or pleated with fullness. Their size is usually determined by sight lines to minimize or eliminate any view to the backstage area. They are usually black as they are meant to become "invisible" when the lights are dimmed. The following are explanations of the different types of masking curtains:

- Borders hide lights and other equipment mounted above the stage. They are finished with fabric ties at the top and hang from the same trussing used for mounting the lights, on the audience side of the truss.

- Legs or wings hide off-stage areas and provide passageways for entrances, change and preparation areas, and areas for sidelights. Their size and location is usually determined by keeping sight lines in mind. They are typically mounted on freestanding pipe and drape hardware as described in Chapter 2.

- Mid-stage travelers or rear travelers are used as stage dividers to create a smaller space or to hide equipment or backdrops near the back wall. They may consist of two panels with a center overlap and open to the sides, or, depending on the available space, a traveler may be one panel and travel off stage on a curved track to one side. Travelers are usually mounted on a special drapery track (like household drapes) in turn mounted to trussing that allows them to be opened with rope pulls.

### 7.4.3 Stage skirting

One other use of stage draping is for skirting stages. Although most staging manufacturers sell matching skirting that is clipped onto the stage surface or attached by Velcro, some designers choose to match other décor by customizing skirting in a specific color or style. For this, they will generally use lightweight material and clip it or staple it onto the stage. Of course, drapery used as backdrops or wings can be further enhanced with lighting or decorations that can be hung from it or over it, such as signs, A-V screens, and other material, fabrics, and objects.

Figure 7.10 illustrates a stage backdrop drape, drapery wing masking curtains, and stage skirting.

### 7.4.4 Front curtains

In special events, due to the temporary nature of the installation and to the fact that front drapes are traditionally very heavy and cumbersome to maneuver and install, they are seldom used unless the event is being held in a theater. However, there are two types of curtains that may be used for short-term events:

- Portable stage and drape system. Some companies are making portable, multi-contour front drape systems that can be installed in temporary situations but that resemble full theater draping. The Sico Insta-Theatre® (www.sicoinc.com/portable_theater.php), for example, is actually a complete portable

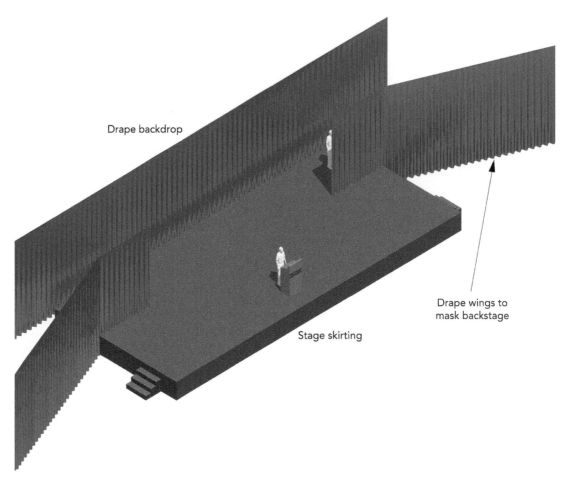

**Figure 7.10** General locations and names of stage drape components

Courtesy of Doug Matthews

stage setup with staging, lighting, and support trussing, drape backdrop, wings, front truss border, and draw-style front curtain.

- Kabuki drop. "The Kabuki drop is a special effect in which a lightweight fabric [usually rigged at or near the front of the stage] is dropped swiftly from above to conceal or reveal a product, space, or performers . . . [Most systems are capable of both single and double kabuki effects.] The single Kabuki consists of either a concealing curtain dropping in, or a revealing curtain dropping to the floor. The double Kabuki is a two-step process which begins with the curtain stored above, out of sight. The first trip releases the curtain into its concealing position. A second trip releases the curtain to the floor for the reveal" (Rose Brand Inc., 2014).

## 7.5 Stage sets and set design

In Chapter 2 on Décor, we briefly discussed the use of sets as part of themed décor in a venue, which may have been stand-alone large set pieces or pieces used on a stage. These would not have been custom designed for the event but would have been existing set pieces available for rental from a prop house or décor provider. In this chapter, we deal with the use of stage sets custom-designed specifically for a given event. Typical events at which these are used are product launches, sales meetings, incentive meetings, awards ceremonies, and association meeting general sessions. In these types of events, the stage and the set are the main, and probably only, focal point in the venue. Often the set and the stage are left in place for the duration of a meeting, which could be up to a week or so. Thus, they have to be attractive, durable, and versatile enough to be easily changed in a small way to create a new "look" for different sessions. Let us now examine the key considerations in achieving effective set design.

## 7.5.1 Design procedure and criteria

The design process typically begins with meetings among the client, set designer, and event producer to lay out the general goals of the design. Unlike a theater set design for which the goals are to establish a time and place, as well as the mood and spirit of a play, the goals of a corporate set design are invariably to reinforce the goals of the event itself and to deliver or emphasize a message. For example, it may require a futuristic design to reinforce a sales meeting's theme of "Selling Effectively in the 21st Century." It may require a giant three-dimensional representation of a company logo in the corporate colors to help motivate a group of employees on an incentive trip. It may require a series of framed screens that allow for the playback of video clips and winners at an awards show. Whatever the client's goal, the set designer must have a clear understanding of it before proceeding.

In addition to establishing the goals of the design, these meetings should also determine what will be happening onstage (e.g. who and what will move on and off stage, and from and to where that movement will be), the exact location of the event (e.g. what room in what venue), how long the setup time will be, and what the budget will be. With this, the designer can further proceed to the initial design phase. In this phase, the designer will:

- establish the size and shape of the set in relation to the stage size and to the location of the stage in the venue (often requiring one or more visits to the venue to take measurements);
- locate entrances and exits to the stage, such as doors, ramps, stairs, or arches, being aware of audience sight lines so that no backstage or unnecessary areas are visible to the audience;
- create a color palette and texture for the general background;
- add logos, graphics, or openings for visual presentations to the set;
- determine the number and location of scenic pieces or additional props if needed;
- draft a *ground* or *floor plan* (top view), *front elevation* (front view), plus possibly an *end* or *side elevation* (from the side of the stage) of the set either by hand or by CADD;
- develop a colored rendering by hand or using CADD.

At some point in this process, the designer and producer will probably consult with the lighting company to ensure that appropriate colors and luminaires will be used to correctly light the set, and also to determine exactly where the luminaires are best placed and/or rigged. Occasionally, the designer may build a miniature three-dimensional model, although this tends to happen more in theater than in special events where time and budget are very limited. With possibly some iterations following until the exact design is found, the next step is for construction of the set, which the set designer has the responsibility to supervise.

## 7.5.2 Construction and installation of the set

The set designer may or may not be the same person or the same company as the set builder. However, once the design is approved, the set must be built. Unlike theater, corporate event sets are usually stationary and are built of any one or more of the following structural components:

- Flats. Flats are lightweight panels attached to frames made of wood or steel tubing and are used to make two-dimensional, painted scenery. They are normally covered with Muslin, plywood, door skin (1/8 in. thick wood paneling), paper, Masonite, velour, or other fabrics and materials. They vary in size from about 2 to 6 ft (0.6 to 2 m) in width, and 8 to 16 ft (2 to 5 m) in height. The frames are normally constructed of 1 in. x 3 in. (2.5 cm x 7.5 cm) wooden sections. For large sets, flats are screwed or hinged together. Often they are painted in perspective or with other *trompe l'oeil* to give the impression of three-dimensional objects. They are often anchored to the stage floor with wooden braces, held up with a combination of braces and weights such as sandbags, or braced with small L-shaped metal feet (brackets) on each side to make them freestanding.

- Cutouts or silhouette flats. A cutout is a piece of thin wood or other firm material that is cut to represent an exterior outline of an object. It may be used on its own or attached to a flat frame; for example, a flat representing the edge of a forest might have a straight edge (the flat) along a tree trunk and then a cutout representing leaves higher up where the foliage begins.

- Platforms. These are used to add levels to stages, whether a few steps up or a higher level representing a different location, and are made out of wood with construction that is similar to, but sturdier than, flats.

- Murals, scrims, and cycloramas. Murals are discussed in Chapter 2 and scrims and cycs in Section 7.4.1 above. They are more often used to augment a theme when onstage rather than convey a corporate message.

- Projections. Projections have been used increasingly as integral parts of set designs. For corporate sets, projections might be still images, like PowerPoint, or moving images shot on video or film. They are typically projected onto a screen surface designed and built into the set. They are discussed in Chapter 4.

Before installation, each flat or individual section of the set is constructed first. The set is then brought in section by section and screwed together. Final paint touchups may be required after construction and often time must be allowed for final painting to dry.

Figure 7.11 shows two examples of finished stage sets. Of interest in the left image are the simplicity and symmetry of the set. Note also the repeated cutout flats on each side covered with stretched fabric, and also the small props decorating the front of the lectern and the back wall. The right image illustrates several elements: a custom stage shape, unique curved flats that dramatically frame the set, several entrance and

Figure 7.11 Examples of stage set design

Images courtesy of: left—Vodafone Crossword Book Awards, Seventy Event Media Group, www.seventyemg.com/; right—South African Film & Television Awards (SAFTAS), Gearhouse SA (Pty) Ltd. and Pieter Joubert

exit stairs from backstage and from the audience, and two large, curved projection screens placed symmetrically on either side of the stage and acting as part of the actual set.

## 7.6 Risk and safety

Because staging supports people—and sometimes automobiles and other heavy inanimate objects—of critical importance is the safe allowable loading for a given stage. Too many event producers and event managers are unaware of the fact that there are currently no North American standards for allowable loading. Why is this important? Consider the fact that, in the last ten years, at least 15 temporary stages have collapsed at special events in various countries around the world, and these were not roof structure collapses, which we will discuss in Chapter 9, but the actual stage decking. In many of these incidents, people were injured. Event producers must be aware of the allowable loading for any given stage design, and since there are no standards, it makes this point even more important because, as part of proper risk management, the stage provider, whether it is a venue or a subcontracted staging company, should be able to provide producers with the deck manufacturer's figures for safe loading limits. In the case of customized staging, the builder should have made proper calculations or should provide proper calculations from a certified structural engineer to prove that the staging will be adequate for the loads anticipated. These limits should state allowable loads of several types:

- Uniformly distributed loads (UDL). Also called the *maximum allowed load*, this means how much weight the entire deck can support overall. This value decreases as stage height increases.
- Pointload. This refers to the maximum weight that a single small point on the deck can support (e.g. a car wheel or a truss tower beam). This is often where problems occur. Typical regulations specify a point loading of 7 kN (kiloNewtons) for a "point" measuring 50 mm x 50 mm (i.e. 2 in. x 2 in.). In North American engineering terms, this load translates into just over 400 psi (pounds per square inch). Of course the upper limit to a pointload will be the UDL if the area of loading is greater than 4 in.$^2$ (2,500 mm$^2$). Note that pointloads are different and usually less over the center portion of a deck than over the edge or corners where there are supporting beams.
- Lateral forces. These forces occur due to movement on the stage such as dancing or jumping people, and moving set pieces, and also by force applied to protective handrails (e.g. someone falling against it). Regulations usually require a deck to be able to absorb 10 percent of the vertical loading on the horizontal plane. In other words, if the deck is stressed to support 4,000 lb UDL, then the allowable lateral force should be 400 lb. Put another way, if there are four supporting legs and the deck is stressed to 4,000 lb, each leg supports 1,000 lb of vertical force and must also support 10 percent of that or 100 lb in lateral force before collapsing.

The only known standards for recommended allowable stage loading (including guardrails) are:

- *EN 13814: Fairground and amusement park machinery and structures – Safety (2004)* incorporates *DIN 4112: Temporary structures: code of practice for design and construction*, originally from Germany. It also applies to some other EU countries, as the name EN (*Euro Norm*) would suggest.
- *Temporary demountable structures. Guidance on procurement, design and use. (Third Edition) (2007)*, in the UK.
- *DIN 15920-11: Entertainment Technology – Practical Types – Part 11: Safety Regulations for Wooden Practicals, Ramps, Steps, Stairs and Stage Balustrades (2011)*. This standard, once again from Germany, provides structural and safety standards for the construction of ramps, railings, and stairs.

The result of not having design safety standards is that staging is not manufactured to consistent load ratings, which means that one manufacturer's staging may not be as strong as another's. This may lead producers to make erroneous assumptions about the strength of a stage and/or its options (e.g. guardrails). Otherwise, for North America, the safety standards that pertain to workers using or building staging are encompassed by the OSHA and WCB (Workers' Compensation Board) standards in the United States and Canada respectively, copies of which should be in the possession of all producers.

## PRODUCTION CHALLENGES

1. Explain to your new employee what the different styles of stages are that have been inherited from the theater, and also what the different stage directions are.

2. A rich client wants to hold a dinner party and dance in his garden, with the band stage placed over the top of a sloping rock garden. Explain to him why a manufactured stage cannot be used and also the circumstances when a custom stage must be used for a special event.

3. You want to place a large Hummer vehicle on four sections of staging with one wheel on each deck as part of a product launch. The Hummer weighs 8,000 lb and each deck has an allowable UDL of 4,000 lb, with an allowable pointload of 400 psi where each of the Hummer wheels will be placed. The Hummer's wheel footprint is 36 in². Will the staging support the Hummer?

4. A client wants to hire a ten-piece show band that includes three lead vocalists, a drummer, a guitarist, a bass player (both electric), a pianist using a full grand piano, two saxophone players, and a trumpeter. Using 4 ft x 8 ft sections of staging, what is the minimum size of stage that is required for this group? Assume that the stage height is 2 ft and that all musicians will be playing downstage of the drummer.

5. You have been asked to create a stage set design for an awards ceremony that will honor pioneers in the logging industry. The set must incorporate a natural look as if it is in the forest with mountains behind. You are not allowed to use live trees and must construct the set out of regular theatrical material, allowing for two backstage entrances and two projection screens on either side of the stage. Describe possible structural components that could be used in the construction and what the final set might look like.

## REFERENCES

DFPNI. (2006). *Technical Booklet H2006*. Department of Finance and Personnel Northern Ireland. Retrieved October 17, 2014, from www.dfpni.gov.uk/technical_booklet_h_2006-2.pdf.

Express Ramps. (2014). ADA Modular Wheelchair Ramp Specifications & Guidelines. *Express Ramps*. Retrieved October 17, 2014, from www.modular-wheelchair-ramps.com/modular-ramps/ada-guidelines.aspx.

Rose Brand Inc. (2014). Kabuki Drop System. *Rose Brand*. Retrieved October 21, 2014, from www.rosebrand.com/.

Scrim (material). (2013, December 10). In *Wikipedia, The Free Encyclopedia*. Retrieved October 20, 2014, from http://en.wikipedia.org/w/index.php?title=Scrim_(material)&oldid=585360958.

# Chapter 8

# Tenting

**LEARNING OUTCOMES**

After reading this chapter, you will be able to:

1. Understand why tents are used for special events.
2. Understand and describe the different styles of tents.
3. Discuss current tent technology.
4. Know when and how to use tent accessories.
5. Describe the basic considerations for tent setups, including site surveys, weather, date, time of day, and installation procedures.
6. Understand the risks associated with tented events and know where to find and how to apply safety standards and regulations in order to apply for an occupancy permit.

Ever since humans developed to the point where they were able to construct their own shelters, they have sought to tame nature. Nomadic peoples were undoubtedly the first to realize that it would be more efficient to create a portable house that required less construction than a permanent one every time they decided to stop on their journeys. Their crude attempts at such shelters were the first known predecessors of today's spectacular tented environments. Over the intervening millennia, tents have appeared in every conceivable situation, and today they enable special events to take place in locations that would have previously been inaccessible.

In this chapter we will explore the use of tents in special events, starting with why they are used today. We will then explain and illustrate the different styles of modern tents used in events, including a look at the latest technology. Following this is an in-depth explanation of fabrics and accessories, followed by a review of setup considerations. We end with a review of risk and safety as it pertains to tenting.

## 8.1 Why use a tent for a special event?

In Chapter 1 of *Special Event Production: The Process*, we examined the underlying reasons why special events are held: political, religious, educational, social, and commercial. These, however, are not necessarily the same reasons why one would choose to use a tent for a special event in today's world. In essence, a tent is an alternative venue, nothing more, nothing less, but one with very special characteristics that sometimes make it more attractive than a traditional venue such as a conference center, a hotel, or another permanent structure. Because so many of today's special event attendees have used traditional venues on a regular basis, they are looking to escape to a unique venue that takes advantage of the geography of the local area. Tents afford them the opportunity to do this, often enabling an event to take place in a locale where no buildings exist but that is an attractive setting in itself. Additionally, some destinations do not have facilities of sufficient size to accommodate larger groups and a tent may provide the only alternative for an event. In forming additional space, a tent can be placed closer to key activities that require support structures to enable them to take place at all. Examples are the large temporary tented corporate pavilions at air shows (e.g. Paris and Farnborough Air Shows) and automobile races.

As a blank canvas, a tent starts with plain bare walls, ceiling, and floor. It therefore permits designers to transform it into a unique environment with décor and lighting, and even to design complete interiors as full working offices, restaurants, clubs, warehouses, and other unique uses such as prisons. The other primary advantage of tents is that they can expand or contract to the required area relatively rapidly and relatively cheaply when compared with more permanent structures.

## 8.2 Styles and configurations of tents

The Tent Rental Division of the Industrial Fabrics Association International (IFAI) defines a tent as "a temporary structure composed of a covering made of a pliable membrane or fabric, supported by such mechanical means as poles, metal frames, beams, columns, arches, ropes and/or cables" (IFAI, 2015a). The word "tent" is sometimes used interchangeably with "pavilion" and "canopy," though a "canopy" can also refer to a tent without sidewalls, a small tent, or even an awning-like structure. In the UK and Australia, the term "marquee" is synonymous with the North American definition of "tent" (meaning a variety of styles and sizes) whereas a "tent" there is typically a small camping tent. A "marquee" in the United States, however, refers to a very specific hybrid style of tent as explained in Section 8.2.2. Indeed, tent styles are constantly changing and improving—generally meaning more user-friendly and practical—as tented events become more popular.

### 8.2.1 Traditional tent styles

The explanations of the following four basic styles of tents are provided by the Industrial Fabrics Association International (IFAI, 2015b), and are used with permission. They are generic in nature and do not constitute an endorsement of a particular tent type, brand, or company.

- Pole-supported tent. This is "a tent that features a set of individual poles arranged beneath the fabric roof to support and define the shape of the structure. The fabric roof is tensioned over the poles and attached to ropes and/or cables at designated spots around the fabric's edges. The ropes or cables are anchored to the ground using stakes, augers, or weights around the perimeter of the tent. Pole-supported tents are the grandfather of the tent industry, and were once the only type of tent available. Although they have lost ground to newer designs, pole-supported tents remain popular in the United States and are still considered an important part of most tent rental inventories."

- Pipe frame-supported tent. This is "a tent with an assembled framework made of aluminum or steel pipes that supports the fabric roof and defines the shape of the structure [and consequently the roof line is usually more rigid and straight than that of a pole tent]. The rigid framework allows the tent to be freestanding without additional support, but requires the same rope or cable anchoring system as a pole-supported tent to hold it in place, as specified by applicable fire or building codes. Pipe frame-supported tents are popular for events that require smaller tents. Most manufacturers make units as small as 10 ft x 10 ft (3 m x 3 m) that are easy to set up and tear down. They are also suitable for smaller events that require few, if any interior obstruction since the frame system makes interior supports unnecessary. Pipe frame-supported tents are available in a wide variety of styles and sizes."

- Box-beam frame-supported (clearspan) tent. This is "a type of tent that features an assembled framework of box beam (or I-beam) arches that support the fabric roof and define the shape of the structure in much the same way as a pipe frame-supported tent. The stronger construction of the aluminum or steelbox-beam frame makes these tents suitable for larger or longer-term applications than other types of tents. The box-beam framework also allows for large areas of unobstructed "clear span" space beneath the fabric roof. The larger structures require heavy equipment because of the size and weight of their parts. Popular in Europe, these tents come in widths ranging from 5–60 m [16–200 ft] wide."

- Tensile tent. This is "a type of tent that shares some characteristics with the pole-supported tent, but which relies more on the tensioning of the fabric roof [over movable poles] for its structural integrity and shape. The use of tensioned fabric to resist applied loads and shape the fabric membrane means less of a traditional support structure is needed to maintain it. One of the more modern tent designs, tensile tents tend to be more curvilinear and sculpted in appearance than traditional tents. This type of tent can be mass-produced or custom-designed as needed." The concept for the tensile tent has been around for centuries in the form of the *Bedouin tent* used by the Middle-Eastern nomads of the same name.

Figure 8.1 illustrates these basic styles.

Pole-supported tent

Pipe frame-supported tent

Clearspan tent

Tensile tent

Figure 8.1  Traditional tent styles

Clockwise from upper left, images courtesy of: Hess Tent Rental LLC, www.hesstentrental.com; Economy Tent International, Miami, FL, http://economytent.com; RHI Tents, www.rhitents.com; JK Rentals, Inc., www.jkrentals.com/

## 8.2.2 Hybrid and unique tent styles

Increased client demand and manufacturers' ingenuity have led to the development of some fascinating hybrid tent styles and some unique approaches to the idea of temporary shelter for special events:

- Peak tent. Depending on the manufacturer and country of origin, this extremely popular style of tent may also be called a *marquee* or *pagoda*. It is a hybrid that combines the smoothly curved, peak roof feature of a pole tent with the structure of a frame tent so that there are no obstructing internal poles supporting the roof. Most of these styles use a design of taut, structural cables that cross from the top corners of the walls to support vertical poles above them that form the roof's shape, so that in a sense, they are also part tensile tents. They may require anchoring *guy wires* under some conditions. Footprints include square, rectangular, hexagonal, octagonal, and more, and all manufacturers design them to be erected as multiple joined units if desired. These are not to be confused with *high peak pole tents*, which are just large versions of the traditional pole tent.

- Pop-up tent. Pop-ups are small, generally consumer tents at the lower end of special event tents. They are essentially frame tents but the frame that forms the roof is collapsible and comes as a single unit. The top is stretched over it and expandable poles attached at the corners. Different manufacturers make them slightly differently and may call them by different names (e.g. the Bumbershoot & Presto!™ Party Tent from Tentnology). They may or may not require anchoring depending on the location, use, and design.

- Saddlespan™ tent. Depending on the manufacturer, this style may also be called *Arabesque*™. This type of design is a unique form of clearspan tent that is in the shape of a saddle and supported by only two points on the ground in addition to guy wires. Specially shaped trussing forms the roof shape over which the roof material is stretched. These tents are designed such that multiple units can be joined together for very unique looks. They are also well designed acoustically and frequently used as stage backdrops.

- Dome tent. A dome tent is based on the *geodesic dome* concept, which is "a spherical or partial-spherical shell structure or lattice shell based on a network of great circles (geodesics) on the surface of a sphere. The geodesics intersect to form triangular elements that have local triangular rigidity and also distribute the stress across the structure. When completed to form a complete sphere, it is a *geodesic sphere*" (Geodesic dome, 2014). For dome tents, the triangular elements (struts) are constructed of steel and are assembled from the top down to the bottom. Particular struts are joined with one screw into five- and six-armed joints or *knots*. (Occasionally these struts are located on the outside of the dome with different manufacturers.) The covering membrane is usually PVC polyester but other materials are available, as are transparent panels. A unique floor system enables mounting of the dome structure to the ground with steel pegs or with ballast weights located beneath the surface of the floor, which eliminates the need for external support. Tunnels designed with the same geodesic principle can be used to attach domes to each other, giving them a similar appearance to igloos. The strength of the frame design of the dome allows audio and lighting to be flown from it. Current dome tent sizes can be up to 700 m² (7,600 ft²) with a 30 m (100 ft) diameter and 15 m (50 ft) height. This specific size can accommodate 500 persons at a seated dinner. Note that these sizes are from Freedomes, at http://freedomes.com.

  Another form of dome tent is a combination of frame and tensile tents, but is really just a variation of the peak tent. A domed roof shape is formed with curved aluminum poles that create the frame, over which the roof is stretched.

**It just kept coming!**

A tented event was being held for 400 of a university's top donors. With one eye on the weather (a rain storm was predicted), we proceeded to install all the elements necessary for a first-class event, including a fireworks finale.

Due to the extreme heat that day, the decision had been made to increase the air-conditioning. Our logistics manager notified us only a few hours before the event that the main generator had failed, and it was necessary to bring in a replacement. Before the failed generator could be removed, smoke started pouring out of it. The smoke quickly turned to fire. Within seconds, our logistics manager was on the phone to 911. The production assistants evacuated the tents. Our executive producer called the client to inform her of the situation. A call was then placed from our office to the communications department. Because of the high-profile nature of this event, the press would most likely be on their way! Our office got in contact immediately with the client's press office to strategize. The technical director and stage managers were sent to another space for script read-throughs. It was vital to maintain focus on the production aspects of the event scheduled to kick off only three hours later!

Within 8 min the fire department and police were on the scene. Within 20 min the fire was largely put out and the immediate danger was over. Unfortunately, a new wrinkle appeared. A diesel fuel leak was discovered to be pouring into the ground underneath the catering tent. HAZMAT technicians took toxicity readings and concluded that the catering tent must be shut down. Hearing this, the president of the university determined the event should be canceled. We asked for a little more time to come up with a solution. With our rain plan in place, we had already erected a marquee tent for guest coverage as they walked to the main tent from the valet area. We enlisted the help of a 15-man crew to lift and carry it to the opposite side of the main tent onto a patio overlooking the campus fountain. Our original plan called for a fireworks finale to be staged there. However, with the diesel leak, that part of the program was canceled for safety reasons and catering was able to move to the newly established location. At 4:20 pm, with 75 min until show time, the main tent was given a clean bill of health, catering and technical staff were brought back to complete the setup, the new generator had arrived, and all technical equipment was back on-line.

At 4:45 pm, the storm, our original worry, hit with a vengeance. Severe thunder, lightning, and a heavy downpour lasted for nearly 20 min. All workers were told once again to evacuate the tent. At 5:05 pm, the storm cleared. Those who had evacuated returned. At 5:30 pm the first guest arrived and cocktails were served as we wrapped up rehearsals in the main tent. The event was a success. Our entire production team, led by the executive producer, maintained focus and pulled off the show beautifully (minus the fireworks). The caterer was able to serve from the new location and the press stories were controlled.

We credit this success to several things: keeping cool no matter what; placing the safety of others first; respecting the authority of safety organizations and working with them as partners; and ultimately, being confident that there is always a solution!

(Courtesy of Paul Wolman, Feats, Inc., Baltimore, USA; www.featsinc.com)

- Yurt. Uncommon in North America but popular in Asia, the round yurt is "a portable, bent dwelling structure traditionally used by nomads in the steppes of Central Asia as their home. The structure comprises a [wooden] crown or compression wheel, usually steam bent, supported by roof ribs which are bent down at the end where they meet the lattice wall (again, steam bent). The top of the wall is prevented from spreading by means of a tension band which opposes the force of the roof ribs. The structure is usually covered by layers of fabric and sheep's wool felt for insulation and weatherproofing" (Yurt, 2014). Although the yurts used in North America tend to be for semi-permanent installation as wilderness or camping lodges because of the length of time required to erect them, some are beginning to enter the more temporary special event market. These are still relatively small as event tents go, the largest currently being about 33 ft (10 m) in diameter and capable of seating about 90+ persons for a dinner, these figures coming from Little Foot Yurts (www.lfy.ca). This tent would take two days to set up, smaller ones a day, because structurally they are the same as the traditional yurts and just as strong, requiring no external support or anchoring. Covering for these is usually canvas.

- Tipi. Both the yurt and tipi are currently most popular in the wedding market but it is surely only a matter of time before they expand to the corporate arena. The tipi—or Nordic *kata*—is constructed with large, straight wooden poles vertically angled in a circle and supported together at their tops to form the framework for a large, high conical tent structure. Most current tipis are covered with canvas and have expandable bottom sections. In some of the larger ones, up to 50 guests can be seated for a dinner. Another similar tent, the *alachigh*, is also round but formed out of curved poles rather than straight ones as in a tipi so that the final shape is more like a slice of a sphere. Originating in Iran, it is basically a cross between a yurt and a tipi. This type of tent has not yet achieved much popularity for special events but has great potential.

- Inflatable tent. Relatively new is a variety of inflatable tents, which are not included in the IFAI definitions of tent styles. These seem to be almost exclusively manufactured in China, and are adaptable to most of the same uses as regular tents. However, they must be connected to a constant flow of air by means of a fan. These inflatables offer several advantages, including easy erection and dismantling, the fact that they are all clearspan, and their low cost. They also lend themselves to easy customization with color and graphics. Stability under wind loads, fire-retardant capabilities, air fan/pump requirements, and anchoring methods for these tents are as yet untested and unknown, although most offer optional guy wire anchoring. They are made of PVC tarpaulin material and come in a variety of sizes and shapes that somewhat mirror the more traditional tents already described.

Figure 8.2 illustrates these hybrid and unique styles (except the pop-up and alachigh).

## 8.2.3 Modern tent technology

Tent manufacturers have risen to the challenge of making tents as versatile and adaptable as possible. Materials have improved. More size options are available. Likewise, the variety of configurations available and the modularity of event tents allow them to be used almost anywhere, both indoors and out, and for almost any number of attendees. Let us examine what makes them so versatile and how best to take advantage of this versatility:

- Materials. It all starts with the material of the tent cover. The primary fabric for tents is a vinyl-laminated polyester, but a small percentage of use is still seen for canvas. The newer polyester fabrics are more durable and resistant to weather effects, including water and sunlight damage. All fabrics are treated with flame-retardants.

  Most event tent sidewalls (pieces of fabric generally attached to the roof structure and used to enclose the sides of tents) are made of lighter-weight vinyl-laminated polyester. They—and the roof structure—can be designed with clear vinyl as windows, and can be as large as the entire tent if desired, although

Peak                                                      Saddlespan

Dome                                                      Yurt

Tipi                                                      Inflatable

Figure 8.2 Hybrid and unique tent styles

Clockwise from upper left, images courtesy of: Muskoka Party Rentals, www.muskokapartyrentals.ca; Tentnology, www.tentnology.com; FM Tents, 2012, www.funkymonkeytent.co.uk; Evolution Dome, www.evolutiondome.co.uk; Peaktipis, www.peaktipis.co.uk/ and Yvonne Lishman Photography; Freedomes, http://freedomes.com

with less strength and durability. However, now walls are also offered in hard material (composites) and real windows instead of fabric.

- Sizing. Tented events have to be comfortable, and overcrowding is one of the serious errors that a producer can commit. Before expanding a tented event with different modules—or with a tent that is, conversely, too large—the first order of business is to determine the minimum size of basic tent(s) required. Depending on the type of event, what follows are some general guidelines and area allowances for doing this. These are also useful for planning indoor events.

- Stand-up reception or cocktail party. 6 ft² (0.5 m²) per person.

- Sit-down dinner. 10–12 ft² (0.9–1.1 m²) per person, depending on whether the tables seat ten or eight persons respectively.

- Buffet table or bar. 100 ft² (9 m²) per 8 ft (2.4 m) long table/bar.

- Auditorium or theater-style seating. 6 ft² (0.5 m²) per person plus 4–6 ft (1.2–1.8 m) width for aisles.

- Dance floor. 2–3 ft² (0.2–0.3 m²) per person, assuming 50 percent of guests are dancing at any given time.

- Speaker stage or platform. 10 ft² (0.9 m²) per person.

- Bandstand. The allowances required for musical groups are outlined in Section 7.3.1 of Chapter 7 and may also be used for calculating tent sizes when such groups are planned to be within the tent.

Obviously, for more complicated events such as trade shows, more specific measurements would have to be made.

- Configurations and modularity. We have already seen how new styles have entered the market, many based on cultural influences (e.g. tipi, yurt, tensile). Astute manufacturers are making tents in a variety of new styles and sizes, and enabling them to mix and mingle. This means that a row of peak tents might very well be mixed with a couple of dome tents and even a large clearspan or tensile tent—and they will all look coordinated. Not only that, but manufacturers are adding components that enable very creative configurations, or *temporary structure systems* as one manufacturer, Höcker, calls them. Curved tent sections, partial sections (e.g. half hexagons), adjoining walkways, roof extensions and wings, and different roof shapes for the same tent (e.g. curved, peak, A-frame) that can also be joined together all increase versatility.

Sizes are going out and up. First, in footprint anything goes. For clearspan tents, for example, size is limited only by width. Most large tent manufacturers make their clearspans in variable widths (e.g. 10–60 m, or 30–200 ft) and sidewall heights (e.g. 2.4–6.0 m, or 8–20 ft). However, the modularity allows for unlimited lengths. Inside, the height at the apex of some of these behemoths is amazing, up to 14 m (46 ft), and for some specialty tents such as the Galaxy tent from De Boer, an incredible 26 m (almost 85 ft) at its highest point. In fact, that particular tent is 60 m (195 ft) wide by 107 m (almost 350 ft) long, dimensions that make it as big as a football field. This is enough space to accommodate 4,000 to 10,000 guests.

Not only are the structures expanding in the two horizontal dimensions, they are also expanding upwards. Tents are now available in multiple levels. Two- and three-storey tents are used frequently at large sporting events and trade shows. Features and options include internal and external stairways, various configurations of covered and uncovered terraces and balconies, picket fencing, railings, doors, and signage systems. See Figure 8.3.

The very large tents, though, are not erected manually. Although portable, they do require large cranes to lift sections into place, and sometimes can take a day or more to fully set up.

- Graphics and colors. Tents provide a blank canvas. Indeed, what better canvas for branding a corporate image than a huge blank white surface in often highly visible locations? Many companies have realized the possible marketing opportunities this presents and are attaching signage to the sides, ends, and tops of tent structures. According to Knight (2005, pp. 173–177), graphics are also being printed right onto tent fabrics, thanks to wide format digital printers: "Graphics do not stop on the outside of the tent either. Interiors utilize extensive graphic merchandising displays, colorful murals, and pop-up displays to reinforce brand awareness . . . For special events on a smaller budget, mass-produced graphic backdrops can be affixed onto tent sidewalls." To add to these options, more tents are appearing with a rainbow of possible colors. See Figure 8.3.

Color and branding

Cultural influence

Modular two-storey with branding

**Figure 8.3** Examples of modern tent technology

Images courtesy of: top left—Tentnology, www.tentnology.com; top right—Craig Adams; bottom—De Boer International BV, www.deboer.com

One area that has to date seen minimal influence is cross-cultural. Certainly, the influence of other cultures in basic tent shapes is beginning to be seen in such designs as yurts, domes, and an increasing variety of stretch tents. However, when it comes to purely decorating the outside and inside of the actual tent walls and roofs with culturally influenced graphics, there has been little seen, at least in North America and Europe. Specific examples here include the beautiful designs of Indian and

Kazakhstan tents, and the near works of art of Tibetan tents. Perhaps it will only be a matter of time. See Figure 8.3.

## 8.3 Tent accessories and options

In keeping with the requirement for a tented environment to be as comfortable as possible, today's tents offer options for styles and accessories that will make a tented event equivalent to a classy hotel ballroom.

### 8.3.1 Tops

Although traditional white is still the norm for most tent tops, various colors and stripes are now making their way into the market in all tent sizes. For all sizes of tents, a clear top is now an option almost universally. Because of the vinyl used, clear tops are not as strong as regular material.

### 8.3.2 Sidewalls

Most tents come with optional sidewalls, which can be installed for weather protection. These can be plain white fabric (or any color nowadays), clear vinyl, clear French windows, screen, mesh, real glass, or rigid PVC. The degree of elegance, fire resistance, or security is up to the user. Manufacturers each have their own method of fastening fabric walls to frames, but most methods involve some sort of strap system. However, for larger tents, a relatively new method of attachment of walls and ceilings to tent frames is known as a *keder* system. In essence, this system allows walls and ceiling components to slide into frame rails rather than lacing up, thus saving considerable setup time and improving tent stability. For hard walls, some manufacturers offer complete interchangeability between hard walls, glass walls, and doors.

### 8.3.3 Gutters

Most tents have optional gutter systems to prevent rain damage. Depending on the tent design, these come in vinyl and lace to the tent frame and some are hard plastic complete with plastic downspouts.

### 8.3.4 Doors

As with walls, fitted doors can be provided to have a finished look that works with the remainder of the tent, or they can be customized. Doors can be single or double, and they can have panic hardware installed. All doors should conform to the code standards for tents, including tempered glass inserts or French panes that may be placed in them. Smoked glass and sliding doors are also available options from some rental companies.

### 8.3.5 Lighting

Standard tent lighting is usually achieved with bowl or globe lights made of PVC resin. They come as single units or as multiples in the form of simple chandeliers, and are used mostly for social events. Other industrial-style lights that use mercury vapor or halogen technology and are very bright are used more for trade shows and general lighting of larger areas. Generally, all styles are able to be mounted from tent frame components and also come as freestanding units. More elaborate chandeliers are available from some rental companies as well as string lights. Theatrical lighting is used extensively for tented events (see Chapter 5), but is normally designed and installed by a lighting company.

Not to be forgotten is site lighting. Tents are often set up in unlit locations and if the event will extend past sunset, it will be necessary to light all access walkways, washroom areas, and paths connecting tents.

As with the inside of tents, industrial-type lights can be used on poles and connected to portable power generators, or lighted helium globes can be used. These are large tethered helium balloons with lights inside that float high over a site thus covering a large area.

### 8.3.6 Liners

According to Tracey (2005, pp. 33–34):

> *liners beautify tent interiors and mask a multitude of sins, including tent mechanics, wiring, out-dated lighting, and soiled tent tops. The tent liner, in effect, acts as a drop ceiling . . . Leg [and pole] drapes can be added to the tent in blouse or tailored styles to match the look of the ceiling liner . . . Liners offer other practical benefits. They help mitigate outdoor temperature fluctuations, so less power is needed to heat or cool the structure. The liner provides a sandwich of air between it and the tent that acts as a blanket of insulation . . . Liners are offered in pleated and smooth styles. Commonly used materials include taffeta polyester, muslin, duvateen, or any flameproof fabric.*

Liners also come in white, black, and up to 50 or more other colors. Most liners are installed and hoisted to the ceiling using a rope and pulley system, then affixed to the tent frame using hooks and tabs. Some are both functional and highly decorative.

### 8.3.7 Flooring

Today's tent flooring comes in a multitude of options. For most special event applications, if there is any doubt whatsoever about weather conditions or if the event is being held on anything but the very firmest and flattest of surfaces, proper flooring should be a consideration. The use of flooring has the advantage of preventing water from accumulating on top of the walking surface by providing a path for drainage underneath it. As well, it provides a level, obstacle-free, and thus safer, surface. The two general categories of flooring are *laydown* and *rollout*. Laydown floors can be either *stick-built* or paneled. "Stick-built" refers to the now almost obsolete method of building a wooden floor using custom lumber construction to a specified height and over any obstacles. It has been replaced by plywood panel systems combined with adjustable aluminum legs that enable large areas to be covered even when the ground is uneven, thanks to the vertical adjustability of the legs. Some companies even have flooring systems that connect directly onto integrated base plates (e.g. Röder HTS Höcker GmbH), ensuring extra stability. A number of manufacturers also provide flat, interlocking plastic panels that are best used directly over paved or cement surfaces. These panels can be installed at roughly half the cost of plywood panels and much faster. Built into them are drainage channels and their modularity permits installation around trees, obstacles, or existing structures. They come in several colors. Most are extremely durable and strong enough for vehicular traffic.

Similar to rigid plastic paneling is the first of the "rollout" options, hinged plastic panels. They literally come in rolls and roll out directly onto the ground, eliminating the intermediate step of physically having to interlock individual panels. The last type of flooring, and one that needs a dry flat surface to begin with, is carpeting. This is normally placed on top of pre-built flooring such as wooden or plastic paneling, or directly on top of pavement or concrete, as long as wet weather is not anticipated, to give a more elegant and finished appearance.

See Figure 8.4 for a general illustration of tent accessories.

### 8.3.8 Heating, ventilation, and air conditioning (HVAC)

Correctly and adequately heating or cooling a tent is more complex than one might imagine at first glance. Prediction of the air conditioning load (in tons [t]) or heating load (usually in British Thermal Units per hour

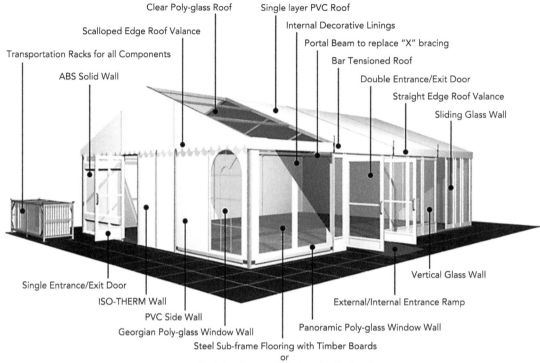

**Figure 8.4** Tent accessories

Image supplied by RÖDER HTS HÖCKER GmbH

[BTU/h]) requirement is based on several factors, including: tent size (volume), number of persons in the tent, the thermal resistance (i.e. insulation) of the tent fabric, number of openings in the tent, the temperature difference between the desired internal tent temperature and the outside ambient temperature, wind speed, and even the number of luminaires in the tent. The results of combining these variables will determine the number of heating or cooling units required to meet the desired inside temperature for the entire tent. Most rental companies will have software or charts that accurately predict the load based on these variable parameters. However, to start with, it is useful to know the following (these are only in Imperial units):

- 1 t of air conditioning equals 12,000 BTU/h.
- One person adds 350 BTU/h of heat.
- 1 W of lighting adds 3.5 BTU/h of heat.
- 1 BTU/h equals 0.00029307111111 kW.

To make this easier to understand, let's look at an example (also in Imperial units) of a tent being used for an event in both winter and summer. We start with some necessary parameters. First, the client wishes to maintain a temperature inside the tent of 70° F no matter what the season. The dimensions of the tent are 100 ft long x 50 ft wide. There will be 100 guests attending the event and it is expected that 5,000 W of lighting will be used. There will also be a 5 mph wind predicted and for the winter event the outside temperature will be 40° F, for the summer event 100° F. How much air conditioning or heating is required?

First, we calculate the area of the tent, which is 5,000 ft² (100 x 50). Next, we check the difference in temperature, which is 30° F in either winter or summer (70 – 40, or 100 – 70 respectively). The next step is to go to a chart based on these parameters. This is what most equipment rental companies will have to assist with determining how many units are required. In this case, I will use a sample chart given by Markel (2007), which states that for these parameters, 95 BTU/ft$^2$ are required. Since the tent is 5,000 ft$^2$, this means that 475,000 BTU/h are required for heating (95 x 5,000) and approximately 40 t of air conditioning for cooling (475,000/12,000). However, we are still not finished. Since there are 100 guests, this means they are adding 35,000 BTU/h of heat (100 x 350), and also the lighting adds another 17,500 BTU/h of heat (5,000 x 3.5). Thus the total heat in the tent in **summer** that must be removed in one hour is 527,500 BTU (475,000 + 35,000 + 17,500), and approximately 44 t of air conditioning is needed (527,500/12,000). Typical special event air conditioning units are rated in tons and come in sizes varying from 1 to 50 t, so at least one 50 t unit would be needed or possibly two 25 t units. It should also be noted that it may be desirable to use more smaller units placed around the perimeter of the tent in order to achieve better air distribution, rather than a single large unit placed at one end of the tent (O'Dell, 2012).

For the **winter** event, since the people and lighting **add** heat, the requirement for heating will be 422,000 BTU/h (475,000 – 35,000 – 17,500). Typical special event heaters are rated in BTU/h and come in sizes from less than 80,000 BTU/h to over 300,000 BTU/h. Mid-range are in the order of 175,000, so probably two 175,000 BTU/h units plus an 85,000 BTU/h unit would cover the heating requirement. Note that this is for a heating unit that runs on fuel (see below) whereas some models run on electricity as radiant heaters and their output is measured in kW. Therefore, using the conversion of earlier, 422,000 BTU/h would convert to a radiant heater output of approximately 124 kW. Electric heaters come in sizes varying from about 10 kW to 150 kW, so this would require either one 150 kW unit or two 50 kW units and one 25 kW unit.

Before renting an air conditioning or heating unit, however, it is also wise to try to minimize heat loss—or cool air loss in summer—by tightening up the actual tent as much as possible. Markel (2007) offers some suggestions:

- Using a keder system of framing.
- Using hard walls and glass doors and windows.
- Sealing valances.
- Using liners.
- Using units that recirculate already heated or cooled air.
- For air conditioning, placing outlet vents up high off the floor and return vents at floor level.
- For heating, placing outlet vents at floor level and return vents higher.

As far as the actual types of heating and air conditioning units, there are numerous options. For heating, there are mainly two options, the first being an electric resistive or radiant heater, and the second being a unit that runs on a fuel such as propane, natural gas, diesel, or kerosene. The fuel-powered units are usually capable of larger loads. These should be operated outside of the tent. Most local fire departments now prohibit the small, mushroom-shaped localized propane heaters and any other types that have the fuel source located within the tent, for safety reasons. Depending on size, radiant heaters usually require 240 V, single-phase or 480 V, three-phase power. Fuel-powered units require 120 or 240 V, single-phase or 208 V, three-phase power.

For air conditioning, besides a simple fan, there are units that operate on a variety of principles, including evaporative, refrigeration, and heat sink. As with heating, the units distribute cool treated air—or warm air in the case of heaters—via white Dacron ducts hung usually in the tent sidewalls, but sometimes in the ceiling. Machines using ducting are positioned outside the tent; however, there are other units that can be flush-mounted into the sidewalls and provide cooling via direct exchange of air within the tent structure (these can be noisier than the others due to fan noise). Air conditioning units, again depending on size, have similar power requirements as heaters, with the very smallest ones needing only 120 V power. It should be noted that many units can provide both air conditioning and heating, depending on the manufacturer.

Other accessories that may be required for a tented event such as fencing, portable washrooms, and temporary power are dealt with in more general terms in Chapter 9 since they also pertain to other areas of events besides just tenting.

## 8.4 Setup considerations

Planning for an efficient, safe, and accessible tent setup begins long before the event. The main considerations include the site itself and conducting a site survey, the weather and time of day of the event, accessibility and safety concerns and the associated permits, and finally, the plan for installation.

### 8.4.1 Site and site survey

Assuming that there is an optimum amount of time before the tented event, the tent rental company should be brought into the initial planning stage about six months prior to the event or sooner. In conjunction with the producer and/or event manager, they will conduct a site survey to determine:

- If the site is large enough to hold the tents and all the activities planned, including stages, tables, chairs, bars, dance floor, catering preparation tent(s), and washrooms.

- The location of fire hydrants, fire and emergency vehicle access routes, access routes for supplier vehicles, existing washroom facilities, and existing power and its specifications. Fire trucks require a minimum of a 10 ft (3 m) wide access road throughout the site. At this time, tentative plans may also be made to augment any emergency services required such as planning for St. John's Ambulance attendants to be onsite, and where they will be located.

- The tentative location and orientation of all tents, any security fencing or barriers needed, entrances and exits to the site, temporary power setup, bus or vehicle drop-off points, and parking.

- If the ground surface is one into which tent anchors can be safely placed. Many companies will test the soil to determine the type of staking required. If the surface is asphalt, gravel, concrete, or wood, special anchoring may be needed in the form of weighted blocks of some sort. Occasionally, the owners of asphalt surfaces may allow temporary holes as long as they are properly patched after the event.

- If tent anchoring will disrupt unseen underground infrastructure such as telephone, gas, water, sewer, and hydro, or if overhead infrastructure will be too close to tents. Any tenting or anchoring must generally be at least 18 in. (45 cm) away from marked utility lines, and at least 10 ft (3 m) away from overhead power lines. Utility companies should be contacted at least two weeks before the event to mark underground lines. Property owners should also be asked to mark private underground lines such as sprinklers.

- If the surface is level and will not present a problem for catering and seating. An uneven surface may require proper leveling and flooring.

- If ground obstructions (e.g. shrubbery, fountains, pavement, trees, buildings, etc.) will get in the way of planned tent locations.

Based on the results of the site survey, a tentative schematic site plan will be drawn up by the tent rental company or the producer. See Figure 8.5 for an example of an actual tent site plan that joins together a

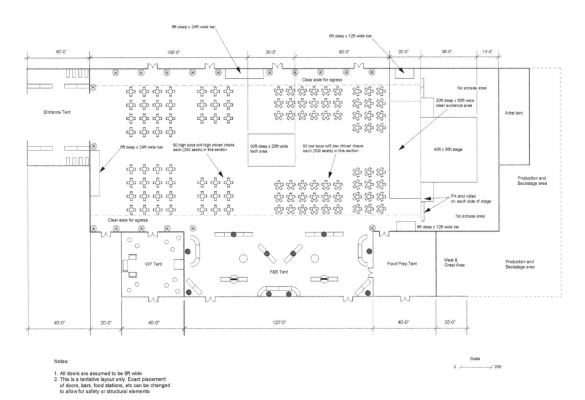

**Figure 8.5** Example of a scaled CADD tent site plan

Courtesy of Doug Matthews

large tent with five other smaller tents around it used for the entrance, VIPs, food and beverage, food preparation, and artist green room.

### 8.4.2 Weather and time of day

The actual date of the event could have an effect on setup. Some climates are prone to rain, some locales are very dry and hot, some are windy, and some combine all of the above, not to mention varying lengths of daylight at different times of the year. As a result, the producer should know clearly what the likelihood is for any of these conditions to exist during the event and also how much daylight will be available without supplementing lighting. Here are the main areas of concern:

- Rain. In any potentially wet climate, there must be an allowance made for proper drainage, either by the use of a certain type of tent (some provide better run-off than others), installing sidewalls and gutters, or providing portable flooring.
- Wind. Pole and frame tents can generally withstand winds of up to 30–35 mph (50–55 km/h or kph), whereas clearspan tents are generally safe in winds up to 70 mph (115 kph). If high winds are a possibility during the event, the choice of tent may have to be changed. Note that in many municipal jurisdictions, the special event department, if there is one, will, by law, require a qualified structural engineer to inspect and certify that the tent setup is structurally sound. This may be required in order to obtain final approval for the event and may not happen until after all tents are set up, so the correct choice of tent is critical ahead of time.

- Heat or cold. This is always a "what if" scenario, like rain. If any doubt exists at all, one should be prepared for the worst in terms of temperature extremes. If the event will go on after sunset, there is a good chance the temperature may also go down and the tent will need heat. If it is during a hot summer day, it will undoubtedly need air conditioning. As described earlier, all-season heating and cooling units may be the answer to wide temperature fluctuations.

- Darkness. Since planning often begins six or more months before an event, the amount of ambient light available for the event may be much more or less than it is during initial planning. As well, sun direction may impact the amount of light and heat in a different way than it does at the time of the initial site survey. Therefore, light for the event should be anticipated ahead of time and the necessary interior tent and exterior site lighting planned using the options mentioned in Section 8.3.5.

### 8.4.3 Installation

Once permits have been approved and site plans drawn up, the critical step of tent delivery and installation takes place. Installation must be done correctly from an engineering point of view or the tent may be unsafe. The Tent Rental Division of the Industrial Fabrics Association International has created a manual for just this purpose, based on significant research, entitled *The IFAI Procedural Handbook for the Safe Installation and Maintenance of Tentage* (IFAI, 2014). It can be obtained from their web site at www.bookstore. ifai.com. Essentially, a correct and safe installation involves proper layout and squaring, staking or anchoring, and erection and tightening of guy wires. For anything except the very smallest and simplest of tents, installation is normally the responsibility of the tent rental company. The explanations that follow are primarily for a simple pole tent; however, similar methods are followed for other tent styles, and IFAI (2014) provides extensive guidelines for those.

- Layout and squaring. A properly squared tent is aesthetically pleasing and is more structurally sound. The purpose of the layout is to make the perimeter of the tent taut and the corners squared. There will always be excess fabric in the interior portion of the tent due to the amount of material needed to make up the pitch of the tent. The basic procedure is to literally lay the tent out on the ground, pull it taut, and then check diagonal dimensions to ensure it is square. This is followed by complete staking.

- Staking and anchoring. Proper anchoring is a prerequisite for a safe tent event. According to IFAI (2014, p. 9), "anchoring is typically accomplished by fastening guy ropes to the tent at the top of the side poles and to stakes which are driven into the ground at some distance outboard from the side poles." Both wind and rain can affect the shape of the tent and hence the forces on the stakes, so safety factors must be employed. Generally speaking, the holding power of stakes is affected by stake diameter (bigger is better), stake design, depth of the stake (deeper is better), soil type (drier is better), stake driving angle, and guy rope angle. Most good tent rental companies take the time to ensure that they are providing more than adequate anchorage for a tent by comparing the required anchor pounds with the total anchor pounds of the specific stakes they are using according to a formula that incorporates a safety factor. If necessary, more stakes should be added to ensure adequate holding power for the entire stake system.

- Erection and guy wire tightening. Once stakes are in place (with guy wires relatively loose), the tent must be physically erected. Traditionally—and still today—smaller tents are erected by using sheer "muscle power." A crew lifts poles and frames into position manually, and then tightens guy wires. However, for large tents, winches and cranes replace muscle power to lift tent panels into place. After the tent has been erected, traditional rope guy wires must be manually pulled and tightened. Once again, however, the tent industry has advanced and is now using ratchet-style tent straps in place of ropes. This makes it much easier and faster to tighten guy wires.

## VOICE OF THE INDUSTRY

### An interview with Mr. Mike Holland and Mr. Tom Markel

Tent Rental Division, Industrial Fabrics Association International (IFAI)
Roseville, MN, USA
www.ifai.com

The IFAI is an international advocacy, educational, and networking organization for companies and individuals working in the various areas of industrial fabrics. One of their divisions, the Tent Rental Division (TRD), represents over 280 tent rental and manufacturing companies from across the globe. Mike Holland, CEO of Chattanooga Tent Company (www.chattanoogatent.com), and Tom Markel, President of Bravo Events Expos Displays (www.bravoeventrentals.com), have well over 60 years of combined experience in the special events industry and sit on the Steering Committee of the division. They are heavily involved with setting directions for the industry with respect to tent installation and the building and fire codes associated with tents.

Figure 8.6  Tented events

Images courtesy of: left—Bravo Events Expos Displays; right—Chattanooga Tent Company

**DM**: What major changes have you seen in both the design and use of special event tents in the last five to ten years?

**MH**: Variety of styles in tents and accessories (e.g. glass, flooring types, etc.) has been one major change. Design criteria in regards to meeting building codes have helped our industry grow by the ability to handle larger and more complex events (e.g. double decker tents).

**TM**: It's gone both ways; more tents have been engineered for wind-rated designs including frame and/or hybrid frame and small pole tents. However, some smaller manufacturers have weakened their designs to lower prices, which makes their frame and pole tents more dangerous.

**DM**: What advances or changes do you see happening in the next five to ten years in both tent design and tent use (rentals), for special events?

**MH**: I hope to see a more realistic look into tents [as] "temporary structures" having their own codes and standards rather than trying to make them fit permanent building codes. I also believe we will see advances in labor savings in design of temporary structures.

**TM**: I see the codes and industry standards changing for the next five to ten years. Standards for non-wind rated tents will be tightening to provide a "number" for wind and therefore an evacuation "number" to clear tents for safety.

**DM**: With respect to safety, there are two areas of concern. The first is in the design of tents. Are most tents now manufactured to common standards in all countries or are there many differences? This may apply, for example, to fire retardancy or strength of materials, to common erection hardware (e.g. keder), or even common anchoring methods and standards.

**MH**: I believe basic design and fabric requirements are pretty much the same on an international basis. It is, however, becoming more common for cities, states, and countries to have their own requirements or seals . . . We need to continue to educate renters and end users on anchoring methods and standards. It is sometimes difficult to explain why you use a 1,000 lb concrete ballast and your competitor is proposing a water barrel.

**TM**: Fire retardancy has not been much of an issue except with code officials . . . Modern vinyls are inherently fire resistant but this fact is not well understood by code officials and they focus on it. The only exception is lower cost fabric from Asia that might not meet fire retardancy standards but is used by smaller manufacturers and rental companies without testing the material properly. For common standards, that really depends on the country and/or jurisdiction's adoption of a code such as the IBC/IFC (International Building Code/International Fire Code) as well as other standards. The most pressing problem is anchoring tents whether staking or ballasting, both for the installer and the code officials. Many installers don't follow industry standards developed by IFAI-TRD and code officials are not educated in proper anchoring requirements.

**DM**: Again with respect to safety, the second concern is regulations. Are there more stringent regulations in place now than say five years ago, and who, in general in most countries, is the controlling jurisdiction? This question could apply to the requirements for occupancy permits, it could apply to wind and weather loading, or it could apply to general site safety in which there may be many tents in place for a given event.

**MH**: Yes, the regulations are getting more stringent, and in most cases that is a good thing. Generally we will deal with building code and fire department officials in acquiring permits. There has also been a move towards having the tent stamped "site specific" rather than just handing the officials your engineering plans.

**TM**: The biggest changes are in Chapter 16 of the IBC and American Society of Civil Engineering (ASCE) Code 7-10 for wind loads for structures which have become more stringent . . . Attempts were made to change the 2015 IFC and would have devastated the industry in the coming years and the same push is still there for change . . . the code changes for 2018 are in the works today . . . We have to be at the table today. The AHJ (Authority Having Jurisdiction) can vary from a state to a town, city, village, or county. On federal property it's the Federal government . . . but some smaller jurisdictions don't want or have resources to deal with events so they opt for state or county oversight. Code officials . . . are concerned with occupants getting out before something happens . . . This will probably evolve into a tier approach where . . . the regulations and the type of tent allowed will change with the increase in occupancy.

**DM**: As a followup to these last two questions, is it becoming harder or easier to obtain liability insurance to stage a special event with tents?

**MH**: Insurance companies ask more questions about what we do and how we do it . . . I have spoken to some of our customers and they have seen rate increases in liability premiums due to exposure and weather-related events seen in the media recently.

**TM**: At this time the marketplace for insurance access has been stable but pricing is outpacing inflation . . . it impacts profitability [in] our industry. The industry has been trending to depressed pricing . . . The result is safety goes out the window which increases insurance rates and regulation because of the increasing accident rates.

**DM**: Do you have any words of wisdom for novice event producers? In other words, what should they probably know as a minimum knowledge base in order to make the job of tent rental companies that much easier?

**MH**: I think it is very important that they know what is required to host the event on the proposed site and [what is required] by the code officials prior to picking their vendors. All vendors that are working on the project should be made aware of the requirements. The best person to make sure all aspects of the event are in compliance is the producer/event manager.

**TM**: Whether novice or old hand, event producers are just as responsible for public safety as any other entity on the "team." The notion that it is solely the tent rental company's "responsibility" to do it right is wrong and dangerous. First they [event producers] are picking the vendor, the lowest price is not always the best vendor and frequently creates a more dangerous install for promoters and occupants at the event . . . Evacuation will, at a large event, be on the producer, not the tent rental company. They [tent rental company] might have some personnel there, but the plans and implementation at a large event are squarely in the promoter's [producer's] domain. The tent rental company is part of that process but not the end decider or implementer for evacuation.

## 8.5 Risk and safety

As already mentioned, tented events have the potential to be highly risky if either the tent is not erected properly or weather causes serious problems. Both the tent rental company and the end user, which could be both the end client (i.e. event manager/planner) and the event producer, may be liable for damages or personal injury suffered as a result of a tent incident.

### 8.5.1 Pre-occupancy inspection

To ameliorate these particular risks, the tent installer (i.e. rental company) should, as a first step, perform the following inspection once the tent has been erected and anchored:

- Ensure all stakes are secure.
- Ensure all guy lines/ropes are properly tensioned and all tent material set for proper drainage.
- Determine that all poles are properly positioned, tied securely, and are structurally sound.
- Ensure all sidewalls are properly secured.
- Address all safety issues as soon as possible.

### 8.5.2 Occupancy permits

There are also extensive safety regulations in effect in most municipal jurisdictions that must be met before an occupancy permit will be issued to hold a tented event. Occupancy permits should be sought no later than about one month before the event. These regulations pertain exclusively to the tents themselves and the interior of the tents. Note that the IBC and IFC, as mentioned in the "Voice of the Industry," may drive tent design and influence the requirements for occupancy permits, but it would still fall to the local authority to decide whether or not to reference these codes (Kaminski, 2012).

Kucik (2004) provides an excellent checklist for producers and event managers who are seeking permits for tent installations. Some of the key questions included are the following, the answers to which producers would do well to have available for any tent permit requests (note that these are for events in the United States):

- Will there be flammable or combustible materials within 10 ft (3 m) of the structure?
- Will fire extinguishers be in clear view and accessible?
- Will the exits, exit aisles, and exit discharge be clear and unobstructed?
- Will there be a fire alarm system, public address system, or alternate method of occupant notification provided for occupant loads exceeding 300?
- Is all tent fabric fire retardant and does it meet the requirements of *NFPA 701: Standard Methods of Fire Tests for Flame Propagation of Textiles and Films, 2010 Edition*?
- Are all tents/membrane structures provided with a minimum of 20 ft (6 m) perimeter space for emergency egress by the occupants and with a minimum 20 ft roadway for access by emergency personnel?
- Are the tops of tent stakes blunt or covered so as to prevent injury?
- Are there a minimum of two separate exits from any point in the structure where the occupant load is fewer than 500 persons; three exits for occupant loads between 500 and 999 persons; or four exits for occupant loads exceeding 1,000 persons?
- Are changes of elevations at exits, exit access, or exit discharge in compliance with code?
- Is panic hardware or an approved equivalent provided on all exit doors that are lockable?
- Will exits remain accessible and unobstructed while the tent is occupied?
- Are exits designed and arranged to be clearly recognizable and distinctly marked as a means of egress?
- Are directional exit signs provided if exits are not readily visible from all points in the structure?
- Is emergency lighting provided in the tent to illuminate the exit access ways?
- Is the occupant load posted?
- Do electrical installations comply with *NFPA 70, National Electrical Code*?
- Are crowd managers/stewards being provided, with a means of emergency forces notification, at a ratio of 1 to 250 persons when occupant loads exceed 1,000 individuals?
- Are cooking and/or open flames being brought into the structure? If yes, explain.
- Are pyrotechnics being used in the structure? If yes, explain.
- Are decorative or acoustic materials such as hay, straw, and woodchips being used in the structure? If yes, explain.
- Are there motorized vehicles being brought into the structure? If yes, explain.
- Is seating for assembly use accommodating more than 200 persons fastened together in groups of not less than three and not more than seven?
- Are distances between tables and chairs in accordance with the local standards?

### 8.5.3 General safety regulations and standards

Other than local regulations for occupancy, which can be very strict, in the United States the main safety standards of concern for tenting are produced by the National Fire Protection Association (NFPA) and include:

- *NFPA 70®: National Electrical Code® (NEC®) Softbound, 2014 Edition*, pertinent to any electrical installations within tents.
- *NFPA 101®: Life Safety Code®, 2015 Edition*, applicable to the egress of people from tents, as well as other aspects of occupant safety and the duties of crowd managers.
- *NFPA 102: Standard for Grandstands, Folding and Telescopic Seating, Tents, and Membrane Structures, 2011 Edition*, which covers the construction, location, protection, and maintenance of tents and air-supported structures.
- *NFPA 701: Standard Methods of Fire Tests for Flame Propagation of Textiles and Films, 2010 Edition*.

In Canada, the equivalent information is covered in:

- *Industry Guide to Canadian Requirements for Tents, 2010 Edition*. Describes test methods for flammability of tent materials.
- *Hazardous Products (Tents) Regulations, SOR/90-245 (Canada Consumer Product Safety Act), 2014*. Similar to the *Industry Guide*.
- *National Fire Code* and the *National Building Code*, both 2010 editions, published by the National Research Council Canada, and the *Canadian Electrical Code* published by the Canadian Standards Association.

In the UK, within the regulatory area, tents are often included in a special category of structures called *temporary demountable structures* (TDS), which include many of the other temporary structures used in special events such as trussing, staging, bleachers, and barriers, most of which are covered in Chapter 9. For now, some of the main documents for tent safety in the UK include:

- *BS EN 13782:2005, Temporary structures. Tents. Safety*. This covers safety, installation, and maintenance.
- *Safe Use and Operation of Temporary Demountable Fabric Structures (2013)* published by the Performance Textiles Association. It covers primarily site safety and public safety and makes reference to all other documents necessary for a tented event.
- *Temporary demountable structures. Guidance on procurement, design and use. (Third Edition) (2007)*. An excellent detailed guide published by the Institute of Structural Engineers.

In Australia, regulations are apparently a state responsibility, although local municipal governments are the approval-granting authorities as in most other countries. One of the better guiding documents is *Guidelines on the Application of the Health (Public Buildings) Regulations 1992*, amended in 2002, and published by the Department of Health of Western Australia. Appendix 2 of this document is quite extensive and covers all safety aspects of a tented event.

Producers from other countries should ensure they understand all applicable equipment and personnel safety standards and regulations from their own jurisdictions.

Humanity's love affair with tents extends back to prehistoric times, yet even though most cultures are well past a nomadic lifestyle, it continues unabated today as a means of remaining close to nature. Now, though, it is for more social and commercial reasons and in more comfortable surroundings. Survival is no longer the driving force for "pitching a tent." Thanks to our inherent ingenuity, the venerable tent is not just getting old, it truly is getting better.

## PRODUCTION CHALLENGES

1. Why are tents used for special events?

2. A large standup reception with heavy hors d'oeuvres is planned for a hot summer evening for 3,000 corporate VIPs and you are producing the event, which is to be in a tent near a local lake. Explain to your client the possible traditional styles and sizes of tents that you might be able to use, including at least one advantage and disadvantage for each type.

3. Research on the Internet and find four variations of the hybrid styles of tents described in Section 8.2.2. Describe their characteristics and explain why you think they would be good for a special event.

4. The weather for the event in question two is predicted to be hot with the possibility of wind and thundershowers. The event will last past sunset. List the possible accessories that will be necessary for this event and why. Keep in mind that the ground surface is a lawn sloping gently down to the lake and that the guests wish to have a good view of the lake throughout the event.

5. Again for the event in question two, outline ten safety and accessibility considerations that you will have to discuss with your client and your tent rental supplier.

## REFERENCES

Geodesic dome. (2014, October 5). In *Wikipedia, The Free Encyclopedia*. Retrieved October 29, 2014, from http://en.wikipedia.org/w/index.php?title=Geodesic_dome&oldid=628364884.

Industrial Fabrics Association International (IFAI). (2014). *IFAI Procedural Handbook for the Safe Installation and Maintenance of Tentage, Fourth Edition*. Roseville, MN: Tent Rental Division, Industrial Fabrics Association International.

Industrial Fabrics Association International (IFAI). (2015a) What is the Difference Between a Tent, Temporary Structure, Marquee and Canopy? *Tent Rental Division IFAI*. Retrieved May 29, 2015, from http://tentexperts. org/education/faq/structuredefinitions.

Industrial Fabrics Association International (IFAI). (2015b). Tent Types & Uses. *Tent Rental Division IFAI*. Retrieved May 29, 2015, from http://tentexperts.org/education/typesanduses.

Kaminski, E.J. (2012, October). Know Your Fire Codes. *InTents*. Retrieved November 18, 2014, from http:// intentsmag.com/articles/1012_qa_fire_codes.html.

Knight, E. (2005, August). Tents Today, Tents Tomorrow: Trends & Options for Experienced Tent Professionals. *Seminar Workbook: 9th Annual Event Solutions Idea Factory*, pp. 173–177.

Kucik, D. (2004). Working with Code Officials: A True Story. *Tent School 2005 Handouts: IFAI Tent Expo*. Roseville, MN: Tent Rental Division, pp. 29–30.

Markel, T. (2007, August). The Principles of Tent Heating and Cooling. *InTents*. Retrieved November 3, 2014, from http://intentsmag.com/articles/0807_f3_principles.html.

O'Dell, H. (2012, August). Chill Out with the Right Cooling System. *InTents*. Retrieved November 4, 2014, from http://intentsmag.com/articles/0812_f3_cooling_devices.html.

Tracey, F. (2005). Making Your Tent Install be the Best! *Tent School 2005 Handouts: IFAI Tent Expo*. Roseville, MS: Tent Rental Division.

Yurt. (2014, June 2). In *Wikipedia, The Free Encyclopedia*. Retrieved October 29, 2014, from http://en.wikipedia. org/w/index.php?title=Yurt&oldid=611241771.

Chapter **9**

# Miscellaneous technical resources

**LEARNING OUTCOMES**

After reading this chapter, you will be able to:

1. Understand and explain how to calculate electrical power requirements for an event.
2. Understand how electrical power distribution works.
3. Understand what constitutes trussing structures and why their design and safety are important.
4. Understand what rigging is, what equipment is used, and why it is used.
5. Understand what scaffolding, bleachers, fencing, and portable toilets are and how they are used for events.

Sometimes neglected in the rush to produce an event are critical resources and technicians that work behind the scenes to make everything else function smoothly. This chapter is devoted to these resources, which include electrical power, trussing, rigging, and temporary structures. If not dealt with knowledgeably, these resources may cause other elements to fail. We therefore want to ensure that producers have as complete an understanding as possible of them.

## 9.1 Electrical power

Virtually everything at a special event nowadays requires electricity, from audio and lighting systems to catering hot plates. Ensuring that adequate power is available for the event is usually one of the duties of the producer. Although calculating the exact power required for all suppliers is not part of these duties, the producer should understand generally how to calculate the electrical power required and what the consequences may be if it is not available. In this section, we will therefore examine how to calculate electrical service requirements, how electrical distribution works, when portable power must be used, and finally safety considerations for working with electrical power. It should be noted that the discussion in this section applies only to electrical power in North America. Due to the complexity of this subject and the large number of connector types in various countries, it is impossible to review them all. This is intended only as a starting point.

### 9.1.1 Determining electrical service requirements

Determining correct electrical service requires matching the power draws of the special event equipment (e.g. lighting, audio, A-V) with the power available in a given venue or at an event site. Power is distributed to large venues such as hotels, arenas, and convention centers in what is commonly referred to as *single-phase* or *three-phase alternating current (AC)*. This power is usually available from venues in several optional "packages." Each of these packages is defined by the voltage or *electromotive force* (E), the amperage or *electrical current* (I), and the *power* (P). Note that "P" can refer to either the power available from the venue or the power consumed by equipment. The key is to match the two and allow for a safety factor. The relationship amongst these variables is given by a derivative of Ohm's Law for alternating current, namely:

$$I = \frac{P}{E \times PF}$$

if a calculation for the amperage is sought, or alternatively:

$$P = I \times E \times PF$$

if a calculation for power draw in watts is sought, where PF is the *power factor*. This is a number less than one that defines, in an alternating current circuit, the *real power* compared to the *apparent power*. Simply put, it reflects the fact that due to the way that alternating current works, the power that a device sees is less than the power that comes into the circuit, and it is device-dependent. Typically, for devices such as lights, this factor is in the order of 0.80 and this is a commonly used number. For purposes of simplicity only, this may be considered our safety factor. The above formula works for single-phase power, and here we need to explain the differences between single- and three-phase power. From this point on, we will be referring to the various electrical terms by their units of measurement: voltage in volts (V), amperage in amps (A), and power in watts (W) or kilowatts (kW).

In North America, most power connection points are 120 V, and are frequently referred to as 120/208 V three-phase, or 120/240 V single-phase. Single-phase power can be either 120 V, or 120/240 V. In 120 V single-phase service, there is only one *leg* of power feeding the service. In this case, the 120 V is known as the *line-to-neutral voltage* and it is found in single wall outlet receptacles in event venues and most North American homes. Since power is also defined by amperage, most common wall outlets deliver 15 A of electrical current and 120 V, thus allowing up to 1,440 W to be drawn safely using the above formula (e.g. the equivalent of a good hair dryer); however, this is insufficient for most special event applications and higher amperage connections must be used to provide enough power.

In a 120/240 V single-phase service, there are two legs of power feeding the service: two wires each carrying 120 V. Because of the way alternating current works, the V in each of these legs is always 180 degrees out of phase with the other leg, making the available V appear as 240 V when the two legs are connected together, which is known as a *line-to-line voltage*.

In a 120/208 V three-phase system, there are three legs of power—or three separate wires—each carrying 120 V. A 120/208 V three-phase power connection actually requires five wires: three *hot* (live) lines each carrying 120 V and a variable number of amps, one neutral wire, and one ground wire. In this system, the three legs are 120 degrees out of phase and the actual available voltage is equivalent to √3 or 173 percent of the single-phase V (i.e. 120 V x 173 percent = 208 V). To account for this, the single-phase formula must be further modified for all calculations involving three-phase power to the following:

$$I = \frac{P}{1.73 \text{ x E x PF}}$$

Now, let us look at how this is all applied for an event. To begin our example, let us consider that a venue offers the following electrical service packages, in ascending order of cost:

- 20 A, 120 V single-phase;
- 30 A, 120/240 V single-phase;
- 30 A, 120/208 V three-phase;
- 60 A, 120/208 V three-phase;
- 100 A, 120/208 V three-phase;
- 200 A, 120/208 V three-phase.

In this example, let us look at two different events using lighting, and we will assume that the lighting is not LED but older and less energy-efficient PAR cans. The first one is for eight PAR64, 500 W luminaires for a small stage show. To determine total power, in simple terms, it is a matter of adding up all the luminaires' total wattage, assuming that we might want to connect them all together on a single dimmer system. For example, eight PAR64 stage luminaires each drawing 500 W will require 4,000 W, or in another term for the same thing, four *kilowatts* (i.e. 4,000 W/1,000 W/kilowatt) of power. Using the above formulas, the lighting designer (LD) will now calculate what electrical service package is required. The first assumption will be the use of the cheapest package, that of 20 A, 120 V single-phase. Knowing the total power draw of the lights, the **required** amperage can be calculated as follows:

$$I = \frac{4,000}{120 \text{ x } 0.80} = 42 \text{ A}$$

Obviously, the package offered is inadequate since it is only 20 A. The LD will now try the next feasible power package of 30 A, 240 V single-phase:

$$I = \frac{4,000}{240 \text{ x } 0.80} = 21 \text{ A}$$

This package will be safe for the intended lighting as the **required** amperage (21) is less than the amperage provided (30). Of course, another option is also the 60 A, three-phase service, but that is more expensive and is overkill.

Now let us consider the second scenario, more of a concert-type show, with forty 1,000 W PAR64 luminaires. The total power draw will be 40,000 W (i.e. 40 kW). The LD might begin by calculating the current required using a single-phase, 240 V service, as follows:

$$I = \frac{40,000}{240 \text{ x } 0.80} = 208 \text{ A}$$

Again, this is higher than any of the options, so three-phase service must be considered. The lowest possible option that may provide sufficient power is 200 A, 208 V, three-phase service. The calculation is:

$$I = \frac{40,000}{1.73 \text{ x } 208 \text{ x } 0.80} = 139 \text{ A}$$

This option will therefore provide sufficient power for the lighting since the **required** amperage of 139 is less than the provided amperage of 200.

Also a consideration for the LD is the voltage drop over their own cables between the luminaires and the dimmers and the console, but they will already have this calculated and have it built into their power requirements. The same holds true for other suppliers such as audio and A-V.

### 9.1.2 Electrical distribution

Now that the amount of electrical power available is known, all that is needed is to connect to the power outlet in the venue using a matching connector and then distribute the necessary power to all equipment. We begin with connection and move to actual distribution.

#### 9.1.2.1 Accessing venue power

Depending on the amount of power required as described above, the decision will have to be made by the equipment supplier (e.g. lighting, audio, A-V) whether single-phase will suffice or whether the load is going to be so great and/or the devices so many that three-phase will be needed. Let us first look at single-phase.

##### 9.1.2.1.1 SINGLE-PHASE CONNECTIONS

The most common connections for taking single-phase power from a venue are:

- NEMA 5 (National Electrical Manufacturers Association). This is also referred to as a Type B, North American 3-pin, and sometimes just a "wall plug," or "Edison." All NEMA 5 devices are three-wire grounding devices rated for 125 V maximum, coming in 5–15, 5–20, and 5–30 versions (the second number refers to the amperage of the circuit). The 5–15 is by far the most common electrical outlet in North America. The Type B plug is used in events only with 120 V single-phase and therefore small electrical loads. See Figure 9.1 (top left; NEMA 5–15).

- NEMA 14. "The NEMA 14 devices are four-wire grounding devices available in ratings from 15 A to 60 A. Of the straight-blade NEMA 14 devices, only the 14–30 and 14–50 are common. The 14–30 is used for electric clothes dryers and the 14–50 for electric cooking ranges. The voltage rating is a design maximum of 250 V . . . All NEMA 14 devices offer two *hots*, a neutral, and a ground, allowing for both 120 V and 240 V (or 120 V and 208 V if the supply system is three-phase rather than split-phase). The 14–30 has a rating of 30 A and an L-shaped neutral blade. The 14–50 has a rating of 50 A and a straight neutral blade sized so that it does not fit in the slot of a 14–30" (NEMA Connector, 2014). For events, the most common is the 14–50, often referred to as a *range plug*. It is used mainly for small audio and lighting systems. See Figure 9.1 (top right; NEMA 14–30 plug and 14–50 receptacle).

- NEMA twist-lock. "Twist-locking connectors were first invented by Harvey Hubbell III in 1938 and 'Twist-Lock' remains a registered trademark of Hubbell Incorporated, although the term is used generically to refer to NEMA locking connectors manufactured by any company. Locking connectors use curved blades. Once pushed into the receptacle, the plug is twisted and its now-rotated blades latch into the receptacle. To unlatch the plug, the rotation is reversed. The locking coupling makes for a more reliable connection in commercial and industrial settings, where vibration or incidental impact could disconnect a non-locking connector. Locking connectors come in a variety of standardized configurations that follow the same general naming scheme except that the designations include an 'L' for 'locking.' Locking connectors are designed so that different voltages and current ratings cannot be accidentally intermated" (NEMA Connector, 2014). See Figure 9.1 (bottom left; NEMA L5–20). For special events,

NEMA 5-15                                      NEMA 14-30 plug and 14-50 receptacle

NEMA L5-20                                                          SPC

Figure 9.1 Single-phase electrical connections

Clockwise from upper left, images courtesy of: www.amazon.com; Doug Matthews [plug] and www.amazon.com [receptacle]; Entertainment Power Systems, www.entertainmentpowersystems.com; and www.amazon.com

twist-lock connectors are used only for single-phase applications, typically in theaters, arenas, and occasionally in hotels and convention centers for relatively small lighting requirements. Twist-lock connectors are more common in Canada than the comparable *stage pin connectors* (SPC) in the United States.

- Stage pin connector (SPC). A stage pin connector is a standard for theatrical lighting, although occasionally they can be used with something else. "These connectors are available in 120V and 250V versions for 20A, 30A, 60A, and 100A service" (Cadena, 2009, p. 9). "The primary advantage of the stage pin connector over the NEMA 5-15 connector (commonly known as an Edison plug) is its ability to lay flat on a stage lessening the likelihood of being a trip hazard. In addition the stage pin connector has an increased durability and resistance to damage due to its more robust construction" (Stage pin connector, 2014). See Figure 9.1 (bottom right; Entertainment Power Systems SP-20 stage-pin connector).

### 9.1.2.1.2 THREE-PHASE CONNECTIONS

Once it is determined that the power requirements are very large, suppliers will request hookup to three-phase power at the venue. This can come in one of two ways:

- Pin and sleeve. Pin and sleeve circular male connectors mate directly with female receptacles that are often present in major hotels and convention centers for high power applications. Depending on the venue, current ratings vary up to about 400 A and voltage ratings vary up to about 600 V AC. Contact arrangements are from three to five pins and differ in different countries. The contacts in the plug are pins and those in the receptacle are simple cylinders (sleeves). These connectors are often referred to as *Blue Hubbell* after a manufacturer, although they come in different colors and configurations. The object of this connection is to take the house power and output it to compatible five-wire *Cam lock connectors* (see Section 9.1.2.2). It is typically the lighting company that will bring the male pin and sleeve connector to the venue and tie it into the female receptacle. In essence, the pin and sleeve connector is really no more than an adaptor.

- Wall box. This situation also occurs in many venues. The three-phase power comes into the venue and is distributed to wall boxes that have five terminal lugs inside instead of a female pin and sleeve connection. For this type of tie-in, a qualified electrician is required (usually from the venue), who connects the lugs with the bare wire ends of female Cam lock connectors for the lighting or audio techs to use. Sometimes, the Cam lock connection has already been made in the venue. With a wall box situation, it is important to ensure that the correct voltage and amperage are present, and that all safety precautions are followed due to the high risk of serious injury or death. Nobody but a qualified electrician should be allowed to make these connections.

### 9.1.2.2 Distributing three-phase power

Once the tie-in has been made to the house three-phase power, connections must be made to *distribution panels* or *boxes*, sometimes also referred to as *distro boxes*, or in many cases, directly into a lighting dimmer pack.

The primary connector for accomplishing this is the Cam lock connector. Cam lock connectors are attached to the ends of the pin and sleeve wiring or the direct wall box wiring. Cam lock connectors come in varying sizes based on amperage loads and are colored. The colors correspond to the different functions of the line, and are not arbitrary, as follows: green (ground); white (neutral); black (phase one); blue (phase two); red (phase three). These are for North America. European colors may differ. Most Cam locks are weatherproof, with their colored rubber boots protecting innocent fingers when open and forming a watertight connection when connected. See Figure 9.2 top left and bottom left.

With the house power now going into a distribution panel (or dimmer pack as illustrated in Figure 9.2), this power must be broken down into smaller circuits of single-phase power for use with the various lighting, audio, or A-V components (and sometimes musical equipment). That is the purpose of the distribution panel (or dimmer pack when specifically for lighting as in this case), which will usually contain a number of different connection options (as described in Section 9.1.2.1.1) as well as individual circuit breakers for each circuit.

Figure 9.2 illustrates generally how house three-phase power is distributed. The upper left image illustrates a Blue Hubbell or pin-and-sleeve connector at one end, which takes three-phase power directly from the venue outlet, and then at the other end the five colored Cam lock connectors that connect into the lighting dimmer pack. The upper right image illustrates a 19-pin Socapex connector that connects with both non-DMX-controllable and DMX-controllable luminaires as described in Section 5.6 of Chapter 5. The bottom two images illustrate the lighting dimmer unit (left—back; right—front). This unit is modular and can incorporate a variety of lighting dimmer circuits, but also a variety of regular single-phase power output options. In this case, the overall unit is designed for lighting power distribution. In the bottom left image note first the Cam lock inputs (green, white, red, blue, black) from house power. Above these are four 19-pin receptacles for the Socapex cables. Each of these connections provides single-phase power to six separate, 20A circuits for non-DMX-controllable luminaires (see Figure 5.14 in Chapter 5). The circuit breakers for these are found on the front of the unit in the middle (Figure 9.2, bottom right). Above these four outlets on the back is another module that provides a separate circuit for the chain motors used to raise the lighting truss, and above this are four more Socapex outlets to provide single-phase power to DMX-controllable luminaires. Finally, above these on the back (bottom left image) are two optical splitters

Blue pin and sleeve and
colored Cam lock connectors

Socapex connector

ProPower® rack panel distribution system
(left—back; right—front)

Figure 9.2  Typical three-phase power connection and distribution equipment

Courtesy of Doug Matthews and Innovation Lighting, www.innovationlighting.net

which extend the number of DMX channels as described in Section 5.6 of Chapter 5. The front of these can be seen at the top of the unit in the bottom right image, along with the DMX dimming channels just below them.

### 9.1.3 Portable power

Whenever an event is held away from one of the standard event venues such as hotels, arenas, or convention centers, and particularly outdoors, there is a high probability that electrical service will not be readily available. In these cases, portable generating units must be brought in. These units are typically trailer-towed and take the place of the house power that would be found indoors, and most come with at least some power distribution breakout. They come from various manufacturers and in various sizes that provide power up to 400 V AC and amperages from 250 to 2,400 (Garber, 2002). Most run on diesel fuel and nowadays, thanks to technological advances driven by the movie industry, are extremely quiet, allowing them to be placed fairly close to event guests—but hidden—without fear of too much noise interference. Two points bear mentioning in the use of portable generators. The first is that fuel levels must be monitored constantly to ensure that fuel does not run out, thus avoiding unexpected power outages. As noted by Garber (2006), some rental companies actually have global positioning systems (GPS) that enable them to monitor their rental units to check the fuel status. The second point is that for large events, a backup unit can act as insurance in case the first one goes down, and also to spread the electrical load more evenly (Wenzel, 2014).

### 9.1.4 Electrical safety considerations

For personnel safety, the appropriate organizations in the United States are the Occupational Safety and Health Administration (OSHA) and the National Fire Protection Association (NFPA), as well as individual states. The NFPA has a safety standard (*NFPA 70E®: Standard for Electrical Safety in the Workplace®, 2015 Edition*) that is the document to which the OSHA adheres. Installation and general design standards for electrical equipment are covered in detail in the *National Electrical Code* (NEC), which in publication form is *NFPA 70®: National Electrical Code®, 2014 Edition*, and although it is not law, most jurisdictions require compliance with the NEC. Additionally, specific design standards come from the National Electrical Manufacturers Association (NEMA) and they "define a product, process, or procedure with reference to one or more of the following: nomenclature, composition, construction, dimensions, tolerances, safety, operating characteristics, performance, rating, testing, and the service for which it is designed" (NEMA, 2014). These are numerous and event producers should ensure that suppliers use equipment that meets these standards whenever there is a standard. Finally for the United States, as a general guide, Chapter 17 of Cooper (2014) has some excellent checklists specifically for electrical safety at outdoor events.

In Canada, responsibility for the electrical safety of personnel rests with the provinces and territories. Every province and territory adopts and enforces the same installation code, promulgated by the Canadian Standards Association (CSA) as *CSA C22.1-12: Canadian Electrical Code, Part I (22nd Edition), Safety Standard for Electrical Installations*. The electrical codes are eventually incorporated into each jurisdiction's regulations for enforcement. With respect to equipment design standards, these requirements are set through *CAN/CSA-C22.2 NO. 0–10: General Requirements – Canadian Electrical Code, Part II (2010 Edition)*. Again, they are adopted (with or without modifications) and enforced by the provincial and territorial electrical safety authorities. This ensures that equipment installed in conjunction with the CEC will be compatible and safe to use under the installation rules. *CEC Part II* contains a myriad of individual equipment standards, and event producers should ensure that the equipment from their suppliers meets the standards wherever applicable. Many are compatible with US standards.

In the UK, standards are extensive, with the British Standards Institute (BSI) being responsible for creating them. Two guiding documents for special events are *BS 7909:2011: Code of Practice for Temporary Electrical Systems for Entertainment and Related Purposes*, and *BS 7671:2008+A3:2015: Requirements for Electrical Installation – IET Wiring Regulations*. In Europe and generally most other countries, the international standard *IEC 60364: Electrical Installations for Buildings*, promulgated by the International Electrotechnical Commission, is the main document. In fact, much of *BS 7671* is taken from it.

In Australia, Live Performance Australia, an advocacy and educational organization for special events, has developed a number of best practices guidelines. Their publication, *Safety Guidelines for Live Entertainment and Events: Electricity (2014 Edition)*, is an excellent overall guide and starting point. It provides several detailed checklists and a list of references to other formal standards and regulations concerning electrical installations in Australia and also New Zealand.

Other countries' standards may vary and producers should ensure they understand all local, state/provincial, and federal standards.

## 9.2 Trussing

Trussing, as we know it, started to develop at the end of the 1970s in response to the entertainment industry's demand for lightweight, strong temporary structures that could span the width of a stage and be used to hang lighting and audio systems. Familiar with the spatial lattice structures found in bridges, scaffolding, and buildings, manufacturers used this as the basis for modern truss design. Today it is ubiquitous in the industry and comes in a wide variety of sizes, shapes, colors, and strengths. While it is the primary method of support for lighting systems, it has gone far beyond that to now also be the primary method of constructing and supporting large roofs and enclosures for outdoor stages. As such—and due to numerous deadly accidents and collapses of such structures regularly around the world—it has become the focus of much attention. This section and the next one on rigging are intended to inform producers and in so doing, help them to plan properly and prevent such accidents from ever occurring.

### 9.2.1 General truss design

Trussing is made of heavy-duty aluminum or aluminum alloy tubing and comes in a variety of sizes and shapes. The most common shapes in cross-section are box, rectangular, and triangular, varying from 12 in. (0.1 m) square to more than 23 in. (58 cm) x 40 in. (101 cm) in rectangular cross-section. Section lengths vary from about 2.5 ft (0.75 m) to more than 118 ft (36 m), with tubing diameters of 1 in. (2.5 cm) to 3 in. (7.5 cm). Generally, different manufacturers make different sizes within these extremes. Lengths can be joined together to make longer, continuous truss lines. Trussing also comes in curved sections and, depending on the manufacturer, a variety of colors, thus enabling a limitless range of shapes and looks. As well, a great many accessories are available to allow different forms of attachment of truss sections, much like Meccano sets for those old enough to remember them.

Trussing must be able to withstand loads imposed on it in shear (i.e. force directed along the cross-section, such as high loads on top of a vertical truss section) and in deflection (i.e. force directed down and perpendicular to its horizontal access, such as too many luminaires clamped in one position). The amount it can withstand depends of course on its size and rated load. Each type and size of truss is rated by the manufacturer for specific maximum loads under these conditions. It is therefore critical that riggers (see Section 9.3) know the exact loads that will be imposed on the truss in these conditions and what the total weight of the loaded truss will be so that the correct choice of supporting wire rope cable, slings, and chain motors may be made. Not only that, but the truss supplier for an event (e.g. the lighting company) is obligated to understand the load rating of their truss and to choose the proper truss accordingly, knowing in detail what the loading will be before the truss is ever rigged into position.

Apart from simple sections of straight truss flown from venue ceilings (see Section 5.4.3.2 of Chapter 5), things get more complicated as truss configurations move to being self-supported from the ground.

### 9.2.2 Ground-supported truss configurations

These types of truss configurations are found in two main scenarios: indoors in large venues such as arenas and stadia for such events as concerts where the venue ceiling is too high or weak for practically rigging and flying truss lines, especially in cases where lighting and set design are complex; and outdoors when large stages are needed, especially for festivals or other public events. While only the imagination of producers limits the different configurations, the following are the most common:

- Single rigging tower. This basically consists of a V-shaped truss base that supports an angled truss mast. The base acts as a stabilizer once the mast is in place. The tower is usually used to support lighting and audio but has no horizontal truss sections.
- Simple support towers and grid. This system is designed to support a grid without the need for suspension points. It is typically set up in a box-like design of four vertical towers, each with outrigger feet for stability. Each vertical tower can support upwards of 2 to 4 tons (4,000 to 8,000 lb) of horizontal truss. The horizontal truss sections are raised and lowered by means of an electric motor and chains built into each tower. This type of system is often found indoors.
- Roofs. This configuration consists of extra truss sections attached to the top of a tower and grid system. This roof structure is then covered with fire-retardant PVC or other material. The entire roof is raised with the remainder of the horizontal truss. Roof systems are used extensively for outdoor events for weather protection. Heights are variable, typically up to 30 ft (approximately 10 m) or so. Roof shapes vary considerably and can be flat, curved, or peaked, depending on the truss sections and accessories used for their construction.
- Tunnel roof. This type of configuration does not rely on a vertical/horizontal grid for support but instead incorporates both into an overall roof design that resembles a tunnel constructed of trussing. It is very strong and compact and can be made from curved truss sections or short straight sections using appropriate connecting hardware.

Figure 9.3 illustrates several different truss configurations.

### 9.2.3  Truss safety

Since many ground-supported truss configurations are used outdoors, particularly important are unique loading scenarios that may be encountered. These include:

- Wind. Wind can cause damage to canopies and walls, it can overload trusses and towers due to the extra load of attached walls, and it can lift all or part of the complete structure.
- Rain or snow. This can make trussing slippery for climbing, it can cause overloading of rooftops due to accumulation of snow or water, it can cause short-circuiting in control systems, and it can cause the support of saturated soils to weaken.
- Lightning. This can cause severe personal safety risk if it hits towers.
- Temperature. Solar heat can cause aluminum to become extremely hot, thus making it unsafe to the touch. It may also cause the safe temperature of any polyester sling covers to exceed their allowable limit (e.g. surface temperature can reach 150°C, greater than the normal safe limit for polyester of 100°C).

It is therefore imperative that such things as roofs be constructed properly and with due consideration of the expected weather conditions. For example, the inclusion of supporting guy wires, base distance frames to minimize compression loads, and adequate ballast is absolutely necessary. Additionally, heights of towers and roofs must be restricted to recommended maximums, both indoors and outdoors.

However, structural problems are not confined to outdoor events. Numerous collapses of truss structures in recent years have occurred indoors as well. As a result of these ongoing problems, increased attention has been paid to the safety of such structures. In particular, in the United States, *The Event Safety Guide* (Cooper, 2014, pp. 192–204) provides an extensive review of safety requirements for truss structures,

Rigging towers

Support towers and grid

Curved roof

Tunnel roof

Figure 9.3 Examples of ground-supported truss configurations

Images courtesy of: upper left, upper right, and lower left, Prolyte Products Group, www.prolyte.com; lower right, Gearhouse SA (Pty) Ltd. and Louise Stickland

including references to some of the most applicable standards. Producers who ever use truss structures for events are strongly advised to become familiar with it. Otherwise, two of the most important standards concerning truss structures in North America are:

- *ANSI E1.2 – 2012: Entertainment Technology – Design, Manufacture and Use of Aluminum Trusses and Towers.* ANSI E1.2 describes the design, manufacture, and use of aluminum trusses, towers, and associated aluminum structural components, such as head blocks, sleeve blocks, bases, and corner blocks, used in the entertainment industry in portable structures.

- *ANSI E1.21 – 2013: Entertainment Technology – Temporary Structures Used for Technical Production of Outdoor Entertainment Events.* This document establishes a minimum level of design and performance parameters for the design, manufacturing, use, and maintenance of temporary ground-supported structures used in the production of outdoor entertainment events. The purpose of this guidance is to ensure the structural reliability and safety of these structures and does not address fire safety and safe egress issues.

In Europe, the following standard applies:

- *CWA 15902-2:2010: Lifting and Load-bearing Equipment for Stages and other Production Areas within the Entertainment Industry – Part 2: Specifications for design, manufacture and for use of aluminum and steel trusses and towers.* Created by the European Institute for Standardisation (CEN), this standard covers design, manufacture, and use of aluminum and steel trusses, towers, and associated structural components such as tower head blocks, sleeve blocks, bases and corner blocks used in the entertainment industry. Trusses and truss constructions are used to support predominantly static loads or to serve purely decorative purposes. They can be hung, ground-supported, permanently installed, or used as a moving construction.

In the UK, the main document is *Temporary demountable structures. Guidance on procurement, design and use (Third Edition) (2007)*. It provides comprehensive details on TDS, including checklists for planning, construction, and use of TDS. Endorsed by the Health and Safety Executive (HSE), it is the industry-accepted guide for the safe management and use of temporary demountable structures.

Suffice it to say, planning to erect a truss structure requires a through understanding and analysis of the risks, a full plan for the design and anchoring of the structure, and almost always a complete analysis of the expected loading on the structure. A properly qualified rigger and the truss supplier should be able to certify compliance with these requirements, although occasionally a qualified structural engineer may have to sign off. This chapter's war story describes the consequences of what can happen when proper design of a truss structure is not completed.

## VOICE OF THE INDUSTRY

**An interview with the Mendip District Council (MDC)**
Licensing Authority for the Glastonbury Festival
Pilton, Somerset, England
www.glastonburyfestivals.co.uk

Considering the critical importance of safety to the public and to event employees, especially at international outdoor festivals at which many major accidents have occurred in recent years, I decided to pose questions about this subject to several of the most prominent festivals in the world. My reasoning was that to be successful, festivals of this magnitude must be conscious of safety and I wanted to determine just how they did it. One, the Glastonbury Festival, responded in detail via their local licensing authority, the Mendip District Council (MDC). By way of introduction, Glastonbury began in 1970 and is now held annually on farmlands in Somerset, England. It attracts upwards of 150,000 or more people each year and is regularly listed as one of the world's biggest music festivals.

**DM**: For temporary structures such as stages, stage roofs, and bleachers, what standards and regulations is the festival required to meet?

**MDC**: We expect event organizers to follow the guidance in the Institution of Structural Engineers publication "Temporary demountable structures. Guidance on procurement, design and use, (Third Edition) (2007)." See this link – http://shop.istructe.org/temporary-demountable-structures.html.

In respect of structures, the Council's building control team works with the festival to ensure compliance, etc. There is no single blanket legislation that covers an event such as Glastonbury, so we utilize best practice from a number of documents, and apply what is most practical and pragmatic depending on each individual venue's use and size. These include:

- The Building Regulations.
- Fifth edition of the Guide to Safety at Sports Grounds ("The Green Guide").

Figure 9.4 Glastonbury Festival

Courtesy of Glastonbury Festivals

- Fire safety risk assessment: open-air events and venues.

- *Safe use and operation of marquees and temporary demountable fabric structures* (Revised March 2011) Performance Textiles Association (MUTA). Endorsed by HSE, it complements the IstructE guidance above and provides comprehensive details and checklists for assembled marquees.

- *BS 9999:2008 Code of Practice for fire safety in the design, manufacture and use of buildings.*

- Fire risk assessment guidance Department for Communities and Local Government.

- *TG20:2008 Guide to good practice for scaffolding with tube and fittings National Access and Scaffolding Confederation (NASC).*

- Selection and use of equipment to support speaker clusters, lights etc. used during outdoor events.

- Identification of safety good practice in the construction and deconstruction of temporary demountable structures.

. . . and, of course, personal and professional experience.

**DM**: Are there specific requirements or configurations for front-of-stage barriers that the festival must follow or use?

**MDC**: The festival site comprises approximately 80 venues and stages ranging from the largest, "the Pyramid," to much smaller and niche venues. There is not a one-size-fits-all approach and the event organizer is required to risk assess each stage and determine the most appropriate front-of-stage barrier for that venue/stage and location. There is also an expectation that each barrier will be supplied, erected, signed off, and regularly checked during the course of the event by competent persons who will be commissioned by the organizer. A range of different barrier configurations is used at Glastonbury Festival. For the last few years an open double barrier has been used at the Pyramid Stage.

The Council in discharging its Public Safety role does not specify or check technical drawings, calculations, or configurations. Rather the onus is on the Festival Organizer to manage TDM's including barriers and the Council carries out an auditing role in terms of the Licensing function. Enforcement of Health and Safety at work for the event is split between the Health and Safety Executive and the Council.

## 9.3 Rigging

In special events, there are frequent occasions when décor pieces, lighting equipment, audio speakers, visual presentation equipment, and even performers must be suspended or *flown* over a stage and/or an audience. Of course, since this may occur both indoors or outdoors and typically from truss structures, rigging goes hand-in-hand with truss design and safety.

To safely rig and fly equipment, a thorough knowledge of rigging hardware and methodology is necessary. If items are improperly rigged and flown, people can be killed! The intent of this section is to present a general overview of rigging, an explanation of some of the equipment that is commonly used in the special event environment, and a brief review of safety.

### 9.3.1 Overview

Rigging involves setting up the necessary physical support system so that equipment and/or people may be raised to a height above the ground. In so doing, the *rigger* or qualified technician must attach support cable and hoisting equipment to hanging points in the ceiling of a venue—and for easier understanding we will consider only indoor events for this section. These are specially strengthened structural locations in the building that permit the hanging of heavy objects up to certain load limits. Usually, the ceiling of a venue is equipped at these locations with bracketry or bolts for this purpose. Riggers need to know the proper methods of securing items like cable (wire rope) to this bracketry and then to other objects (e.g. trussing for lighting) without the possibility of slippage or cable or bolt breakage.

Overloading a line (e.g. cable) poses a serious threat to the safety of personnel, not to mention the heavy losses likely to result through damage to material. To avoid overloading, the rigger must know the strength of the rigging system and components used in it. This involves three factors: *breaking strength, safe working load,* and safety factor. Breaking strength refers to the tension at which a line will part when a load is applied. Breaking strength has been determined through tests made by cable manufacturers, and tables have been set up to provide this information. The *safe working load* (SWL) of a line is the load that can be applied without causing any kind of damage to the line. A wide margin of difference between breaking strength and SWL is necessary to allow for such factors as additional strain imposed on the line by jerky movements in hoisting or bending over sheaves in a pulley block. The safety factor of a line is the ratio between the breaking strength and the SWL. Safety factors will vary, depending on such things as the condition of the line and the circumstances under which it is to be used. The safety factor is usually between four and ten.

Rick Smith, the president of Riggit Services Inc. in Vancouver, Canada, a certified rigger with over 25 years of experience in event rigging, notes that before rigging begins, the load rating of the venue hanging points has to be in writing from either the venue or from an engineer. He cautions that too often the somewhat hazy corporate memory of either venue staff or older technicians is the source of a load rating, and that is neither professional nor safe (R. Smith, personal communication, September 7, 2006).

## 9.3.2 Rigging equipment

Rigging and its ancestry derive from the theater world and go as far back as the ancient Greeks, with a myriad of ropes, cables, pulleys, and lifting equipment designed for that environment. For simplicity of understanding, we will restrict our discussion to basic attachment hardware and flying methods.

### 9.3.2.1 Basic attachment hardware

The most common hardware used for events includes:

- Wire rope. "Often called cable, this is the most common method of attaching gear to ceilings. Wire rope is a material made [of several strands] of thin steel wire groups. Different types of wire rope exist, the main differences being the arrangement of the wires, and the type of steel used. One type of wire rope used frequently is called *hoisting cable*, and is typically of *6 x 19* construction. This means that there are 6 larger strands of 19 wires each. Hoisting cable is often used in fly systems, as it is strong and flexible. *Aircraft cable* is another type of wire rope that is used often in theater applications. It is usually *7 x 19* construction, and is more flexible and stronger than hoisting cable. Aircraft cable is made out of specially processed steel that has a very high tensile strength" (Richardson, 2000).

- Thimbles, wire rope clips, and swages. "Any time the wire rope needs to be attached to a hang point that would cause the cable to sharply bend, a device called a *thimble* must be used. Thimbles simply guide the cable into a natural curve shape and offer a degree of protection to the cable in the loop. To secure the end of the rope, wire rope *U-clips* are used. These clips provide an effective means for terminating cables . . . Another method for securing the ends of wire rope is through the use of *swages*, or *nicopress sleeves*. Small metal sleeves are pressed on to the wire rope with a special tool. These sleeves are permanent, but act much in the same way that clips do. When properly applied, swages can hold the full rated working load of the cable they are attached to" (Richardson, 2000).

- Shackles, turnbuckles and hooks. "A wide variety of additional rigging hardware exists for various tasks. *Turnbuckles* are used in situations where small adjustments need to be made in the length of a cable. Usually turnbuckles are not used to bear load, but rather in tensioning guy wires. *Shackles* are often used with locking *hooks* to connect between wire rope and nylon harnesses or rope" (Richardson, 2000).

- Chain. Chain is typically used in conjunction with pulleys or chain motors to raise trussing on which luminaires, audio speakers, or other equipment may be attached. It is important to note that only welded-link steel chain should be used to bear loads, and the load capacity of the chain should be verified to ensure it can carry the anticipated load.

- Slings. "One of the most common ways to hang truss for flying is through the use of slings made of a synthetic material such as polyester. A modern sling consists of a synthetic fiber core encased in a woven synthetic casing, [although slings may also be made of wire rope]. Slings of this nature tend to be very strong and quite durable, and by nature conform to the shape of the load they are carrying . . . There are many acceptable methods for attaching slings to the truss to fly it. The most common involves the use of four slings. When the truss is flown point-down, a *choker* scheme is used, whereby the sling wraps through itself and around the truss" (Richardson, 2000).

### 9.3.2.2 Flying methods

There are generally two main methods used to fly equipment or people in special events:

- Chain and pulleys. In certain situations with relatively light loads, a pulley system is attached to the ceiling hanging point and a heavy-duty chain as described above is run through the pulleys. There are usually two pulleys or more on a length of truss if the length is a long one. The pulley system is mechanically advantaged which means that when it is pulled by hand to raise the trussing, the actual weight pulled is much less than the weight of the truss.

- Chain motor. Likewise, a motor may be substituted for the pulleys. "A chain motor is simply a large electric motor with a gearbox and a chain drive mounted in one chassis. The chassis of the motor generally has a large hook mounted on its underside, to which loads are attached. An extremely heavy gauge chain with a hook at one end passes through the motor and into a chain bag. The hook of this chain is generally clipped to the shackle of a wire rope sling [or other type], which is attached to a load-bearing overhead beam [or hanging point, usually an *eye-bolt*]. Once the attachment has been made to an overhead hang point, the motors can have loads attached for flying" (Richardson, 2000). The motor is then controlled to raise or lower the truss by handheld controls, sometimes called *pickles*, located on the floor. It is important, notes Smith of Riggit Services in Vancouver, to ensure that all phases of a chain motor are in synch. Otherwise the motor may inadvertently reverse when the switch is pushed, causing older motors with no safety mechanism to literally "eat" the chain and hook.

See Figure 9.5 for an example of rigged trussing. Several points are worth noting in this example. In the top image, this rear truss (the stage is to the right of, or in front of, the truss) has already been fitted with chain motors. Three motors out of four total, along with their chain bags, can be seen above the truss with the chains extending to the ceiling. Note also that three A-V screens can be seen already attached via wire rope slings to the truss, in addition to some luminaires that are harder to see, and black masking drape on the front side of the truss. In the lower image, this long truss line can be seen fully raised at the rear of the stage and the four chain motors, five A-V screens, luminaires, two long drape sections, and masking drape that it supports are clearly visible. As well, there is a front truss with multiple luminaires and masking drape that was raised using only chains and pulleys, four of which can be seen mounted above the truss.

When working with chain motor/truss combinations, technicians and producers must understand the exact definition of trim height, which is the final height above the ground or floor that the rigged equipment (e.g. lighting truss) must reside. There are as many as three different interpretations of the term and it is important that everyone involved understands the definition being used. As shown in Figure 9.6, the *venue trim* is the height above the floor to the lowest attachment point in the ceiling, the *highest trim to truss* or *low trim* is the distance from the floor to the bottom of a standard 16 in. (40 cm) truss, and the *lighting trim* is the distance from the floor to the lights or, in some cases, A-V equipment (e.g. projectors). Those involved have to understand that there must be space allowed for the wire ropes, hooks, chain motors, and chains between the ceiling and the truss.

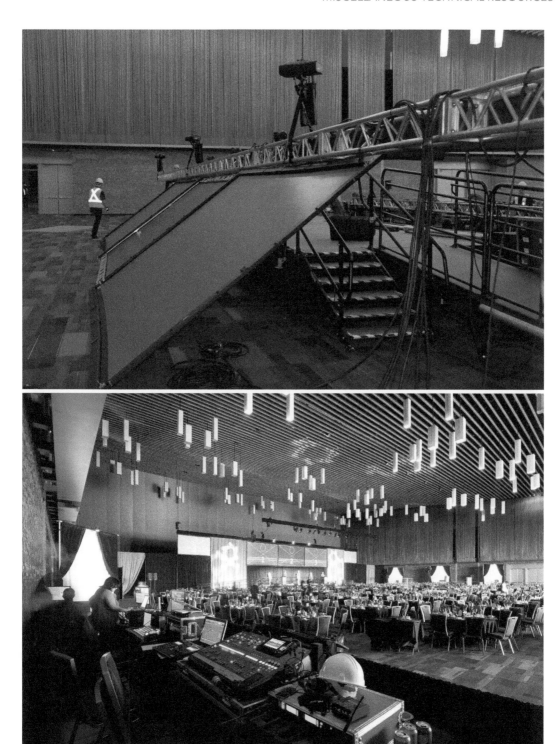

Figure 9.5  Rigged truss lines

Courtesy of Doug Matthews and Innovation Lighting, www.innovationlighting.net

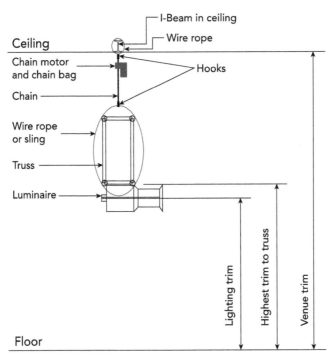

**Figure 9.6** Rigging trim heights

Courtesy of Doug Matthews

**Stage roof collapse in Turkey**

When the roof first started going up for a multi-day festival in Turkey, I noticed a few things that worried me about the setup. Since all my rigging experience had been in ballrooms, tents, and convention centers and I had never worked with a self-climbing truss stage roof before, I didn't feel qualified to raise issue with the setup. However, some things that seemed unsafe included:

- The tower feet were placed on 6 in. x 6 in. pieces of ½ in. ply, not much bigger than the feet themselves.
- Truss was Thomas Supertruss and the crew wasn't using the safety clips on the truss pins.
- The roof was supported only at the peak. There were no support beams running from the peak to the sides, only a couple of steel cables in an "X." Thus the roof sagged and collected water. The crew used a pole to push the roof up so that the water would run off!

On the opening day of the festival, about an hour before the start, there was a sudden thunderstorm. There were massive lightning strikes in the mountains all around us (imagine my anger when I found the grounding stake was attached to the generator with 12-gauge wire!), and a massive amount of water started coming down. Everyone around the stage immediately got under the roof as the water coming down was as intense as anything I'd ever seen, including my times in the

Amazon basin. Within minutes there were large puddles of water all over the field and everything not under the roof was soaked.

This went on for about 4–5 min. Suddenly, the rain turned to hail, about the size of dimes. And it was coming down hard! A cry went out to look at the roof. We looked up and there was a small lake on the roof, which was growing rapidly, with another on the other side but smaller. The sticks the crew was using earlier to clear water were now too short to reach the roof at trim, so they sent a couple of guys up into the truss to attempt to relieve the strain somehow. Within minutes the lake had grown to what I would estimate to be about 400 gal. The tarp was stretching between the peak and the side truss to allow this. One of the guys in the truss went to cut the tarp, but the company owner told him not to. It looked as if the tarp was going to break and dump a ton of water onto the stage.

Suddenly, there was a "grrrunnnk" sound from the truss. I looked up to see that the truss piece creating the side of the roof had bent. At either end, near the corner blocks, the truss had bent, allowing the center section of the truss to pull inward about 2–3 ft. The upside-down boil on the tarp just kept growing as it stretched and filled with water and hail. At this point I decided to abandon ship and took a flying leap off the front of the stage. I turned around to see at least half the people still under the roof staring at the boil! I started screaming, "The roof is going to fall! Get out of the way," but they didn't listen. Thirty seconds later the roof collapsed on them. The bent section of truss gave way and we ended up with a huge mess. Amazingly, nobody died or was even hurt! And remember the two guys who were climbing the truss? They both jumped to safety! Thank God they weren't wearing safety harnesses.

(Courtesy: Name withheld by request)

### 9.3.3 Rigging safety

As already mentioned, every year serious accidents occur around the world, from workers falling off platforms to trussing collapses, many resulting in serious injuries or death. In a lot of these cases, truss loads were not calculated properly, risks were not assessed, and standards were not followed, leading to lawsuits and frequently considerable grief. The person at the leading edge of ensuring that equipment is safely lifted above the ground is the rigger. Everything he or she does must be of the highest quality and must adhere to all safety regulations and standards.

If equipment is to be rigged and flown at an event, it will often fall within the producer's responsibility area to hire the rigging company either directly or through a subcontractor and to ensure that they are qualified. Indeed, everyone in the chain of command must ensure that correct safety factors are used, and that they incorporate the manufacturer's design loading for the equipment, the truss supplier's calculations for truss loading, the rigger's calculations for safety factors and choice of supporting material that ensures the right factor, and finally, the producer's guarantee that this has been done correctly. To avoid potential liability, this implies that the producer should demand a paper trail from the rigger and trussing supplier for all calculations and equipment load limits, preferably contractually, following the methodology explained in Chapters 6 and 8 of *Special Event Production: The Process*.

Fortunately, the rigging qualification process has improved from what it was ten years ago. There is now a North American, industry-wide certification program by the Entertainment Services and Technology Association (ESTA, http://etcp.plasa.org). This program, called the Entertainment Technician Certification Program (ETCP), requires that riggers pass a knowledge exam as well as accumulating a specific number of experience-based points. Most knowledge is acquired by experience in this field although some training programs are starting to emerge (Tilson, 2014). There are two certification categories: *ETCP Certified Rigger – Arena* and *ETCP Certified Rigger – Theatre*. For the special events industry, the arena certification is the desired one. It encompasses rigging that employs chain hoists and truss systems to temporarily suspend objects from overhead structures in any environment. ETCP recognizes that these methods and hardware are used throughout the entertainment industry in arenas, convention and trade show spaces, and in theatrical venues. It is strongly recommended that producers only work with such qualified individuals.

Otherwise, there are numerous standards and guidelines that have been developed over recent years to ensure safety in rigging operations. These include:

- Chapter 18 of Cooper (2014) on Rigging. This provides an excellent overview of what is involved in generating a rigging plan and what a producer should be aware of. It is applicable to the United States but is informative for other countries.
- *ANSI E1.1 – 2012: Entertainment Technology – Construction and Use of Wire Rope Ladders.*
- *ANSI E1.4-2014: Entertainment Technology – Manual Counterweight Rigging Systems.*
- *ANSI E1.6-1 – 2012: Entertainment Technology – Powered Hoist Systems.*
- *ANSI E1.6-2 – 2013: Entertainment Technology – Design, Inspection, and Maintenance of Electric Chain Hoists for the Entertainment Industry.*
- *ANSI E1.6-3 – 2012: Selection and Use of Chain Hoists in the Entertainment Industry.*
- *ANSI E1.6-4 – 2013: Portable Control of Fixed-Speed Electric Chain Hoists in the Entertainment Industry.*

The above are US standards, and also apply to Canada. Interestingly, in Canada, only the province of Ontario appears to have developed unique safety guidelines that apply to the live performance industry (see Ontario Ministry of Labour, 2013). Europe and the UK have also developed similar standards as follows:

- *CWA 15902-1:2010: Lifting and Load-bearing Equipment for Stages and other Production Areas within the Entertainment Industry – Part 1: General requirements (excluding aluminium and steel trusses and towers).* Created by the European Institute for Standardisation (CEN), this document applies to machinery and machinery installations with guided or unguided load bearing and load carrying equipment used in places of assembly and in staging and production facilities for events and theatrical productions (stage machinery, for short). Such facilities include: theaters; multi-purpose halls and exhibition halls; film, television, and radio studios; concert halls; schools; bars and discotheques; open-air stages; and other rooms for shows and events.
- *DIN 56950-1:2012: Entertainment technology – Machinery installations – Part 1: Safety requirements and inspections.* This is also a European standard (originally German). Machinery installations are designed for use in events and the production setup of technical equipment and facilities which are used for lifting and lowering, holding and driving of loads (e.g. decorative parts, trusses, lighting, sound, and visual technology equipment). At least part of this standard may be included in the CWA 15902 standards.
- *BS 7905-1:2001: Lifting equipment for performance, broadcast and similar applications. Specification for the design and manufacture of above stage equipment (excluding trusses and towers).* This is a British standard and at least part of it may be included in the CWA standards.
- *Construction Design and Management (CDM) Regulations 2015.* These are regulations created by the HSE in the UK. They lay down the general responsibilities and competencies for health and safety for all levels of construction projects. Those responsible include clients, designers, supervisors, contractors, and workers. Important to note is that these are **regulations**, and as such, are enforceable by law.

Although still in draft form at the time of this book's writing, it is expected that they will be promulgated with few changes. They implement a European directive and expand on the previous regulations from 2007 to now include the entertainment industry and hence special events. The ramifications could be far-reaching and serious for those companies not following strict risk management policies as far as temporary structures are concerned (e.g. truss structures and the rigging that is entailed). However, in the HSE's own words, "duty-holders who currently have effective arrangements in place to manage risk arising from construction activities will need to do little more to comply with CDM 2015" (HSE, 2014). Whether similar regulations are put into place in other countries, including North America, remains to be seen.

## 9.4 Other temporary structures

For outdoor events, there is one final technical area that occasionally falls under the supervision of the event producer and that is temporary structures (other than tents, stages, and truss structures that have already been covered). For this section, we will reserve discussion to scaffolding, bleachers, fencing or barricades, and portable washrooms, including a review of safety and design standards for each. By definition, the term demountable structures is often used in conjunction with temporary structures, particularly sectionalized ones, that can be assembled and disassembled easily and quickly for portability (e.g. stages, tents, fencing, scaffolding, box truss arrangements, and bleachers).

### 9.4.1 Scaffolding

Although the term is used in other contexts, scaffolding in our industry is a temporary framework used to support people and equipment. Some of these structures include stages with or without roofs (similar to truss structures but with different components), catwalks, bleacher seats, seating risers, audio speaker towers (capped if necessary), camera platforms, towers, ramps, and jumps. See Figure 9.7 for examples.

#### *9.4.1.1 Construction*

Scaffolding is usually a modular system of metal pipes and wooden boards, although it can be made out of other materials. Pipes are either steel or aluminum. If steel they are either black or galvanized. The pipes come in a variety of lengths and a standard diameter of 1.90 in. (known as *1.5 NPS pipe* in North America), or 48.3 mm. *Couplers* are the fittings that hold the pipes together. *Boards* provide a working surface for users of the scaffold. They are made of seasoned wood and come in various thicknesses and widths. As well as boards for the working platform, there are *sole boards* that are placed beneath the scaffolding if the surface is soft or otherwise suspect.

> *The key elements of a scaffold are standards, ledgers and transoms. The standards, also called uprights, are the vertical tubes that transfer the entire mass of the structure to the ground where they rest on a square base plate to spread the load. The base plate has a shank in its centre to hold the tube and is sometimes pinned to a sole board. Ledgers are horizontal tubes which connect between the standards. Transoms rest upon the ledgers at right angles. Main transoms are placed next to the standards, they hold the standards in place and provide support for boards; intermediate transoms are those placed between the main transoms to provide extra support for boards.*

> *As well as the tubes at right angles, there are cross braces to increase rigidity. These are placed diagonally from ledger to ledger, next to the standards to which they are fitted. If the braces are fitted to the ledgers they are called ledger braces. To limit sway a facade brace is fitted to the face*

*of the scaffold every 30 m [100 ft] or so at an angle of 35°–55° running right from the base to the top of the scaffold and fixed at every level.*

*(Scaffolding, 2014)*

### 9.4.1.2 Safety

In the United States, the OSHA has very specific standards for the construction and use of scaffolding in the workplace, and many large commercial and government construction projects require all workers to have scaffold training and OSHA certification. The main standards applying to general industry (i.e. special events) are *Title 29 Code of Federal Regulations (CFR) Part 1910.28: Safety Requirements for Scaffolding* and *Title 29 Code of Federal Regulations Part 1926, Subpart L: Scaffolds*. There are also a number of others that pertain to specific industries and producers should ensure that the correct standards are being followed by consultation with their subcontractors and the OSHA. Some of the OSHA regulations regarding construction of scaffolding include using specific types of lumber when not using steel, weight limitations based on the design of the scaffolding, and regular checks for weakened or broken sections.

In Canada, the responsibility for scaffold safety rests with each province and each one has individual standards that require compliance, although SIAC (2011) provides an excellent and detailed checklist as a starting point. General safety guidelines are given by the Canadian Centre for Occupational Health and Safety (CCOHS), but these are not enforceable, unlike the provincial standards. Producers should obtain copies of their provincial standards to ensure compliance.

In the UK, there are several publications that cover both safety and design:

- *HSG 150: Health and Safety in Construction (2006)* published by the HSE is the main standard for safety.
- *BS EN 12811 – 1:2003 – Temporary works equipment. Scaffolds. Performance requirements and general design.* This is both a UK and European standard for the construction of scaffolding.
- *TG20:13 Good Practice Guidance for Tube and Fitting Scaffolding.* This is a set of technical guidelines published in 2014 by the National Access and Scaffolding Confederation in the UK that incorporates an operational guide and a design guide. It is intended to facilitate compliance with *BS EN 12811* and is backed by the HSE.

In Australia, the guiding document for safety is the *General guide for scaffolds and scaffolding work (2014)* published by Safe Work Australia. It provides information for persons conducting a business or undertaking on how to manage the risks associated with scaffolds and scaffolding work at a workplace. It is also supported by specific guidance material for: common types of scaffolds and scaffolding, suspended (swing stage) scaffolds, and scaffold inspection and maintenance. As well, a separate information sheet, *Tower and mobile scaffolds*, provides advice for small businesses and workers on managing the risks associated with tower and mobile scaffolds and related scaffolding work.

### 9.4.2 Bleachers

Bleachers used for outdoor events can be easily transportable, even with wheels attached, in small versions of three or four rows only, or transportable using a specially designed trailer in larger versions of up to about ten rows. Other higher capacity versions must be constructed in place (see Figure 9.7). They are not to be confused with the chair and riser combination that is used indoors mentioned in Chapter 7.

### 9.4.2.1 Construction

Although not completely consistent with all manufacturers, bleachers generally have a rise of 8 in. (20 cm) and seats have a rise above the tread or *foot plank* of 17 in. (43 cm). *Low rise* bleachers have a rise of 6 in.

Stage roof

Bleachers

Figure 9.7 Examples of scaffolding structures for events

Images courtesy of: top—Doug Matthews; bottom—Euro Arena Sport, www. euroarenasport.com

(15 cm). The *run* is the distance between seats, typically being 24 in. (60 cm), and is affected by the number of foot planks. Foot planks or rests for feet can be either single or double meaning that there is more room for one's feet on a double plank. Seat sizes are 1.5 to 2.0 in. x 9.5 to 10.0 in., all usually constructed of anodized aluminum with end caps. Guardrails are usually anodized pipe, 1.5 to 1.675 in. (3.75 to 4.2 cm) diameter and 42 in. (106 cm) high. These are normally fitted to the backs, sides, stairs, and fronts of bleacher sections. Sections also come in more or less standard sizes of 3, 5, 10, and 15-row x 15 ft (4.5 m) sections, *elevated* or *non-elevated*, with various guardrail options, as well as accessibility options (i.e. ramps)

to meet Americans with Disabilities Act (ADA) requirements. Note that non-elevated bleachers are a type of bleacher that when seated on the first row, one's feet are at ground level, whereas elevated bleachers have the first row elevated above the ground and accessible by stairs and/or a ramp. Supporting bleacher superstructure is generally of a scaffolding-type construction.

### 9.4.2.2 Safety

The current guiding standard for the design, construction, and inspection of portable bleachers in the United States is contained in *ICC/ANSI 300-2012: Standard for Bleachers, Folding and Telescopic Seating, and Grandstands*. The International Code Council (ICC) initiated the development of this stand-alone standard to address bleacher safety, after the issue was highlighted when two US congressional representatives petitioned the Consumer Product Safety Commission to develop such regulations, following a study of deaths and injuries resulting from falls from bleachers. For example, in 1999 in the United States, there were an estimated 22,100 bleacher-associated injuries treated in hospital emergency rooms. Approximately 6,100 of these injuries were a result of the person falling from, or through, bleachers onto the surface below. Approximately 4,910 of these falls involved children under the age of 15 (US Consumer Product Safety Commission, 2000). In particular, the standard addresses the need for a solid *riser plank* to be mounted vertically under the seats and behind the foot plank in order to close the opening that would enable small children to fall to the ground. Also, any bleacher seats above 30 in. (75 cm) require guardrails. Obviously, event producers must be aware of and meet the requirements of this standard to avoid liability.

One other important standard is *NFPA 102: Standard for Grandstands, Folding and Telescopic Seating, Tents, and Membrane Structures, 2011 Edition*, which covers the design of bleachers from a safety point of view.

In Canada, the *National Building Code of Canada 2010* covers bleacher safety. Accessibility for persons with disabilities is covered by standards in both countries listed below, and must be followed for bleachers:

- *2010 ADA Standards for Accessible Design* for the United States.
- *Canadian Standards Association (CSA) B651-12 – Accessible design for the built environment* for Canada.

In the UK, the main document would again be *Temporary demountable structures. Guidance on procurement, design and use (Third Edition) (2007)*.

In Australia, there appear to be no detailed guidelines, although the *Employer Guide to Occupational Health and Safety (2004)* published by the Australian Entertainment Industry Association (AEIA) further refers to *HSG195* from the UK, *The Purple Guide to Health, Safety and Welfare at Music and Other Events*.

### 9.4.3 Fencing and barriers

For special events, especially those outdoors, temporary fencing and barriers are generally utilized for crowd control. Even for large indoor events, they can be critical to providing an organized, less stressful experience for guests and attendees. We will briefly look at the various types of fencing and barriers and then at safety.

### 9.4.3.1 Categories and construction

Crowd control fencing and barriers come in many designs but can be fitted into three main categories:

- Low height. This category of fence is most often used within an event space to delineate exhibits, ticketed sub-events, VIP areas, concessions, and such. There are generally two models, one regular and constructed of steel. Sections for this type are 8+ ft wide x 43 in. high (2.4 m x 108 cm). The second type is an upscale model usually constructed of steel supports and wood, or steel supports and PVC. Sections are typically 6 ft (1.8 m) wide and 32 to 48 in. (80–120 cm) high. The sections of both types are designed to interlock.

● Perimeter. The second category of crowd control fence is a higher, more durable design, used primarily as event perimeter fencing. This type is constructed of welded steel mesh and steel tubing of varying designs. Section heights are fairly standard at 7 ft 6 in. (2.25 m) and widths vary from 4 to 10 ft (1.2–3 m). Accessories include interlocking clamps, heavy bases, gates (with wheels), and privacy screens that can be installed over the entire fence surface. These screens are made of a PVC-coated nylon mesh with an open weave to allow wind to pass through.

● Barrier. Originally designed in Europe, the third category is often called a barrier and is used for heavy-duty crowd control typically at outdoor rock concerts in front of a stage. In this case it is called a *front-of-stage barrier* (FOSB), *stage barrier*, or *crowd barrier*. Barriers can come in lightweight or heavy-duty versions, usually constructed of aluminum or steel respectively, the steel type being used for larger events where higher spectator loading is anticipated. Modern barriers are of A-frame construction in profile, and rely on a *tread plate* (ideally with a tapered lip to prevent tripping) in front to maintain their stability and to withstand the forces associated with crowd crushes and surges. They are normally freestanding but if used outdoors, they may be fixed to a stage using couplers, providing the stage is also built to withstand the lateral crowd forces. The rear of the barrier is usually fitted with a step to enable crowd control officials (called *event stewards*, who require certification in Europe) to monitor crowd activity and to assist with lifting crowd surfers and audience members in distress out of harm's way if necessary. Dimensions are nominally 4 ft (1,200+ mm) high x 43 in. (1,070+ mm) wide x 50 in. (1,242+ mm) deep, although there might be slight differences amongst manufacturers. Railings should be rounded or covered to prevent injury to persons leaning on them or being lifted over them. Lightweight aluminum barrier sections usually weigh in the order of 35–38 kg (77–83 lb) and can withstand horizontal forces of 2 kN (450 lb) or more, whereas heavy-duty steel barrier sections weigh about 65 kg (145 lb) and can withstand horizontal forces of up to 8 kN (1798 lb) or more. Sections lock together and fold up for easy storage and transport.

See Figure 9.8 for examples of the different categories of fencing and barriers.

### 9.4.3.2 Safety

For fencing and barriers, there are no current specific safety or design standards in North America, although most fencing is manufactured using approved steel or aluminum products. Chapter 23 of Cooper (2014)

Low height fence          Perimeter fence          Front-of-stage-barrier

Figure 9.8 Examples of fencing and barriers

Courtesy of Doug Matthews

does, however, discuss the basics of working with fencing and barriers in the United States. The European design standard, *EN 13200-3:2005: Spectator facilities – Part 3: Separating elements – Requirements*, appears to lead the way in this regard in Europe. As well, the *Event Safety Guide* (see Säterhed et al., 2011) from Sweden goes into extensive detail about barriers in particular.

In addition, in the UK, there are several key references that offer guidance:

- *Temporary Demountable Structures: Guidance on design, procurement and use* forms the basis for design and use of fencing and barriers.
- *HSG195: The Purple Guide*, also called *The Event Safety Guide: A Guide to Health, Safety and Welfare at Music and Similar Events*, published by the HSE.
- HSG154, *Managing crowds safely: A guide for organisers at events and venues (2014)*. This publication addresses very well how to manage crowds including the use of fencing and barriers. Also published by the HSE.
- The HSE web site itself has a one-page summary of how to use stage barriers that is quite detailed (visit www.hse.gov.uk/event-safety/stage-barriers.htm).

In Australia, the document *Guidelines for concerts, events and organised gatherings (2009)* published by the Department of Health in the Government of Western Australia provides extensive detail about crowd control including specifics about barriers, especially stage barriers and their allowable loading.

Indeed, the most concern for crowd—and event worker—safety is associated not with the first two types of fencing described, but with stage barriers and their use at live music events, especially rock concerts. Rutherford-Silvers (2013), Van Der Wagen and Carlos (2005), Tarlow (2002), and Fruin (1993), in particular, discuss crowds and the types of disasters that can result from crowd mentality. To put the seriousness of the potential for disaster in perspective, Fruin (1993, p. 103) states:

> *Crowd forces can reach levels that are almost impossible to resist or control. Virtually all crowd deaths are due to compressive asphyxia and not the 'trampling' reported by the news media. Evidence of bent steel railings after several fatal crowd incidents show that forces of more than 4500 N (1000 lb) occurred. Forces are due to pushing, and the domino effect of people leaning against each other . . . Horizontal forces sufficient to cause compressive asphyxia would be more dynamic as people push off against each other to obtain breathing space . . . Experiments to determine concentrated forces on guardrails due to leaning and pushing have shown that a force of 30% to 75% of participant weight can occur. In a US National Bureau of Standards study of guardrails, three persons exerted a leaning force of 792 N (178 lb) and 609 N (137 lb) pushing. In a similar Australian Building Technology Centre study, three persons in a combined leaning and pushing posture developed a force of 1370 N (306 lb). This study showed that under a simulated 'panic,' five persons were capable of developing a force of 3430 N (766 lb).*

Suffice it to say, crowd disasters are a very real and serious risk at live events where music or other entertainment generates psychological pressures as well as physical ones. In Europe, studies have been ongoing for years about the best configuration for FOSB and have resulted in the optimum configuration—to date—of a convex barrier arrangement in front of the stage, often with two or three layers of barrier (Upton, 2004 and updated by Upton, 2010). The minimum distance between the stage and the first barrier layer must, according to current regulations in many jurisdictions, be at least 1.0 to 1.5 m (3 to 5 ft) to permit event stewards, security, and emergency personnel free access and to permit the fast extraction of crowd members in distress. This shape also permits escape routes at either end of the convex shape and minimizes the locations where concentrated points of force may occur as would happen in a straight or concave shaped barrier. Figure 9.9 illustrates a simple single convex barrier configuration. The optional straight barrier may be used when low crowd pressure is anticipated.

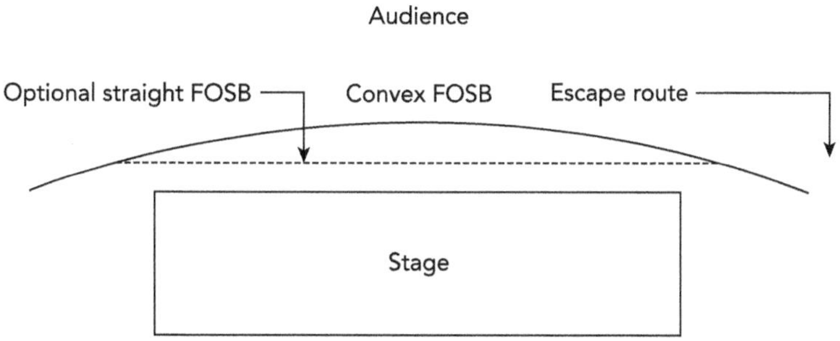

Audience

Optional straight FOSB ⎤     Convex FOSB     Escape route ⎤

Stage

Figure 9.9  Simple FOSB configuration

Courtesy of Säterhed et al., 2011—redrawn by author

However, there is more than just pressure **toward** the stage to be concerned about. According to Petter Säterhed from Sweden, one of the most potent dangers in a large audience is side-to-side movement. If crowd density exceeds approximately 7 persons/m², parrying a crowd surge (i.e. by taking a side step) gets difficult, resulting in the crowd *cratering* (i.e. many people falling, in a crater-like fashion). When the fallen audience gets up again, the crowd closes. This has historically trapped slow members of the crowd who are still lying down, putting them in severe danger of being trampled. In these cases, designing the FOSB with a *wave-breaker*—sometimes called a *finger* or *pier*—in the middle can be very effective (Säterhed et al., 2011, p. 100 and P. Säterhed, personal communication, March 16, 2015). See Figure 9.10.

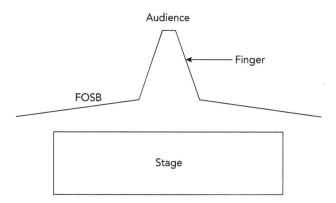

Audience

Finger

FOSB

Stage

Figure 9.10  FOSB with finger

Courtesy of Säterhed et al., 2011—redrawn by author

For larger crowds, wave-breakers are combined with splitting up the crowd by creating enclosures, also called *cages* or *pits*, for smaller numbers of people and using double or multiple barriers. However, it is important to calculate the angles of the barrier correctly so that no audience member gets trapped in a dead-end against the barrier (P. Säterhed, personal communication, March 16, 2015, and Säterhed et al., 2011, pp. 100–101). This concept is illustrated in Figure 9.11, which shows the cages along with the barriers and walkways/escape routes between them. Also, according to Säterhed, it is important to limit the size of any enclosure for the audience in order to avoid *crowd turbulence* or *quake*, as reported by Helbing and Mukerji (2012). This is a situation in which the dense crowd is subjected to unpredictable forces from varying directions that can build up and result in audience members falling and piling up, which in turn exacerbates the problem.

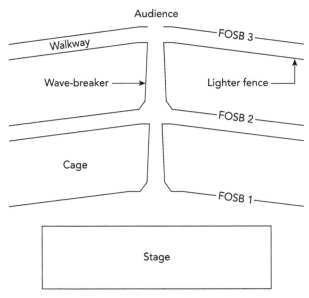

Figure 9.11  Example of cages and wave-breakers

Courtesy of Säterhed et al., 2011—redrawn by author

The number and spacing of FOSB arrangements is largely dependent on the total audience size and demographics as well as the nature of the event, and event stewards or security professionals with experience in this type of event should be consulted before producers make the final decision on FOSB arrangements.

### 9.4.4  Sanitary facilities

Creature comforts, or rather the lack thereof, can form a lasting negative impression in the minds of event attendees. To prevent this, adequate sanitary facilities must be provided, no matter where the event is held. For outdoor events—and even large indoor ones—portable toilets may be rented on a short-term basis where sewer-connected sanitation and water are not readily available or adequate. It is often the responsibility of the event producer to estimate toilet needs and to make arrangements for their delivery, placement, and servicing.

#### 9.4.4.1  Equipment, location, and servicing

The basic equipment consists of the portable toilet units and service trucks. The toilet unit is a small toilet room built over a water-tight waste holding tank. The service truck has a pump and a large tank which is divided into two compartments, one for fresh charge for use in cleaning the units and the other for receiving and transporting the effluent for proper disposal. At special events, toilet units are placed on a site and picked up when the event is completed. For big events with a large number of units, the service truck may remain onsite to provide continuous standby maintenance service, especially if the duration is long.

Portable toilets are large enough for a single occupant, usually about 90–118 cm (35–46 in.) on a side by 210–236 cm (7–8 ft) high. They are held upright by the weight of the disinfectant liquid in the holding tank at the bottom. Nearly all include both a seated toilet and a urinal. Most include lockable doors, ventilation near the top, and a stovepipe vent for the holding tank. Single-sex units and larger units for wheelchair access compatible with ADA requirements are available. All are available in different colors and designs, depending on the manufacturer. Plastic, freestanding hand-washing units with four wash stations (one on each side) and equipped with paper towels and soap are now part of most portable toilet orders. Luxury units with more amenities are popular for smaller or VIP audiences. These incorporate separate stalls with doors, vanities and make-up areas, washbasins, and towels, all packaged within an attractive interior design.

The keys to the successful incorporation of portable toilets into an event are:

- Correct estimation of the number of units needed. HSE (1999) recommends that, when estimating the number of units required at an event, consideration should be given to the duration of the event, the perceived consumption of food and beverages (particularly alcohol) by the audience, timing of breaks in entertainment performances, provision for children or elderly who make take longer to use a facility, and weather conditions and temperature. In addition, the ratio of women to men is essential to correctly estimating numbers.

Determining the number of toilets required for an event is far from an exact science and numbers vary considerably, depending on the source. As would be expected, suppliers' numbers are much higher than those coming from unbiased sources. To provide reasonably accurate estimates, for the purposes of this book, five different sources have been consulted and the resulting numbers averaged. Figures 9.12 and 9.13 represent these combined averages of the sources (Cooper, 2014; Government of Western Australia, 2009; PSAI, 2013; White House Sanitation, 2011; United Site Services, 2014), and can be used for general estimates of toilet units required when alcohol is or is not being served at the event. Note that the straight lines in these graphs are the trend lines of the averages and it is these lines that should be used. The graphs assume that: the event lasts 8 h, there is a 50/50 mix of men and women, one unit provides approximately 200 uses with 4 h between uses by a single person, and there is no pumping service provided. Thanks to mathematics, we can derive equations from these trend lines that can be used to more exactly predict the number of toilets needed, where $y$ represents the number of toilets and $x$ the attendance, so that for less than 30,000 attendees, the equations are:

- $y = 0.0071x + 2$, for an event with no alcohol; and
- $y = 0.0096x + 3$, for an event with alcohol.

For an event with up to 100,000 attendees, the equations would be:

- $y = 0.0079x + 14$, for an event with no alcohol; and
- $y = 0.0091x + 11$, for an event with alcohol.

In addition to the number of toilet units, hand-wash stations should be provided in the ratio of approximately 20 percent of the total number of toilets (i.e. for 100 toilets, 20 hand-wash stations are needed), although many deluxe toilets now incorporate a station into every unit. The Government of Western Australia (2009), in its extensive event guidelines, also further recommends that for events with different durations, the following changes in numbers should be made:

- More than 8 h, 100 percent increase over graph values.
- 6–8 h, 80 percent of graph values.
- 4–6 h, 75 percent of graph values.
- Less than 4 h, 70 percent of graph values.

By way of an example to illustrate, let us assume that a festival is expecting an attendance of 25,000 people at a 7-h event in which alcohol will be available at a beer garden. The number of toilets needed would therefore be:

- $y = 0.0096x + 3$, or $0.0096 (25,000) + 3 = 243$ toilets, less 20 percent if one follows the Australian suggested guidelines for a 7-h event rather than an 8-h event, for a total of 194 toilets.

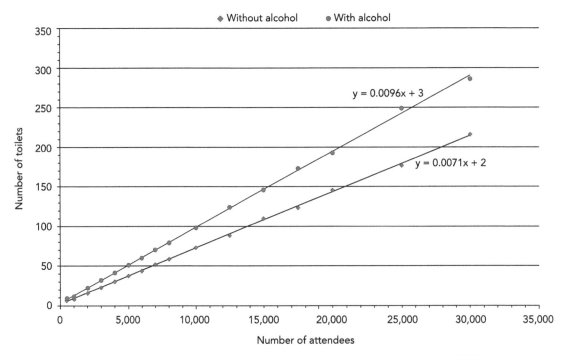

Figure 9.12 Portable toilet requirements for an 8-h event (total attendance up to 30,000)

Courtesy of Doug Matthews

According to National Construction Rentals (2014), in the United States, federal and state guidelines also require one ADA toilet unit for each "cluster" of toilets, which works out to approximately 10 percent of the entire order that should be disabled units. Event workers and employees must have their own dedicated facilities that should be located near work areas, specifically backstage, near the mixer tower, next to catering areas and car parks, and near first aid and children's areas. Toilets with hot and cold hand-washing facilities should be provided for food handlers and should be at least 50 m from the vendors but no more than 20 m from a service road (Säterhed et al., 2011, p. 126).

- Correct location of the units. Where possible, toilets should be located at different points around the event site to minimize crowding and queuing problems. Attention should be given to accessibility for servicing and emptying. This may include temporary roadways and dedicated access routes, subject to the site layout.

- Regular servicing schedule. Depending on the type, portable toilet units have waste storage tank capacities ranging from about 150 l (40 gal) to 250 l (65 gal). On average, a single usage will deposit approximately 1.4 l (0.37 gal) of waste. Based on another average of 54 to 75 seconds per use (men versus women), smaller units may therefore require major service and emptying of toilet receptacles as frequently as every 2 h, or as infrequently as 4 h, but this may need to be monitored if some units receive heavier usage than others due to their location. At a minimum, units should be cleaned and checked for supply replenishment (e.g. toilet paper) at 2-h intervals, and a plumber should at least be on call for short events and onsite for longer events. Major service procedure involves driving the service truck to within approximately 20 ft (6 m) of the portable toilet, pumping or evacuating the effluent from the portable toilet receptacle into the truck holding tank, recharging the portable toilet receptacle, and performing minor repairs to the portable toilet as needed.

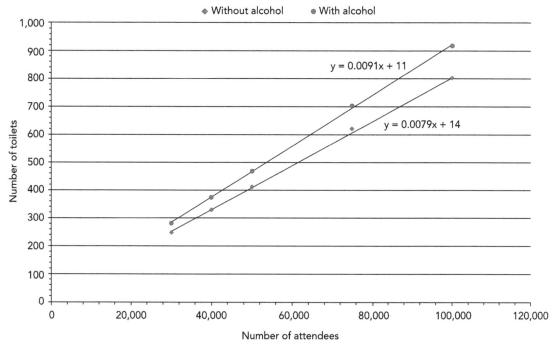

**Figure 9.13** Portable toilet requirements for an 8-h event (total attendance 30,000 to 100,000)

Courtesy of Doug Matthews

### 9.4.4.2 *Safety and health considerations*

There are no known specific standards for portable toilets used at events; however, standards do exist for portables used on construction sites. Some state and provincial jurisdictions now classify all portable toilet waste as *septage* (untreated waste that has not gone through a stabilization process, such as processing at a sewage treatment plant), and any group or organization that has portable toilets onsite must use a licensed waste hauler to dispose of their waste. Clients have the right to demand that a waste hauler produce proof of a license.

As well, some jurisdictions (HSE, 1999) require stable and non-slip surfaces, protection from trip hazards, and adequate lighting (80 to 100 lux, depending on the jurisdiction).

In general, Cooper (2014), Government of Western Australia (2009), and HSE (1999) provide good overall advice on the use of portable toilets at events.

Even with the estimates of required numbers of toilets as described in this section and the above safety considerations, producers should check with local authorities for the correct interpretation of local regulations, if any, for the numbers, locations, and servicing requirements of sanitation facilities.

> **PRODUCTION CHALLENGES**
>
> 1. You want to check the calculations of your lighting designer who has called for 100 A, three-phase service out of the following options presented by a venue in which you are producing a stage show:

- 20 A, 120 V single-phase;
- 30 A, 120 or 208 V single- or three-phase;
- 60 A, 120 or 208 V three-phase;
- 100 A, 120 or 208 V three-phase;
- 200 A, 120 or 208 V three-phase.

The lights he plans to use are older and include 20 PAR64s @500 W, 16 PAR64s @1,000 W, ten Source Four ellipsoidals @500 W for gobo projection, and eight automated Vari-lites @1,200 W for excitement. He plans to use a single dimmer system. Did he choose the correct option for electrical service?

2. Research online any two major accidents at events in which truss structures have collapsed over the last two years anywhere in the world. Explain what you think might have gone wrong and what, if anything, you would do to prevent the accidents if you had been the event producer.

3. You are producing an aerial ribbon act above a 3 ft high stage in a venue that has a 30 ft high ceiling. The ribbon must be suspended from a 16 in. square truss section that will be rigged from the ceiling using chain motors. The ribbon is 20 ft long and the performer needs a clear 16 ft of ribbon to work on. The chain motor, chain, and hooks require 4 ft of vertical space once they are fully trimmed. Will there be enough vertical space for the performer to work and what is the final highest trim to truss?

4. You are to produce a large outdoor festival for about 20,000 alternative music fans in a farmer's open field with a single road access. There will be six musical acts performing on a mobile stage during the festival which lasts for 4 h on a Sunday afternoon. It will be a non-alcoholic event. Consider what you might need in terms of scaffolding, bleachers (if any), fencing, FOSB, and portable toilets. Describe how these would all be used, how much or how many of each you might need, and where they might all be placed.

5. As a producer, you must be concerned with the safety both of your workers and of the audience. List at least one safety standard or guideline for each of the technical resources discussed in this chapter and describe for whom it is relevant.

## REFERENCES

Cadena, R. (2009). *Electricity for the Entertainment Electrician & Technician*. Oxford: Focal Press.

Cooper, D.C. (Ed.). (2014). *The Event Safety Guide: A Guide to Health, Safety and Welfare at Live Entertainment Events in the United States*. New York: Event Safety Alliance of USA, Inc./Skyhorse Publishing.

Fruin, J.J. (1993). The Causes and Prevention of Crowd Disasters. In R.A. Smith and J.F. Dickie (Eds.) *Engineering for Crown Safety: Proceedings of the International Conference on Engineering for Crown Safety, London, UK, 17–18 March 1993* (pp. 99–108). Amsterdam; New York: Elsevier Science & Technology Books.

Garber, N. (2002, October 1). Tools of the Trade: Fresh Juice. *Special Events Magazine*. Retrieved November 17, 2014, from http://specialevents.com/supplies/meetings_fresh_juice/index.html.

Garber, N. (2006, May 1). Tech Tips: Power Launch. *Special Events Magazine*. Retrieved November 17, 2014, from http://specialevents.com/eventtools/events_power_launch_20060516/index.html.

Government of Western Australia. (2009, December). *Guidelines for Concerts, Events and Organized Gatherings*. Department of Health.

Helbing, D. and Mukerji, P. (2012). Crowd Disasters as Systemic Failures: Analysis of the Love Parade Disaster. *EPJ Data Science* 2012, 1:7. Retrieved March 13, 2015, from www.epjdatascience.com/content/1/1/7.

HSE. (1999). *The Event Safety Guide: A Guide to Health, Safety and Welfare at Music and Similar Events*. Norwich: Health and Safety Executive.

HSE. (2014, November 21). CDM Update November 2014: Construction (Design and Management) Regulations 2015 ("CDM 2015"). *Association of British Theatre Technicians*. Retrieved November 18, 2014, from www.abtt.org.uk/cdm-update-november-2014-construction-design-and-management-regulations-2015-cdm-2015/.

National Construction Rentals. (2014). ADA Restrooms. *National Construction Rentals*. Retrieved December 2, 2014, www.rentnational.com/ada-portable-toilets.aspx.

NEMA. (2014). About NEMA Standards. *NEMA*. Retrieved November 18, 2014, from www.nema.org/Standards/About-Standards/Pages/default.aspx.

NEMA Connector. (2014, November 11). In *Wikipedia, The Free Encyclopedia*. Retrieved 19:44, November 14, 2014, from http://en.wikipedia.org/w/index.php?title–EMA_connector&oldid=633405042.

Ontario Ministry of Labour. (2013, October). Safety Guidelines for the Live Performance Industry in Ontario. *Performance Industry*. Retrieved March 2, 2015, from www.labour.gov.on.ca/english/hs/topics/performance.php.

PSAI. (2013). Special Event Chart: Extended Breakdown. *Portable Sanitation Association International*. Retrieved December 2, 2014, from http://psai.org/wp-content/uploads/2014/07/PSAI-Extended-Chart.pdf.

Richardson, S.S. (2000, July 6). Rigging. *WPI Technical Theatre Handbook*. Retrieved November 15, 2014, from www.gweep.net/~prefect/pubs/iqp/node43.html.

Rutherford-Silvers, J. (2013). *Risk Management for Meetings and Events*. Abingdon and New York: Routledge.

Säterhed, P., Hansson, M., Strandlund, J., Nilsson, T., Nilsson, D., Locken, D., and Meimermondt, A. (2011). *Event Safety Guide*. Sweden: Swedish Civil Contingencies Agency.

Scaffolding. (2014, November 24). In *Wikipedia, The Free Encyclopedia*. Retrieved November 24, 2014, from http://en.wikipedia.org/w/index.php?title=Scaffolding&oldid=635199024.

SIAC. (2011). Codes of Safe Practice Ontario. *Scaffold Industry Association of Canada*. Retrieved November 24, 2014, from www.scaffoldaccess.ca/pdf/Codes%20of%20Safe%20Practice%20Ontario-2011.pdf.

Stage pin connector. (2014, August 19). In *Wikipedia, The Free Encyclopedia*. Retrieved 21:21, November 14, 2014, from http://en.wikipedia.org/w/index.php?title=Stage_pin_connector&oldid=621931263.

Tarlow, P.E. (2002). *Event Risk Management and Safety*. New York: John Wiley & Sons, Inc.

Tilson, K. (2014, August 11). Taking Entertainment Rigging Training to New Heights. *Columbus McKinnon Corporation*. Retrieved November 18, 2014, from http://blog.cmworks.com/taking-entertainment-rigging-training-to-new-heights/.

United Site Services. (2014). *Portable Toilet Event Planning Tool*. United Site Services. Retrieved December 2, 2014, from www.unitedsiteservices.com/uses-and-planning/special-events/planning-tool.

Upton, M. (2004, January/February). *Front of Stage Barrier Systems*. Paper presented to the Cabinet Office Emergency Planning College, Easingwold, UK.

US Consumer Product Safety Commission. (2000). *Guidelines for Retrofitting Bleachers, Pub. No. 330-000011*.

Van Der Wagen, L. and Carlos, B.R. (2005). *Event Management for Tourism, Cultural, Business, and Sporting Events*. Upper Saddle River, NJ: Pearson Education, Inc.

Wenzel, C. (2014, May 14). Event Planning 101: Keeping the lights on. *Special Events Blog; Special Events Magazine*. Retrieved November 17, 2014, from http://specialevents.com/blog/event-planning-101-keeping-lights.

White House Sanitation. (2011). Portable Toilet Calculator. *White House Sanitation*. Retrieved December 2, 2014, from www.whitehousesanitation.com/portable_toilet_calculator.php.

# Index

2D or 3D CADD *see* CADD
3D and 4D mapping *see* projection mapping
4K or 8K ultra-high-definition (UHD) video *see* ultra-high-definition video or television (UHDTV)

**A**
*accessory*, in design theory 56
acrylic 75
acting 1, 6–7, 19–21
additive color mixing 198–9
Advanced Television Systems Committee (ATSC) 153
advertising: as a reason for entertainment 8–9
aerials, laser 239
airburst effect 247–8
*aircraft cable* 315
Airtubes® 90
allowable load: of stage barriers 326; of staging 277
aluminum, as material for: A-V screen framing 180; choral riser frames 266; dance floor edges 265; drape support hardware 72; fencing 325; *lighting trees* 219; scaffolding 321, 323; sign substrate 75; stage deck frames 261; tension fabric support 82; tent flooring legs 289; tent support framework 280–2; trussing 309–12
ambience: creating through décor 86, 94; creating through entertainment 9; creating through lighting 215–16
American National Standards Institute (ANSI) 142, 229–30, 238, 241, 311, 320, 324
Americans with Disabilities Act (ADA) 264, 324, 329–30
*analog-to-digital converter* (ADC) 122
analyzing performance: athletic and physical 23–4; dance 22–3; musical 17–19; technology as entertainment 24–7; theater and speaking 19–22

animation projection *see* aerials, laser
applications, mobile: used in audio 122; used as décor 90–2; used in entertainment 24–5; used in lighting 225; used in visual presentations 167–8
appliqué 75, 77, 80
app(s) *see* applications, mobile
aquascreen *see* atmospherics: water curtain, or water screen or *water scrim*
*Arabesque*™ tent *see* Saddlespan™ tent
*architectural mapping see* projection mapping
arena stage 259–60
*Art-Net* or ArtNET 225
aspect ratio 154, 160, 172–4, 181–2, 184
asymmetrical balance 61, 195
athletic acts or entertainment 3–4, 9, 17, 23–4, 32, 36, 46–7
atmospherics, types of special effects: bubbles 233, 253–5; foam 253–4; laser *see* aerials, laser; snow (artificial) 233, 253–4; water curtain, or water screen or *water scrim* 147, 255
attire, of performers *see* costuming
audience blinder *see* luminaires: audience blinder
audience participation or interaction 9, 12–13, 15, 24–6, 36, 50, 147, 149
*audience response software* and/or systems (ARS) 167
audio console *see* mixer, audio
*Audio-over-Ethernet* (AoE) 125
audio/video interleaved (AVI) 156
automated fixtures, for lighting: control and programming 221, 225; of décor 87; designing with 215–18; features of 210–11; setup of 226
automated lighting *see* automated fixtures, for lighting

**B**

backdrops: balloons as 88; blowups as 90; drapery as 71–2; florals as 85; lighting of 158, 195–6, 201, 207, 215; as room décor 19, 54, 62–6; screens as 149–50, 177, 184–5; setup and strike of 96; for stage 71–2, 258, 272–4, 282; tension fabric structures as 82; water curtains as 255

balance, as a principle of design: asymmetrical 61; in color 59; in lighting 195–6, 214; radial 61; in space 54; symmetrical 61

ballet 4, 265

balloons, decorative see inflatables: balloons as décor

band risers 266, 268

banners and signs: appliqué on 80; computer-cut vinyl on 80; digital printing on 79–80; filling space as décor 54; flexible substrates for 75; as focal points 63; general requirements for graphic artwork 81; hand-painting 80; materials 74–6; as props 75; methods of suspension 81–2; rigid substrates 75–6; screen printing 80; specialty fabrics 74–5; used with drape 273; as warnings 241, 298

barn doors, accessory for luminaires 203, 210

barrier see fencing and barriers: barrier or front-of-stage barrier (FOSB)

bars, as décor see lounge furniture and bars, as décor

bass bins 105–6; see also speakers, audio: woofers or subwoofers

Bayonet Neill–Concelman connector (BNC) see BNC connection

Bedouin tent 281

beltpack 115–16, 135

bi-directional microphone see microphone(s): bi-directional

blacklight see luminaires: blacklight

bleachers: construction of 322–4; low rise 322–3; safety of 324

blinders see luminaires: audience blinder

blocking, in theater 19–20

blowups see inflatables: other blowups and air-supported décor

Blue Hubbell see pin and sleeve electrical connector

Bluetooth 118–19

Blu-ray 156–7, 188

BNC connection 157–8, 164, 176

borders: to mask lighting 273; as screen dressing 181

box-beam, frame-supported tent see clearspan tent

breaking strength, in rigging 314

brightness: lasers 239; LED screens 149, 186; luminaires 197, 208, 216, 229; monitors 183; projectors 149, 152, 163, 172–5, 177; video 154, 159, 176; videowalls 184

British Standards Institute (BSI) 243, 308

bubbles, type of special effect see atmospherics, types of special effects: bubbles

buffet: area required for 286; as location for décor 62–3, 84–7, 93

**C**

CADD: décor layout 95; lighting plot or plan 221; projector resolution for 173; screen size required for projection 181; stage set design 275; tented event plan 293

cage, for crowds 327–8

cake, type of low-level firework 246

camera control unit (CCU) 159

Cam lock connector 306–7

Canadian Centre for Occupational Health and Safety (CCOHS) 322

Canadian Electrical Code (CEC) 142, 230, 299, 308

Canadian Standards Association (CSA) 142, 229, 308, 324

candles 93

canons, choreographic 22

canvas 64–5, 74, 80, 272, 284

CAT5, or CAT5e, or CAT6 124–5

cathode ray tube (CRT) 154

CD see compact disk (CD)

celebrity talent, or celebrities 4, 7–9, 40, 48–9, 148

certification and/or licensing: audio equipment 142; event stewards 325; fireworks and proximate pyrotechnics 249–51; rigging 319–20; scaffold workers 322

chain and pulleys, method of flying equipment 316

chain motor 132, 143, 180, 220, 228, 306, 309–10, 315–16

chair covers 56, 61, 68–9, 71

chairs, as décor see dining tables and chairs

chair sashes 69, 71

changing rooms see green rooms

charge-coupled device (CCD) 153

charisma 11–13, 18–19, 21

choice and interpretation of material, in performance 14–16

choral risers 266

choreography 3, 19, 22–3, 31, 46

chorus, as audio effect 123, 139

chroma see chrominance

chrominance 155, 157, 176

clearspan tent 281–2, 284, 286, 293

clipping, in audio 138

CMYK color format, for printing 81

codec (coder-decoder) 155–6, 160

color: as an element of design for décor 56–9; as a quality of light 197–200

color encoding, in video 155

color meaning 57–8

color schemes, for décor 58–9

color wheel: in DLP projector 171–2; in moving luminaires 210

comedy: as genre of entertainment 3–5; lighting for 217; performance of 12, 14–15, 18–19, 21–2, 24, 38–9, 41; setup for 31; staging for 34

comet, type of low-level firework 246

commando cloth 73, 272

Commedia Dell'arte 259

compact disk (CD): backup for digital pre-sets in lighting 263; backup for entertainment 29, 31, 46; input to audio system 107, 120–1, 136, 143; input to digital lighting console 230; input for visual presentations 146, 153, 156, 190

*complementary metal oxide semiconductor* (CMOS) 153

component video 176

composite video 176

compositing, in video 168

*compression*, video 155–6

compressor, audio effect 122–4, 126

computer aided design and drafting *see* CADD

computer-cut vinyl 75–6, 80

concentration, in performance 14, 20

condenser microphone *see* microphone(s): condenser

confetti *see* streamers and confetti, as special effects

connected play 168

connecting with the audience, in entertainment 11–16

connections or connectivity: for audio 125; for projectors 175–6

console, audio or house console *see* mixer, audio

console, lighting *see digital multiplex* (DMX) or DMX512: control console

Consumer Product Safety Commission 324

*continuance*, in design 63

contour curtain 273

contrast, in: choreography 22; design 56, 58–9, 62; lasers 238–9; LED screens 184; lighting 194, 216; monitors 183; ratio, in projectors 172, 174–5; screen surfaces 180; visual presentations 152, 158

Coroplast 75

costuming 3, 12, 24, 29, 49, 83

*cratering*, of crowd 327

crossover, audio 125–7, 135, 137–8

crowd control 324–8

*crowdsourcing* 24

*crowd turbulence* or *quake* 327

CRT *see* cathode ray tube (CRT)

*cryo jet* 235

cultural acts or entertainment 4–6, 18, 47

cutouts, as part of stage set 276

*cyclorama* or *cyc* 207, 272, 276

**D**

dance, or dancers: analysis of 14–16, 22–3; flooring for 265; as genre of entertainment 3–4; lighting for 195, 217, 225; in pacing a show 37–9, 41; staging of 29, 31–2, 45, 268; used as decoration 7–8; used to educate 6; used to emotionally move people 7; used to motivate people 148; used to physically move people 6; used to reward performance 9

dance band 5, 18, 29–30, 34, 44, 46, 269

dance floor 26, 34, 62, 112, 265, 286, 292

deck, as a component of staging 261, 264–6, 277

decoration, as a reason for entertainment 7–8

delay, audio effect 122–3

delay speakers 106, 130–1

*demountable structures* or *temporary demountable structures* (TDS) 277, 299, 312–13, 321, 324, 326

DI *see* direct input box (DI)

*dichroic mirror* 171

*diffraction grating* 239

digital lighting *see* luminaires: digital

*digital light processing* (DLP) projectors *see* projectors: DLP

digital mixer *see* mixer, audio: digital

*digital multiplex* (DMX) or DMX512: *base address* 223, 225; control console 225; control protocol 222–5; for conventional luminaires 207; *daisy chain* connection(s) 205, 223–4, 253; for digital lighting 211; for LED luminaires 205, 208–9; power for 306–7; safety 229–30; setup of, for lighting 228; for special effects 234, 236, 248, 253, 255; *splitter/repeater* or *opto-isolator* for 223, 306–7; for *star drop* 272; universe 223, 225

digital printing 74–6, 79–80

Digital Terrestrial Multimedia Broadcast (DTMB) 154

*digital-to-analog converter* (DAC) 124

digital versatile disk (DVD): backup for digital pre-sets in lighting 230; input to audio system 107, 118, 120, 136, 143; storage medium for visual presentations 146, 153, 156–7, 159, 169, 172, 177, 188, 190

Digital Video Broadcasting (DVB) 153–4, 156

digital video mixer *see* switcher or switching, video

*Digital Visual Interface* (DVI) 164, 176–7

dimming, for lighting 204, 209–10, 221–2

dining tables and chairs: category of furniture 67–9; focal points for décor 63; placement of 35, 84–5

*direct input* or *injection box* (DI) 118–19, 120, 123

display fireworks *see* fireworks and pyrotechnics: display fireworks

*distributed system*, of audio speakers 105, 129

*distribution amplifier see* video distribution amplifier

*distribution panel* or *box* 306

*distro box see distribution panel*

*divine proportion* or *golden proportion* 60

DLP projectors *see* projectors: DLP
DMX or DMX512 *see digital multiplex* (DMX) or DMX512
dome tent 282
*dominance*, in design *see* emphasis, as a principle of design
*donut*, accessory for luminaires 203
*dots per inch* (DPI) 80–1
drama: analysis of 20–2; as an entertainment genre 3
drapery or draping: dressing for A-V screens 181, 188; fabrics 72–4; method of support 72, 82; a room 63, 72–4; stages 71–2, 79, 272–4
drop point 70–1
*dry ice* fog 234–7
DVD *see* digital versatile disk (DVD)
dye sublimation printing 79–80
dynamic microphone *see* microphone(s): dynamic
dynamics: of dance performance 22; of musical performance 17; physical, or gestures, as control of technology 25

**E**

echo: in acoustic theory 102; as audio effect 122–3
*edge blending*, in projection *see* projectors: *edge blending* and *warping*
Edison plug 304–5
education, as a reason for entertainment 6
effects, audio 37, 120–4, 127, 135–9, 148
*ellipsoidal reflector spotlight* (ERS) *see* luminaires: *ellipsoidal reflector spotlight* (ERS or Leko or *profile* or *Source Four*)
emotionally moving people, as a reason for entertainment 6–7
emphasis, as a principle of design 62–3
Encore, type of drapery 72–3, 272
encore, in performance 41
Entertainment Services and Technology Association (ESTA) 319
Entertainment Technician Certification Program (ETCP) 319–20
*equalization* or EQ, in audio 102, 120–1, 125–7, 135, 137–9
*Ethernet* 124–5, 164, 211, 225, 230
ethnic acts or performers *see* cultural acts or entertainment
European Institute for Standardisation (CEN) 312, 320
event space: acoustics 100–6, 143; décor 54, 60–1, 66–7, 79, 82, 84, 86, 88, 90; entertainment within 7, 19, 32–3, 37; fencing 324–5; lighting 201–2, 210, 216; location of audio equipment in 115, 119, 122, 124, 126–7, 129–33, 135–7; location of lighting control equipment in 220–2; logistical details and/or physical characteristics 95, 218; placement of stages within 34–5; using floor space as a performance area 36; using vertical space as a performance area 36–7; wide-screen projection in 177
*event stewards* 325–6, 328
excitation transfer 18–19, 21
*experiential events* 6, 24, 77, 83, 267
Explosives Regulatory Division (ERD) 244, 249, 251
*eye line*, in dance 23

**F**

fabrics: as backdrop material 272–4; as banner and sign material 74–5; effect of colored lighting on 198–9; as drapery material 71–3; as form in design 55; as inflatable material 90; for linens and napery 69–70; printing on 80; as projection surfaces 146, 149, 179; as screen material 180–1, 186; tension fabric structures 82–3; as tent material 279–81, 284–6, 288–90, 294, 296, 298–9
Fast-Fold®, type of projection screen *see* screen(s), for visual presentations: Fast-Fold®
fencing and barriers: barrier or *front-of-stage barrier* (FOSB) 325–8; low height 324–5; perimeter 325; safety of 325–8
FHD *see* full high-definition video (FHD)
fiber optics 125, 141, 212
*finger see wave-breaker*
fire, as a live special effect 15, 46–7, 248
fireworks and pyrotechnics: classifications 242–3; definitions 242; display fireworks safety 249–50; *ground-level* display fireworks 246; *high-level* display fireworks 245; *low-level* display fireworks 246; in multimedia presentations 147–8, 161; proximate pyrotechnics 247–8; proximate pyrotechnics safety 250–2
flame effects (*flame bars, flame cannons, flame projectors*) 248
flanging, audio effect 123, 139
Flash (Adobe), as a visual presentation source 156
flash drive (USB): input to audio system 107, 118, 136, 230; input to visual presentations 150; storage of digital audio mixer settings 122; storage of digital still images 153; storage of edited videos 156–7; storage of performer's music 29, 31
flash effects (*flash paper, flash pot,* flash powder) 247
*flats*, as components of décor or a stage set 65, 276
floodlight *see* luminaires: floodlight
floral décor or floral design: general guidelines for integrating florals with event production 86–7; part of event focal points 84–6; on people 86; total environment 86
*flow*: of entertainment show 37, 150; as psychological state 11, 14, 44

flown system: attachment hardware 315–6; for audio 35, 103–4, 106, 130–3, 135, 142; for A-V or visual presentation equipment 35, 149, 180, 188, 190; description 220; design 309, 314, 316–19; for lighting 35, 219–20, 230; methods of flying 316; for special effects equipment 234, 253
flying *see* flown system
foam, type of special effect *see* atmospherics: foam
*Foamcore* 66, 75, 88
fog, as a special effect 216, 234–9
fog machine 234–5
followspot *see* luminaires: followspot
form, as an element of design 55–6, 60, 62, 202
format, of entertainment shows 29–30
fountain, type of ground-level firework 246
*frame rate*, in video 154, 160,
frequency, of sound *see* sound: frequency
*frequency modulation* (FM) 115
Fresnel *see* luminaires: Fresnel
front lighting 200–1, 207, 217
*front-of-house* (FOH): for audio 39, 125, 127, 134, 136–7; for A-V 150, 158, 188; for lighting 220, 272
*front-of-stage barrier* (FOSB) *see* fencing and barriers: barrier or *front-of-stage barrier* (FOSB)
front projection *see* screens, for visual presentations: front projection
full high-definition video (FHD) 160, 170, 173
*full-range* or *mid-high*, audio speakers *see* speakers, audio: *full-range* or *mid-high*

**G**
*gain before feedback* 105, 115, 143
*gamification* and gaming 24–5, 27, 167, 175, 183, 233, 267
gatorboard 75
*gel*, for luminaires 199, 203, 208
*General Packet Radio Service* (GPRS) 167
Genie lift 220
*Genie® Super Tower™* or *lift* 220
*geodesic dome* 282
gerb, type of firework 246, 248
gesture recognition 167–8
GIF 81, 152
global positioning system (GPS) 25, 27, 308
gobo or *go-between*, accessory for luminaires 197, 201, 203, 206–7, 210, 216, 218, 221, 273
*God-voice see* voiceover
*golden proportion see* divine proportion
GPRS *see* general packet radio service (GPRS)
GPS *see* global positioning system (GPS)
green rooms 31, 43, 46, 48, 293
*ground-to-air fireworks see* fireworks and pyrotechnics: *ground-level* display fireworks
guardrails *see* railing, safety, for stages
*guy wires* 282, 294, 310, 315

**H**
handheld microphone *see* microphone(s): handheld
*handheld projectors see* projectors: *handheld* or *pico*
hand painting 74–6, 80
*hanging points* 95, 187, 219–20, 314–15
harmony: in music 17; as a principle of design 63, 79, 196
haze, as a special effect 195, 197, 236–9
HDTV *see* high-definition television (HDTV)
*headroom see* gain before feedback
headset microphone *see* microphone(s): headset
*head spot*, in dance 23
Health and Safety Executive (HSE) 142, 249, 251, 312–13, 320–2, 326, 329, 331
*High-Definition Multimedia Interface* (HDMI) 157, 164, 177
*high-definition television* (HDTV) 154–6, 176, 181, 184
*highest trim to truss* 316
holding back, in performance 16
hologram 79
*hotspotting* 180
house power (mains) 95, 207, 228, 306, 308
*hue*, in color 59, 62, 171, 197–8, 253

**I**
*illuminance* 197
*image magnification* (IMAG): camera locations 157–8, 187; cameras 157; lighting for 158, 218; as part of multimedia presentation, general 147, 153; personnel for 158–9, 190; *timecode* on video 160; used with edge blending 177
*impedance*: of microphone 109–11, 118; in *snake box* 124
incentive or rewarding performance, as a reason for entertainment 9–10
Industrial Fabrics Association International (IFAI) 280, 284, 294–6
*in-ear monitor* (IEM) *see* monitor system, for audio: personal and/or *in-ear*
inflatables: Airtubes® as décor 90; balloons as décor 87–9; as forms 55; other blowups and air-supported décor 63, 90–1
inflatable tent 284
*infra-red* (IR) 167, 219
inspiration or inspiring people, as a reason for entertainment 7
instrument microphones *see* microphone(s): instrument
insurance, liability 50, 66, 229, 244, 249–52, 296–7
Integrated Services Digital Broadcasting (ISDB) 154, 156
intelligent lighting *see* automated fixtures, for lighting
interactive acts or entertainment 5, 7, 26, 83, 90–2, 167–8

interactive content *see* audience participation or interaction

*interlaced scanning*, in video *see scanning*

International Code Council (ICC) 324

introductions, for entertainment shows 39–40

IR *see infra-red* (IR)

*isolation*, in design 63

**J**

JPEG 81, 152

**K**

Kabuki drop 79, 233, 274

*keder*, framing system for tents 288, 291, 296

keynote speaker: analyzing performance of 19–21; audio for 115, 143; A-V for 148, 151, 156, 168, 177; as genre of entertainment 3–4; lighting for 194; staging for 31

keystone correction 177

*kinetic instruments see* luminaires: moving

**L**

lance, type of ground-level firework 278

laser(s): light source of 239; performance interaction with 4, 15; pointer 190; projector 171–2, 239; safety 240–2; software for projection of 239–40; as used in multimedia presentations 147–8, 195, 212, 233, 238–40, 255

lavalier microphone *see* microphone(s): lavalier

layout and squaring, of tents 294

LCD *see liquid crystal display* (LCD)

LCD projector *see* projectors: LCD

LED *see light-emitting diode* (LED)

LED lighting *see* luminaires: LED

LED projector *see* projectors: LED

LED screen(s): brightness 186; design technology 184; pixel density 185–6; pixel pitch 185; refresh rate 186; resolution 185–6; setup 188; specifications and features 185–6

legs *see* wings, to mask backstage areas

Leko *see* luminaires: *ellipsoidal reflector spotlight* (ERS or Leko or *profile* or *Source Four*)

*lenticular* surface, of projection screen 180–1

licencing or licensing *see* certification and/or licensing

lift *see Genie® Super Tower™* or *lift*

light amplification by the stimulated emission of radiation (LASER or laser) *see* laser(s)

*light-emitting diode* (LED): backdrop 272; dance floor 62, 265; for décor lighting 82, 87, 89; OLED monitor 183; projection screens *see* LED screen(s); projector *see* projectors: LED; tables and chairs 67, 69, 75

lighting color wheel 198

lighting console *see digital multiplex* (DMX) or DMX512: control console

lighting control *see digital multiplex* (DMX) or DMX512

lighting director or designer (LD) 79, 87, 149, 158, 193, 214, 303

lighting instruments or fixtures *see* luminaires

*lighting plot* or *plan* 221–2

lighting support 219–20

lighting trim 316–8

lights *see* luminaires

limiter, audio 125–7, 135, 137

line, as an element of design 56, 62

line array *see* speakers, audio: line array

*line art* 81

*line level*, in audio 109, 118, 120, 127

line rocket or *grid rocket*, type of proximate pyrotechnic 248

*line-to-line voltage* 302

*line-to-neutral voltage* 302

linen sizing 70–1

*liquid crystal display* (LCD) 153, 170–1, 176–7, 182–4, 205

live video *see image magnification* (IMAG)

losing concentration, in performance 14

lounge furniture and bars, as décor 67–8

low height fencing *see* fencing and barriers: low height

low trim *see* highest trim to truss

*lumens* 164, 172–5, 197

luminaires: audience blinder 207, 209, 212; automated fixtures *see* automated fixtures, for lighting; blacklight, 212; box flood 207; construction of 202–5; conventional 206–7; digital 210–11; DJ club effects 208–10, 212; *ellipsoidal reflector spotlight* (ERS or *Leko* or *profile* or *Source Four*) 197, 203, 206–7, 210, 217, 222; floodlight 207, 209; followspot 32, 36–7, 201, 207, 209, 217, 219, 221, 228–9; Fresnel 206, 208, 210, 217, 219; LED 207–10; moving 209–10; neon *see* neon; PAR can 206, 208–10, 223; pinspot 207–8, 210, 212; rope light 89; scoop 207; searchlight 212; specialty 212; string or pin lights 84, 89, 212; strobelight (*strobe*) 195, 210, 212

*luminance* 155, 176

**M**

mains power *see* house power (mains)

*Marley* carpet 265, 271

*marquee*, as alternate term for tent 280, 282

Masonite 75, 276

mesh, as substrate for signs 75

microphone(s): *bi-directional* 108–9; choral 112; condenser 107–8, 111–14; directionality 108–9; dynamic 107–8, 111–14; electrical output of

109–10; frequency response 108, 110–12; general rules for placement 114–15; handheld 31, 105, 110–11, 116, 143; headset 31, 105, 110–11, 115; instrument 106, 112–14, 136; lavalier 31, 105, 110–11, 115, 120, 143; *omnidirectional* 108–9, 111–12; operating principle 107–8, 110; overhead 110–12; physical design 110–14; placement and technique 110–15; stand-mounted 110, 114; surface-mounted 110; *unidirectional* 108–9, 111–14; wireless *see* wireless microphone
mine, type of low-level firework 246
*mini beamers see* projectors: *handheld* or *pico*
mirror ball 195, 212
mixer, audio: analog 120–1, 124, 134; digital 122, 124–5, 127, 137–9; location 136–7; and monitor system 134–5; role of 109, 116, 118, 120–1, 124, 127, 138–9; setup and operation 138–9; and visual presentation equipment 188–9
mixer, video *see switcher* or switching, video
*mixing color wheel* 58
mobile device(s): as a projector 175; as storage medium for edited video 157; used for décor 90–2; used for entertainment 3–4, 24–5, 47, 166–8, 267; as visual presentation source 147, 149, 153, 169
*mobile projectors see* projectors: *handheld* or *pico*
*monitor engineer* 106, 135, 137, 139
monitors, display, for A-V and visual presentations: *confidence monitors* 186–7; connections 176–7; LCD 182–3; location 146, 149, 168–9, 187; organic light-emitting diode (OLED) 183; plasma 183; resolution 152, 154; setup 187–8; size 181–2; touchscreen 183; for videowalls 184
monitor system, for audio: main 32, 106, 125, 133–5, 137; personal and/or in-ear 32, 106, 134, 139
*mortar*, to launch fireworks 245–7
motivation, as a reason for entertainment 7, 9, 148
*moving head*, principle of moving LED luminaire operation 210
moving luminaires or lights: *see* automated fixtures, for lighting; *see also* luminaires: moving
*moving mirror*, principle of moving luminaire operation 210
moving people, as a reason for entertainment 6
Moving Picture Experts Group (MPEG) 156
*moving yoke*, principle of moving luminaire operation 210
murals 54, 63–4, 86, 194, 201, 272, 276
music: analysis of performance 17–19; choice of material for performance 14–16, 22, 25, 37–8; as genre of entertainment 3–5; presentation 18–19; psychology of 18; setup for performance 32, 35–7; staging for 266, 269; technique and technical proficiency 14, 17–18
musical variety, as a classification of entertainment 5

Muslin 73, 272, 276, 289
Mylar 87, 234

**N**
napkins 69
*National Building Code* 299, 324
*National Electrical Code* (NEC) 299, 308
National Electrical Manufacturers Association (NEMA) 304–5, 308
*National Fire Code* (NFC) 299
National Fire Protection Association (NFPA) 249–50, 298–9, 308, 324
National Television Standards Committee (NTSC) 155
*native resolution*, of projectors *see* projectors: *native resolution*
neon 212
noise, unwanted: from air conditioning units 291; ambient 9, 102; in audio equipment 109–12, 118, 120, 143; during décor setup 95; from LED screen equipment 186; from portable power units 308; of projection mapping show 163; from projectors 171, 179
noise effect, proximate pyrotechnic 247
noise gate, audio effect 123
NTSC *see* National Television Standards Committee (NTSC)
nylon 71, 75, 80, 82, 87, 90, 315, 325

**O**
Occupational Safety and Health Administration (OSHA) 142, 230, 264, 278, 308, 322
*omnidirectional* microphone *see* microphone(s): *omnidirectional*
organic light-emitting diode (OLED) 166, 182–4
*ornament*, in design 56, 195
*output level*, of microphone 109
overhead microphone *see* microphone(s): overhead
overhead projector 151
overpreparation, in performance 14

**P**
pageant wagon 259
*pagoda*, as alternate term for peak tent 282
pantone matching system (PMS), or *PMS number* 81
parabolic aluminized reflector (PAR) *see* luminaires: PAR can
peak tent 282
performance, analysis of: comedy 21–2; dance 22–3; musical 17–19; physical entertainment 23–3; theatrical 19–22
perimeter fencing *see* fencing and barriers: perimeter
permits: for fireworks and pyrotechnics 250–1; occupancy, for tents 297–8
photographs, for visual presentations *see* still images, as source for visual presentations

*pico* projectors *see* projectors: *handheld* or *pico*
*pier see wave-breaker*
*pigment color wheel* 58–9
pin and sleeve electrical connector 305–6
pin lights *see* luminaires: string or pin lights
pinspot *see* luminaires: pinspot
pipe and drape 45, 64, 72, 82, 96
pipe frame-supported tent 280–1
*pit*, for crowds *see cage*, for crowds
pitch, in music 17, 20, 105
placemats 69
placement, to create emphasis with décor
    62–3
PLASA 142, 230, 238, 319
plasma monitor *see* monitors, for A-V and visual
    presentations: plasma
plywood 65, 76, 261, 276, 289
*pocket projectors see* projectors: *handheld* or *pico*
pointload 277
pole-supported or pole tent 280–2, 294
polycarbonate 76
polyester: backdrops 64, 272; balloons 87; banners
    and signs 74–5; drapery 72–4; linens 70–1; rigging
    sling covers 310, 315–16; tent liners 289; tents
    282, 284
polyethylene 75, 87, 245
polyvinyl chloride (PVC): décor 82, 88–9; fencing
    325; signs 75–6; stage decks 265; tent covering
    282, 284, 288; truss roof covering 310
pop-up tent 282
portable toilet(s) *see* sanitary facilities
potential acoustic gain *see gain before*
    *feedback*
power amplifier 127–8
*power factor* 302
PPI 79–81, 152
printing: appliqué; color standard for 58; computer-
    cut vinyl 80; digital, for signs 74–6, 79–80; dye
    sublimation 80; graphic artwork for 81; hand
    painting *see* hand painting; inkjet or UV 79–80;
    photo 79–80; screen 74–6, 80; *variable-data*
    *printing* (VDP) 80
*progressive scanning*, in video *see scanning*
*projection mapping*: 4D mapping 161; budget 164;
    definition 161; projectors 175; show content and
    objectives 150, 162; software and equipment
    164–5, 179; structure to be mapped and its
    location 162–4
projection screens *see* screen(s), for visual
    presentations
projectors: aspect ratio 172–3; brightness 173–4;
    choice of, for multimedia show 149; connectivity
    of *see* connections or connectivity: projector;
    contrast ratio 174–5; DLP 171; *edge blending* and
    *warping* capability 177–9; front or rear projection
    capability 177; *handheld* or *pico* 171, 175;

keystone correction 177; laser, for laser shows
    239–40; laser, for regular visual presentations 172;
    LCD 170–1; LED 171–2; *native resolution* 172–3;
    power consumption 177; remote control 177;
    setup 187–90; weight and portability 175; zoom
    lens 177
proportion, as a principle of design 60–1, 84, 195,
    268–9
props: with balloons 88; considerations during setup
    96; with décor vignettes 54, 63–4; with florals
    86; hand or *small* props, as décor 66; lighting of
    215–16, 228; as part of entertainment act 3–4,
    19, 46; as part of stage sets 275–6; set props, as
    décor 66; using drapery with 71; using to achieve
    balance in design 61
proscenium stage 258–9
Proust effect 93
proximate pyrotechnics *see* fireworks and
    pyrotechnics: proximate pyrotechnics
*proximity*, in design 63
psychology, of music 18
pulleys, for rigging 220, 228, 314–16
*punch line*, in comedy 21
pushing, in performance 14, 16
PVC *see* polyvinyl chloride (PVC)
pyrotechnics *see* fireworks and pyrotechnics:
    proximate pyrotechnics

**Q**
*quake see crowd turbulence*
QuickTime (MOV) 156

**R**
radial balance 61
*radio frequency interference* (RFI) 116
*radio frequency* (RF) 118, 167, 219
railing, safety, for stages 35, 261, 264, 266, 277
*rain curtain see* atmospherics: water curtain, or water
    screen or *water scrim*
*rain lights see* luminaires: pinspot
*raked* stage 259
ramp, for stage 264
raster files 81
RCA connection 176
rear lighting 195, 200–1
rear projection *see* screens, for visual presentations:
    rear projection
rehearsal 10–11, 13–14, 28–32, 41, 47–8, 150,
    188
remote control 177, 187–8, 219, 225, 230
resolution: conversion for projection 168; digital
    video 154; LED screens *see* LED screen(s):
    resolution; projectors *see* projectors: *native*
    *resolution*; monitor *see* monitors, display, for
    A-V and visual presentations: resolution; still
    images for printing 79–81; still images for

projection 149–50, 152; ultra-high-definition (UHD) video 160, 188; videowalls 184
reverberation: in acoustic theory 102–3, 105, 112, 130; as audio effect (reverb) 123
RF see radio frequency (RF)
RGB color wheel 58, 198
RGB format, for printing 81
RGBHV, analog connection 176
rhythm, as a principle of design 61–2
rhythm, in music 17–18
rigging tower 220, 310
risers, band and choral 266
robotics 24, 26, 233
Roman candle, type of low-level firework 246
roof system, type of supporting truss configuration over stages 220, 310–11

**S**
Saddlespan™ tent 282
safety factor, for: electrical power 302; number of décor setup personnel 96; rigging and trussing 314–15; tent stakes 294
safety railing, for stages see railing, safety, for stages
Safe Work Australia 142, 322
safe working load (SWL) 314
sand, as décor 63, 87, 93
sanitary facilities: calculation for number of units needed, 329–30; description 328–9; location 330; safety and health considerations 331; servicing 330
satin 75
saturation, in color 152, 197, 239
scaffolding: construction 321, 323–4; part of form in décor 55, 90; safety 313, 322; support for projection equipment 151, 164, 188
scale, in design 60–1
scaler or scaling see video scaler
scan conversion, in video 168
scanning, in video 154
scissor lift 95–6, 226
screen printing 75, 80
screen(s), for visual presentations: blowup 90; determining screen size 174, 181–2; dressing 181; Fast-Fold® 180; front projection 179; gain 181; LED see LED screen(s); location 63, 149, 187–8; modular 180; part of stage set 275–7; pullup or floor 180; rear projection 179; surface and material 180–1; tripod 180; types of support and mounting 180; wide or ultra-wide 90, 160, 166, 173, 175, 177–8, 180, 267; viewing angles 181
scrim, theatrical 150, 163, 197, 272–3, 276
script or scripted: cues, lighting for 229; format for a show 6, 19, 29, 39–40; on teleprompter or confidence monitor 186; written 6, 29, 40, 148, 150–1

SD or SDTV see standard definition television (SDTV)
searchlight see luminaires: searchlight
segues 32, 37, 39–41
sensitivity, of microphone 108–9, 111–12
separate video (S-Video) 176
septage 331
serial digital interface (SDI) 157–8, 176
serpentine tables 70
shade, in color 57, 197
shader 150, 159
sheers 73
shell, container for fireworks 245–6
showcard 76
show taffeta 73
side lighting 200–1
sight lines: general 72, 105–6, 141, 187, 190, 219, 273, 275; for seated audience 84–5, 270–1; for standing audience 270
signs or signage see banners and signs
similarity, in design 63
single-phase power 302, 304–6
Sintra 76
site lighting 289, 294
site or venue survey and/or visit 95–6, 164, 218–21, 292, 294
sizing, of tents 285–6
skill, of performers 24
skirting, for stages 273
smartphone see mobile device(s)
smell, as décor 93
smoke, as a special effect 195, 197, 236–7
snake, audio 107, 109, 118–20, 122, 124–6, 134–7
snow, type of special effect see atmospherics, types of special effects: snow (artificial)
Socapex or Soca 224, 228, 306
sonic entrainment 18–19
sound: absorption 102–3; diffraction 103; frequency 100–3; loudness 100–2; reflection 102; refraction 103–4; wavelength of 100–3
sound check 30–2, 137–9
soundscaping 94
space, as an element of design 54–5
speakers, audio: active, 128; delay see delay speakers; design of and types 127–9; distributed see distributed system, of audio speakers; equalization 126; full-range or mid-high 126–30, 135, 229; line array 131–3; monitor system 133–5; placement 129–31; powered 128; rigging for 314–15; signal flow to 135–6; tweeters 127; woofers or subwoofers 128, 130–2, 135
spiking, as in marking of stage 30
stage pin connector (SPC) 305
stage plot 47, 134
stage presence see charisma
stage size: height for seated audience 270–1; height for standing audience 270; horizontal 268–9

stairs, for stages 259, 263–4
staking and anchoring, of tents 292, 294, 296
*standard definition television* (SDTV) 154, 157, 176
Standards Development Organization (SDO) 142
*standing wave* 102
*star drop* 272
still images, as source for visual presentations: file format 152; improvements 152–3; resolution 152; size 151–2; storage 153; text and non-photographic material 152
*stings*, musical 30
streamers and confetti, as special effects 234
string lights *see* luminaires: string or pin lights
strobe or strobelight *see* luminaires: strobelight (strobe)
Styrene 76
subtractive color mixing 198–9
*sub-woofers see* speakers, audio: *woofers or subwoofers*
Sunbrella 75
Supervel 72
*switcher* or switching, video 168–9, 188–9
SXGA 173
symmetrical balance 61

**T**
table linens: cloths 69–71; overlays 61, 69–71; runners 69; skirting 69–71
tables, as décor *see* dining tables and chairs: category of furniture
tablet *see* mobile device(s)
technical proficiency, of performers 14
technique: dance 22–3; musical 17–19
technology: as décor 79, 90–2; as entertainment 3–4, 24–7, 32
tempo, in performance 17, 20–1, 38
*temporary demountable structures* (TDS) *see* demountable structures or *temporary demountable structures* (TDS)
tensile or tension fabric structures 54–5, 82–3, 179
tensile tent 281–2, 286
texture, as an element of design 56, 62, 195–7, 275
theater: analyzing performance in 20–1; curtains for 274–5; direction in 19–20; experience of director in 39; as a genre of entertainment 3–4, 15, 17; rigging for 315–16; seating style for 270; terminology in 258–9; use of audio in 111; use of introductions in 40; use of lighting in 207; use of props in 66; use of vertical performing space for 36–7
*theater-in-the-round see* arena stage
theme event 9, 53, 253
three-phase power 291, 302–7
three-to-one or 3-to-1 rule 114–15
thrust stage 258–9
*timbre*, in music 112

timecode *see image magnification* (IMAG): *timecode on video*
*tint*, in color 197
tipi, type of tent 284–6
toilets, portable *see* sanitary facilities
tonal sensitivity 18
tone: in color (*tone*) 197; in music 17, 112
top lighting 200–1
touchscreen 4, 26, 147, 149, 182–3
*traveler*, type of stage curtain 273
tray stand covers 69
trees, lighting *see* lighting support
*trim height* 229, 316
tripod, type of projection screen *see* screen(s), for visual presentations: tripod
tunnel roof *see roof system*, type of supporting truss configuration over stages
*tweeters see* speakers, audio: *tweeters*
*twist-lock*, electrical connector 304–5

**U**
ultra-high-definition video or television (UHDTV) 160–1, 164, 183
underpreparation, in performance 14
Underwriters Laboratories Inc. (UL) 142, 229, 238
*unidirectional* microphone *see* microphone(s): *unidirectional*
uniformly distributed load (UDL) 277
Universal Serial Bus (USB) *see* flash drive (USB)
up lighting 72, 82, 200–1, 206, 216, 228
UV printing 80

**V**
value: as an element of design (*value contrast*) 56, 61–2; in color 61–2, 197
variety acts or entertainment 4, 20, 47
vaudeville 39
vector files 81
velour 70, 72, 103, 195, 272, 276
venue, or event site *see* event space
*venue trim* 316, 318
video *compression see compression*, video
*video distribution amplifier* 168
*Video Graphics Array* (VGA) 164, 176
video home system (VHS) 151, 176
*video scaler* 168
videowalls 184, 186
vinyl: balloon material 88; cut-out graphics 80; dance floor surface 265; drapery material 73; laminate for tents 284; sign material 75–6; tent gutters 288
visibility, audience 10, 32, 36, 149, 157, 261, 270–1
*visual color wheel* 58
*visual weight see* balance, as a principle of design
voiceover 29, 39–41, 136, 139, 156

**W**

wall box, electrical 306
*warping*, in projection *see* projectors: *edge blending* and *warping* capability
water curtain, or water screen or *water scrim see* atmospherics, types of special effects: water curtain, or water screen or *water scrim*
waterfall, type of firework 246, 248
*wave-breaker*, 327–8
*wedges see* speakers, audio: monitor system
wheel and driver, type of ground-level firework 246
WiFi 157, 167–8, 223, 225
Windows Media Video (WMV) 156
wings, to mask backstage areas 273–4
wireless microphone: connectivity 125; description of system 115–16; handheld 31, 105, 111; headset 31, 105, 111; as input to audio mixer 107, 120, 136; lavalier 31, 105, 111; need for 36, 143
*wiring configuration*, of microphone 109–10
*woofers see* speakers, audio: *woofers* or *subwoofers*
Workers' Compensation Board (WCB) 96, 142, 230, 278
WUXGA 173
WXGA 173

**X**

XGA 172–3

**Y**

yurt, type of tent 284, 286–7

**Z**

zoom lens 171, 177, 205, 210